The Wiley Blackwell Companion to Religion and Ecology

The Wiley Blackwell Companions to Religion

The Wiley Blackwell Companions to Religion series presents a collection of the most recent scholarship and knowledge about world religions. Each volume draws together newly-commissioned essays by distinguished authors in the field, and is presented in a style which is accessible to undergraduate students, as well as scholars and the interested general reader. These volumes approach the subject in a creative and forward-thinking style, providing a forum in which leading scholars in the field can make their views and research available to a wider audience.

Recently Published

The Blackwell Companion to Nineteenth Century Theology
Edited by David Fergusson
The Blackwell Companion to Religion in America
Edited by Philip Goff
The Blackwell Companion to Jesus
Edited by Delbert Burkett
The Blackwell Companion to Paul
Edited by Stephen Westerholm
The Blackwell Companion to Religion and Violence
Edited by Andrew R. Murphy
The Blackwell Companion to Christian Ethics, Second Edition
Edited by Stanley Hauerwas and Samuel Wells
The Wiley Blackwell Companion to Practical Theology
Edited by Bonnie J. Miller-McLemore
The Wiley Blackwell Companion to Religion and Social Justice
Edited by Michael D. Palmer and Stanley M. Burgess
The Wiley Blackwell Companion to Chinese Religions
Edited by Randall L. Nadeau
The Wiley Blackwell Companion to African Religions
Edited by Elias Kifon Bongmba
The Wiley Blackwell Companion to Christian Mysticism
Edited by Julia A. Lamm
The Wiley Blackwell Companion to the Anglican Communion
Edited by Ian S. Markham, J. Barney Hawkins IV, Justyn Terry, and Leslie Nuñez Steffensen
The Wiley Blackwell Companion to Interreligious Dialogue
Edited by Catherine Cornille
The Wiley Blackwell Companion to East and Inner Asian Buddhism
Edited by Mario Poceski
The Wiley Blackwell Companion to Latino/a Theology
Edited by Orlando O. Espín
The Wiley Blackwell Companion to Ancient Israel
Edited by Susan Niditch
The Wiley Blackwell Companion to Patristics
Edited by Ken Parry
The Wiley Blackwell Companion to World Christianity
Edited by Lamin Sanneh and Michael J. McClymond
The Wiley Blackwell Companion to Politics and Religion in America
Edited by Barbara A. McGraw
The Wiley Blackwell Companion to Religion and Ecology
Edited by John Hart

The Wiley Blackwell Companion to Religion and Ecology

Edited by

John Hart

WILEY Blackwell

This edition first published 2017

Registered Offices
John Wiley & Sons, Inc., 111 River Street, Hoboken, NJ 07030, USA
John Wiley & Sons Ltd, The Atrium, Southern Gate, Chichester, West Sussex, PO19 8SQ, UK

Editorial Office
9600 Garsington Road, Oxford, OX4 2DQ, UK

For details of our global editorial offices, customer services, and more information about Wiley products visit us at www.wiley.com.

Wiley also publishes its books in a variety of electronic formats and by print-on-demand. Some content that appears in standard print versions of this book may not be available in other formats.

Library of Congress Cataloging-in-Publication Data

Names: Hart, John, 1943– editor.
Title: The Wiley Blackwell companion to religion and ecology / edited by John Hart.
Other titles: Wiley-Blackwell companions to religion.
Description: Hoboken, NJ : John Wiley & Sons, 2017. | Series: Wiley Blackwell Companions to Religion | Includes bibliographical references and index.
Identifiers: LCCN 2016052012 (print) | LCCN 2016057682 (ebook) | ISBN 9781118465561 (cloth) | ISBN 9781118465547 (epdf) | ISBN 9781118465530 (epub)
Subjects: LCSH: Ecology–Religious aspects. | Ecology–Moral and ethical aspects.
Classification: LCC BL65.E36 W55 2017 (print) | LCC BL65.E36 (ebook) | DDC 201/.77–dc23
LC record available at https://lccn.loc.gov/2016052012

Cover Image: Playa Negra by Moira Gil, www.sincronizarte.com
Cover Design: Wiley

Set in 10/12.5pt Photina by SPi Global, Pondicherry, India

Printed in the UK

Contents

List of Contributors

Nawal H. Ammar is a professor of criminology and Dean of the Faculty of Social Science and Humanities, University of Ontario Institute of Technology. Previously, Nawal was a professor at Kent State University, Ohio. Her research areas include environmental justice in Islam, violence against immigrant women, and Muslims in the criminal justice system. Nawal's recent publications include an edited volume, *Muslims in US Prisons* (2015).

Francisco J. Ayala is a university professor and Donald Bren Professor of Biological Sciences at the University of California, Irvine. He has published over 1,000 articles and is author or editor of 50 books. He is a member of the US National Academy of Sciences and the American Philosophical Society. In 2001 he received the US National Medal of Science and in 2010 the Templeton Prize. The *New York Times* named him "Renaissance Man of Evolutionary Biology."

Whitney A. Bauman is an associate professor of religious studies at Florida International University, Miami. He is the author of *Religion and Ecology: Developing a Planetary Ethic* (2014) and *Theology, Creation and Environmental Ethics* (2009), and editor of *Grounding Religion: A Field Guide to the Study of Religion and Ecology* (with Kevin J. O'Brien and Richard Bohannon, 2011) and *Science and Religion: One Planet Many Possibilities* (2014). He was a Fulbright Fellow in Indonesia (2014: "Religion and Globalization") and a Humboldt Fellow in Germany (2015–16: "The Religious Underpinnings of Ernst Haeckel's Understanding of Nature").

Christopher Key Chapple, Doshi Professor of Indic and Comparative Theology and Director of the MA in Yoga Studies at Loyola Marymount University, Los Angeles, has published more than 20 books, including *Yoga and Ecology* (2008), *Jainism and Ecology* (2000), and *Nonviolence to Animals, Earth, and Self in Asian Traditions* (1993). He serves on several advisory boards, including the Forum on Religion and Ecology (Yale University) and the Jain Studies Centre (London), and edits the journal *Worldviews.*

John Chryssavgis, Archdeacon of the Ecumenical Patriarchate, is special theological advisor to the Office of Ecumenical and Inter-Faith Affairs of the Greek Orthodox Archdiocese of America, coordinates the Social and Moral Issues Commission of the Orthodox Churches in America, and serves as ecological advisor to Ecumenical Patriarch Bartholomew I. His books include *Light Through Darkness: the Orthodox Tradition* (2004) and *Beyond the Shattered Image: Insights into an Orthodox Christian Ecological Worldview* (1999); he is editor of *On Earth as in Heaven* (2011) on Patriarch Bartholomew's ecological vision and activities and, with Pope Francis, of *Bartholomew: Apostle and Visionary* (2016).

John B. Cobb, Jr. was born in Japan of Methodist missionary parents from Georgia. He earned a PhD from the Divinity School of the University of Chicago. Most of his teaching career was at Claremont School of Theology, California where, with David Griffin, he founded the Center for Process Studies. Among his books are *Christ in a Pluralistic Age* (with Charles Birch, 1999), *The Liberation of Life* (1982), and *For the Common Good* (with Herman Daly, 1994).

Heather Eaton is Full Professor of Conflict Studies, Saint Paul University, Ottawa. Her doctoral studies at the University of Toronto integrated ecology, feminism, theology, and religious pluralism. Heather's publications include *The Intellectual Journey of Thomas Berry* (2014), *Ecological Awareness: Exploring Religion, Ethics and Aesthetics* (with Sigurd Bergmann, 2011), *Introducing Ecofeminist Theologies* (2005), *Ecofeminism and Globalization* (with Lois Ann Lorentzen, 2003), and numerous articles. Her most recent work covers religious imagination, evolution, Earth dynamics; peace and conflict studies on gender, ecology, and religion.

Dianne D. Glave is on the staff of the Western Pennsylvania United Methodist Conference Center as coordinator of diversity development. She completed her MDiv degree at the Candler School of Theology, Emory University, Druid Hills, Atlanta. She has served at two churches in Pittsburgh. Dianne's doctorate in history emphasized African-American and environmental history, and experience as a professor informs her current position. Her publications include *Rooted in the Earth: Reclaiming the African American Environmental Heritage* (2010).

Tom B. K. Goldtooth, Diné Nation, is executive director of the Indigenous Environmental Network (IEN). He has been a social activist for almost 40 years promoting, in his speeches, writing, and nonviolent protest, justice for indigenous peoples and the wellbeing of Mother Earth and all life. He is a member of the International Indigenous Peoples' Forum on Climate Change and the Steering Committee of Climate Justice Alliance. He was awarded the Gandhi Peace Award in 2015, and in 2010 was selected as the Sierra Club and NAACP "Green Hero of Color."

Roger S. Gottlieb is a professor of philosophy at Worcester Polytechnic Institute, Massachusetts, and the author or editor of 18 books and over 125 articles on environmentalism, political philosophy, spirituality, the Holocaust, and disability. Among his recent works are the Nautilus Book Award winners *Spirituality: What it Is and Why it Matters* (2012), *Engaging Voices: Tales of Morality and Meaning in an Age of Global Warming* (2011), and *Political and Spiritual: Essays on Religion, Environment, Disability and Justice* (2014).

Allison Gray is a doctoral student at the University of Windsor, Ontario pursuing a range of interests in the areas of social justice, criminology, and food studies. She is currently working on projects involving the experiences of contemporary food activists in a consumerist culture, exploring the connections between population demographics and the use of Canada's Food Guide, and the governance of children's brown-bag school lunches in Ontario.

Tallessyn Zawn Grenfell-Lee was awarded a doctorate from Boston University School of Theology; her MS in biology from Harvard University, and BS in biology from the Massachusetts Inistitute of Technology. She contributed a chapter on Creation empathy and Christian mission to *Ecology and Mission* (2015), and has published articles in the *Journal of Faith and Science Exchange* and *James Nash: A Tribute: Environmental Ethics, Ecumenical Engagement, Public Theology* (2010); and in the scientific journals *PNAS*, *Molecular and Cellular Biology*, and *Neuron*.

John Grim teaches religion and ecology at Yale University. With Mary Evelyn Tucker he directs the Yale Forum on Religion and Ecology, which arose from a series of ten conferences they organized at Harvard University and ten edited volumes. John specializes in Native American religions. He is the author of *The Shaman* (1988) and editor of *Indigenous Traditions and Ecology* (2001). With Mary Evelyn he edited *Worldviews and Ecology* (1994), *Ecology and Religion* (2014), and Thomas Berry's essays, *The Christian Future and the Fate of Earth* (1994). John is president of the American Teilhard Association, with Mary Evelyn as vice president.

Melanie L. Harris is an associate professor of religion and ethics at Texas Christian University, Fort Worth. She teaches environmental ethics, womanist ethics, African-American religion, and Africana studies. She is the author of *Gifts of Virtue, Alice Walker and Womanist Ethics* (2013). She is editor of *Faith, Feminism and Scholarship*. (with K. Ott, 2011). Melanie serves on the board of KERA-TV; her academic leadership positions include member advocate, American Academy of Religion; and board member, Society of Christian Ethics.

John Hart is Professor of Christian Ethics, Boston University School of Theology. His books include *Cosmic Commons: Spirit, Science, and Space* (2013), *Sacramental Commons: Christian Ecological Ethics* (2006), *What Are They Saying About ... Environmental Theology?* (2004), *Ethics and Technology: Innovation and Transformation in Community Contexts* (1997), and *The Spirit of the Earth—A Theology of the Land* (1984). He has written more than 100 articles, essays, and book chapters, and presented invited lectures on socioecological ethics on five continents, in eight countries, and 35 US states.

John F. Haught is Distinguished Research Professor, Theology Department, Georgetown University, Washington, DC, where he was formerly a professor and Chair. His area of specialization is systematic theology, with a particular interest in issues pertaining to science, cosmology, evolution, and ecology and religion. He has authored 20 books, most on topics in science and religion, including *Science and Faith: A New Introduction* (2013) and *Making Sense of Evolution: Darwin, God, and the Drama of Life* (2010), as well as numerous articles and reviews. He lectures internationally on issues related to science, ecology, and religion.

Kapya John Kaoma is a visiting researcher at Boston University's Center for Global Christianity and Mission, and Adjunct Professor, St. John's Anglican University College, Zambia. He holds degrees from Evangelical University College, Zambia; Trinity College, England; the Episcopal Divinity School; and Boston University, Massachusetts. He is author of *The Creator's Symphony: African Christianity* (2015), *Raised Hopes, Shattered Dreams* (2015), *God's Family, God's Earth* (2013), and numerous peer-reviewed articles and book chapters, and is editor of *Creation Care in Christian Mission* (2015).

Fazlun M. Khalid is the founding director of the Islamic Foundation for Ecology and Environmental Sciences (IFEES/EcoIslam). He was named one of 15 leading eco-theologians in the world (*Grist* magazine, July 24, 2007) and listed among the "500 Most Influential Muslims in the World" by the Royal Islamic Strategic Studies Centre of Jordan. He received the 2004 award for Excellence in Engineering, Science and Technology by the London-based *Muslim News* for developing a scientific approach to Islamic environmental practice.

Heup Young Kim is Professor of Theology, Kangnam University, Yongin, South Korea. He was a moderator of the Congress of Asian Theologians, president of the Korean Society for Systematic Theology, and a founding member of the International Society for Science and Religion. He has published numerous works in the areas of East Asian theology, interreligious dialogue, and religion and science, including *Christ and the Tao* (2010) and *Wang Yang-ming and Karl Barth: A Confucian–Christian Dialogue* (1996).

Robin Wall Kimmerer is SUNY Distinguished Teaching Professor of Environmental and Forest Biology at the SUNY College of Environmental Science and Forestry in Syracuse, New York, and founding director of the Center for Native Peoples and the Environment. She is an enrolled member of the Citizen Potawatomi, a mother, scientist, and writer. Her publications include *Braiding Sweetgrass: Indigenous Wisdom, Scientific Knowledge, and the Teachings of Plants* (2015) and *Gathering Moss: A Natural and Cultural History of Mosses* (2003).

Winona LaDuke is executive director of Honor the Earth, and an Anishinaabe from Round Lake, White Earth reservation, Minnesota. She received her BA in native economic development, Harvard University in 1981, participated in the Community Fellows program, MIT, 1982, and earned her MA in rural development at Antioch University, Yellow Springs, Ohio, in 1986. She received the Thomas Merton Award

(1996), the Ann Bancroft Award for Women's Leadership Fellowship, and was named the *Ms.* magazine Woman of the Year in 1998. She is author of *Recovering the Sacred: The Power of Naming and Claiming* (2016) and *All Our Relations: Native Struggles for Land and Life* (2016).

Bill McKibben, author and environmentalist, founded 350.org to combat global heating; it has organized 20,000 climate-related events around the world. He is the Schumann Distinguished Scholar in Environmental Studies at Middlebury College,Vermont, a fellow of the American Academy of Arts and Sciences, and has been awarded the Right Livelihood Prize (2014), the Gandhi Prize (2013), and the Thomas Merton Prize (2013). He has written numerous books, including *Deep Economy: The Wealth of Communities and the Durable Future* (2008) and *The End of Nature* (2006), and articles for *The New Yorker, New York Review of Books, National Geographic,* and *Rolling Stone.*

Ian S. Mevorach holds a BA in philosophy from Middlebury College, Vermont, and an MDiv and PhD in theological ethics and constructive theology from Boston University, Massachusetts. He represents the American Baptist Churches USA on the board of Creation Justice Ministries, which is affiliated with the National Council of Churches. He authored "Stewards of Creation: A Christian Calling for Today's Ecological Crisis," *For Such a Time as This: Young Adults on the Future of the Church* (2014).

Cynthia Moe-Lobeda is Professor of Theological and Social Ethics at Pacific Lutheran Theological Seminary and the Graduate Theological Union, Berkeley, California. She is author or co-author of five books, most recently *Resisting Structural Evil: Love as Ecological–Economic Vocation*, and numerous articles and chapters. Her research focuses on climate justice related to race and class, moral agency, hope, public church, faith-based resistance to systemic injustice, economic globalization, and the ethical implications of resurrection and incarnation.

Seyyed Hossein Nasr, world-renowned scholar on Islam, is University Professor of Islamic Studies at George Washington University, Washington, DC. He earned his undergraduate degree in physics and mathematics from Massachusetts Institute of Technology, and studied geology and geophysics at Harvard University, where he earned his PhD in the history of science and philosophy. He has published over 50 books and hundreds of articles in numerous languages and translations, and is editor-in-chief of *The Study Quran* (2015).

Michael S. Northcott is Professor of Ethics in the School of Divinity, University of Edinburgh, an episcopal priest, and a keen gardener. His books and papers are principally in the interdisciplinary area of ecology, religion, and ethics. His most recent books include *Place, Ecology and the Sacred: The Moral Geography of Sustainable Communities* (2015), *A Political Theology of Climate Change* (2013), and *A Moral Climate: The Ethics of Global Warming* (2007). He is editor of *Systematic Theology and Climate Change: Ecumenical Perspectives* (with Peter Scott, 2014).

Kōō Okada, spiritual leader of Sukyo Mahikari, graduated from Kokugakuin University, Tokyo in 1970 with a major in Shinto archeology. After graduating, he joined the staff of Sukyo Mahikari, while also commencing his formal training in the art of calligraphy under his late father, Yuhkei Teshima, a renowned master calligrapher and designated Person of Cultural Merit by the Japanese government. He is now, under his pen name, Tairiku Teshima, an internationally renowned calligrapher. In 2015, Kōō was appointed by the Agency of Cultural Affairs (Japanese government) as a member of the Religious Juridical Persons Council.

Naomi Oreskes is Professor of the History of Science and Affiliated Professor of Earth and Planetary Sciences at Harvard University. Her research focuses on the Earth and environmental sciences, with a particular interest in understanding scientific consensus and dissent. Previously she was Professor of History and Science Studies at the University of California, San Diego, and Adjunct Professor of Geosciences at the Scripps Institution of Oceanography. She is the author of *Merchants of Doubt: How a Handful of Scientists Obscured the Truth on Issues from Tobacco Smoke to Global Warming* (with Erik M. Conway, 2011), and a novel, *The Collapse of Western Civilization: A View from the Future* (2014).

Yongbum Park is an assistant professor of Christian ethics at Honam Theological University and Seminary, Gwangju, South Korea, and concurrently serves as a youth group pastor in Gwangju Bethel Presbyterian Church. He studied philosophy, theology, and ethics in the Master of Sacred Theology program, and theological ethics in the PhD program, at Boston University, Massachusetts. He focuses on the areas of ecological ethics in multicultural contexts, and envisions the construction of a socioecological community in a local area.

Larry L. Rasmussen is Reinhold Niebuhr Professor Emeritus of Social Ethics, Union Theological Seminary, New York City. His books include *Earth-Honoring Faith: Religious Ethics in a New Key* (2013), which received the Nautilus Book Award as the Gold Prize winner for Ecology/Environment and as the Grand Prize winner for best 2014 book overall, and *Earth Community Earth Ethics* (1996), which won the prestigious Grawemeyer Award in Religion in 1997.

David Mevorach Seidenberg teaches ecology and Judaism throughout North America and internationally. He is the author of *Kabbalah and Ecology: God's Image in the More-Than-Human World* (2015), and created and directs neohasid.org, which disseminates eco-Torah, liturgy, and Hasidic nigunim (religious songs). He was ordained by the Jewish Theological Seminary (doctorate in Jewish thought) and by Rabbi Zalman Schachter-Shalomi. His research interests include midrash (interpretation or commentary on Hebrew scripture) and the Talmud, Nachman of Breslov, Martin Buber, and the theurgy of dance.

Myrna Perez Sheldon, historian of evolutionary theory, holds a joint appointment as an assistant professor of gender and American religion in the Department of Classics and World Religions, and the Women's, Gender and Sexuality Studies Program, at Ohio University, Athens, Ohio. She received her PhD in the history of science from Harvard University and was a postdoctoral fellow at the Center for the Study of Women, Gender and Sexuality Studies at William Marsh Rice University, Houston, Texas.

Vandana Shiva, quantum physicist, environmental activist, and social justice proponent, has promoted awareness of the adverse impacts of climate change, seed patents, and globalization. Her master's degree is from Guelph University (1976), and her doctorate from the University of Western Ontario (1978). She founded the Research Foundation for Science, Technology, and Ecology, and received the Right Livelihood Award in 1993. Her books include *Globalization's New Wars: Seed, Water, and Life Forms* (2005) and *Earth Democracy: Justice, Sustainability, and Peace* (2005).

Elizabeth Theokritoff is an independent scholar, freelance theological translator, and occasional lecturer at the Institute for Orthodox Christian Studies, Cambridge (England). She is editor of *The Cambridge Companion to Orthodox Christian Theology* (with Mary B. Cunningham, 2008), and author of *Living in God's Creation: Orthodox Perspectives on Ecology* (2009), as well as numerous articles.

Hava Tirosh-Samuelson is Irving and Miriam Lowe Professor of Modern Judaism at Arizona State University, Phoenix. She is the author of *Happiness in Premodern Judaism: Virtue, Knowledge and Well-Being* (2003), *Between Worlds: The Life and Work of Rabbi David ben Judah Messer Leon* (1991), and numerous essays. She edited *Judaism and Ecology: Created World and Revealed World* (2002), six collections of essays, and the Library of Contemporary Jewish Philosophers.

Rabbi Zalman Schachter-Shalomi, a founder of the Jewish Renewal Movement, was its much-beloved spiritual guide. His roots were in the Chabad-Lubavitch tradition, an offshoot of Hasidism. He welcomed insights from all religious and spiritual traditions; promoted women's equality in Judaism, social justice, and environmental wellbeing. He earned an MA degree in the psychology of religion at Boston University and a doctorate in theology at Hebrew Union College-Jewish Institute of Religion. His books include *A Heart Afire* and *From Age-Ing to Sage-Ing.*

Mary Evelyn Tucker with John Grim, teaches religion and ecology at Yale University, and directs the Yale Forum on Religion and Ecology. Mary Evelyn specializes in Confucianism, is the author of *Worldly Wonder: Religions Enter Their Ecological Phase* (2003) and *Moral and Spiritual Cultivation in Japanese Neo-Confucianism* (1989), and is translator of *The Philosophy of Qi* (2007). With Brian Swimme, she wrote *Journey of the Universe* (book and film, 2014). She edited Thomas Berry's books, *The Great Work, Evening Thoughts,* and *The Sacred Universe.*

Arthur Waskow is a rabbi and founder director of The Shalom Center, focused on peace and ecojustice for the Earth, humanity, and all living beings. His books include *Seasons of Our Joy* (rev. ed., 2012), and *Freedom Journeys: The Tale of Exodus and Wilderness Across Millennia* (with Rabbi Phyllis Berman, 2011). His latest arrest was during interfaith climate action at the White House before Passover and Palm Sunday, 2013.

Foreword

His All-Holiness Ecumenical Patriarch Bartholomew

In its foremost and traditional symbol of faith, the Christian Church confesses "one God, maker of heaven and earth, and of all things visible and invisible" (Nicene-Constantinopolitan Creed). If the Earth is created by a loving God, then it is sacred; and if Creation is sacred, then our relationship with the world is sacramental.

From this fundamental principle of the sacredness and sacramentality of all Creation, the Orthodox Church articulates its vital concept of cosmic transfiguration, which is especially evident in its liturgical expressions and spiritual classics. The breadth and depth of cosmic vision implies a humanity that is a part of this transfiguration; at the same time, this worldview is greater than any one individual. Indeed, Orthodox theology takes a further step in recognizing that Creation is inseparable from the destiny of humanity, inasmuch as every human action leaves a lasting imprint on the body of the Earth. Moreover, human attitudes and behavior toward Creation directly impact on and reflect human attitudes and behavior toward other people, toward our brothers and sisters.

In this respect, it is clear that only a cooperative and collective response—by religious and civil leaders, theologians and scientists in dialogue, as well as political authorities and financial corporations—can appropriately and effectively address the challenging issues of climate change in our time. For this reason, on September 1, 1989, Ecumenical Patriarch Dimitrios issued an encyclical to all Orthodox churches throughout the world, establishing that day, being the first day of the ecclesiastical year, as a day of prayer for the protection and preservation of the natural environment. This dedication was later embraced by the European Council of Churches and, in turn, the World Council of Churches; more recently, Pope Francis formally adopted it for the Roman Catholic Church worldwide, and Archbishop Justin Welby followed suit for the Church of England. Over the past 25 years, we have endeavored to maintain the same sense of urgency with regard to environmental concerns in order to raise popular awareness and render international consciousness more sensitive to the irreversible destruction that threatens our planet today. One lesson that we have learned and repeatedly emphasized over the past decades is the realization that we are all faced with the same predicament: we are all in the same boat! The truth is that none of us—no individual or institution, no segment of society or field of discipline, no religion or race, neither East nor West—can either be blamed or burdened to solve this problem. We must all—together, in partnership and collaboration and communion—humbly accept our responsibility for exploiting and destroying natural resources, while at the same time embracing our vocation to "serve and preserve" (Gen. 2: 15) God's gift of Creation.

Therefore, it has been encouraging to witness the same conviction and commitment expressed by a diverse group of individuals and wide range of institutions on the relationship between religion and ecology, as well as on the responsibility of religious thought and practice in ecological awareness and action. In this regard, we were deeply moved by the clear and compassionate message conveyed by our beloved brother Pope Francis, with the publication of his encyclical *Laudato Si*. Similarly, the present anthology of contributions by distinguished scholars of religion and ethics brings together many voices from seemingly divergent fields and contexts, albeit all of them converging on the same teaching and truth —namely, that it is only when we work together for the common good that we can bring about change for a caring world.

"Common commons" is the title of one of the concluding chapters in this volume, composed by its editor, John Hart. It is precisely the approach that we must assume if we are to envisage and expect "a new heaven and a new earth."

Preface

People around the Earth have an ever-greater understanding of the interconnectedness, interdependence, and interrelationships among the diverse species that comprise the biotic community, the community of all living beings in the web of life. They understand better, too, how the biotic community—as species and individuals—lives in relation to the Earth, its shared home. Humankind, even without expressing these relationships as ecological, has come to recognize how important local and global ecologies are for conserving, in a sometimes delicate balance, life on Earth.

Accomplished German scientist Ernst Heinrich Philipp August Haeckel (1834–1919) coined the term "oecology" in 1866. The term comes from two Greek words: *oikos* ("house") and *logos* ("science"). Ecology is the scientific study of the Earth's household. The science of ecology is about relationships—among biota, and between biota and their environment, the place in which they live.

Faith Traditions and Ecology

People globally in the twenty-first century who are members of a specific faith tradition, whether theists (who believe in a meta-material Being who—or that—is distinct from the material, physical world), or atheists (who believe that there is no meta-material Being), are exploring their respective traditions to find teachings or doctrines about human relations with and responsibilities toward the Earth and its biota. Theists, for example, might discover or rediscover religio-ecological instructions that originated millennia or generations ago; or they might formulate or reformulate religio-ecological understandings that originated not in ages past but in the past century (or decade). Believers, then, are becoming conscious or more conscious of the relationship between beliefs and moral norms that seemingly transcend origins in or interactions with the world. Perceptive believers recognize and acknowledge that there is no abrupt break between material and meta-material realities: the latter emerge on Earth in specific times and places. The meta-material is formed in part by the physical setting of its origin: if only in the believers' faith, of giving verbal expression to a spiritual experience in which a transcendent or transcendent-immanent Spirit provides, through words heard or visions seen, teachings about spiritual matters or conduct in community on Earth. People's faith expresses insights received through and for what they consider to be their religion or their spiritual way, which they describe often as their "spirituality."

The Wiley-Blackwell Companion to Religion and Ecology, in its title but not its intent, gathers all these belief systems under the umbrella of religion. Volumes of elaboration would be needed to discuss the nature and function of "religion," more appropriately called "religions" since they have different understandings of God, Allah, Yahweh, Wakantanka (Lakota), Masau'u (Hopi), and "spirituality" because of their respective origins from, and later historical development within, diverse social, cultural, and geographic locales. In the title and text of the *Companion*, therefore, the term "religion" should be understood to refer generically to any kind of body of belief, structured or unstructured, institutionally organized or not, that provides a foundation for individuals' and social groups' spiritual or Spirit-derived or Spirit-oriented way of life.

Religions across the world have diverse understandings of a transcendent sacred Presence. It might be a conscious, independent divine Spirit or a present energy; identified with the world or the cosmos, or developing with the world or cosmos; a companion Being solicitous of other beings, or an observer of what transpires with them—alone or when engaged with others—and sometimes or never intervening; an immanent existence-permeating Spirit, a transcendent Spirit, or an immanent-transcendent Spirit. Other possibilities, beyond number, exist among peoples of Earth.

Creation Stories and Inspiration

Religions that have Creation stories provide distinctive narratives about how the Earth and cosmos came into being. People within a particular faith tradition often think that theirs is the only story about the origins of existence, or that it is the only "true" account of how this transpired. People open to stories from traditions other than their own come to understand that all such stories are narratives from a particular cultural understanding in a particular geographical place at a particular time in human history. This knowledge enables each and all to have an ecumenical appreciation of the richness of the heritage of distinct traditions that seek to understand, in their own way and to the extent possible in their time and place, the origins of all that is.

Two decades ago students' reactions to my presentation of Creation stories from diverse traditions around the world was particularly instructive. I was teaching an undergraduate course on the Hebrew scriptures at a Catholic college. I decided to discuss Creation stories complementary to but decidedly distinct from the Genesis Creation stories. Many of the students were amazed: they had believed that the Genesis biblical story (actually, two complementary stories that originated in different historical eras and cultural periods) was the only Creation story, and that it was literal truth, provided to the ancient Hebrews by divine inspiration, having been directly dictated by God to a revered leader. They came to learn and then appreciate, over time, that religion- or spirituality-based Creation stories were told in diverse cultural and historical contexts.

Each story was distinct, since it originated from a specific culture, but every story first emerged from sincere people seeking cosmic truth: to understand and express, from the knowledge and beliefs of a particular time and place, the creative work of a transcendent Being or Beings, understood in diverse ways.

The storytellers (originally speaking, later writing) shared a common purpose: to narrate for a particular people, in their own language (and therefore culturally conditioned, since language conveys and is limited by the culture in which it emerges and evolves) speculation about origins: their own, their world's, and the vast cosmos seen at night. In order for the insights revealed in Creation (and other) sacred stories from diverse traditions to be understood and appreciated by people in later eras, biblical (and other) religious inspiration cannot be understood as or believed to be divine dictation, or express scientific understandings, or relate historically accurate events. On the contrary, both science and history continue to be enriched, enhanced, and enabled to be more accurate over time, as new data are found. The Bible and other sacred texts are not science or history books; they are expositions of religions' or spiritual traditions' beliefs and values; they originate and develop when culturally distinct people ponder and interact with the world and wonder about the mysteries of the distant stars. In the earliest science available, for example, where visual observation provided most information that served as a foundation for exposition, the Sun was thought to orbit the Earth, while stars and other "heavenly bodies" were thought by some to be lights in the solid vault of the sky, the heavens, that followed certain tracks around this material "ceiling" for the Earth, and kept cosmic waters above separate from Earth water below; everything visible in the sky was believed to circle the Earth, which was perceived to be the center of the universe around which all revolved—until Copernicus and Galileo proved otherwise with their mathematical calculations and optical telescopes.

If inspiration is not dictation in sacred stories, what is it? Inspiration might be defined or described in this way: "Inspiration is a religious insight, given to an historical person, for people of their era (a particular time and place with its culture, language, and religious/spiritual beliefs) to understand, and for future generations to discern." This inspiration might be revealed in direct or symbolic language to the revered person, but in either case it can only be conveyed to the community in their own language, using a seer's setting, their local environment's natural phenomena—rocks, mountains, trees, desert, animals, rivers, and so on—historical events (present or past), and religious beliefs. Its original meaning might best be understood in that place and time. It might carry over, in whole or in part, to future generations living in a variety of places and historical moments, and perhaps having their own religious traditions and stories (some biblical stories, for example, are based on older Babylonian myths).

Dissemination of Faith Traditions

In contemporary social contexts, faith-based thinkers, whether theists who believe in a divine Being or transcendent Being, or atheists who believe that there is no divine or transcendent Being, are enabled to present their beliefs and ideas globally via emails or social media. This is a benefit of our communications-laden and influenced era, since religious beliefs, speculative thinking, and teachings can be globally and thoughtfully engaged with and considered. Sometimes, however, it seems that no opinion, however well- or ill-founded, goes unexpressed. "Everyone is entitled to their opinion" is fine, but when opinion becomes "fact" that transition can be problematic. The ideas and beliefs of religions, which are founded in faith and reason culturally expressed, are particularly vulnerable in such a communication milieu when aspects or segments of their broader array of religious thought are derided, without reference to historical context or mode of elaboration.

In recent decades this has been the case with regard to religions' teachings on social justice and ecological responsibility. When people are challenged by these teachings they can reflect deliberatively on their own consciousness and conduct vis-à-vis particular teachings, or they can dismiss them outright, especially but not exclusively in individualism-based, consumption-oriented, religious psychological wellbeing and security, and economic comfort-seeking nations and communities.

Resistance to Religions' Ecological Teachings

Earth is in an ever-growing ecological crisis. When leaders or believers in specific faith traditions call for humans to accept responsibility for what they have been doing to the air, soil, and water in the name of "growth" and "progress," and their supposed individual "right" to consume the Earth's natural goods at an alarming rate, despite how this impacts people, the planet, and all biota today and intergenerationally, their teachings are dismissed as just opinions, no matter the state of the Earth and no matter that science provides evidence of global and regional ecological deterioration. Such irresponsibility might well relegate their progeny and their planet to an undesirable state. The global warming deniers (including energy corporations determined to keep burning fossil fuels, prioritizing profits over people, and the politicians and scientists whom they fund) have succeeded, through supposed "science" research, propaganda, and press releases in an organized disinformation campaign, to manipulate people's thinking and continue "business as usual" for the most part. However, calls to conversion from consumption to conservation have increasingly met with some success. Climate heating, for example, has been assessed by groups as diverse as the World Council of Churches, the Islamic Foundation for Ecology and Environmental Sciences, the National Association of Evangelicals, the Coalition on Environment and Jewish Life, and the Vatican. Faith traditions are complemented by the Union of Concerned Scientists, United Nations agencies, the US National Oceanic and Atmospheric Administration, and Nobel Peace Laureate, science-based Intergovernmental Panel on Climate Change. As with the prophets of ancient Israel, religious thinkers' and leaders' voices may be ignored or rejected by many people, but are heard by some; a critical mass is developing that could catalyze change. In this *Companion*, the voices of people from diverse religious and spiritual traditions from around the world call on their co-believers and others, and the public at large, to see what is transpiring as a consequence of human acts harmful to the Earth and all life, and to strive to transform human consciousness, culture, and conduct such that people care for their common home. Current global warming is a particular event that calls for a response and action, since every year is hotter than its predecessor, and species are being extincted by humankind at an alarming rate. (Several contributors in this volume address climate change directly or indirectly.)

Space Limitations on Religions' Consideration

In *The Wiley-Blackwell Companion to Religion and Ecology* a diversity of religions and spiritual understandings is represented by culturally distinct thinkers. Space limitations restricted the extent to which a single religion, let alone all religions, could be represented. In order for readers to have a deeper understanding of insights from a particular religion, when possible several authors from multiple cultures and generations have contributed to the volume. Scores of other potential authors were invited to submit a chapter but reluctantly declined and expressed their regret about not being able to do so because of particular current writing projects to which they were committed (often by contract), or by personal or professional obligations and constraints.

Religions or spiritual ways represented here include Buddhism, Hinduism, Islam, Judaism, Eastern Christianity, Western Christianity (Catholic and Protestant), indigenous peoples, and Shintoism. All authors were invited to approach an ecological issue from within the perspective of their tradition, particularly by exploring a new insight or a new approach to an existing teaching. All chapters are original, whether authors are familiar names in or newly arrived on the religion–ecology scene, or senior or early-career scholars. Some authors' professional lives are principally involved with academic institutions and scholarship, while others are primarily community-engaged; all have insights that address religion–ecology constructively.

An especially gratifying experience for me as editor was to renew contact with several old friends and acquaintances when I asked them to contribute a chapter. I was particularly moved when I reconnected with Rabbi Zalman Schachter-Shalomi, whom I had last seen in 1992 at the Earth Summit in Rio after he spoke and led prayer at the dusk-to-dawn all-religions service. Previously, he had accepted my invitation to speak at a conference, "Religion in the 21st Century," which I had organized in 1987 for Carroll College, Helena, Montana. I had his email address from our conversations in years past, and wrote to him. I knew he was approaching 90 years of age, but I decided that it would be good to communicate with him again, whether or not he contributed a chapter. After a brief exchange of emails, he suggested that we Skype, and so we did. He sent me an article he had written a decade before and suggested that I find someone in the Jewish tradition to revise it. When I read it, I knew that we had complementary and at times identical spiritual–social understandings. I spent six hours making revisions to update his paper, as I thought about how he might develop further ideas he had elaborated. I sent the revised paper to him; he liked it a great deal and suggested that we continue working together. We had warm and wonderful conversations. He said at one point that he had not thought that he might make contact with friends after many years' separation and how good that would be, and so he was happy when I contacted him. After I declined to be listed as co-author, he decided that the paper should be published as a conversation between us. And so it is. One week after he sent final revisions, he passed on to another dimension of reality. He remains very much a part of me.

Environment, Ecology, and Economics

The words environment and ecology are sometimes used interchangeably. They do, however, have distinct meanings. Environment is a place, a discrete context for abiota and biota. When places are contiguous, they might be viewed as particular regions within the Earth's place: an ecosystem or a watershed, for example. Ecology is the relationships in a place: Earth–biota, biota–biota, humankind–other biota, as elaborated earlier. So, ecology studies the relationships that exist in a particular environment, a particular earth-place on Earth. Environments change, due to external and internal factors (earthquakes, floods, fires; human-caused private property divisions, river diversions, forest clearcuts, and climate changes). Ecologies similarly change (species extinction through biological evolution, human extinction of species, invasive species disrupting relationships, species with a swelling population, or a new migration competing with other migrating species or native species for equally desired or needed available natural goods).

The ecological cannot be separated from the economic or, for many thinkers, from the spiritual. In an issue such as global climate change, for example, many religions' representatives have criticized, from a base in their specific tradition, what is happening to the Earth and people, especially the most vulnerable populations. Many have responded to the Earth's heating by demanding a change in perspective and doctrine(s); a new reading or a new understanding of ancient texts, as they are or as they might come to be used to address issues which did not exist when they originated and developed; and possible concrete actions in a place or places, based on their tradition, to confront injustices to the Earth, people, and the extended community of all life.

Philosophical Ethics and Ethics-in-Context

In a related volume, *The Blackwell Companion to Religious Ethics*, editor William Schweiker has assembled an impressive collection of chapters by notable scholars. That book complements well this volume. It explores a diverse array of more traditional philosophical and theological ethical systems as its authors probe the meanings of moral inquiry, moral traditions, and moral issues. It elaborates diverse ethical systems' various approaches to ethics and society, and their distinct philosophical bases. In this text, the ethical focus is on consideration of the interrelated areas of social justice and ecological wellbeing. As most of the writers point out, these areas cannot be disentangled. The integration of the social and the ecological cannot be done well or exclusively by transcendent thinking, or solely abstract thought and theory, as if the thinkers were disembodied, angel-like beings; it must be deeply related to contexts immersed in and related to the places where and the times in which it is pondered and developed. Even the tallest ivory tower has its foundation deep in the clay and rocks of the Earth, and the knowledge acquired within its walls is related to its physical environs, the society in which it is constructed, and the communities of scholars and individual scholars with whose ideas it is in discussion or debate. Socioecological ethics is not contextual (moral principles are solely place-originated, not universal norms), deontological (focused on normative rules, principles-based), or teleological (moral principles focused on a desired end, consequentialist). Socioecological ethics is ethics-in-context: theorized in and from places, offered for discussion in society, and, even while written with the hope that its principles will be acceptable and incorporated in diverse places, open to be continually evolving, at least in part, as new events or newly engaged people challenge its assumptions, principles, and proposals in diverse settings.

A thread running throughout the *Companion*, then, is socioecological praxis ethics: justice within and among human communities integrated with the wellbeing of the Earth and all biota. Ecological ethics is, by definition, about principled relationships. These include the relationship between thinkers and the particular social context of their thought. Principles cannot ordinarily be considered "universal" or "absolute," since they might have to be adapted to context in different cultures or include insights from them. There are non-negotiable, core, essential principles that are thought to be operative in all places, and adaptable secondary principles. The distinctions are evident in several of the chapters in this *Companion* when contributors, even when not discussing ethics, express diverse views on ethical aspects of ecology. They provide glimpses of socioecological praxis ethics, since they consider their religious or humanist tradition and sociocultural settings when presenting possibilities for principles of right conduct—ethics— obliquely at times.

The Contributors'Approaches to Religion and Ecology

The *Companion* is divided into four parts. I: Religions and Ecological Consciousness presents perspectives from nine traditions: Islam, Hinduism, Judaism, Catholicism, Shintoism, Anishnaabe, womanist Christianity, Buddhism, and Daoism. II: Care for the Earth and Life places religions' teachings in conversation with real-life, distinct socio-ecological contexts. III: Ecological Commitment contextualizes religion–ecological teachings in particular settings, at times in dialogue with each other. IV: Visions for the Present and Future Earth considers ways in which religion/ecology-inspired dreams and concrete projects "on the ground" might transform human consciousness and conduct and catalyze a restored, renewed, and conserved Earth milieu. This would benefit the planet, people, and the integrated, interdependent, and interrelated biotic community. The themes of the various parts are not exhaustive or exclusive categories. Several chapters would fit into multiple parts; retaining some balance of the number of chapters in each part meant a chapter that might be seen to have been a good fit in one part is situated in another. All four parts are, however, interrelated.

The Contributors' Insights

The summary presentation that follows provides a hint of what is to come. It cites parts of individual contributors' views on current teachings on ecology from their tradition, or creatively proposes for their tradition new teachings or adaptation of traditional teachings to new settings.

Foreword: Orthodox theology recognizes that "Creation is inseparable from the destiny of humanity, inasmuch as every human action leaves a lasting imprint on the body of the Earth. Moreover, human attitudes and behavior toward Creation directly impact and reflect human attitudes and behavior toward our brothers and sisters." Patriarch Bartholomew I, head of the Orthodox Church

Part I: Religions and Ecological Consciousness

1. "Religion in its universal reality is thus essential for an in-depth revival of ecological consciousness," Seyyed Hossein Nasr
2. "Women and indigenous communities, the excluded of the industrial world, are the real custodians of biodiversity-related knowledge," Vandana Shiva
3. "Maimonides and various Kabbalists envisioned a reality in which the highest moral good transcended human needs and was measured by diversity, abundance, and wholeness in the cosmos itself," David Mevorach Seidenberg
4. Pope Francis' encyclical *Laudato Sí* "integrated human communities' economic wellbeing with the ecological wellbeing of humankind, all biota (living beings), and the Earth, their common home," John Hart
5. "Everything in heaven and on earth is the voice of God. It overflows with the divine principles," Kōō Okada
6. "In the time of Thunderbeings and Underwater Serpents, it was understood that a constant balance with the universe beyond this material world, a universe to whom we would belong always, needed to be maintained," Winona LaDuke
7. In African ecotheology, "as with creation care, Earth and her goods are treated with great respect and solicitude," Dianne D. Glave
8. "By engaging earth, water, fire, air, and space, one cultivates states of connectivity and bliss that result in an abiding sense of wellbeing. This practice is being reconsidered in light of its potential for establishing a foundation for the cultivation of concern and care for the environment," Christopher Key Chapple
9. "If theo-logy is a perspective from above and if theo-praxis is that from below, then theodao is a perspective from an entirely different dimension, theanthropocosmic intersubjectivity," Heup Young Kim

Part II: Care for the Earth and Life

10. "[T]he excesses of a consumer culture: we are trying to squeeze the infinite from what is in fact finite, namely, our own little planet," John F. Haught
11. "We are required to care for and manage the Earth in a way that conforms to God's intention in Creation: it should be used for our benefit without causing damage to the other inhabitants of planet Earth who are communities like ourselves," Fazlun M. Khalid
12. "Science and religion are like two windows for looking at the world. The two windows look at the same world, but they show different aspects of that world," Francisco J. Ayala

13. "[In] Africa, the serpent was and is the most visible symbol of the deities, ancestors, and other spirits. It is this symbol that comes to mind when some Africans hear the word God," Kapya John Kaoma
14. "The most distinctive feature of Jewish environmental ethics is the causal connection between the moral quality of human life and the vitality of God's creation," Hava Tirosh-Samuelson
15. "According to an ecowomanist vision, the values of interconnectedness and interdependence that serve as a new base for shaping ecological reparations emerge by validating African, indigenous, and fourth world cultural perspectives," Melanie L. Harris
16. "Caused overwhelmingly by the world's high-consuming people, climate change is wreaking death and destruction first and foremost on impoverished people who are also, disproportionately, people of color," Cynthia Moe-Lobeda
17. "[Maximus teaches that] All things at their core express divine will and purpose; the unifying web of the *logoi* of things pervades the physical universe no less than the spiritual, intellectual, and moral aspects of human life," Elizabeth Theokritoff

Part III: Ecological Commitment

18. "A new era of deep human impact on the planet—the Anthropocene—renders problematic any notions of justice as intra-human only. Yet since climate change visits its worst on human populations that contribute least to it, social justice is more urgent than ever," Larry L. Rasmussen
19. "The relevance of ecofeminism, and the combination of gender, religion, and ecology, are crucial for the further development of the field of religion and ecology," Heather Eaton
20. "The Orthodox Church retains a 'eucharistic' view of Nature and the environment, proclaiming a world imbued by God and a God involved in the whole world," John Chryssavgis
21. "[P]resent-day humans are consuming and polluting in the first three months of each year what the Earth can sustainably provide without being systematically degraded for future generations. The remaining nine months of consumption would require three planets the size of the Earth to sustain indefinitely," Michael S. Northcott
22. "There is no doubt that an Islamic environmental ethics perspective sees a direct relationship between the maltreatment of women and the degradation of the environment. This relationship is clear in ideas on respecting all God's creatures," Nawal H. Ammar and Allison Gray
23. "Taking the ecological crisis as a starting place opens a new dialogical space for Christians and Muslims. The central epiphany of ecological consciousness—that human beings and all beings are interdependent parts of the same web of life—can serve as its centering theme," Ian Mevorach
24. "Humans discover their earthly place by first rediscovering their own inward cosmic consciousness and inner mysteries of the cosmos itself," Yongbum Park

25. "Natural theology holds that there are in effect two books of revelation, God's word and God's work. The natural world is the second book of God's revelation, to be read and revered alongside the first book, the revelation of scripture," Naomi Oreskes and Myrna Perez Sheldon
26. "We are surrounded by teachers and mentors who come dressed in foliage, fur, and feathers. There is comfort in their presence and guidance in their lessons... Let us hold a giveaway for Mother Earth, spread our blankets out for her and pile them high with gifts of our own making... Gifts of mind, hands, heart, voice, and vision all offered up on behalf of the Earth. Whatever our gift, we are called to give it and to dance for the renewal of the world. In return for berries. In return for birds. In return for the privilege of breath," Robin Wall Kimmerer

Part IV: Visions for the Present and Future Earth

27. "[If] human beings follow the sacred teachings that indeed the Divine is One, then the rivers will run, the rains will fall, the heavens will bless the Earth, and the Earth will be abundantly fruitful in feeding human beings, in making the harvest abundant, and in making the land flourish," Arthur Waskow
28. "Teilhard's and Berry's aim was to evoke the psychic and spiritual resources to establish a reciprocity of humans with the Earth and of humans to one another. They believed that with a comprehensive perspective regarding our place in this extraordinary unfolding of universe and Earth history there would emerge a renewed awareness of our relation to and responsibility in evolutionary processes at this crucial point in history," Mary Evelyn Tucker and John Grim
29. "Permaculture requires an attitude of great humility and respect for the land and all its creatures; it incorporates care of the Earth and care of the people, which includes equitable sharing and distribution of natural goods ('resources') ... [M] inistry works better when we empower the voices of both marginalized communities and marginalized Creation," Tallessyn Zawn Grenfell-Lee
30. "[W]e should eliminate gross economic inequity, gross inequality in sharing the eco-social benefits and ills that result from our ways of becoming ... when we have access to the technologies that would enable us to survive and thrive on renewable and more democratic forms of energy," Whitney A. Bauman
31. "[T]he dimensions and intensity of our global environmental crisis are real, terribly frightening, and in the view of many the most daunting challenge our civilization has ever faced ... one hopeful development of the last three decades is the emergence of a specifically *religious* environmentalism," Roger S. Gottlieb
32. "In a world where we're literally building our own hellfire—where more of the US burned this past hot summer than any year on record—the pope's ethical choices also become physical imperatives. God is no longer larger than we are, which means that we will need to rein ourselves in," Bill McKibben
33. "The modern world cannot achieve economic sustainability without environmental and economic justice and without a strong environmental ethic that recognizes the human relationship and responsibility to protect the sacredness and integrity of Mother Earth... The indigenous worldview perceives that all Creation

is alive and imbued with the intelligence of the Creator ... we are all part of an integrated whole ... where all parts of Creation care for all of the other parts," Tom B. K. Goldtooth

34. "Earth's religions have an important role to play vis-à-vis ecology: to imagine today and actualize toward tomorrow the new Earth that is envisioned in and by a community of communities. Social justice and ecology, the interdependent wellbeing of humankind, and the wellbeing of the Earth and all living beings, are integrally interrelated and intertwined," John Hart
35. "Religion can have a profound impact on ecology in our time and places. People in faith traditions must look to their sacred texts for insights that affirm the divine Spirit's solicitude not only for all humans, but for all living beings and Earth ... and human responsibilities for God's Creation as humans seek to image God with a like solicitude," Zalman Schachter-Shalomi

Afterword: "We have done much to overcome the obstacles to cooperation among the world's great wisdom traditions. Now let us direct our thought and energy to the task for which we have prepared ourselves—working together to ameliorate the now inevitable disasters and constructing an integral ecology to replace our suicidal society," John B. Cobb, Jr.

What is evident in these insights is their complementarity and their seeds of collaborative thought which could carry them to another stage of development: a shared spiritual–socioecological consciousness, and consequent cooperative writing or community projects in selected settings.

The *Companion* in Context

The intent of *The Wiley-Blackwell Companion to Religion and Ecology* is to provide religious and spiritual insights into the most pressing issue of our time: human destruction and consequent continual deterioration of the Earth's places and systems. Such devastation—and, in some places, desertification—continues because relatively wealthier individuals, groups, and nations exploit the Earth, and the poor, waste natural goods, adversely impact the socioeconomic wellbeing of people of all social classes, promote racism and manipulate common people to express racism, legalize sexism in various forms that harm women and those with an alternative sexual orientation, drive species into extinction, and ensure that the global climate becomes hotter every year.

Religions throughout the world have diverse understandings of "Nature." Among them, a living being in whole or in part, a sacred Mother Earth solicitous about and nurturing her children, or the interplay of the Earth, biota, geophysical dynamics, meteorological events, and types of energy. These distinct but, at times, complementary or overlapping understandings are present in several of the chapters of the *Companion*.

The *Companion* is intended, too, to provide an alternative consciousness and conduct: the contributors express this in a variety of ways, with hope and proposals for projects "on the ground" so that these will become the new reality. Finally, the *Companion* is intended to be a stimulus for people around the world, from diverse cultures and religions, to learn about and appreciate insights from traditions not their own, and initiate conservations toward development of common perspectives, principles, and practices that open closed doors to religious, spiritual, and humanist traditions, and promote collaborative thought and action. Efforts made in the present will provide the foundation for a better future world—ecologically and socially—for today's children and their children, and generations to come and all members of the community of life on Mother Earth, our shared home and the common ground of our being.

Acknowledgments

The Wiley-Blackwell Companion to Religion and Ecology would not have been written without the creativity, scholarship, dedication, and community engagement of the 35 distinguished authors whose creative and complementary chapters are the heart of the book. They contributed generously their perceptions and passion, their knowledge and inquisitiveness, and their congeniality and collegiality. All are noted for their professional work in diverse and distinct geographical places around the world. Their original insights and perceptive contributions provide the core of the book's reasoned discussion and analysis of the relationship between religion and ecology; the contributors are the mind, heart, and soul of this volume. I am grateful to His All Holiness Bartholomew I, Ecumenical Patriarch, who is acclaimed as the "Green Patriarch," for writing the Foreword; and to John B. Cobb, Jr., Professor Emeritus, Claremont School of Theology, California for writing the Afterword at short notice.

I am grateful to Rebecca Harkin, religion editor and now publisher, *Humanities*, for her unexpected but much appreciated invitation to be editor of this volume, and for her patience as deadlines came and went and the book stayed "in process."

The professional support and personal friendship of faculty colleagues at Boston University were invaluable while I worked on the *Companion*. I have especially appreciated the periodic encouraging social presence, conversations, and friendship, sometimes at crucial moments, of Norm Faramelli, Walter Fluker, Andrew Shenton, Bryan Stone, and Elie Wiesel.

I thank my daughter, Shanti Morell-Hart, and son, Daniel Morell-Hart, respected professionals in their respective fields, for their love and encouragement from faraway places. I especially thank my wife, Jane Morell-Hart, for her love, patience, encouragement, and support over the past four years while I labored on the *Companion* with few breaks and minimal vacation time. We can catch up now.

I. Religions and Ecological Consciousness

Ecology Perspectives from Diverse Religious and Spiritual Traditions

CHAPTER 1

God is Absolute Reality and All Creation His *Tajallī* (Theophany)

Seyyed Hossein Nasr

Introduction

One can hardly avoid the conclusion that as long as religion was central to human life, there was no ecological crisis even if there were minor degradations of the natural environment. The environmental crisis that we face today is due most of all, if not wholly, to the desacralization of both man and Nature and the preeminence of science and technology in which the religious and spiritual significance of Nature is considered irrelevant or even unreal and scientifically meaningless. The crisis is the result of man trying to "live by bread alone." To cure the fatal disease that is causing the present crisis, it is necessary first to discover the cause of this disease and then seek a cure. The major cause is the marginalization of the spiritual dimension of human life, combined with the rejection of the spiritual dimension of Nature, which is then relegated to the status of a complex machine. The regimen is the rediscovery of the lost spiritual dimension of both man and Nature. Moreover, this rediscovery is only possible by returning to the full message, and not only the moral and social aspects, of traditional religions and the wisdom embedded in them. This wisdom is none other than traditional metaphysics and cosmology understood in its symbolic and not only its literal sense. Only this wisdom can reveal to us who we are and why we are here, what Nature is in its total and not only material aspect, and what our relation should be and must be to Nature in order not only for the natural order to survive, but also for humans to survive as a species. Religion in its universal reality is thus essential for an exhaustive revival of ecological consciousness. With this truth in mind we turn to the Islamic tradition and the wisdom it contains as it pertains to the present environmental or ecological crisis.

The Wiley Blackwell Companion to Religion and Ecology, First Edition. Edited by John Hart.

The Metaphysical Foundation

Wisdom in Arabic is called *al-ḥikmah*, which is concerned first and foremost with God and second with both macrocosmic and microcosmic Creation, in light of the Divine Metacosmic Reality. According to the teachings of this tradition, the Divine Reality or God is both absolute and infinite. In fact, God is *the* Absolute and *the* Infinite. To say that God is absolute means that all otherness and relationality are excluded from Him. In fact He alone *is*. Metaphysically speaking, there is no reality but the Divine Reality. God is the only abiding Reality, beyond all becoming and relativity. But God is also infinite, which means that the roots of all cosmic reality are to be found in the Divine Order. It is as the Infinite that the Divine Reality generates the world. Metaphysically speaking, the Infinite encompasses all possibilities and so must include the possibility of the negation of itself. Here can be found the root of all cosmic manifestation. And yet the Divine is present in all its manifestations, and in reality all manifestation is a stage of the Divine Presence. Nature is theologically created by God, but metaphysically, although it "negates" the Divine Reality by being a veil (*ḥijāb*) that covers it, it also reveals that Reality, being the manifestation of the Divine Principle and locus of the Divine Presence. Nature, therefore, is sacred but it is not divine. Moreover, although not divine but sacred, it must be respected and loved as such by those who believe in God and who love Him. As the Sufis have said, the wisdom of God is written on every page of the cosmic book and He is present everywhere in His Creation. The whole of Creation is the theophany (*tajallī*) of His Names and Qualities.

While Islamic theology, going back to the Qur'an, speaks of Creation, Islamic metaphysics, also going back to the Qur'an, but especially to its inner meaning, speaks (along with theophany) of manifestation, emanation, and similar terms when talking of the appearance of multiplicity from Unity. Sufis also speak of the very substance of all Creation being the Breath of the Compassionate (*nafas al-Raḥmān*), which God "blew" on the archetypes (*al-'ayān al-thābitah*) of all things, thereby generating the world. According to this doctrine, the very substance of the cosmos is ultimately a single reality which, moreover, is associated with the mercy and compassion of God. Nature is therefore to be seen as a mercy emanating from the Divine Mercy and is to be treated as such.

Sufi doctrine, as formulated by Ibn 'Arabī and many others, also speaks of the unity of Being (*waḥdat al-wujūd*), a doctrine that has been interpreted in multiple ways by Muslim sages over the centuries and has been misinterpreted by many Western scholars as pantheism. However, *waḥdat al-wujūd* does not mean that the world in its totality is God or even that God is only immanent without being transcendent. Rather, in the words of Frithjof Schuon, it means that "the world is mysteriously plunged in God" and that all being (*wujūd*) belongs ultimately to Him; nothing has an independent *wujūd*. This doctrine can be interpreted as *wujūd* having grades (*marātib al-wujūd*) like the rays of the Sun, which radiate from the Sun to become the light that illuminates the sky and the road on which we walk; all are rays of the same Sun and nothing other than the rays of the Sun, but with different degrees of intensity and weakness. Or it can be interpreted as a single light reflected on the myriad of mirrors that constitute cosmic existence. The Persian poet Rūmī (1207–1273) summarized this doctrine in a famous verse:

> We are non-existence reflecting being,
> Thou art Absolute Being and our being besides.

This interpretation of *waḥdat al-wujūd* brings us back to the question of theophany (*tajallī*) and the symbolism of the mirror. Ibn 'Arabī wrote that God created the mirror so that we could understand the nature of His Creation and speak about His relation to it. The surface of a mirror is nothing in itself but reflects what is placed in front of it. The image of the object in the mirror is reflected in the mirror and in a sense is that object, and yet the object is not identical with its reflected image. If we break the mirror, the object is untouched. All beings we see and experience in this world are reflections of God's names and qualities reflected on the mirror of nothingness. Moreover, if we look directly and solely at an object that appears in a mirror as an image, we do not see the mirror; if we try to look only at the mirror, we do not see the object that appears as an image in that mirror. And if we understand the image as reality instead of seeing it for what it is, a reflection of reality, we suffer from the sin of "false attribution," that is, attributing independent reality to something that does not possess it.

This is the root of the sin of modernism which attributes to Nature an independent reality that is at the same time distinct from the higher orders of being. Nature is then treated as a purely material reality to be used and plundered at will, unaware of the spiritual and even natural consequences of the error of this false attribution. Nature is not, however, an independent order of reality confined to the material and the quantitative. To treat it as such is to destroy its harmony and balance, and bring about the environmental crisis that is now threatening not only the natural world but also the existence of humanity, which has brought about this unprecedented crisis. Our responsibility toward Nature must include not only utilitarian and practical considerations, which of course have a role to play, but above all the rediscovery of the authentic knowledge of Nature in its spiritual aspects and its role not only in the sustenance of our earthly life, but also in its spiritual and even psychological function in our existence here on Earth as fully human beings.

The Role of Religion

The ideas briefly outlined above reveal why religion is so important in creating ecological consciousness in Islam and, one could say, elsewhere. But in order for religion to play its role, it cannot be confined to its social and moral aspects only; its metaphysical, cosmological, and spiritual teachings must also be brought into play. One should not forget that the Christian tradition is not only the Sermon on the Mount, but also the *Summa* of St. Thomas Aquinas and the theological and metaphysical writings of St. Bonaventure, St. Gregory of Palamas, and Nicholas of Cusa, not to speak of many early medieval figures such as Erigena and other very early authorities, such as Clement of Alexandria and Origen. All that these men wrote about the natural order belongs to the Christian religious tradition. Similarly, the *Upanishads*, the *Bhagavad-Gita*, and the works of many Hindu sages who wrote about the spiritual significance of Nature in Hinduism all belong to the Hindu tradition. The same holds true *mutatis mutandis* for Islam. To speak of religion and ecological consciousness one must expand the meaning of religion to include its universal sense and not consider it only in the restricted and limited connotation it has gained in most circles today. One must also pay full attention to the relevant metaphysical and cosmological teachings that have developed in each traditional religious universe over the ages. In the case of Islam, therefore, religion must include not only the Qur'an and ḥadith, but also the writings of such seminal figures in the exposition of Islamic metaphysics and philosophy of Nature as Ibn 'Arabī, Rūmī, Shabistarī, and Mullā Ṣadrā, along with those teachings of the *Sharī'ah* (Islamic law) that concern Nature and our relation to and responsibility toward it, not to speak of nature poetry.

Although this chapter deals primarily with the metaphysical foundation for ecological consciousness based on religion seen from an Islamic perspective, a word must also be said about the role of the *Sharī'ah* in this context. In fact, many Muslim authors confine themselves to the *Sharī'ah*, which contains many teachings pertaining to Nature, but not to cosmological issues. According to it, every creature has rights (*ḥuqūq*) that must be respected. Animals must be used by man with full consideration of their rights. Trees are not to be felled without the reasons cited in the Divine Law. Running water should not be polluted and human beings should never be wasteful. These are just a few examples. In addition, the teachings of the *Sharī'ah* and Prophetic instructions created an area around Makkah and Madinah where flora and fauna were to be protected and hunting was forbidden, an early model for today's national parks and other protected areas. There are numerous other teachings of this kind that could be mentioned. Since most people in the Islamic world are pious and respect the *Sharī'ah*, emphasis on such teachings, which many Muslims especially those living in urban areas do not heed, could certainly ameliorate the environmental crisis, but the crisis cannot be overcome by such considerations alone. What is needed is an in-depth critique of the modern worldview that has led to the crisis and the reassertion of the traditional Islamic metaphysical, cosmological, and ethical doctrines about both man and Nature.

Man and the Natural Order

Returning to the metaphysical and cosmological teachings that must be considered if an ecological consciousness can be developed that is capable of diverting or at least ameliorating the looming environmental crisis, it must be remembered that according to traditional cosmogenesis, the natural world or primordial Nature was created before man. We find this assertion in both the biblical and the Qur'anic accounts of Creation. This doctrine should not be confused with the teachings of many traditions according to which it is man—not earthly man, but Universal Man—who is the source and principle of the cosmos, as seen in teachings on Puruśa in Hinduism and Universal Man (*al-insān al-kāmil*) in Islam. What we have in mind here is the creation of earthly man, who then becomes the central being of the terrestrial domain.

The precedence in the genesis of the natural order before man in the order of Creation has an important bearing on the environmental crisis. Unlike Christianity, Islam does not believe in original sin, but it does believe in the fall of man from his state of primordial perfection, a fall in which the natural order has also participated to some extent but not to the same degree as man. In Islam, paradise is called *jannah* or *firdaws*, meaning the Garden. In fact, both the English word paradise and the Arabic *firdaws* are derived from the Middle Persian word *pardīs*, meaning garden. This does not mean, however, that paradise is simply the idealization of the earthly garden as many modern scholars of religion claim. Rather, it means that the earthly (traditional) garden and virgin Nature are reflections of the celestial Garden or paradise. We have fallen from the Edenic state which was paradise, and nature too has fallen from its state of primordial Edenic perfection, but not to the same extent as we have. Something of that paradisal quality survives in what remains of virgin Nature on Earth and this paradisal presence reveals itself to those whose inner eyes and heart are open to Nature's spiritual reality.

Since men and women also carry that paradise deep within their being, even today many still turn to Nature for spiritual sustenance, even those who claim to be agnostics and not interested in religion, and encounter and experience Nature "religiously," with awe and wonder. To the extent that modern man destroys Nature, what remains of virgin Nature becomes evermore precious as both a refuge from human folly and a living presence and reminder of what we carry in the deepest recesses of our being. The fact that Nature has not fallen to the extent that we have means it can provide spiritual sustenance and remind us who we really are—beyond the veil of the state of the fall and the ordinary consciousness with which, as fallen beings, we mistakenly identify ourselves. Our inner being is woven from the strands of harmony and beauty that virgin Nature displays before our eyes. We need Nature not only physically to sustain our biological life, but also spiritually to nourish our soul and inner life, to remain truly human, true to our inward reality.

The correspondence between man (meaning here both male and female) and the cosmos, that is, between microcosm and macrocosm, is not simply the naïve teaching of various religions and philosophies in the East and West in past ages, as those who consider only the material and quantitative dimensions of things claim. Rather, it is a truth of a most profound order. The Gospel of John asserts, "In the beginning was the Word" by which the world was created, while the Qur'an, referring to how the world was created, states "God said, 'Be!' and there was." The world began with the Divine Word, which means consciousness at the highest level. Therefore, one could say, "In the beginning was consciousness." We did not evolve into a state of consciousness, as metaphysically absurd theories of human evolution assert. We began with a state of consciousness; and so did Nature.

Consciousness

Many today recognize that plants too have a mode of consciousness and not only animals. Hinduism in fact sees the whole of the cosmos, including rocks and water, as consisting of degrees and modes of consciousness. The school of Vedanta goes a step further and claims that there is only in reality one consciousness, associated with *Ātman*. In the Abrahamic understanding the world is seen as degrees and states of being rather than consciousness; ultimately, however, the two cannot be separated. It is interesting to note in this context that the word in Arabic for both existence and being is *wujūd*, which comes from the root *wjd*, which in the form *wajada* means "to find," and therefore contains within itself the element of consciousness. Man cannot find without knowing, and man cannot know without consciousness. Ecological consciousness therefore requires our becoming aware that it is not only we who possess consciousness; Nature is also conscious in its own way. Usually, one speaks of inanimate, animate, and conscious beings. However, in a deeper sense we live in a universe that is alive, a *living* universe extending from the galaxies and the stars to the depths of the oceans. It is, too, a *conscious* universe, with varying modes of consciousness that manifest at different levels according to the nature of various beings. As for man, in principle he contains all levels of consciousness, being the theophany of all the Divine names and qualities that relate to Creation or manifestation.

The Face of God

At various points, the Qur'an speaks about the Face of God (*wajh Allāh*). It mentions that everything perishes except His Face, but also that wherever we turn, there is the Face of God. Most Muslim sages interpret the Face of God as referring not to the metacosmic aspect of the Divine Reality, which does not participate in the creative act, but to that aspect of God's names and qualities, or cluster of Divine names and qualities, whose theophany constitutes the cosmos, both the macrocosm and the microcosm. Everything in the created order is a reflection of the Divine Face. Moreover, the Face that God turns toward us is ultimately the face that we turn toward Him; that face is our inner reality. So, when the Qur'an asserts that everything perishes but His Face, it is not referring only to an eschatological reality but also to a metaphysical truth that everything that appears as something is non-existent in itself. It is only a reflection of His Face. In destroying Nature, modern man is thus "defacing" the Face of God, which is turned toward His Creation. More precisely, we do not destroy the Face itself—we do not have the power to destroy it; we destroy its sacred reflection in Nature and even within ourselves. Our face turned to God defines us in the most profound sense as human beings, and our destruction of the reflection of the Divine Face in Nature not only destroys the natural order, but ultimately dehumanizes, "defaces," and destroys us.

The Role of Man in Relation to Nature

One might ask how it is possible for one species, which according to modern thinking is nothing more than the product of the evolution of purely earthly elements through the agency of simple physical forces, to destroy the natural environment that has given rise to it. The deeper answer to this question alone demonstrates that man is not simply and only an earthly being. Rather, he is the microcosm that contains all possibilities within himself by virtue of which there is no limit to his worldly knowledge, and he can dominate the earthly domain. But if his will is not surrendered to God and he falls short of the goal for which he was put on Earth, then he can use his warped will and cunning to play a God-like role and destroy the world of Nature in a way that no other species can—even species that are physically far more powerful, numerous, or diversified than *Homo sapiens.*

Traditionally, in Islamic metaphysics as well as in other wisdom traditions, man is seen as a channel of grace (*barakah*) for Nature. Since *barakah* flows "through the arteries of the universe," Nature is seen as a source of *barakah* for man. The role of man in this exchange, however, is more active while that of Nature more passive. This is because man, having free will, can rebel against Heaven, whereas Nature cannot but necessarily reflects paradisal realities. That is why it was the darkness of the soul of secularized man that "darkened" Nature and caused the destruction of so much of the natural environment, not vice versa. The environmental crisis is an externalization of the darkness of the soul of modern man and the resulting eclipse of man's intuitive and spiritual faculties, along with the loss of the symbolist spirit. To overcome the present environmental crisis we must rediscover these lost elements and faculties within our souls. We must once again become a channel of grace for Nature, the window through which the light of grace illuminates the natural order. Then we shall discover that Nature will also help us through the *barakah* that manifests itself still so strongly in it, and it will be our spiritual companion in our journey on Earth.

To accomplish this task, we need first to remove the obstacles that the prevailing worldview has placed on the road to recovery of the sacred within ourselves; then we can realize the presence of the sacred in Nature. On the human and subjective side, we must set aside the current view of man as simply an earthly creature endowed mysteriously through evolutionary processes with cleverness and what is now called intelligence but is, however, but a shadow of real intelligence. On the objective side, we must rediscover the sacred character of Nature, but that cannot be done without rediscovering the sacred within ourselves and criticizing in depth the current ideology of scientism, a belief that is widespread (although rejected by some scientists).

The Obstacle of Scientism

Scientism, currently widespread in the West but also accepted without much thought and, in a sense, "unconsciously" by many modern Muslims, even some pious ones, is a totalitarian ideology that generalizes the worldview derived from modern science to embrace the whole of reality and knowledge of it. According to its tenets, anything that modern science cannot study is either unreal or irrelevant. It brushes aside in cavalier fashion the spiritual dimension of man and Nature and considers the sacred reality in man and virgin Nature to be devoid of reality, or at best simple subjectivism. Theoretically, one could conceive of a world in which modern science would exist as a legitimate but limited form of knowledge of the natural world, existing alongside other sciences of Nature that are concerned with its non-material dimensions, all integrated into a universal hierarchy of knowledge. But this is not what has happened, at least not so far. Rather, many today consider modern science to be the only legitimate knowledge of Nature, and thereby claim that science is what it can never be. Scientism is, therefore, one of the greatest obstacles, along with the current truncated image of human reality, itself related to this false ideology, which stands against the restoration of an authentic view of Nature and man's relation to it.

In this context it is important for Muslims to know that during the past century many profound criticisms of scientism have been made in the West by twentieth-century scientists such as Arthur Eddington and James Jeans, and contemporary philosophers and social critics such as Theodore Roszak and Jacob Needleman, not to speak of expositors of traditional doctrines such as René Guénon, Frithjof Schuon, and Titus Burckhardt. Beyond the traditionalist group, Muslim scholars who have provided a profound philosophical critique of scientism have been few indeed, although there are rare but significant figures such as Muzaffar Iqbal. It is important for Muslims, therefore, to familiarize themselves with criticisms of scientism in the West and to formulate their own criticisms based on Islamic sources.

An Islamic Philosophy of Nature

Once the ground has been cleared, Muslims must turn to a contemporary formulation of the Islamic philosophy of Nature and science, as well as of the role of man in relation to the natural environment. To achieve this requires thorough familiarity with traditional Islamic sources, a task made difficult by the fact that the Islamic philosophy of Nature and of science are not treated as separate subjects in classical Islamic sources, as are, for example, logic, physics, and psychology. One must draw instead from diverse sources of the Islamic teachings. There is the Qur'an itself, a large part of which concerns the natural world and the relation of human beings to it. The same could be said about the ḥadith. Commentaries on the Qur'an, therefore, are also a valuable source, especially theological, philosophical, and Sufi commentaries such as those of Fakhr al-Dīn al-Rāzī, Mullā Ṣadrā, 'Abd al-Razzāq Kāshānī, and Rashīd al-Dīn Maybudī. Then there are philosophical works dealing with natural philosophy (*al-ṭabī'iyyāt*), parts of which deal directly with the philosophy of Nature and science as we see at the beginning of the *ṭabī'iyyāt* of Ibn Sīnā's *Kitāb al-shifā'* ("The Book of Healing"), in the section titled *Fann al-samā' al-ṭabī'ī*. Similarly, treatments of this subject can be found in other schools of Islamic philosophy such as the Illuminationist School (*ishrāqī*) founded by Suhrawardī, who developed an elaborate physics based on light; or the School of Transcendent Theosophy (*al-ḥikmat al-muta'āliyah*), founded by Mullā Ṣadrā; it contains another version of the philosophy of Nature related to what came before but with new elements, especially trans-substantial motion (*al-ḥarakat al-jawhariyyah*).

Another rich source for the Islamic philosopher of Nature is general works that deal with natural history, such as the writings of al-Mas'ūdī and Ibn Qutaybah, or with such sciences as botany and zoology, such as the works of al-Jāḥiẓ, the Ikhwān al-Ṣafā', and al-Damīrī. There is also a whole genre of literature, in Arabic, Persian, and other Islamic languages such as *al-Kalīlah wa'l-dimnah*, which contains valuable material concerning the natural environment and the relation of human beings to it. There are, too, many poetical works dealing with this subject. Many of these works reflect not only the sciences of Nature but also, to one degree or another, the *Sharī'ite*, philosophical and/or Sufi teachings about Nature and man's role in relation to God's Creation.

For the needs of Muslims today seeking to reformulate a philosophy of the natural environment and to waken ecological consciousness, nothing is more important after the Qur'an itself than Sufi sources, in both poetry and prose. Works such as *al-Futūḥāt al-makkiyah* ("The Makkan Openings") of Ibn 'Arabī written in Arabic prose, or the *Mathnawī* of Jalāl al-Dīn Rūmī in Persian poetry, are inexhaustible sources for the formulation of this philosophy. The poetic opus of Maḥmūd Shabistarī, *Gulshan-i rāz* ("The Secret Garden of Divine Mysteries") contains in synthetic form the basic principles of Islamic metaphysics and philosophy of Nature and of man, as well as the relation between the two.

Such sources, along with others that we do not have space to mention here, are available to all those interested in developing an authentic, indepth formulation of an Islamic philosophy of Nature, and of man in his relation to it. Making use of such sources, Muslims must seek to strengthen their ecological consciousness through their religion, that is, Islam. There is no more urgent matter for the Muslim intelligentsia. If the task is not accomplished, there will be no future in the long run to deal with anything else. Let us hope and pray, then, that the necessity and urgency of raising the ecological consciousness of Muslims through recourse to the very rich resources of the Islamic tradition will be recognized by all those who are seriously interested in the future of the Islamic community and of the human family as a whole.

Further Reading

Bakar, O. 1991. *Tawhid and Science*. Kuala Lumpur: Centre for Civilisational Development.

Bakar, O. 2007. *Environmental Wisdom for Planet Earth—The Islamic Heritage*. Kuala Lumpur: Centre for Civilisational Development.

Foltz, R., Denny, F., & Baharuddin, A. (Eds.). 2003. *Islam and Ecology—A Bestowed Trust*. Cambridge, MA: Harvard University Press.

Foltz, R. (Ed.). 2002. *Worldviews, Religion and the Environment: A Global Anthology*. Belmont, CA: Wadsworth Publishing.

Izzi, Dien, M. 2000. *The Environmental Dimensions of Islam*. Cambridge: Lutterworth Press.

Khalid, F., & O'Brien, J. (Eds.). 1992. *Islam and Ecology*. London: Cassel.

Nasr, S. H. 1996. *Religion and the Order of Nature*. New York: Oxford University Press.

Nasr, S. H. 1997. *Man and Nature*. New York: Oxford University Press.

CHAPTER 2

Swaraj

From *Chipko* to *Navdanya*

Vandana Shiva

Introduction

Swaraj for me has a multitude of meanings. It is, of course, Gandhi's word for a deep freedom of self-rule and self-governance, of political self-organizing beyond colonialism, transcending electoral and representative democracy. His little book *Hind Swaraj* (*Indian Home Rule*) articulates the difference between *swaraj* and electing someone to rule through the structures of Empire.

Because I am a scientist and an ecologist, *swaraj* also means self-organization in Nature—from the organism to ecosystems to Gaia. And I see the freedom of Nature, and of humans as part of Nature, as a continuum. That is why my philosophy is based on Earth Democracy—the democracy of all life, practiced in our everyday thoughts and lives. More than five decades ago my *swaraj* journey started with the Chipko movement. For the past three decades it has continued with *Navdanya*.

Chipko and the Story of the Forest

In 1972, women living in a high-altitude village, Reni, blocked logging operations, giving rise to the Chipko (literally, "to cling") movement. The name was given to the movement by Ghanshyam Raturi (Shailani) who composed folk songs which were sung by every child, woman, and man in Garhwal. In 1972, the most widespread organized protests against commercial exploitation of the Himalayan forests by outside contractors erupted, in Uttarkashi on December 12, and in Gopeshwar on December 15. It was

The Wiley Blackwell Companion to Religion and Ecology, First Edition. Edited by John Hart.

during these two protest meetings that Raturi composed his famous poem describing the method of embracing the trees to save them from being felled:

> Embrace the trees and Save them from being felled;
> The property of our hills, Save it from being looted.

Before leaving for Canada to do my PhD on the foundations of quantum theory, I wanted to visit my favorite places in the Himalayas. I discovered that the forests and streams had disappeared in the insane rush to build dams and roads, and to cultivate apple orchards by felling rich oak forests which had absorbed the monsoon rains and then released the water slowly as streams.

I decided in 1974 that, while pursuing my PhD, I would volunteer with Chipko every vacation. And that is what I did. Chipko was clearly my university for ecology. While my parents provided my embedding in a forest culture and an appreciation of natural, mixed forests, it was Chipko that made me realize, in fine detail, how biodiversity is at the heart of sustainable economies, and how Nature provides the basic needs of the large majority of people around the world. As I worked with peasant women, transferring fertility from the forest to the field, I learnt my first lessons in organic farming: sustainable societies rely on humus. In those early years, as I moved between quantum physics and protecting the Himalayan forests, I learnt to respect both the best of modern ecological science and the best of traditional knowledge. I developed humility about my doctoral studies, recognizing how much I did not know and how much knowledge illiterate village women with no formal education possessed. That is why I find the term "knowledge society" as a description of computer-based societies so inaccurate and misleading, implying that non-industrialized, non-computerized societies lack knowledge. In the case of biodiversity, of forest species and plant species, this is clearly not true; women and indigenous communities, the excluded of the industrial world, are the real custodians of biodiversity-related knowledge.

I realized during the great drought in Karnataka in 1984 that the way we practice agriculture is flawed. That year also saw the peak of militancy in Punjab. I wrote about the violence of the Green Revolution that gave rise to a non-sustainable form of agriculture, purporting to create more food but actually destroying Nature and farmers' sense of self, and fomenting war within society. What was really a sustainability and democracy issue was politicized and communalized.

In 1987, during a meeting at the United Nations (UN), I thought, "Mahatma Gandhi used a *charkha* [spinning wheel] to spin freedom as *swaraj* and *swadeshi*." I came up with the idea of the seed as an equivalent of the *charkha* for our modern *swaraj*, *swadeshi* ("self-sufficiency"), *satyagraha* ("truth-force," usually nonviolent action) against the appropriation and patenting of seeds, and control of agriculture by multinational corporations (MNCs). Navdanya was born in that moment of awareness; but it did not become a fully-fledged organization until 1991. The conservation farm was started about five years later, with the aim of inspiring farmers to come and see 250 varieties of rice and 800 species of plants growing in the same field.

When Satish Kumar, editor of *Resurgence*, asked me to set up in India something along the lines of the Schumacher College I hesitated, because I preferred building movements to constructing buildings. But he convinced me that it was time for an institution like *Bija* ("seed"), and so we came up with *Bija* mainly because the university was going to be developed at the Navdanya farm, which was a seed bank, and also because a seed is an inspiration for renewal and an example of the small embodying the whole. Bija Vidyapeeth had really become a *bija*; instead of buildings, I could see the progression of a dialogue and mutual growth. And so we both continued to hold courses with Schumacher College, and the best of people agreed to come to teach: the physicist Fritjof Capra, Body Shop founder Anita Roddick, and Satish himself.

Navdanya and the Story of the Seed

In 1984, a number of tragic events took place in India. In June, the Golden Temple was attacked because it was harboring terrorists; by November, Indira Gandhi had been assassinated; and in December, the worst industrial disaster took place in Bhopal, when Union Carbide's pesticide plant leaked toxic gas into the environment. Thirty thousand people died in the terrorism in Punjab, and a further 30,000 have died in the "industrial terrorism" of Bhopal. This is equal to twelve 9/11 s. I was forced to ask why agriculture had come to resemble war. Why did the Green Revolution, which received the Nobel Peace Prize, breed extremism and terrorism in Punjab? This led me to write *The Violence of the Green Revolution* and *Monocultures of the Mind*. Blindness to diversity and self-organization in Nature and society were clearly a basic problem in the mechanistic, Cartesian, industrial paradigm. This blindness led to false claims that industrial monocultures in forestry, farming, fisheries, and animal husbandry produced more food and were necessary to eradicate hunger and poverty. On the contrary, monocultures produce less and use more inputs, thereby destroying the environment and impoverishing people.

In 1987, the Dag Hammarskjold Foundation organized a meeting in Geneva on biotechnology entitled "Laws of Life," to which I was invited because of my book on the Green Revolution. At the conference, the biotechnology industry laid out its plans to patent life, to genetically engineer seeds, crops, and life-forms, and to gain full freedom to trade through the General Agreement on Tariffs and Trade (GATT) negotiations, which culminated in the World Trade Organization (WTO). This led to my focus on intellectual property rights, free trade, globalization—and to a life dedicated to saving seeds and promoting organic farming as an alternative to a world dictated and controlled by corporations. Having dedicated myself to the defense of the intrinsic worth of all species, I found abhorrent the idea of life-forms, seeds, and biodiversity being reduced to corporate inventions and hence becoming corporate property. Further, if seeds become "intellectual property," then saving and sharing them become intellectual property theft! Our highest duty, to save seeds, becomes a criminal act. I found the legalization of the criminal act of owning and monopolizing life through patents on seeds and plants morally and ethically unacceptable. So I started Navdanya ("nine seeds"), a movement that promotes biodiversity conservation, as well as seed-saving and seed-sharing among farmers.

Navdanya has created more than 20 community seed banks through which seeds are saved and freely exchanged among our three *lakh* (1 *lakh* = 100,000) members.

Through this we have brought back forgotten foods like jhangora (barnyard millet), *ragi* (finger millet), *marsha* (amaranth), *naurangi dal* (a lentil dish with nine dal), and *gahat dal*. These crops are not only more nutritious than globally traded commodities, they are more resource-prudent; they require only 200–300 mm of rain compared to 2,500 mm for chemical rice farming. Millets could increase food production 400-fold, using the same amount of limited water. These forgotten foods are the foods of the future.

Farmers' seeds similarly are the seeds of the future. For the farmer, the seed is not merely the source of future years' plants and food; it is the storehouse of culture, of history. Seed is the first link in the food chain, the ultimate symbol of food security. The free exchange of seeds among farmers has been the basis of maintaining biodiversity as well as food security, and is founded on cooperation and reciprocity. A farmer who wants to exchange seeds generally gives an equal quantity of seeds from his field in return for the seeds he obtains. But this exchange goes beyond seeds: it involves the exchange of ideas and knowledge, of culture and heritage. It is an accumulation of tradition, of knowledge, of how to work the seeds. Farmers gain knowledge about the seeds they want to grow by watching them grow in other farmers' fields, by learning about drought, disease, and pest resistance.

In saving seeds and biodiversity we are protecting cultural diversity. Navdanya means not only nine seeds; it also means "new gift" in the face of the extinction of species and the extinction of small farmers. The nine seeds and their respective *navgrahas* (nine cosmic correlates) are these:

1. *Yava* (barley) represents the Sun
2. *Shamaka* (little millet) represents the Moon
3. *Togari* (pigeon-pea) represents Mars, which is responsible for controlling the nervous system
4. *Madga* (moong) represents Mercury and stimulates intelligence
5. *Kadale* (chickpea) represents Jupiter
6. *Tandula* (rice) represents Venus
7. *Til* (sesame) represents Saturn and is characterized by oil
8. *Maasha* (black gram) represents Rahu (an imagery planet representing the head without a body)
9. *Kulittha* (horse-gram) represents Ketu (an imagery planet representing the body without a head)

Contrary to the myth of industrial agriculture, biodiverse systems produce more food and higher incomes than industrial monocultures. Our *baranaja* (12 seeds) system yields twice as much output and incomes three times higher than a monoculture of corn. The 12 crops are:

1. *Phapra* (Fagopyrum tataricum)
2. *Mandua* (Eleusine coracana)
3. *Marsha* (Amaranthus frumentaceous)
4. *Bhat* (Glycine soja)
5. *Lobia* (Vigna catiang)
6. *Moong* (Phaseolus mungo)

7. *Gahat* (Dolichos biflorus)
8. *Rajma* (Phaseolus vulgaris)
9. *Jakhia* (Cleome viscose)
10. *Navrangi* (Vigna umbellate)
11. *Jowar* (Sorghum vulgare)
12. *Urad* (Phaseolus mungo)

Our conservation of heritage rice varieties has led to the protection of the original, authentic basmati as part of a slow food presidium. We have saved more than 3,000 rice varieties, including over 30 aromatic rice varieties. The saline-tolerant seeds we have saved helped farmers in Orissa recover from the super-cyclone of 1999 which killed 30,000 people. These seeds were also distributed by Navdanya in rehabilitation after the 2005 tsunami. We are now creating "Seeds of Hope" seed banks to deal with climate chaos. Heritage seeds that can survive droughts, floods, and cyclones will be collected, saved, multiplied, and distributed. Farmers' seed-breeding is far ahead of scientific breeding and genetic engineering in providing flood-resistant, drought-resistant, and saline-resistant varieties.

In the context of farmers' heritage, genetic engineering is, in fact, a laggard technology. Not only are corporate, industrial breeding strategies incapable of dealing with climate change, genetically engineered seeds are resulting in the suicide of farmers. In India, according to a debate in parliament, more than 200,000 farmers have committed suicide because of debt caused by high costs and unreliable seeds they bought from corporations. Suicides are concentrated in areas that have become dependent on commercial seeds, and are most intense where genetically engineered Bt cotton has been sold. These are the seeds of suicide and seeds of slavery. There are no suicides where farmers use heritage seeds and their traditional varieties.

Like Gandhi's salt *satyagraha*, we have undertaken a seed *satyagraha*—a commitment not to cooperate with patent laws and seed laws which prevent farmers from saving and exchanging seed. Seed freedom is our birthright; without seed freedom there is no food freedom.

In May 2006, Navdanya undertook a seed pilgrimage (*Bija Yatra*) to prevent farmers' suicides and create an agriculture of hope. We are building a movement to stop the genocide of our farmers and reclaim our seed and food sovereignty. The *Yatra* started from Gandhi's ashram in Sevagram, District Wardha, Maharashtra, and ended on May 26 in Bangalore. It covered Amravati, Yavatmal, and Nagpur in Vidarbha region of Maharashtra; Adilabad, Warangal, Karimnagar, and Hyderabad in Andhra Pradesh; and Bidar, Gulbarga, Raichur, Hospet, Chitradurg, and Bangalore in Karnataka. These are the regions where farmers have been locked into dependence on corporate seed supplies in order to grow cash crops integrated into world markets, which has led to a collapse in farm prices due to subsidies of $400 billion in rich countries.

I have just returned from a soil pilgrimage through the heart of India to celebrate the International Year of Soil as a year of renewing our commitment to a nonviolent relationship with the Earth and with Earth's earth, and within society. We started the pilgrimage at Bapu Kutir, at the Sewagram Ashram on October 2, the Day of

Non-Violence. My fellow pilgrims were the Navdanya family and colleagues who have contributed nearly half a century of their lives to build the Organic Movement: Andre Leu, president of IFOAM; Ronnie Cummins, director of the Organic Consumers Association of the US; and Will Allen, a professor and longtime organic farmer.

At Gandhi's mud hut we made a pledge to stop the violence done to the soil by the use of chemical fertilizers and poisons, and promote organic *Ahimsic Kheti* ("nonviolent farming"). We dedicated ourselves, and our communities, to a move away from a violent chemical industrial agriculture that is destroying soil fertility and trapping farmers in debt through exorbitant seeds and chemicals. Vidarbha has emerged as the epicenter of debt-induced farmers' suicides. It is also the region with the highest acreage of GMO (genetically modified organism) Bt cotton.

We visited Navdanya organic farmers and saw fields of non-Bt native cotton, totally pest- and weed-free, that give greater yields than Bt cotton. The Bt fields are being doused in pesticides because of pest outbreaks, because Bt is failing farmers as a tool to control pests. Bt cotton fields are also being sprayed with Monsanto's Round Up, a known carcinogen, to control the weeds. There is no regulation of the poisons being used. Most of the GMO cotton seed is being blended and labeled for sale as vegetable oil. Indians are being fed GMO cotton seed oil, even though GMOs are not permitted in food in our country. And while toxic oils spread without regulation, the new Food Safety rules have shut down the *Ghaani* (virgin oil press), which produced healthy, safe oils such as flax, groundnut, sesame, and mustard.

The oilcake is being fed to our sacred cow, our *Gau Maata*. Those who kill others in the name of cow protection are silent on the fight against the toxic giants who are poisoning *Gau Maata*, and through her, her milk and us, and killing all life, some instantly, some slowly.

We ended the pilgrimage at the Agriculture College in Indore, which started as Albert Howard's Institute on organic farming, which contributed to the famous Indore process of composting. Gandhi came to know of the Indore process when he visited London for a Round Table Conference. Gandhi and Howard are two major influences on my ideas and work. They have shown me that we can have a peaceful and respectful relationship with the soil and with each other.

Howard was sent to India in 1905 by the British government to introduce chemical farming. When he arrived, he found the soils were fertile and there were no pests in the fields. He decided to make the Indian peasant his tutor, and wrote *The Agricultural Testament*, which is known as the bible of organic farming. Organic farming is the original example of #MakeInIndia. Howard's book helped spread the organic movement to the US through the Rodale Institute and to the UK through the Soil Association, and so found its way to the far corners of the world.

The soil pilgrimage was our expression of gratitude to sources of organic farming in India—our fertile and generous *Bhoomi* (soil) and *Maati Maa*, who has sustained us for millennia. The traditions of compassion and nonviolence defined Indian agriculture, and were rejuvenated by Gandhi and Howard.

Ecological, regenerative agriculture is based on recycling organic matter, and hence recycling nutrients. It is based on the law of return and on giving nutrients back to the soil, not simply taking nutrition out of it until it is sterile. As Howard wrote in *The Soil and Health*:

> Taking without giving is a robbery of the soil and a banditry; "a particularly mean form of banditry", because it involves the robbing of future generations which are not here to defend themselves.

In taking care of the soil, we also produce more food on less land. Fertile soils are the sustainable answer to food and nutrition security. And organic agriculture is the only real answer to climate change.

The air pollution that has built up in the atmosphere since the beginning of the use of fossil fuels in the eighteenth century is roughly 400 parts per million (ppm) carbon dioxide today. This is what is causing the greenhouse effect and climate chaos, including the temperature rise. To cap the rise of temperature at 2 °C we need to reduce the carbon build-up to 350 ppm. This demands reducing emissions and phasing out of fossil fuels, but it also requires a reduction of the excess carbon from the atmosphere and returning it to the soil where it belongs; organic, regenerative agriculture offers us a way to achieve this. In the process, it also addresses food insecurity and hunger, it reverses desertification, it creates livelihood security by creating ecological security, and so creates the path to peace. Above all, it allows a transition from the violent paradigm, structures, and systems of capitalist patriarchy to the nonviolent paradigm, structures, and systems based on *Ahimsa*, which include the wellbeing of all people and all species.

An increase in soil organic matter (SOM) increases the water-retaining capacity of soil:

- 0.5% SOM can hold 80,000 liters
- 1% SOM can hold 160,000 liters
- 5% SOM can hold 800,000 liters

Organic farming is the answer to drought and climate change. It is also a peace solution. As we have written in our "Manifesto Terra Viva on Our Soils, Our Commons, Our Future," the Syrian uprising and Boko Haram have their roots in dying soils. If we do not respect the soil and cultural diversity, if we do not collectively commit ourselves to *Ahimsa*, we will rapidly disintegrate as a civilization.

Organic agriculture is the *Dharma* ("path of righteousness") that sows the seeds of peace and prosperity for all. It helps us break out of the vicious cycle of violence and degeneration, and create virtuous cycles based on nonviolence and regeneration.

Just as humus binds soil particles and prevents soil erosion, it also binds society and prevents violence and social disintegration. Since humus provides food, livelihood, water, and climate security, it can contribute to peace. Just as wet straw cannot be set alight with a match, communities that are secure cannot be set on fire by violent elements that feed on the insecurity created by an economic model that is killing *Swadeshi* and is designed purely for global economic powers to extract what they want.

We forget that we are soil. In taking care of the soil, we reclaim our humanity.

Our future is inseparable from the future of the Earth. It is no accident that the word human has its roots in *humus*, the Latin word for soil. Adam, the first human in the Abrahamic traditions, is derived from *Adamah*, meaning soil in Hebrew.

Gandhi wrote: "To forget how to dig the earth and tend the soil is to forget ourselves."

We must never forget that Ahimsa *must be the basis of our relationship with the Earth and each other.*

CHAPTER 3

Eco-Kabbalah

Holism and Mysticism in Earth-Centered Judaism

David Mevorach Seidenberg

Judaism has always viewed the world from a Creation-centered perspective, beginning with God's declaration at the end of Genesis 1 that the entire Creation is "very good." Even its very notion of time, in both biblical and rabbinic Judaism, is structured around the weekly celebration on the Sabbath of Creation. The Torah, and the rabbis afterward, raised the idea of original blessing, found the purpose of human existence in what happens here in this life-world, and honored both God as Creator and God's Creation as good and holy. For modern eco-theology, especially as it has emerged in Christian circles, this notion of an original blessing is an important foundation. It is moreover true that finding redemption and salvation in this world can be a basis for right action and right living.

These ideas fit with a holistic view of the Earth and all life where redemption, the human good, and moral value are grounded in the redemption and good of Creation itself. Yet Jewish and other theistic communities have often honored Creation not as a good in itself, but only as the "Creator's handiwork," which reveals God's wisdom. A theistic holism, which as we shall see may be rooted in concepts from Maimonides and Kabbalah, can go beyond this, envisioning Creation as a moral end in itself, imbued not only with the holiness and presence of the Divine, but also with the potential to fully become a revelation of divinity. Two dimensions may be discerned here: seeing the whole of Creation as the greatest moral good imaginable, which goes along with true gratitude to the Creator, and seeing in the diversity of Creation the fullest revelation of God's infinity.

Creation-centered theologies must also touch on the foundations of our ethics. Most importantly, this may entail seeing the value of each human being as a reflection of the value of Creation itself. Though this conclusion may seem to go directly against the anthropocentrism of biblically-based traditions, it is already hinted at in the rabbinic

The Wiley Blackwell Companion to Religion and Ecology, First Edition. Edited by John Hart.

statement that "one who destroys a single human life destroys a full world" (Mishnah, *Sanhedrin* 4: 5; Seidenberg, 2015, 114–116). Moreover, much of the anthropocentrism we read into biblical tradition is a product of medieval and modern thought, native neither to the Torah nor to the rabbis (Seidenberg, 2015, Part 1).

Challenging anthropocentrism may seem radically new, but once we bracket the modernist and humanist assumptions we bring to the texts the seeds for transfiguring our experience of this more-than-human world we call Nature can be readily found, most importantly, within those streams of Jewish thought that questioned the strictly human focus of most ethics. Here I examine the two most important streams: the thoughts of Moses Maimonides and the images in Kabbalah. In many ways these two visions pull in opposite directions; Maimonides rejected the anthropocentric universe while Kabbalah projected the *anthropos* onto every aspect of the universe. Yet both Maimonides and various Kabbalists envisioned a reality in which the highest moral good transcended human needs and was measured by diversity, abundance, and wholeness in the cosmos itself.

Maimonides

Moses Maimonides (Rabbi Moshe ben Maimun, 1135–1204, also called the Rambam) is arguably the premier philosopher and theologian of Jewish history, and one of the most influential thinkers, Jewish, Christian, or Muslim, of the medieval period. The ecological depth of his work is only beginning to be understood. Maimonides, uniquely in all of Jewish thought, challenged the primacy of humanity within the order of Creation, asserted that there is complete equivalence between human and animal emotions, and believed that Creation as a whole is the only dimension of being that has intrinsic value.

In his most important work *The Guide for the Perplexed* or *Moreh N'vukhim*, which reflects his mature thought, Maimonides espoused a model of the cosmos that parallels Gaia theory, which posits that the Earth is most accurately understood to be a living and self-regulating organism. Maimonides admonished his reader, "Know that this whole of being is one individual and nothing else," adding that the whole of Creation "has the same status as Zayid or Omar"—a person, endowed with a heart and a soul (1963a, 1: 72, 184). For Maimonides, the idea that the universe is an organic whole was a fundamental scientific fact, which led to a direct understanding of God's relation to the world, for "the One has created one being" (1: 72, 187; see also 2: 1, 251).

The ethical and metaphysical implications of this model were tremendous. Fundamentally, Maimonides rejected the idea that humanity was the final end of Creation and rejected also the idea that other creatures exist to serve human pleasure: "It should not be believed that all the beings exist for the sake of the existence of man. On the contrary, all the other beings too have been intended for their own sakes" (3: 13, 452). Maimonides held that this view was delineated within Genesis itself, explaining the word "good" in Genesis 1 to mean that each creature has something akin to what modern philosophers call intrinsic value (3: 13, 453). He wrote in the same passage: "the individuals of the human species, and all the more so the other species, are things of no value at all in comparison with the whole [of Creation] that exists and endures" (452). Scripture's use of the phrase "very good" (Gen. 1: 31) to describe Creation indicates this overwhelming value of "the whole," which surpasses all individuals and species.

Maimonides arrived at this interpretation after concluding that there can be no *telos* for Creation: "[E]ven according to our view holding that the world has been produced in time, the quest for the final end of all the species of beings collapses" (452). In a later chapter, he derived a remarkable conclusion from this idea: "[T]he entire purpose [of God's actions] consists in bringing into existence the way you see it everything whose existence is possible" (3: 25, 504). This is fundamentally congruent with Baruch Spinoza's cosmology as well as with biocentrism; it is also compatible with those who understand evolution to be "directed" toward diversity.

Maimonides believed that the highest revelation of God came from understanding the diversity of Creation itself, all its creatures and all their interrelations. Even God's revelation to Moses (after the Israelites made the golden calf, when Moses was absent on Mt. Sinai), was of this nature:

> When [Moses] asked for knowledge of the attributes ... he was told: "I will make all My goodness/*kol tuvi* pass before you" [Exod. 33: 19] ... All My goodness—alludes to the display to him of all existing things (creatures) of which it is said: "And God saw everything that He had made, and behold, it [is] very good/*tov m'od*" [Gen. 1: 31]. By their display, I mean that he will apprehend their nature and the way they are mutually connected so that he will know how [God] governs them in general and in detail. (1: 54, 124)

While here the subject is revelation, Maimonides also believed that one could develop an understanding of the truth intellectually, by studying the more-than-human world in its wholeness.

> I have already let you know that there exists nothing except God, may He be exalted, and this existent world, and that there is no possible inference proving his existence, may He be exalted, except those deriving from this existent taken as a whole and from its details. (1:71, 183)

Maimonides' approach to natural theology in *The Guide* laid the foundation for the development of scientific method in the West. In contrast with the Kalam and with most theology of his time, Maimonides asserted that "demonstrations ... can only be taken from the permanent nature of what exists, a nature that can be seen and apprehended by the senses and the intellect" (1: 76, 231; see also 1: 71, 179). But for Maimonides, as we find today among some of the spiritual interpreters of Gaia theory, the living, organic whole of being was more than a scientific truth. It was the supreme source of value and measure of all meaning, and it was our path to knowing God (Seidenberg, 2015, 71–72, 268–271).

Maimonides' ideas about the wholeness of Creation profoundly influenced the Church, especially Thomas Aquinas, as *Summa Theologica* (1920, 1: 47, 246) and *Summa Contra Gentiles* (1955, 3: 64) confirm. His rejection of anthropocentrism contrasted sharply with nearly every other medieval Jewish thinker—those before him, such as Saadyah Gaon and Bachya ibn Pakuda, and those after him. In fact, the entire *Guide* can be interpreted as a polemic against the extreme anthropocentrism of Saadyah Gaon, who wrote in *Emunot v'Dei'ot*, "When we see the many created beings, we should not be perplexed [*n'vukhim*] about what among them is the goal ... for the goal is humanity" (1970, art. 4, Introduction).[1] Just the opposite, Maimonides teaches that we should be perplexed if we think the goal is humanity, and this should lead us toward the right, non-anthropocentric understanding of Creation and humans' place in Creation.

This overarching principle also transformed the way Maimonides understood ethics and the significance of animals' lives.[2] In general, Maimonides minimized differences between humanity and other animals, and in the *Guide* he always refers to humanity in contrast with "the other animals." He taught that the instruction to "dominate" in Genesis 1 was neither a commandment nor an imperative, but merely a description of human nature (3: 13, 454). Maimonides also explained that instrumental reason, what gives us the power to dominate other creatures with our tools and machinations, is not a mark of human excellence or divine blessing, but merely something that makes human beings very dangerous animals (1: 7, 33). Moreover, he held that animals and humans could have equal capacity to feel and imagine. This understanding was integral to his interpretation of the prohibitions concerning slaughtering or taking animals and their young (Lev. 22: 27, Deut. 22: 6–7):

> It is forbidden to slaughter [an animal] and its young on the same day, this being a precautionary measure to avoid slaughtering the young animal in front of its mother. For in these cases animals feel very great pain, there being no difference regarding this pain between [humanity] and the other animals. For the love and the tenderness of a mother for her child is not consequent upon reason, but upon the activity of the imaginative faculty, which is found in most animals just as it is found in [humanity]. (3: 48, 599; see also 1: 75, 209; 2: 1, 245)

Some modern interpreters incorrectly play down this passage by emphasizing Maimonides' statement elsewhere that the prohibition on causing pain to animals has as its purpose the object of perfecting people (3: 17, 473). However, Maimonides is clear there, just as he is here, that compassion is enjoined for individual animals; his concern in the latter passage is to show that Divine Providence does not operate in the lives of individual animals.

For Maimonides, the uniqueness of human nature is found in the capacity to apprehend the Divine. This is humanity's perfection. Its attainment, which only a few individuals attain, is what constitutes being in God's image (1: 1–2, 23–24). Yet even this quality, along with the "hylic intellect" (1: 72, 190–191), makes human beings "merely the most noble among the things that are subject to generation," since he believed like other Aristotelians that the spheres and the heavens far surpassed humanity in their capacity to contemplate the Divine (3: 12, 443).

Maimonides' rejection of anthropocentrism and his espousal of a holistic cosmology are starting points for any eco-theology rooted in biblical traditions. Much in Maimonides may also be problematic for contemporary ecological thinkers. As an Aristotelian, Maimonides had a strongly negative attitude to the sense of touch (2: 56, 371; 3: 8, 432–433), which is incompatible with the phenomenological approach to the Earth taken by many eco-philosophers. His writings also made dualism between the intellect or soul and the body a fundamental part of Jewish thought. In the same vein, he emphasized that imagination is inferior to reason, and espoused an intellectual elitism that remains controversial. In contrast with Maimonides' explicit philosophy, so much of our encounter with Nature is based on feeling, empathy, and imagination. In order to locate an eco-theology that embraces the imagination, we must turn to the masters of the imagination, the Kabbalists.

Kabbalah and Eco-theology

If Maimonides rejected the sensuousness of physical being, many Kabbalists embraced it with a passion barely restrained by rabbinic norms. Kabbalistic literature spans many centuries and is highly diverse and complex. In my examination of the themes in Kabbalah I focus on only a few dimensions of that complexity.

Jewish mysticism has taken many forms throughout its history, but the tradition we call Kabbalah became fully crystallized in the thirteenth century with the publication of the *Zohar* (*The Book of Radiance*). While the literature of Kabbalah is vast, certain themes run through them all. Jewish mysticism is fundamentally concerned with cosmology and cosmogony, the origins and the process through which God created the world, the holism of Creation in all its aspects, and the processes within Divinity that sustain the world.

The mystical traditions most associated with the term Kabbalah started with *Sefer Bahir*, which goes back at least to the eleventh century. The *Bahir*, and all subsequent Kabbalah, is characterized by several motifs that are relevant to eco-theology. These include the idea that the human body in its physical details, and not just the soul, is in the image of God—a direct rejection of the dualism of Jewish philosophy. They also include the idea that the commandments of the Torah were given to us for the sake of restoring or healing the whole cosmos and reuniting it with the Infinite.

In fact, Kabbalah is the primary thread within Jewish tradition and imagines that one purpose of the Jewish covenant, and hence an intention of the Divine Will, is to redeem the more-than-human world, beyond both Israel and humanity. In short, God's abundance appears as a cosmic blessing, and it is the human task to increase the flow of cosmic blessing into the world. As Seth Brody wrote, "The Kabbalist's goal is to become a living bridge, uniting heaven and earth, so that God may become equally manifest above and below, for the healing and redemption of all" (1993, 153).

Moshe Cordovero (1522–1570, Palestine) elucidated the meaning of this principle in his work *Or Ne'erav* (*Sweet Light*):

> Being involved in this wisdom, a person sustains the world and its life and its sustenance. And this is what Rabbi Shimon bar Yochai (the main protagonist of the Zohar) explained, and he said that "the world is blessed because of us" ... for involvement with Divinity causes cleaving, and when the human cleaves to the One who flows/guides the world, he causes the flow [of divine energy] necessarily, and ... causes to flow upon the world a great flow. (1965, 32)

One of Cordovero's most popular works, *Tomer D'vorah* (*The Palm Tree of Deborah*), sums up the human task as follows: "This is the principle: he should cause life to stream forth to all" (from the Hebrew, 1969, 21; 1974, 82). The fundamental principle that "the whole world is blessed because of us" (*kol alma mit'barekh b'ginan*) means that the actions of the righteous bring blessing to the whole of Creation and to the Earth and all its creatures, as well as to God. This is fertile ground in which to root contemporary Jewish eco-theology.

Another fundamental kabbalistic principle, that "there is no place empty of God [*leyt atar panui miney*]," that is, the presence of God can be found in every creature and being, also provides a foundation for eco-theology. In addition, several areas in Kabbalah may be drawn on to develop an ecological ethics, including the holism of Creation, the ethical treatment and moral standing of other animals and other species, the contemplation of the natural world as a revelation of the Divine Presence, and the extension of the idea of God's image from humanity to Creation itself.

One way to understand the holism of Kabbalah in modern terms is through the concept of the more-than-human world. This term was coined by David Abram (1996) to remind us that human society is part of the natural world—"Nature" is not only "out there," but also within—and at the same time to caution us that the world is far beyond our needs and our understanding. But conceptually, both God and Nature are more than human; in certain moments, the distinction between the two is dissolved in the overwhelming power of being. This is effected in Kabbalah through the sanctification of the world around us by holy actions. Every deed is an act of compassion for Creation, as well as a fulfillment of *tzorekh gavoha* (the need on high) in the divine realm.

On the cosmological level, other characteristics of Kabbalah are also significant for contemporary ecological thought. The holographic complexity that characterizes Creation according to Kabbalah is resonant for any theology of Nature that attempts to incorporate contemporary science. For eco-feminism, the kabbalistic emphasis on balancing or uniting male and female at all levels, and an acknowledgment of the feminine aspect of the Divine, are also intriguing, even though many texts on this maintain a gender hierarchy. Finally, the sensuous way that Kabbalah understands cosmogony, and the significance of playfulness in God's relation to Creation, are echoed in contemporary eco-psychology.

Sefirotic Play

The *Sefer Bahir* (*Book of Brightness*), the earliest articulation of what we now think of as Kabbalah, is the first book to begin to delineate the characteristics of the *Sefirot*. The *Bahir* describes the parable of a king who began building a palace (that is, when God began creating the world), and a spring gushed forth. When he saw the spring, he said, "I will plant a garden, then I will delight (or 'play') in it, and so will all the world" (Margaliot, 1994a, §5; Kaplan, 1989, 3). Creation is here both God's act of delight or play, and a gift of delight to all creatures.

The playful garden that the king planted is described later in the *Bahir* as the Tree of Life. This Cosmic Tree is defined in later Kabbalah as a particular pattern called the

Sefirot (singular: *Sefirah*), which together are the image of God, or what Gershom Scholem (1991) called "the mystical shape of the Godhead." The *Sefirot* are regarded alternately as divine attributes, essence, emanations, instruments or vessels; various perspectives are emphasized by different Kabbalists. The Kabbalists in general found God by tracing the pattern of God's unfoldment (to borrow David Bohm's term) through the levels of emanation, from one *Sefirah* to the next, and from one world to the next. These levels represent the way in which divine energies such as love and judgment, male and female, hidden and manifest, and so on, are balanced to emanate and create this reality. Everything that exists has within it the essence and image of those supernal levels. Thus each "holon" manifests the *Sefirot* and so bears witness to the image of God. ("Holon" is Ken Wilber's term for the way the nature of every being reflects the whole of what he calls "the Kosmos.") At each level and within each entity, the Kabbalists saw the pattern of the *Sefirot* in a manner we might call fractal or holographic.

Holism

Kabbalah, like most mysticisms, embraced a holistic view of the universe where the more visible and physical levels of reality depend on the spiritual and invisible. "Implicit [in Kabbalah] is a notion of sacred cosmology... The Kabbalists' faith involves a hierarchy of worlds that are ontologically higher than the material world" (Krassen, 1999, 137). Kabbalah called for the expansion of divinity into the physical world, and the work of the Kabbalist was to draw the higher worlds into the lower and to unite the lower with the higher, thereby uniting all the worlds, including dimensions of God and Nature, into one realm or one whole.

This tendency is most pronounced in the radical cosmogony some texts propose: the universe is composed of shards of an original Creation that shattered while it was still in the realm of the Divine, carrying "sparks" of divinity into what became the physical realm. Each of these sparks is a part of the Divine that has been alienated from its root. (Cf. chapter 17 on Maximus the Confessor whose writings parallel this in some ways, though he writes not of a "shattering," but of the divine *Logos* and of *logoi*, who have sparks of the Divine within them.) Human beings are the vehicle to repair this rupture and reunite the sparks with the whole. Equally important, the process that begins Creation is understood to be a contraction of God, called *tzimtzum*, which makes space for the world to emerge. Isaac Luria (1534–1572, Palestine) in particular used images of birth to describe this process, suggesting that the universe or Nature is somehow commensurable with God in the way that a child is with its mother (Seidenberg, 2015, 276–277).

These tropes teach us that the human purpose in Creation is to unify all realms of being with and within the Divine. The *kavanot* (opening incantations) that the Kabbalists added to their prayers expressed this purpose: "for the sake of the unification of the Holy One and the Shekhinah." One of its most beautiful expressions can be found in the opening prayer of the original Tu Bish'vat seder (the kabbalistic ritual meal in honor of the Mishnaic New Year for the trees, interpreted by the Kabbalists as the New Year for the Cosmic Tree). This prayer, from the *P'ri Eitz Hadar*, was first published in the seventeenth-century *Chemdat Yamim* (*Delight of Days*):

> O God who makes, and forms, and creates, and emanates the upper/supernal worlds, and in their form and pattern you created their model on the earth below—You made them all with wisdom, upper ones above and lower ones below, "to join the tent [together] to become one" (Exod. 36: 18). (Seidenberg, 2015, 357)

The purpose of wisdom (i.e., Kabbalah) is to recognize and re-establish the pattern of the Divine Image, here denoted by "joining the tent to become one." This phrase is taken from the verse describing how Moses put together the desert sanctuary called the *Mishkan* or Tabernacle. In other words, God created upper and lower realms as reflections of each other in order to make out of Creation a holy temple. It is the Kabbalist's work to serve as priest in that Temple, as the *P'ri Eitz Hadar* describes:

> May it be Your will, through the strength of the merit of eating the fruit which we will eat [on Tu Bish'vat], and our blessing over them now, and our meditating on the secret of their roots above upon which they depend, to cause the flow of desire and blessing and free gift to flow over them, to return again to make them grow and bloom...for good and for blessing, for good life and for peace ... And may the Whole return now to its original strength ... and may all the sparks that were scattered by our hands, or by the hands of our ancestors, or by the sin of the first human against the fruit of the tree, be returned to sustain in might and majesty the Tree of Life. "Then the trees of the forest will sing out," (Ps. 96: 11) and the tree of the field will raise a branch and make fruit. (357–358)[3]

That priestly function includes bringing blessing to the physical fruit that will be set by the trees in the spring months leading up to the Shavuot festival of the first fruits. But this same process is a physical model of what must happen cosmologically, which is the restoration of those sparks from the Tree of Life that we and our human ancestors have scattered. There is also a profound resonance between this mystical Tree of Life and the evolutionary Tree of Life that unites all living things, whose sparks we have also scattered and extinguished.

The Earth or Cosmos as Divine Body and Image

There are several themes in Kabbalah that relate to nature as a whole participating in divinity. *Shekhinah*, the "indwelling presence" which is the feminine dimension of divinity, is also called "the image which includes all images," that is, the images of all creatures above and below (*Zohar*, Margaliot, 1984, 1: 13a). As the source of all divine *shefa* (overflow) that reaches the lower worlds, *Shekhinah* is the image of God that is closest to the Earth:

> R' Eliezer said to him: Father, is it so above, as they learned, that there is no body and no substance? He said to him: My son, about the world-to-come it was said, for that is a supernal [i.e., purely immaterial] mother, but below there is the body of this world, which is the *Shekhinah* below. (*Tikunei Zohar* §70, Margaliot, 1994a, 131a)

The *Shekhinah* in some sense represents "Nature." The Kabbalah's concept of Nature, however, is vastly different from both science and Gaia spirituality. Compared to classical scientific determinism, Nature in Kabbalah is potentially free and self-willing, and corresponds to the name *Elohim*, usually translated as God. But, unlike the simpler understanding of Nature as Mother-Goddess, in Kabbalah Nature as *Shekhinah* must be united with the worlds above and hence with the transcendent. Thus, Nature is creative but it is not self-creating.

Whatever these images mean on a practical level, they also imply that the natural world needs to be redeemed along with the divine feminine. According to some texts, this unification ends with the feminine being reabsorbed into the masculine, while others depict the feminine attaining equal stature, "eye-to-eye" with the masculine. Because of the former motif, Elliot Wolfson (2002) doubts whether Kabbalah has any value for eco-theology. However, Seth Brody, Daniel Matt, Arthur Green, Arthur Waskow, and I, among others, find these tropes powerful grounds for creating an "eco-Kabbalah."

Kabbalah also conceptualized Creation not only as a Cosmic Tree and as *Shekhinah*, but also as *Adam Kadmon* (the "primordial human," sometimes translated as "divine anthropos"), thereby connecting the Divine Image, the Tree of Life, and the cosmos itself through the mediation of Adam. While some texts connect *Adam Kadmon* primarily with the upper or originary realms only, others see it as the macrocosm that represents the Divine Image in the whole of Creation. The former dualistic perspective (discussed below) and the latter holistic perspective can sometimes be found in the same text. This complexity means that before we can carry out a wholesale adoption of kabbalistic cosmology for a theology of Nature, we must first reread these texts.

Nevertheless, some Kabbalists consistently emphasized the inclusion of the Earth and its creatures in the Divine Image. Yosef ben Shalom Ashkenazi (thirteenth-century Spain), for example, calls this "the secret of *Adam HaGadol* [the great Adam]," explaining:

> The human being should be called a small world, for in his form he is like all [the creatures of the world]—the human, formed of "the dirt from the ground" [Gen. 2: 8], included in himself the seal and structure and likeness and image of all ten *Sefirot* and all that is created and formed and made from them. (1974, 36)

The dirt of the Earth itself includes the seal, structure, and image of God, which became part of Adam. Shneur Zalman of Liady (founder of Lubavitcher Hasidism, 1745–1813), one of the few Hasidic rabbis to systematically treat Kabbalah, even more pointedly asserted that the very substance of the Earth manifested the greatest revelation of divinity. In the very last letter he wrote, published as *Igeret Hakodesh* 20, he described the growth from year to year of plants from the soil as the completion of *Adam Kadmon* and as the most visible expression of the pure *Chesed* (originary love), which gave birth to Creation (1972, 512; Seidenberg, 2015, 255–260).

Ashkenazi also wrote in his commentary on *Sefer Yetzirah* (the *Book of Formation*, an early mystical tract where the term *Sefirot* first appears) that the heavens and the Earth together (i.e., the cosmos itself) was God's image:

> All the existences ... whether silent or growing or moving or speaking (rock, plant, animal, human) ... every one of them, all of which are His, is in the structure of His seal—understand this for it hints at the truth, as it is said "Let us make a human being (adam) in our image as our likeness," and it says "the heavens rejoice and the earth sings out [*yism'chu hashamayim v'tagel ha'aretz*"] (Ps. 96: 11)—the first letters [of these four words] spell out *YHVH* and the last letters (read backwards) spell out "His image [*tzalmo*]." (Ashkenazi, 1961, *ad* 1: 12, 67–68)

The universe is God's image, and not just the image of *Elohim*, the name for God used in Genesis 1, which is the template for humanity, but an image of *YHVH* (the Tetragrammaton, often translated as "Lord"). *YHVH* alludes to a higher dimension of God than *Elohim*, and the letters of the Tetragrammaton, *Yud Heh Vav Heh*, represent the structure of the *Sefirot*.

On the largest scale, the four letters of the name *YHVH* were seen as corresponding to the multi-level process of emanation that creates and sustains all, which was characterized according to "the four worlds" or stages of being: emanating (*Yud*), creating (*Heh*), shaping (*Vav*), and acting (*Heh*). From this perspective, emphasized in Cordoveran Kabbalah, the whole of Creation, embracing all levels, was conceived as an image of God.

God's Image within the World

If the *Sefirot* are the image of God and the soul of the world, then the elements of Creation are sometimes also treated as the embodiment and manifestation of that image and that soul:

> The ten *Sefirot* ... are clothed in ten things that were created on the first day, and these are: skies and land, light and darkness, abyss and chaos, wind and water, the measure of day and the measure of night. (*Tikunei Zohar* §70, Margaliot, 1994a, 120a–b)

In rhythmic language, the author surveys the whole of Creation, discerning ten elemental parts that correspond to the ten *Sefirot*, which function as an analogue for God's image.

God's image in Adam also unites the whole of Creation, in part because it carries within itself each created species and individual, that is, the entire diversity of Creation. Isaiah Horowitz (1562–1630) even taught that God's purpose in creating humanity was to unite the diversity of Creation with God's image: "'The end of the thing' [Eccl. 12: 13] is Adam, who was created last ... Adam was created at the end so that he could include everything in his image and likeness" (1996, 216). Similarly, we have seen how

Ashkenazi included all the creatures in God's seal, which is God's image. So humanity's place as the last to be created was not in order for humanity to rule over everything, but rather to enable humanity to serve everything. Moreover, for Ashkenazi, idolatry was forbidden not because it falsely attributed divinity to an object of worship, but rather because by worshiping a piece of the whole, one removes that piece from its rightful place within divinity (see below).

At the same time, the pattern of the *Sefirot* at the highest level is the guarantor that every subsequent level is also an image of God. The *Sefirot*, the angels, the animals of Ezekiel's chariot (human, lion, eagle, and ox), and the four elements are seen as manifestations of the same pattern but at different levels (Horowitz, 1996, 152). This highlights another motif in Kabbalah, which is that anything that represents the whole of reality, such as the four elements, also represents the image of God.

Since Kabbalah uses the letters of the Tetragrammaton to represent the structure of the *Sefirot*, seeing these letters in a creature or thing also expresses the idea that God's image is manifest through it. For example, in *Tikunei Zohar* (a series of meditations on the first verse of Genesis) each limb of the human body is an image of this name; each human being as a whole person is understood to be an image; and the diversity of humanity as one species is also an expression of God's image, mapped onto *YHVH* (Margaliot, 1994a, 146a).

This trope, however, was not limited to the human realm. The human species as a whole is further seen as one letter in the name formed by the spectrum of animal species represented in the chariot. Correspondences with *YHVH* were also drawn to the bodies of other creatures such as birds and fruit trees, and to other dimensions of the physical and supernal worlds such as the colors of the rainbow, thereby relating various senses, spectrums, and dimensions to *YHVH*.[4] In general, those creatures which were seen as uniting the upper and lower worlds represent an image of God in the world, along with those symbols of human culture whose explicit purpose was to create unification, like the Torah and the *Mishkan* (Seidenberg, 2015, 217–231).

While all Creation in general is part of God, some texts emphasize the role of the lower creatures as an essential part of God's name. For example, *Zohar Chadash* explains the final *Heh* of God's name in *Sitrey Otiyot* (*Secrets of the Letters of Creation*):

> In the secret of the ten *Sefirot* ... all is included in this image of *Heh* (the fourth letter of God's name)... [I]n this secret were created and ordered all these lower ones. For this [reason] it's written: "Elohim said: Let us make [*na'aseh*] Adam in our image as our likeness ..." "*Na'aseh/N'SH*"—certainly this [refers to the letter] *Heh*, literally, and all these that are existing below and are united in her, in her image, truly. (Margaliot, 1994b, 2a)

When the physical dimension of being is not conjoined with the higher levels, the final letter of God's name, the *Heh*, is as it were missing, and the image of God is diminished. While Kabbalah mostly focused on specific manifestations of the *Sefirot* and God's image, the image of God ultimately embraced the breadth and diversity of Creation.

Rabbinic Roots and Modern Branches

Many elements found in Kabbalah are rooted in classical rabbinic texts. At the same time, the mythical elements that Kabbalah inherited from biblical and rabbinic traditions were transformed and systematized (Liebes, 1993). The raw material for kabbalistic cosmology includes the animism of the rabbis and the Torah before them, the personification of the land as a covenantal partner in the Torah, the midrashic idea that the upper beings or heavens were created in God's image, and the idea that the human body is a complete microcosm of the Earth. Even the expression "there is no place empty of God" is Talmudic in origin.

A second-century esoteric teaching known as *Shiur Komah* (*The Measure of the Body*), which described God's body as similar in structure to the human body but measured in the ancient equivalent of light-years, also provided a critical element that allowed Kabbalah to connect God's image and the physical cosmos. The classical rabbinic texts, however, never made a connection between the structure of the cosmos, the human microcosm, and the image of God, and they explicitly stated that the lower beings or the creatures of the Earth were not created in God's image. Kabbalah penetrated the boundaries between Heaven and Earth and between upper and lower realms, projecting the image of God onto the "lower beings."

Contemporary scholars such as Green (2002) and Brody (1993) understand these texts to be the product of imaginations that embraced the diversity of Creation; a parable from the *Zohar* related to this theme has been translated by Matt (1996, 134). Krassen explains:

> For the Kabbalists, nature is neither a source to be exploited for utilitarian benefits nor a sentimental vestige of the past to be romanticized by poets and naturalists. It is rather an ultimate link in a chain of divine manifestation that directly emerges from the divine source of life. (1999, 137)

Others, such as Hava Tirosh-Samuelson (2002), have questioned whether the intention of Kabbalah goes beyond the play of textuality and linguistic interpretation. While I support the former view, in either case Kabbalah provides a powerful model that we can use to express the religious meaning of our encounter with the diversity of life.

Dualism and Repairing the Cosmos

According to some cosmologies, especially within Lurianic Kabbalah, the human of the Genesis story is born into an already shattered universe. This perspective led some Kabbalists to a dualistic understanding of Creation in which the connection between the Earth and *imago dei* was rejected. In one Zohar passage, we read, "*Adam Kadmon*, even though his body is made from dirt, it's not from the dirt here ... *Adam Kadmon* has nothing from this world at all" (*Zohar* 3: 83a).

Here the element from which the primordial human is created is entirely derived from an anti-physical (or ante-physical) Earth. Nevertheless, even though the image of God is not expressed through the originary physical universe, our human bodies still have the potential to express the divine pattern, and this can only happen in completeness in the physical world. (This position radically divided all Kabbalah from medieval Jewish philosophy, which completely dissociated the body from God's image.) In Lurianic doctrine, this is described as raising the sparks to their root in divinity and purifying them from their materiality, *berur han'tzotzot*. Through this process, the original shattering of Creation could be repaired, and this is the purpose of our existence. Thus, unlike Gnostic dualism, even within the most dualistic interpretations of Kabbalah the purpose of humanity is to be engaged with the physical world and to bring redemption to the whole of Creation.

Ethics

Because Kabbalah saw the redemption of the cosmos as something that could come about through every interaction with the world, we find Kabbalists who developed an acute sensitivity concerning other creatures and how we use them[5] (Seidenberg, 2015, 162–165). The seeds for these ideas can be found in the classical rabbinic understanding that everything has a place and one should despise nothing in the world (*Mishnah Avot* 4: 3). Cordovero, who developed this rabbinic principle further than any other Kabbalist, wrote that a person must

> honor the creatures entirely, since he recognizes in them the exalted quality of the Creator [*ma'alat haborei'*] who "formed the human with wisdom" and so [it is with] all creatures—the wisdom of the One who forms [them] is in them, and he sees himself that they are so very very honored, for the One who forms [them] cares for all ... And it is evil in the eyes of the Holy One if they despise any creature of His creatures, and this is [why] it says: "How manifold/diverse/*rabu* are Your works" (Ps. 104: 24) ... *rabu* [like] the language "*rav beito*/ important in the house [of the king]" (Esther 1: 8)—very important. (1969, 19–20; 1974, 78; cf. 1969, 16; 1974, 71)

Cordovero stressed that showing mercy and respect, and bringing beneficence to every aspect of Creation, is what it means to become like the Creator: "One's mercies should be distributed to all the creatures, not destroying and not despising them. For so is the highest Wisdom distributed to all the creatures, silent, growing, moving and speaking [i.e., mineral, plant, animal, and human]" (1974, 83).

The wisdom of the Creator is bestowed according to the pattern of the *Sefirot*. When a person imitates this pattern, he or she allows the influx of divinity to reach each and every being, according to Cordovero. He wrote that this principle has strong practical implications:

> [A person should] not uproot a growing thing except for need, nor kill any animal except for need. And he should choose a good death [*mitah yafah*] for them, with a carefully examined knife, to show mercy however is possible. This is the principle: compassion [should be] over all existences, to not hurt them ... unless [it is] to raise them from level to level/high to higher, from growing to living, from living to speaking, for then it is permitted to uproot the growing thing and to kill the animal, the debt [being outweighed] by the merit. (1969, 20; 1974, 84)

Differing broadly from normative *halakhah* or Jewish law, Cordovero understood other creatures not in terms of human need, but in terms of the need of all living things to fulfill their divine purpose. More subtly, when Cordovero used the term *mitah yafah*, he was referencing the Talmud's use of this term as an embodiment of the Levitical principle "Love your neighbor as yourself" (Bavli, *Sanhedrin* 45a, 52b), intentionally applying a human ethical principle to non-human animals.

This deep understanding of ethics extended even to the interpretation some Kabbalists gave to the prohibition against idolatry. Yosef Ashkenazi, quoted above, explained that the sin of idolatry is that it separates the worshiped entity from the divinity that comprises the whole:

> Since all the existences from the upper and lower ones are all of them tied into [God's] great, mighty and awesome name, therefore He warned [Israel] to not worship them in separation from His name—[but] only [to worship] through the name of *YHVH* [as] one. (1984, 148)

Here as elsewhere, the unity of being, which is concomitant with the presence of divinity in all being, is the root of the extraordinary proto-ecological sensibility displayed in Kabbalah. Applying these principles to eco-theology, if the image of God is an image of the diversity of life, then we might say that God's image is diminished every time human beings cause another extinction (Seidenberg, 2015, 239).

Contemplation and Ritual

Kabbalists reconciled the unity of being with the diversity of Creation by seeing every aspect of the world as simultaneously cloaking and revealing the Divine. They found the *Sefirot* and the letters of God's explicit name everywhere, and reached the spiritual dimension of things by engaging with the traces of the Divine in the physical world. This engagement was realized principally through the projection of language and text onto the world, and thus focused on ideas at least as much as it focused on phenomena. The implication of kabbalistic theurgy (ritual or magic which operates on or affects divinity) was that proper intention and consciousness could reveal the divinity underlying all phenomena and unify phenomena with their source. This engendered a deeper respect for the intrinsic value of other creatures and things than one finds in normative Judaism.

The potential to create a phenomenology of holiness was further developed from Kabbalah by Hasidism in the eighteenth century. These ideas also inspired many other Jewish thinkers, in both the Renaissance and the early modern period, to use Kabbalah to reconcile theology and science.

Some modern Kabbalists also gave full expression to the power of contemplating and understanding Nature as hinted at in Kabbalah. Abraham Isaac Kook (1865–1935, Palestine) wrote:

> Contemplate the wonders of Creation, the divine dimension of their being, not as a dim configuration that is presented to you from the distance but as the reality in which you live ... [F]ind the source of your own life, and of the life beyond you, around you, the glorious splendor of the life in which you have your being. The love that is astir in you—raise it to its basic potency and its noblest beauty, extend it to all its dimensions, toward every manifestation of the soul that sustains the universe. (1978, 207)

For Kook, the meaning of Kabbalah is found in the lived experience of the natural world. He wrote that from the knowledge of God, "there radiates ... a love for the world, for all worlds, for all creatures, on all levels of their being. A love for all existence fills the hearts of the good and kindly ones among creatures, and among humans" (1978, 226). Kook's theology may be called biocentric in the broadest sense (as further evidenced by his impassioned embrace of the theory of evolution). Kook's spiritual directives may be realized in contemporary work that ties together Kabbalah and ecology.

Conclusion

Together, Maimonides and Kabbalah provide the basis for a robust Jewish eco-theology and ecological ethic. Looked at over the course of its history, Kabbalah is a process that has led to an increasing embrace of the more-than-human world as divine in all its aspects. Equally importantly, Maimonides rejected anthropocentrism and embraced the whole of Creation. Both teach us to see ourselves in relation to the whole and to regard the whole as the ultimate ethical end.

The road to healing this physical world and living responsibly and sustainably in it may even depend on more fully developing holism as the ground of morality. We cannot expect religion to serve its societal purpose—the purpose of shaping a right way of life—if our theologies leave human beings at the center and pinnacle of Creation, here to serve God and to be served by the rest of Creation. A Hasidic master taught that one should always remind oneself of two dictums: "The whole world is created for my sake" and "I am nothing but dirt and ashes," and that the key to righteousness is to know when to take which dictum to heart (Seidenberg, 2015, 118). Keeping this lesson in mind, we could rewrite these dictums to reflect our two sources of teaching: for Kabbalah, "I was created for the sake of the whole world"; and for Maimonides, "I am nothing but conscious dirt and ashes." Holding these truths close to our hearts, encountering this manifold universe with both humility and responsibility, we can develop a Judaism that is closer to the sources of the tradition than the religion we live today. That same Judaism, and that same reading of biblical tradition, is one that can carry us forward into a world that is both more redeemed and more vivid, and is sweetened by the human presence.

Notes

1 In fact, Maimonides held this position as a young man (1963b, 21–22).
2 It was also determinative for how he understood the problem of evil. See 3: 12 and 3: 25.
3 For a complete translation of this prayer, see Krassen (1999, 148–151).
4 In the example of the bird, *Tikunei Zohar* describes the head as the *Yud*, the body the *Vav*, and the two wings the two *Hehs* of God's name (Margaliot, 1994a, 82b).
5 One seminal concept in Kabbalah engendering this sensitivity was reincarnation; for many Kabbalists this included the possibility that human beings could reincarnate as animals or even plants. In another vein, many Kabbalists asserted that only one knowledgeable in the Torah and raising the sparks should be allowed to eat meat.

References

Abram, David. 1996. *The Spell of the Sensuous*. New York: Random House.

Aquinas, Thomas. 1920. *Summa Theologica* (2nd ed.). Transl. Fathers of the English Dominican Province. http://www.newadvent.org/summa/1047.htm.

Aquinas, Thomas. 1955. *Summa Contra Gentiles, book 3, transl.* Vernon Bourke. http://www.dhspriory.org/thomas/ContraGentiles3a.htm.

Ashkenazi, Yosef ben Shalom. 1961. Perush Hara'vad. In *Sefer Yetzirah*. Jerusalem: Monzon. http://www.hebrew.grimoar.cz/jecira/ravad_jecira.htm.

Ashkenazi, Yosef ben Shalom. 1984. *Perush L'parshat B'rei'shit* [Commentary on Creation in Genesis], Moshe Hallamish (Ed.). Jerusalem: Magnes Press.

Brody, Seth. 1993. "Human Hands Dwell in Heavenly Heights: Contemplative Ascent and Theurgic Power in Thirteenth-Century Kabbalah" (123–158). In R. Herrera (Ed.), *Mystics of the Book: Themes Topics and Typologies*. New York: Peter Lang.

Cordovero, Moshe. 1965. *Or Ne'erav [Sweet Light]*. Jerusalem: Kol Y'hudah. http://www.hebrew.grimoar.cz/kordovero/or_neerav.htm.

Cordovero, Moshe. 1969. *Tomer D'vorah [Palm Tree of Deborah]*. Jerusalem: Or Yiqar. http://www.daat.ac.il/he-il/mahshevet-israel/yesod/mahshava/tomer-dvora.htm.

Cordovero, Moshe. 1974. *The Palm Tree of Deborah*. Transl. Louis Jacobs. New York: Sepher Hermon Press. http://www.digital-brilliance.com/contributed/deborah/deborah.htm.

Green, Arthur. 2002. "A Kabbalah for the Environmental Age" (3–15). In Hava Tirosh-Samuelson (Ed.), *Judaism and Ecology*. Cambridge, MA: Harvard University Press. Originally published in *Tikkun*, 14, 5, 33–40.

Habahir, Sefer. http://www.hebrew.grimoar.cz/anonym/sefer_ha-bahir.htm.

Hazohar. Sefer. http://www.hebrew.grimoar.cz/zohar/zohar_vilno_1.htm.

Horowitz, Isaiah. 1996. *The Generations of Adam*. Transl. Miles Krassen. New York: Paulist Press.

Kaplan, Aryeh (Transl.). 1989. *The Bahir*. York Beach, ME: Weiser.

Kook, Abraham Isaac. 1978. *Abraham Isaac Kook*. Transl. Ben Zion Bokser. New York: Paulist Press.

Krassen, Miles. 1999. "*Peri Eitz Hadar*: A Kabbalist Tu B'shvat Seder" (135–153). In Ari Elon, Naomi Hyman, & Arthur Waskow (Eds.), *Trees, Earth, and Torah: A Tu B'Shvat Anthology*. Philadelphia, PA: Jewish Publication Society.

Kook, Margaliot, Reuven (Ed.). 1994b. *Zohar Chadash and Shaarei Zohar*. Jerusalem: Mossad Harav Kook.

Liebes, 1993. "*De Natura Dei*: On the Development of Jewish Myth" (1–64). In *Studies in Jewish Myth and Messianism*. Transl. Batya Stein. Albany, NY: SUNY Press.

Maimonides, Moses (Rambam). 1963a. *The Guide for the Perplexed*, 2 vols. Transl. Shlomo Pines. Chicago, IL: University of Chicago Press.

Maimonides, Moses (Rambam). 1963b. *Mishnah Im Peyrush Harambam*, vol. 1. Jerusalem: Mosad Harav Kook.

Maimonides, Moses (Rambam). 1980. *The Guide for the Perplexed*. Transl. Moses Friedlander. New York: Dover Books.

Margaliot, Reuven (Ed.). 1984. *Sefer Hazohar*, 3 vols. Jerusalem: Mossad Harav Kook.

Margaliot, Reuven (Ed.). 1994a. *Sefer Habahir and Tikunei Hazohar*. Jerusalem: Mossad Harav.

Matt, Daniel (Ed.). 1996. *The Essential Kabbalah*. San Francisco, CA: HarperCollins.

Saadyah Gaon. 1970. *Emunot v'Dei'ot*. Transl. Yosef Kafich. Jerusalem: Makhon Sura. http://www.daat.ac.il/daat/mahshevt/kapah/4-2.htm.

Scholem, Gershom. 1991. *On the Mystical Shape of the Godhead*. Transl. Joachim Neugroschel. New York: Schocken Books.

Seidenberg, David. 2015. *Kabbalah and Ecology: God's Image in the More-Than-Human World*. New York: Cambridge University Press.

Shneur Zalman of Liady. 1972. "*Igeret Hakodesh* 20" (497–513). In *Likutei Amarim (also called Tanya)*. Transl. Nissan Mindel et al. London: Otzar Hachasidim. http://www.chabad.org/library/tanya/tanya_cdo/aid/7965/jewish/Epistle-20.htm.

Tirosh-Samuelson, Hava. 2002. "The Textualization of Nature in Jewish Mysticism" (389–396). In Hava Tirosh-Samuelson (Ed.), *Judaism and Ecology: Created World and Revealed Word*. Cambridge, MA: Harvard University Press.

Waskow, Arthur. 2001. "The Emergence of Eco-Kabbalah." Philadelphia, PA: Shalom Center. https://theshalomcenter.org/node/170.

Wolfson, Elliot. 2002. "The Mirror of Nature Reflected in the Symbolism of Medieval Kabbalah" (305–331). In Hava Tirosh-Samuelson (Ed.), *Judaism and Ecology: Created World and Revealed Word*. Cambridge, MA: Harvard University Press.

CHAPTER 4

Laudato Sí in the Earth Commons—Integral Ecology and Socioecological Ethics

John Hart

Greetings, all my relations. Greetings to all the two-legged people. Greetings to all the four-legged people. Greetings to all the winged people. Greetings to all the finned people. Greetings to all the rooted people. Greetings, all my relations.

In the first International Indian Treaty Council conference in which I participated almost 40 years ago, every morning and afternoon session began with a prayer by a traditional Indian spiritual leader. In the morning of the opening day, the elder began with "Greetings, all my relations," and continued in his native language. At that time, I had looked around and observed the diversity of peoples of distinct colors, ages, and cultures, and appreciated the elder welcoming everyone as relatives each to the other. In the afternoon, another elder initiated the session; he began with the greeting above. This elder's prayer elaborated the fullness of the greeting and I realized then that the earlier version had implicitly included, too, the diversity of all living creatures with which humans are related.

The two elders expressed independently but complementarily a consciousness that had not developed from biologists' research on biotic evolution from a single-cell organism to humankind, as theorized by Charles Darwin in the nineteenth century, or resulted from physicists' exploration of cosmic complexification from a "primeval atom" to an expanding universe, as proposed by Georges LeMaître in the early twentieth century. Rather, the elders voiced an oral tradition-originated, Mother Earth-formed spiritual and social consciousness. It had developed in cultural milieux related intimately to and permeated and shaped deeply by their natural abiotic and biotic environment over millennia. It recognized that all living beings emerged through divine creativity: they are children of the Creator, of sacred Mother Earth, of their parents, and of the family of all living beings, and are integrally related.

The Wiley Blackwell Companion to Religion and Ecology, First Edition. Edited by John Hart.

In May 2015 Francis I published an encyclical, *Laudato Sí*, to Catholics and "all people of good will." The document integrated human communities' economic wellbeing with the ecological wellbeing of humankind, all biota (living beings), and the Earth, their common home. It includes the concept and teaching of integral ecology. This theme complements well a prior concept and ethical practice related to ecological wellbeing which had emerged from Christian social thought a few years earlier: socioecological praxis ethics. Ecological-economic thought elaborated in the encyclical and current Christian socioecological ethics complement not only each other, but also perspectives that have emerged in the stories, traditions, and prayers of indigenous peoples throughout the world.

Pope Francis, in his references throughout the encyclical to previously published bishops' and papal documents and other Catholic Church statements on social and economic justice, has emphasized his continuity with and within the Catholic tradition. Subsequent analyses of the encyclical have noted its expression of existing Catholic social teaching (CST), including from his papal predecessors. (For a summary discussion of previous Catholic Church environmental thought, see Hart, 2004.) This chapter complements those elaborations of *Laudato Sí*. It discusses and integrates ideas presented in *Laudato Sí*, Christian social thought augmented by complementary religious and humanist thinking, representative Muskogee and Wanapum indigenous traditions, and the Earth Charter. These culturally diverse ideas from distinct contexts, when interrelated and integrated in the Earth commons, will benefit humankind, all biota, and the Earth.

Laudato Sí: Insights from the Earth Community Commons

A dialogic relationship in Earth contexts bridges the social and spiritual dimensions of reality. It emerges from personal transcending moments, when visions are seen or voices are heard, and in reflection on sacred texts, insights from spiritual leaders, mystics, scholars, social thinkers, and community activists, and immersion in the wonders of Creation. St. Francis and Pope Francis, in different eras and creative modes, elaborate this dialogic relationship. Pope Francis uses, as the title of his twenty-first-century encyclical, words that St. Francis used throughout his celebrated thirteenth-century canticle *Laudato Sí*: "Praised be" begins each verse in Francis's song about the voices of all creatures praising their Creator.

In the *Canticle of All Creation*, St. Francis joyfully sang that all beings—living and non-living—continually praise God. The words in the *Canticle* celebrate *non-living*, or abiotic, beings. The melody to which St. Francis sang was from a then-familiar Italian romantic ballad that celebrated *living*, or biotic, beings. The words and melody together provide a holistic view of all biotic and abiotic beings in Creation praising their Creator. In his song, St. Francis exults in "my lord Brother Sun, through whom you give us day and light"; "Sister Moon and Stars," created bright, precious, and beautiful in the heavens; "Brother Wind, and air and cloud and calm and all weather" that sustain God's creatures; "Sister Water," who is helpful, humble, precious, and pure; "Brother Fire, through whom you brighten the night, who is beautiful and playful, and sinuous and strong"; "our Sister Mother Earth, who sustains us and guides us, and provides varied fruits with colorful flowers and herbs." St. Francis concludes by praising and blessing God, and urging gratitude and service to God.[1]

While St. Francis is known primarily for his love of and affinity for all creatures and rightly acknowledged as a "Nature mystic," he expressed, too, in his words and actions, his compassion for and commitment to "the least of these" in Assisi's environs and beyond: the poor and outcasts of his era, especially the most oppressed, the lepers (Hart, 2009, 2015). The first community work he had his Friars Minor do was to care for them in an encampment outside Assisi.

In *Laudato Sí*, Pope Francis acknowledges St. Francis's mystical moments and community compassion, and complements them with a call for people today to "go and do likewise."

Francis of Assisi and Francis I

A hint of what is to come in the encyclical is revealed in the title itself, *Laudato Sí*. This opening phrase of the *Canticle of All Creation* is reiterated throughout. St. Francis's song celebrates all creatures: biota (indirectly) and abiota (directly), calling each of them "brother" or "sister." Earth is "our sister, Mother Earth," a phrase Francis I uses in *Laudato Sí*. The pope, who chose his papal name to honor the saint, frequently addresses injustices toward the poor oppressed while relating them to injustices toward the Earth. He states that St. Francis "shows us just how inseparable the bond is between concern for Nature, justice for the poor, commitment to society, and interior peace" (10).[2] He not only notes St. Francis's compassion for the "least of these," but urges that this attitude be mirrored in human communities today.

Laudato Sí Themes

Pope Francis discusses social, environmental, and ecological issues throughout *Laudato Sí*. All three relate to his thinking on integral ecology, a concept that he proposes and develops, and simultaneously, as will be discussed, to the complementary theory and practice of socioecological praxis ethics.

Climate Change

On climate change, Francis declares that

> The climate is a common good, belonging to all and meant for all... At the global level, it is a complex system linked to many of the essential conditions for human life. A very solid scientific consensus indicates that we are presently witnessing a disturbing warming of the climatic system ... a number of scientific studies indicate that most global warming in recent decades is due to the great concentration of greenhouse gases (carbon dioxide, methane, nitrogen oxides and others) released mainly as a result of human activity. (23)

Francis counters here those who defend fossil fuel consumption and deny the reality of climate change—even as the Earth grows ever hotter, devastating storms increase in number and ferocity, drought becomes extensive in some areas and harms or destroys agricultural lands and thereby food supplies, flooding increases, and people's lives and livelihoods are imperiled globally. Some who acknowledge climate heating deny human culpability: they claim that this is a recurring cycle and humankind has little to do with it. Yet climate change denial and rejection of human responsibility for it fly in the face of overwhelming evidence to the contrary. Their assertions likely indicate the extent to which behind the scenes Big Oil is influencing some politicians and scientists just as Big Tobacco did in the past, fighting science to safeguard profits. Despite the succession of years in which each year and every decade is hotter than its predecessor, and despite the consequences evermore harmful altered climate impacts have had on people and the planet, transnational corporations' striving for profit maximization seems to be prioritized over people's health and the Earth's wellbeing. The more than 3,500 scientists from 195 nations and diverse ideologies who are members of the Intergovernmental Panel on Climate Change (IPCC) disagree. They provided data on conditions on the Earth for the IPCC Fifth Assessment Report (AR5), issued in 2014. Their data include both dire warnings about climate change events and hope in the form of proposals to mitigate it. Recent newspaper headlines and articles highlight some climate change issues and impacts: "Seas Are Rising at Fastest Rate in Last 28 Centuries" (*The New York Times*, February 22, 2016); and "2015 Was Hottest Year in Historical Record, Scientists Say" (*New York Times*, January 20, 2016). At the time of writing, 2016 was on track to surpass 2015.

Francis rightly describes, in words that complement UN documents and statements from numerous religious traditions, including the Vatican, the World Council of Churches, the Coalition on Environment and Jewish Life, and the National Association of Evangelicals, how *ecological devastation disproportionally impacts the poor*: "[T]he excluded ... are the majority of the planet's populations ... [often] treated merely as collateral damage... [A] true ecological approach *always* becomes a social approach; it must integrate questions of justice in debates on the environment, so as to hear *both the cry of the earth and the cry of the poor*" (49). (The italicized phrase mirrors the writings of pioneer Brazilian theologian of liberation Leonardo Boff, who wrote a book with that title.) Francis links, too, biblical images of God with social and ecological realities: "In the Bible, the God who liberates and saves is the same God who created the universe, and these two divine ways of acting are intimately and inseparably connected" (73). He comments that it is doubtful that people are really in a profound relationship with the Earth and Earth's biota if they are not also concerned, and engaged socially, with the "least of living beings": "A sense of deep communion with the rest of nature cannot be real if our hearts lack tenderness, compassion and concern for our fellow human beings ... Concern for the environment thus needs to be joined to a sincere love for our fellow human beings and an unwavering commitment to resolving the problems of society" (91). Poverty and social suffering result from ideologies of greed and individualism that contradict traditional Christian (and other religions') teachings. The anti-biblical prioritization of private property over communal property, and admiration of human greed and selfishness over religions' attitudes of communal sharing to meet community needs are particularly problematic:

> the Earth is essentially a shared inheritance, whose fruits are meant to benefit everyone. For believers, this becomes a question of fidelity to the Creator, since God created the world for everyone. Hence every ecological approach needs to incorporate a social perspective which takes into account the fundamental rights of the poor and the underprivileged... The Christian tradition has never recognized the right to private property as absolute or inviolable, and has stressed the social purpose of all forms of private property ... there is always a social mortgage on all private property, in order that goods may serve the general purpose that God gave them. (74)

Francis reiterates and reinforces this point: "[E]very ecological approach needs to incorporate a social perspective which takes into account the fundamental rights of the poor and the underprivileged. The principle of the subordination of private property to the universal destination of goods, and thus the right of everyone to their use, is a golden rule of social conduct and 'the first principle of the whole ethical and social order'" (71).[3]

Anthropocentrism and Human Domination

Laudato Sí rejects *historical anthropocentrism and human domination*: "This sister [Earth] now cries out to us because of the harm we have inflicted on her by our irresponsible use and abuse of the goods with which God has endowed her... [T]he Earth herself, burdened and laid waste, is among the most abandoned and maltreated of our poor; she 'groans in travail'" (2). Abuses of the Earth, the result of human anthropocentrism, have been at times based on misinterpretations of Genesis Creation stories, whose themes express, in reality, humanity's responsibilities to God, neighbor, and the Earth: "The Creation accounts in the book of Genesis contain, in their own symbolic and narrative language, profound teachings about human existence and its historical reality. They suggest that human life is grounded in three fundamental and closely intertwined relationships: with God, with our neighbor and with the earth itself" (66). Other Genesis stories "full of symbolism, bear witness to a conviction which we today share, that everything is interconnected, and that genuine care for our own lives and our relationship with nature is inseparable from fraternity, justice and faithfulness to others" (70).

Biodiversity

Francis deplores loss of biodiversity, one of whose causes is that people act as if species have only instrumental value, to be used by humans as they please, to satisfy not only their needs but also their wants, and not intrinsic value (inherent integrity): "It is not enough ... to think of different species merely as potential 'resources' [I suggest using 'natural goods' rather than 'resources'; Hart, 2006, 150–152] to be exploited, while overlooking the fact that they have value in themselves... The great majority become extinct for reasons related to human activity" (33). I have proposed that while through millennia species ordinarily "go extinct" through natural evolutionary processes when they cannot adapt to a new or altered ecosystem, today species are rendered extinct by people who do not respect them, but alter or drastically reduce the environment they need for survival, and hunt or fish them to oblivion (Hart, 2006, 107–108).[4] The loss of biodiversity would be diminished or eliminated if humankind were to acknowledge species interdependence: "Because all creatures are connected, each must be cherished with love and respect, for all of us as living creatures are cherished with love and respect, for all of us as living creatures are dependent on one another" (42). Francis notes further that "The German bishops have taught that, where other creatures are concerned, 'we can speak of the priority of *being* [intrinsic value] over that of *being useful* [instrumental value]'" (69). Along these lines, *Laudato Sí* reflects on the intrinsic value of ecosystems:

> Ongoing research should ... give us a better understanding of how different creatures relate to one another in making up the larger units which today we term "ecosystems." We take these systems into account not only to determine how best to use them, but also because they have an intrinsic value independent of their usefulness. Each organism, as a creature of God, is good and admirable in itself; the same is true of the harmonious ensemble of organisms existing in a defined space and functioning as a system ... we depend on these larger systems for our own existence. (140)

In "Beyond the Sun," the last section of *Laudato Sí*, Francis makes the novel papal theological statement that "Eternal life will be a shared experience of awe, in which *each creature*, resplendently transfigured, will take its rightful place..." (243; emphasis added). This refutes some traditional theological views that only humans will take their "rightful place" in a heavenly hereafter.

Dialogue and Collaboration

In order to eliminate a variety of environmental injustices, a science, religion, and ecological movements dialogue, and collaboration on common ground, are important. Religions should "dialogue among themselves for the sake of protecting nature, defending the poor, and building networks of respect and fraternity. Dialogue among the various sciences is likewise needed... An open and respectful dialogue is also needed between the various ecological movements... The gravity of the ecological crisis demands that we all look to the common good..." (201)

The Precautionary Principle

The scientific precautionary principle is helpful to protect the most vulnerable places and populations:

> The Rio Declaration of 1992 states that "where there are threats of serious or irreversible damage, lack of full scientific certainty shall not be used as a pretext for postponing

cost-effective measures" (132), which prevent environmental degradation. This precautionary principle makes it possible to protect those who are most vulnerable and whose ability to defend their interests and to assemble incontrovertible evidence is limited. If objective information suggests that serious and irreversible damage may result, a project should be halted or modified, even in the absence of indisputable proof. Here the burden of proof is effectively reversed, since in such cases objective and conclusive demonstrations will have to be brought forward to demonstrate that the proposed activity will not cause serious harm to the environment or to those who inhabit it. (186)

Appropriate Energy Technology

Francis advocates replacing polluting fossil fuels and their delivery systems with appropriate energy technology: "We know that technology based on the use of highly polluting fossil fuels—especially coal, but also oil and, to a lesser degree, gas—needs to be progressively replaced without delay" (165). Community efforts are addressing the urgent need to eliminate pollution emissions that contribute to global warming: "In some places, cooperatives are being developed to exploit renewable sources of energy which ensure local self-sufficiency and even the sale of surplus energy" (179).

In a comment on flaws in urban architecture that impede a human relationship with Nature, Francis comments that "Many cities are huge, inefficient structures, excessively wasteful of energy and water. Neighbourhoods, even those recently built, are congested, chaotic and lacking in sufficient green space. We were not meant to be inundated by cement, asphalt, glass and metal, and deprived of physical contact with nature" (44).

Complementary Socioecological Teachings from Eastern and Western Christianity

On an ecumenical note, Francis states that Orthodox Patriarch Bartholomew I, known as the "Green Patriarch" for his ecological teachings and his actions around the world to combat eco-social injustices, challenges us to acknowledge our sins against creation: "For human beings ... to destroy the biological diversity of God's creation; for human beings to degrade the integrity of the earth by causing changes in its climate, by stripping the earth of its natural forests or destroying its wetlands; for human beings to contaminate the earth's waters, its land, its air, and its life—these are sins" (15). And "to commit a crime against the natural world is a sin against ourselves and a sin against God" (16).

Indigenous Peoples' Rights

Francis calls for the recognition of indigenous peoples' rights. This has been a constant papal theme since it was introduced by John Paul II: "The disappearance of a culture can be just as serious, or even more serious, than the disappearance of a species of plant or animal" (145): native peoples' cultures are being rendered invisible by dominant societies. Therefore,

> in this sense, it is essential to show special care for indigenous communities and their cultural traditions. They are not merely one minority among others, but should be the principal dialogue partners, especially when large projects affecting their land are proposed. For them, land is not a commodity but rather a gift from God and from their ancestors who rest there, a sacred space with which they need to interact if they are to maintain their identity and values. When they remain on their land, they themselves care for it best. (146)

Similarly, the United Nations, in its 2007 *Declaration on the Rights of Indigenous Peoples*, strongly advocated restoring and sustaining traditional native cultures; for pressing nations to fulfill their obligations to honor treaties signed with Indians, First Nations, *indios*, and other indigenous peoples; and for returning native peoples' land to them or agreeing with them an acceptable equivalent to atone for the theft of native lands and natural goods over the past five centuries. A dire and continuing consequence in the present century of the harmful impacts made from the fifteenth to the eighteenth centuries has been native peoples' physical and cultural genocide worldwide.

Teachings that emerge from native peoples' traditions illuminate and complement what Francis states. The spiritual wisdom of twentieth-century elders Phillip Deere and David Sohappy are especially significant.

Muskogee elder Phillip Deere (1926–1985) and Wanapum Dreamer David Sohappy (1925–1991) were traditional Indian spiritual leaders, human rights activists, and healers. From their respective traditions they provided knowledge of and insights into humans' relationships with Mother Earth. Teachings such as theirs express the "integral ecology" consciousness Pope Francis advocates; their conduct expresses "socioecological praxis ethics."

Phillip Deere was a Muskogee elder from Okemah, Oklahoma. He was raised in a traditional family, some of whose members were Methodists. As an adult, he served for some two decades, until he was about 40 years old, as a Methodist teacher and pastor. Then, he returned to traditional ways and became a respected spiritual leader, healer, and Indian activist fighting for Muskogee and other peoples' treaty rights. He was the spiritual guide for the American Indian Movement (AIM) and the International Indian Treaty Council (IITC), which was in effect the international arm of AIM. It was the first native peoples' non-governmental organization (NGO) recognized by the United Nations, almost 40 years ago.

As he viewed the degradation of Mother Earth caused by Euro-American ideologies and practices based in colonialist attitudes and lacking both spiritual values and respect for Creation, Phillip urged a change of mindset—a socioecological-spiritual conversion and acceptance of responsibility that would lead to Earth- and community-beneficial conduct:

> So we have to turn around and respect Mother Earth. We cannot say that "I am just a pilgrim passing through," so I have no use for the Missouri River. We cannot say that "I am a Baptist," "I am a Methodist," or "I am a Catholic," so I have no use for this tree. We have to

> understand who we are, what we are, where did we come from. We are the caretakers of this land and we are part of this creation. So we must respect Mother Earth.
>
> We believe in natural laws of love, peace and respect. We learned this thousands of years ago and this was the life of our people. When we destroy anything within the creation, we feel that we destroy ourselves... So we must preserve what we have... We have felt ourselves to be a part of the creation: not superiors, not the rulers of the creation, but only part of the creation. If we understand those natural ways, natural laws of love, peace and respect, we will be able to get along with everyone. We will learn to love and share with everyone.
>
> When we learned about Christianity we heard about the Father. We learned to pray to the Father, and in the churches every Sunday we heard about Father. To this day we still hear about Father. But we never hear anything about Mother... But every Indian knows what you mean when you say, "Mother Earth." Traditional people know what you're talking about... We must all learn to say "Mother" as well as we say "our Father." And in this way of life we will have balance.
>
> Native religion to us is a way of life. That religion is based upon this creation and its sacredness. In this religion every day was a sacred day to us. Religion did not take place just on Saturdays or Sundays. Every day of our life was a holy day.[5]

Deere continues to be remembered and revered today in Indian Country and beyond.

David Sohappy, Sr. was a Wanapum (River People) fisherman, spiritual leader, healer, and human rights activist. He was a Dreamer who received dreams and visions to guide his people. He focused on enforcement of federal and state governments' responsibilities expressed in treaties; upholding native peoples' fishing rights; and safeguarding traditional spirituality. Like many social activists around the world, at times he used nonviolent civil disobedience to protest against unjust laws or to demonstrate for the enforcement of existing laws that benefited people and the planet but were ignored, allowing a few in the dominant society to benefit from violating them. Like other activists, he was arrested, convicted, and imprisoned for his actions to promote justice. In a prison interview, David reflected on the insights given in spiritual moments:

> When a person believes in the religion he goes to Mother Earth so he can get the good teachings that the Creator gives to the believers... If the Creator wants you to know something he'll tell you. We never see God, only hear him. I was asleep at one time and I heard this voice tell me "Listen to this, here is a chant you have to repeat all the time." I have been following my dream all these years.

As a Dreamer, David was called on to guide his people: "We're told in a dream what's going to happen. You hold services and tell people, 'Here's what I dreamt, here's what we have to do next.'"

The Wanapum have followed an oral tradition since long before the Europeans arrived in the region of Che Wana ("Great River," now called Columbia River). For David Sohappy, the ancient oral laws of native peoples take precedence over the new, written laws of the river's newcomers: "Lots of people couldn't understand what I was talking about when I told them that I follow unwritten laws. They didn't understand. I told them I follow a law that is higher than any written law." In the Christian Bible, the same perspective was presented millennia ago by Peter, as described in Acts, when he and John were ordered to discontinue teaching about Jesus. Peter replied that the priests should decide whether Peter and John should obey the priests or God (Acts 4: 19).

In his role as a traditional healer, David used spiritual power rather than herbs to cure his people: "When we go to our services to help heal people we pull down the power of the universe. People that can see, can see it coming." The Dreamer, without expectation of remuneration, must use the healing power that comes from the Creator for whoever needs it, even their "worst enemy."

The Wanapum have a perpetual concern for and special relationship with the salmon and are solicitous for their wellbeing: "The salmon were created for the people to have for their own food... We are taught that if we honor our food, it will come back. If we stop, it won't come back."[6]

David's spirit lives on in his Wanapum people, in other human rights and ecological wellbeing activists, and in the salmon people—"all our relations."

Integral Ecology

Consciousness of integral ecology permeates *Laudato Sí*, to which the whole of Chapter 4 (paras. 137–162) is devoted. The section titles of this chapter indicate aspects of integral ecology it elaborates: environmental, economic, and social ecology; cultural ecology; ecology of daily life; the principle of the common good; and justice between the generations.

Francis teaches that "Ecology studies the relationship between living organisms and the environment in which they develop... It cannot be emphasized enough how everything is interconnected" (138). "When we speak of the 'environment,' what we really mean is a relationship existing between Nature and the society which lives in it. Nature cannot be regarded as something separate from ourselves or as a mere setting in which we live. We are part of Nature, included in it and thus in constant interaction with it... We are faced not with two separate crises, one environmental and the other social, but rather with one complex crisis which is both social and environmental. Strategies for a solution demand an integrated approach to combating poverty, restoring dignity to the excluded, and at the same time protecting nature" (139). Biota are interrelated in ecosystems, which "have an intrinsic value independent of their usefulness" (their instrumental value). Humankind depends on ecosystems for its existence. Discussion of an ecosystem's "sustainable use" must always consider "each system's regenerative ability" (140). Ecology and economics are closely related. Consequently, "economic ecology" is needed. Protection of the environment is an "integral part" of economic development processes (141). Culture is a "living, dynamic and participatory present reality," which must be included in discussions about how humanity and environment are related (143). For this reason, no uniform "regulations" or "technological interventions" should be imposed in all situations as they might overlook "the complexities of local problems which demand the participation of all members of the community." "New processes" imported from without do not fit into every social setting: "they need to be based in the local culture itself ... our care for the world must ... be flexible and dynamic" (144). Similarly, as noted below, the core principles of socioecological praxis ethics are retained in context, but secondary principles, often originating in a specific culture, are negotiable and can be adapted to context.

Francis declares that the way humans are integrated in and interrelated with the places in which they live, and are guided by moral teachings such as those expressed in an awareness of human ecology, should be linked to promoting the common good among people and peoples: "Human ecology is inseparable from the notion of the common good, a central and unifying principle of social ethics" (156). The "common good" calls for "social peace," which can be achieved only with a "particular concern for distributive justice." Communities and governments should advocate and act for the common good: "Society as a whole, and the state in particular, are obliged to defend and promote the common good" (157). Further, "the principle of the common good immediately becomes, logically and inevitably, a summons to solidarity and a preferential option for the poorest of our brothers and sisters. This option entails recognizing the implications of the universal destination of the world's goods" (158). (The "universal destination" hearkens back to Thomas Aquinas' teaching in his *Summa Theologica* that by natural law, all things are in common; human law, not divine law, developed the practice of private property.) Orientation toward the common good is intergenerational: "The notion of the common good also extends to future generations... We can no longer speak of sustainable development apart from intergenerational solidarity... Intergenerational solidarity is not optional, but rather a basic question of justice, since the world we have received also belongs to those who will follow us" (159).

Along these lines, Indian activist and poet John Trudell, at an Indigenous Environmental Network meeting in Montana several years ago, denounced genetic manipulation as an irreversible alteration of living beings: He declared that "D'n'A" stands for "descendants and ancestors": every living being has received the core of who they are from their ancestors and will pass on their traits intergenerationally, beginning with their offspring. Thus, genetic intervention in any present era and social milieu will change forever future generations of humanity, potentially with dire consequences which will result from impacts as yet unforeseen. Francis adds that *inter*generational solidarity considerations should remind people of needed *intra*generational solidarity (162).

The Earth Charter

Pope Francis cites affirmatively the internationally developed Earth Charter. He declares that "The Earth Charter asked us to leave behind a period of self-destruction and make a new start, but we have not as yet developed a universal awareness needed to achieve this. Here, I would echo that courageous challenge: 'As never before in history, common destiny beckons us to seek a new beginning'... Let ours be a time remembered for the awakening of a new reverence for life, the firm resolve to achieve sustainability, the quickening of the struggle for justice and peace, and the joyful celebration of life" (207). (I have been involved in Earth Charter events and dissemination efforts since 1999; Hart, 2004, 126–128, 2006, 153–156, 2013.)

The Earth Charter is an idea and document originally developed by Canada's Maurice Strong in preparation for the 1979 UN Conference on Environment and Development (UNCED), commonly called the Earth Summit, and held in Rio de Janeiro. Its efforts expanded when Steven Rockefeller, Ruud Lubbers, and Mikhail Gorbachev joined Strong. The Earth Charter's core themes and principles[7] are compatible, in whole or in part, with the teachings of all religions that are presented in this *Companion*, and with ideas of integral ecology elaborated by Pope Francis.

In its Preamble, the Earth Charter declares:

> [W]e stand at a critical moment in Earth's history, a time when humanity must choose its future ... which at once holds great peril and great promise. To move forward we must recognize that in the midst of a magnificent diversity of cultures and life forms we are one human family and one Earth community with a common destiny. We must join together to bring forth a sustainable global society founded on respect for nature, universal human rights, economic justice, and a culture of peace ... it is imperative that we, the peoples of Earth, declare our responsibility to one another, to the greater community of life, and to future generations.

The Earth Charter elaborates 16 principles, each with corresponding subprinciples. Several of these principles complement especially well the integral ecology narrative set out in *Laudato Sí*:

> 1. Respect Earth and life in all its diversity; Recognize that all beings are interdependent and every form of life has value regardless of its worth to human beings. 2. Care for the community of life with understanding, compassion, and love. a. Accept that with the right to own, manage, and use natural resources comes the duty to prevent environmental harm and to protect the rights of people. b. Affirm that with increased freedom, knowledge, and power comes increased responsibility to promote the common good. 3. b. Promote social and economic justice, enabling all to achieve a secure and meaningful livelihood that is ecologically responsible. 4. Secure Earth's bounty and beauty for present and future generations. a. Recognize that the freedom of action of each generation is qualified by the needs of future generations. 5. Protect and restore the integrity of Earth's ecological systems, with special concern for biological diversity and the natural processes that sustain life. 6. Prevent harm as the best method of environmental protection and, when knowledge is limited, apply a precautionary approach. a. Take action to avoid the possibility of serious or irreversible environmental harm even when scientific knowledge is incomplete or inconclusive. b. Place the burden of proof on those who argue that a proposed activity will not cause significant harm, and make the responsible parties liable for environmental harm. 7. b. Act with restraint and efficiency when using energy, and rely increasingly on renewable energy sources such as solar and wind. 8. Advance the study of ecological sustainability and promote the open exchange and wide application of the knowledge acquired. a. Support international scientific and technical cooperation on sustainability, with special attention to the needs of developing nations. 9. Eradicate poverty as an ethical, social, and environmental imperative. a. Guarantee the right to potable water, clean air, food security, uncontaminated soil, shelter, and safe sanitation, allocating the national and international resources required. 10. a. Promote the equitable distribution of wealth within nations and among nations. 11. Affirm gender equality and equity as prerequisites to sustainable development and ensure universal access to education, health care, and economic opportunity.

12. Uphold the right of all, without discrimination, to a natural and social environment supportive of human dignity, bodily health, and spiritual well-being, with special attention to the rights of indigenous peoples and minorities. b. Affirm the right of indigenous peoples to their spirituality, knowledge, lands and resources and to their related practice of sustainable livelihoods. 13. f. Strengthen local communities, enabling them to care for their environments, and assign environmental responsibilities to the levels of government where they can be carried out most effectively. 14. d. Recognize the importance of moral and spiritual education for sustainable living. 15. Treat all living beings with respect and consideration.16. f. Recognize that peace is the wholeness created by right relationships with oneself, other persons, other cultures, other life, Earth, and the larger whole of which all are a part.

In its concluding section, "The Way Forward", the Earth Charter states that "we must find ways to harmonize diversity with unity, the exercise of freedom with the common good, short-term objectives with long-term goals."

Earth Commons

In most religious traditions, even if not expressed in precisely these words, the Earth is a commons. Prior to the development of European and Euro-American notions of private property, and continuing in some cultures contemporaneous to ideologies expressing and advocating economic globalization and property privatization around the world, people and peoples have lived in communal societies.

The *commons* is the place in which dynamic natural history evolves, diversifies, and complexifies, and the base from which cultural history develops in all its intricacy. Human natural history and human cultural history develop together. Human property in land and goods is part of a human commons that is to provide for human needs. In a complementary way, Earth is a commons: a shared space that is the source of life-providing common goods for all creatures. The Earth commons is not intended solely for humans' use and enjoyment, although as part of the biotic community they are to share in its goods. Earth provides for all creatures as they live related to and dependent on each other in integrated bioregions. It is also a shared space whose common goods should equitably provide for the needs of those creatures. (Hart, 2006, 62)

[Earth is] naturally a commons: a home shared by all the members of the community of life in which their food and habitat needs are integrated, their competitive needs are balanced, their relationships are interdependent, and their associations are consciously or unconsciously collaborative. (Hart, 2006, 62–63)

Mindfulness of the common good should permeate human societies sharing the Earth's commons:

In the commons, human communities are called to pursue the common good ... [The commons provides], through the evolutionary dynamics of the biotic community and the complementary availability of air, land, and water, a sufficiency of goods—when they

> are justly distributed—to meet everyone's needs... Ecojustice is the act of linking responsibility for the natural world with responsibility for the neighbor. The good of the revelatory commons and the common good of the revelatory poor are inseparable. The commons good and the common good are woven together. (Hart, 2006, 63)

> Earth as *commons* is an area shared by all of the members of the community of life. It provides for their needs while humans sustain or renew its integrity, as needed (to remediate or repel human practices of despoliation of context and diminution of creatures). (Hart, 2006, 63–64)

Social justice should characterize life in the Earth commons:

> The commons must provide justly for the needs of all humans, a distribution that requires that the basic needs of all take priority over the wants of a few. The land of the Earth commons that is required as human space, to sustain life and enable livelihood, must be shared equitably among humans. The goods of the commons—also called "resources," which can imply anthropocentrically that these goods are intended solely for humans—must be equitably shared among human communities and individuals. (Hart, 2006, 65)

Solicitous sharing of Earth's natural goods, and of human-manufactured products made from Earth goods, historically has exemplified and expressed community consciousness and values, societal ethics, and ecological ethics.

Socioecological Praxis Ethics

In *Laudato Sí* Pope Francis provides a theological foundation and socioeconomic-ecological vision, and proposes that people should strive to restore and conserve the Earth and responsibly relate to each other in human communities. His thinking is well complemented by socioecological praxis ethics, which in turn complements integral ecology thinking and elaborates ways in which it might be translated into community thought and action.

Socioecological praxis ethics (Hart, 2013, 184–190) is a consciousness expressed in contexts and a method for socioecological transformation and conservation. It is the integration of social justice within and among human communities with the wellbeing of the Earth and all living beings.

Ethics presents principles for right conduct. These principles embody values that underlie thinking and action oriented to justice and the common good of the interrelated, interdependent, intergenerational, and integral community of the Earth, all biota, and human societies. Ethics has core principles, understood to be non-negotiable or absolute, and derivative principles, regarded as negotiable when confronted by alternate compelling ideas or situations not previously encountered or considered.

Praxis is the locus of dialogic (or alternately dialectic) engagement between ethical theory and ethical practice. It is a place where theories can be adapted to a context in context or adopted by a community in context, or a place that can catalyze changes in attitudes and actions brought to or present in that context.

"Socio-" represents one or several human societies, groups, or communities that ideally are principally oriented to the common good rather than primarily or solely to individual selfishness (which is not to be confused with self-interest).

"Ecological" has to do with relationships in a particular environment or a cluster of environments which may be contiguous in a single place or widely separated in their respective places.

Socioecological praxis ethics is ethics-in-context. It envisions a common good and suggests ways to achieve it. It presents a four-step method to stimulate social, ecological, and environmental wellbeing. First, socioecological analysis of a specific context—seeing from the points of view of the "least of these" in *this* place: racially, sexually, ethnically, religiously, economically, and politically oppressed human beings; endangered species; threatened Earth and its abiotic entities. Second, social and spiritual reflection related to the analysis—considering historical perspectives which, in diverse contexts, have provided principles of justice contradictory to the prevailing unjust contextual perspectives that promote or allow harm to people, other biota, and the planet; sources include religions' sacred texts or oral teachings, and humanist insights. Third, social vision—formulating a socioecological vision of what might be if the contradictions between "what is" and "what ought to be" were overcome, such that this place will evermore closely correspond to accepted social and ecological values, which might be adapted to or modified for this context. Fourth, social project—embarking on a course of action that will strive to realize, over time, aspects of the socioecological vision; each vision or vision component realized provides a base for formulating a new vision from a new context (cf. Hart, 2013, 189).

Dialogic Relational Community in the Common Commons

In religious traditions around the world, a spiritual-social consciousness might view Mother Earth as a sacred commons. In sacred commons consciousness and conduct, a divine Spirit might be understood to be transcendent-immanent, or transcendent but yet a Presence-in-context, a metaphysical Presence in which is present all material reality. Mother Earth is a microcosm of the universe macrocosm. The sacred cosmos is localized in the sacred commons. Earth, a small planet in the vastness of space, shares with space and the stars and species being part of a cosmic commons.

Humans live simultaneously in multiple dimensions of reality, and at sacred moments they have holistic experiences of the totality of reality. In their mind and spirit they transcend physical reality, they are meta-material while still in their material form. They become immersed in an experience of the integral being of the cosmos, seeing beyond what is possible to see with their eyes.

The sacred commons is a place of mediation between the visible and invisible, between material and spiritual dimensions of reality. Earth, Earth lives, and the starry cosmos are not solely mediations of and to an unseen Spirit, but are themselves sacred realities and material beings worthy of consideration and admiration in their own right. They can lead people to be aware of and ponder meta-material realms, and they can also lead us to celebrate beauty and being in material reality. Meditation on what is being mediated can enable socioecological spiritual understanding and social engagement to foster integral ecology.

The interrelated, integrated, interdependent, and intergenerational biotic community in which the divine Spirit is immanent has intrinsic value. In this community each species, and any individual member of that species, has intrinsic value within an ecosystem that has intrinsic value. As need arises for food, clothing, shelter, medicine, and other essential elements of survival, some members of the biotic community might regard others—or individuals within others—necessary to meet their needs. These others become instrumentally valued for a brief or long time, and used by the species in need, in this place (or several places) in the ecosystem. Such predator–prey interaction is a natural part and process of biota dynamics in evolutionary contexts.

Integral Ecology and Socioecological Consciousness and Conduct

Human consciousness of integral ecology, expressed in human conduct embedding socioecological praxis ethics in a transforming relational Earth community, would effect a just and ecologically beneficial future for the Earth and all biota. Consequently, humankind and other-than-humankind will come to live in a future where what humanity envisions and works for today will have been achieved. In the dialogue between theory and practice, between a present vision of a new Earth and its actualization on Earth, integral ecology and socioecological praxis ethics in conversation will be continually mutually enriched and stimulate the socioecological and spiritual well-being of the Earth, and of present and future generations of the community of all life.

Notes

1 Transl. John Hart from the Italian text of Ms. 338 in the Assisi library, cited in Fortini (1981, 566–567).
2 Numbers in brackets indicate paragraph numbers in *Laudato Sí*.
3 Paragraph 71 has a footnote reference to a similar statement made by John Paul II in *Laborem Exercens*, 1981, 19: AAS 73 (1981), 626. John Paul had declared even earlier, in Cuilapán, Mexico in 1979, that all property had a "social mortgage" and that redistribution of land should be used to provide for the needs of the poor.
4 This occurred to me while I pondered historical atrocities committed in right-wing Latin American dictatorships. They catalyzed people to develop a new verb: to "disappear" someone. Relatives and friends did not know what had happened to a loved one, who had vanished and might have been murdered, or was imprisoned and being tortured. The "disappeared" were not returned alive.
5 Interview with John Hart, Great Falls, MT, 1984. The teachings of Phillip Deere are discussed in greater depth in Hart, 2006, chapter 3, "Native Spirits," 41–57.
6 Interviews with John Hart, Geiger Federal Correctional Institution, Spokane, WA, 1988, and letters from prison to John Hart. The life and teachings of David Sohappy are described more extensively in Hart, 2006, chapter 6, "Species Survival," 101–107. David Sohappy was the

most extraordinary person I ever met. We became friends because of my Treaty Council work and our shared spiritual consciousness; we are kindred spirits.

7 See the EC site: http://earthcharter.org. Information is updated periodically on EC activities around the world.

References

Fortini, Arnaldo. 1981. *Francis of Assisi*. Transl. Helen Moak. New York: Crossroad, 566–567.

Francis I. 2015. Encyclical Letter *Laudato Sí*, of the Holy Father Francis, "On Care for Our Common Home." http://w2.vatican.va/content/francesco/en/encyclicals/documents/papa-francesco_20150524_enciclica-laudato-si.html; © Libreria Editrice Vaticana.

Hart, John. 2004. *What Are They Saying About ... Environmental Theology?* Mahwah, NJ: Paulist Press.

Hart, John. 2006. *Sacramental Commons: Christian Ecological Ethics*. In the series "Nature's Meaning." Roger Gottlieb (Ed.). Lanham, MD: Rowman & Littlefield.

Hart, John. 2009. St. Francis for the 21st Century. In Cynthia Ho, John Downey, & Beth Mulvaney (Eds.), *Finding Francis: Remembering Il Poverello*. Basingstoke: Palgrave Macmillan.

Hart, John. 2013. *Cosmic Commons: Spirit, Science, and Space*. Eugene, OR: Cascade Books/Wipf & Stock.

Hart, John. 2015. Creation and Community Consciousness—*Il Poverello*'s Intercultural and Intergenerational Insights and Inspiration. In Bradley Franco & Beth Mulvaney (Eds.), *The World of St. Francis: Essays in Honor of William R. Cook* (The Medieval Franciscans Series). Leiden, The Netherland: Brill.

The New York Times. "2015 Was Hottest Year in Historical Record, Scientists Say." http://www.nytimes.com/2016/01/21/science/earth/2015-hottest-year-global-warming.html?emc=edit_th_20160121&nl=todaysheadlines&nlid=60714615&_r=0.

The New York Times. "Seas Are Rising at Fastest Rate in Last 28 Centuries." http://www.nytimes.com/2016/02/23/science/sea-level-rise-global-warming-climate-change.html?emc=eta1.

CHAPTER 5

神の大経綸

The Great Divine Plan: Kotama Okada's Vision for Spiritual Civilization in the Twenty-First Century

Kōō Okada

Everything in Heaven and on Earth is the voice of God. It overflows with the divine principles.

So begins *The Holy Words*, a compendium of the revelatory teachings of Kotama Okada, who founded the Mahikari movement in 1959. *Sukyo* means the universal laws established by God at the time of the Creation so that all things throughout the universe can prosper eternally. *Mahikari* means True Light, the Light of the Creator God, which purifies all things. This True Light is the common source of all religions and is available to return to today.

Okada established the Mahikari movement with the goal of enabling people to experience a higher dimension by experiencing the art of True Light. One objective is to help people awaken to the universal (divine) principles and to encourage people to return to a more spiritually-oriented way by practicing these principles in their daily life, including using material resources with a spiritual way of thinking.

The fundamental teaching of Mahikari is: "The origin of the world is one, the origin of humankind is one, and the origin of all religions is one." This origin or source—from which everything emanates—is the Creator God. All people are brothers and sisters, children of the Parent God. Inspired by their experiences with True Light and the teachings of Mahikari, people find joy in learning how to develop spiritually by cultivating love and harmony all around them—in their families, workplaces, schools, and communities—for this is the first step to achieving true happiness and world peace.

As the voice, or emanation, of God, everything in the universe was originally created in a state of purity. Out of great love, the Creator established immutable laws or principles to ensure the eternal perfection and flourishing of everything in Creation. These universal laws govern and unite all the spiritual realms. God also imbued Creation with natural mechanisms to correct any disorder or imbalance resulting from occurrences that run contrary to these divine laws.

The Wiley Blackwell Companion to Religion and Ecology, First Edition. Edited by John Hart.

It is the Parent God's wish that humans, who are God's children, create a Heaven-like civilization on Earth—a physical manifestation of the divine realm—where people live in harmony with the universal will and enjoy eternal health, harmony, and prosperity. God endowed the Earth with the bountiful gifts of Nature and abundant natural goods—"material resources"—for humans to cultivate and use in creating this heavenly civilization. It is also the Creator's will that humans share these natural goods fairly according to need, and always express their innate character as children of God with generosity. This heavenly civilization will be a society that is peaceful, just, and environmentally sustainable. From God's point of view, humans have an important and highly responsible role to fulfill in relation to the Earth and as part of its ecology.

How have we fulfilled this role? As a result of significant achievements in the fields of science and technology over the past few centuries, human society has made tremendous strides, making it possible for many to enjoy unprecedented levels of comfort. Yet there is growing concern and mounting evidence that this has come at an unsustainable cost. Humans have harnessed science, technology, and other aspects of human knowledge for geopolitical and material purposes. We have focused on physical resources, money, and making a profit, rather than on fulfilling our God-given purpose. The lack of spiritual values guiding much of modern society is the fundamental factor eroding both the natural environment and the foundation of society, the family.

There is nothing inherently wrong with accumulating money and material possessions. What is important is the manner in which people obtain and use them. In a spirit-centered civilization, which Mahikari teaches will ultimately be established, a spiritual outlook based on universal principles and an understanding of the true nature of human beings inspires and guides people to use science, technology, and other aspects of human knowledge altruistically, with an understanding of our highly accountable God-given role.

Okada cautioned that if people continued to focus on material progress at the expense of human values such as respect and compassion for others, morals and ethics, and compassion, then society would begin to show signs of collapse by the end of the twentieth century. Unfortunately, at the start of the twenty-first century, such signs are evident in many parts of the world.

Okada first taught about the potential threat of environmental pollution in 1959 and the early 1960s, at a time when relatively few were aware of it. Among his many predictions, he said that if people continued to pollute the environment with toxic chemicals, the land would become infertile and people's health would suffer. He warned that a lack of discretion in the use of the Earth's natural goods, including oil, would result in shortages or scarcity. He cautioned that the indiscriminate consumption of fossil fuels could lead to air pollution and poor air quality, acid rain, and global warming.

While some believe that extreme weather, natural disasters, and societal ills signal the end of the world, Mahikari teaches that we are witnessing a transitional period of intense challenge at all levels for individuals, families, communities, organizations, countries, and the planet to prepare for a coming, spiritually-oriented civilization. We are, in effect, witnessing the end of the world as we know it—the end of a material-centered civilization. Okada's foundational teaching on how to survive and thrive during this transition—even to advance ushering in of the heavenly civilization—is twofold: to close the gap between the Creator and humans, and to close the gap between humans and Nature. We must therefore enable humankind to redirect themselves from being material-centered to being spiritually oriented. At the same time, we must protect the ecosystem, conserve precious natural goods, and be grateful for and cherish what we have and use each day.

We all have our origin in God or the Source and are here on Earth to bring about a peaceful and harmonious civilization. One reason why people do not cooperate with or respect each other is that they have forgotten, ignored, or have not been educated about their common origin and true purpose. Okada often said that society could avoid calamity by choosing a path that places spiritual values ahead of material values, while still pursuing and enjoying the benefits of science and technology. He envisioned such a society coming into existence in the twenty-first century, a spiritually-oriented civilization—a peaceful, just, and sustainable society.

In addition to altruism and kindness, we need to build a culture of moderation, a civilization that observes rules and limits. No matter how much science may progress, humankind must never forget the need for humility and moderation. Humankind urgently needs to cultivate the ability to make spiritual distinctions. Without this, we will not be able to establish a culture of moderation. All of us, whether we are scientists, religious leaders, economists, educators, and so on, need to observe limits and exercise moderation. Only then will we be able to maintain the health of Nature and human society and achieve true prosperity. In the present time of crisis, we need to give consideration to spiritual values and how we can promote and maintain them.

The actions people are making to conserve Earth's resources are to "reduce, reuse, recycle, and repair" as much as possible. Spiritually, the universal principles emphasize sharing and generosity, a kind and loving attitude toward everyone as brother and sister, and an appreciation of all living beings and Earth's materials. With this kind of spiritual consciousness, conservation is raised from a negative experience—having to make sacrifices—to a perspective of positive moderation, and having desires and ways of living that are more moderate materially, but richer in the personal satisfaction of having all that is really needed, materially and in interpersonal and spiritual relations.

Larger-scale actions for the Earth that go beyond the individual are made in the community, scientific, and international arenas. People who practice Sukyo Mahikari are active in environmental projects in their communities, in researching innovative, environmentally-sound ways of doing business, and in speaking at and sponsoring international forums. For those who garden or farm Earth's soil, organic farming principles have been shown to revitalize the condition of the soil and the atmosphere, while the light available through Sukyo Mahikari purifies and revitalizes its spiritual aspect.

In this new civilization, whose beginning we are presently witnessing, science and spirituality are no longer at odds. Thanks to research in modern physics into the subatomic world, scientific understandings of the nature of existence are now converging with spiritual understandings. Because the observed world, including science, medicine, and the environment, has its origins in the spiritual principles that govern the universe, there is a spiritual aspect to all these fields. Professionals and scholars are looking increasingly to the spiritual dimension of being to gain a deeper understanding of the unanswered questions in their fields.

Sukyo Mahikari understands human beings as simultaneously physical, mental, social, and spiritual beings. Scholars, academics, medical professionals, environmentalists, and politicians are turning to Sukyo Mahikari to increase their understanding of their work. Sukyo Mahikari connects with professionals in science, medicine, and the environment to help support the burgeoning interest in understanding the spiritual aspect of the phenomena observed in the world.

It is of paramount importance that all scientific developments to date converge with the spiritual essence of Nature. Instead of existing separately, science and religion should be united in a state of harmony. Humankind must give rise to a new civilization by combining cutting-edge science with the spirituality found in Nature.

Okada believed that as the foundations for a spiritually-oriented civilization are already established, it will prove to be so successful that humanity will begin to enjoy eternal peace. His predictions and teachings make him both a visionary and a pioneer for the twenty-first century.

Many believe that science, medicine, economics, and other disciplines will eventually bring happiness to everyone by helping humanity reach a "summit of truth." Sukyo Mahikari holds that scientists, doctors, and other professionals will only reach the ultimate Truth when they elevate themselves and their professions to a spiritual level that enables them to perceive spiritually-oriented science, medicine, economics, and so on. At this level of spiritual discernment, professionals will recognize that everything has its origin in God or the Source and that the underlying unity that binds all disciplines is embraced by the divine principles that govern the universe. Albert Einstein coined the phrase "cosmic religious feeling" to express his concept of spiritual experience and asserted that "it is the most important function of art and science to awaken this feeling and keep it alive" (*Ideas and Opinions*, 38).

Humans and the environment need to flourish together in harmony—and they can. Now is the time when both small, individual, and local decisions as well as larger institutional, scientific, and governmental decisions must be made with a view to the whole of Earth's ecological system so that the young today will have a positive, healthy future. There is hope, but everyone's collaborative action is urgently needed.

A Vision for the Twenty-first Century as a Holy Century

The Parent God revealed to Okada a vision of the future, which he gave to humankind. He predicted that the twenty-first century would be the "holy *(hijiri* 聖) century." What does this mean? That a new and creative age will commence, one where a high-dimensional divine science, of a kind that humanity has never seen before, will become commonplace.

To fully understand what the "holy century" means, we need to know the true spiritual meaning of the Japanese word for "holy"—"*hijiri*, 聖." We can understand what it means by studying the ideogram shown in Figure 5.1.

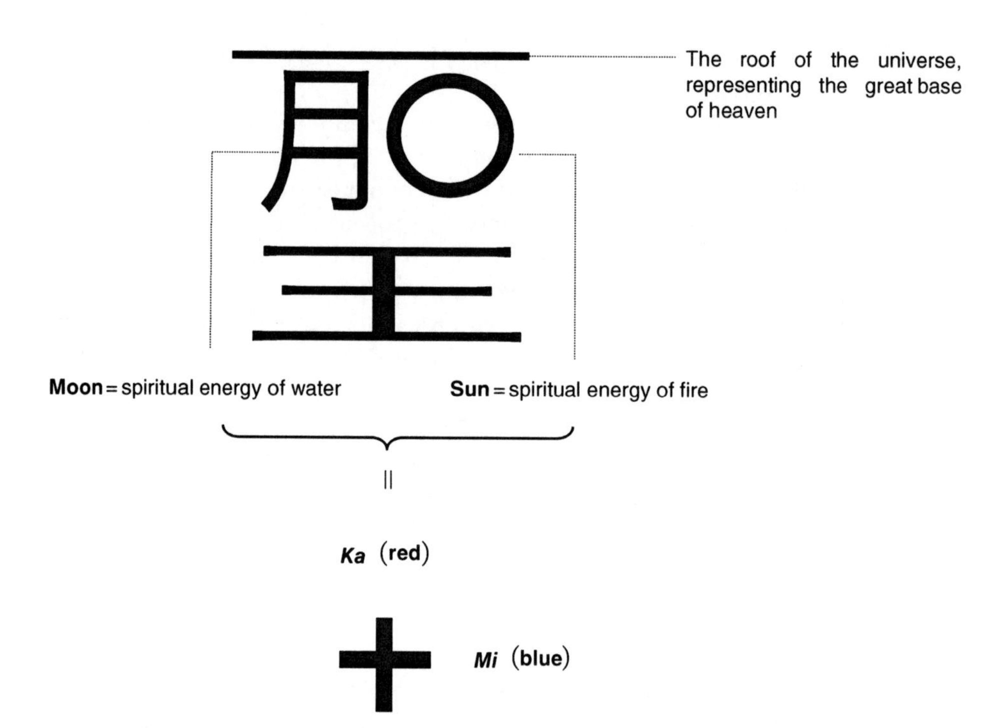

The top part of the ideogram for *hijiri* 聖 shows the moon and sun embracing each other under the roof of the universe. The moon represents the spiritual energy of water, and the sun represents the spiritual energy of fire. *Ka* is "fire" and *mi* is "water." When combined, *Kami* means "Creator," ultimately the Creator physically manifesting on earth, or "one who has attained divine nature." Under the moon and sun is the ideogram 王, which represents "king" or "one who governs." The entire ideogram means "the one who is qualified to govern humankind under the roof of the universe, one who has gained knowledge of the plan of the Creator and principles governing the universe and who has mastered the Creator's great love and truth.

Figure 5.1 The Significance of the Ideogram of Hijiri.

Okada wrote in "The Dictionary of Words" a section of an article published in the journal of the Mahikari movement:

> The spiritual meaning of the word *hijiri* is "spiritual wisdom." *Hi* means "fire," "yang," and "spirit," and *jiri* means "spiritual knowledge."
>
> Gautama Buddha, a historical figure from India, was an exemplar of *pāramitā*, a person who has a deep understanding of the spiritual realm. Jesus was also such a person, as too was Mokuren [his Sanskrit name is Maudgalyayana], Buddha's principal disciple. A person who has knowledge of the spiritual realm (at least, of the Buddhist spiritual realm) could be called a saint or sage, but such a person, in the context of the true spiritual meaning of

the word *hijiri*, may not necessarily be someone considered as *hijiri*. In other words, there is a difference between the Buddhist meaning of the word *hijiri* and the true meaning of the word *hijiri*.

The Pannyachi of the Heart Sutra also means Pannya wisdom (般若智). Under the ideogram of *chi* (知), there is the ideogram of *hi* (日). The original power of God that created all things is the soul of fire (ball of fire) = fire = sun = positive = spirit. Therefore, *chi* (spiritual wisdom) is to have knowledge of the true aspect of the spiritual realm and a radiant soul.

What we can deduce from this passage is that the holy century will see the establishment of a civilization whose foundation is influenced by spiritual energy. Until now, civilization has been based on knowledge without spiritual wisdom. Now we are entering a spiritual age, that is, a civilization of the holy century, based on spiritual wisdom.

The twentieth century, in name and reality, is of the past. As pioneers at the dawn of the new, holy century, we need to understand what is happening in the universe, as Okada explained.

The civilizations of the age that is now ending focused on materialism. This was particularly the case in the twentieth century, when we seem also to have lost our common understanding of what it means to be human, and when people became so enamored of materialism that we now are on the brink of self-destruction. The holy twenty-first century will be a new age which will witness a revival of our common humanity and understanding of what it means to be human and will witness the establishment of a spirit-centered, three-dimensional civilization—a harmonious civilization, brought about by uniting seemingly opposing elements—where seemingly disparate fields will find common ground and be united.

A spirit-centered civilization is on the threshold of replacing the material-centered civilization that has existed for a very long time. The new civilization will be a high-dimensional civilization of light, filled with "spiritual fragrance."

Okada predicted the advent of the spiritual civilization in terms of the holy twenty-first century. The twenty-first century is still in its infancy. Just beyond the chaotic confusion of our materialistic civilization the daybreak of the spiritual civilization beckons. This new spiritual civilization (in Japanese, the "yoko civilization," meaning a civilization of positive energy with a bright, sustainable, and just future for all) will put the spiritual aspect at the forefront, unlike the present civilization, where money and material things are of primary importance. The establishment of the spiritual civilization is a marvelous destiny for people who are doing their utmost to overcome the baptism by fire.

The Fundamental Principle for the Yoko Civilization is "The Origin of the World is One"

The origin of the earth is one
The origin of the world is one
The origin of all humankind is one
The origin of all religions is one

A door into the holy twenty-first century is now being opened and Okada's grand vision that "the origin of the world is one; the origin of all humankind is one" is gradually being embraced around the world. His vision was to make eternal world peace possible for everyone by discovering the principle of eternal stability by respecting each other's beliefs and putting this principle into practice.

A yoko civilization is not about imposing the ideas of a particular religion or sect on anyone. It is a peace movement that aims to create Heaven on Earth, based on love and harmony, and that unites diverse and even seemingly contradictory cultures and civilizations.

Every one of us has been given life by our parents, and they in turn were given life by their parents. If we follow our ancestral lineage, we will eventually arrive at our common ancestor. Who created the ancestors? The "who" is none other than the life-giving Creator, the common ancestor of all human beings. To recognize this fact, and to accept its ramifications, is the first step toward awakening to the principle that the origin is one and only one. We need to fully acknowledge that the five races of different skin color of humankind are brothers and sisters who share a single bloodline. Our mission as human beings is to unite and cooperate with one other, with love and harmony, so that together we can establish everlasting world peace. This is what it means to be spiritually united. As is written in Revelation, Heaven on Earth will be established when all are united as one.

From an Age of Religion to an Age of Sukyo

When Okada established the Mahikari movement in 1959, he predicted that the twenty-first century would see the emergence of an age of *sukyo*. (*Sukyo* means "the universal laws established by God at the time of the Creation so that all things in the universe can prosper eternally.") In other words, he predicted that in the twenty-first century, the age of religions, which is replete with the ideologies of different religious sects and denominations, will end, and a brilliant age of *sukyo* will begin. However, he stated that "If religions continue to be in conflict with each other in the twenty-first century, it will be a truly deplorable situation. God is lamenting the current condition of religions" (August 20, 1961).

Why are religions necessary? Were religions not created for the purpose of giving people peace of mind and saving their souls? However, is it not true that established religions have failed to bestow true happiness on humankind? Moreover, has modern society not been excessively focused on materialism and has it not tried to substitute science for religion in its quest for happiness? And has scientific technology not been used to create highly destructive weapons, and have not major wars been waged over and over again? If this continues, those who sacrificed themselves in wars will not receive salvation.

Our age cries out for a living spirituality that can help humankind save itself from this endless cycle of war and revenge. This new spiritual direction will need to transcend all barriers of sect and denomination and will actively promote unity among all people.

The following question is bound to be asked when people talk about the demise of religions: "Do we repudiate or deny religions that already exist?" No, we do not.

Let us consider the situation in Japan. From quite early on, Japan had an indigenous religion, ancient Shinto. People expressed their gratitude for the blessings of Nature and lived a life according to the laws of God. Later, a new Shinto emerged and gradually embraced various rituals that now are part of Shinto. Nonetheless, its approach to the Divine has remained firmly polytheistic, in contrast to the monotheistic approach of the West.

Following the introduction of Buddhism to Japan, by way of the Korean Peninsula during the Kofun period (c. 250–538 AD), people began to venerate the Buddha. Then, in the second half of the sixteenth century, during the Warring States Period—an extended state of military conflict that lasted from about the middle of the fifteenth century to the beginning of the seventeenth)—Father Francis Xavier arrived and introduced Christianity. Gradually, Christianity spread throughout Japan, and even some warlords converted and became fervent adherents. Father Xavier was surprised and remarked: "The Japanese do not feel shame in being poor. A poor samurai is more respected than a merchant."

At the time *bushido* was practiced, which has parallels with the Christian practice of pure poverty. *Bushido* is a Japanese code of conduct that evolved during the samurai period. It emphasized loyalty, honor, duty, filial piety, and self-sacrifice. A true samurai upheld justice and despised cowardice. The spirit of *bushido* was experienced at all levels of society.

Japan embraced a polytheistic attitude but was quite open to religions from other countries. It was this openness that eventually led to the coexistence and even integration of Shinto and Buddhism. In other words, the ability to embrace a different religion and unite it with an existing religion has been one of the wonderful characteristics that the land of the origin of spirit possessed from ancient times.

Okada did not repudiate Christianity, Buddhism, or any religion. In fact, he explained that the age of *sukyo* was necessary so that all religions could develop further. He also said that in the early days of Buddhism and Christianity, when Gautama Buddha and Jesus were alive, many of their followers were convinced that they were in the presence of holy men. They must have stirred the souls of those who heard them. These holy men must also have followed a long and arduous path as they strove to bring salvation to the suffering and afflicted through their practice of True Light. If what they practiced is considered to be a religion, then their religion was a true one, filled with the living power of salvation. In Okada's opinion unless we overcome the barriers that exist between religions, we will not be able to bring true salvation to the people.

Sukyo (universal principles) elaborates a process for overcoming religious divisions. First, people need to transcend the barriers that separate the denominations and sects, and promote unity in their place. They need to understand that if they cannot do so, they will not be able to overcome the unprecedented global crisis that humankind currently faces. It is impossible for any one denomination or sect to save humanity alone. Indeed, the only way to surmount the crisis is through the spiritual unification of all humankind.

Second, if all religions, denominations, and sects can transcend the barriers that exist between them, and if they can unite under the umbrella of *sukyo*, then people will naturally wish to cooperate and create harmony for all. In other words, a spirit of harmony will prevail, similar to that expounded long ago in Japan by Prince Shotoku, a legendary regent and politician of the Asuka period (573–621 CE). Many agree with the *sukyo* principles that Okada advocated, including the principle that "the origin of the earth is one; the origin of the world is one; the origin of all humankind is one; the origin of all religions is one," which describe a vision imbued with foresight. The twenty-first century is the age of the advent of universal laws. We should be confident that a brilliant and shining holy century awaits us.

A Spirit-Centered Civilization and "The Principle of the Two-Dimensional Cross"

What kind of vision should people have of the new, spiritually-oriented civilization that will be established in the holy twenty-first century? One of Okada's fundamental teachings is that the coming spiritually-oriented civilization will be a manifestation of "the principle of the two-dimensional cross." This underpins God's great plan for the universe. When creating the universe, God used the principle of the two-dimensional cross as the fundamental principle of Creation. It is a supreme example of God's arrangements according to the laws laid down by his hand (*okite*).

The Principle of the Cross

When two opposite elements are combined in a cross, the power of *ma*, that is to say, the power of Creation, or power of production, is generated. Examples are shown in Figure 5.2. The fundamental characteristic of the principle of the two-dimensional cross is to bring together two opposite qualities and combine them. For example, when fire and water are united, a most mysterious power is generated and hot water is produced. Okada explained that the principle of the two-dimensional cross has functioned ever since the time of Creation and controls everything in the universe, including the rise and fall of nations, civilizations, and ideologies—in other words, of history.

Elaborate arrangements, including the weather, are manifested depending on how fire and water are combined and what kind of power is generated. So, if a spiritual civilization (fire) and a material civilization (water) are united in a harmonious way, a heavenly civilization will be the outcome.

Since the principle of the two-dimensional cross affects all aspects of Heaven and Earth, everything will progress smoothly if the principle is applied in a positive and constructive way. For example, if a parent and child unite, then the family will be blessed with love and harmony. The same is true for the relationship between business owners and workers, teachers and students. On the other hand, if the two aspects are in conflict, the result is destructive.

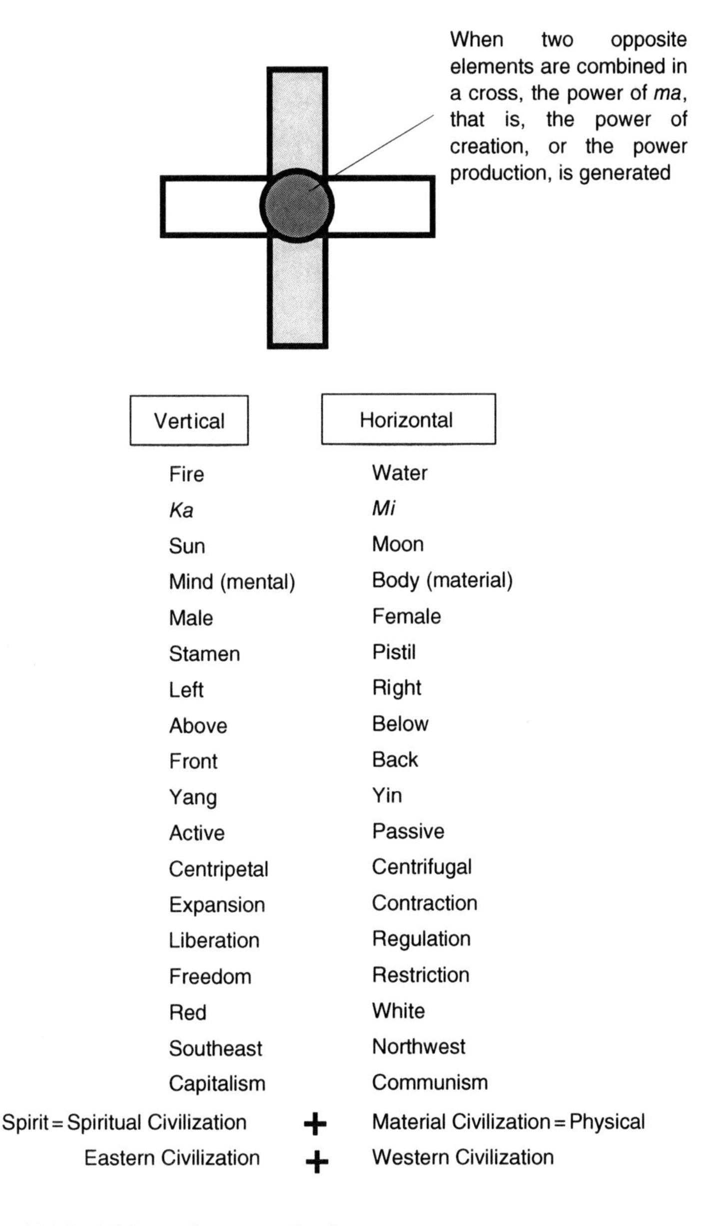

Excerpt from the Sukyo Mahikari Primary Course textbook

Figure 5.2 The Principle of the Cross.

A spiritually-oriented civilization becomes possible when two opposites combine in a spirit of unity and cooperation. In such a civilization, fire (*ka*) and water (*mi*) are able to unite, and the result is a civilization of God (*kami*).

For a very long time, the relationship between fire and water has been the reverse of what it should be. In other words, "water" has taken the lead, which is a vertical function, and "fire" has taken a supporting role, which is a horizontal function. As a result, material civilizations have been able to flourish while spiritual civilizations have become weak, or even have failed. For a spiritual civilization to flourish, fire needs to be the vertical function and water the horizontal function. What this means is that the best of both spiritual and material civilizations will be shared to create such a society and civilization. In no way does it mean that the "spiritual civilization" will dominate the "material civilization." What it does mean is that spiritual wisdom will govern materialism. One such example would be the unity of science and religion, where spiritual wisdom will govern and guide the progress of scientific study and its application.

The Convergence of Science and Religion

This does not mean that Okada denied or repudiated science. More than 50 years ago he said that science and religion will eventually be integrated. It is a remarkable prophecy about how things will develop in a spiritually-oriented, three-dimensional civilization in the holy twenty-first century. In Europe during the Middle Ages, the dominant religion, Christianity, held absolute power and influence. Scientific reasoning of any form had to be kept private in the face of religious fervor. This situation gradually began to change in the sixteenth century when Copernicus and Galileo arrived on the scene. In the nineteenth century, science made rapid progress, and the relative position of religion and science was reversed. Science gained absolute trust, and the belief developed, mistakenly, that science would be able to explain everything in the universe.

With the introduction of quantum mechanics in the twentieth century, the notion of a boundary between existence and non-existence was gradually accepted. In other words, the nature of the "other world," which had been the domain of religion, now became a subject of research.

Charles H. Townes, who was awarded the 1964 Nobel Prize for physics, predicted that advances in physics would eventually lead to a convergence of science and religion: "Finally, if science and religion are so broadly similar, and not arbitrarily limited in their domain, they should at some time clearly converge. I believe this confluence is inevitable. For both represent man's efforts to understand his universe and must ultimately be dealing with the same substance" ("The Convergence of Science and Religion," p. 7).

Okada was a pioneer in introducing this same thesis to the world of religion. His thoughts about this appeared in the March, April, and May 1967 issues of the journal of the Mahikari movement (nos. 55–57). Whenever he had the opportunity, Okada studied the latest advances in the field of physics and predicted that in the future the realm of minute, infinitesimal particles would be discovered.

Some years ago, a report issued by the Fermi National Accelerator Laboratory confirmed that there was evidence for the existence of the elementary particle, the quark. As a result, work began on proving the existence of a new and even more esoteric elementary particle, a virtual particle called the Higgs boson.

Well-known literary critic James Lipton lamented: "More minute things are appearing one after the other, and ultimately there is no end to it." This perceptive remark, I feel, sums up the underlying nature behind the science of elementary particles.

In the early 1960s, Okada had said that beyond the atom was the realm of elementary particles. He also anticipated that ultimately the "vacuum realm" would be discovered and that quantum mechanics by itself would not be able to explain it. He predicted that science and religion would integrate in order that phenomena such as the vacuum realm could be explained.

The astral particles to which Okada was referring can be discovered now that the existence of the Higgs boson has been confirmed. He said that within the astral particles there exist spiritual particles, and within the spiritual particles exist infinitesimal spiritual particles. The nature of the spiritual particles cannot be explained in physical terms; all we can say is that they exist in the spiritual realm.

Today, cutting-edge research in quantum mechanics is reaching the threshold of the spiritual realm, and some scientists are concluding that everything in this world has been created by consciousness. And behind consciousness exists a vast spiritual realm. Now some scientists are extending their research into the realm of the "unseen world," which until quite recently was regarded as the domain of religion. This shows that religion and science are indeed beginning to converge.

The Forum of the Cross and the Yoko Civilization

Shortly after he established the Mahikari movement, Okada explained his vision for the forum of the cross. He said that this forum should be a place where the guiding principles for the coming yoko civilization are defined. He spoke eloquently about the principles for the coming civilization and predicted that, if various specialized fields work in concert, the process of creating unity would stimulate research and new ways of thinking.

In promoting the concept of a spiritually-oriented yoko civilization, Okada made clear that the forum of the cross should be a place where science and religion find common ground. This should be a holy place where the vertical (fire) and horizontal (water) unite and where God's will $(^{\text{God}}_{+})$ manifests itself. Furthermore, it should be a place where all presently existing forms of love based on self-centered attitudes are abandoned, and where unity based on altruistic love and sincerity is nurtured.

Until now science, religion, philosophy, medicine, art, politics, and economics have attempted to bring happiness to humankind. However, Okada said, by and large what we have today is deadlock in each of these fields. He explained the situation in the following way:

> In various ways, the modern age places a great emphasis on specialization and analysis. Indeed, there is constant specialization and analysis. However, paradoxical as it may seem, specialization and analysis are important steps in paving the way to integration. We are now entering an age when we need to make greater efforts to cooperate with each other, to unite and to direct ourselves toward establishing new principles for an integrated civilization.

And further:

> The age of a united global civilization that I speak about will be an age of a cross civilization. In other words, it will be about establishing principles for a holy century rather than just about principles for another century. I think there will be a significant step forward in establishing a new civilization in the coming holy twenty-first century.

Okada ignited the spiritual fire for this vision, based on his great love for humankind. He explained that if science takes itself seriously it will reach out to religion, and if religion takes itself seriously it will reach out to science. What he said is now happening. The Yoko Civilization International Conferences, sponsored by Sukyo Mahikari, are the embodiment of Okada's profound philosophy that religion and science must inevitably converge.

The Great Opportunity for the Renaissance of Sukyo

For a long period in human history, people have lived in a way fundamentally contrary to the divine principles, and salvation during this period has been mainly by dim light, white light, and weak light (*yin* light). However, we are now in an era where the world of *yin* light and tranquil light is coming to an end and where divine principles are brilliantly shining. True Light and *yang* Light have finally arrived. The unique appearance of the divine principles heralds a new dawn in human history and a great opportunity for the renaissance of religion.

The present materially-oriented civilization is hanging on a precipice, spaceship Earth continues to be poisoned, and many species are on the verge of extinction. Everything—animals, fish, mountains, rivers, trees, and grasses—is being contaminated. The Himalayas, often referred to as the rooftop of the world, and Mount Fuji in Japan are also being contaminated—indeed, they have become mountains of trash.

Our propensity to be destructive does not stop here. Nuclear weapons are heinous weapons of mass destruction, which powerful nations use to intimidate or threaten other countries. Despite an outcry about the potential contamination of the environment if such weapons were to be used, and despite much talk that they should be banned, they continue to be accumulated. Temporary peace, itself always in imminent danger of being broken, is maintained throughout the world by exercising a so-called balance of power. The reality, however, is that there are more than 10,000 nuclear warheads, and what we regard as peace may well be transitory.

In a world of darkness, daybreak will surely come. The imminent daybreak is the "daybreak of human history" and heralds the great transition from a *yin* era to a *yang* era. When this miraculous time arrives, people will find that they will have to make a U-turn in how they live, because the age of darkness will be making way for the dawn of God's brilliant Light.

New divine principles that are totally different from those taught in the past have now been revealed. We need to focus on activities that are in tune with the divine plan and that can lead to true salvation for others. All religions need to wake up and go out into the fields, mountains, and cities to help those who are suffering as they are ignorant of the advent of a spiritually-based way of life.

The word renaissance means "revival, rebirth." The Renaissance began in Italy at the end of the fourteenth century. It was a tremendous reform movement in the arts and other fields of human endeavor. It then spread throughout Europe and flourished until the mid-seventeenth century. The catalyst for this movement was a revival in interest in ancient Greek and Roman culture, and it influenced not only the arts but politics and religion too, and brought fresh insights and opportunities to these fields.

The Renaissance transformed the Middle Ages and made possible the modern era. In many respects, it was a response to the impasse that Christian culture was experiencing, and what it led to was a redefinition of what it means to be human, as expressed through art and various scholarly disciplines. Interestingly, Leonardo da Vinci, the great Renaissance genius, after completing a drawing of a dissected human body, remarked: "The soul is present in the center of the skull." Sukyo Mahikari teachings explain that each person has a soul that is derived from God's soul. Like da Vinci, they state that a person's soul is located about 10 cm (4 in.) behind the forehead in the area of the pineal gland.

Today, some four centuries since the Renaissance came to an end, an era of a spiritually-oriented, three-dimensional civilization is about to supersede the materially-oriented, reductionist scientific civilization that has prevailed for many years. This new era will be revolutionary in that it will be an age for new, true religions.

The purpose of religions is to save souls by salvation. Therefore, true practitioners of religion need to be those who can establish a holy twenty-first century, revive the Garden of Eden, and help others to restore their true nature as children of God. It is the age of Heaven, when we must collaborate in an attitude of mutual respect, unity, and cooperation to achieve the goal of a renaissance of religions, which will be also a renaissance of the Earth. It will benefit not only the planet but all living beings. Religion and ecology here are integrally intertwined.

Eventually, the mystery of humankind's true history, which has been hidden, will be revealed, and the history of religion will be rewritten. As awareness of the universal principles grows, people will unite under the Creator of the universe and humankind. There will be a revival in faith directed toward God. When a God-centered and spirit-centered civilization is established new, true human beings will live in a world of art, enveloped by love, virtue, and sincerity, where the trinity of the spirit, mind, and body is noble, pure, and bright.

The renaissance of religions is the path to salvation, that is, transformation for everyone. The path to salvation has to be universal, accessible, and open to anyone and everyone. In order to save humanity, people need to transcend all barriers of race, nationality, ideology, and philosophy. They must construct a spiritual network that spreads across the five major continents. When the entire planet is bathed in a network of Light, the Earth will once again radiate brilliant spiritual Light.

The following is a summary of a spiritual vision for the holy twenty-first century that Okada predicted more than 50 years ago:

1. In the twenty-first century, the field of electronics and interconnectivity will develop dramatically. There will be a radical change in the way people live due to the widespread use of computerized machines and robots.
2. As a result, time spent working as we have hitherto will be greatly reduced.
3. People will have more discretionary time to enjoy sports and the arts.
4. Money will become redundant. Instead of using cash, payments will be made using a point system.
5. Science and religion will converge, and a new, high-dimensional, true science—divine science—will quickly develop.
6. The use of natural energy, such as solar energy and wind power, as a substitute for fossil fuels will greatly expand, and alternate forms of energy will be discovered.
7. A non-polluting, silent car will be invented. Eventually, flying cars will appear.
8. There will be a greater focus on the natural environment. Desalinization technology will enable seawater to be converted into fresh water on a large scale. Nature and the new, true science (divine science) will unite, and a society where both can flourish in harmony will be established.
9. People will respect a spirit-centered way of life and develop a deeper understanding of the relationship between mind and spirit.
10. The Parent God common to all humankind and the Parent God's children will unite and work toward advancing a society that truly reflects the fact that the origin of the world is one and only one.

After the world has overcome hardship and onerous difficulties, a brilliant new world will be established. We are children of God, and every one of us has at least one strong point. It is essential that we nurture these strong points in this lifetime.

From now on, living to offer service will become the way a true child of God lives. A person who lives life in the understanding that life has a deep meaning and purpose will shine brilliantly. Living a life focused on altruistic love, acceptance of God's will, and a sincere inner attitude will save us and allow us to save others.

We need to understand that "all natural resources are lent to us by the Earth." It is vital that we practice energy conservation and make a diligent effort to develop systems of harnessing clean energy sources. People today need to have a fundamental change of heart. It is urgent that people devote themselves to developing renewable energy as quickly as possible and thus bring about an environmental revolution.

We have a wonderful opportunity to create pure and shining cities—"eco-friendly, spiritually-oriented cities"—all around the world. It is the Creator God's will that we promote eco-friendly economics as a field of study and orient society toward recycling Nature's goods and conserving energy. Establishing eco-friendly cities by harnessing clean energy will help us to usher in a new, true, holy century that shines brightly with the Light of God.

Scientists, politicians, religious leaders, and, indeed, all those who are concerned about the future of humankind need to work toward establishing a spirit-centered civilization that harmoniously combines science and spiritual values.

As the euro crisis in Europe and the economic crisis in the United States show, economic conditions are deteriorating. Now is the time for us to develop environment-friendly industries and encourage people to buy environment-friendly products. A pillar or key part of the effort to create environment-friendly industries would be to establish construction companies that build "eco-houses of Light" and "eco-condominiums of Light." Using technologies that utilize renewable natural resources, people need to change civilization, which has emphasized the consumption of non-renewables as a virtue, into one that emphasizes the recycling of Nature's goods. To promote the rapid rise of the new civilization in Japan, as a first step people can work on constructing eco-towns on high ground when building near the coast.

People need to refrain from ineffective methods of recycling. In everyday life, they are inundated with all sorts of material goods. All of us need to reassess our lifestyles and determine what we really need to support daily life. The new civilization will need to develop high-quality durable products that do not place a heavy burden on the environment, and people will need to look after these products so that they can be used for as long as possible. All of us, without exception, need to be more aware of environmental issues, work hard at changing our consciousness, and follow a way of life that gives priority to spiritual values.

Today, it is of particular importance that we build a highly advanced industrialized society that incorporates the positive innovations of science and technology. Thus, we are presented with a divine opportunity to conduct our lives and our professional endeavors in all spheres in a way that is in harmony with the Creator God, who created and sustains us, Earth, and all living beings.

Sukyo Mahikari is now working to put some forested areas it owns to practical use. When it comes to the development of renewable energy, people should not rely solely on the government or utility companies. They need to become pioneers and help to pave the way in developing renewable energy. With the support of the authorities of Takayama City and Gift Prefecture, Sukyo Mahikari has embarked on a project to use the Morimo forested area it owns in Kiyomicho, Takayama City, to construct a hydroelectric power plant and thus play a part in producing renewable energy. Takayama City itself has already been working on energy conservation for many years. The Sukyo Mahikari vision is to harness the natural resources of light, water, and forests to promote self-sufficiency in the supply of electricity, with the aim of acting as a pioneer in promoting an environmental revolution. Next, Sukyo Mahikari plans to pursue three objectives:

- Promote and spread the use of natural energy: construct low-head hydroelectric power.[1]
- Promote and spread the utilization of new forms of energy: work to establish a clean, pollution-free society using hydrogen fuel.
- Improve the local environment and conserve land: promote education on the proper maintenance and thinning of forests

Sukyo Mahikari started by building two low-head hydroelectric power plants. After closely monitoring the results, it will consider building another two. With this facility, electricity will be supplied to 1,200 households annually. For the time being, this natural energy will be sold to the local electric power company. A few years on, if all proceeds as planned, energy will be supplied to Sukyo Mahikari facilities in the Takayama area. Finally, any surplus energy will be sold to facilities in Takayama and elsewhere.

In the future, Sukyo Mahikari hopes to cooperate with the authorities of Takayama City to introduce a harmonious combination of low-head hydroelectric power, solar power, biomass power, and others. It is Sukyo Mahikari's earnest wish that it will be able to contribute significantly to the environmental revolution to help realize the spiritual vision Kotama Okada had for the advent of a spiritually-based, ecologically-conscious civilization in a holy twenty-first century.

Note

1 "Head" is a measure of the pressure of falling water. Hydroelectric sites are broadly categorized as low- or high-head sites. Low head typically refers to a change in elevation of less than 10 ft (3 m). http://www.oregon.gov/ENERGY/RENEW/Pages/hydro/Hydro_index.aspx.

References

Einstein, Albert. 1954. *Ideas and Opinions*. New York: Crown Publishers.

Townes, Charles. The Convergence of Science and Religion. *Think* (March–April 1966), 32, 2, 7.

CHAPTER 6

In the Time of the Sacred Places

Winona LaDuke

It's not like a church where you have everything in one place. We could describe how sacred sites are the teachers... We don't want the American Dream... We want our prayer rocks.

Calleen Sisk, Interview, August 15, 2013, Winnemun Wintu Territory

Minwenzha

For as long as there are memories, the traditional peoples of Turtle Island have narrated sacred stories and lived in sacred places. The stories guided our lives, reinforced our values of community wellbeing and respect for our sacred Mother Earth, and fostered our spirituality. The places provided us with sites for our homes, for our agriculture and fishing, and for engaging with the Creator Spirit and other spirits. Turtle Island is now called "America" by descendants of the aggressive immigrants who began to trespass on these shores shortly after Christopher Columbus was discovered by indigenous peoples as he disembarked from his foreign ship and trespassed on native peoples' land. Despite this foreign invasion, resulting in the aliens' oppression of native peoples, seizure of our lands, and degradation of the natural world, the sacred stories continue to be told. We dream of the time foretold by our ancestors when the Earth will be made whole and known by all people to be holy.

Sacred Stories

In the time of Thunderbeings and Underwater Serpents the humans, animals, and plants conversed, carried on lives of mischief and wonder, and fulfilled everyday tasks. The prophets told of trying times ahead, explained the causes of the deluge of the past,

The Wiley Blackwell Companion to Religion and Ecology, First Edition. Edited by John Hart.

and predicted two possible paths of the future—one scorched, one green—from which the Anishinaabeg would have to choose.

In the time of Thunderbeings and Underwater Serpents it was understood that a perpetual balance with the universe beyond this material world, a universe to whom we would belong always, needed to be maintained.

The Anishinaabe people live within distinct, land-based universes, and oscillate between these worlds. The light of day and the deepness of night remain; the parallel planes of spirit world and material world coexist in perpetuity. All remains, despite the jackhammer of industrial civilization, the rumble of combustion engines, and the sanitized white of a dioxin-bleached day. That was then, but it is also now. Teachings, ancient as the people who have lived on a land for five millennia, speak of a set of relationships to all that is around, predicated on respect, recognition of the interdependence of all beings, understanding of humans' absolute need to be reverent and to manage our behavior, and awareness that this relationship must be reaffirmed through lifeways and acknowledgment of the sacred.

A millennium after that time of the Thunderbeings and Underwater Serpents, those beings still emerge: lightning strikes unexpectedly, seemingly unending fires of climate change scorch Mother Earth, frequent tornadoes flatten buildings, King Tides and river deluges flood the land, and copper beings abound in the midst of industrial society. So it is that we come to face our smallness in a world of mystery and our responsibilities to all life that surrounds us.

> We are a part of everything that is beneath us, above us and around us. Our past is our present, our present is our future, and our future is seven generations past and present.
>
> Oren Lyons, Haudenosaunee oral history

In the midst of the now-time, land-based peoples work to continue a lifeway, or follow simply the original instructions passed on by Gichi Manidoo, the Creator, and others who instruct us. This path often is littered with the remnants or threat of a fossil fuel and nuclear economy—a uranium mine, a big dam project, or tar sands oil extraction. People still work, however, to restore or retain their relationship to a sacred place and to a world, and to tell and retell sacred stories. In many places, for instance, people hold Earth renewal ceremonies or water-healing ceremonies; perhaps these are how, in an indigenous philosophical view, people are able to continue to exist. This chapter narrates some of these stories.

This is also a story of a different society, one based on the notion of "frontier." America is that society. It was born of a fifteenth-century-origin Doctrine of Discovery, a papal-justified European claim to entitlement to vanquish and destroy that which was indigenous, and an accompanying assertion that indigenous territories were *terra nullius* ("empty land") because no Europe-like civilization existed there.[1] America was framed in the mantra of Manifest Destiny. This settler relationship to this North American continent has been historically one of conquest, of utilitarian relationship—an anthropocentric taking of Mother Earth's and native peoples' wealth to make more things for empire. That society has named and claimed for its empire one mountain after another: Mount Rainier, Washington; Harney Peak, South Dakota; Mount

McKinley, Alaska; Mount Lassen, California; Pikes Peak, Colorado. But naming and claiming with a flag does not mean relationship, it means only naming and claiming.[2]

This process denudes relationship, particularly when it names sacred mountain spirits after mortal men, who trample through for a few decades. Americans have developed a sense of place related to empire, with no understanding that for indigenous peoples the Holy Land is not Israel: it is here.

Americans are also, by the social norm of the country, transient. This attitude and practice teach them the notion and enduring illusion of an American dream of greener pastures, always elsewhere. This, too, belittles a relationship to place. It does not teach responsibility, only entitlement: mineral rights, water rights, and private property, as enshrined in the Constitution.

In the times in which we find ourselves, with ecosystems crashing, bees, fish, and trees dying, climate change rampant, and consequently, destabilization continuing, our relationship to place and to our relatives—whether they have wings, fins, paws, or roots—merits reconsideration.

Sacred Places

Since the beginning of time, the Creator and Mother Earth have given our peoples places to learn the teachings that will allow us to continue to be, and to reaffirm our responsibilities and ways to be on the lands from which we have come. Indigenous peoples are place-based societies,[3] and at the center of those places are the most sacred of our sites, where we reaffirm our relationships.

Everywhere there are indigenous people, there are sacred sites, there are ways of knowing, there are *relationships*. The people, the rivers, the mountains, the lakes, the animals, and the fish are all related. In recent years, the US courts have challenged our right to be in these places, and indeed our ability to protect them. In many cases, we are asked to quantify "how sacred it is" or "how often it is sacred," baffling concepts in the spiritual realm. Yet we do not relent, we are not capable of becoming subsumed.

Related Peoples: *Nur* and Human

In northern California, the Winnemem Wintu people have known since time immemorial of their relationship to the *Nur*, the salmon people. They have known that they have a sacred responsibility to protect and care for the salmon that have sustained them on the slope of *Boyum Patuk*, the sacred mountain now known as Mount Shasta. The *Nur* gave the Winnemem their voice and taught them to sing. The Winnemem were told long ago that if the salmon disappeared so, too, would they.

Legends tell of the time when the *Nur* people took pity on the Wintu people and gave them their voice. In return, the salmon only sing as they course the rivers of the northwest, and only the Wintu can hear them. The Wintu, in turn, are to care for the *Nur* always and to sing. And so they try to fulfill this responsibility a millennium later. The people believe that "when the last salmon is gone, humans will be gone too," Caleen Sisk, traditional spiritual leader of the Winnemem Wintu, explains (2013 interview, as cited above):

A millennium on the river did well for both the people and the salmon, who inhabited an area whose remoteness from white civilization was its protection.

Although they were signatories in good faith to what would be an unratified 1851 treaty, and later identified as the tribe many of whose members would be drowned in the aftermath of the 1941 Federal Act which created the Shasta Dam, the Winnemem Wintu ceased to exist as "Indians" under federal law. This strange irony, that the government created by the settlers and intruders who took your land and killed your people gets to determine if you are still an Indian, even if you exist, remains particularly bitter to many tribes. The Winnemem Wintu are particularly caught in this quagmire.

In 1941, the Shasta dam drowned more than 26 miles of the lower McCloud River system. It submerged sacred sites, villages, and history under a deep pool of water destined to benefit cities far away, provided agriculture for the world, and invited to this altered land new occupants and transient tourists who could afford the new way of life. The dam drowned much of the history of the Winnemem Wintu; the dam blocked the passage of the salmon people—the McCloud River *Nur.* The *Nur* either interbred with the Sacramento River salmon or died out in California.

Fish Rock was blown up to make room for a railroad track in 1914, which was, like so much else, drowned by the waters that would become known as Lake Shasta. What is left of Dekkas Rock, a prayer site, now protrudes from the reservoir as, one reporter notes, "a malformed atoll." It was here, on the banks of the river, that the Winnemem held what other native peoples in the region call "Big Times," where disputes were adjudicated, songs were sung, ceremonies were held, and marriages were arranged.

The Wintu grieved the loss of their salmon, their sacred doctoring rocks, and their river. Yet, "Our old people said that the salmon would be hidden behind a river of ice. Indian doctors and prophets had been with the Wintu long ago, and prophesied the time when the salmon would disappear," Caleen Sisk tells me. That was almost unimaginable to the Wintu or to those who had "discovered the salmon" of the McLeod or Middle River.

More than a century ago Livingston Stone, a fish culturist, arrived in Wintu territory. He said that the spawning Chinook were so plentiful he could have walked across their backs from one side of the river to the other. In the 1870s, he established the Baird Hatchery on the McCloud, originally in an attempt to breed a Pacific salmon to replenish the now dwindling and overfished Atlantic salmon stocks. The Winnemem Wintu were initially opposed to the fishery, but made peace with the White men of the fisheries on the condition that the salmon would always be able to come home.

In a strange turn of events, in 1890 Stone decided to attempt to transplant the Wintu *Nur* to another world, Aotearoa (now called New Zealand). There, in the Rakaia River on the South Island, moved over a vast ocean to be among sphagnum moss, the *Nur* salmon people came to live.

So it was that the salmon of the McLeod, the *Nur*, disappeared from the Wintu world. However, just as had been prophesied, they returned—but elsewhere. The Rakaia River is a River of Ice, emerging from a glacial mountain in the south of Aotearoa. In 2008, the Wintu went to Aotearoa to visit their salmon for the first time since the dams destroyed their relatives. And the Wintu sang once again for the *Nur*. It is 50 years since the dam destroyed the homeland of the salmon and much of the sacred world of the Wintu, but the Wintu believe that through prayer, prophecy, and hard work, the *Nur* will return.

Copper and Iron, or Wild Rice and Water

> Sometimes it seems like people aren't interested in sticking around for another thousand years.
>
> Mike Wiggins, Bad River Anishinaabe tribal chairman

On the shore of Gichi Gummi, Lake Superior, 2,000 miles to the East, "copper was said to belong to the Underwater Manitouk... One often finds at the bottom of the water pieces of pure copper... I have several times seen such pieces in the Savage's hand, and since they are superstitious, they keep to them as so many divinities, or as presents which the gods dwelling beneath the water have given them and on which their welfare is to depend," one European explorer would record.

The Underwater *Manidoowag* and the *Miskaabik* (spirit of copper) and *Biwaabik* (spirit of iron ore) live here, *omaa akiing*, on this land. The Anishinaabeg Akiing ("the land to which the Anishinaabe people belong") extends across the Great Lakes region in a territory of lakes, rivers, and wild rice.

The Underwater Manidoowag, Miskwaabik, and Biwaabik were viewed not as spirits by the US government, but as objects of empire. The government never claimed to hold or control Anishinaabeg land by "right of conquest"; rather, it claims to have legally acquired Anishinaabeg and other Native lands by mutual agreement. Between 1785 and 1923, the US, England, and Canada entered into more than 40 treaties with the Anishinaabeg. These treaties are the bases for some of the largest land transactions in world history.

Some of the first incursions onto Anishinaabeg land were to secure access to iron and copper deposits. By 1800, representatives of both the British monarch and the emerging United States had "discovered" a 2,500 lb boulder of naturally occurring copper called the "Ontonogan Boulder." It rested on the southern shore of Lake Superior in Anishinaabeg territory in what is now known as the Keewanaw Peninsula. By the 1820s, the federal government had tried to undertake a comprehensive study of "mineral assets" in the Lake Superior area, and a corresponding study of Indian title to the land there. Within a very short period, four treaties were signed by the US, each providing for mining in Anishinaabeg territory. These treaties covered both the Kewanee Peninsula and the Mesabe "Sleeping Giant" iron ore belt in northern Minnesota.

By mid-century, more than 100 copper companies had been incorporated in Michigan, Wisconsin, and Minnesota Territories. As early as 1849, copper production at Keewenaw Peninsula in Anishinaabe territory led the world. Similarly, beginning in 1890, mining at northern Minnesota's Mesabe accounted for 75% of all US iron ore production. Many of today's US-based transnational mining companies were founded in this era on the wealth of the Anishinaabeg. They include Kennecott and Anaconda Copper, and 3 M.

After the Miskwaabik (the copper) came the Biwaabik (iron). In the time of Thunderbeings wild rice also grew here, called by the Anishinaabe *manoomin* ("seed of the Creator"). Wild rice is the only grain endemic to North America; it is one of the greatest gifts imaginable to the land and waters. Indeed, it has been part of the Anishinaabeg migration story and is found in a set of prophecies in which the people are instructed to "go to the place where the food grows upon the water." There are few other places in the world where such a bountiful gift is delivered to those who live there, whether they have wings or hands. The lakes and rivers, owing to the unique nature and adaptability of the *manoomin*, offer a wild rice crop somewhere in the region each year. That is an amazing food security for people, and for the waterfowl that nest and eat in these same waters.

Thanks to this bounty, where there is wild rice there are Ojibwe or Anishinaabeg people and where there are Anishinaabeg, there is wild rice. Indeed, *Manoominike Giizis* is the wild rice-making moon. It is seen during the late summer to early fall when the Anishinaabeg move to the lakes of the north and begin a harvest. This is a sacred food and a keystone of the ecosystem of the Great Lakes region (the Anishinaabe Akiing).

Similarly, the most spiritual of all traditions and history is the Anishinaabeg relationship to *ma'iingan*, the wolf. It is said that the first friend of our half-man/half-human being, *Naanaaboozhoo*, walked with the *ma'iingan*. In Anishinaabeg prophecies that which befalls the wolf will befall the Anishinaabeg. The decimation of the Anishinaabeg by epidemics, starvation, and federal policies closely mirrored the annihilation of the *ma'iingan*. Reducing Anishinaabeg territories to reservations, and confining the wolves to a few sanctuaries and a few sparse patches in the northern woods, occurred simultaneously. However, both have returned to the northland. Today, 19 Anishinabeg reservations span the north country, from Michigan to Montana. This same territory—from northern Minnesota to northern Michigan—is today home to the largest wolf population in the lower 48 states. There are 60,000 Anishinaabeg and 5,000 wolves. Both are recovering from near-extinction and are relatives—one with two legs, one with four.

The Predator Returns

The companies forged from empire in the 1850s are returning home, having ravaged the world, fortified their empires, and left memorials in the form of deep pits to the copper that once was. New mines are proposed throughout this region—Anishinaabe Akiing—from the Yellow Dog mine in the Keewenaw Penninsula to the Polymet and Franconia mines of the Boundary Waters. In the center is the proposed Gogebic Penokee Mine, thus far successfully opposed by citizens and tribal opposition. Yet, the region remains incredibly challenged, as Ojibwes note in a letter to the United Nations requesting assistance:

> Currently, an aggressive mining boom throughout Anishinaabeg territory, of present-day Michigan, Wisconsin, Minnesota and Ontario, threatens the water quality and ecosystem of almost every sub-watershed of Lake Superior. This is due to our region's valuable geology, increases in global metal market prices, and friendly political administrations at state government levels—whose political representatives are focused primarily on short-term job prospects.

Eagle Rock, known as the "Home of the White Wolf," is a sacred place and prehistoric navigation site on the Keewenaw. The Rock correlates to the Bighorn Medicine Wheel and other rock formations and sacred sites in Wisconsin and east of the Mississippi River. The Rock is considered sacred not only by the Anishinaabeg, but also the Hochunk and Cheyenne peoples. Today, the Keewenaw Bay Band of Anishinaabeg and the Lac Vieux Desert bands of Anishinaabeg live in this territory, and the tribes, as well as the National Congress of American Indians, have requested that the Rock be protected as a site of religious worship.

Beneath the Rock in a world below is *Miskaabik Aabinoojiins*, the Copper Child. The copper ore body appears in geographic information systems (GIS) imaging as a baby, and awaits its scheduled demise, like a convict on death row. Rio Tinto Zinc, a UK-based mining company, through its subsidiary Kennecott, plans to mine the copper deposit adjacent to the sacred place. A seven-year battle has been fought for this sacred site, marked by arrests and legal actions. A petition was presented to the UN in 2012 by tribal members of the Keewenaw Bay community for intervention under the UN Declaration on the Rights of Indigenous Peoples, not only to protect the people's sacred sites, but to protect Anishinaabe Akiing. Mineral exploitation would destroy the water ecosystems of wild rice and the rich land on which the Anishinaabeg have lived for five millennia.

The Michigan regulatory authorities which have assumed jurisdiction over the area have ruled against the tribes, the water, and the sacred site. They claim, essentially, that the site could not be sacred or did not have spiritual significance because a place of worship "must be a building." On these grounds the state approved the mining permit. In response, the leadership of the HoChunk Tribal Court, in present-day Black River Falls, Wisconsin, asserted:

> [C]onsultation should include learned tribal members who are the leaders of our ancient societies. Their knowledge spans the time prior to Christianity and Christopher Columbus. It is this understanding that makes who we are. There is no other place where tribal people can gain this understanding...

Relationships are now changing. It is ironic that the two largest barriers to the wholesale mining of the north may be *manoomin* and the *ma'iingan*.

Proposals in both Wisconsin and Minnesota would eviscerate water quality laws, causing serious harm to the wild rice of the north. In a related development, the recent delisting of the wolf by US Fish and Wildlife seems synchronized with the interests of new mining companies in the region. Tribal communities, joined increasingly by northern residents, have opposed the threats to water and wild rice throughout the North Country; regulatory battles are underway in Minnesota. Although the wolf has been delisted from the Endangered Species Act, tribal communities are opposing the delisting in their territories. This is significant: in Minnesota, Wisconsin, and Michigan the remaining wolf territory, delisting has allowed the issuing of hunting permits in the North Country. Wolf territories are on reservations and in the areas surrounding reservations, all of which are still under tribal jurisdiction according to treaties and court decisions.

Tribal governments and inter-governmental agencies in the north have pledged to retain their relationship and responsibility to the *ma'iingan*, and our communities remain vigilant in working to protect the sacred beings from the mines of the predator.

Doko'oosliid, Kachinas Mountain, and Recycled Ski Areas

To the far south, in the realm of the sacred mountains of the Diné (Navajo) people, *Dine Bii Kaya*, four sacred mountains are again facing threats. Mount Taylor is once again proposed as a site for uranium mining, and *Doko'oo'sliid*, the Navajos' Sacred Mountain of the West, is being desecrated for the pleasure of skiers.

This volcanic highland area of Arizona began to form over 6 million years ago with the eruption of nearly 600 volcanoes. The most dramatic of those eruptions created a place sacred to 13 tribes, a cluster of three 12,000-ft mountain peaks, known as a place where the Kachina spirits emerge, and the sacred Mountain of the West, one of four cornerstones marking the borders of *Dine Bii Kaya*, the land of the Diné. In the vain vernacular of American empire, the sacred mountains are called the San Francisco Peaks.

On the highest point in Arizona, the only arctic-alpine vegetation in the state grows in a fragile 2-square-mile zone. Arizona's best examples of Ice Age glaciation can be found here. It is here that sacred herbs have been gathered and religious ceremonies held since the dawn of time.

In 1984, the US Congress recognized the fragile ecosystem and cultural significance of the area and designated the Kachina Peaks a wilderness. Yet, in this unlikely place, in an ostensibly protected wilderness in the desert, the current conflict is over a ski resort. Its developers plan to pipe treated sewage water from Flagstaff to make and spray artificial snow on the sacred mountain. There is no water source on the mountain other than what falls from the sky.

Ironically, on the Navajo Reservation, "water is so scarce and inaccessible that some 40 percent of the tribe's 190,000 residents have no potable supply, and many receive their water out of the back of trucks... A 2006 water-pricing analysis by the tribe found that 3,800 liters (1,000 gallons) of hauled water carried a price tag of $US133, compared to $US2.73 for the same quantity of water delivered directly to homes via water infrastructure in nearby Flagstaff. The high cost of water is a contributing factor to the reservation's poverty rate—more than 40%—which is among the highest in the country," according to a 2010 article in the *Navajo-Hopi Observer*, a tribal paper.

Despite the acknowledged ecosystem, archeological and cultural issues, and determined opposition from Native nations and conservation organizations, the 9th US Circuit Court of Appeals recently allowed the Arizona Snowbowl Recreation project to proceed. Flagstaff's treated sewer water will be trucked to Snowbowl until a 14.8-mile pipeline is constructed, and then some 180 million gallons a year of treated effluent from Flagstaff will be pumped up the sacred mountain to the ski area to make snow. The treated sewage has been shown to contain contaminants such as pharmaceuticals and hormones. Snowbowl hopes to attract ski-starved desert dwellers to its resort with clever marketing; it remains to be seen how enticing a mouthful of Snowbowl effluent will be.

The Snowbowl owners have already clear-felled some 74 acres of rare alpine forest for new ski runs. A 10-million gallon retention pond and another 12 miles of pipeline will be built to distribute reclaimed sewer water along the ski runs, all desecrations in the eyes of the Diné people. In the Summer of 2012 protests continued in defense of a sacred place and ultimately at some level in a questioning of priorities, and access to water for people and the land. Yet, the project went ahead, and was installed.

This is the difference between a worldview where one society, an industrial society, views a land as a rich ore body or a playground, and another that views it as a source of great spiritual and cultural wealth. This is the story of the time in which we find ourselves.

The Auction of the Sacred

As the wind breathes out of Wind Cave and in my face I am reminded of the creation of humans and my own small place in this magnificent world. Wind Cave National Park is named for the Cave itself, called *Washun Niya* (The Breathing Hole of Mother Earth) by the Lakota People. In this Creation story, it is where the people emerged into the world.

It is a complex cave system. According to scientists, we may have an appreciation of only 5% of the cave's volume and breadth, and likely even less of its power. In the vernacular of some, it is the "known unknown." Most indigenous peoples understand there is a Great Mystery, that which is much larger than our human presence and our anthropocentric understanding of the world. There is, too, an understanding that there is more than one world surrounding people.

So it is that in 2012, the time of change and transformation in a US election year, and according to the Mayan calendar, the smallness and greatness of humans in a world around us, came face to face with us in the Black Hills. A most sacred place, *Pe'Sla*, in the center of the Lakota Universe, came up for sale, and values and questions clashed.

As Lakota scholar Chase Iron Eyes explains:

> Pe'Sla, to the Lakota, is the place where Morning Star, manifested as a meteor, fell to earth to help the Lakota by killing a great bird which had taken the lives of seven women; Morning Star's descent having created the wide open uncharacteristic bald spot in the middle of the forested Black Hills [on American maps, called "Old Baldy] ... the Morning Star placed the spirits of those seven women in the sky as the constellation "Pleiades" or "The Seven Sisters." ("Last Real Indians," August 2012)

This is the "Center of the Heart of Everything that is ... one of a small number of highly revered and geographically-cosmologically integral places on the entire planet," explains Iron Eyes. Sacred places, recognized under federal judicial review Presidential Executive Order (1996), and international law are to be protected.

On August 25, 2012, the Center of the Heart of Everything was to be placed on the auction block in Ramkota Inn, Rapid City, South Dakota. It was destined to be diced into 300-acre tracts, proposed for ranchettes, and the site of a possible road through the heart (and more divisions) of what has been, until now, a relatively undesecrated sacred site. "We didn't even know it was going to be sold," Debra White Plume from Manderson told me." We heard nothing about it until we saw the auction announcement."

The Brock Auction Company of Iowa and South Dakota announced in mid-July, 2012, when offering the Reynolds Ranch: "this story begins in 1876 just two short years after General George Armstrong Custer led his historic expedition through the then almost unknown Black Hills in the Dakota Territory... In 1876 Joseph Reynolds filed his first claim & homesteaded ...'Reynolds Prairie!' He was followed by three more generations ..." Brock promotes the property noting, as some solace for potential buyers,

> As you sit in quiet solitude, with only the whispering of the wind gently easing through the pines, let your mind wander back in time & imagine the Native Americans, the Homesteaders & Pioneers who passed across this land that is now a part of yours & your families' legacy forever!

Ironic, perhaps insulting, to a Lakota.

While other religions have revered and protected sacred sites, the Lakota continue to struggle to protect their most sacred places. These include *Mahto Paha*, Bear Butte, where numerous challenges made to the annual Sturgis Motor Cycle Rally have met with some success; and Grey Horned Butte ("Devil's Tower"), which has been protected to preserve its sacred space from recreational rock climbers.

The US is a country where private property is enshrined as a constitutional right, but the rights of Nature, of the natural world, and of future generations, are not enshrined. In the time of the sacred sites and the collapse of ecosystems and worlds, it is not worth making a commodity out of all that is revered. As a 2005 editorial in the *Rapid City Journal* points out, protecting Lakota sacred sites is of interest to all:

> Non-Indians have little to fear if familiar sites are designated as sacred; visitors are still allowed at Bear Butte, Devil's Tower, and Rainbow Bridge, even though they are being managed as Indian sacred sites. And in fact, expanding non-Indians' knowledge and appreciation of the Indian lore surrounding such sites could lead to greater cultural understanding...

That is generous for the usually very conservative *Rapid City Journal*.

So it was that with less than two weeks remaining before Pe'Sla was to be auctioned, word spread: through communities (three of which are the economically poorest counties in the country, all on Lakota reservations), via Facebook, the internet, and the media—from the *Huffington Post* to the *Seattle Times*. The story of the Lakota, their sacred site, and the proposed auction was repeated in whispers, and then in rallies and in outrage. Using the internet, the communities raised over half a million dollars, which was then matched by tribal money originating with the Rosebud Sioux Tribe, and other donations. The auction was cancelled and the Lakota have begun to negotiate for the purchase of their sacred site.

It remains exceptionally ironic, however, in many ways. This is particularly true considering that *Paha Sapa*, the Black Hills, was illegally taken from the Lakota by the US with the advent of gold mining and Hearst empire support; the land has never been purchased. In legal settlements of North American Native land titles, this one remains the largest and the most resisted: over $105 million was allocated for the Black Hills by Congress to pay the Lakota for the illegal seizure, but that money has never been accepted. Hence, the irony: the people must buy back land they have never considered was held by someone else. And the price tag—$12 million—represents just 10% of the sum originally proposed to be paid to the Lakota for the entire Black Hills region. Most of five states—North and South Dakota, Montana, Wyoming, and Nebraska—were all included in the 1868 treaty; the Lakota reserved them as their territory in the treaty.

Return to Sacred Lifeways

Even in periods of great injustice there is always hope; for those of us who remain involved in our ceremonies, there is also faith. That faith is reaffirmed when small miracles of spirit occur and the world changes.

On the banks of the McLeod River in northern California, the Wintu gather, despite citations and legal opposition by the state and others, to hold their sacred coming of age ceremonies for their young women. This is how life continues.

And one day, not too far away, the salmon will return from Aotearoa and the *Nur* and the Wintu will celebrate.

In the north woods, the Anishinaabeg celebrate one round of opposing the Beast—the huge Gogebic Taconite, LLC (GTAC) mine proposed for the Penokee Mountains of Wisconsin, which wants to desecrate and pollute the headwaters of the Bad River. The Penokee Mountains and Bad River are at the heart of the Bad River tribal community of Anishinaabeg. In 2012 the proposal for that mine, like another four before it in Wisconsin, was rejected. That may be a temporary victory, but it provides breathing room for Mother Earth.

In 2012, it seemed that Pe'Sla would be protected from being turned into luxury ranchettes and might continue to be a place where a people pray and reaffirm their relationship to Creation. In 2013, the Pe'sla site was purchased by a coordinated effort between the Lakota tribes, led by the Rosebud Tribe and the Indian Land Tenure Foundation. The land remains protected.

Then, too, a renaming or recovery of names is occurring. Several decades ago, Mount McKinley was renamed Mount Denali. On the other side of the world, Australia's Ayers Rock reverted to its original name, Uluru. Ayers Rock was the name the White man gave it who found what native people already knew was there. In 2010, in Canada, the Haida homeland was formally renamed Haida Gwaii, erasing Queen Charlotte Island, named for a queen who had never visited that land and probably did not understood Haida traditions. Further south, the Salish Sea is likely to be the name for what has been called Puget Sound. Other reaffirmations of place and history are reframing our understanding of the holy land which is here. These stories merge with stories of a people and their allies who have come to live on this land.[4]

On a larger scale, the New Zealand Courts, a judicial system which emerged from colonial and church authorities, recently affirmed the rights of a river to exist. The Whanganui River became a legal entity, and in 2012 was given the same status as a person under New Zealand law. In an agreement in parliament between the Crown and the Maori (represented by the Whanguanui Iwi), the river was given its legal status with the name *Te Awa Tupua*. Two guardians, one from the Crown and one from the Whanganui River Iwi, were assigned to protect the river. Brendon Puetapu, the spokesman for the Whanganui Iwi, explained: "Today's agreement which recognizes the status of the river as Te Awa Tupua (an integrated, living whole) and the inextricable relationship of Iwi with the river is a major step towards the resolution of the historical grievances of Whanganui Iwi and is important nationally."

The Living Industrial Predator

The industrial predator, however, is remorseless. Voracious in appetite and greed, and lacking any heart, it sees all as prey for profit.

If 57% of the energy produced in the US is wasted through inefficiencies, people might want to become less wasteful to survive. If two-thirds of our materials end up in waste dumps relatively quickly, we may want to reduce our consumption. These are economic choices, political choices, and personal choices. Ultimately, all have to do with empire and the need for new frontiers, or making peace, *omaa akiing*, here on this land.

In the clamor of crashing worlds, it is possible to watch and breathe. In the massive deluge of the city of Duluth in 2012, rain fell constantly for two days on a city with aging infrastructure. The Anishinaabeg remember a great flood from the earliest of memories, after which the world was made anew. The Anishinaabeg watched the flood from reservations, an island at a safe distance from the deluge and crash.

The tally in economic terms of the flood was in the region of $100 million. That represented just the beginning of climate change-related costs that year. World insurance agencies project that we will be spending 20% of GDP worldwide on climate change-related disasters. By March, 2012, there had been over 129,000 recorded weather records worldwide.

Freed by the Duluth deluge, a polar bear escaped from Duluth Zoo. As it headed north, we Anishinaabeg knew that the time was changing. We watched and we understood that we, as sacred beings in this millennium, have an opportunity to do a righteous and *pono* thing—follow a righteous path.

Today, we must challenge fossil fuel transnational corporations to leave coal, oil, tar sand, and gas where they are: underground. Most of these fuels are on indigenous peoples' lands. Our Anishinaabe Akiing territories in northern Minnesota have become focal points for pipeline battles. We need clean, local, renewable energy and organic food to conserve our territories and protect our people and all beings—today and in the future. We must have intergenerational responsibility, looking toward the wellbeing of those who will come seven generations from now: not just humankind, but all living beings, including Mother Earth.

Periodically, hope for protecting Mother Earth and the health and livelihoods of native peoples is generated anew. The Lummi people in Washington State began to protest strongly against proposals to construct six massive coal export terminals, including on Lummi lands in Washington, as reported in *The New York Times* in "Tribes Add Potent Voice Against Plan for Northwest Coal Terminals" (October 2012). In September, "the Affiliated Tribes of Northwest Indians, a regional congress of more than 50 tribes in seven states, passed a resolution demanding a collective environmental impact statement for the proposed ports." Lummi elder Mary Helen Cagey, who had fished at Cherry Point in years past, opposed the construction. She said that building the gigantic shipping terminal to export coal overseas is "something that should not come about." The Lummi joined environmental groups and "green" politicians who opposed the chain of export terminals along the Pacific northwest coastline in Washington through Oregon. The resolution was backed by the Columbia River Inter-Tribal Fish Commission.

The Lummi brought a powerful Indian voice to the struggles of environmental groups. They added to previous environment-focused discussions issues of treaty rights, adverse economic and environmental impacts on traditional Indian village and fishing sites, and degradation of sacred lands and burial sites. (Years earlier, President Clinton had issued an Executive Order to federal agencies "to allow tribal access to sacred sites and to take into account religious practices in federal decision making.")

In 2016, the Lummi people of Washington State succeeded in stopping the construction of the $665 million Gateway Pacific Terminal, some 90 miles north of Seattle, which would have been the biggest coal export terminal in the US. The massive facility would have been located on Lummi traditional fishing grounds. *The New York Times* reported in "U.S. Denies Permit for Coal Terminal in Washington State" that the US Army Corps of Engineers, which had jurisdiction over such projects, agreed with the Lummi claim that their access to water would have been curtailed. Its District Commander stated that "the corps may not permit a project that abrogates treaty rights," and therefore is not permissible. This was an important victory for the Lummi and all Indian peoples. We will continue our work supporting similar efforts across the US.

In our Honor the Earth movement, we have been working on solar and wind projects to provide alternate energy sources. We have supported the Lubicon Cree in Alberta in their solar energy efforts, particularly the Pitapan ("sunrise") Solar Project. On the White Earth reservation where I live, we hope to install solar thermal panels on our homes. Our work is barely beginning, given the magnitude of the problems we face. But we will press on—for ourselves and for our children. We are working to create the place our prophets told us would be, in the time of the eighth fire, the world we make.

Sacred Places Renewed, Sacred Stories Retold, Sacred Lives Relived

In the time of Thunderbeings and Underwater Serpents, humans, animals, and plants conversed, carried on lives of mischief and wonder, and fulfilled everyday tasks. The prophets told of times ahead, explained the deluge of the past, and predicted two possible paths in the future—one scorched and one green—from which the Anishinaabeg would have to choose.

All of us have the same choice. Somewhere in this time, the potential exists to take the right path. Let us choose that path and help to change the course of our history and renew the wellbeing of Mother Earth as we walk toward a bright—solar bright—new future. The new yet old path will carry forward the hopes and dreams and lives of our ancestors.

Notes

1 An extensive discussion of the Doctrine of Discovery is found in Miller (2006); and Newcomb (2008).
2 This is elaborated in LaDuke (2005).
3 Osage scholar and spiritual leader George Tinker describes the distinction between Indian peoples' primarily *spatial* focus on place and Euro-Americans' primarily *temporal* focus on chronological time. See Tinker (2008, 7–9).
4 See LaDuke (2005).

References

LaDuke, Winona. 1999. *All Our Relations: Native Struggles for Land and Life*. London: Haymarket Press. (2nd ed., 2015.)

LaDuke, Winona. 2005. *Recovering the Sacred: The Power of Naming and Reclaiming*. London: Haymarket Press. (2nd ed., 2016.)

LaDuke, Winona. 2016. *LaDuke Chronicles*. Ponsford: MN: Spotted Horse Press.

Miller, Robert J. 2006. *Native America, Discovered and Conquered: Thomas Jefferson, Lewis and Clark, and Manifest Destiny*. Westport, CT: Praeger.

New York Times. 2012 (October 11). Kirk Johnson, "Tribes Add Potent Voice against Plan for Northwest Coal Terminals." https://www.nytimes.com/2016/05/10/us/washington-state-army-corps-denies-permit-coal-terminal.html?emc=eta1.

New York Times. 2016 (May 9). Kirk Johnson, "U.S. Denies Permit for Coal Terminal in Washington State." http://www.nytimes.com/2012/10/12/us/tribes-add-powerful-voice-against-northwest-coal-plan.html?emc=eta1.

Tinker, George. 2008. *American Indian Liberation: A Theology of Sovereignty*. Maryknoll, NY: Orbis Books.

Further Reading

Newcomb, Steven T. 2008. *Pagans in the Promised Land: Decoding the Doctrine of Christian Discovery*. Golden, CO: Fulcrum.

CHAPTER 7

Eco-Theology in the African Diaspora

Dianne D. Glave

My most visceral memory of "having church" outdoors was on a chilly day in December 2009 at Sweet Water Creek State Park in the suburbs of Atlanta, Georgia. The temperature was in the 30 °F, but with the exertion of hiking I had shed my jacket and was down to a T-shirt. Suddenly, I found myself surrounded by birches. The silvery trunks were shedding their bark in the sun's warm light, seemingly just as I had shed an outer layer of protection against the cold. The branches shot upward to Heaven as if they were reaching out to God. And I had church alone in the woods in a glimmering sanctuary of trees under the winter sun.

Consider the contradictions of being inside an African-American church surrounded by walls and being in the natural backdrop of the woods in which I reconnect in more than one way with God and remember the ancestors. The connection to God through Nature can be found outdoors in a more tactile way than indoors. In both settings, I remember the ancestors—invoking the spirits of those gone—through African spirituality. Some of the ancestors of the African-American historical record knew Nature. Harriet Tubman trekked from the South to the North with runaway slaves using the North Star and moss on trees to find her way. Booker T. Washington, president of the now historically black Tuskegee Institute from 1881 to 1915, recounted that as a child he feared the woods when running an errand for a slaveholder (Glave, 2005, 41).

Through worshiping outdoors and indoors and recounting the African-American past in the context of Nature, my own theology has evolved as an African-American woman rooted in Protestantism and African spirituality. My history, my DNA, are irrevocably tied to an African style of worship that includes honoring the ancestors—invoking the name of that church mother or remembering that much loved deacon. My own theology is also drawn from faith, through the words and experiences of the African-Americans who knew Nature intimately.

The Wiley Blackwell Companion to Religion and Ecology, First Edition. Edited by John Hart.

Two strands, sometimes competing, at times entwined, of my Protestant religious experience and African spirituality had already triggered some theological thinking while I was hiking in those Georgia woods, but it was yet to be articulated. Layers of eco-theology inform how African-Americans view and treat the Earth, natural goods ("resources"), and people: eco-theology; Creation care from the Book of Genesis; dominion of the Earth and her goods—an African eco-theology paralleling Creation care; and an African-American eco-theology, one of whose strands is Black Environmental Liberation Theology (BELT).

Part of the foundation of African-American experiences with Nature is in Christianity, which is very much Western, European, Euro-American, or White in scope. The foundation has its origins in colonial-era first contact between Whites and Africans in Africa. During the European maritime discovery, which included the Middle Passage in which millions were captured and relocated to the Americas, seamen and missionaries brought the sword along with the Bible. African lives and spirituality were transformed within the nexus of clinging to their spirituality and being indoctrinated into Christianity when captured (initially by the Portuguese, followed by other Whites), forced to journey from the shores of Africa, shipped like cattle to the Americas, and compelled to work in the fields in a new, frightening place.

A strand of modern eco-theology is rooted in White Christianity, but other faith traditions, such as Hinduism, have their own complementary interpretations. Christian eco-theology is the relationship between the tenets of Christianity and the meaning and perception of Nature. Interpretations are derived from scripture, rational thought or analysis, practice, and an evolving and deepening understanding of God. The theology is often driven by a pressing need to respond to the destruction of the planet. So it makes sense that the theology is transformed through practice, specifically through activism on behalf of the Earth and its inhabitants.

Creation care is a strand of eco-theology, caring for God's Creation. Eco-theology is based initially in Genesis, in whose Creation and Flood stories God entered into a covenant with humanity—a mutually reciprocal agreement—of good stewardship of the Earth. God agreed to give humankind, starting with Adam and Eve, responsibility for Nature. Adam and Eve were bound to Nature by naming every living being. Later, in their part of the agreement, the first woman and man cared for the land, plants, and animals. To reiterate, Adam and Eve consented to care for Nature; the covenant did not direct them to use and abuse it (Glave, 2005, 63; Merchant, 2013, 12–19).

Unfortunately, Christians and those influenced by Christianity, have practiced biblical dominion—the foundation of modern sensibilities toward Nature in Christian and secular circles in the United States, exploiting rather than caring for nature (Glave, 2005, 63; Merchant, 2013, 26, 40–41, 55).

Eco-Theology

Africans and African-Americans are not exempt from responsibility for exploiting the natural goods (resources) of the planet, though the practice of dominion through scriptural interpretation was sadly forged out of enslavement and colonialism or Christian eco-domination (Merchant, 2013, 125). Whites drove the exploitation of people of African descent working the land and its natural benefits. Whites colonized the minds and resources of Africans and African-Americans, often working hand-in-glove with Christian missionaries and their exploitative doctrines. For example, slaves were expected to honor their master by working the cotton fields without question (this was justified at times by citing the teaching in Ephesians 6:5).

Today, many, particularly First World nations, are culpable for the decline of the Earth typified by the global warming that continues in the twenty-first century (White, 1967, 1287). Developing nations, often populated by people of color, want the same goods that First World nations have long possessed. They want modern cars fueled by petrochemicals—even though these are destructive of the planet—a very modern and common First World convenience.

African eco-theology, paralleling Creation care, brings another sort of sensibility of the planet. As with Creation care, the Earth and her goods are treated with great respect and solicitude. In this vein, African scholar Kapya J. Kaoma, author of *The Creator's Symphony: African Christianity, the Plight of Earth and the Poor*, describes his own experience based on African spirituality and Anglican Christianity: "I grew up believing that Creation was sacred. We were seriously warned never to despise any creature we encountered in the forest—doing so was inviting the wrath of the Creator and the ancestors. All these lesson built in me the sense of my interconnectedness to the natural world—something my Franciscan spirituality later confirmed" (Kaoma Location 83, Amazon ebook).

In much the same way, Wangari Maathai's sense of Nature was based on the duality of African spirituality and Christianity. In 1977, she organized The Greenbelt Movement, which planted trees to combat deforestation and soil erosion in Kenya. Her people brought their perceptions as both Christians and Africans to Nature ("Transcript of Wangari Maathai"). In one example of the perceptions of some Kenyans, Maathai recounted how Western missionaries felled the woodlands, counter to the experiences of Maathai and other Kenyans who saw the trees as sacred ("Transcript of Wangari Maathai"). Her great act of rebellion as an African who embraced both her Christianity and African spirituality was to fight for the trees to be replanted, as a prayer to the Earth through action.

BELT reflects the historical and contemporary experiences of people of African descent like Maathai. Eco-theology is based on black liberation theology, which denounces the oppression of African-Americans based on biblical principles. BELT is a nascent theology, forged from environmental justice and activism rooted in Christian experience, worship, and theology by and of African-Americans, a branch of black liberation theology ("Black Environmental Liberation Theology," in Glave & Stoll, 2005, 190: and Glave, 2017).

Nat Turner, an African-American who was enslaved, was emblematic of BELT. He led enslaved and free African-Americans in a rebellion against slaveholders in Southampton County, Virginia in 1831. Both African-Americans and Whites were killed, and ultimately Turner was captured and executed.

Turner's eco-theological or nascent BELT reflections are detailed in Turner, "The Confessions of Nat Turner, The Leader of the Late Insurrection in Southampton VA" (1831).

He had visions before embarking on a revolt. Turner's visions were based on his understanding of the Bible: he was literate, which was unusual for the enslaved. He was a true believer, who incited a rebellion because of his faith in a Christian God, while fighting for African-Americans as an enslaved man. In "The Confessions of Nat Turner," he wrote:

> I then found on the leaves in the woods hieroglyphic characters, and numbers, with the forms of men in different attitudes, portrayed in blood, and representing the figures I had seen before in the heavens. And now the Holy Ghost had revealed itself to me, and made plain the miracles it had shown me.

Turner worshiped God, he conversed with God, he was a prophet of God—all in the context of Nature and revolt. His theology—an analysis of scripture, faith, and practice—galvanized him to rebel against Whites because of his vision of blood, characters, figures, and heaven. He prepared to act first through quiet contemplation and conversation with God, and only then took action (Glave, 2016).

Taken together, Creation care, dominion, African and Black eco-theology, and BELT led Kaoma to suggest through the lens of faith that Nature be treated and celebrated as a sacrament, a Christian ritual like baptism or communion (Kaoma, Location 48). Whether from the perspectives of African spirituality or Westernized faith traditions—often dueling perspectives and theologies for African-Americans—Nature must be seen and treated in a different and better way to save the Earth and humanity (DuBois, 1903, 2–3). For those of African descent, will this dual and internally dueling consciousness lead to care for or destruction of Nature? Answers should bear in mind the lessons of history, and be mindful of the racial and at times the racist complexities of eco-theology, including Black eco-theology, while creatively envisioning and developing a holistic spiritually, socially, and ecologically renewed Earth and Earth biotic community.

I still "have church" outdoors, sometimes intentionally, sometimes spontaneously. I visited Glacier National Park in 2010. We took the Road to the Sun highway to higher ground. At our last stop, my friend left me in order to clamber up the icy mountain along a narrow pass, clinging to the rock face. I stayed at the lower elevation, watching and waiting. Suddenly an icy snowstorm descended. I experienced God in the theophany the storm presented: for me, it was the appearance of God through Nature. I was relatively safe but stood for an hour in the snow, worried and wondering about my friend as God swirled around me. She arrived back safely but shocked because she had feared she would not get back and the cold had left her frozen. Though we were both daunted, I knew God had been there with me in the ice and the snow.

Note

1 Part of this chapter is reproduced with permission from *Sojourners*, https://sojo.net/.

References

DuBois, W. E. B. 1903. *The Souls of Black Folk*. New York: Dover Publications.

Fanon, Franz. 1961, 2005. *The Wretched of the Earth*. New York: Grove Press.

Glave, Dianne D. 2005. Black Environmental Liberation Theology: The Historical and Theological Roots of Environmental Justice Activism by the African American Church. *The Griot: The Journal of Black Heritage*. 25, 61–70.

Glave, Dianne D. 2010. *Rooted in the Earth: Reclaiming the African American Environmental Heritage*. Chicago, IL: Chicago Review Press.

Glave, Dianne D. 2016. The Green Confessions of Nat Turner—The Rich and Varied Roots of Black Environmental Liberation Theology. *Sojourners*, May. https://shar.es/1jXl0U.

Glave, Dianne D. & Stoll, Mark. 2005. *To Love the Wind and the Rain: African Americans and Environmental History*. Pittsburgh, PA: University of Pittsburgh Press.

Kaoma, Kapya J. 2015. *The Creator's Symphony: African Christianity, the Plight of Earth and the Poor*. Kindle ed. Pietermaritzburg, South Africa: Cluster Publications.

Merchant, Carolyn. 2013. *Reinventing Eden: The Fate of Nature in Western Culture*. New York: Routledge.

Transcript for Wangari Maathai—Planting the Future. 2011 (September 2). On Being, with Krista Tippett. http://www.onbeing.org/program/planting-future/transcript/530.

Turner, Nat. 1831. The Confessions of Nat Turner, the Leader of the Late Insurrection in Southampton, Va. *Documenting the American South*, Chapel Hill, NC: University of North Carolina. http://docsouth.unc.edu/neh/turner/turner.html.

White, Jr. Lynn. 1967. The Historical Roots of Our Ecologic Crisis. *Science*, March 10, 155, 3767.

CHAPTER 8

Buddhist Interdependence and the Elemental Life

Christopher Key Chapple

The Study of Buddhism and Ecology

The study of Buddhism and ecology in some ways began with Western and Asian Buddhists linking the Asian tradition of engaged Buddhism with the development of an eco-friendly life, such as advanced by Alan Badiner (1990) and Martine Batchelor and Kerry Brown (1992). It continued with the convening of a major conference on Buddhism and Ecology at Harvard University in 1996. This event, the first in what became a series of 12 gatherings sponsored by the Forum on Religion and Ecology, helped launch a sustained inquiry into ecology and the world's religions by more than 600 scholars. Ten volumes (1997–2002) resulted from these conferences. The Buddhist volume, *Buddhism and Ecology: The Interconnection of Dharma and Deeds* (1997), suggests various paradigms for environmental activism which have been developed in Buddhist communities worldwide, from the protection of trees, through Buddhist monks' initiation in Thailand, to the recycling strategies employed at Zen Mountain Monastery in Idyllwild, California.

A number of subsequent books on religion and ecology have been published. These include volumes on Buddhism, among them *Deep Ecology and World Religions* (2001), *A Companion to Environmental Philosophy* (2001), the *Encyclopedia of Religion and Nature* (2005), and *The Oxford Handbook of Religion and Ecology* (2006), to name a few.

Several focused studies of Buddhism and ecology were published in the first decade of the twenty-first century. Stephanie Kaza (2000, 2005) edited two volumes on this topic. The first, *Dharma Rain*, examines textual resources for developing a Buddhist environmental ethic. The second, *Hooked!*, includes essays by contemporary Buddhists on the need for lifestyle adjustment. Pragati Sahni (2008) discusses what he characterizes as a conservational and cosmological approach to Buddhist ecology in *Environmental Ethic in Buddhism*. He opts for a Buddhist, vow-based virtue ethics. David Edward Cooper,

The Wiley Blackwell Companion to Religion and Ecology, First Edition. Edited by John Hart.

in *Buddhism, Virtue, and Environment* (2005), emphasizes the centrality of compassion, equanimity, and humility as Buddhist virtues that accord well with the sorts of virtue valued by Western environmental ethicists. In *Buddhism, Ethics, and Society*, Padmasiri deSilva (2002) notes that, according to Buddhism, harm to the environment has its roots in egoism and greed. He cites the Buddha's objection to animal sacrifice as an indication of the need to overcome anthropocentrism.

Other studies see Buddhist environmentalism as one of the social issues being taken up by Buddhist communities worldwide. *Action Dharma: New Studies in Engaged Buddhism* (Queen, Prebish, & Keown, 2003) includes an essay by Susan Darlington on Buddhism and development in Thailand, which she further developed in *TransBuddhism* (Bhushan, Garfield, & Zablocki, 2009), where she discusses an update on environmental actions undertaken by Thai Buddhist monks, who during the 1990s initiated the practice of ordaining trees to prevent their being felled. Both Tibet and Thailand are taken up by Sallie King in *Socially Engaged Buddhism* (2009). She states that Chinese land-use policies have been harmful to the Tibetan plateau. She writes about four leaders of Engaged Buddhism, Joanna Macy, John Seed, Gary Snyder, and Thich Nhat Hanh, whom she views as deep ecologists. Buddhist activist-practitioners, both Western and Asian, continue to publish treatises urging a connection between Buddhist philosophy and ecological values. Ken Jones fully embraces a Buddhist-inspired "socially radical culture of awakening" in *The New Social Face of Buddhism* (2003). David Loy, a professor for many years in Japan, advocates a Buddhist approach to ecological healing. He examines in *The Great Awakening: A Buddhist Social Theory* (2003) and *Money, Sex, War, Karma* (2008) the poisons of greed, ill-will, and delusion as the root causes for the current state of environmental degradation. Thai Buddhist activist Sulak Sivaraksa gives examples of monastic and lay Buddhism advocacy for the preservation of Thailand's endangered forests and waters, especially lakes, in *Conflict, Culture, Change: A Buddhist Social Theory* (2005). Bodo Balsys, in *Ahimsa: Buddhism and the Vegetarian Ideal* (2004), writes extensively of the need to be wary of food impurities; he advocates vegetarianism and veganism as the best options for human and environmental health.

These and other works indicate the range of approaches Buddhist scholars and activists are using to engage contemporary issues related to ecological concerns. These studies include social analysis, direct action on behalf of particular ecosystems, and the dissemination of Buddhist teachings in a manner that emphasizes the importance of inner stability, but with an eye on the common good.

The Buddhist Worldview

The Buddha lived approximately 500 years before the birth of Christ. Born into a princely family, he nonetheless was deeply moved by the sufferings of the sick and the elderly, and, when confronted with his own mortality, decided to seek *nirvana*, freedom from all suffering (*duḥkha*). For six years he trained with two meditation teachers, perfecting their yogic teachings. Eventually, he sat under a Bodhi tree, achieved his goal of perfect freedom, and developed his own system of teaching. The Buddha eventually was reconciled with his family, who entered the monastic orders that he established.

The Buddha taught for 45 years, largely in northeast India. Following his death, 18 schools of thought developed that helped spread Buddhism throughout the subcontinent and into Southeast Asia and beyond. The primary surviving form of Buddhism from the early period, the Theravada, is practiced today in Sri Lanka, Myanmar, Cambodia, Laos, and Thailand. Around the first century of the Common Era (CE), a second form of Buddhism, the Mahayana, arose, which added new teachings that emphasize the Bodhisattva vow to return to life after life to help all sentient beings. This form of Buddhism can be found today in China, Japan, Vietnam, and Korea, as well as through the worldwide network of Zen and other forms of Buddhist practice. In the seventh century a third major school emerged, the Vajrayana, adding meditative practices and rituals. This form became popular in East Asia and found a lasting home in the Tibetan cultural region.

For Buddhism, the psyche must be purified of hatred, greed, and delusion in order for one to live the good life, a life free from suffering. Ego causes the clinging that results in pain. By entering into community life, by putting societal values ahead of personal desires, by cultivating meditative and devotional states that calm the mind, a lightness of ego can be attained, allowing one to emerge from a state of suffering (*duḥkha*), due to the perception of impermanence (*anitya*), and into a state of blissful no-self (*anātman*).

Buddhist Practice: Elemental Meditations

Many identify the practice of Buddhism with quiet meditation, as found in the Vipassana practice of the Theravada and the Zen school of the Mahayana. In addition to focusing on the breath, early Buddhist literature prescribes a form of concentration on the elements that can result in self-transformation. Meditation can alter the relationship of human self-conception, allowing one to see interdependence between the elements and utter reliance of the human on their presence. By engaging earth, water, fire, air, and space, one cultivates states of connectivity and bliss that result in an abiding sense of wellbeing. This practice is being reconsidered in light of its potential for establishing a foundation for the cultivation of concern and care for the environment, and for the interdependent networks within Nature.

The *Visuddhi Magga* of Buddhaghosa (c. 430 CE, tr. 1976) provides instructions for the practice of elemental meditation. The text lists ten objects of meditation (*kasinas*), starting with earth, water, fire, and air; moving through four colors (blue, yellow, red, and white); and then moving to light, and finally space. These meditations, as will be seen, hold the potential for inspiring a sense of connection through the senses with the external world.

A very precise description is given for the monk to create a disk the size of a bushel (*suppa*) or saucer (*sarava*) (IV: 22, 127). This disk is to be crafted from "clay like that in the stream of the Ganga, which is the colour of the dawn" (IV: 24, 127). It is to be constructed in a screened place away from public view or under "an overhanging rock or in a leaf hut," "either portable or as a fixture." To create a portable *kasina*, one smears the clay onto rags, leather, or four sticks; a fixed one will be created on top of stakes pounded into the ground. In either case, one uses a stone trowel to "make it as smooth as the surface of a drum" (IV: 25, 128). The text goes on to say that one should take a seat approximately 30 in. away so that it comes into sufficient focus without revealing too much detail, and one does not need to flex the neck to gaze on it, and in order that one is sufficiently raised (approximately 10–20 in.) to prevent the knees from aching.

One then gives mental homage to the Buddha, his teachings (*Dharma*), and the community of Buddhists (*Sangha*). Following this, one begins to focus the gaze on the circle of dry, yellowish clay. The eyes are not to be opened too wide, as they "get fatigued and the disk becomes too obvious," nor too little, as the "disk is not obvious enough" and the "mind becomes drowsy" (IV: 28, 129). The ideal is to gaze lightly, as if looking at one's image in a mirror. The mind is not to dwell on the color of the clay, but to review various names that indicate the earth, including "earth (*pathavīi/prthivi*), Great One (*mahī*), Friendly One (*medinī*), ground (*bhūmi*), the Provider of Wealth (*vasudhā*)," and so forth (IV: 29, 130). By gazing and invoking these words "a hundred times, a thousand times" one develops "the learning sign," which indicates that one can re-create the visualization of the *kasina* whether the eyes are opened or closed. The monk is then urged to go into a private space and "go on developing it there ... striking at it with thought and applied thought" (IV: 30, 130).

The benefit of this concentration is that it serves to reduce hindrances in the mind: "the hindrances eventually become suppressed, the defilements subside, the mind becomes concentrated with access concentration, and the counterpart sign arises." This latter phenomenon is described as a purified visualization of the *kasina*, appearing "like a looking-glass disk drawn from its case, like a mother-of-pearl dish well washed, like the moon's disk coming from behind a cloud, like cranes against a thunder cloud" but with "neither colour nor shape" (IV: 31, 130).

In the first *Jhana* or meditative state cultivated by concentration on the earth *Kasina*, one experiences applied thought and sustained thought leading to happiness, bliss, and unification of the mind (IV: 150, 164). In the second *Jhana*, one abandons applied and sustained thought, automatically dwelling in happiness, bliss, and unification of the mind. In the third *Jhana*, one abandons happiness, replacing it with equanimity. In the fourth *Jhana*, one moves beyond the dualities of pleasure/pain, joy/grief that adhere to bliss. This fourth is characterized as "purity of mindfulness due to equanimity" (IV: 195, 175).

The remaining *kasinas* are to be regarded similarly with regard to the cultivation of progressive states of *Jhana*, starting with water. For one who has undertaken this practice in a past life, it will arise spontaneously when one is near "a pool, a lake, a lagoon, or the ocean" (V: 2, 177). The example is given of Elder Cula-Siva, who entered this state while on board an ocean-bound ship. Otherwise, one should "fill a bowl or a four-footed water pot to the brim with water uncontaminated by soil, taken in the open through a clean cloth strainer, or with any other clear unturbid water" (V: 3, 177). One should take it to a place as described earlier, and sit comfortably. Without focusing on specific details, one begins to repeat various names for water (*āpo*), such as rain (*ambu*), liquid (*udaka*), dew (*vāri*), fluid (*salila*): water, water" (V: 3, 177). One then obtains the "learning sign" when the presence can be detected as with the counterpart sign, "like a crystal fan set in space, like the disk of a looking-glass made of crystal" (V: 4).

For the third *kasina*, the meditator focuses on fire. For those with experience with this practice in a past life, "it arises in any sort of fire ... as one looks at the fiery combustion in a lamp's flame or in a furnace or in a place for baking bowls or in a forest conflagration" (V: 5, 178). The text cites the examples of Elder Cittagutta, who entered this *Jhana* while looking at a lamp. Others have work to do: "split up some damp heartwood, dry it, and break it up into short lengths ... go to a suitable tree root or to a shed and make a pile in the way done for baking bowls and have it lit. Make a hole a span and four fingers wide in a rush mat or a piece of leather or a cloth, and after hanging it in front of the fire, sit down in the way already described. Instead of giving attention to the grass and sticks below or the smoke above, one should apprehend the sign in the dense combustion in the middle" (V: 6, 178). The words used to support this form of fire concentration are: fire (*tejo*), Bright One (*pāvaka*), Leaver of the Black Trail (*kanhavattani*), Knower of Creatures (*jātaveda*), Altar of Sacrifice (*hutāsana*) ... fire, fire (V:7). One becomes reminded of this practice and carries the learning sign when seeing "any firebrand or pile of embers or ashes or smoke... The counterpart sign appears motionless like a piece of red cloth set in place, like a gold fan, like a gold column" (V: 8, 179).

To develop the air *kasina*, one need not create a disk of dried clay, or collect clean water in a bowl, or build a fire to be viewed through a hole in a mat. One merely "notices the tops of growing sugarcane moving to and fro, or the tops of bamboos or of trees, or the ends of the hair" (V: 9, 179). The text also advises that one can "establish mindfulness where the wind strikes a part of the body after entering by a window or a crack in a wall, using ... names for wind (*vāta*) (such as) breeze (*māluta*), blowing (*anila*) ... and air, air" (V: 10, 179).

The next sequence of *Jhanas* moves beyond the elements to the realm of color. Buddhaghosa first advises the meditator to notice the color blue as it manifests in flowers or textiles and even suggests forming a disk as with the earth *kasina*, coloring it blue. The same instructions are given for cultivating awareness of the colors yellow, red, and white. The ninth *Jhana* specifies mindfulness of how light penetrates "a hole in a wall, or in a keyhole, or in a window opening" (V: 21, 181). The tenth *kasina* provides a description of how to contemplate space (*ākāśa*). The text states that one who has had a previous life experience reflects on the hole created in instances above rather than on the light that passes through, and that those who are new to the practice "should make a hole a span and four fingers broad in a well thatched hut, or in a piece of leather, or in a rush mat" (V: 25, 181).

This section of the *Visuddhi Magga* ends with praise for what is to be accomplished through these practices. Through the earth *kasina*, "Having been one, he becomes many" (V: 27) and acquires the "bases of mastery." The water *kasina* allows one to dive in and out of the waters, as well as "causing rain storms, creating rivers and seas, making the earth and rocks and palaces quake" (V: 29). The author goes on to state:

> The Fire Kasina is the basis for such powers as smoking, flaming, causing showers of sparks, countering fire with fire, ability to burn only what one wants to burn, causing light for the purpose of seeing visible objects with the divine eye, burning up the body by means of the fire element at the time of attaining nibbana.

The description of the air *kasina*, though no less powerful, is brief: "The air *kasina* is the basis for such powers as going with the speed of the wind, causing wind storms." The four colors and light are given correlating abilities, with light enabling one in the arts of "creating luminous forms, dispelling darkness, causing light for the purpose of seeing visible objects with the divine eye." The space *kasina* "is the basis for such powers as revealing the hidden, maintaining postures inside the earth and rocks by creating spaces inside them, traveling unobstructed through walls, and so forth" (V: 32–37, 183).

The practice of these ten *kasinas* has been instituted by ecologically engaged American Buddhist meditators in California at Insight, LA. This organization is affiliated with Spirit Rock, a Vipassana meditation center established by Jack Kornfield, a well-known author and psychotherapist who trained at a Thai monastery for many years. Through a program known as Mindful Nature, meditation teachers and school teachers have been trained in the concentration techniques described above as a means to make meditation more interesting and meaningful. By experiencing the earth, water, fire, and air for extended periods, thoughts and feelings arise that inspire deepening care for the natural world. Some of the people trained in this technique are introducing the practice to students in private and public school settings to enhance their field studies of ecological systems.

Seeing the Buddha

One aspect of the Buddhist religion entails gazing on the image of the Buddha. He serves as the exemplar for the faith. His narrative of questioning, seeking, entering freedom, and returning to teach others has become paradigmatic for the spiritual seeker. Although he abjured his depiction during his lifetime, within a couple of hundred years of his death statues and paintings proliferated that depict his many narratives, including stories of the hundreds of past lives that he recalled during the night of his awakening under the Bodhi tree.

Most Buddhas are depicted in the lotus pose, or *Padma Asana*. Buddha images often exhibit signs of physical perfection, including pendulous ear lobes, long arms, short ringlets, and a peaceful expression. The hands of a Buddha reflect his state of mind, gesturing peace, or teachings, or generosity, or love. By imitating the Buddha's bodily symmetry and palpable sense of inner peace, the meditator might be inspired toward greater levels of self-improvement. Gazing on the Buddha image, one experiences a sense of balance and serenity, perhaps catching a glimpse of the goal of Buddhism: freedom from the bonds of karma.

Similarly, seeing the sculptures and frescoes that depict the life of Siddhartha Gautama and the many lives that preceded his birth as a prince in Kapilavastu can inspire one to reflect on the Buddhist assessment that all things are contingent and depend on multiple causes. The Buddha named karma as the culprit that causes attachment and hence suffering (*duḥkha*). He posited a 12-fold chain reaction, beginning with ignorance that traps hell beings, animals, humans, ghosts, titans, and gods in the cycle of birth, old age, death, and rebirth (*saṃsāra*). As proof of this cosmology, the Buddha told stories of his past births and how they interacted with the current state of his disciples and companions. According to Buddhism, the cause is to be found in careful observation of current habits and remembrance of instigating events earlier in this life and in past lives.

Past Life Stories of the Buddha

The Buddhist worldview presupposes that every sentient being has existed in prior forms over the course of countless lifetimes. The Buddha told many stories of his own past births in the collection of narratives known as the *Jataka Tales* (c. 300 BCE). These stories include references to more than 70 species of animal. The Buddha himself took many animal forms, including monkeys, elephants, jackals, lions, crows, deer, birds, and fish (Chapple, 1997, 135).

The Buddhist *Jataka Tales* include narratives that describe the destruction of forests and consequent ecological upheaval due to the rapid expansion of trade and of cities. Buddhism emerged in northwest India during a time of economic growth which involved the expansion of both agriculture and trade. As noted by Lewis Lancaster, "it was a time when deforestation of the Ganges region was taking place, population growth was sizable, urban centers were the important hubs—urban islands in a sea of rain forests" (Lancaster, 1997, 11–12). In the *Vyaddha Jataka*, the Buddha relates that the tree spirits of one forest were repelled by the stench of rotting meat left repeatedly by an overzealous lion and tiger. They arranged to scare away the predators. However, the villagers who were previously too afraid to enter the forest noticed that the felines were gone and quickly chopped down the forest and put it under cultivation, depriving the forest spirits of their habitat. Due to their folly, the denizens of the forest were expelled from their native habitat (*Jataka* 272, in Cowell, 1900, 3, 244–246). This fable, like many of the rebirth stories, speaks of human greed and the inevitability (and sorrow) of change. It also gives testimony to the tremendous changes wrought on the landscape by the advance of agriculture and human settlement.

Though later transcendentalist and Orientalist thinkers tended to develop a grand romantic narrative from early materials such as these, the texts themselves are actually quite earthy and practical. A tree is seen as a tree, a forest as a forest, and a field as a field, in contrast to the later poetry of William Wordsworth and Walt Whitman and the elevated prose of Ralph Waldo Emerson and Henry Thoreau, which rhapsodize about Nature over and beyond the reality of Nature itself. In Asia, people tend not to romanticize Nature but seek to survive within it.

In earlier studies, I explored ways in which select *Jataka* tales can be interpreted as ecological parables (Chapple,1986, 1997). This chapter focuses on one exemplary tale that shows two aspects of what might be termed a nascent ecological sensibility: a careful description of a natural environment and a moral exhortation against the temptation of greed.

The Ruby-Eyed, Silver-Clawed Blue Bear

Landscape and all that it contains and implies, including the animals and humans that populate it, provides a frame through which to view the religious traditions of India. By examining a story drawn from the Himalayan landscape, a sense of intimacy with the elements and other-than-human animals can be gleaned that remains instructive beyond its historical, geographic, and religious origins. The Blue Bear tale starts in the deeply forested mountains, moves to the city, and then returns to the mountains again. In this story, place plays an important part, as well as placement within society. The story of the Blue Bear offers sage advice on royal rule, advice that carries particular relevance to the world's environmental situation today.

The 550 past-life *Jataka* tales of the Buddha include stories of 225 prior animal births. One story in particular seems to speak to the topic of ecological displacement, deception, and, eventually, justice. Retold by Rafe Martin (2010), this narrative, though illustrated in the caves of Ajanta, is only found in written form in the Khotanese *Jatakastava*, a tenth-century Central Asian text discovered in one copy in the Tunhuang Caves and translated by Mark Dresden in 1955.

In this story, the future Buddha lived in the Himalayas as a "bear with blue fur, silver claws, and ruby-red eyes" (Martin, 2010, 57). Legends circulated about this magnificent beast, the color of lapis lazuli, the world's most precious gem. His pelt and claws would bring a small fortune and his flesh would bestow long life. However, no one could find where the bear lived.

One day a lost hunter, trapped in a blinding snowstorm, called out for help. The great blue bear rescued him, carried the half-dead man back to his cave, and then "revived him with the warmth of its own body and breath." The bear protected the man for the duration of the storm, feeding him roots and dried berries, with the understanding that the man would never reveal the location of the bear's cave.

At the end of the storm, the hunter departed and safely reached an inn where he took shelter. All night long he tossed and turned, fantasizing about the fortune he would amass if he let others know about the whereabouts of this legendary blue bear. Despite his promise, he went to the king and told him of the bear's location, neglecting to mention the bear's kindness and his own pledge not to betray his savior. The king's huntsmen traveled into the mountains, found the bear's den, and sounded their horns, jolting the bear from his slumber into their nets.

Once delivered to the palace, the bear requested a meeting with the king and told the king how he had been betrayed by the huntsman whose life he had saved. With great wisdom, the bear addressed the king: "Good actions lead to happiness, selfish ones to disaster. Kindness is greater than cruelty. Do not strike back but develop the fortitude of patience. If you practice these virtues diligently you will find happiness without limit" (Martin, 2010, 60). The huntsman who betrayed the bear was summoned to the court. The king castigated him for his bad behavior and banished him from the palace. The bear, now garlanded by the king, was escorted safely back to the mountains. He took up residence in a new cave, never again to be discovered.

The hunter descended into a life of subsistence, hunting wild game and eating roots and berries. His hair became unkempt and his eyes were reddened from campfire smoke.

One day he caught a glimpse of his reflection in a slow-flowing stream. He exclaimed that he had taken on the appearance of a bear. From this jolt, he saw his own kinship with the bear that he had betrayed. From that time onward, he stopped hunting, stopped eating meat, and became a beacon of safety, "lending a helping hand to man or beast" (Martin, 2010, 62).

The Blue Bear, when wrenched from his happy home, haplessly begs to be returned safely, away from the bustle and danger of the palace. The story-teller conveys a sense of profound difference between the safety of the Blue Bear's cave and the dangers of the king's court. Yet, despite his captivity, the bear's innate qualities prevail. The Blue Bear lumbers, moving slowly toward outrage, and then with gravitas sets things right. Bears inspire fear, awe, and respect. The compassion manifested by the bear toward the lost hunter presaged the later compassion manifested by the Buddha.

In the Indian system of reincarnation, all beings are said to be equal. The preparatory lessons from past lives shape and guide an individual into the present and future lives. The regal and just nature of the Blue Bear demonstrated the great capacity for animal behavior to be seen in human qualities and the reverse. Recognition of innate animal impulses can work for good and for ill; a good animal might be regarded as superior to a bad human. To have been an animal and to have recalled past animal experiences indicates a sign of greatness, an acknowledgment of one's ongoing connections and kinship with other species.

The Ruby-Eyed Silver-Clawed Blue Bear carries himself with such dignity and aplomb that even in the worst of circumstances he prevails. One cannot hear this story without feeling embarrassed by the greedy, selfish hunter and relieved once the just king sets the bear free. Comportment wins over conniving. Gravitas trumps duplicity. This story calls out for the development of a new ethic, an ethic of gravitas and comportment rooted in a quiet moral outrage that simmers until appropriately expressed and adjudicated.

Human beings sometimes innately know the correct path to follow. This story suggests that from the classical Indian perspective this knowledge arises from lessons learned in this life and in prior lives. Tenderness paved the way for a life dedicated to nonviolence and the protection of life in all its forms.

Buddhist Ecological Leaders and the Gyalwa Karmapa

Many contemporary Asian Buddhists have pioneered specialized forms of environmental activism. These include Thai monks such as Buddhadāsa Bhikkhu, Phra Prajak, Ajahn Pongsak, and Somneuk Natho; Thai lay intellectual Buddhists including Chatsumarn Kabilsingh and Sulak Sivaraksa; and Dr A. T. Ariyaratne, a lay leader in Sri Lanka. In Japan, the work of the Kyoto School holds ecological implications for that country. Nishida Kitarō (1870–1945) developed the concept of *basho* (relational field), which can be interpreted to include person, interpersonal relations, and one's place in Nature. Watsuji Tetsurō (1880–1960) developed the notion of relational field into a theory of climate (*fūdo*). More recent representatives of the Kyoto School, such as Masao Abe and Masatoshi Nagatomi, introduced ecological themes into their later works. The most prominent Asian Buddhist teachers, the Dalai Lama and Thich Nhat Hanh, have taken on ecological concerns, as have American Buddhist leaders such as Philip Kapleau, Joanna Macy, Joan Halifax, Gary Snyder, and Robert Aitken (Chapple, 2001). The present chapter concludes with a description of the work of an emerging Buddhist leader, Ogyen Trinley Dorje, seventeenth Gyalwa Karmapa, who is deeply dedicated to the protection of animals and other environmental causes.

At the 2011 Global Buddhist Congregation held in New Delhi, the seventeenth Gyalwa Karmapa, as recognized by the Dalai Lama, convened a day-long seminar on "Environment and the Natural World: A Buddhist Response." Chaired by Vivek Menon, executive director of the Wildlife Trust of India, the seminar included presentations by research biologists, activists, and scholars.

His immediate prior incarnation loved parrots. He had gone into exile from Tibet by the impending threat of Chinese invasion in the late 1950s and moved his entire monastic entourage by foot into Sikkim, then an independent kingdom. There he took up residence in Rumtek. Anticipating the eventual move to the West predicted long ago, in the 1970s he sent one of his young charges, Lama Tenzin, son of a Tibetan former prime minister, to Stony Brook, New York, where he learned English and worked in the Institute for Advanced Studies of World Religions at the university. When the sixteenth Karmapa visited New York, he stayed at Bodhi Field, the former Tinker Estate in Poquot, New York, on the north shore of Long Island, where the young Lama Tenzin lived before establishing Karma Triyana Dharmacakra in Woodstock, New York.

Some 30 years later, in 2008, the seventeenth Gyalwa Karmapa was formally enthroned as the rightful successor at that same monastery in New York State. Having been identified at the Tsurphu Monastery at the age of seven as an important reincarnation in a search party headed by Tai Situ Rinpoche in 1993, Ogyen Trinley Dorje fled Tibet in disguise in 2000, frustrated by his inability to gain a proper education. Since that time he has lived at McLeod Ganj, Dharamsala, and is providing a new style of leadership to the Kagyu School of Tibetan Buddhism. This particular branch of Buddhism, founded by Milarepa, emphasizes the practice of Dzogen meditation.

The seventeenth Karmapa, due to the chance of receiving tutelage from George Schaller, has introduced profound attitudinal and dietary changes to the Karma Kagyupa community. Schaller, winner of the National Book Award, traveled in the Tibetan Plateau for 17 years in search of the breeding grounds of the chiru, a rare Himalayan antelope under threat. Its fine wool was used to make delicate, warm, and beautiful shawls known as *shatoosh*. However, tens of thousands of these beautiful animals were being slain for the sake of their wool in the 1990s, and the species was near extinction. During his yearly travels to Tibet, he visited the Tsurphu Monastery and befriended the young, newly discovered Karmapa, and taught him about the wildlife of the fragile high-elevation plateau. Schaller eventually prevailed: *shatoosh* shawls have been banned, and four countries, Afghanistan, Pakistan, China, and Tajikistan, are working cooperatively to establish a vast preserve. Schaller also made a deep impression on the young Karmapa, who has now decreed that all members of his denomination must observe a vegetarian diet. Before leaving Tibet, the Karmapa forbade the use of animal skins in religious ritual, holding mass burnings of the once-prized pelts.

At the 2011 Global Buddhist Congregation in New Delhi, the Karmapa summarized his 2001 paper, "Walking the Path of Environmental Buddhism through Compassion and Emptiness." He described his uncanny attunement to the environment from an early age. In the paper he makes an appeal to engage Buddhist ethics, noting that "we now have over 40 Kagyu monasteries and nunneries across the Himalayas implementing environmental projects to address issues such as forest degradation, water shortages, wildlife trade, climate change, and pollution" (Dorje, 2011, 1097). Quoting Shantideva's *Bodhicaryavatara*, he notes that "we are not isolated individuals but one whole made up all life on Earth" (Dorje, 2011, 1095). He describes the plight of the tigers whose numbers have been reduced by 95%, and has taken up nature protection as a central cause.

The Blue Bear with silver claws, red eyes, and a pelt like lapis lazuli stands as a metaphor for endangered species and endangered cultures. Animals, just as in the time of the Buddha, become apt survival metaphors. The Karmapa helped save the chiru, the endangered Himalayan antelope, and stands firmly in the camp of compassion for all animals. He serves as a symbol of survival under duress, holding up a beacon of hope that, just as the Blue Bear was restored to his cave of safety and inspired the transformation of the greedy hunter from rapacious to guardian, so also the animals and the people of the Himalayas might survive and eventually thrive, with their way of life protected and cherished.

Conclusion

Buddhist environmentalism has taken many forms since its emergence in the latter part of the twentieth century. The Buddhist worldview, which emphasizes interdependence and, in the words of Thich Nhat Hanh, inter-being, makes a good starting point for ecological conversations such as those initiated by David Loy, who stresses the need to rise above trivial consumerist practices in quest of a higher meaning. However, some Buddhist practices such as the release of captured animals, which at first glance might seem to stem from compassion, might foster suffering, as suggested by Duncan Ryuken Williams (1997). Ian Harris, citing some of the world-negating aspects of Buddhism and monks' practice of exploiting natural resources in ninth-century China (Harris, 1997, 386), suggests that great care must be exerted in conflating the values of traditional Asian Buddhists, which are rooted in the performance of monastic vows, and the romance of modern environmentalism.

In this chapter we have explored some of the modes of discourse being undertaken by scholars and activists, including direct action to protect trees and develop "green" practices in monastic and meditative contexts. As seen in the analysis of the *Kasina* meditations in the *Visuddhi Magga*, mindfulness of the natural world in its most elemental forms has long been part of the Buddhist tradition. By gazing on the substances of earth, water, fire, and air, one can gain an intimacy with the rhythm of one's own corporeal reality. By slowing down to consider each of the elements, control can be gained over the mind, resulting in an ability to focus. One can imagine that the skills taught by field biologist George Schaller to his young protégé included surveying the horizon for signs of movement and the need for keen observation. This steady practice can result in the cultivation of intimacy with the landscape and its residents. By knowing how animals move in their natural habitat, one automatically enters a point of focus. In the focus on the chiru, for example, an endangered species cherished for its wool, a sense of responsibility can arise, as it did for Schaller and the Karmapa.

Buddhist teachings on interdependence prompted the Karmapa to extend his concern for animals to all the species that had previously been hunted for their pelts. By organizing the monasteries under his control and rallying them to the cause of animal protection and vegetarianism, he has signaled a willingness to challenge long-standing traditions and advocate change.

Buddhists in the twenty-first century, in both Asia and the West, are coming to a realization of the interconnectedness of human action worldwide. Pollution and diversion of rivers, clear-cutting of forests, overfishing of the oceans, and myriad other problems arise from complex motivations and causes. From a Buddhist perspective, all such actions are caused by human greed (*tṛṣṇa*), which must be addressed by entering into a deep and profound ethical reflection. Only by confronting devastation and its consequent suffering (*duḥkha*) can proper corrective action be taken. The Buddhist Eightfold Path presents several ways in which recovery can begin. Through a right view, one can realize the damage caused, for instance, by climate change. This could lead to right thinking, speech, and conduct through which one assesses consequences and undertakes remediation. The corrective action might lead, for instance, to the installation of solar panels, supporting an entire livelihood dedicated to a noble cause. One maintains this commitment through effort and mindfulness, leading to elevated states of awareness to the benefit of others.

In the Mahayana tradition, one works for the welfare of all, putting the needs of others before one's own. Shantideva writes:

> For all those ailing in the world,
> Until their every sickness has been healed,
> May I myself become for them
> The doctor, nurse, the medicine itself.
> (Shantideva, 2006, III: 8, 48)

As one takes stock of the many ills wrought by humans on the soil, waters, and air, the problems seem endless. One of the Buddhist perfections, patience (*kṣānti*), may prove useful here, but be responsibly combined with sufficient effort and strength (*vīrya*) to effect change.

By reordering intention away from selfish consumerism and self-aggrandizement toward concern for other beings and the elements themselves, one might undertake a Tantric restructuring of the self within the world. If one visualizes banishing the burdens of pollution that damage the soil, poison the waters, and darken the air, creative engagement may take place that will lessen attachment to things manufactured and redirect human endeavor toward a place of greater peace, attained through wisdom and not driven by greed.

For Buddhists, answering the following questions might be seen as the gateway to environmental repair: How did this pollution arise? How might it be removed? The answer to the first is somewhat simple: pollution has been caused by carelessness and greed. This chapter has given two answers in regard to the latter question. Meditation on earth, water, fire, and air can help establish intimacy and care for the Earth. Buddhist leaders such as the Gyalwa Karmapa can provide leadership and inspiration for the constant vigilance and patience needed to undo the damage inflicted on the planet.

References

Badiner, Alan. 1990. *Dharma Gaia: A Harvest of Essays in Buddhism and Ecology*. Berkeley, CA: Parallax Press.

Batchelor, Martine & Brown, Kerry. 1992. *Buddhism and Ecology*. London: Cassel.

Balsys, Bodo. 2004. *Ahimsa: Buddhism and the Vegetarian Ideal*. Delhi: Munshiram Manoharlal.

Barnhill, David Landis & Gottlieb, Roger S. 2001. *Deep Ecology and World Religions: New Essays on Sacred Ground*. Albany, NY: SUNY Press.

Bhushan, Nalini, Garfield, Jay L., & Zablocki, Abraham. 2009. *TransBuddhism: Transmission, Translation, Transformation*. Amherst, MA: University of Massachusetts Press, 2009.

Buddhaghosa. 1976. *The Path of Purification: Visuddhimagga. A Classic Textbook of Buddhist Psychology*. Transl. Bhikkhu Nyanamoli. Boulder, CO: Shambhala.

Callicott, J. Baird & Ames, Roger T. 1989. *Nature in Asian Traditions of Thought*. Albany, NY: SUNY Press.

Chapple, Christopher Key. 1986. Nonviolence to Animals in Buddhism and Jainism (213–235). In Tom Regan (Ed.), *Animal Sacrifices: Religious Perspectives on the Use of Animals in Science*. Philadelphia, PA: Temple University Press. Reprinted in Kenneth Kraft (Ed.). 1992. *Inner Peace, World Peace: Essays on Buddhism and Nonviolence*. Albany, NY: SUNY Press.

Chapple, Christopher Key. 1997. Animals and Environment in Buddhist Birth Stories (131–148). In Mary Evelyn Tucker & Duncan Ryuken Williams (Eds.), *Buddhism and Ecology: The Interconnection of Dharma and Deeds*. Cambridge, MA: Harvard University Center for the Study of World Religions.

Chapple, Christopher Key. 2001. Jainism and Buddhism (52–67). In Dale Jamieson (Ed.), *A Companion to Environmental Philosophy*. Malden, MA: Blackwell.

Cooper, David Edward. 2005. *Buddhism, Virtue, and Environment*. Aldershot: Ashgate.

Cowell, E. B. (Ed.). 1895–1907. *The Jataka or Stories of the Buddha's Former Births*. 6 vols. London: Pali Text Society.

De Silva, Padmasiri. 2002. *Buddhism, Ethics, and Society: The Conflicts and Dilemmas of Our Times*. Clayton, Australia: Monash Asia Institute.

Dorje, Ogyen Trinley Dorje, 17th Gyalwang Karmapa. 2011. Walking the Path of Environmental Buddhism through Compassion and Emptiness. *Conservation Biology*, 25, 6, 1094–1097.

Dresden, Mark D. 1955. The Jatakastava or Praise of the Buddha's Former Births: Indo-Scythian (Khotanese) Text, English Translation, Grammatical Notes, and Glossaries. *Transactions of the American Philosophical Society. New Series*, 45, 5, 397–508. Philadelphia, PA: The American Philosophical Society

Gottlieb, Roger S. 2006. *The Oxford Handbook of Religion and Ecology*. New York: Oxford University Press.

Harris, Ian. 1997. Buddhism and the Discourse of Environmental Concern (377–402). In Mary Evelyn Tucker & Duncan Ryuken Williams (Eds.), *Buddhism and Ecology: The Interconnection of Dharma and Deeds*. Cambridge, MA: Harvard University Center for the Study of World Religions.

Jamieson, Dale. 2001. *A Companion to Environmental Philosophy*. Malden, MA: Blackwell.

Jones, Ken. 2003. *The New Social Face of Buddhism: A Call to Action*. Boston, MA: Wisdom Publications.

Kaza, Stephanie. 2000. *Dharma Rain: Sources of Buddhist Environmentalism*. Boston, MA: Shambhala.

Kaza, Stephanie. 2005. *Hooked! Buddhist Writings on Greed, Desire, and the Urge to Consume*. Boston, MA: Shabhala.

King, Sallie B. 2009. *Socially Engaged Buddhism: Dimensions of Asian Spirituality*. Honolulu, HI: University of Hawaii Press.

Lancaster, Lewis. 1997. Buddhism and Ecology: Collective Cultural Perceptions (3–20). In Mary Evelyn Tucker & Duncan Ryuken Williams (Eds.), *Buddhism and Ecology: The Interconnection of Dharma and Deeds*. Cambridge, MA: Harvard University Center for the Study of World Religions.

Loy, David R. 2003. *The Great Awakening: A Buddhist Social Theory*. Boston, MA: Wisdom Publications.

Loy, David R. 2008. *Money, Sex, War, Karma: Notes for a Buddhist Revolution*. Boston, MA: Wisdom Publications.

Martin, Rafe. 2010. *Endless Path: Awakening within the Buddhist Imagination: Jataka Tales, Zen Practice, and Daily Life*. Berkeley, CA: North Atlantic Books.

Queen, Christopher, Prebish, Charles, & Daniel Keown. 2003. *Action Dharma: New Studies in Engaged Buddhism*. London: RoutledgeCurzon.

Sahni, Pragati. 2008. *Environmental Ethics in Buddhism*. London: Routledge.

Schaller, George. 2012. *Tibet Wild: A Naturalist's Journey on the Roof of the World*. Washington, DC: Island Press.

Shantideva. 2006. *The Way of the Bodhisattva. Padmakara Translation Group*. Boston, MA: Shambhala.

Sivaraksa, Sulak. 2005. *Conflict, Culture, Change: Engaged Buddhism in a Globalizing World*. Boston, MA: Wisdom Publications.

Williams, Duncan Ryuken. 1997. Animal Liberation, Death, and the State: Rite to Release Animals in Medieval Japan (149–164). In Mary Evelyn Tucker & Duncan Ryuken Williams (Eds.), *Buddhism and Ecology: The Interconnection of Dharma and Deeds*. Cambridge, MA: Harvard University Center for the Study of World Religions.

CHAPTER 9

Theodao

Integrating Ecological Consciousness in Daoism, Confucianism, and Christian Theology

Heup Young Kim

Ecology is without doubt a pressing issue for contemporary global Christianity. A half-century ago, Lynn White criticized Christianity as the "historical root" of the ecological crisis because it endorsed human domination over Nature (White, 1967, 1204). This criticism motivated theologians and religious scholars to re-examine the exclusive attitude of Christianity in its interaction with the natural world and explore an alternate wisdom and "new models of ecological wholeness and reciprocity" in other religious traditions (Tucker & Grim, 1994, 11). The series editors of *Religions of the World and Ecology*, Mary Evelyn Tucker and John Grim (2000, xxiv), wrote: "[W]e are currently making macrophase change of the life systems of the planet with microphase wisdom. Clearly, we need to expand and deepen the wisdom base for human intervention with nature and other humans."

In a subsequent conference on Christianity and Ecology,[1] most Western participants, including Elizabeth Johnson, Sallie McFague, and Mark Wallace, agreed that three theological revisions are necessary to construct a proper Christian theology in the present age of ecological crisis: a shift of the fundamental vision from anthropocentrism to cosmo- or earth-centrism, a reconsideration of theological metaphors and symbols, and a shift of focus from orthodoxy and christology to orthopraxis and pneumatology. Nevertheless, theological discourses do not seem to achieve these revisions, conceivably due to their inherent traditions of Western thought.

As Gordon Kaufman (2000) pointed out, they seem not to overcome sufficiently the long-standing convention of anthropomorphism, personifying God in human form, and the tendency to reductionism in Enlightenment mentality, reducing everything to human cognition and reasoning. Anthropomorphism and reductionism, therefore, are root causes for ecological crises. With anthropomorphism Western Christianity lost the Earth, by reductionism it lost Heaven, and hence too lost Creation. Reductionism as the

The Wiley Blackwell Companion to Religion and Ecology, First Edition. Edited by John Hart.

basis for modern science produced static worldviews, such as the Newtonian. However, discoveries by contemporary scientists disclose that the universe is not so much reducible as emergent, not so much fixed as ever-evolving and creative. This vindicates the argument that Western cosmologies based on anthropocentric, reductionist, and static worldviews are scientifically mistaken (Kauffman, 2008, ix–xiii).

East Asian traditions are less prone to narcissistic attachment to the human body and more interested in staying in harmony with Nature in the form of mountains, waters, and trees (compare Greek sculptures with East Asian landscapes). Grounded in the harmony and symbiosis of humanity with Nature, East Asian thought is co-friendly and life-affirming. As Tucker and Grim (2000, xxiv) put it: "The East Asian traditions of Confucianism and Taoism remain, in certain ways, some of the most life-affirming in the spectrum of world religions." Furthermore, contemporary sciences suggest that East Asian holistic cosmologies are more accurate than reductionist worldviews. The universe is interdependent (relational) rather than independent (essential), circular not linear, flexible not static, diverse not uniform. Correspondingly, Fritjof Capra (1996, 297–304), author of *The Tao of Physics*, proposed interdependence, recycling, partnership, flexibility, and diversity as the five principles of ecology. In dialogue with East Asian traditions and liberation (*minjung*) theology, this chapter proposes East Asian alternatives to three revisions for a proper Christian theology in an age of ecological crisis: a theanthropocosmic vision (cosmology), theodao (theology of dao), and pneumatosociocosmic narratives of the exploited life (pneumatology of *ki* [氣; *qì*]).[2]

A Theanthropocosmic Vision: Both a New and an Ancient Cosmology

A theanthropocosmic vision (God, humanity, and the cosmos in communion) is a fitting cosmology for Christianity in an age of ecology and science. Tucker and Grim (2000, xxiv) state: "If [Western] religions have traditionally concentrated on divine–human and human–human relations, the challenge is that they now explore more fully divine–human–earth relations." Influenced by salvation history and modern historical consciousness, Christianity became anthropocentric and history-centered. For the last 500 years, Earth, Nature, and the cosmos "got lost" in Christian theology, with an exclusive focus on God and the human, as Elizabeth Johnson (2000, 4–9) elaborated. The ecological disaster made Western theologians aware of the devastating results of "such amnesia about the cosmic world" and eager to find Creation in the Christian tradition.

The loss of Creation or amnesia about the Earth is a modern phenomenon; it did not happen for the first 1,500 years of Christianity. The Bible respects the religious value of the Earth. The Jewish scriptures speak of an Earth filled with the glory of God. The Christian scriptures are also Earth-affirming, expressed in the notion of the Incarnation, resurrection of the body, eucharistic sharing, and eschatological hope. Early and medieval theologies treated humanity in association with the natural world as the common creation of God. "God–world–humanity: these form a metaphysical trinity." And "cosmology, anthropology, and theology of God formed a harmonious unity," as expressed in Hildegard of Bingen, Bonaventure, and Aquinas (Johnson, 2000, 6). Hence, the theanthropocosmic vision is nothing new, but an ancient cosmology for Christianity.

Nevertheless, both Catholic and Protestant theologies "focused on God and human self, leaving the natural world to the side" (Johnson, 2000, 8). The Reformation's doctrines of Christ alone, faith alone, grace alone, and scripture alone gave Protestant theology, and subsequently Catholic theology, "an intensively anthropocentric turn." "The center of gravity shifts to the human subject." However, reformers such as John Calvin were affirmative toward Nature, regarding it as the locus of divine glory. The anti-natural views of modern science, philosophy, and history accelerated this shift (Johnson, 2000, 9). The Cartesian view of the self and the Kantian turn to the subject divorced the human person (the internal, active subject) from Nature (the external, passive object). The modern emphasis on history reinforced this division. History was viewed as actual events in chronological, linear time and the locus of God's salvific work, whereas Nature, in cyclical time, was seen as the realm of paganism. Most twentieth-century theologies, including existentialist theology, neo-orthodoxy, political theology, and early liberation theologies, did not take Creation seriously.

Finally, the ecological crisis has prompted Western Christians "to incorporate the natural world as part or even the center of their work." The geocentric, unchanging, hierarchical medieval cosmology and a deterministic, mechanistic worldview are mistaken. Rather, the natural world discovered by contemporary science is "surprisingly dynamic, organic, self-organizing, indeterminate, chancy, boundless, and open to the unknown." Furthermore, the "rape of the Earth" is closely linked with "male hierarchy over women and nature," that is, "violent sexual conquest of women, and of virgin forest." Accordingly, Johnson argued for an ecofeminist approach: "To be truly effective, therefore, conversion to the earth needs to cut through the knot of misogynist prejudice and shift from the worldview of patriarchal hierarchy to a holistic worldview of relationships and mutual community" (2000, 11, 13, 17).

Ecofeminist theology is an important movement with legitimate correctives to Western theologies. However, from an East Asian perspective, it is still questionable whether ecofeminist theology sufficiently transcends the either/or way of thinking (anthropocentrism vs. cosmocentrism) or monistic dualism, which is not unrelated to essentialism, substantialism, and reductionism, though ecofeminist theology tries to avoid them. By monistic dualism, one cannot achieve a genuine holistic, mutual, and reciprocal relationship. The theanthropocosmic vision presupposes an entirely different paradigm that is both/and, pluralistic (triadic), and concentric.

According to Raymond Panikkar (1993), the history of world religions presents three great visions: ancient cosmocentrism, medieval theocentrism, and modern historico-anthropocentrism. All three are flawed, one-sided, reductionist views (monocentrism) of reality. God, humans, and the cosmos constitute three indivisible and concentric axes of the one reality. Early and medieval theologies maintained this anthropocosmic or cosmotheandric vision. Moreover, the genius of the doctrine of the Trinity lies in its capacity to articulate the pluralistic and concentric reality of the Triune Godhead beyond Greek monistic dualism. Nevertheless, the Western either/or division remains problematic, selecting either God or Earth, humans or Nature. True humanity can be realized only through the right relationship with Heaven (God) and the Earth (cosmos). A theanthropocosmic vision refers to this triadic communion of God, the cosmos, and humans, the ontologically indivisible reality.

East Asians have long believed in the triadic reality of heaven, Earth, and humanity, by calling it the Trinity (三才) or the Triune Ultimate (三極). The ideographic structure of the Korean language embodies this vision. It also appears in the trigrams and the hexagrams of *Yìjīng*, a cornerstone of East Asian thought (Wilhelm, 1977). One Confucian scholar suggested that East Asians "might see God the Son as the ideal human, God the Father would be Heaven (the creative spirit), and God the Holy Spirit the earth (the receptive co-spirit), or agent of the world which testifies to the accomplishment of the divinity" (Cheng, 1998, 225).

Furthermore, in East Asian Christianity, the theohistorical vision of Christianity has encountered the anthropocosmic vision of East Asian religions (neo-Confucianism). Simply put, an anthropocosmic vision refers to the Confucian idea of the unity of Heaven and humanity (天人合一), whereas a theohistorical vision refers to the Christian view of salvation history (God in history). This encounter leads to a fusion of hermeneutical horizons to form a theanthropo-cosmic vision (Kim, Heup Young, 1996, 176–178, 183–184; Tu, 1989). In East Asian Christianity, Christian theology, East Asian religions, and ecology meet. Thematizing this fusion of hermeneutical horizons may bring about a new paradigm of theology, anthropology, and cosmology in an age of ecology and science. Christian theology presents a considered view of God (Heaven, the Father); East Asian religions offer a profound wisdom of humanity and life (the Son); and ecology (natural sciences) submits the most recent understanding of the Earth (the Holy Spirit). Together, Christian theology, East Asian religions, and ecology constitute the triadic polarities that entail a Triune Great Ultimate (三太極). A theanthropocosmic paradigm of Christian theology can be constructed with these three great resources in a Triune Great Ultimate. These relations can be illustrated as follows.

The Triune Great Ultimate of Theology of Dao

Christian theology:	*Theos,*	Heaven,	*ki* (*pneuma*),	Father,	emancipation.
East Asian religions:	*Anthropos,*	human (life),	*society,*	Son,	dialogue.
Ecology (natural sciences):	*Cosmos,*	Earth,	*Cosmos,*	Holy Spirit,	ecology.
		theanthropocosmic vision,		*pneumato-socio-cosmic narratives*	

Theodao (Theology of Dao): A New Paradigm of Asian Theology

The theology of dao (theodao) refers to a new paradigm of Christian theology in the theanthropocosmic vision, constructed in dialogue with East Asian religions. It searches for the theanthropocosmic dao, the Way of the Triune Great Ultimate, where the heavenly way (天道), the human way (人道), and the earthly way (地道) are in communion. It seeks a way to embody the trinity of theology, life, and ecology, in and through interreligious and interdisciplinary dialogues among Christianity, East Asian religions, and natural sciences. It is a theology of learning how to participate in this holistic trajectory of theanthropocosmic dao.

The dominant root metaphor of Christian theology for the last two millennia has been the *Logos*. However, it was rooted in Greek hierarchical dualism and further reduced to technical reason by modernism. *Logos* has become an inappropriate root metaphor for Christian theology. Dao could be a more appropriate root metaphor in this ecological age. For dao is not only "the most life-affirming" but also more biblical. Jesus said, "I am the way, truth, and life" (John 14: 6a) and identified himself not so much as the *Logos* incarnate as the ultimate way (dao) to God (John 14: 6b). Moreover, the first name for Christianity in the New Testament was *hodos* (way), translated as dao in the Korean Bible (Acts 9: 2; 19: 9; 22: 4; 24: 14, 22).

The term theodao was coined to contrast with the traditional theology (*Logos*) and its modern alternative, theopraxis (praxis) (Kim, Heup Young, 2003, 135–254). Just as its Chinese character (道) consists of two ideographs, meaning head (首 being) and vehicle (辶 becoming), dao means both the source of being (*Logos*) and the way of becoming (praxis). It denotes the being in becoming or the *Logos* in transformative praxis. Dao does not refer to either/or, but embraces the whole of both/and. It does not force one to stay at the crossroads of *Logos* (being) and praxis (becoming), but actualizes participation in a dynamic movement to be united in the cosmic track. The dao as the ultimate way and reality embodies the transformative praxis of the theanthropocosmic trajectory of life in the unity of knowing and acting (知行合一).

If theology is a perspective from above and theopraxis is that from below, then theodao is a perspective from an entirely different dimension: theanthropocosmic intersubjectivity. Theodao as a theology of life is neither *Logos*-centric (knowledge) nor praxis-centric (action), but dao-centric (*sophia* in action). Theodao can be reduced neither to an orthodoxy (a right doctrine of the Church) nor to an orthopraxis (a right practice in history), but embraces holistically the right way of life (orthodao), the transformative wisdom of living in a theanthropocosmic trajectory. What theodao pursues is neither a metaphysical debate for church doctrines nor exclusively an ideological conscientization for social action, but a holistic way of life. Its key issue is whether it is the right way to participate in the loving process of theanthropocosmic reconciliation and sanctification.

While orthodoxy emphasizes faith and orthopraxis underscores hope, orthodao focuses on love (1 Cor. 13: 13). If the traditional theology (theo-*Logos*) focuses on the epistemology of faith and modern theopraxis (liberation theology) focuses on the eschatology of hope, the cardinal theme of theodao is the pneumatology of love. If the classical definition of theology is faith-seeking understanding (*fides quaerens intellectum*) and that of theopraxis is hope-seeking action, then theodao takes the definition of *love-seeking dao* (way). If theology (God-talk) focuses on the right understanding of the Christian doctrines and theopraxis (God-walk) on the right practice of Christian ideologies, then theodao (God-live) searches for the way and wisdom of Christian life.

The teachings of Jesus were not an orthodox doctrine, a philosophical theology, a manual of orthopraxis, or an ideology of social revolution, but the dao of life and living. Christ cannot be divided between the historical Jesus (theopraxis) and the kerygmatic Christ (theologos). In fact, the fusion of hermeneutical horizons toward a theodao in a theanthropocosmic vision appeared as soon as Christianity landed on the neo-Confucian soil of Korea. The first Korean Catholic theologian, Yi Pyŭk (1754–1786), conceived

Christ as the intersection of the heavenly dao and the human dao, that is, neither Christo-*logos* nor Christo-praxis, but Christo-dao (Kim, Heup Young, 2003, 153–182; Ri,1979). Christo-dao comprehends Christ as both the dao of the Crucifixion (the way of theanthropocosmic reconciliation) and the dao of resurrection (the way of theanthropocosmic sanctification).

Ryu Yŏng-mo (1890–1981), a seminal Korean Christian thinker, envisioned the cosmogonic Christ from the deepest heart of the East Asian hermeneutical universe of dao. He believed that in Christ, the Non-Ultimate (無極; *Wú jí*) and the Great Ultimate (太極; *Tài jí*) were united. In neo-Confucianism, this unity denotes the ultimate complementary and paradoxical opposites of the ineffable Vacuity (the Non-Ultimate) and the Cosmogony (the Great Ultimate) (Chan, 1963, 463–465). From the vantage point of this supreme cosmogonic paradox, Ryu understood

> the cross as both the Non-Ultimate and the Great Ultimate... Jesus is the one who manifested the ultimate in Asian cosmology. Through the sacrifice of himself, he achieved genuine humanity (仁; *rén*). That is to say, by offering himself as a sacrifice, *he* saved the human race and opened the kingdom of God for humanity. (Kim, Heung-ho, 1994, 299)

Further, Ryu articulated the Cross as "the blood of the flower" in which the Son reveals the glory of the Father, and the Father the glory of the Son. Seeing the blossom of this flower of Jesus (at the Cross), he envisioned the glorious blossom of the cosmos (cosmogony). "[T]he Cross is a rush into the cosmic trajectory, resurrection is a participation in the revolution of the cosmic trajectory, and lighting up the world is the judgment sitting in the right-hand side of God" (Kim, Heung-ho, 1994, 301). Accordingly, the Crucifixion and the Resurrection do not refer to a narrow story about God's salvation work exclusively for *Homo sapiens* in a linear history of a minuscule planet, Earth, in the solar system. Rather, these events signify a grand narrative of the theanthropocosmic drama that Jesus, true humanity, has successfully inserted into the cosmic trajectory to achieve a cosmotheandric union, illuminating the entire universe, and thus becoming the christic-dao of true life (cf. Col. 1: 16–17; John 1: 3).

Furthermore, Ryu conceived the Crucifixion and Resurrection as the events that make the Being in Non-Being. Western christologies, preoccupied by being (substantialism), neglect the dimension of non-being. In fact, the core of christology is in the paradoxical mystery of creating the being (Resurrection) from the non-being (Crucifixion), which is God's cosmogonic principle (*creatio ex nihilo*). From this vantage point, he conveyed a fascinating Korean apophatic christodao. Jesus is the One who "Is" in spite of "Is-Not"; that is to say, "Being-in-Non-Being (*Ŏpshi-gyeshin nim*)." Whereas we are non-being-in-being, He is the One of Being-in-Non-Being. Whereas we are the "forms" that are "none other than emptiness" (*Heart Sutra*), He is the "emptiness" that is "none other than form" (Kim, Heung-ho, 1985, 68). Christian theology needs to embody this cosmogonic principle of being-in-non-being if it is to be ecological and life-affirming. Here is the significance of the medieval tradition of negative theology (*via negativa*) and *kenosis* (emptiness).

Dàodéjīng describes dao in basically feminine metaphors—"mother of all things," "the root," "the ground" (of Being), "the uncarved block" (original Nature), "the mystical female."

This vision is based on Lǎozǐ's principle of "reversal." Lǎozǐ always preferred the strategy of *yin* (weak, soft, small, empty) over *yang* (strong, hard, big, full), as Graham (1989, 223) noted. The *yin* principle of reversal is closely connected with the principle of return.

> Attain complete vacuity, maintain steadfast quietude. All things come into being, and I see thereby their return. All things flourish, but each one returns to its destiny. To return to destiny is called the eternal (Dao). To know the eternal is called enlightenment. (Chan, 1963, 147)

The principle of reversal and radical return entails the spirituality of dao with the paradoxical power of weakness and emptiness.

Pneumatosociocosmic Narratives of the Exploited Life: A New Pneumatology of *Ki*

The spirituality of dao can bolster Christianity in our age of ecological crisis. The *yin* principle of reversal and radical return with the paradoxical power of weakness and emptiness can empower Christianity to resist the merciless process of genocide, biocide, and ecocide. In fact, the *yin* principle accords with the life-act of Jesus. The life-saving mystery of His Resurrection entails a Christian principle of radical return—the victory of life over death. The Crucifixion denotes a Christian principle of reversal with the paradoxical power of weakness and emptiness (cf. Isa. 53: 5, Luke 6: 20f, 1 Cor. 1: 18), while the *yin* strategy resonates with the biblical "preferential option for the poor," a well-known idiom of liberation theology. However, the preferential option is related not only to the poor, women, and *minjung* (the oppressed), but is extended to the suffering ecosystem as a whole, including endangered species.

Minjung theology argues that the social biography (the underside of history) of *minjung* is a more authentic historical point of reference for theological reflection than doctrinal discourses (official history) superimposed by the Church in its Western rationality orientation (Kim, Yong-bock, 1984–1985). This was important for Asian theology to realize *minjung* as the subject of history, correcting traditional theology, primarily based on autobiographical (psychological) or church (official) narratives. Nevertheless, its exclusive focus on the political history of God, and subsequently on anthropocentric history, hinders Asian theology's embrace of the full profundity of Asian religious and ecological thought. Asian theology needs also to include the underside histories of whole life-systems on Earth. It needs to thematize sociocosmic narratives of the exploited life, to be a creative crossover between the social biography of *minjung* and the East Asian anthropocosmic vision.

By embodying the spirituality of reversal and return, theology can achieve a sociocosmic transformative praxis (i.e., the dao), healing wounded Mother Earth. In Christianity, this spirituality implies a pneumatology empowered by the paradoxical power of the Cross with the eschatological hope of resurrection. The East Asian notion of *ki* (氣) is very helpful to articulate this pneumatology. Christianity needs to focus on sociocosmic narratives of the exploited life in spiritual communion with *ki*.

Kim Chi Ha (1992, 188–192), a Korean Catholic poet, presented an insightful parable, "the Ugŭmch'i Phenomenon," to illuminate this *ki* spirituality.[3] To cure his sickness, the result of a long term of imprisonment under the military dictatorship, he retired to a provincial city. The once pristine stream that flowed in front of his house was heavily polluted by industrial waste. However, when it rained, the rain flushed away the waste and he was surprised to see small fish swimming upstream against the flood of water! How could such feeble fish swim against such a turbulence?

Through meditation, he realized that it could happen thanks to *ki*. When the primordial *ki* of a weak fish becomes united with that of water, it can swim against even a mighty flood. Furthermore, as *ki*, "energy," always consists of *yin* and *yang*, the *ki* of water moves in the direction of *yin* and *yang*. From the exuberant palpitation of the primordial *ki* of many fish in union with the *yin* movement of the water, he discovered the key to understanding the mystery of the Ugŭmch'i War,[4] in which the feeble *minjung*—several hundred thousand Korean peasants—fought forcefully against Japanese troops armed with powerful mechanized weapons. Their collective *ki* inspired and empowered the *minjung* to participate courageously in the movement and to be united with the primordial *ki*, in the same way that the feeble fish swim forcefully upstream against the formidable flood to be in union with the *yin* movement of the water. The fierce palpitation of the *minjung* against the turbulent flood of historical demons is a great cosmic movement united with the *yin–yang* movement of *ki*. He called it the ugŭmch'i phenomenon.

The first realization in this parable was an ecological insight that Nature, in the form of rain, has a self-saving power to bring forth life in a hostile environment (polluted water). He saw hope for life in this spiritually fragmented and ecologically destructive world spawned by developmental ideology. A more important realization, however, was that from the dao world he found the key to transcending historical dualism and the real source of life energy which gives such vitality to fish and the *minjung* in ugŭmch'i. This marked a turning point for his thought as he formulated a creative Korean hermeneutics of suspicion from the perspective of *han*, "the suppressed, amassed and condensed experience of oppression" (Suh, 1981, 65). He argued that *minjung* must escape the vicious circle of *han*-riddenness to resolve their *han*. This inspired Korean theologians to arrive at *minjung* theology. Some even argued that theologians are charged to become priests of *han* to motivate and participate in the movement of *hanpuri* (a collective action to release *han*) of *minjung*, including women.

Finally, he returned to the old dao world. This implies a paradigm shift in his thought from a Korean version of the dualistic mode of contradiction (*han*) to the East Asian corresponding mode of complementary opposites (*yin–yang*). This shift involves his enlightenment to the true source of the life-empowering force manifested by the feeble fish in the floodwater and the multitude of *minjung* in the Ugŭmch'i War. The key to revealing the mystery of the ugŭmch'i phenomenon is the notion of *ki*, which is very similar to *pneuma*. *Ki* is not so much dualistic and analytic as holistic and embracing. It is both the source and the medium of empowerment. This insight enables the substantiation of a theology of life in the East Asian theanthropocosmic vision with a pneumatology of *ki*.

The new horizon in the unity of Heaven (God), Earth (the cosmos), and humanity can be further extended through the spirit (*ki, pneuma*), namely, "a pneumatoanthropocosmic vision" (Kim, Heup Young, 2003, 142–148). This pneumatoanthropocosmic vision can cultivate a symbiosis of the life network through the communication of *ki*, which fosters humans' relationship with other lives more holistically.

The ugŭmch'i phenomenon is an example of the sociocosmic narratives of the exploited life, telling the story of the two exploited lives in the metaphors of the feeble fish and the host of *minjung* in the Ugŭmch'i War. In addition, *ki* as both spirit and matter offers a clue to the mystery of the Incarnation. While the Nativity refers to the pneumatoanthropocosmic vision *par excellence*, the Passion narrative of Christ tells the sociocosmic biography of the exploited life *par excellence*. Christ as the theanthropocosmic dao entails the life-breathing *pneumato-sociocosmic trajectory* of the primordial (holy) *ki*.

Finally, the theology of dao as a new paradigm of theology of life invites Christians to participate in rehabilitating exploited life, including *minjung* and women as well as endangered life-systems and polluted Nature, by the power of *ki*. As the ugŭmch'i phenomenon shows, it requires the spirituality of dao, which empowers the principle of radical return and reversal with the paradoxical power of weakness and emptiness. Thus, a primary task of the theology of dao as a new paradigm of Christian theology is to rehabilitate our planetary and cosmic habitats—"our" home (*oikos*) in the universe—with the re-visioning of the true com-union of God, humanity (life), and Earth (cosmos), and by the outpouring power of the cosmic Spirit, the holy *ki*.

The theology of dao as a new theology of life based on a proper cosmology and ecology in and through dialogue with East Asian religions and *minjung* theology demands not just an inter-Christian or an inter-religious dialogue, but also a theanthropocosmic com-union to embody the transformative praxis in the pneumatosociocosmic trajectory, the dao, by the outpouring power of the holy *ki*. This notion of *ki* is well supported by contemporary sciences, as it "bears the most striking resemblance to the concept of quantum field in modern physics" (Capra, 1983, 212). Therefore, a trialogue among Christianity, Asian religions, and the natural sciences is an esssential conversation for Asian and global Christianity to have in the years to come (Kim, Heup Young, 2006).

Notes

1 The conference was held at Harvard University's Center for the Study of World Religions, Cambridge, MA, April 16–19, 1998. See *Christianity and Ecology*.

2 *Ki*, a Korean romanization of 氣 (*qì* in the Pinyin Chinese [*ch'i* in the Wade-Giles]) is a key East Asian notion, very similar to the Greek word *pneuma*. It has various meanings—energy, vital force, material force, and breath. This chapter romanizes this word mainly as *ki* due to the contextual consideration.

3 For a full English translation, see Kim, Heup Young (2003, 138–142).

4 The last and most ferocious battle during the second uprising of Tonghak peasants, which broke out on the Ugŭmch'i Hill of Gongju, Korea, in December 1894.

References

Capra, Fritz. 1983. *The Tao of Physics: An Exploration of the Parallels between Modern Physics and Eastern Mysticism* (2nd ed.). Boulder, CO: Shambhala.

Capra, Fritjof. 1996. *The Web of Life: A New Scientific Understanding of Living System.* New York: Doubleday.

Chan Wing-tsit (Transl. and Comp.). 1963. *A Source Book in Chinese Philosophy.* Princeton, NJ: Princeton University Press.

Cheng Chung-ying. 1998. The Trinity of Cosmology, Ecology, and Ethics in the Confucian Personhood (211–235). In Mary Evelyn Tucker & John Berthrong (Eds.), *Confucianism and Ecology: The Interpretation of Heaven, Earth, and Humanity.* Cambridge, MA: Harvard University Press.

Graham, A. C. 1989. *Disputers of the Tao: Philosophical Argument in Ancient China.* La Salle, IL: Open Court.

Johnson, Elizabeth. 2000. Losing and Founding Creation in the Christian Tradition (3–21). In Dieter T. Hessel and Rosemary Radford Ruether (Eds.), *Christianity and Ecology: Seeking the Well-Being of Earth and Humans.* Cambridge, MA: Harvard University Press.

Kauffman, Stuart A. 2008. *Reinventing the Sacred: A New View of Science, Reason and Religion.* New York: Basic Books.

Kaufman, Gordon. 2000. Response to Elizabeth A. Johnson, 23–27. In Dieter T. Hessel and Rosemary Radford Ruether (Eds.), *Christianity and Ecology: Seeking the Well-Being of Earth and Humans.* Cambridge, MA: Harvard University Press.

Kim, Chi Ha. 1992. *Saengmyung [Life].* Seoul: Sol.

Kim, Heung-ho. 1985. *Jesori [The Words of Yu Yŏng-mo].* Seoul: Pungman.

Kim, Heung-ho.1994. Yu Yŏng-mo's View of Christianity from the Asian Perspective (293–325P). In Park Young-ho (Ed.), *Dasŏk Yu Yŏng-mo.* Seoul: The Sungchun Institution.

Kim, Heup Young. 1996. *Wang Yang-ming and Karl Barth: A Confucian–Christian Dialogue.* Lamham, MD: University Press of America.

Kim, Heup Young. 2003. *Christ and the Tao.* Hong Kong: Christian Conference of Asia.

Kim, Heup Young. 2006. Asian Christianity: Toward a Trilogue of Humility: Sciences, Theologies, and Asian Religions (121–133). In Fraser Watts and Kevin Dutton (Eds.), *Why the Science and Religion Dialogue Matters: Voices from the International Society for Science and Religion.* West Conshohocken, PA: John Templeton Press.

Kim, Yong-bock. 1981. Theology and the Social Biography of Minjung. *CTC Bulletin,* 5, 36, 1, 66–78.

Panikkar, Raymond. 1993. *The Cosmotheandric Experience: Emerging Religion Consciousness.* Maryknoll, NY: Orbis Books.

Ri, Jean Sang. 1979. *Confucius et Jesus Christ: La Première Théologie Chrestienne en Corée d'après l'oeuvre de Yi Piek lettre Confucèen 1754–1786.* Paris: Editions Beauchesne.

Suh Nam-dong. 1981. *Minjung Theology: People as the Subjects of History.* Hong Kong: Christian Conference of Asia.

Tu Wei-ming. 1989. *Centrality and Commonality: An Essay on Confucian Religiousness* (rev. ed.). Albany, NY: SUNY Press.

Tucker, Mary Evelyn & Grim, John (Eds.). 1994. *World Views and Ecology: Religion, Philosophy, and the Environment.* Maryknoll, NY: Orbis Books.

Tucker, Mary Evelyn & Grim, John. 2000. Series Foreword (xv–xxxii). In Dieter T. Hessel & Rosemary Radford Ruether (Eds.), *Christianity and Ecology: Seeking the Well-Being of Earth and Humans.* Cambridge, MA: Harvard University Press.

White, Lynn, Jr. 1967. The Historical Roots of Our Ecological Crisis. *Science*, 155, 1203–1207.

Wilhelm, Hellmut. 1977. *Heaven, Earth, and Man in the Book of Changes*. Seattle, WA, and London: University of Washington Press.

Further Reading

Hessel, Dieter T. & Radford Ruether, Rosemary (Eds.). 2000. *Christianity and, Ecology: Seeking the Well-Being of Earth and Humans*. Cambridge, MA: Harvard University Press. Provides various examples of Christian eco-theology.

Kim, Heup Young. 1996. *Wang Yang-ming and Karl Barth: A Confucian–Christian Dialogue*. Lamham, MD: University Press of America. Offers a solid Confucian–Christian dialogue and basic insights for theodao.

Kim, Heup Young. 2017. *Solely: A Theology of Dao*. Maryknoll, NY: Orbis Books. Provides a general introduction to the constructive, dialogical, and practical scopes of theodao, a new paradigm of Christian theology.

Tucker, Mary Evelyn & Berthrong, John (Eds.). 1998. *Confucianism and Ecology: The Interpretation of Heaven, Earth, and Humanity*. Cambridge, MA: Harvard University Press. Provides a stimulating introduction to ecological insights from East Asian worldviews.

Tucker, Mary Evelyn & Grim, John (Eds.). 1994. *World Views and Ecology: Religion, Philosophy, and the Environment*. Maryknoll, NY: Orbis Books. Provides an excellent overview of the foundation of ecological study with important global religious and philosophical traditions.

II. Care for the Earth and Life

Traditions' Teachings in Socioecological Contexts

CHAPTER 10

Science, Ecology, and Christian Theology

John F. Haught

Christian theologians paid little attention to ecological issues until late in the twentieth century. By 2015, however, a considerable body of official and unofficial Christian writings by Catholic, Protestant, and Orthodox theologians on the importance of ecological concern as a moral and religious issue had appeared (e.g., Barbour, 1972; Birch et al., 1990; Christiansen and Grazer 1996; Edwards, 1995; John Paul II, 1990; McDonagh, 1990; Nash, 1991; Ruether, 2000; Santmire, 1985; Zizioulas, 1989–1990). What these three branches of Christianity hold in common is a sense of a Creator who declares all of Creation good. They each have a sense that God loves life, diversity, and the intercommunion of all creatures. And they hope for the final fulfillment of the cosmos in the compassionate and everlasting embrace of God.

This shared emphasis is significant since it responds to the accusation by some secular environmentalists that Christianity, generally speaking, is so otherworldly in its preoccupations that it cannot provide a secure foundation for an ecologically moral lifestyle in the here and now. Australian philosopher John Passmore, for example, has claimed that Christianity is too preoccupied with the afterlife to inspire Christians to care for the natural world. Christianity's obsession with the supernatural, he asserts, persuades its devotees to focus so one-sidedly on hope for their survival in the "next world" that they remain indifferent to the dire conditions of the present natural environment (Passmore, 1974, 184). Secular criticism of Christianity also typically cites the simplistic thesis of historian Lynn White, Jr., that by giving humans "dominion" over life (Gen 1: 26) the Bible has permitted Christians to exploit and ruin their natural environments (White, 1967).

As a Christian theologian, I agree that traditional Christian ethics has not been sufficiently concerned with the integrity of the nonhuman natural world. However, I also believe that Christian tradition and the biblical writings from which it draws the

The Wiley Blackwell Companion to Religion and Ecology, First Edition. Edited by John Hart.

substance of its faith and moral traditions provide the framework for a worldview that can ground a robust ecological ethic. Indeed, I propose that Christianity can do so more reasonably and consistently than the inherently fatalistic visions espoused by purely secular interpretations of Nature. After all, contemporary scientific naturalists such as Passmore claim that Nature—by which they mean the world available to experience and scientific inquiry—is all there is. Since for scientific naturalism God does not exist, there can be no transcendent reality and meaning that might ground the value of worldly reality or save it everlastingly. If scientific naturalism is right in its assumption that nothing is imperishable, then there can be no everlasting realm of "rightness" that could judge our abuse of Nature or ground human values consistently and *permanently*. So, all human valuations, including ecological value judgments, would be purely natural, and hence impermanent.

In contrast, I propose that the posture of hope for what is imperishably good and beautiful, a theological view that has its roots deep in Christianity and many other traditions, is a reasonable foundation for intergenerational commitment on the part of perishable human beings to the long-term care of Nature in general and life in particular. This does not mean that the Bible and other classical sources of Christian thought possess specific prescriptions for contemporary ecological ills. Instead, what they can inspire is a promissory, future-oriented worldview, without which it is unlikely that the natural world's wellbeing will be a consistent concern for countless generations to come. I call this Christian perspective an *anticipatory* vision of Nature, and I outline it below in a way that takes fully into account new scientific ways of understanding the natural world, especially those of biology and cosmology. Before developing my argument, however, I summarize two other ways in which Christian thought may defend its ecological relevance. I call these the *traditional* and the *sacramental* approaches to Christian ecological theology

The Traditional Approach

The tradition-centered approach to Christian ecological theology is based on the belief that the Christian scriptures, creeds, and theological reflection provide adequate resources for cultivating ecological concern. I am referring here not only to the call in Genesis 2: 15 for human beings to exercise responsible stewardship in their tending of the garden of life, but also to the need to practice the religious virtues that quite naturally discourage our indulging in practices that place undue stress on the natural world. Adhering to the virtues of moderation, humility, justice, gratitude, and compassion is a salutary—and indeed necessary—response to the greed, arrogance, inequity, and apathy that have led to the ruination of Nature and the life-world in many places. A tradition-centered—and hence characteristically text-based—retrieval of Christian resources directly contradicts the immoderate consumption, ingratitude, and economic injustice that underlie the degradation of so much of Earth's ecological diversity and richness. Without a massive popular return to the pursuit of time-tested virtues, humans will have great difficulty restoring the planet to health. The question, then, is how to motivate people to adopt an ecologically virtuous way of life.

Environmental abuse, the traditional approach claims, is the consequence not of Christian faith but of disobedience to Christianity's challenging moral precepts. This approach responds to accusations such as Passmore's by pointing out that whatever ecological damage has occurred in Christian countries is not due to theoretical or moral weaknesses in that faith itself, but in a failure to ground moral and practical life in an authoritative Christian vision of Creation. Moreover, this admittedly apologetic response would consider Lynn White's thesis—that the Bible's granting humans "dominion" over the Earth is the main historical cause of the ecological crisis—an instance of mistaken biblical exegesis. Even though Christians may sometimes have interpreted dominion to mean domination, biblical scholarship has now shown that to "have dominion" in fact means that humans should assume a nurturing and protective attitude to Nature. Furthermore, the real causes of ecological problems are too complex to blame on any one religious tradition.

In response to White's thesis, to be more specific, contemporary biblical scholars point out that the Hebrew verb often translated as "to have dominion" originally had the sociopolitical connotation of "functioning as a vice-regent." Because a kingdom's territories were often too extensive to be governed directly, the potentate appointed deputies to oversee the remoter corners of his kingdom. It was expected, however, that these subordinates were commissioned as local conveyors and representatives of the ruler's *generally* benign disposition toward the inhabitants of the entire realm. On this analogy, therefore, the biblical injunction misread by White really means that humans—God's viceroys—should cultivate the same nurturing disposition toward Creation as the Creator does. In other words, dominion does not mean domination or exploitation at all. Unfortunately, Christians through the ages have not always interpreted dominion in its original biblical sense.

The most fundamental theological reason Christianity can cite for promoting ecological responsibility, however, is its own radical monotheism. Belief in God means that all finite beings, including humans, are gifts of the infinite creative love of God, that all beings are embraced by God, and that their destiny is communion with the infinite love and source of life that graciously gives them their being and invites human trust. Because of our finite human participation in the infinite resourcefulness from which we draw our being, Christians believe that human hearts are restless until they rest in God, as St. Augustine famously put it. Only our encounter in faith with the infinite can relieve our anxiety and bring us peace. However, our relationship with the infinite God who creates and embraces us is often a troubled one, for we are also idolaters who constantly need to be reminded of our tendency to identify the infinite with what is merely finite (Niebuhr, 1960).

Our current environmental crisis, therefore, at least from the perspective of radical monotheism, is the consequence of an idolatrous religiosity that currently underlies the excesses of a consumer culture: we are trying to squeeze the infinite from what is in fact finite, namely, our own little planet. To address this idolatry, only a radical monotheism will prove to be consistently effective. Secularism is not the answer since, by insisting that Nature is *all* there is, it lacks the constraints that might prevent us literally from making Nature function as our *All*. In principle, by contrast, radical monotheism is inherently opposed to the acquisitiveness and greed underlying all instances of idolatry.

When modern secular culture wiped the horizon clean of divine transcendence, it did nothing to banish the longing for infinity that pulls on every human heart. As a result, we have irrationally expected from our finite planet the limitless resourcefulness that could conceivably come only from what is infinite. Only a thoroughgoing monotheism, logically speaking, can liberate our hearts from the allure of idolatry and shield the Earth from the unrealistic demand that it function as the full and final satisfaction of human desire.

Monotheism is taken for granted also by the two theological alternatives. Before describing these in more detail, however, I must add that contemporary Christian theologians generally agree that a judicious understanding of our environmental predicament requires a plurality of levels of analysis and reparative intervention. Considered from an ethical point of view, for example, the current crisis is in great measure the result of injustice and lack of compassion. From an economic point of view, Earth's ecological decline is due to widespread poverty and the general maldistribution of wealth. Politically speaking, the situation is due to an oppressively nationalistic exercise of force that across the planet squeezes the life out of the poor and, consequently, of their environments as well. From the point of view of sociohistorical analysis, the death of Nature can be viewed as the result of male dominance buttressed for many centuries by patriarchal cultures (Merchant, 1980). From a biological point of view, the crisis can be understood as a breakdown of biodiversity, which can be addressed appropriately only within the framework of a scientifically informed understanding of the mutual dependence of systems of life on one another. From a chemical point of view, the present crisis comes down to the transforming of organic into inorganic physical units. And from the perspective of physics it is an expression of the second law of thermodynamics, which states that the total entropy of an isolated system always increases over time.

Any appropriate theological response to the ecological crisis must be informed by all these perspectives and more. However, according to the traditional approach I am summarizing here, the most fundamental contribution Christianity can make to understanding and responding to the present situation is to highlight the idolatrous character of humanity's current relationship to the natural habitat and, second, to show how the redemptive good news given in Christ can in principle restore a proper relationship of human creatures to their Creator. Below, I examine how recent developments in science, especially biology and cosmology, provide the intellectual setting for a fresh Christian perspective on the task of accounting for and responding theologically to our ecological problems.

The Sacramental Approach

A second type of Christian motivation for ecological responsibility stems from Christianity's doctrine of God's Incarnation and the *sacramental vision* of Nature implied in the teaching that God became flesh (John 1). Sacramentalism, as I call it, is an approach more typical of Roman Catholic and Eastern Christianity than of Protestantism, but the doctrine of the Incarnation—that in Christ God has become human—painfully worked out in early church councils and eventually codified especially in the Nicene and Apostles' Creeds, is still fundamental for most branches of Christianity. It has profound ecological implications. The incarnational, sacramental approach emphasizes the religiously revelatory value of Nature to a degree that the traditional approach summarized above might consider dangerous. Sacramentalism takes Nature to be essentially good, not only because it participates in, but also because it reveals or makes manifest, the infinite being, goodness, and beauty of the world's Creator.

Sacramentalism's response to the present ecological predicament is not so much text-based and tradition-centered as focused on the inherent value of Nature itself. The fundamental reason for our respecting Nature is that the natural world is revelatory of the Divine. Although sacramental Christianity embraces biblical narratives and prophetic faith, its main emphasis is on Nature as a manifestation of God. Christian sacramentalism, moreover, embodies and encourages a style of religious awareness that goes back historically to the earliest of human religions. Nature, primordially, is inherently symbolic of what is sacred. The Roman Catholic priests Michael and Kenneth Himes express the sacramental point of view succinctly: "The essence of a sacrament is the capacity to reveal grace, the agapic self-gift of God, by being what it is. By being thoroughly itself, a sacrament bodies forth the absolute self-donative love of God that undergirds it and the entirety of creation." Accordingly, "every creature, human and non-human, animate and inanimate, can be a sacrament" (Himes & Himes, 1990, 45).

By emphasizing the natural world's transparency to the Divine, sacramentalism discourages devotees from transforming Creation into purely human projects. Since the natural world participates to one degree or another in God's own life, sacramentalism gives a numinous meaning to Nature which serves to protect it from impoverishment by economically and technologically exploitative attitudes and efforts. "By its Nature," the Himes brothers reflect, "a sacrament requires that it be appreciated for what it is and not as a tool to an end. " As far as these two Catholic theologians are concerned, the sacramental vision of Catholic tradition "provides the deepest foundation for reverencing creation" (Himes & Himes, 1990, 45).

I think it is important to add that in terms of contemporary Western intellectual assumptions the sacramental vision is also countercultural, especially in its resistance to secularism's denial that Nature is transparent to an infinite transcendent reality. The academically endorsed materialist vision of Nature, after all, reduces Nature ontologically to mindless and lifeless material matter, thus draining it of inherent value and leaving it vulnerable to being subjected to human engineering projects (Commoner, 1974, 44). Sacramentalism's emphasis on Nature's ontological participation in infinite being, goodness, and beauty, on the contrary, endows the natural world with intrinsic value which, at least in principle, arouses in people of faith an instinct to protect it from human abuse. Advocates of a sacramental ecological spirituality are sometimes skeptical about the effectiveness of the biblical injunction to practice faithful stewardship or embrace the life of virtue, since these do not necessarily acknowledge the God-revealing value of Nature in the explicit way that sacramentalism does. The traditional approach's advocacy of the practice of virtue, necessary though this may be, does not provide a sufficiently protective defense against ecological recklessness here and now. What is needed, according to the proponents of a sacramental Christian ecological theology, is a recovery of the dispositions of primal and native religions that thrived in closer proximity to the rhythms and cycles of Nature and that took Nature to be revelatory of an encompassing sacred mystery. This is a style of religiousness that a purely prophetic biblical perspective might find suspect.

The traditional, biblically-based ecological theology summarized above, generally speaking, is more Protestant than Catholic. It emphasizes the primacy of the "word" of God more than the sacredness of Nature as the point of encounter of humans with ultimate reality. If the traditional approach emphasizes the transcendence and infinity of God, the sacramental approach highlights the sacredness of Nature and God's love of diversity. A word-oriented faith warns Christians of the dangers of sacramentalism because of the latter's tendency to slip into shallow idolatry. Nevertheless, the Nature-focused sacramental posture is now becoming more acceptable to non-Catholics (McFague, 1987, 1993; Santmire, 1985). One reason for this is that science itself, as I develop in the next section, is increasingly presenting the cosmos as an unfinished epic that promises to reveal the Divine in surprising new ways in future chapters of the ongoing cosmic process. The fact that Nature is narrative to the core invites us all to pay closer attention to where it might be going, and hence to grant it a more dramatic significance than static, pre-scientific cosmologies seem to allow. (More on this below.)

In summary, the sacramental approach to ecological theology makes a respectable argument that Christian faith is essentially, and not just accidentally, obliged to respect the inherent goodness of Nature and take action for its conservation. The loss of Nature, after all, would lead directly to a diminution of our sense of God. It is instructive here to ask, along with the Catholic ecologist Thomas Berry, what our sense of God would be, and what our religions would look like, if we humans lived on a lunar landscape (Berry, 1988). The question is worth considering since, from the beginning of religious history, the mystery of the sacred has been apprehended by religious people through such natural phenomena as clean water, fresh air, fertile soil, clear skies, bright light, thunder and rain, trees, plants, animals, and sexual fertility. Nature, viewed in sacramental perspective, is not primarily raw material to serve human purposes, but essentially the revealing of divine goodness and generosity. And since God is infinite being, a human sense of God's limitless goodness and beauty requires an endless array of revelatory media, as found in biodiversity, whose manifold richness is indispensable to the disclosure of divine plenitude. All of this, at least according to sacramentalism, requires from Christians a gratitude and reverence that a purely secularistic view of reality cannot support.

Since I am associating the sacramental approach primarily with Catholicism, I should say more here about Catholic tradition and its distinctive way of looking at the world. All Christians profess belief in a "holy Catholic Church," where the term "Catholic" means "universal," a term pointing to the shared hope that people everywhere may share in the blessing of God's self-revelation in Christ. After the Protestant Reformation, however, "Catholicism" has come to refer mainly to Christians united to the Church of Rome and its bishop, the Pope. Roman Catholicism today includes more than half of the Christians in the world and around 17% of the Earth's population.

Catholics constitute a minority of North American Christians, but they are the largest single denomination in that part of the world.

Catholics, like other Christians, profess belief in one God in three "persons": Father, Son, and Holy Spirit. God the Father is the Creator of all things visible and invisible. But since the Creation is in some sense still estranged from God, it requires redemption. In the person of Jesus Christ, God the Son, by his incarnation, death, and resurrection, reconciles a sinful world to the Father through the power of the Holy Spirit. The Holy Spirit, all Christians confess, has been poured out over the face of the Earth and promises the renewal of all Creation. The belief that God has become incarnate in Christ, and is always present in the Holy Spirit, means that God loves the physical world to the point of taking it bodily into the divine life, and thus grounding Nature's value everlastingly. If God so loves the world, Christians have no excuse not to love the natural world that has given birth to Christ and to our own bodily existence.

These are parts of the common creed that all Christians may formally embrace. Roman Catholicism, however, is distinct from Protestantism in its special emphasis on sacramental life. It sculpts Christian identity by means of seven sacraments: baptism, confirmation, reconciliation, Eucharist, marriage, holy orders, and final anointing. The sacrament of the Mass, known as "Eucharist" (which means thanksgiving), is of central significance. In the Mass Catholics believe that bread and wine, which have their origin in the products of the Earth's fertility and the work of human hands, are transformed into the body and blood of Christ. By consuming these elements, Catholics believe they commune bodily with God and that God embraces us fully in our corporeal existence, and, along with us, *all* of Creation.

Catholicism's emphasis on sacramental life has ecological implications simply by virtue of the fact that its liturgical life integrates the natural world into the very center of its worship. A sacrament is anything—for example, water, bread, wine, oil, sunlight, rain, soil, and fertility—through which the "sacred" is manifested. From the beginning of human life on Earth, people have experienced the sacred through the mediation of natural phenomena, through the sun that expels darkness, through running water that cleanses, through fresh air that restores breath and life, and through sexual communion that brings new life. Sacramental rituals may, at least in principle, inspire an ethical posture of caring for the integrity of Nature. Catholic sacramentalism, therefore, makes an essential contribution to the grounding of a contemporary ecological ethic (Gibler, 2010).

If Nature is a sacramental disclosure of God, moreover, it follows that God is much more intimately related to the natural world than an exclusively text-based and tradition-centered version of Christianity seems to permit. Preserving a robust sense of God, according to sacramentalism, depends on our unceasing concern for the integrity of the natural world. In the twentieth century the Catholic visionary Thomas Berry became widely revered by ecologically sensitive Christians, especially in North America, for his claim that by destroying Nature we lose God. By poisoning the water, air, and soil we run the risk of losing contact with the divine mystery that has revealed its infinite goodness and beauty through the natural world (1988).

Berry, a priest, feminist, and professor of religious studies, shocked some of his fellow Christians by declaring that the universe rather than sacred scripture offers us the "primary" revelation of God. Such a claim inevitably raised suspicion on the part of other Christians. They wondered if Berry was recommending a reversion to paganism (e.g., Smith, 1993). By deliberately challenging a Bible-centered approach to ethics, Berry placed himself at the center of an ancient squabble within the wider world of religions over the respective merits of priestly versus prophetic traditions. Insisting, however, that his approach is in harmony with Catholic tradition, including the thought of St. Thomas Aquinas, Berry attracted a good number of disciples. His adventurous ideas are supportive of the ecological thought of some Christian feminist theologians who, like Berry, see a causal connection between the social and political oppression of women on the one hand and the death of Nature on the other. According to some Christian feminists, the contemporary ecological predicament has been legitimated by patriarchal cultures and their institutions, including, ironically, the hierarchical Catholic Church. Consequently, sacramental ecologists argue that Christians must learn to think of God in terms of female rather than exclusively male imagery (McFague, 1987, 1993).

Finally, It should be stressed that the importance of the Catholic emphasis on the sacramentality of Nature emerges most significantly not so much in its tension with a purely Bible-centered approach to ethics and theology as in its opposition to the radically secularist ideology of scientific materialism, which still deeply influences contemporary culture and intellectual life.

The Promissory Approach

Without minimizing the ecological significance of the tradition-based and sacramental types of Christian ecological theology, I want to propose now that the natural sciences offer Christian theology a whole new framework for connecting faith to ecological concern. First, an important implication of recent science is that we humans truly *belong* to the universe. The total cosmic process, as we now understand it with the help of biology, astrophysics, and cosmology, has entered into the formation of each living and conscious being. The billions of years during which the world has labored to produce life and mind are not incidental to, but are constitutive of, our own lives and the life-systems that sustain us. Recent astrophysics has even shown that the mathematical values assumed by physical reality at the time of cosmic origins fall within the exceedingly narrow range that can allow for the eventual arrival of living and conscious organisms. Life and the cosmos, science has demonstrated, are a package deal.

Second, science has shown that the universe remains a work in progress, and this new picture of a world-in-process opens up a future horizon for continuous cosmic creativity, which had not been previously noticed (Haught, 1993, 2015). I call this new setting the *anticipatory* vision of Nature. Even the briefest survey of astrophysics, biology, and cosmology instructs us that the universe is still coming into being. If so, it is not unreasonable to hope that it has a future. What this means for an ecological theology is that the whole of Creation, from the beginning until now and into the future, and from the closest to the remotest galaxies, is set within the ambience of a momentous promise.

And if all of Nature shares in this promise, then a scientifically informed Christian faith offers fresh reasons for our taking care of Creation here and now as we wait "in joyful expectation" for its fulfillment in God.

In contrast to the ancient, especially Hellenistic, metaphysical traditions that have shaped Christian theology and philosophy for centuries, the natural sciences have woven our mental, moral, and spiritual existence seamlessly into the larger epic of a natural world that is still in the making. Familiarity with recent scientific discoveries, therefore, challenges fixed fatalistic assumptions that the universe is fundamentally indifferent to life and mind. Contrary to the materialism and cosmic pessimism of so much modern thought, empirical science today does not require that thoughtful people consider it self-evident that our own existence is essentially unconnected to Nature, a severance depicted starkly by the academically celebrated biochemist Jacques Monod in his popular book *Chance and Necessity* (1972). In strict opposition to contemporary materialist and now obsolete mechanistic assumptions about Nature, a future-oriented or anticipatory vision of Nature, in keeping with biblical faith's openness to a new future, requires that we revise the meaning of human stewardship of Creation. If Nature is not only a sacrament but also the promise of more being, stewardship is no longer reducible to acts of preservation, but consists also of *preparation*, that is, of making the world ready to host creative new developments in the long-term future.

The new scientific view of the cosmos as a work in progress is confluent with Christianity's hope for future fulfillment. Lest we forget, Christianity is a religious tradition born in the belief that the whole world, and not just human history, is shaped by promise. Technically speaking, in other words, Christianity is an "eschatological" religion. Eschatology, a term derived from the Greek word *eschaton*, literally means "last." Narrowly understood, eschatology means concern with the "last things," particularly with what happens to human beings at death: entry into Heaven, Hell, or Purgatory. More broadly speaking, eschatology is best understood simply as a reflection on what we may hope for. Biblically speaking, moreover, Christian hope anticipates not only human redemption, but also a whole "new Creation." That is, hope includes concern not only for our personal salvation but also for the renewal of the entire universe in God.

If Christianity is eschatological through and through, then all Christian theology, including ecological theology, must be grounded in hope for a final redemption and fulfillment of all things. Theologian Jürgen Moltmann writes:

> From first to last, and not merely in the epilogue, Christianity is eschatology, is hope, forward looking and forward moving, and therefore also revolutionizing and transforming the present. The eschatological is not one element of Christianity, but it is the medium of Christian faith as such, the key in which everything in it is set, the glow that suffuses everything here in the dawn of an expected new day... Hence eschatology cannot really be only a part of Christian doctrine. Rather, the eschatological outlook is characteristic of all Christian proclamation, of every Christian existence and of the whole Church. There is therefore only one real problem in Christian theology ... the problem of the future. (Moltmann, 1965, 16)

The pastoral letter *Renewing the Earth*, issued by the American Catholic Bishops (1991), therefore, rightly affirms that the fundamental Christian ecological virtue is hope. I am proposing here that recent developments in scientific cosmology open up both spiritual and intellectual space for Christian thought to link ecological concern more tightly than ever to the biblical hope for a new future.

Scientific cosmology allows Christians to care for the integrity of Nature precisely because of their hope for the word's future fulfillment. To support this notion, let us start with the empirically-demonstrable scientific claim that the universe is still in process and that it has hosted a series of increasingly complex emergent developments throughout its long history, including the awakening to life and mind. This universe may at present still be open to surprising new developments in the future as well. Our new sense of an unfinished universe, therefore, offers contemporary, scientifically educated Christians the opportunity to connect ecological concern more intimately than ever to the basic biblical themes of promise and hope. In principle our unfinished, still-emerging universe allows an opening to future creative outcomes that have been inconceivable to the cosmic pessimists and otherworldly optimists of pre-scientific and early modern thought. Furthermore, the new picture of an unfinished universe allows Christian ecological theology to pull together into a fertile new synthesis the most important contributions of both the traditional and sacramental perspectives summarized above.

As I have noted, however, ecological ethicists are sometimes critical of any hope for future fulfillment since they believe, wrongly in my opinion, that hope leads people to lose interest in the present age and its problems. No doubt some interpretations of biblical expectation, when taken in isolation from the incarnational aspect of Christian faith, seem at least initially to be so disposed, ecologically speaking. Apocalyptic writings, when interpreted independently of other forms of anticipation represented in the Bible, and when we fail to consider the political and social context of their literary genesis, seem to expect a final cosmic catastrophe: "The heavens will pass away with a mighty roar and the elements will be dissolved by fire" (2 Peter, 3: 10). In interpreting such formulations, contemporary Christian theology must attempt to show that biblical faith's looking toward a new Creation and our longing for the "coming of God" are not impediments to Christian ecological concern, but its very heart. In the Mass Roman Catholics express a hope "to enjoy forever" the vision of God's glory, but theology needs to make it clear that this liturgical sentiment is compatible with the fundamental Christian imperative to make Earth ready for the coming of God.

At first sight, making this connection may seem a little strained. An early Christian prayer was "Maranatha: come Lord Jesus (Rev. 22: 12)." So how can this foundational Christian petition motivate followers of Jesus here and now to nurture Earth's life-systems rather than preside over their destruction? In responding to these questions Christians need to be reminded that, in a biblical perspective, Nature is as much promise as it is sacrament. The good and beautiful things in Nature are not mere analogies of an eternal present—not merely vertical participations in a timelessness beyond all becoming—but promises or *anticipations* of what is yet to come. And what is a promise if not something that opens up the future? We are grateful to promises because they give us a future. We do not seize a promise as though it were an end in itself, but we cherish it and hold on to it because it is pregnant with a still unrealized future that allows space and time for hope.

Consequently, if gratitude is the fundamental virtue for a sacramental ecology, then hope is the fundamental virtue for a promissory ecological vision. The point is, if we lose touch with the promissory aspect of Nature—that is, if we instrumentalize Nature or excessively sacramentalize it—we may fall into the disastrous idolatry that tries to make Earth itself the final fulfillment of our native longing for the infinite. This is why a pure naturalism, the dogma that Nature is all there is, is an unsatisfactory, and possibly even disastrous, metaphysical setting for ecological ethics in the long run. It provides no good reason why, in the absence of God, we should not divinize Nature. On the other hand, if we are permitted to interpret Nature as a promise open to future creative surprises, we are enjoined to respect it here and now with a degree of disciplined reserve that leaves it open to the arrival of "fuller being" in the future. In this sense expectation and hope deliver us of any obligation to worship Nature as though it were already completed. We do not realistically expect perfection from the beautiful things that presently carry a promise. We may expect perfection from the final *fulfillment* of a promise, but not from the promise itself. Holding a promise close to our hearts, in other words, does not mean that we suffocate it in the limitlessness of our desiring, but that we allow it to turn our attention and affection toward a flowering yet to come.

I believe the greatest "gift of the Jews" to human wisdom on Earth is the bold belief that the whole of finite being is enfolded in, and enlivened by, a gracious promise that opens up the future. Christianity was made possible only because it was prepared for by the ancient Hebraic sense of the futurity of being, a quality that allows time to be irreversible and every single event to be unrepeatable. Instead of settling either for the timeless absolute of Platonic philosophy or the essentially lifeless cosmos of materialist pessimism, an anticipatory Christian vision looks for "more being" and a richer life ahead (Teilhard, 1964). Christian faith, above all, refuses to reconcile itself to any ideology that insists on the eventual sinking of all things toward the bottomless abyss of non-being. And instead of resting quiescently in a sacramentalist or analogical theology that connects the finite world to an eternal now, a promissory theological vision liberates Creation from the burden of having to be presently the final and ultimate satisfaction of our own needs and desires.

To sum up, Christian hope allows Nature to be anticipatory rather than exclusively sacramental. Yet, at the same time, it allows us to greet Nature with reverence because of what it makes provisionally present—the Coming of God. Again, a promissory vision reinterprets faithful stewardship as caring for the world in such a way that it remains open to emergent new being ahead. Caring for what Nature has already become is necessary too, of course, and it seems religiously right to celebrate the long drama of evolutionary creativity that has left us with such an ecologically rich environment as Earth. But an eschatologically enriched theology invites us to care for the natural world because it is pregnant with the promise of incalculable future outcomes that far outreach our own narrow predictions and deepest desires. An anticipatory theological vision does not give us a clear vision of the cosmic future, but it does inspire confidence that Creation contains in seedling form the promise of indeterminate future outcomes and new chapters of creativity. Such a world is well deserving of our persistent love and care.

References

Barbour, Ian G. (Ed.). 1972. *Earth Might Be Fair: Reflections on Ethics, Religion, and Ecology*. Englewood Cliffs, NJ: Prentice-Hall.

Berry, Thomas. 1988. *The Dream of the Earth*. San Francisco, CA: Sierra Club Books.

Birch, Charles, Eakin, William, & McDaniel, Jay B. (Eds.). 1990. *Liberating Life: Contemporary Approaches to Ecological Theology*. Maryknoll, NY: Orbis Books.

Christiansen, Drew & Walter Grazer (Eds.). 1996. *"And God Saw That It Was Good": Catholic Theology and the Environment*. Washington, DC: United States Catholic Conference.

Commoner, Barry. 1961. In Defense of Biology. *Science*, 133, 1745–8.

Edwards, Denis. 1995. *Jesus the Wisdom of God: An Ecological Theology*. Maryknoll, NY: Orbis Books.

Gibler, Linda. 2010. *From the Beginning to Baptism: Scientific and Sacred Stories of Water, Oil, and Fire*. Collegeville, PA: Liturgical Press.

Haught, John F. 1993. *The Promise of Nature*. New York: Paulist Press.

Haught, John F. 2015. *Resting on the Future: Catholic Theology for an Unfinished Universe*. New York: Bloomsbury.

Himes, Michael J. & Kenneth, R. 1990. The Sacrament of Creation. *Commonwealth*, 117 (January), 42–49.

John Paul II. 1990. Peace with God the Creator—Peace with All of Creation. World Day of Peace Message, January 1. *Origins, CNS Documentary Service* 19 (December, 14), 465–468.

McDonagh, Sean. 1990. *The Greening of the Church*. New York: Orbis Books.

McFague, Sallie. 1987. *Models of God: Theology for an Ecological, Nuclear Age*. Philadelphia, PA: Fortress.

McFague, Sallie. 1993. *The Body of God: An Ecological Theology*. Minneapolis, MN: Fortress Press.

Merchant, Carolyn. 1980. *The Death of Nature: Woman, Ecology, and the Scientific Revolution*. San Francisco, CA: Harper & Row.

Moltmann, Jürgen. 1965. *Theology of Hope: On the Ground and the Implications of a Christian Eschatology*. Transl. James W. Leitch. New York: Harper & Row.

Monod, Jacques. 1972. *Chance and Necessity: An Essay on the Natural Philosophy of Modern Biology*. Transl. Austryn Wainhouse. New York: Vintage Books.

Nash, James. 1991. *Loving Nature*. Nashville, TN: Abingdon Press.

Niebuhr, H. Richard. 1960. *Radical Monotheism and Western Culture*. Louisville, KY: Westminster/John Knox Press.

Northwest US/Southwest Canada Catholic Bishops Pastoral Letter. 2001. The Columbia River Watershed: Caring for Creation and the Common Good.

Passmore, John. 1974. *Man's Responsibility for Nature*. New York: Scribner.

Ruether, Rosemary Radford (Ed.). 2000. *Christianity and Ecology: Seeking the Well-Being of Earth and Humans*. Cambridge, MA: Harvard University Press.

Ruether, Rosemary Radford. 2007. Ecofeminist Philosophy, Theology and Ethics (77–93). In Laurel Kearns & Catherine Keller (Eds.), *Ecospirit: Religions and Philosophies for the Earth*. New York: Fordham University Press.

Santmire, Paul. 1985. *The Travail of Nature*. Philadelphia, PA: Fortress Press.

Smith, Samantha. 1993. *Goddess Earth: Exposing the Pagan Agenda of the Environmental Movement*. Lafayette, LA: Vital Issues Press.

Teilhard de Chardin, Pierre. 1964. *The Future of Man*. Transl. Norman Denny. New York: Harper & Row.

White, Lynn, Jr. 1967. The Historical Roots of Our Ecologic Crisis. *Science*, 155, 3767 (March 10), 1203–1207.

US Conference of Catholic Bishops, Renewing the Earth (1991). Drew Christiansen, S. J. & Walter Grazer (Eds.),"*And God Saw That It Was Good*" (Washington, DC: United States Catholic Conference, 1996).

Zizioulas, John.1990. Preserving God's Creation: Three Lectures on Theology and Ecology. Parts 1–3. *King's Theological Review*, 12, 1 (Spring), 1–5; 12, 2 (Autumn 1989), 41–45; 13, 1 (Spring), 1–5.

CHAPTER 11

Exploring Environmental Ethics in Islam

Insights from the Qur'an and the Practice of Prophet Muhammad

Fazlun M. Khalid

A Disrupted Tradition—Some Uncomfortable Thoughts

Faith traditions have customarily been responsible for protecting the natural world. This was not a conscious matter, as faith-based environmentalism did not appear as a special subject; rather, it was interwoven into the texts and practices which we have come to describe as holistic. The advent and advance of secular education ensured the demise of the holistic approach as faith and tradition were relegated as simply matters for individual conscience. At the same time, individuals and society were progressively drawn into a type of education almost exclusively focusing on economic advancement which viewed the natural world not as an entity to be cherished, but as a resource to be exploited.

This is a very recent event in human development. The transition from hunter-gatherer to a lifestyle we describe as sedentary is said to have begun over 14,000 years ago. There is no denying humanity's aggressive tendencies, but through highs and lows, progress and decline, war and peace, our species did manage to get as far as about the seventeenth century when, environmentally speaking, we were in reasonable shape. There was, however, an intellectual buzz in sixteenth-century Europe, known as the Enlightenment. As it matured over the following two centuries it brought about a "radical shift in psychological alliance from the divine to humankind" (Tarnas, 1996, 275–281). Cartesian dualism, Newton's clockwork universe, and Adam Smith's economics were some of the major influences that drove a wedge between humankind and Nature. Having intellectually established their position of dominance, humans never ceased to seduce Mother Nature in the name of progress and prosperity.

The post-Cartesian world has managed to destroy in just 300 years or so what our ancestors preserved for millennia. We are now witnessing a panic over climate change.

The Wiley Blackwell Companion to Religion and Ecology, First Edition. Edited by John Hart.

While this issue clearly needs to be addressed, other equally important issues are being pushed down our list of priorities, if not ignored altogether. Climate change is but one lethal cause among many that will continue to degrade the planet, the tip of the iceberg (if this metaphor is not inappropriate). But what lies submerged—as the push for economic growth takes precedence over all other human affairs—is continuing species extinction, biodiversity destruction, deforestation, air, land, and sea pollution, population disruption, and, indeed, population growth.

Faith communities have been overtaken by events which they themselves have been culpable of creating by acts of omission if not commission. As they wake up to their responsibilities they face up to the monumental but necessary task of changing the behavior of their adherents from consumerism to conservationism. This is a daunting task, but it must be done.

There is no gainsaying the fact that faith communities have much to offer in this field of human endeavor; Islam is no exception to this. But, there has been a shift in emphasis. The textual tradition in Islam is deep and profound, but current Muslim practice is shallow as priority is now given to economic drivers. What follows is an exploration of the Islamic teaching on the relationship between *Homo sapiens* and the natural world.

Earth—A Sacred Site

Fitrah—The Natural State

Open the Qur'an[1] almost anywhere and there is some kind of reference to the natural world. Its approach is holistic and it deals with Nature on the basis that the human is integral to it. However, we have taken this for granted and have created such a rupture between ourselves and the natural world that we treat it as the "other." We have become observers of the life-experience we are integral to and have formed an imaginary subject/object dichotomy between ourselves and the natural world. This gap is more acute than ever and we almost invariably see Nature as a resource to be exploited. We once took from it for our survival, but now we take from it for our aggrandizement. Paradoxically, the gap widens as we come to know and understand more about natural phenomena, from subatomic particles to the distant galaxies.

The term *fitrah* in the Qur'an describes an original natural state in which humankind was brought into being. Some translators describe this as the natural pattern, others the original state or pattern, and yet others simply as Nature. Some scholars describe *fitrah* as the pure state or the state of infinite goodness and point to the possibility that everything in Creation has the potential for goodness, the conscious expression of which rests uniquely with humankind. We often say that children are born in a state of *fitrah*, unspoilt and pure.[2] It is commonly held that the real meaning of the Qur'an in Arabic cannot be translated into any other language, but we may conclude that *fitrah* denotes the original and natural state of purity, which applies to all of Creation, including the human in its newborn state. The term *fitrah* is derived from the Arabic root F T R and is found once in the Qur'an and in its verb form, *fatarah*, 14 times.

The key verse in the Qur'an in which both the noun and the verb form occur tells us, "Allah originated you in His original Creation. There is no changing Allah's Creation" (30: 30). Arberry translates *fitrah* here as original and *fatarah* as originated. Abdalhaqq and Aisha Bewley translate *fitrah* as natural pattern and *fatarah* as made, while Yusuf Ali's translation reads, "The nature in which Allah has made mankind"; *fitrah* is translated here as Nature and *fatarah* as made. *Fitrah* is a feminine noun which allows us to consider Nature as mother. As the translators grapple to convey the meaning of this verse, there is simplicity inherent in this message that conveys a sense of where we belong in Allah's Creation. The human race, like all other sentient beings, originated in the bosom of the Creation that Allah originated.

The verse continues, "There is no changing Allah's Creation. That is the true *Deen*[3] but most people are unaware of it." Humankind was brought into a vast universe functioning within a natural, primordial, unchanging pattern, but most people do not understand this. This is like someone with basic mechanical knowledge trying to modify a nuclear reactor, but the scale is beyond comparison. This verse, taken with the other verses on Creation, lays the foundation for the deep ecological insights of the Qur'an. An appreciation of this would lead us to address today's environmental concerns at their root.

Fatarah—Echoes of the Big Bang

In the Qur'anic narrative, "The stars and the trees all prostrate themselves [to Allah]" (55: 6). Thus, we draw the conclusion that the natural world works because it submits to the will of the Creator. "The sun and the moon both follow exact paths" (55: 5) and by submission the celestial bodies give us warmth, the seasons, the tides, and the myriad other benefits that accrue to us. Then "He [Allah] created man and taught him comprehension" (55: 3) so that man's submission would be an act of conscious worship. The Qur'an tells us that a stable, harmonious environment is the result of the natural world obeying the laws of Creation to remain in balance (*mizan*). "He [Allah] created Heaven and established the balance, so that you would not tip the balance" (55: 7, 8). Everything is held together for us, but we are the only sentient beings that can, through the very gift of reasoning, choose not to submit, and destroy everything around us by our presumed ingenuity. "He created man from a drop of sperm and yet he became an open challenger" (16: 4). This geological epoch is now coming to be known as the Anthropocene—the human species has become a force of Nature.

We understand from this that as the Earth's systems work and remain in balance they are in submission (in Islam) to the will of the Creator. As the only intelligent beings who can give meaning to this, humans need to be reminded of their responsibilities. The Qur'an says, "He is the Lord of the heavens and the Earth and everything between them, so worship Him and persevere in His worship." The word the Qur'an uses for worship is '*ibadah* and this has a wide meaning in that it does not confine itself to ritual. In its narrowest sense it means the five daily ritual prayers and in its widest it means being always conscious of one's responsibilities to the rest of Creation. Thus, caring for the environment and protecting it from abuse is integral to worship.

The five daily prayers, which are offered in the direction of Mecca, are reminders. They have a cyclical pattern, and each cycle is performed standing, bowing, prostrating, or sitting. The dawn prayer contains two cycles, the noon prayer four, the afternoon prayer four, the dusk prayer three, and the night prayer four. Each prayer starts while standing. The following verse from the Qur'an is recited at the beginning of the standing position in the first cycle, "I have turned my face to Him who originated the heavens and the Earth, a pure natural believer" (6: 79).

In the translation of "originated" we again encounter the term *fatarah*; as discussed earlier, it emerges from the root F T R from which the following terms are also derived (Kassis, 1983, 451):

- *Futur*—a rent, fissure, flaw: "return thy gaze; seest thou any fissure? (67: 3)
- *Tafattara*—to be rent asunder: "the heavens well nigh are rent above them" (42: 5)
- *Infatara*—to split open, be cleaved asunder: "when heaven is split open" (82: 1)

The Qur'an tells us that Creation occurs by splitting, like the seed that splits to produce plant life and like the sperm that splits the egg to produce a sentient life-form. When the Qur'an says that Allah "originated the heavens and the Earth" could it be telling us that the universe came into existence when the heavens were rent asunder? The Big Bang perhaps? This is a matter to ponder.

The Signs

The term in the Qur'an used to describe the verses it contains is *āyah* (plural *āyāt*). It means signs. The term is also applied to everything in the natural world, as in "There are signs on the Earth for people who are certain" (51: 20). There are also signs of the Creator in the self, "and in yourself as well. Do you not then see?" (51: 21). This allows us to say that abuse of the natural world and one's self is hardly worse than abusing the Qur'an itself. As Nasr (1968, 94, 95) observes:

> In Islam the inseparable link between man and nature, and also between the sciences of nature and religion, is to be found in the Qur'an itself... As such it is both the source of the revelation which is the basis of religion and that macrocosmic revelation which is the universe. It is both the recorded Qur'an ... and the Qur'an of Creation ... which contains the "ideas" or archetypes of all things. That is why the term used to signify the verses of the Qur'an or *āyah* also means events occurring within the souls of men and phenomena in the world of nature.

These verses indicate the integration of the soul with the cosmos. In times gone by when human beings did not differentiate between the self and the natural world nature was integrated into the human psyche. There was no separate environmentalism. Having once been unconscious environmentalists we now need to become conscious of the fact that we are deeply and irrevocably interwoven into the fabric of the natural world, that we are causing it grievous bodily harm and that we have to contend with the consequences of our actions. We need to relearn what the sources, the Qur'an and the Sunna of the Prophet, tell us about Creation, the Creator's expectation of us and the responsibilities we have to shoulder. There is a way out of this dilemma and our approach involves two layers. The first is a layer we will call Knowledge of Creation (*Ilm ul Khalq*) and the second the Rules Governing Islamic Environmentalism (*Fiqh al Bi'ah*) which can alternatively be referred to as Islamic Natural Resources Management.

The Qur'an describes the creational process in many ways and the first revelation[4] came in the words of Archangel Gabriel to Prophet Muhammed, "Read: In the name of your Lord who created; Created man from clots of blood" (96:1, 2). In recounting this Özdemir (2003, 7) reminds us that the Prophet responded by saying he did not know how to read; tradition has it that he was illiterate. That there was no text to read but this, as Özdemir observes, signifies a different way of looking at the world. "The key notion is that this reading should be in the name of our Sustainer" who gives existence and meaning to everything. The reading is from texts found in the natural world. All life emerges from the Creator and all natural phenomena are to be read as if they were from the book of the Creator. The revealed Qur'an signposts the ontological Qur'an thus:

The cosmos: "It is He who appointed the sun to give radiance; and the moon to give light, assigning it in phases; in the alteration of night and day and what Allah has created in the heavens and earth there are signs for people who have awareness" (10: 7, 7).

Domestic animals: "And He created livestock. There is warmth for you in them, and various uses and some you eat" (16: 5).

Animals created out of water: "Allah created every animal from water, some of them go on their bellies, some of them on two legs and some on four. Allah creates whatever He wills" (24: 45).

Every living thing is part of a community: "There is no creature crawling on the Earth, or flying creature, flying on its wings, that are not communities like yourself" (6: 38).

Water: "And we send down water from the sky and make every generous species grow in it" (31: 10).

Plants and crops: "It is He who produces gardens, both cultivated and wild, and palm-trees and crops of diverse kind" (6: 141).

The Qur'an also reminds us:

Allah sends down water from the sky
And by it brings the dead earth back to life.
There is certainly a *sign in that for people who hear.*

There is instruction for you in cattle.
From the contents of their bellies,
From between dung and blood,
We give you pure milk to drink,
Easy for drinkers to swallow.

And from the fruit of the date palm and the grapevine
You derive both intoxicants and wholesome provision.
There is certainly a *sign in that for people who use their intellect.*

Your Lord revealed to the bees:
"Build dwellings in the mountains and the trees,
And also in the structures which men erect."

Then eat from every kind of fruit
And travel the paths of your Lord,
Which have been made easy for you to follow.

From inside them comes a drink of varying colors,
Containing healing for mankind.
There is certainly a *sign in that for people who reflect.*
(16: 65–69)

The Doctrine of Divine Unity

Tawhid

Tawhid is the doctrine of divine unity. It is the foundation of Islam and the first of the five articles of faith to which all Muslims subscribe. Understanding the primary aspect of *Tawhid* leads us to recognize that the Creator is One and His Creation is a unified whole. It is the essence of Islam and the first expression on the tongue of every Muslim and a constant reminder of faith. This expression *shahada* is in two parts. The first is *La ilaha illal lah* (there is no God but God),[5] which is an affirmation of the unity of the Creator from which everything else flows; and the second, *Muhammadur Rasulullah* (Muhammad is the Prophet of Allah) whose example we follow.

Tawhid has three dimensions:

1. *Tawhid ar Rububiyyah*—belief in Allah the one and only Creator
2. *Tawhid al Asma was Sifat*—belief that the names and attributes of Allah are uniquely His alone
3. *Tawhid al Ibadah* —belief that only Allah merits worship

We have dealt with the third dimension, *Tawhid al Ibadah*, in the previous section under *Fatara*; we now turn to the first and second dimensions.

Tawhid ar Rububiyyah

The chapter *al-Ikhlas* (Sincerity) in the Qur'an lays down the basis for understanding *Tawhid ar Rububiyyah*:

Say: *He is Allah, the One.*
Allah the Eternal.
He neither begets nor is He begotten.
And no one is comparable to Him.
(112: 1–4)

This is the bedrock of Islamic monotheism and is the heart of the Qur'anic message. As Nasr (1985, 311) observes:

> At the heart of the Qur'anic message lies the full and plenary doctrine of God as both transcendent and immanent, as both majesty and beauty, as both the One and the Source of the manifold, as both the Origin of Mercy and the Judge of all human actions, as the Originator and Sustainer of the cosmos and the goal to which all beings journey, as the supra personal Essence beyond all Creation, and as the personal Deity Whose Will rules over all things, Whose love for knowledge of Himself is the cause of Creation, and Whose Mercy is the very substance of which the threads of His Creation are woven.

There is in Islamic theology a line of thought that attempts to describe the nature of God. The term *tanzih* is used to describe God's otherness and distance from the human and *tashbih* to describe similarities and proximity. The first is akin to transcendence and the second to immanence.

> The perspective of *tanzih* affirms God's oneness by declaring that God is one and God alone is Real. Hence everything other than God is unreal and not worthy of consideration. God's single reality excludes all reality. In contrast, the perspective of *tashbih* declares that God's oneness is such that his one reality embraces all creatures. The world, which appears as unreality and illusion, is in fact nothing but the One real showing his signs. Rather than excluding all things, God's unity includes them. (Murata & Chittick, 1996, 70–74)

God is incomparable, transcendent (*tanzih*), and capable of being compared, immanent (*tashbih*) with the created world. Some caution is advisable here because of fear of *shirk*. This is an absolute taboo against associating or comparing anything with Allah. It is the "unforgivable wrong action of worshipping something or someone other than Allah or associating something or someone as a partner with Him" (Bewley, 1998, 21). It is noted that without *tanzih* Nature would literally be God and without *tashbih* the signs of God could not appear in Nature (Upton, 2006, 21). The Qur'an deals with this in the following manner.

Tanzih (Transcendence)

> God has no earthly connections with the flesh: "He neither begets nor is He begotten" (112: 3).
>
> He is ever wakeful. He ensures that the world functions for us: "It is He Who originates and regenerates [Nature]. He is the ever-forgiving ever-loving" (85: 13, 14).
>
> He is incomparable: "There is nothing like Him. He is the all-hearing all-seeing" (42: 11).

Tashbih (Immanence)

> God is everywhere and He is constantly in your presence: "Both East and West belong to Allah, so wherever you turn is the face of Allah" (2: 115).
>
> He is closer to you than you think and He is aware of every secret in your soul: "We created man and we know what his soul whispers to him. We are nearer to him than his jugular vein" (50: 16).
>
> He surrounds everything: "What is in the heavens and the Earth belong to Allah. Allah encompasses all things" (4: 125).

Tawhid al Asma was Sifat

This is the second of the three dimensions that define the doctrine of divine unity; it describes the attributes of the Creator and the names by which He is known and which are uniquely His. Islamic theologians have defined seven attributes in the Qur'an (Surti, 1990, 101–108). They are:

> *Hayat* (life)—He has life. "Allah, there is no God but Him, the living, the self sustaining. He is not subject to drowsiness or sleep" (2: 255).
>
> *'Ilm* (knowledge)—"Do you not see that Allah knows all that is in the heavens and the earth?" (58: 7).
>
> *Qudrah* (power)—" [A]m I to desire other than Allah as Lord when He is the Lord of all things?" (6: 164).
>
> *Iradah* (will)—"Lord of the throne, the All-Glorious. Doer of what He will" (85: 15–16).
>
> *Sam'* (hearing)—"He is the All-Hearing, the All-Knowing" (6: 13).
>
> *Basr* (seeing)—"Vision cannot perceive Him, but He takes in all vision. He is the All-Penetrating, the All-Aware" (6: 103).
>
> *Kalam* (speech)—"He spoke directly to Moses" (4: 164).

Allah is both transcendent and immanent, "He is the first and the last, the Outward and the Inward; He has knowledge of all things" (57: 3). Prophet Muhammad is reported as having said in a *hadith*,[6] "Allah has ninety-nine names, that is, one hundred minus one. Who so ever counts them and believes in their meanings and acts accordingly will enter Paradise."[7] There are 99 terms in the Qur'an known as the *al Asma al Husna*, the most beautiful names: "To Allah belong the most beautiful names, so call on Him by them" (7: 180). These names range from the purely transcendent—*Ar Rahman* (the Compassionate), *Ar Rahim* (the Merciful), *Al Quddus* (the Divine), to names that manifest immanent qualities —*Al Wadud* (the loving), *Al Latif* (the Gentle), and *Ar Ra'uf* (the Kind).

Among the divine names revealed in the Qur'an is *al-Hayy*, the "Ever Living" or, quite simply "Life." Eaton (2006, 340) explains:

> Since the Creator lends His attributes (and names) to everything that He creates, there can be nothing in existence that does not possess a kind of life, even if we do not understand in what sense to take this. Like all other rigid distinctions which apply in this world, that between the animate and inanimate is provisional, not absolute.

The three dimensions of *Tawhid* are uniquely integrated. "Know yourself to know your Lord" is a common Muslim saying, but this knowing comes from knowing your Lord. It is a virtuous circle—the more one knows oneself, which is achieved through an understanding of the names and attributes of Allah, the more one knows Allah. Islam in its totality amounts to living in harmony with the divine reality in its essence: "Praise belongs to Allah the Lord of the worlds" (1: 2); its names: "He is Allah the Creator, the Originator, the Giver of form" (59: 24); and its attributes: "Do you not see that Allah knows all that is in the heavens and the Earth?" (58: 7).

Responses to Change

Environmental Ethics and Ecojustice

Allah "gives each thing its created form and then guides it" (20: 50); the guiding principles for life on Earth are clearly stated in the Qur'an. The basis of Islamic social action is to establish the good and prohibit the bad: "Let there be a community among you who calls for what is good, urges what is right, and forbids what is wrong; those are the ones that achieve success" (3: 104). This establishes a caring relationship with the natural world. Conservation in Islam is associated with good behavior, which is the principle by which Muslims are expected to conduct their affairs and manage their surroundings. "Eat of their fruits when they bear fruit and pay their due on the day of their harvest. And do not be wasteful. He [Allah] does not love wastefulness" (6: 141).

The human species is the primary beneficiary of the Creator's handiwork. The Qur'an tells us to "be thankful" (45: 12) as "He has subjected all that is in the heavens and the Earth for your benefit as a gift from Him" (45: 13). But Creation is not a playground as "We did not create heaven and Earth and everything between them as a game" (21: 16). There was a purpose in Creation since "We did not create the heaven and the earth and everything between them to no purpose" (38: 27). This purpose is to test believers: "He wanted to test you regarding what has come to you. So compete with each other in doing good" (5: 48).

Khalifa is the name given to someone who deputizes for or stands in for someone else (Bewley, 1998, 12). This is usually translated as steward, guardian, successor, and other similar expressions; "It is He who appointed you *khalifs* on the earth" (6: 165). The Creator "offered the trust to the heavens, the Earth and the mountains, but they refused to take it on and shrank from it. But man took it on. He is indeed wrong-doing and ignorant" (33: 72). The immensity of this trust is expressed metaphorically: the heavens and the Earth and the mountains refuse to undertake it. And yet there is a seeming paradox here. The humblest of God's Creation—"The Creation of the heavens and the earth is far greater than the Creation of mankind" (40: 57)—has been given the weightiest of all responsibilities. This can be seen as the price we pay for the gift of intelligence: "He created man and taught him understanding" (55: 3), which is the exclusive privilege of humankind, giving our species the capacity to communicate and change the environment.

'Adl (justice) is the principle by which we are required to execute this trust: "weigh with justice and skimp not in the balance. He set the Earth down for all beings. With its fruits, its palm trees with clustered sheaths" (55: 9, 10, 11). The role of *Khalifa* is a sacred duty handed down to the human species, as no other sentient being in Creation can perform this role. We are called to care for and manage the Earth in a way that conforms to God's purpose in Creation: it should be used for our benefit without causing harm to the other inhabitants of planet Earth, which are communities like ourselves (see below). The relationship we have with the natural world is not a right to do with as we please, but a responsibility that carries with it accountability. The discharge of our responsibilities should be tempered by justice and kindness with the intention always to

do good. This is *ihsan*, doing what is pleasing to Allah who is ever-present and ever-watchful; the ultimate reward is goodness itself. "Will the reward for doing good be anything other than good?" (55: 60).

What we now call Islamic environmentalism was a natural way of life when Muslims lived in a way that emulated the example of the Prophet. The Prophet is regarded as the Qur'an walking. The following verses demonstrate how he exemplified this:

On waste: "and do not be wasteful. He [Allah] does not love the wasteful" (6: 141).

The Prophet discouraged any wasteful action among his companions, as this *hadith*[8] affirms:

> When the messenger of Allah passed by Sa'd as he was performing his ablutions he said, "What it is this extravagance?" Sa'd asked, "Can there be any extravagance even in ablution?" The messenger of Allah replied, "Yes, even if you are on the bank of a flowing river."

The Qur'an emphasizes the value of trees and other vegetation, "the stars and the trees all prostrate [to Allah]" (55: 6). The lesson that is driven home by the Prophet regarding this is contained in the following *hadith*:[9]

> Those amongst you who plant a tree or sows seeds that ultimately benefit a bird, or a person or an animal, is regarded as having contributed a charitable gift.

On the treatment of animals:

> There is no creature crawling on the Earth or those that fly, that are not communities like yourself. (6: 38)

The following *hadith* narrates an incident that took place near a well:[10]

> A thirsty man went down a well to quench his thirst. On his return to the surface he saw a dog licking mud to quench its thirst. The man felt sorry for the dog and returned to the well and came back up again with some water for the dog in his shoes. The companions asked the Prophet about the merits of this action and if there was recompense for serving the dog. The Prophet replied that there was a reward in serving all living beings.

These examples demonstrate the depth of the material in the texts and remind us how much has been lost. The task now is not just to re-examine the material, but to present it in a way that can be readily understood, absorbed, and applied. This work has been pioneered by the UK-based Islamic Foundation for Ecology and Environmental Science (IFEES/EcoIslam),[11] which has designed a teaching template, *Ilm ul Khalq* (Knowledge of Creation), based on four themes or principles:

1. *Tawhid*—the principle of divine unity
2. *Fitrah*—the principle of primordiality
3. *Mizan*—the principle of balance in Nature
4. *Khalifa*—the principle of human responsibility

In addition to providing literature on this model IFEES/EcoIslam has pioneered workshops worldwide,[12] the results of one of which we examine next.

Misali—The Sacred Island

The people of Zanzibar are almost all Muslim and it is part of the United Republic of Tanzania. It is composed of two main islands, Unguja and Pemba. The latter, famous for its cloves, is the smaller of the two and lies north of Unguja. The Misali Island Marine Conservation Area (MIMCA), which was the location of our project, lies off the west coast of Pemba and is flanked by mainland Africa. MIMCA is 8.5 square miles in area and has at its center a small, uninhabited island of coral rag (rubble) known as Misali. This island is forested and is surrounded by some of the finest coral slopes in the entire Indian Ocean. It is also a turtle nesting ground.

Local people claim that Misali derives its name from a corruption of the word *masalla*, which means prayer mat. Tradition has it that in times past a Muslim holy man lived on this island and treated the island like his mosque. It is now a base for fishermen who work there. Apart from its practical uses, they treat it with reverence in memory of the mystic who once dwelt on the island. This would partly explain why the fishing community supported by local people resisted efforts by a hotel chain to turn the island into a tourist resort.

Fishing in this conservation zone provided direct livelihood support to an estimated 11,500 people on the island of Pemba, scattered over 36 villages. The problems these people experienced were the classic ones familiar to traditional communities worldwide. They are an expanding population with rising expectations, few employment opportunities, dwindling resources, and threats from industrial development, in this case tourism.

Additionally, this area of the Indian Ocean is subject to the scourge of overfishing by fleets of international trawlers equipped with the latest fishing technology; they have caused drastic depletion of fish stocks. This in turn has forced local fishermen to dynamite the coral reefs which act as spawning grounds for the fish that once provided them with the protein they needed. Given a choice between alleviating hunger and long-term conservation, dynamite appeared to be the option that resolved their immediate problems. This was the last desperate measure for some fishermen in the struggle to maintain the number of their ever-dwindling catches.

It was becoming apparent that many years of trying conventional conservation practices was not having the desired effect. As the situation appeared to be deteriorating the Islamic Foundation for Ecology and Environmental Sciences (IFEES)/EcoIslam was invited by CARE International, an American-based non-governmental organization (NGO), to develop an Islam-oriented environmental education program for the fishing communities, religious leaders, and government officials, and to canvass the support of local institutions to enhance the management and protection of MIMCA. This part of the project was funded by the US-based MacArthur Foundation. It was seen as supporting a community-run (Janet Chernala, 2002, 31–34) protected area initiative to reduce illegal fishing practices, promote awareness among the fishing communities, and emphasize the importance of sustainable practices in the designated conservation zone. This project was also supported by the World Wide Fund for Nature International (WWF) and the UK-based Alliance of Religions and Conservation (ARC).[13]

IFEES/EcoIslam's training program lasted 13 months from November 1999 to January 2001. The resource used for the introductory workshop in 1999 was a pack of

24 photographic slides, accompanied by an instruction manual, the *Qur'an, Creation and Conservation* (Khalid, 1999).[14] Workshop participants included fishermen, local government officials, madrasa (Qur'an school) teachers, senior government officials from the Ministry of Agriculture, Livestock and Natural Resources, and senior members of the Mufti's Office. These workshops were a great success and representatives of the international NGOs who participated in them were of the view that the use of the Qur'an as a teaching resource sensitized stakeholders to conservation issues overnight compared with the poor results achieved in previous years using established conservation approaches. The fishermen stopped dynamiting the coral reefs almost immediately.

The initiative was known as the Misali Islamic Environmental Ethics Project. Its objectives were to:

- Explore Islamic environmental stewardship principles
- Sensitize marine resource users to the Islamic conservation ethic
- Implement these teachings within the parameters of an integrated conservation and development project bearing in mind sustainability issues

In one of the brainstorming sessions toward the end of the workshop the participants identified responsibility, moderation, conservation, stewardship, trusteeship, and kindness as the core messages inherent in the material they were working with. The participants also identified a wide variety of choices regarding the methods of dissemination and the groups and institutions that should be targeted. They ranged from Friday sermons for adults to lessons in the madrasas for children. Other methods proposed were a poster campaign, local radio, and street theater. There were also requests for an instruction manual (Khalid & Thani, 2008) which could be used by imams as a basis for sermons, by teachers in both mainstream and madrasa, and by community leaders for their own edification.

This is probably the first time that a body of knowledge from the Qur'an on Creation, which we refer to as *Ilm ul Khalq* (see under Signs in Sacred Earth, above) and developed by IFEES/EcoIslam was used to positive effect anywhere.

A second tier was essential and that was an implementation framework, alongside that of the technical parameters, to enable this initiative to succeed. This is the emerging body of law within the *Sharī'ah*,[15] now being referred to as *Fiqh al Bi'ah* (see under Signs in Sacred Earth, above) which was used to complete the project. It was proposed that MIMCA be designated a *hima* in accordance with the conservation and sustainability principles embodied in the matrix of *Sharī'ah* law.

The *hima* is a flexible conservation management system that enables the establishment of land and marine conservation zones in designated areas. *Hima* means a place that is guarded or one that is forbidden to enter. In practice a *hima* could broadly be defined as a reserve or a conservation zone. It is pre-Islamic in origin, dating to when powerful tribal leaders reserved pasture and grazing land for their exclusive use and allowed only limited access to others. The Prophet abolished these practices when he established the first *hima* in Islam: "There are no reserves except for Allah and His messenger" (Dien, 2000); in other words, *himas* were for the people.

The initiative in Zanzibar was a pioneering project in the sense that it is possibly the first time that Islamic environmental themes were used by a community to protect their resources by changing what they did.[16] While it brought to the surface recognition of the wide gap that has opened up between behavior and knowledge of the texts, it also demonstrated the speed and effectiveness with which they could be taught to good effect in real situations. But this story is not over yet, as Misali Island is now part of the Pemba Channel Conservation Area (PECCA), a major regional project supported by the World Bank. Whether the fisherman of Misali will be allowed to continue with their newfound faith in Islamic environmental ethics is a question we have all been asking.

Some Concluding Thoughts

Muslims now live like the rest of the human race, willingly or unwillingly, in a hegemonic, secular-driven regime. The challenge facing Muslims is how to implement the teachings and practices of their worldview within an institutional framework that has a fundamentally opposing outlook. This is not a rejection of materialism; Islam is not anti-materialist, "It is He who created everything on this earth for you" (2: 29). But we have breached the limits that restrained us from overindulgence: "Do not overstep the limits, Allah does not love people who overstep the limits" (5: 87). The Qur'an and the practice of the Prophet provide us one vital boundary that has been defined for us thus: "Those who practice usury will not rise from the grave except as someone driven mad by Satan's touch" (2: 274).

The Qur'an prohibits usury/interest, which would make it impossible for the fractional reserve banking system to control our lives as it does today. We are all in thrall to the banks, and "There is something quite magical about the way money is created. No other commodity works quite the same way. The money supply grows through use; it expands through debt. The more we lend, the more we have. The more debt there is, the more there is" (Kurtzman, 1993). This discussion is for another time and another place. Suffice it to say here that the evidence for this is unfolding in front of us as a result of the recent global banking crisis. Our analysis leads us to the inevitable conclusion that the looming global environmental collapse is a direct result of the system of financial intermediation which supports our global civilization. The Qur'an teaches that we can—and must—do otherwise in our financial structures for our communities and for the well-being of our environment, Allah's Creation, for which we are responsible.

Notes

1 Qur'an is the phonetic spelling of Islam's holy book which is used rather than the anglicized Koran in this chapter. It is generally accepted that the essence of the Arabic Qur'an cannot be translated into any other language. To assist us with its nuances we have had recourse to the following translations: Abdullah Yusuf Ali, *The Holy Qur'an*. A standard work first published in1934, available in numerous imprints; A. J. Arberry, *The Koran Interpreted*. London: George Allen & Unwin, 1955. Recognized for its rhythm and consistency; Muhammad Asad, *The*

Message of the Qur'an. Gibraltar: Dar Al-Andalus, 1980. Gives access to wider sources; A. & A. Bewley, *The Noble Qur'an*. Norwich: Bookwork, 1999. A modern translation, very readable, but watch out for the slight modifications in the numbering system; M. A. S. Abdul Halim, *The Qur'an*. London: Oxford University Press, 2004. Another modern translation; Mohammed Marmaduke Pickthall. *The Meaning of the Glorious Qur'an*. Hyderabad: Government Central Press, 1938. Another classical translation on a par with Yusuf Ali's. The numbering system in Yusuf Ali's translation is used when quoting references to the Qur'an. The chapter and verse numbers are given in parenthesis. The names of the chapters have been left out as there are minor variations from one translation to another.

2 For an exposition of *fitra* from the perspective of human nature, see Mohamed Yasien. 1996. *Fitrah: The Islamic Concept of Nature*. London: Ta Ha.

3 The word used in the Qur'an for religion is *deen*, which describes an integrated code of conduct which deals with personal hygiene at one end of the spectrum and our relationships with the natural world at the other. It provides a holistic approach to existence; it does not differentiate between the sacred and the secular; nor does it make a distinction between the human world and the world of Nature.

4 Arberry observes, "These revelations were supernaturally received, in circumstances of a trance like nature, over a considerable number of years intermittently." See Arberry (1964).

5 The terms God and Allah are used interchangeably.

6 Report of a saying, teaching, or action performed by Prophet Muhammad. There are six collections of *hadith* literature recognized by Islamic scholars.

7 Sahih Bukhari 52, 910. See http://ahadith.co.uk/searchresults.php?page=1&q=99+names&rows=10. Accessed May 2016.

8 Sunan Ibn Majah, 2, 425. See http://ahadith.co.uk/searchresults.php?pto%252520at%252520aage=3&q=wudu+river&rows=10" http://ahadith.co.uk/searchresults.php?pto at aage=3&q=wudu+river&rows=10, accessed May 2016.

9 Sahih Bukhari 40, 518. See http://ahadith.co.uk/searchresults.php?page=3&q=trees&rows=10. Accessed May 2016.

10 Sahih Bukhari 45, 656. See http://ahadith.co.uk/hadithsearchfilter.php?id=1&q=thirsty+dog+panting. Accessed May 2016.

11 See www.ifees.org.uk.

12 http://www.ifees.org.uk/trainingstory.

13 This was one of the projects that received the Sacred Gift for a Living Planet award at a WWF international gathering in Nepal, 2000.

14 Islamic Foundation for Ecology and Environmental Sciences. 1999. *Qur'an, Creation and Conservation*. http://www.ifees.org.uk/wp-content/uploads/2015/04/1380144345.pdf.

15 The basis of Islamic law and jurisprudence.

16 For a documentary made about this project, see http://video.pbs.org/video/1874606186.

References

Bewley, Aisha. 1998. *Glossary of Islamic Terms*, London: Ta Ha.

Chernela, Janet M. & others, 2002. Innovative Governance of Fisheries and Ecotourism in Community-Based Protected Areas. *Parks*, 12, 2 local communities and protected areas Cambridge and Geneva: International Conservation Union (IUCN).

Dien, M. Izzi, 2000. *The Environmental Dimensions of Islam*. Cambridge: Lutterworth.

Eaton, Gai. 2006. Remembering God. In Camille Helminski (Ed.), *The Book of Nature: A Source Book of Spiritual Perspectives on Nature and the Environment*. Bristol: The Book Foundation.

Kasis, Hanna E. 1983. *A Concordance of the Qur'an*. Berkeley, CA: University of California Press.

Khalid, Fazlun M. 1999. *Qur'an, Creation and Conservation. Islamic Foundation for Ecology and Environmental Sciences*, Birmingham: Islamic Foundation for Ecology and Environmental Sciences.

Khalid, Fazlun & Thani, Ali Kh. 2008. *Teachers' Guidebook for Islamic Environmental Education: Promoting Conservation in Misali Island, Zanzibar*. Birmingham: Islamic Foundation for Ecology and Environmental Sciences.

Kurtzman J. 1993. *The Death of Money*. Boston, MA: Little, Brown.

Murata, Sachiko & Chittick, William C. 1996. *The Vision of Islam*. London: I. B. Tauris.

Nasr, Seyyed Hossein. 1968. *Man and Nature—The Spiritual Crisis of Modern Man*. London: George Allen & Unwin.

Nasr, Seyyed Hossein. 1985. God. In Seyyed Hossein Nasr (Ed.), *Islamic Spirituality: Foundations*. London: SCM Press.

Özdemir, Ibrahim. 2003. Toward an Understanding of Environmental Ethics from a Qur'anic Perspective. In Richard Foltz, Frederick M. Denny, & Azizan Baharuddin (Eds.), *Islam and Ecology: A Bestowed Trust*. Harvard, MA: Harvard University Press.

Surti, Muhammad Ibrahim H. I. 1996. *The Qur'an and of Al-Shirk (Polytheism)*. London: Ta Ha.

Tarnas, Richard. 1996. *The Passion of the Western Mind*. London: Pimlico.

Upton, Charles. 2006. The Signs of God in Mathematics and Geometry: An Islamic Perspective. In Camille Helminski (Ed.), *The Book of Nature: A Source Book of Spiritual Perspectives on Nature and the Environment*. Bristol: The Book Foundation.

Further Reading

Ahmad, Ali. 2001. *Cosmopolitan Orientation of the Process of International Environmental Law Making: An Islamic Law Genre*. Lanham, MD: University Press of America. Makes a case for international environmental law with a particular emphasis on Islamic law.

Arberry, Arthur J. 1972. *The Koran Interpreted*. London: Oxford University Press. This version gives many readers a fresh and exciting glimpse of the original.

Bagadeer, A. A. & others (Eds.). (1994). *Environmental Protection in Islam*. IUCN Environmental Policy and Law Paper 20 (second rev. ed.). Gland, Switzerland and Cambridge. (First published 1983.)

Foltz, Richard. 2005. *Environmentalism in the Muslim World*. New York: Nova Science. An excellent introduction to environmental activism in the Muslim world.

Foltz, Richard, Denny, Frederick M., & Baharuddin, Azizan (Eds.). 2003. *Islam and Ecology: A Bestowed Trust*. Harvard, MA: Harvard University Press. A comprehensive introduction to the Islamic environmental ethic.

Khalid, Fazlun & O'Brien, Joanne (Eds.). 1992. *Islam and Ecology*. London: Cassell. An introductory work.

Sachiko, Murata & Chittick, William C. 1996. *The Vision of Islam*. London: I. B. Tauris. An excellent introduction to Islam written by two university lecturers.

Nasr, Seyyed Hossein, 1968. *Man and Nature—The Spiritual Crisis of Modern Man.* London, George Allen & Unwin.

Ibrahim Özdemir. 2008. *The Ethical Dimension of Human Attitude towards Nature —A Muslim Perspective.* Istanbul: Insan Press. An excellent introduction to understanding the ethical and philosophical roots of current environmental problems.

Suleiman, Majda K. & others (Eds.). 2012. *Towards an Implementation Strategy for the Human Integrated Management Approach Governance Systems: Theories, Concepts, Methodologies, Case Studies and Action Plans.* Kuwait: Institute for Scientific Research. http://www.kisr.edu.kw/pubs/en/conf-sem-sym/HIMAProceedings.pdf. A comprehensive, theoretical, and practical treatment of the land management system in Islam with a focus on the *hima* system.

CHAPTER 12

Science and Religion

Conflict or Concert?

Francisco J. Ayala

Aristotle (384–322 BCE) is known as one of the great philosophers of Antiquity for his works on logic, epistemology, metaphysics, ethics, rhetoric, politics, and others, but he is also the first world-class biologist and expert in natural history. In his 18th year he entered the Academy, the school of Plato (428–348/347 BCE) in Athens, where he remained until Plato's death. In 343, appointed by Philip II of Macedonia, Aristotle became the tutor until 336 of the future Alexander the Great, then 13 years old. In 345, Aristotle moved to Lesbos, where he remained until 342 and where, as D'Arcy Thompson put it, "Aristotle began the great work of charting, and understanding the world of living things" (Leroi, 2014, 32). In Lesbos, Aristotle investigated all sorts of marine and freshwater organisms, from coral reefs and molluscs to fish, as well as land animals. In his numerous zoological works, such as *The Generation of Animals*, Aristotle mentions 500 animal species, a large number relatively to the knowledge at the time (Ross, 1964, 112). He makes frequent references to natural history and describes in detail the development of the chicken embryo from egg to hatching, which he dissected, as well as other animals. None of his botanical writings has been preserved; they are known only through the writing of his follower Theophrastus, particularly a treatise on the morphology, natural history, and therapeutic use of plants (Ross, 1964). Contradicting what later would be called preformism, Aristotle asserts that the parts of the developing animal are not performed in the germ but are successively produced by epigenesis. Aristotle developed a system of classification of animals, recognizing two higher categories: animals with blood and without blood. He classified the animals with blood into five groups: mammals, birds, amphibians, reptiles, and fish, and the animals without blood into cephalopods, crustaceans, insects, and a fourth group that would include the rest. This compares favorably with Carl Linnaeus' classification 21 centuries later, who divided animals into six kinds: mammals, birds, reptiles, fish, insects, and worms. One of Aristotle's remarkable accomplishments is

The Wiley Blackwell Companion to Religion and Ecology, First Edition. Edited by John Hart.

the binomial method of nomenclature, often attributed to Linnaeus, although used in Antiquity, through the Middle Ages, and into modern times for the classification of all sorts of entities, not only animals and plants. Aristotle defines each animal with two words: its "genus" (encompassing interrelated animals or other entities) and its "difference" (the distinctive characteristics of the species or particular entity). No wonder toward the end of his life in 1882, on reading Aristotle's *The Parts of Animals*, Darwin would write: "Linnaeus and Cuvier have been my two gods, though in very different ways, but they were mere school-boys to old Aristotle" (cited in Leroi, 2014, 275).

Nevertheless, Aristotle believed in the immutability of species, not in their evolution. The world was eternal, and so any sort of change or motion would be attributed to an "unmoved mover," also of eternal existence. Among the philosophers of Ancient Greece, some traces of evolutionary thinking can be found in Anaximander (610–c. 547 BCE), who proposed that animals could be transformed from one kind into another. A trace of natural selection can be imagined in Empedocles (490–430 BCE), who speculated that animals were made up of various combinations of pre-existing parts, so that successful combinations would result in the animals we know, while unsuccessful ones would not persist.

Christian Authors

Traditional Judaism, Christianity, and Islam explain the origin of the world, and in particular the origin of living beings and their adaptations to the environment—wings, gills, hands, flowers—as the handiwork of an omniscient God. Among the early Church Fathers, a hint of evolutionary thinking can be detected in Gregory of Nazianzus (329–390) and Augustine of Hippo (353–430), who maintained that not all species of plants and animals were created as such by God; rather, some had developed in historical times from creatures created earlier by God. Their motivation was not biological but religious. Some species must have come into existence only after the Flood because it would have been impossible to hold representatives of all species in a single vessel such as the Ark.

Christian theologians of the Middle Ages did not directly explore the notion that organisms may change by natural processes, but the matter was, usually incidentally, considered as a possibility by many, including Albertus Magnus (1200–1280) and his student Thomas Aquinas (1225–1274). Aquinas concluded, after detailed discussion, that the development of living creatures like maggots and flies from non-living matter like decaying meat was not incompatible with Christian faith or philosophy. But he left it to experts to decide whether this was what actually happened.

Argument from Design

Theologians and other religious writers have over the centuries argued that the order, harmony, and design of the universe are incontrovertible evidence that the universe was created by an omniscient and omnipotent Creator. Augustine wrote in *The City of God* that the "world itself, by the perfect order of its changes and motions and by the great beauty of all things visible, proclaims ... that it has been created, and also that it could not have been made other than by a God ineffable and invisible in greatness, and ... in beauty." Thomas Aquinas advanced in his *Summa Theologiae* five ways to demonstrate, by natural reason, that God exists. The fifth way derives from the orderliness and designed purposefulness of the universe, which evince that it has been created by a Supreme Intelligence: "Some intelligent being exists by which all natural things are directed to their end; and this being we call God."

This manner of seeking a natural demonstration of God's existence later became known as the "argument from design," which is two-pronged. The first prong asserts that the universe evinces that it has been designed; the second that only God can account for the complexity and perfection of the design. A forceful and elaborate exposition of the argument from design was *The Wisdom of God Manifested in the Works of Creation* (1691) by English clergyman and naturalist John Ray (1627–1705). Ray regarded as incontrovertible evidence of God's wisdom that all components of the universe—the stars and the planets, as well as all organisms—are wisely contrived from the beginning and perfect in their operation. The "most convincing argument of the Existence of a Deity," writes Ray, "is the admirable Art and Wisdom that discovers itself in the Make of the Constitution, the Order and Disposition, the Ends and uses of all the parts and members of this stately fabric of Heaven and Earth."

The argument from design was advanced, in greater or lesser detail, by a number of authors in the seventeenth and eighteenth centuries. Ray's contemporary Henry More (1614–1687) saw evidence of God's design in the succession of day and night and of the seasons: "I say that the Phenomena of Day and Night, Winter and Summer, Springtime and Harvest ... are signs and tokens unto us that there is a God ... things are so framed that they naturally imply a Principle of Wisdom and Counsel in the Author of them. And if there be such an Author of external Nature, there is a God." Robert Hooke (1635–1703), physicist and Secretary of the Royal Society, formulated the watchmaker analogy: God had furnished each plant and animal "with all kinds of contrivances necessary for its own existence and propagation ... as a Clock-maker might make a Set of Chimes to be a part of a Clock" (Hooke, 1665, 124). The clock analogy, among others, such as temples, palaces, and ships, was also used by Thomas Burnet (1635–1703) in his *Sacred Theory of the Earth* and would become common among natural theologians of the time. Dutch philosopher and theologian Bernard Nieuwentijdt (1654–1718) developed, at length, the argument from design in his three-volume treatise *The Religious Philosopher*, where, in the Preface, he introduces the watchmaker analogy. François-Marie Arouet Voltaire (1694–1778), like other philosophers of the Enlightenment, accepted the argument from design. He asserted that in the same way that the existence of a watch proves the existence of a watchmaker, the design and purpose evident in Nature prove that the universe was created by a Supreme Intelligence.

Natural Theology

William Paley (1743–1805), one of the most influential English authors of his time, formulated in his *Natural Theology* (1802) the argument from design, based on the complex and precise design of organisms. Paley was an influential writer of works on

Christian philosophy, ethics, and theology, such as *The Principles of Moral and Political Philosophy* (1785) and *A View of the Evidences of Christianity* (1794). With *Natural Theology*, Paley sought to update Ray's *Wisdom of God* of 1691. But Paley could now carry the argument much further than Ray, by taking advantage of one century of additional biological knowledge.

Paley's keystone claim is that there "cannot be design without a designer; contrivance, without a contriver; order, without choice ... means suitable to an end, and executing their office in accomplishing that end, without the end ever having been contemplated." *Natural Theology* is a sustained argument for the existence of God based on the obvious design of humans and their organs, as well as the design of all sorts of organisms, considered by themselves and in their relations to one another and to their environment. Paley's first analogical example in *Natural Theology* is the human eye. He points out that the eye and the telescope "are made upon the same principles; both being adjusted to the laws by which the transmission and refraction of rays of light are regulated." Specifically, there is a precise resemblance between the lenses of a telescope and "the humors of the eye" in their figure, their position, and the ability to converge the rays of light at a precise distance from the lens—on the retina, in the case of the eye.

Natural Theology has chapters dedicated to the human frame, which displays a precise mechanical arrangement of bones, cartilage, and joints; to the circulation of the blood and the disposition of blood vessels; to the comparative anatomy of humans and animals; to the digestive tract, kidneys, urethra, and bladder; to the wings of birds and the fins of fish; and much more. After detailing the precise organization and exquisite functionality of each biological entity, relationship, or process, Paley arrives again and again at the same conclusion: only an omniscient and omnipotent deity could account for these marvels of mechanical perfection, purpose, and functionality, and for the enormous diversity of inventions that they entail.

The Bridgewater Treatises

Francis Henry Egerton (1756–1829), eighth Earl of Bridgewater, bequeathed in 1829 the sum of £8,000 sterling with instructions to the Royal Society that it commission eight treatises that would promote natural theology by setting forth "The Power, Wisdom and Goodness of God as manifested in the Creation." Eight treatises were published in the 1830s, several of which artfully incorporate the best science of the day and had considerable influence on the public and among scientists. *The Hand, Its Mechanisms and Vital Endowments as Evincing Design* (1833), by Sir Charles Bell, distinguished anatomist and surgeon, and famous for his neurological discoveries, examines in considerable detail the wondrously useful design of the human hand, but also the perfection of design of the forelimb used for other purposes in different animals, serving in each case the needs and habits of that species: the human's arm for handling objects, the dog's leg for running, and the bird's wing for flying. He concludes that "Nothing less than the Power, which originally created, is equal to the effecting of those changes on animals, which are to adapt them to their conditions." William Buckland, Professor of Geology at Oxford University, noted in *Geology and Mineralogy*

(1836) the world distribution of coal and mineral ores, and pointed out that they had been deposited in a remote area, yet obviously with the anticipation of serving the larger human populations that would come much later. Later, another geologist, Hugh Miller, in *The Testimony of the Rocks* (1858), would formulate what may be called the argument from beauty, which allows that it is not only the perfection of design, but also the beauty of natural structures found in rock formations, mountains, and rivers that manifests the intervention of the Creator.

Creationism and Intelligent Design

In the 1990s, a new version of the argument from design was formulated in the United States, known as Intelligent Design (ID), which refers to an unidentified Designer who accounts for the order and complexity of the universe, or who intervenes from time to time in the universe to design organisms and their parts. The complexity of organisms, it is claimed, cannot be accounted for by natural processes. According to ID proponents, this Intelligent Designer could be, but need not be, God, but an alien from outer space or some other creature, such as a "time-traveling cell biologist," with amazing powers to account for the universe's design. Explicit reference to God is avoided, so that ID "theory" could be taught in public schools as an alternative to the theory of evolution without coming into conflict with the Constitution, which bans the endorsement of any religious beliefs in public institutions. This new version of the design argument came after Darwin's theory of evolution by natural selection had provided a scientific explanation of the design of organisms. It is nothing but a caricature that denies science and parodies religion by substituting some unknown "Intelligent Designer" for God. It came also in the aftermath of so-called "creationism," which had been repudiated by the Supreme Court in 1987 as a subject that could be taught as science in public schools.

The word "creationism" has many meanings. In its broadest and traditional sense it is a religious belief, the idea that a supernatural power, God, created the universe as well as everything that exists in the universe, including humans. In a narrower sense it has come to mean the doctrine that the universe and all that is in it was created by God, essentially in its present form, a few thousand years ago. It is a doctrine largely formulated in reaction to Darwin's theory of evolution and is based on a literal interpretation of the Bible. Creationism, in this sense, denies the discoveries of astronomy concerning the origin of the universe and those of biology concerning the evolution of humans.

Opposition to the teaching of evolution in public schools can be traced in the United States to two movements with nineteenth-century roots, Seventh-Day Adventism and Pentecostalism. Consistent with their emphasis on the seventh-day Sabbath as a memorial of the biblical Creation, Seventh-Day Adventists insist on the recent creation of life. This interpretation of Genesis became the hard core of "creation science" in the late twentieth century. Many Pentecostalists, who generally endorse a literal interpretation of the Bible, have also adopted and endorsed the tenets of creationism, including the recent origin of Earth. They differ from Seventh-Day Adventists and other creationists in their tolerance of diverse views and the limited import they attribute to the evolution/creation controversy. During the 1920s, biblical fundamentalists helped to persuade more than 20 state legislatures to debate anti-evolution legislation, and four states—Arkansas, Mississippi, Oklahoma, and Tennessee—prohibited its teaching in their public schools.

In 1968, the Supreme Court declared as unconstitutional any law banning the teaching of evolution in public schools (*Epperson v. Arkansas* 393 US97, 1968). Thereafter, Christian fundamentalists introduced legislation in a number of state legislatures ordering that the teaching of "evolution science" be balanced by allocating equal time to "creation science." Creation science, it was asserted, propounds that all kinds of organisms abruptly came into existence when God created the universe, that the world is only a few thousand years old, and that the biblical Flood was an actual event survived by only one pair of each animal species. The legislatures of Arkansas in 1981 and Louisiana in 1982 passed statutes requiring the balanced treatment of evolution science and creation science in their schools, but opponents successfully challenged the statutes as violations of the constitutionally mandated separation of church and state. The Arkansas statute was declared unconstitutional in federal court in 1982 after a public trial in Little Rock. The Louisiana law was appealed all the way to the Supreme Court, and in 1987 was ruled unconstitutional on the grounds that, by advancing the religious belief that a supernatural being created humankind, it endorsed religion.

More recently, on October 28, 2004, the Dover (Pennsylvania) Area School Board of Directors adopted the following resolution: "Students will be made aware of gaps/problems in Darwin's theory and of other theories of evolution including, but not limited to, intelligent design." The constitutional validity of the resolution was challenged in the Federal District Court for the Middle District of Pennsylvania. The case was heard over several weeks, and, on December 20, 2005, Federal Judge John E. Jones III issued a 139-page decision declaring that "the Defendants' ID Policy violates the Establishment Clause of the First Amendment of the Constitution of the United States" and that the "Defendants are permanently enjoined from maintaining the ID Policy."

As mentioned earlier, in the 1990s several American authors advanced a theory of ID similar to the argument from design advanced over the centuries by Christian authors as a rational demonstration of the existence of God. The ID argument calls for an Intelligent Designer to explain the supposed irreducible complexity in organisms. An irreducibly complex system is defined by Michael Behe (1996) as an entity "composed of several well-matched, interacting parts that contribute to the basic function, wherein the removal of any one of the parts causes the system to effectively cease functioning." ID proponents have argued that irreducibly complex systems cannot be the outcome of evolution. According to Behe, "An irreducibly complex system cannot be produced directly." Therefore, he affirms, "If a biological system cannot be produced gradually it would have to arise as an integrated unit, in one fell swoop."

The argument asserts that unless all parts of the eye, for example, come simultaneously into existence, the eye cannot function; it does not benefit a precursor organism to have just a retina or a lens if the other parts are lacking. The human eye, according to this argument, could not have evolved one small step at a time, in the piecemeal manner by which natural selection works. This is, of course, the same argument advanced by Paley and other Christian authors before Darwin published the *Origin of Species* in 1859.

As evolutionists have explained again and again, with supporting evidence, organs and other components of living beings are not "irreducibly complex"; they do not come about suddenly, or in one fell swoop. They have shown that the organs and systems claimed by ID proponents to be irreducibly complex are not irreducible at all; rather, less complex versions of the same systems have existed in the past and can be found in today's organisms.

The human eye, the octopus eye, or the insect eye did not appear suddenly in their present complexity. Eyes have repeatedly evolved in different animal lineages because sunlight is a pervasive feature of the Earth's environment, to which different animals have adapted in different ways, depending on their physiology and way of life, but always starting from something very simple, even single cells with light-sensitive enzymes. Scientists have shown that the evolution of the eye has occurred by gradual advancement of the same function—seeing. The process is impelled by natural selection's favoring over time individuals that exhibit functional advantages over others of the same species.

Other instances of alleged irreducible complexity advocated as evidence for ID include the bacterial flagellum, an organ consisting of three components used by some bacteria for swimming; the blood-clotting mechanism in mammals; and the origin of the immune system. How these organs and functions have come about in evolution by natural selection has been satisfactorily explained by scientists (Ayala, 2007).

Darwin's Design

Darwin is deservedly credited as the pre-eminent author of the theory of evolution. In *The Origin of Species*, he laid out the evidence demonstrating the evolution of organisms. However, he accomplished something much more important for intellectual history than demonstrating evolution. Darwin's *Origin of Species* is, first and foremost, a sustained effort to solve the problem of how to account scientifically for the design of organisms. Darwin explains their design, complexity, diversity, and marvelous contrivances as the result of natural processes.

There is a version of the history of the ideas that sees a parallel between the Copernican and Darwinian revolutions. In this view, the Copernican revolution consisted in displacing the Earth from its previously accepted locus as the center of the universe, moving it to a subordinate place as just one more planet revolving around the Sun. In congruous manner, the Darwinian revolution is viewed as consisting of the displacement of humans from their exalted position as the center of life on Earth, with all other species created for the service of humankind. According to this version of intellectual history, Copernicus accomplished his revolution with the heliocentric theory of the solar system. Darwin's achievement emerged from his theory of organic evolution.

What this version of the two revolutions says is correct but misses what is most important, namely that they ushered in the beginning of science in the modern sense of the word. These two revolutions together may be seen as one scientific revolution in two stages, the Copernican and the Darwinian.

The Copernican revolution was launched with the publication in 1543, the year of Nicolaus Copernicus's death, of his *De revolutionibus orbium celestium* (On the Revolutions of the Celestial Spheres), and gained recognition with the publication in 1687 of Isaac Newton's *Philosophiae naturalis principia mathematica* (The Mathematical Principles of Natural Philosophy). The discoveries by Copernicus, Kepler, Galileo, Newton, and others, in the sixteenth and seventeenth centuries had gradually ushered in a conception of the universe as matter in motion governed by natural laws. It was shown that Earth is not the center of the universe, but a small planet rotating around an average-sized star; that the universe is immense in space and in time; and that the motion of the planets round the Sun can be explained by the same simple laws that account for the motion of physical objects on our planet. These and other discoveries greatly expanded human knowledge. The conceptual revolution they brought about was more fundamental yet: a commitment to the postulate that the universe obeys immanent laws that account for natural phenomena. The workings of the universe were brought into the realm of science: explanation through natural laws.

The advances of physical science brought about by the Copernican revolution had driven mankind's conception of the universe to a split personality state. Scientific explanations, derived from natural laws, dominated the world of nonliving matter, on the Earth as well as in the heavens. However, supernatural explanations, which depended on the unfathomable deeds of the Creator, were accepted as explanations of the origin and configuration of living creatures. Writers such as Paley argued that the complex design of organisms could not have come about by chance or by the mechanical laws of physics, chemistry, and astronomy, but was accomplished by an Omniscient and Omnipotent Deity, just as the complexity of a watch, designed to tell time, was accomplished by an intelligent watchmaker. It was Darwin's genius to resolve this conceptual division. He completed the Copernican Revolution by drawing out for biology the notion of Nature as a lawful system of matter in motion, which human reason can explain without recourse to supernatural agencies.

The conundrum Darwin faced can hardly be overestimated. The strength of the argument from design to demonstrate the role of the Creator had been forcefully set forth by philosophers and theologians. Wherever there is function or design, we look for its author. It was Darwin's greatest accomplishment to show that the complex organization and functionality of living beings can be explained as the result of a natural process—natural selection—without any need to resort to a Creator or other external agent. The origin and adaptations of organisms in their profusion and wondrous variations were thus brought into the realm of science.

Organisms exhibit complex design, but it is not, in current language, "irreducible complexity," emerging spontaneously in full bloom. Rather, according to Darwin's theory of natural selection, the design has arisen gradually and cumulatively, step by step, promoted by the reproductive success of individuals with incrementally more adaptive elaborations.

Natural selection accounts for the "design" of organisms, because adaptive variations tend to increase the probability of the survival and reproduction of their carriers at the expense of maladaptive, or less adaptive, variations. Paley's arguments against the improbability of chance accounts of the adaptations of organisms are well taken as far as they go. But neither Paley nor any other author before Darwin was able to discern that there is a natural process, natural selection, that is not random, but rather is oriented and able to generate order or "create." The traits that organisms acquire in their evolutionary histories are not fortuitous but are determined by their functional utility to the organisms, "designed" as it were to serve their life needs.

Evolution and the Bible

To some Christians and other people of faith, the theory of evolution seems to be incompatible with their religious beliefs because it is inconsistent with the Bible's Creation narrative. The first chapters of Genesis describe God's creation of the world, plants, animals, and human beings. A literal interpretation of Genesis seems incompatible with the gradual evolution of humans and other organisms by natural processes. Even independent of the biblical narrative, Christian beliefs in the immortality of the soul and in humans as "created in the image of God" have appeared to many as contrary to the evolutionary origin of humans from non-human animals.

In 1874, American Protestant theologian Charles Hodge published *What Is Darwinism?*, one of the most articulate assaults on evolutionary theory. Hodge perceived Darwin's theory as "the most thoroughly naturalistic that can be imagined and far more atheistic than that of his predecessor Lamarck." Echoing Paley, Hodge argued that the design of the human eye reveals that "it has been planned by the Creator, like the design of a watch evinces a watchmaker." He concluded that "the denial of design in nature is actually the denial of God."

Some Protestant theologians saw a solution to the apparent contradiction between evolution and Creation in the argument that God operates through intermediate causes. The origin and motion of the planets could be explained by the law of gravity and other natural processes without denying God's Creation and providence. Similarly, evolution could be seen as the natural process through which God brought living beings into existence and developed them according to His plan. Thus, A. H. Strong, president of Rochester Theological Seminary, New York State, wrote in his *Systematic Theology* (1885): "We grant the principle of evolution, but we regard it as only the method of divine intelligence." He explains that the brutish ancestry of human beings was not incompatible with their excelling status as creatures in the image of God. Strong drew an analogy with Christ's miraculous conversion of water into wine: "The wine in the miracle was not water because water had been used in the making of it, nor is man a brute because the brute has made some contributions to its creation." Arguments for and against Darwin's theory came from Roman Catholic theologians as well.

Gradually, well into the twentieth century, evolution by natural selection came to be accepted by the majority of Christian writers. Pius XII, in his encyclical *Humani generis* (*Of the Human Race*, 1950), acknowledges that biological evolution is compatible with the Christian faith, although he argues that God's intervention was necessary for the creation of the human soul. John Paul II, in an address to the Pontifical Academy of Sciences on October 22, 1996, deplored interpreting the Bible's texts as scientific statements rather than religious teachings. He added: "New scientific knowledge has led us to realize that the theory of evolution is no longer a mere hypothesis. It is indeed remarkable that this theory has been progressively accepted by researchers, following a series of discoveries in various fields of knowledge. The convergence, neither sought nor fabricated, of the results of work that was conducted independently is in itself a significant argument in favor of this theory."

Similar views have been expressed by other mainstream Christian denominations. The General Assembly of the United Presbyterian Church in 1982 adopted a resolution stating that "Biblical scholars and theological schools ... find that the scientific theory of evolution does not conflict with their interpretation of the origins of life found in Biblical literature." The Lutheran World Federation in 1965 affirmed that "evolution's assumptions are as much around us as the air we breathe and no more escapable. At the same time theology's affirmations are being made as responsibly as ever. In this sense both science and religion are here to stay, and ... need to remain in a healthful tension of respect toward one another."

Similar statements have been advanced by Jewish authorities and leaders of other major religions. In 1984, the 95th Annual Convention of the Central Conference of American Rabbis adopted a resolution stating: "Whereas the principles and concepts of biological evolution are basic to understanding science ... we call upon science teachers and local school authorities in all states to demand quality textbooks that are based on modern, scientific knowledge and that exclude 'scientific' creationism."

Christian denominations that hold a literal interpretation of the Bible have opposed these views. A succinct expression of this opposition is found in the Statement of Belief of the Creation Research Society, founded in 1963 as a "professional organization of trained scientists and interested laypersons who are firmly committed to scientific special creation": "The Bible is the Written Word of God, and because it is inspired throughout, all of its assertions are historically and scientifically true in the original autographs. To the student of nature this means that the account of origins in Genesis is a factual presentation of simple historical truths."

Many Bible scholars and theologians have long rejected a literal interpretation as untenable, however, because the Bible contains mutually incompatible statements. The very beginning of Genesis presents two Creation narratives. Extending through chapter 1 and the first verses of chapter 2 is the familiar six-day narrative, in which God creates human beings—both "male and female"—in his own image on the sixth day, after creating light, earth, firmament, fish, fowl, and cattle. In verse 4 of Chapter 2, a different narrative starts, in which God creates a male human, then plants a garden and creates the animals, and only then proceeds to take a rib from the man to make a woman.

Which one of the two narratives is correct and which one is in error? Neither contradicts the other if we understand the two narratives as conveying the same message, that the world was created by God and that humans are God's creatures. But both narratives cannot be "historically and scientifically true," as postulated in the Statement of Belief of the Creation Research Society.[1]

Faith and the Problem of Evil

There are numerous inconsistencies and contradictions in different parts of the Bible, for example, in the description of the return from Egypt to the Promised Land by the Chosen People of Israel, not to mention erroneous factual statements about the Sun circling the Earth and the like. Biblical scholars point out that the Bible should be held inerrant with respect to religious truth, not in matters that are of no significance to salvation. Augustine wrote in his *De Genesi ad litteram* (Literal Commentary on Genesis): "It is also frequently asked what our belief must be about the form and shape of heaven, according to Sacred Scripture... Such subjects are of no profit for those who seek beatitude ... What concern is it of mine whether heaven is like a sphere and earth is enclosed by it and suspended in the middle of the universe, or whether heaven is like a disk and the Earth is above it and hovering to one side." He adds: "In the matter of the shape of heaven, the sacred writers did not wish to teach men facts that could be of no avail for their salvation." Augustine is saying that Genesis is not an elementary book of astronomy. The Bible is concerned with religion, and it is not the purpose of its authors to settle questions about the shape of the universe that are of no relevance to how to seek salvation.

In the same vein, John Paul II said in 1981 that the Bible itself "speaks to us of the origins of the universe and its makeup, not in order to provide us with a scientific treatise but in order to state the correct relationships of man with God and with the universe. Sacred Scripture ... in order to teach this truth, it expresses itself in the terms of the cosmology in use at the time of the writer."

Christian scholars for centuries struggled with the problem of evil. Scottish philosopher David Hume (1711–1776) set out the problem succinctly and with brutal directness: "Is he [God] willing to prevent evil, but not able? Then he is impotent. Is he able, but not willing? Then, he is malevolent. Is he both able and willing? Whence then evil?" If the reasoning is valid, it would follow that God is not all-powerful or all-good. Christian theology accepts that evil exists, but denies the validity of the argument.

Traditional theology distinguishes three kinds of evil: moral evil or sin, the evil originated by human beings; pain and suffering as experienced by human beings; physical evil, such as floods, tornados, earthquakes, and the imperfections of all creatures. Theology has a ready answer for the first two. Sin is a consequence of free will; the obverse of sin is virtue, also a consequence of free will. Christian theologians have expounded that if humans are to enter into a genuinely personal relationship with their Maker, they must first experience some degree of freedom and autonomy. The eternal reward of Heaven calls for a virtuous life as many Christians see it. Christian theology also provides a good account of human pain and suffering. To the extent that pain and suffering are caused by war, injustice, and other forms of human wrongdoing, they are also a consequence of free will; people choose to inflict harm on one another. On the other side are good deeds by which people choose to alleviate human suffering.

What about earthquakes, storms, floods, droughts, and other physical catastrophes? Enter modern science into the theologian's reasoning. Physical events are built into the structure of the world itself. Since the seventeenth century, humans have known that the processes by which galaxies and stars come into existence, the planets are formed, the continents move, weather and seasons change, and floods and earthquakes occur, are natural processes, not events specifically designed by God to punish or reward humans. The extreme violence of supernova explosions and the chaotic frenzy at galactic centers are outcomes of the laws of physics, not the design of a fearsome deity. Before Darwin, theologians encountered a seemingly insurmountable difficulty. If God is the designer of life, whence the lion's cruelty, the snake's venom, and the parasites that secure their existence only by destroying their hosts? Evolution came to the rescue. John Haught (1998), a Roman Catholic theologian, has written of "Darwin's gift to theology." Protestant theologian Arthur Peacocke has referred to Darwin as the "disguised friend," by quoting the earlier theologian Aubrey Moore, who in 1891 wrote that "Darwinism appeared, and, under the guise of a foe, did the work of a friend" (Peacocke, 1998). Haught and Peacocke are acknowledging the irony that the theory of evolution, which at first had seemed to remove the need for God in the world, now has convincingly removed the need to explain the world's imperfections as failed outcomes of God's design.

One difficulty with attributing the design of organisms to the Creator is that imperfections and defects do pervade the living world. A major burden was removed from the shoulders of believers when convincing evidence was advanced that the design of organisms need not be attributed to the immediate agency of the Creator, but rather is an outcome of natural processes. If we claim that organisms and their parts have been specifically designed by God, we have to account for the incompetent design of the human jaw, the narrowness of the birth canal, and our poorly designed backbone, which is less than fittingly suited for walking upright. Imperfections and defects pervade the living world.

Consider again the human eye. The visual nerve fibers in the eye converge to form the optic nerve, which crosses the retina in order to reach the brain and thus creates a blind spot, a minor imperfection, but an imperfection of design, nevertheless; squids and octopuses do not have this defect. Did the Designer have greater love for squids than for humans and thus exhibit greater care in designing their eyes than ours? It is not only that organisms and their parts are less than perfect, but also that deficiencies and dysfunctions are pervasive, evidencing incompetent rather than intelligent design. Consider next the human jaw. We have too many teeth for the jaw's size, so that wisdom teeth need to be removed and orthodontists can make a decent living straightening the others. Would we want to blame God for this? A human engineer would have done better.

ID: Imperfect Design, not Intelligent Design

Evolution gives a good account of these imperfections. Brain size increased over time in our ancestors; the remodeling of the skull to allow for the larger brain entailed a reduction of the jaw, so that the head of the newborn would not be too big to pass through the mother's birth canal. The birth canal is much too narrow for the easy passage of the infant's head, so that thousands upon thousands of babies and many mothers die during delivery. Surely we do not want to blame God for this dysfunctional design or for stillbirths. The theory of evolution makes it understandable, a consequence of the evolutionary enlargement of our brain. Females of other primates do not experience this difficulty. Theologians in the past struggled with the issue of dysfunction because they thought it had to be attributed to God's design. Science, much to the relief of theologians, provides an explanation that convincingly attributes defects, deformities, and dysfunctions to natural causes.

Consider the following. About 20% of all recognized human pregnancies end in spontaneous miscarriage during the first two months of pregnancy. This misfortune amounts at present to more than 20 million spontaneous abortions worldwide every year. Do we want to blame God for the deficiencies in pregnancy? Many people of faith would rather attribute this mishap to the clumsy ways of the evolutionary process than to the incompetence or deviousness of an Intelligent Designer.

Evolution: Religion's Disguised Friend

Evolution makes it possible to attribute these mishaps to natural processes rather than attributing them to the direct creation or specific design of the Creator. The response of some critics is that evolution by natural selection does not discharge God's responsibility for the dysfunctions, cruelties, and sadism of the living world, because for people of faith God is the Creator of the universe and thus is accountable for its consequences, direct or indirect, immediate or mediated. If God is omnipotent, the argument goes, God could have created a world where such things as cruelty, parasitism, and miscarriages would not occur.

One possible religious explanation goes along the following lines. Consider, first, human beings, who perpetrate all sorts of misdeeds and sins, even perjury, adultery, and murder. People of faith believe that each human being is a creation of God, but this does not entail that God is responsible for human crimes and misdemeanors. Sin is a consequence of free will; its opposite is virtue. The critics might say that this account does not absolve God, because God could have created humans without free will (whatever these "humans" would have been called and been like). But one could reasonably argue that "humans" without free will would be a very different kind of creature, one much less interesting and creative than humans in fact are. Robots are not a good substitute for humans; robots do not perform virtuous deeds.

This line of argumentation can be extended to the catastrophes and other events of the physical world and to the dysfunctions of organisms and the harms caused to them by other organisms and environmental mishaps. However, some authors do not find this extension fully satisfactory as an explanation that would exonerate God from moral responsibility. The point made again is that the world was created by God, so God is ultimately responsible. God could have created a world without parasites or dysfunctionalities. But a world of life with evolution is much more exciting; it is a creative world where new species arise, complex ecosystems come about, and humans have evolved. These considerations may provide the beginning of an explanation for many people of faith, as well as for theologians.

Some Christian authors go further. Anglican theologian Keith Ward (2008) has put the case in strong terms, arguing that the creation of a world without suffering and moral evil is not an option even for God: "Could [God] not actualize a world wherein suffering is not a possibility? He could not, if any world complex and diverse enough to include rational and moral agents must necessarily include the possibility of suffering... A world with the sorts of success and happiness in it that we occasionally experience is a world that necessarily contains the possibility of failure and misery." Physicist and theologian Robert J. Russell (2007) goes even further, making the case why there should be natural (physical and biological) evil in the world, "including the pain, suffering, disease, death, and extinction that characterize the evolution of life."

An additional point is that physical or biological (other than human) events that cause harm are not evil actions, because they are not caused by moral agents but are the result of natural processes. If a terrorist blows up a bus carrying schoolchildren, that is moral evil. If an earthquake kills several thousand people and destroys their homes and livelihood, there is no morally responsible subject, because the event was not committed by a moral agent, but was the result of a natural process. If a mugger uses a vicious dog to brutalize a person, the mugger is morally responsible. But if a coyote attacks a person, there is no moral evil that needs to be accounted for. In the world of nature, physical and biological (again excluding human deeds), no morality is involved. This claim may or may not satisfy everyone, but it deserves to be explored by theologians and people of faith.

Science and Religion in Concert

Evolution and religious beliefs need not be in contradiction. Indeed, if science and religion are properly understood, they *cannot* be in contradiction because they address different matters. Science and religion are like two windows on the world. The two windows look at the same world, but they show different aspects of it. Science concerns the processes that account for the natural world: how planets move, the composition of matter and the atmosphere, the origin and adaptations of organisms. Religion concerns the meaning and purpose of the world and of human life, the proper relation of people to the Creator and to each other, the moral values that inspire and govern people's lives. Apparent contradictions only emerge when either the science or the beliefs, or often both, breach their own boundaries and wrongfully encroach on one another's subject matter.

The scope of science is the world of Nature, the reality that is observed, directly or indirectly, by our senses. Science advances explanations concerning the natural world, explanations that are subject to the possibility of corroboration or rejection by observation and experiment. Outside that world science has no authority, no statements to make, no business whatsoever taking one position or another. Science has nothing decisive to say about values, whether economic, aesthetic, or moral; nothing to say about the meaning of life or its purpose; nothing to say about religious beliefs, except in the case of beliefs that transcend the proper scope of religion and make assertions about the natural world that contradict scientific knowledge; such statements cannot be true.

Science is a way of knowing, but it is not the only way. Knowledge also derives from other sources. Common experience, imaginative literature, art, and history provide valid knowledge about the world; and so do revelation and religion for people of faith. The significance of the world and human life, as well as matters concerning moral or religious values, transcend science. Yet these matters are important; for most of us, they are at least as important as scientific knowledge per se.

The proper relationship between science and religion for people of faith can be mutually motivating and inspiring. Science may inspire religious beliefs and religious behavior, as we respond with awe to the immensity of the universe, the glorious diversity and wondrous adaptations of organisms, and the marvels of the human brain and mind. Religion promotes reverence for the Creation, for humankind, as well as for the world of life and the environment. Religion often is, for scientists and others, a motivating force and source of inspiration for investigating the marvelous world of the Creation and solving the puzzles with which it confronts us.

Note

1 William P. Brown (2010) has pointed out that a careful reading of the Bible shows seven Creation stories which, literally interpreted, are incompatible with one another. In addition to the two Genesis narratives, the Bible describes the creation of the world in Job 38: 1–41: 6; Psalm 104; Proverbs 8: 22–31; Ecclesiastes 1: 2–11; and Isaiah 40–55. Brown makes the point that the Bible's descriptions of Creation can and should be interpreted, accordingly, with what we know from the natural sciences.

References

Aquinas, Thomas. 1905. Of God and His Creatures (pp. 241–368). In Joseph Rickaby (Ed.), *Summa contra Gentiles*. London: Burns & Oates.

Augustine. 1982. *The Literal Meaning of Genesis (De Genesi ad Litteram)*, Vol. 1. New York: Newman/Paulist Press.

Augustine. 1998. Ed. Richard Dyson. *The City of God*. Cambridge: Cambridge University Press.

Ayala, Francisco J. 2007. *Darwin's Gift to Science and Religion*. Washington, DC: Joseph Henry Press.

Ayala, Francisco J. 2010. *Am I a Monkey? Six Big Questions about Evolution*. Baltimore, MD: Johns Hopkins University Press.

Behe, Michael J. 1996. *Darwin's Black Box. The Biochemical Challenge to Evolution*. New York: Touchstone.

Brown, William P. 2010. *The Seven Pillars of Creation. The Bible, Science, and the Ecology of Wonder*. New York: Oxford University Press.

Darwin, Charles. 1859. *On the Origin of Species by Means of Natural Selection*. London: John Murray.

Haught, John F. 1998. Darwin's Gift to Theology (pp. 393–418). In Robert J. Russell, William R. Stoeger, & Francisco J. Ayala (Eds.), *Evolutionary and Molecular Biology: Scientific Perspectives on Divine Action*. Vatican City State: Vatican

Observatory Press; and Berkeley, CA: Center for Theology and the Natural Sciences.
Hooke, Robert. 1665. *Micrographia*. 2014. (Facsimile edition). South Yarra, Victoria, Australia: Leopold Publishing.
Leroi, Armand M. 2014. *The Lagoon: How Aristotle Invented Science*. New York: Viking.
Miller, Hugh. 1858. *The Testimony of the Rocks*. Amazon facsimile reprint, 2012.
Paley, William. 1802. *Natural Theology, or Evidences of the Existence and Attributes of the Deity Collected from the Appearances of Nature*. New York: American Tract Society.
Peacocke, Arthur R. 1998. Biological Evolution: A Positive Appraisal (357–376). In Robert J. Russell, William R. Stoeger, & Francisco J. Ayala (Eds.), *Evolutionary and Molecular Biology: Scientific Perspectives on Divine Action*. Vatican City State: Vatican Observatory Press; and Berkeley, CA: Center for Theology and the Natural Sciences.
Ross, David. 1964. *Aristotle*. London: Methuen, University Paperbacks.
Russell, Robert J. 2007. Physics, Cosmology, and the Challenge to Consequentialist Natural Theology (109–130). In Nancey Murphy, Robert J. Russell, & William R. Stoeger (Eds.), *Physics and Cosmology: Scientific Perspectives on the Problem of Natural Evil*. Vatican City State: Vatican Observatory Press; and Berkeley, CA: Center for Theology and the Natural Sciences.
Ward, Keith. 2008. *The Big Questions in Science and Religion*. West Conshohocken, PA: Templeton Foundation Press.

Further Reading

Ayala, Francisco J. 2012. *The Big Questions. Evolution*. London: Quercus Publishing. A readable introduction to the theory of evolution and related controversies.
Ayala, Francisco J. & Arp, Robert (Eds.). 2010. *Contemporary Debates in Philosophy of Biology*. Malden, MA: Wiley-Blackwell. Del Ratzsch, a professor of philosophy at Calvin College, Grand Rapids, MI, argues that "There is a place for intelligent design in the philosophy of biology." F. J. Ayala argues that there is not; Intelligent Design is not science.
Harris, Mark. 2013. *The Nature of Creation. Examining the Bible and Science*. Durham, NC: Acumen. A critical investigation of the Creation texts of the Bible and how they relate to scientific ideas of beginnings.
Haught, John F. 2010. *Making Sense of Evolution. Darwin, God, and the Drama of Life*. Louisville, KY: Westminster John Knox Press. A Catholic theologian's defense of the theory of evolution and a critique of creationism and intelligent design.
Lesos, Jonathan B. (Ed.). 2014. *The Princeton Guide to Evolution*. Princeton, NJ: Princeton University Press. A large volume in which 103 experts explore all the major issues concerning the theory of evolution and its implication for modern society.
Miller, Kenneth R. 1999. *Finding Darwin's God: A Scientist's Search for Common Ground*. New York: HarperCollins.
National Academy of Sciences and Institute of Medicine. 2008. *Science, Evolution, and Creationism*. New York: National Academy of Sciences Press.
Numbers, Ronald L. 1998. *Darwinism Comes to America*. Cambridge, MA: Harvard University Press. A wonderful narrative of the background and origins of creationism in the United States.
Reznick, David N. 2010. *The Origin Then and Now. An Interpretive Guide to the Origin of Species*. Princeton, NJ: Princeton University Press. A readable and updated account of

the Origin of Species' revolutionary contributions to modern science.

Ruse, Michael. 2012. *The Philosophy of Human Evolution*. Cambridge: Cambridge University Press. A distinguished scholar provides a discussion of human evolution from a philosophical perspective.

Russell, Robert J., Stoeger, William R., & Ayala, Francisco J. (Eds.). 1998. *Evolutionary and Molecular Biology: Scientific Perspectives on Divine Action*. Vatican City State: Vatican Observatory Press; and Berkeley, CA: Center for Theology and the Natural Sciences. Scientists, philosophers, and theologians elucidate the theory of evolution's implications for faith and theology.

Slack, Gordy. 2008. *The Battle over the Meaning of Everything*. New York: Wiley.

CHAPTER 13

The Serpent in Eden and in Africa

Religions and Ecology

Kapya J. Kaoma

Introduction

On April 21, 2003, the *African Church Information Service* carried a story with the headline, "Threats to Burn Omieri Put Christian Views to Test" (Obonyo, 2003). It turns out that Omieri (meaning something revered and adored) was a 14-foot python that had been seen in Nyando District in Kenya's Lou-land. The test was clear: what attitude should the Luo community take toward Omieri? According to local Anglican priest Shadrack Owuor, "Omieri is a devil which should not be adored or worshipped but destroyed" (Obonyo, 2003). Based on his reading of Genesis 3: 14–19, Kenya Anglican Bishop Peter Njoka concurred: "[It] is clear that the serpent misled man to rebel against God, and so Christians should view it as an enemy of man" (Obonyo, 2003).

A 79-year-old local elder, John Gome Sarari, understood things differently: "This is a sign that we are going to have a good harvest this season. If someone takes her, then it would spell doom for us because there would be severe starvation" (Yeir, 2003). Among the many blessings attributed to Omieri is an abundant harvest, children's academic excellence, and the peaceful political transition in Kenya. Agai Yier (2003) asserts:

> The harbinger of good fortune, bounty harvests and a basket of other blessings, is back after 16 years of bad luck and waiting. The messenger of good tidings is none other than a 14-foot python, believed by the Luo community to be a sign that their luck is about to take a turn for the better.

Kenyan politician Peter Odoyo, then assistant Minister of Labor, shared this opinion—the serpent is a blessing.

The Wiley Blackwell Companion to Religion and Ecology, First Edition. Edited by John Hart.

The Lou community had enjoyed a similar visitation in 1987. Sadly, Omieri then died on a veterinary surgeon's operating table, after being set on fire by a child. The community did not just mourn Omieri, but also "slaughtered animals to appease the spirit of the snake" (Yeir, 2003). This time, people were determined to defend Omieri from all harm. Oscar Obonyo (2003) writes:

> Omieri, which three months ago appeared and received friendly treatment ... was recently in danger following threats by a section of Christians to burn it, saying it was "a symbol of the devil." The threat on the serpent's life has invoked sharp differences in opinion between old-time foes, Christians and traditionalists.

The perception of the serpent in Eden and in Africa explains this ideological war. The conflict is between traditional views of serpents as sacramental avenues through which humanity encounters the sacred, and the Christian interpretation of Genesis 3: 14–15 in which the serpent is said to be the devil. However, the fact that the assistant minister and Sarari have English Christian names and yet identify with Omieri hints at the dual lives of many Africans: they identify with modernity but remain rooted in traditional cultures.

Can the intercultural interpretation of the serpent in Genesis bridge these differences? To answer this question, we begin by exploring the interpretation of the serpent in Eden, African beliefs about sacred serpents in popular literature, anthropological, and historical works, and end with a discussion of the intercultural interpretation of the serpent in our life-threatening ecological crisis.

The Serpent in Eden—Confronting the Myth

In an attempt to explain the origin of evil, Genesis presents the serpent (*nahesh*) as responsible for human disobedience to YHWH. Immediately thereafter, the serpent is cursed:

> Cursed are you above all livestock and all wild animals! You will crawl on your belly and you will eat dust all the days of your life. And I will put enmity between you and the woman, and between your offspring and hers; he [woman's seed] will crush your head, and you [snake] will strike his heel. (Gen. 3: 14–15)

The woman and man, however, are not cursed but punished. To the woman, God said,

> I will make your pains in childbearing very severe; with painful labor you will give birth to children. Your desire will be for your husband, and he will rule over you. (Gen. 3: 16)

As for the man, God cursed the ground and then reminded him that "for dust you are and to dust you will return" (Gen. 3: 17–19). Read in conjunction with Genesis 1: 28—"Be fruitful and increase in number; fill the earth and subdue it. Rule over the fish in the sea and the birds in the sky and over every living creature that moves on the ground"— Christians have employed Genesis to define human–Nature relations.

Yet, despite this disobedience, humanity still possesses inherent natural rights to life to be protected and defended (Genesis 4: 15). Such rights, however, are denied the serpent; it is the symbol of Satan and is to be destroyed, as Bishop Njoka argued.

The story of Eden is a myth; hence many interpretations exist. Some scholars view it as the myth of maturation as humanity moved from infancy into adulthood. Rather than interpreting every actor separately in this myth, the entire story must be interpreted as one (Bechtel, 1995; Walker-Jones, 2008). Others, however, seek to interpret the events and actors in this myth. Key to this story is *nahesh* (serpent). So, where did it come from?

The story of Eden was composed in the cultural context in which serpents were prominent in religious mythology (Davidson, 1973). In both the Egyptian and Mesopotamian cultures, for example, certain serpents were regarded as representatives of the Deity and other spiritual powers. According to Joines (1968, 250), "the cultic significance of the serpent in the Ancient Near East ... was that of fertility and the return of life." In these cultures, the "serpent symbolized life, death, wisdom, nature, chaos and fertility" (Kvam et al., 1999). Serpents were also "images of the serpent-goddesses" (Sarna, 1966, 26). Hence, in addition to being symbols of female power, serpents were symbols of royalty. This cultural history may explain the encounter between the serpent and the woman in Eden.

Regardless, Genesis 3 seeks to answer one important question: if God created a very good world, how did evil enter it? Unlike other Near East religions which perceived the world as full of evil forces fighting among themselves, the Hebrew Bible demotes all forces by presenting God as above all other gods and creatures; YHWH has no equal. But this conviction leads to another question: How did evil come into God's very good Creation? It is this question that the story of Eden seeks to answer. God created a very good world, but humanity by its conduct and desire to be like God corrupts the Creation. In short, humanity brought "evil into the world as a result of its corruption" (Cassuto, 1961). Understood from an ecological perspective, the Eden story shows how human disobedience threatens and destroys God's very good Creation.

However, in various traditions, serpents are said to bring human prosperity and wisdom. The Ancient Near East was no exception: serpents were associated with wisdom, life, and knowledge. Among the Egyptians, serpents were used "in divining the truth" (Gilboa, 1998) and were the manifestation of deities—one reason why Moses' rod turned into a snake (Ex. 4: 3; 7: 10). This tradition explains the qualification of the serpent in Eden as a creature of God. As Davidson (1973, 39) rightly notes, like many other poetic passages in the Old Testament, the Eden story echoes

> an ancient cosmological story in which God does battle against primordial forces of chaos symbolized by a sea-serpent (Isa. 27: 1). But just as the Creation hymn in Gen. 1 is remarkably restrained in the use of creation mythology, so here the serpent seems to be demoted. He is merely one of the world creatures the Lord God had made, different only in that he is ... *crafty* [more than other creatures].

Aside from noting the serpent symbolized the deity and fertility in the Near East, Sarna (1966, 26) concludes that the "serpent symbolism in this situation has most likely been conditioned by the place of the serpent in the old cosmic combat."

The Near East's association of the serpent with wisdom is reflected in the story of Eden. The serpent possessed more special intelligence than any other animal, to which most Africans would shout, "Amen!" Although verses 14 and 15 put the serpent and humanity in conflict, biblical scholars agree that the serpent in Eden has little to do with today's snake (Bechtel, 1995; von Rad, 1972). Besides, the association of the serpent in Eden with all snake species ignores some illogical aspects of this myth. Since all creatures die, does human punishment apply to all bio-kind? What about the role of giving birth? Is Eve's punishment on behalf of all female species? Using God's curse on the serpent, Hamilton (1990, 196–197) writes:

> Snakes do not eat dust, and no ancient writer ever thought they did. One has to take this passage symbolically, not literally. Therefore, it is fruitless to see in this particular verse an etiology of why snakes no longer walk on legs and why they lost their legs. If one is prepared to see in this decree *On your belly shall you crawl* a change in the snake's mode of locomotion, then to be consistent one must see the decree *dust shall you eat* as a change in the snake's diet.

From Hamilton's observation, one can add other crawling species to this list. Moreover, eating dust and crawling on the belly, Jewish scholar Cassuto (1961: 160) argues, is a metaphor for humiliation—something expected of conquered foes. In this regard, the curse points to human humiliation that comes with disobedience or a desire to be like God; it is not intended to define the serpent at all.

Kvam and colleagues (1999) rightly argue that the interpretation of the serpent "as Satan or one of the Satan's minions" is a post-biblical concept that goes against the original meaning of the text. Accordingly, Sarna (1966) argues that the serpent "is an independent creature; it possesses no occult powers; it is not a demonical being; it is not even described as evil; merely as being extraordinarily shrewd." von Rad (1972) rejects attempts to link the serpent in Eden to Satan. The serpent, he concludes, "is not the symbol of demonic powers and certainly not Satan." Vawter (1977) equally cautions against the interpretation of the serpent as the devil or Satan in both Judaism and Christianity since it disregards Yahwist thought in which "dualism of supernatural agents is foreign." Not until "approximately the third century BCE" was the snake in this text understood as Satan (Gilboa, 1998). Moreover, Davidson (1973, 39) writes:

> Certainly there is no suggestion in the narrative that he is a supernatural, demonic figure to be equated with Satan. This development comes much later in Jewish and Christian thinking. The serpent indeed is almost incidental to the central thrust of the story. In the dialogue between the serpent and the woman we are overhearing a struggle which is going on in the mind of the woman, a struggle between innocence and temptation.

Similarly, Cassuto (1961, 139) dismisses the link between the serpent in Eden and today's snakes. He writes: "The interpretation reflected in the New Testament and in later rabbinic literature, according to which the serpent is none other than Satan ... introduces into the text concepts that are foreign to it." This is because "according to ancient Talmudic sources, the primeval serpent is just a species of animal, although differing in character from the serpent of today, and resembling man in his upright stature and in his manner of eating—that is, "half serpent and half man."

To show the inconsistency of equating the serpent in Eden with today's snakes, Gilboa (1998) writes: "True enough the snake bites, so do other creatures." To Gilboa's point, one can add that less than 20% of snake species are harmful. Thus the serpent in Eden is innocently symbolic, as Westermann (1974) argues. Further, the identification of the serpent in Eden as Satan views the snake as the opposite of God, which the Hebrew faith totally rejects. God has no opposite, hence the serpent in Eden is certainly not Satan; it is a product of the Creator's creativity. Unfortunately, the story of Eden influences and to some extent justifies the negative attitudes toward snakes. But just as feminist interpretations of the story of Eden aided a paradigm shift in gender relations, the snake and the ground must be redeemed from the curse of Genesis amid the mounting ecological crisis.

The Serpent in Africa: The Ambiguous Premise of Snakes

Near East attitudes to serpents are similar to those found in Africa. Across the continent, the serpent occupies a critical role in African life-worlds. From San (Bushmen) paintings to contemporary Africa, the image of the serpent is multifaceted. While Africans understand that snakes can be dangerous and can be used negatively, they also believe that some snakes are sacred (Kaoma, 2015, 61–79). San paintings in Southern Africa seem to address this paradox. In one, the snake is being offered a buck; in another it is being confronted with an assegai (spear). Woodhouse (1979, 94) writes:

> Very few paintings of snakes are straightforward representations. Many are associated with people. [The painting of the snake] at Gulubahwe [in the Matopo hills of Zimbabwe] has people on its back. In the Bethlehem district a man offers the corpse of a buck to a serpent and in the Floukraal district a man confronts a snake with an assegai. This particular example is a masterpiece of tension, caught at the moment before the projectile is launched. It is also unusual in that it is painted in three colors and the snake has spines along its back. While some snakes are painted fully extended, others are in complicated convolutions or simple coils. In one instance ... the fangs are painted in detail.

Woodhouse's hypothesis is that the fangs seem to point to the San's skill of milking poison for hunting and inoculations from snakes—something we see in Moses' use of the Bronze Serpent in the book of Numbers. Other paintings show snakes with horns, which, as Woodhouse argues, points to a six-meter long serpent believed to live in water.

In line with Woodhouse, it is hard to present just one logical explanation to all the paintings. In retrospect, the San paintings express the ambiguous premise of snakes in African cosmologies: some snakes are harmful, while others are benign. Accepting this premise is fundamental to understanding the role of the serpent in Africa. Together, these paintings propose different roles associated with snakes. The one confronted with the assegai is not the same one being offered a buck; it is an evil snake, which, like the magical snake *ilomba* in Bemba, Chishinga, and Ushi cosmologies, is viewed negatively (Kaoma, 2015).

A similar belief is found among the Xhosa, Ndau, and Zulu of Southern Africa. The snake *mamlambo* is said to bring abundant blessings (*divisi*)—wealth as well as the ability to syphon money secretly from others. Wood's (2004) study of Khotso Sethuntsa, a powerful, wealthy, uneducated native who owned Cadillacs and boasted of having millions of Rands in apartheid South Africa, shows how local people employed this belief to explain his wealth. In addition, Sethuntsa's association with the snakes has made him a very powerful and feared diviner to this day.

The Serpent in Popular Literature

Although African theologians generally ignore this phenomenon, the serpent is widely discussed in African literature, such as in Wilson Katiyo's *A Son of the Soil* (1976) and Chunua Achebe's (1959) *Things Fall Apart.* While these authors represent two distinct communities—the Shona of Southern Africa and the Igbo of West Africa, respectively—they articulate the potent conflict between Christianity and traditional religions with regard to snakes.

In Katiyo's novel, after a married couple, Rugare (peace) and Tendayi (be thankful), convert to Christianity, they view all African beliefs and customs as evil. When Tendayi suffers repeated miscarriages, the couple seek the help of Sekuru, a spiritual medium and traditional healer. Initially, Rugare denounced Sekuru's healing powers as the work of the devil, but as is often the case in contemporary Africa, their problem forces the couple to seek traditional help. Before helping them, Sekuru blames the miscarriages on Rugare's disrespect for the ancestors:

> The spirits of the ancestors are already aware of this [miscarriages]. They are not pleased Rugare... You can't go on defying their will any longer. You have to mend your ways. Take this as a warning. If you persist, my child, they are going to take you... I saw it quite clearly... They will take you without any hesitation. (1976, 30)

After issuing this stern rebuke, Sekuru performs a healing ritual and predicts that Tendayi will give birth to a son. Sekuru dies immediately thereafter. When Tendayi gives birth to a son, they name him Alexio Chikomborero (blessing), abbreviated to Chiko. Despite Sekuru's successful intervention, the couple reverts to ignoring their ancestors.

One day, Rugare and Tendayi are happily working in their field and Chiko is playing under the Msasa tree. Katiyo writes:

> A tropical shower began falling. Ma Chiko [mother of Chiko] and Baba wa Chiko [father of Chiko] hurried to take shelter under the Msasa tree. But when they got there, their child wasn't playing alone. A medium-sized black snake was coiled around the child. It was licking Alexio's face with its fangs. The boy was laughing and warding off the snake's kisses

with his short chubby arms. In her shock, Ma Chiko screamed before she froze silent with fear. The snake uncoiled. The child began to cry. Baba wa Chiko rushed from behind the snake and snatched the child away... The snake slowly begun moving towards a thicket at the edge of the field. Armed with an axe, Baba wa Chiko pursued the black snake. As he tried to kill it, a flash of lightning tore the sky. It was a blind flash. When she recovered from being blinded Ma Chiko looked around and saw her husband... He was dead. (1976, 34)

Behind this story is the Shona belief that the ancestors visit their people through snakes and other natural phenomena. The boy's relationship with the black snake suggests his connectedness to the ancestral world. Although the author does not say it explicitly, the serpent is an important avenue through which the Shona ancestors communicate their will to their people.

Chinua Achebe reflects on this point in *Things Fall Apart*, too. In this novel, Enoch is like Rugare. After converting to Christianity, Enoch, whose father was a snake-cult priest, falsely boasts of killing a python, which the Igbo community considers to be the emanation of the powerful goddess Idemili. It was his Christian friend, Okoli, who actually killed one. Achebe (1959) explains:

The rainbow was called the python of the sky, thus the royal python was the most revered animal in the Mbanta and all surrounding clans. It was addressed as "Our Father," and was allowed to go wherever it chose, even into people's beds. It ate rats in the house and sometimes swallowed hens' eggs. If a clansman killed a royal python accidentally, he made sacrifice and performed an expensive burial ceremony as was done for a great man.

This situation brought the new religion and local people into serious conflict. As the community deliberated what to do with him, Okoli fell sick during the night and died the following day.

Ifi Amadiume's (1997) study of the Igbo people of Nigeria speaks to Achebe's story. As in the Egyptian and Mesopotamian cultures, Idemili is the Supreme Mother who presides over all aspects of life, from fertility to socioeconomic activities. She writes, Idemili "reigned above all the other deities and the ancestors. She provided an overall administrative system, embracing the organization of the periodic markets, the days of the week, and the seasonal festivals" (Amadiume, 1997).

In 1940 the worship of Idemili was outlawed, probably due to the European interpretation of the serpent in Eden. Nathaniel, a Christian convert, took advantage of this law and "deliberately killed the holy symbol of Goddess Idemili, a python" (Amadiume, 1997). His act was considered an abomination; hence the community demanded the execution of the python killer. When the District Officer refused, the community took the law into their own hands—they destroyed Nathaniel's house and cursed him. The next day, Nathaniel was found dead.

Achebe could have based his story on this historical event, so Nwabueze (2000) argues. While Achebe is reconstructing the story to fit the colonial, male-dominated society, the association of the goddess with women follows smoothly in Amadiume's analysis. The worship of Idemili was not only dominated by women, it influenced how the deity was comprehended. To this day, deliberately killing Idemili, the mother goddess, is a taboo even among Christians.

The Serpent in Anthropological Literature

Complementary to novelists who have explored the role of snakes in African societies, anthropologists, and historians have documented the serpent in Africa. The Edo people of Benin perceive snakes as consumers and destroyers of illness. Among the Dogon of Cameroon, a serpent represents the Supreme Being, Lebe. Some African Creation myths even attribute the Creation to the python (de Heusch, 1994). Among many African cultures in Central and Southern Africa, it is said that some people have the capacity to tap the powers of serpents for various reasons. This was the case with King Hintsa Sarhili in colonial South Africa, whose reign was associated with a python during the prophetess Nongqawuse's great Xhosa cattle-killing movement of 1856–1857 (Peires, 1989).

The Bemba, Nguni, Lamba, Tonga, and Chishinga people of Zambia are among the many who attribute sacredness to some snakes. Various high god cults, such as the Chisumpi and Mbona cults of Malawi, the Mwari cult of Zimbabwe, and the Makumba cult of the Ushi, have a special relationship with serpentine spirits. In the Chisumpi and Mbona cults, for example, the central ritual animal is the python, Thunga (*nsato*). This snake is the ultimate sacred image of the deity. If killed unintentionally, like Idemili, Thunga must be buried with the utmost respect. Failure to do so will destabilize the ecological harmony of the land.

In addition, many African communities "associate snakes with the living-dead or other human spirits, and such snakes are given food and drinks when they visit people's homes" (Mbiti, 1975). The Bemba, Chishinga, and Ushi peoples of Zambia believe in *insoka shamipashi* (snakes of spirits), which are showered with gifts (Kaoma, 2015). Nkabinde and Morgan (2006) document an encounter in South Africa in which a serpent prevented a male *sangoma* (medium) consummating his marriage. As the couple was preparing to be intimate, the snake was seen on the woman's belly. The *sangoma* immediately took it as an ancestral prohibition of that marriage—something that allowed the woman to be given to a female *sangoma* as an ancestral wife.

As in the Near East, many African cultures assign healing powers to certain snakes. Zulu diviners in Southern Africa are expected to live among water serpents at the bottom of pools or river beds. This is because *inhlwathi* (the great pythons) control diviners' healing skills. Anthropologist (later a diviner) Bernard (1998) attributes her mentor *baba*'s [father's] healing powers to the red zigzag-patterned and spotted water serpent, which "wrapped itself around his [*baba's*] waist four times and with its head above his, [and] rode with him through the sea. After his visit to his ancestors, he returned with a dolphin and a snake accompanying him." To become a *sangoma*, Bernard had a similar snake encounter, first through her daughter's dream and later her own dream. What is interesting in these encounters is the role of the natural world in the diviner's life. This relationship might represent what scholars have long identified—the relationship between human health and that of the natural world.

Although Bernard's encounter dates to the 1990s, Kinjikitile Bokero Ngwale (died August 4, 1905), the primary architect of the 1905 *Maji Maji* rebellion in colonial

German East Africa (today's Tanzania), built his movement chiefly from his "sacred encounter" with the serpent. Gwassa (1972, 211), explains:

> A huge snake of a size never seen before, and having a head of a small black monkey, paid a visit to the house of one Mzee Machuya Nnundu of Lihenga near Ngarambe. The occupants of the house moved out in favor of the visitor. The snake was too big for the house so that its coils overflowed outside while it kept its head above the coils at the entrance into the house. It had large red glowing eyes and looked at people ... in a fearsome manner. It was colored like the rainbow—one of the commonest attributes of the divinity, Hongo. On the third day, the snake disappeared miraculously.

According to Iliffe (1979, 169), what Jesus is to God so *hongo* was to Bokero. Since the deity Bokero was believed to be a great water serpent, the snake's disappearance coincided with Kinjikitile vanishing underwater:

> [People] tried to get hold of his legs and pull him but it was impossible, and he cried out that he did not want [to be pulled back] and that they were hurting him. Then he disappeared in the pool of water. He slept in there and his relatives slept by the pool overnight waiting for him. Those who knew how to swim dived down into the pool but they did not see anything. Then they said, "If he is dead we will see his body; if he has been taken by a spirit of the waters we shall see him returned dead or alive. So they waited, and the following morning, at about nine o'clock again, he emerged unhurt with his clothes dry and as he had tucked them the previous day. After returning from there he began talking of prophetic matters. He said, "All dead ancestors will come back; they are at Bokero's in Rufiji Ruhingo. No lion or leopard will eat men." (Gwassa, 1972, 211–212; Iliffe, 1979, 169)

After this encounter, Kinjikitile became Bokero's prophet. Using his new identity, Kinjikitile recruited masses to rebel violently against German rule. He also assured his followers that the sacred *maji* (water) from Bokero's cultic center would turn the White man's bullets into water, shielding them from European guns. Kinjikitile's rebellion failed to oust the Europeans, but it showed the powers of serpents in Africa's self-understanding.

The Serpent and the Waters

As in the Near East, the serpent in Africa is not just the guardian of the land but of the waters too. Bodies of water—from waterfalls to pools to river sources—are said to be inhabited by sacred serpents. Among the Tonga people of Zambia, the serpentine spirit Nyami-Nyami is believed to reside in the waters. While Clements (1959) identifies Nyami-Nyami as "the all-powerful god of the river," the Tonga people consider Nyami-Nyami a spirit (Kaoma, 2013, 38). Gibbons (1904) first documented Nyami-Nyami in 1904, but the spirit's prominence surfaced during the construction of the Kariba Dam, which led to the forced removal of the Tonga people from the Zambezi valley in 1957. The floods which destroyed cofferdams (temporary water enclosures), the suspension footbridge, and the road bridge between colonial Zambia and Zimbabwe, and the deaths of many workers were all attributed to this snake.

While water serpents are believed to live below the water, like Hongo, they surface occasionally, especially during a social crisis. In addition to during the time of the socio-anthropology insults of the forced resettlement, Nyami-Nyami was said to appear during famines, offering his own body as food to his starving people.[1] To this day, Nyami-Nyami's sightings are regularly reported, among them in 2012 and 2006 (Chara, 2012; *The Herald*, 2007).

The association of sacred serpents with water is also recorded by Hudson, then District Commissioner in colonial Zambia. Hudson (1999, 72) writes about two White British South Africa Company (BSAC) assistant collectors, John A. Drysdale and A. C. R. Miller, who died after killing sacred snakes at Nyala in colonial Zambia.[2] Hudson writes:

> In 1898 Drysdale noticed a pair of black snakes at the stream which was the source station's water supply. Ignoring the advice of local people, who warned him that the snakes were spirits and that he would die if he harmed them, Drysdale shot one. He died shortly afterwards on, possibly of black water. His replacement Miller, also disregarded the warning and shot the other snake. He too died within a few days. After this the station was abandoned. (1999, 72)

The prominence of serpent deities, ancestors, and spirits across the continent demands theological reflection. From the smallest to the largest creature, God is sacredly present—which is understood only when people relate to them with reverence and awe.

The Serpent in God's Creation

The flawed interpretation of the serpent in Eden and the assumption that native peoples were serpent worshipers explain the exploitation of snakes in Christian-influenced cultures. It is understandable that missionaries, given their biblical literalist backgrounds, found it hard to accept snakes as symbols of divine revelation.

As in the biblical world, in Africa the serpent was and is the most visible symbol of the deities, ancestors, and other spirits. It is this symbol that comes to mind when some Africans hear the word God. Unless Christians interacting with such cultures accept this reality, religious conversion is artificial. Importantly, too, the reinterpretation of the snake in Eden can transform attitudes toward snakes and the Earth as a whole. Infield (2001, 801) advocates planting ecological responsibilities and actions in people's worldviews. In his words, "managing protected areas to reflect local values may help build support for and reduce resistance to them and allow governments to justify and explain conservation in terms that have real meaning to local communities." Infield's observation has great implications for Christian theology. Specifically, African theologies that link Christ to our ancestors ought to reflect on this subject. As noted, in the Lou and Igbo cultures the snake, not Jesus, receives credit for abundant life.

The association of snakes with the Supreme Being, the ancestors, and various spirits implies revisiting African christologies that seek to interpret Christ as our ancestor.

Arguably, when certain community cultures speak of the Supreme Being, ancestors, and the Spirit, they have in mind the beings symbolized by snakes. In traditions where snakes can symbolize the Supreme Being and ancestors, it is difficult for the Church to speak of Jesus as our ancestor without addressing the manifestations of these spiritual beings in snakes. Unless Jesus our ancestor is explained in light of how the ancestors are experienced in the life-worlds of Africans, the relevance of the ancestor christology will remain superficial. I propose that Christ our ancestor ought to take the functional role of Omieri among the Luo, Nyami-Nyami among the Tonga, and Idemili among the Igbo. A Jesus planted in African worldviews and Nature has a better chance of meeting land-dwellers' needs as opposed to the one hanging in Christian cathedrals in sub-Saharan Africa. Besides, amidst the life-threatening ecological crisis, the Genesis story needs to be reinterpreted. Just as teachings on the dominion of Earth and women's exploitation have been critiqued and rejected, the curse of the serpent and of the Earth must be rejected.

The rationale for God's involvement in Creation is needed. For Christians, the doctrine of general revelation teaches that God is revealed in the Creation. Christianity does not sanction the worship of Nature, but it holds all creatures as potential sacramental avenues for God's grace (Kaoma, 2015). When people respect snakes, they are not putting their trust in the snake but in what the snake represents. That the Omieri rather than Jesus receives credit for academic excellence, good harvests, and political stability suggests how limited current christologies in African theological discourse are. But as Linera (2010) writes: "The Incarnation of Jesus brings to fulfilment the whole plan and process of Creation, revealing how God shares His love with all creatures since all eternity." In other words, just as Moses brought the snake cult under the authority of YHWH, the Christian Church needs to do the same.

African scholars have good reason to demonize this phenomenon; after all, missionaries presented the snake as Satan. Such a view is still confirmed by countless Jesus movies that present Satan as the black serpent in the temptations of Jesus (Matthew 4: 1–11) as well as in the betrayal of Jesus by Judas Iscariot (Mark 14; Matt 26; Luke 22). Yet, the biblical God is the God of the earth. Like Western theologies, African christologies rushed to remove the triune God from the earth and located God in urban settings. This God has little to do with farming, rains, rivers, and the ecological balance of village life in which many Christians live. Whereas in the past people experienced God in Nature, this understanding was replaced with cerebral experiences of the Divine, inculcated by the study of the Bible. However, YHWH remains the God of earth.

Like YHWH, African deities were and are ecological in application; hence the need for an ecological theology that interprets God, the ancestors, and spirits from the locus and perspectives of the peoples of the earth. Since sacred snakes are associated with the natural world—river sources, pools, mountains, and forests—it is necessary to build on such beliefs in conservation and Creation care efforts. By linking the sacred to the natural world, Christians are likely to attract support from local communities in earth-preserving activities. This is because African cults and rituals "issue and enforce directives with regard to a community's use of its environment" (Schoffeleers, 1979, 2).

The Serpent in Christian Ecological Theology

Despite the Christian tendency to deny the manifestation of God in natural phenomena, Eichrodt (1967, 16) notes that the Israelites believed differently:

> That God can without detriment to his majesty give visible evidence of his presence on earth is a conviction taken as much for granted by Israel as by other nations. Their sharing the common view on this point is shown by the fact that they regard it as perfectly possible for the deity to manifest himself both in the forces of Nature and in human form.

Despite our acceptance of the doctrine of natural revelation, misunderstanding the serpent of Eden informs human attitudes toward snakes in Western-influenced cultures. But as this study shows, Christianity has failed to distance the serpent from the African mind—both on the continent and in African communities across the world, especially those associated with voodoo (Mulira, 1990).

Biblical faith does not accord divinity to any creature. The Torah prohibits the worship of any creature, including humanity, but it accords sacredness to Creation. In this regard, it is necessary to move beyond the serpent in Eden to the serpent in the entire Bible in which the snake is a sacred creature of God. From God's perspective, snakes have natural rights to be protected and defended. Wittenberg (2008) argues that, in the Torah, animals and plants have rights. Specifically, the biblical covenant demands that even an enemy's animals are to be protected: "If you come across your enemy's ox or donkey wandering off, be sure to return it. If you see the donkey of someone who hates you fallen down under its load, do not leave it there; be sure you help them with it" (Ex. 23: 4–5). In war, the Torah prohibits the destruction of innocent trees. Deuteronomy 20: 19 reads, "When you lay siege to a city for a long time, fighting against it to capture it, do not destroy its trees by putting an ax to them... Do not cut them down. Are the trees people, that you should besiege them?" Commenting on these texts, Wittenberg (2008, 75) writes: "The Cartesian dichotomy between sentient beings, persons and non-sentiment things, between subjects and objects, is totally foreign to Old Testament thinking. An animal is not a thing, but a subject of law which is also liable, like other human beings."

Olupona (2009, 63) argues that in Africa, "wild animals are the most pure expression of God's power." But as Mbiti (1970) observes, the deification of non-human creatures does not mean worship of the "object or phenomenon as such"; rather, the reverence is directed to God or the Spirit represented in them. In this regard, the Christian God only makes sense to the Luo, Tonga, and many African cultures once God is interpreted and associated with the natural world on which their livelihoods depend.

Historically, all Bible-influenced and promoted oppressive systems self-select biblical texts to justify their actions. The negative interpretation of the serpent in Eden, for example, was meant to validate the destruction of snakes and perhaps, by implication and extension, the exploitation of the natural world. As the ecological crisis mounts, we must reject such texts and acknowledge the entire biblical testimony which presents the whole of Creation as both very good and sacred. In this regard, just as humanity possesses natural rights, the Creation—including snakes—has intrinsic rights to be protected and defended.

It is important to note that biblical writers did not ignore the snake cult of the Near East. Rather, they brought it under the authority of YHWH. Moses' staff turned into a snake and then back into a staff (Ex. 4: 2–4) to prove God's power over the Pharaoh. Again, when the people of God sinned, God sent snakes to bite them. To address their plight, God instructed Moses to make "a bronze snake and put it up on a pole. Then when anyone was bitten by a snake and looked at the bronze snake, he lived" (Numbers 21: 7–9).[2] By raising the bronze serpent, God used the snake as a healing symbol—a popular remedy in the Near East communities including Israel. As Gilboa (1998, 106) asserts: "The Biblical remedy for its bite was its own icon (Numbers 21: 8–9) which, in this case, renders the snake as a symbol of salvation, and that is why it took place in Israelite rituals until the middle of the eighth century B.C. (2 Kings 18: 4)."

The deconstruction and the intercultural interpretation of the serpent in Eden reveal that the snake is a creature of God, which the Creator used and can still employ to reveal the Godself, as was the case with Moses and in many African cultures. In the New Testament, Jesus identifies with the serpent when he interprets his own death: "As Moses lifted up the serpent in the wilderness, even so must the Son of Man be lifted up, that whoever believes in Him should not perish but have eternal life" (John 3: 14–15). It is not surprising that Christian thinkers find it easy to theologize around humanity and the tree in Eden, but have deliberately ignored the snake.

If the first Adam failed, it is argued, the second Adam passed the test. An argument can be made that while the first snake led us to death, the second snake saves us. In christological terms, Jesus is the archetype of the snake that Moses raised in the desert, whose role is now fulfilled in the death of the incarnate God, who heals us from eternal death. Once sin is understood as sickness, the role of Jesus as the archetype of the healing serpent becomes evident.

Moreover, every creature is related to the Creator. This conviction enhances the doctrine of general revelation on one hand, and confirms the sacramental nature of the covenanted Creation (Gen. 9: 8–17) on the other. Accepting this theology of Creation obliges us to accept that all creatures—snakes, humans, dogs, rats, and so on—are sacramental expressions of the Creator's love and presence. As Oduyoye (1979, 110) asserts, the identification "of the divine spirit in nature and the community of the spirit between human beings, other living creatures and natural phenomena could reinforce the Christian doctrine of creation as well as contribute to Christian reflection on ecological problems."

Indeed, our negative attitude to snakes reflects attitudes toward the Earth in general. Amidst the mounting ecological crisis, the religio-intercultural interpretation of the story of Eden informed by the African traditional religious understanding of sacred snakes can transform our perception of Creation as a whole. Ignoring the snake in theological discourse in an environment where people have high regard for the serpent is self-defeating. The fact that evil people exist does not justify withholding rights from the human race; and the same is true of the natural world. To deny natural rights to all snakes and other creatures on the basis of their being harmful is immoral. The Creation is sacred before the Creator and we need to see the world with the Creator's eyes: God loves snakes just as the Creator loves the whole cosmos (John 3: 16).

As the ecological crisis mounts, global Christianity should engage other cultures in understanding, appreciating, and relating to the Creation. Africans do not need to study Near East mythology to accept the feminine nature of God. As this study reveals, some African cultures held the Supreme Being to be the mother and the guardian of the land and the waters. Likewise, Africans knew that the Creation is the reflection of the Creator long before the Bible and Thomas Aquinas's theology reached them. African Christianity and religions have much to contribute to global theological discourse. But this will only occur through mutual intercultural interpretation of Christian beliefs, in context, as this study shows.

Notes

1 It was believed that people would cut off chunks of meat from the body of Nyami-Nyami and that the body would heal instantly (Kaoma, 2013, 35).

2 Karen R. Joines (1968, 253) argues that "the ancient Egyptians did not use bronze serpents in their cult, but the practice of repelling serpents by a serpent image was very common to them, a practice which apparently was not performed in Palestine and Mesopotamia. On the other hand, the bronze serpent as a symbol of fertility was a part of the cults in Canaan and Mesopotamia, but seemingly not in Egypt."

References

Achebe, Chinua. 1959. *Things Fall Apart.* New York: Fawcett Crest.

Amadiume, Ifi. 1997. *Reinventing Africa: Matriarch, Religion and Culture.* New York: Zed Books.

Bechtel, Lyn M. 1995. Genesis 2.4b–3.24: A Myth about Human Maturation. *Journal for the Study of the Old Testament* 67, 1, 3–26.

Bernard, P. 1998. *Rituals of the River: Convergence of Baptism and River Spirits in Isangoma Cosmology in Natal Midlands.* Rhodes University, South Africa, unpublished paper.

Cassuto, U. 1961. *A Commentary on the Book of Genesis.* Transl. Israel Abrahams. Jerusalem: Manes Press.

Clements, Frank. 1959. *Kariba: The Struggle with the River God.* London: Methuen.

Davidson, Robert. 1973. *Genesis 1–11.* Cambridge: Cambridge University Press.

de Heusch, Luc. 1994. Myths and Epic in Central Africa (229–238). In Thomas D. Blakely, W. E. A. van Beek, & Dennis L. Thomson (Eds.), *Religion in Africa: Experience and Expression.* London: J. Curry.

Eichrodt, Walter. 1967. *Theology of the Old Testament*, Vol. 2. Philadelphia, PA: Westminster Press.

Gibbons, Major A. S. H. 1904. *Africa from South to North through Marotseland.* London: J. Lane.

Gilboa, R. 1998. *Intercourses in the Book of Genesis: Mythic Motifs in Creator–Created Relationships.* Lewes: Book Guild.

Gwassa, G. C. K. 1972. Kinjikitile and the Ideology of Maji Maji (202–217). In T. O. Ranger & I. N. Kimambo (Eds.), *Religious Symbols in East and Central Africa: Historical Study of African Religion.* Los Angeles, CA: University of California Press.

Hamilton, Victor P. 1990. *The Book of Genesis Chapters 1–17.* Grand Rapids, MI: Eerdmanns.

Hudson, John. 1999. *A Time to Mourn: A Personal Account of the 1964 Lumpa Church Revolt in Zambia.* Lusaka: Bookworld.

Iliffe, John. 1979. *A Modern History of Tanganyika*. Cambridge: Cambridge University Press.

Infield, Mark. 2001. Cultural Values: A Forgotten Strategy for Building Community Support for Protected Areas in Africa. *Conservation Biology*, 15, 3, 800–802.

Joines, Karen R.1968. The Bronze Serpent in the Israelite Cult. *Journal of Biblical Literature*, 87, 3: 245–256.

Kaoma, Kapya J. 2013. *God's Family, God's Earth: Christian Ecological Ethics of Ubuntu*. Zomba: Kachere.

Kaoma, Kapya J. 2015. *The Creator's Symphony: African Christianity, the Plight of Earth and the Poor*. Dorpspruit: Cluster.

Katiyo, Wilson. 1976. *A Son of the Soil*. London: Collins.

Kvam, Kristen E., Schearing Linda S., & Ziegler, Valerie H. 1999. *Adam and Eve: Jewish, Christian, and Muslim Reading of the Genesis and Gender*. Bloomington, IN: Indiana University Press.

Linera, Fr. Carlos Rodríguez. 2010. *Creation at the Heart of Mission*. http://www.edinburgh2010.org/fr/ressources/papersdocumentse4aa.pdf?no_cache=1&cid=33877&did=22391&sechash=613255d3.

Mbiti, John. 1970. *Concepts of God in Africa*. London: Praeger.

Mbiti, John. 1975. *Introduction to African Religion*. London: SPCK.

Mulira, Jessie G. 1990. The Case of Voodoo in New Orleans (34–68). In Joseph E. Holloway (Ed.), *Africanisms in American Culture*. Bloomington, IN: Indiana University Press.

Munro, John. 2003. The Establishment and Early Days of the Northern Rhodesia Police. *Western Cape Outpost*, 74, 43–47. http://www.bsap.org/pdfbin/WesternCapeOutpost_November2013.pdf.

Nkabinde, Nkunzi N. & Morgan, Ruth. 2006. This Has Happened since Ancient Times … It's Something That You Are Born with: Ancestral Wives among Same-Sex Sangomas in South Africa. *Agenda: Empowering Women for Gender Equity, 67, African Feminisms*, 2, 3, 9–19.

Nwabueze, Bons O. 2000. Our Ancestors and the Oracle they Left Behind. *Africa Economic Analysis*. www.afbis.com.

Obonyo, Oscar. 2003. Threats to Burn Omieri Put Christian Views to Test. African Church Information Service, April 21, 2003. www.allafrica.com.

Oduyoye, Mercy Amba. 1979. The Value of African Religious Beliefs and Practices for Christian Theology (109–116). In Kofi Appiah-Kubi & Sergio Torres (Eds.), *African Theology en Route: Papers from the Pan African Conference of Third World Theologians, December 17–23, 1977, Accra, Ghana*. Maryknoll, NY: Orbis Books.

Olupona, Jacob. 2009. Comments on the Encyclopedia of Religion and Nature. *Journal of the American Academy of Religion*, 77, 1, 60–65.

Peires, J. B. 1989. *The Dead Will Arise: Nongqawuse and the Great Xhosa Cattle-Killing Movement of 1856–57*. Johannesburg: Ravan Press.

Sarna, Nahum M. 1966. *Understanding Genesis*, Vol. 1. New York: Jewish Theological Seminary of America.

Schoffeleers, Matthew. 1979. *Guardians of the Land: Essays on Central African Territorial Cults*. Gwelo: Mambo Press.

The Herald. 2007. *Was the River God Nyaminyami Angry? The Herald*, January, 12.

Vawter, Bruce. 1977. *On Genesis: A New Reading*. New York: Doubleday.

Von Rad, Gerhard. 1972. *Genesis: A Commentary*. London: SCM.

Walker-Jones, Arthur W. 2008. Eden for Cyborgs: Ecocriticism and Genesis 2–3. *Biblical Interpretation*, 16, 3, 263–293.

Westermann, Claus. 1974. *Genesis 1–11*. London: SPCK.

Wittenberg, Gunther. 2008. Plant and Animal Rights—An Absurd Idea or Ecological Necessity: Perspective from the Hebrew Torah. *Journal of Theology for Southern Africa*, 131, 72–83.

Wood, Felicity. 2004. Snakes, Spells, Cadillacs and Kruger Millions: Oral Accounts of the Extraordinary Career of Khotso Sethuntsa. *Kronos*, 30, 167–183.

Woodhouse, H. C. 1979. *The Bushman Art of Southern Africa*. Cape Town: Purnell.

Yeir, Agai. 2003. Good Luck Python Brings Hope and Joy to Nyanza. *The Nation*, March, 6. http://www.allafrica.com.

Further Reading

Baxter, T. W. 1950. Slave Raiders in North-Eastern Rhodesia. *The Northern Rhodesia Journal*, I, 1, 7–17.

British South Africa Company. 1892–1903. *Reports on the Administration of Rhodesia: 1889/92–1900/02*. London: British South Africa Company.

Chara, Tendai. 2012. *Nyaminyami Reappears, Disappears. The Herald*, December, 23.

Gouldsbury, Cullen & Sheane, Hubert. 1969. *The Great Plateau of Northern Rhodesia, Being Some Impressions of the Tanganyika Plateau*. New York: Negro Universities Press.

Joines, Karen R. 1967. Winged Serpents in Isaiah's Inaugural Vision. *Journal of Biblical Literature*, 86, 4, 410–415.

CHAPTER 14

Jewish Environmental Ethics

The Imperative of Responsibility

Hava Tirosh-Samuelson

We live in the Anthropocene Age (Crutzen, 2006; Zalasiewitz et al., 2010), an epoch in which human activity profoundly and, in many cases, irreversibly impacts all ecosystems. While humans have always impacted their natural environment, modern industrialization and technological advances have come at the expense of the very physical environment that sustains life on Earth, including human life. Under the banner of "progress" and the desire to improve the quality of human life, humanity has exploited natural resources for its own benefit, damaging the natural environment and the wellbeing of non-human life. Most scientists today agree that human activities have caused a massive ecological crisis manifested in the heating of the climate, extreme weather events, soil erosion, deforestation, desertification, mass extinction of species, loss of biodiversity, pollution of air and water, and depletion of natural resources. Life on Earth, including human life, is now severely threatened, requiring us to rethink our attitudes and conduct toward the physical environment.

Human beings' awareness that they are indeed responsible for the ecological crisis gave rise to the discourse of environmental ethics in the early 1970s (e.g., Passmore, 1974). However, as environmental ethics became theoretically more sophisticated and refined, the value of responsibility has receded in importance. One need only consult influential reference books on environmental ethics (e.g., Jamieson, 2001, 2008; Light & Rolston III, 2003) to note the conspicuous absence of the value of responsibility. If responsibility is discussed at all, it is framed either in terms of obligations to future generations (e.g., Partridge 1981) or in the context of the debate about "stewardship" (Attfield, 2014, 101–137). The secular version of stewardship is the argument that "human beings do not own the Earth, but hold it as a trust not least for the sake of future generations" (Attfield, 2014, 20). But even when responsibility to future generations is acknowledged, the secular interpretation of stewardship has given rise to

The Wiley Blackwell Companion to Religion and Ecology, First Edition. Edited by John Hart.

environmental science (e.g., Chapin III et al., 2009) dominated by the very instrumental attitudes toward Nature that brought about the ecological crisis in the first place.

Whereas secular environmental ethics and managerial environmental science have failed to mobilize humanity to address the ecological crisis, world religions can make a difference because they appeal to ultimate norms and values. The religious version of stewardship states that God has commanded humans to care for the Earth and that they are answerable to God for their actions. Within a religious worldview responsibility means both responsibility to God and responsibility for the world that God has created (Huber, 1993). Within a religious tradition environmental ethics is defined by sacred texts, and its norms and values relate not just to humans and natural entities but to the ultimate source of value: God. Religiously oriented environmentalists have generated the discourse of religion and ecology that has recovered environmental resources of religious traditions, critiqued and reinterpreted these traditions in light of environmental sensibilities, or replaced existing beliefs and practices with environmental spirituality (e.g., Gottlieb, 2006; Grim & Tucker, 2014; Jenkins, 2008; Oelschlaeger, 1994). This chapter discusses the distinctive Jewish contribution to the discourse of religion and ecology by elucidating the value of responsibility in Jewish environmental ethics.

Jewish Religious Environmentalism

Jewish religious environmentalism emerged in the 1970s in response to the charge of Lynn White Jr. (1967) that the Bible, and the Judeo-Christian tradition it sanctioned, was the primary cause of the ecological crisis. The biblical command to "be fruitful and multiply and replenish the earth and subdue it, have dominion over ... every living thing" (Gen. 1: 28), so he charged, gave human beings a license to dominate and exploit the Earth's resources.[1] Rejecting this charge, Jewish theologians, religious leaders, and educators began to explore Judaism from an environmental perspective, showing that this verse by no means summarizes the Jewish approach to the environment. Scripture does not sanction human domination of the Earth because it severely curtails human activities in regard to the natural world. Moreover, scripture entrusts humanity "to till and protect" the Earth (Gen. 2: 15) by specifying how to treat the soil, vegetation, and animals in order to ensure the fecundity of the Earth. As religiously committed Jews began to interpret Judaism in light of environmentalism, they demonstrated that the sacred texts of the Jewish tradition articulate not only a deep concern for the wellbeing of God's created world but also an obligation to protect the world from human destruction (Benstein, 2006).

Jewish environmental ethics is grounded in three foundational beliefs: Creation, revelation, and redemption, which are framed within the Jewish sacred narrative. Accordingly, God created the physical world and all its inhabitants, and God continues to sustain the world in His goodness forever. The created world is good, but not perfect, and its numerous creatures are structured hierarchically, in accordance with their capacity to perfect the created world. At the top of the hierarchy of beings stands the human who was created "in the divine image" (*Tzelem Elohim*). Whether the "image of God" was identified as the power to reason, personhood, or subjectivity, Jewish thinkers have viewed the human being as a creature that stands between animals and God.

As a created being, the human being is subject to temporality, materiality, and death, but because created in the divine image, the human being is able to transcend creatureliness and imitate God. Precisely because the human is created in the "divine image," the human is able to act in accordance with God's will by observing God's commands. Creation in the image of God, then, entails responsibility: the human being is responsible to God and responsible for the world.

All human beings are accountable to God for their actions, but one group of human beings—Israel—is particularly chosen to enter into a covenant. To Israel, the Chosen People, God has revealed His will in the form of the Torah (literally, "instruction"). The revealed Torah spells out how Israel is to conduct itself in all aspects of life, including conduct toward the physical environment: the Earth, vegetation, and animals. Expressing the unbound and unconditional love of God to Israel, the Covenant makes Israel, collectively and individually, responsible to God, who rewards or punishes human deeds. The Covenant between God and Israel is a contract whose collateral is the Land of Israel: so long as the People of Israel observe the revealed God's will, the Land of Israel is fertile and fecund and the people of Israel flourish; but, when Israel sins by not observing God's will, the Land of Israel loses its fertility and the people of Israel suffer. When the sins of Israel become too egregious, God exiles the people from the Holy Land. In the Jewish sacred myth, the condition of the Land of Israel manifests the dynamics of the relationship between God and Israel. In both the Land of Israel and in the diaspora, Israel's task is to perfect the world through actions in accordance with divine commands that sanctify the world. Such an ongoing process culminates in redemption (*geulah*), although how it operates remains a mystery that is open to conflicting interpretations.

For the past few decades Jewish religious environmentalists have produced a growing body of literature (e.g., Tirosh-Samuelson, 2002, 2015; Yaffe, 2011) and many environmental organizations. In Israel secular environmental activists have influenced public policies and practices, and some organizations (e.g., Adam, Hayim ve-Sevivah, Sevivah Israel, Teva, Teva Ivry, and ve-Din) have shown that environmentalism is compatible with the teachings of Judaism. In the diaspora, where Jews as a minority do not frame environmental policies, several Jewish organizations and initiatives (e.g., Aytzim: Ecological Judaism, COEJL, Hazon: Jewish Inspiration, sustainable communities) encourage Jews to cultivate an environmentally moderate lifestyle inspired by the Jewish textual tradition (Tirosh-Samuelson, 2012). Jewish environmentalism has explicated the ecological dimension of Jewish sacred texts, rituals, customs, and ethics, and has articulated an ecotheology inspired by Kabbalah and Hasidism (Seidenberg, 2015), even though these strands of thought initially had little to do with environmentalism. Although Jewish environmentalism is represented by a numerically small group, it has become an important and influential strand in contemporary Judaism.

Principles of Jewish Ethics of Responsibility: Normative Ethics

The Bible recognizes the tension between the human capacity to control the natural world and human responsibility to take care of the natural world. Gen. 1: 28 and 2:15, respectively, articulate this tension: the first verse authorizes human control over the

Earth; the second imposes the obligation to cultivate and guard the Earth. The two verses are complementary rather than contradictory: the human being has the creative ability that make it possible to benefit from Nature as well as to transform Nature and even destroy it (Soloveitchik, 1965, 10–16). Therefore, human creative capacities must be curtailed. The Bible limits human action in regard to Nature: humans must act in accordance with divine commands that specify how to treat the natural environment; human actions are to be undertaken for the sake of improving the created world. And, humans must regularly cease their creative activities by resting on the Sabbath, emulating God who rested on the seventh day of Creation. By acting responsibly toward the Earth and its inhabitants, humanity functions as a "caretaker" or "steward" of Creation, increasing order in the created world and protecting it from destruction.[2]

Land Management

The underlying assumption is that God is the true proprietor of the Earth. In Leviticus 25: 23 where the laws of the sabbatical year are promulgated, God proclaims "the land is mine," an assertion that is restated poetically in the Psalms: "the Earth is the Lord's and the fullness thereof" (Ps. 24: 1). Since the Creator is the true owner of the Earth, humans are viewed as no more than temporary tenants: they are to care for the Earth rather than exploit it for their own needs. Since God is viewed as the rightful owner of the Land of Israel, God's tenant-farmers are obliged to return the first portion of the land's yield to its rightful owner in order to ensure the land's continuing fertility and the farmers' sustenance and prosperity. Accordingly, the first sheaf of the barley harvest, the first fruit of produce, and two loaves of bread made from the new grain are to be consecrated to God. Some of the consecrated produce is to be given to the priests and Levites; the rest is to be eaten or used by the farmer. Land-based commandments pay special attention to trees: Leviticus 19: 23 commands that during the first three years of growth, the fruits of newly planted trees and vineyards are not to be eaten (*orlah*), because they are considered to be God's property. If Israel observes these divine commands, the Land of Israel is abundant and fertile, producing grain, oil, and wine, the basic necessities for human life. Biblical land legislation evolved in the rabbinic period but its basic principles remained the same.

Protection of Biodiversity

The goodness of the created world is manifested in its diversity: the created world is an organized cosmos in which creatures are grouped together, "each according to its kind" (*min le-minehu*) (Gen. 1: 31). Leviticus 19: 19 protects diversification in stating, "You shall not let your cattle breed with a different kind; you shall not sow your field with two kinds of seeds" (repeated in Deut. 22: 9–11). Scripture prohibits the mixing of different species of plants, fruit trees, fish, birds, and land animals, and this prohibition is clarified and further elaborated by the rabbis in Mishnah, Tractate Kilayim, and in the Palestinian Talmud on that tractate. Other biblical sources (Ps. 148, 104; Job 38–41) offer an even better foundation for "new Jewish ethics for the preservation of species and ecosystems" because these sources teach that humans "are part of a larger community of life" and that "God revels in its variety" (Troster, 2008, 15).

Limits on Human Consumption

Food is the primary point of contact between humans and animals. The Jewish tradition places stringent limits on human consumption of animals and regulates all food sources. The production and consumption of food is governed by divine commands which sanctify natural entities, declaring them to be either ritually pure or impure for the priesthood and for individual Israelites. Scripture prohibits eating the meat of certain creatures that are classified as impure or unclean, the ingestion of blood of any animals, the consumption of animal fat (*helev*), the eating of meat from the carrion (*nevelah*) of animals and fowl. The differentiation between "clean" and "unclean" animals, which is the core of the Jewish dietary laws (*kashrut*), has generated many theories about the origin of the system; it is possible to explain the prohibition on consuming certain animals as ecologically motivated. Many of the forbidden species were common in the Land of Israel, so these prohibitions can be seen as extended protection of birds that are important to "maintaining the ecological equilibrium and serve as the most efficient biocontrol agents of species" (Hütterman, 1999, 78).

Concern for Future Generations

The richness of the created world must be protected for the sake of future generations. Deuteronomy 22: 6–7 attests to biblical concern with the perpetuation of the life of non-human animals. If one finds a nest on the ground or on a tree with chicks or eggs in it and "the mother sitting upon the young or upon the eggs, you shall not take the mother with the young; you shall let the mother go, but the young you make take to yourself, that it may go well with you and that you may live long." By saving the mother, the law enables the species to continue to reproduce itself and avoid potential extinction. Elaborated by the rabbis (e.g., Deuteronomy Rabba VI, 5; Babylonian Talmud Hulin 138b–142a; Sifre Deuteronomy, 227), this law specifies that the person who finds the nest is only allowed to take the nestlings if they have not fledged. The concern for future generations demonstrates the Jewish notion of sustainability, also documented by the later rabbinic prohibition on rearing sheep and goats, to enable the Land of Israel to recover from the devastation of the Bar Kochba War (132–135 CE). While this legislation was justified by appealing to the intrinsic holiness of the Land of Israel, it demonstrated too rabbinic attention to the wellbeing of the physical environment.

Prevention of Wanton Destruction ("Do Not Destroy")

The main principle of Jewish environmental ethics concerns the protection of plant life, especially fruit-bearing trees. In wartime, fruit-bearing trees must not be chopped down while a city is under siege (Deut. 20: 19). This commandment indicates that scripture recognizes the interdependence between humans and trees, on the one hand, and the capacity of humans to destroy natural things on the other. To ensure the continued fertility of the land, human destructive tendencies are curbed by scriptural law. In the Talmud and later rabbinic sources, the biblical injunction "do not destroy" is extended to cover all destruction, complete or incomplete, direct or indirect, of all objects that may potentially benefit humans (Schwartz, 2001 [1997]). A sweeping number of environmental regulations specifies the meaning of the principle "do not destroy": the prohibitions on cutting off water supplies to trees; overgrazing; unjustifiably killing animals or feeding them noxious foods; hunting animals for sport; species extinction and the destruction of cultivated plant varieties; pollution of the air and water; overconsumption of anything; and squandering mineral and other resources. These environmental regulations indicate that the Jewish legal tradition requires that one carefully weigh up the ramifications, for every interaction with the natural world, of all actions and behavior; it also sets priorities and considers conflicting interests and permanent modification of the environment.

Prevention of Distress of Living Creatures (Tza`ar Ba`alei Hayyim)

Although responsibility for management of God's Creation is placed in human hands, the tradition also recognizes the wellbeing of non-human species: humans should protect other species and be sensitive to the needs of animals (Shochet, 1984). Cruelty to animals is prohibited because it leads to other forms of cruelty. The ideal is to create a sensibility of love and kindness toward animals in order to emulate God's attribute of mercy and fulfill the commandment "to be Holy as I the Lord am Holy" (Lev. 19: 2). Thus Deuteronomy 22: 6 forbids the killing of a bird with her young because it is exceptionally cruel and can affect the perpetuation of the species. This commandment is one of seven given to the sons of Noah and is therefore binding on all human beings, not just Jews. Deuteronomy 22: 10 prohibits yoking an ass and an ox together: their uneven size could cause unnecessary suffering. The command "you shall not cook a kid in its mother's milk" (Ex. 23: 19; 34: 26; Deut. 14: 21), which is the basis for an elaborate system of ritual separation of milk and meat products in rabbinic Judaism, is explained by the rabbis as an attempt to prevent human cruelty (Deut. Rabbah 6: 1). While Scripture does not forbid slaughtering animals for consumption or sacrifice, or using eggs for human use, it curtails cruelty. Kindness to animals is a virtue of the righteous man which is associated with the promise of heavenly rewards (Prov. 12: 10). The tradition prescribes particular modes of slaughter which are swift, because they are performed with a clean, sharp blade, in order to minimize pain. (This concern about unnecessary suffering of animals is applied today to farming animals for human consumption and using animals in scientific experiments; Bleich, 2001 [1999]).

Social Justice and Ecological Wellbeing

The most distinctive feature of Jewish environmental ethics is the causal connection between the moral quality of human life and the vitality of God's Creation. Conversely, the corruption of society is closely linked to the corruption of Nature. In both cases, injustice arises from human greed and failure to protect the original order of Creation. From a Jewish perspective, the just allocation of Nature's resources is a religious matter of the highest order. The treatment of the marginalized in society—the poor, the hungry, widows, orphans—must follow scriptural legislation. Thus, parts of the land's produce—the corners of the field (*peah*), the gleanings of stalks (*leqet*), the overlooked sheaf (*shikhekhah*), the separated fruits (*peret*), and the defective clusters (*olelot*)—are to be given to those who do not own land. When people observe such particular commandments the soil itself becomes holy, and the person who obeys these commandments ensures the religio-moral purity necessary for residence in God's land. Failure to treat other members of society justly, to protect the sanctity of their lives, is integrally tied to acts extended toward the land.

The connection between land management, ritual, and social justice is most evident in the laws regulating the Sabbath and the sabbatical year (*shemittah*). The Sabbath, as Jonathan Sacks put it succinctly, is "the most compelling tutorial in human dignity, environmental consciousness and the principle that there are moral limits to economic exchange and commercial exploitation" (Sacks, 2005, 169). On the Sabbath, creative action is prohibited to enable humans to devote time to reflection and recognition of human subservience to a greater power (Schorsch, 1992). Rest is imposed not only on humans but also on the domestic animals in their service, thus indicating that even though animals do not receive divine commands directly, environmental legislation impacts the quality of their life. The principles of the Sabbath were extended to the Land of Israel every seventh year, during which it is forbidden to plant, cultivate, or harvest grain, fruit, or vegetables; in the sixth year, it is forbidden to plant in order to harvest during the seventh year. Crops that grow untended are not to be harvested by the landlord but are to be left ownerless (*hefqer*) for all to share, including the poor and animals. The rest imposed during the sabbatical year facilitates the restoration of nutrients and the replenishment of the soil, promotes diversity in plant life, and helps maintain vigorous cultivars. On the seventh year debts contracted by fellow countrymen are to be remitted (Lev. 25–33; Deut. 15: 3), providing temporary relief from these obligations. In the sabbatical year as well as in the Jubilee year (the 50th year) all Hebrew slaves are freed, regardless of when they were acquired (Lev. 25: 39–41), in order to teach that slavery is not a natural state. The laws of the sabbatical years were practically reversed in the rabbinic period when a written document (*prozbul*) assigned the debt to the court prior to the sabbatical year with the intention of collecting the debt as a later date. In modern Israel, the return to land cultivation by religious Jews has revived the practices of the sabbatical year (Riskin, 1974), justified by a unique fusion of Judaism and socialism (Chayne, 2010).

Eco-Kosher: Jewish Social Justice

Jewish normative environmental ethics is best summarized by the concept "Eco-Kosher." Coined in the early 1970s by the late Rabbi Zalman Schachter-Shalomi and popularized by Arthur Waskow (1976), this term pertains not just to ritual cleanliness but to a range of practices related to food production: food can become ritually unclean if produced by unjust exploitative practices involving, for example, child labor or adult exploitation, or animals, such as in industrial animal farming. Eco-Kosher specifies in legal terms what it means to treat animals justly and what the connection is between justice for animals and justice for humans. Going beyond the ideals of the environmental justice movement, eco-justice insists on a global commitment on behalf of all creatures. Seeking to build ecological ethics applicable to the entire world and instructive for all persons, eco-justice rallies the global community round an ideal of harmonious coexistence throughout the community of life. The underlying value in ecojustice is responsibility. In short, Jewish normative environmental ethics is religious, law-governed, pragmatic, and relational.

Theorizing the Ethics of Responsibility: Meta-Ethics

Although Jewish religious ethics of responsibility supports conservation and preservation policies, today the majority of Jews do not see themselves as obliged by Jewish law even though they define themselves both ethnically and culturally as Jews. Can the Jewish ethics of responsibility be relevant to non-observant or secular Jews? Can Jews theorize responsibility without justifying it by appeal to divinely revealed scriptures? Can the Jewish religious ethics of responsibility be relevant to non-Jews? Two Jewish philosophers—Martin Buber (1878–1965) and Emmanuel Levinas (1906–1995)—allow us to answer these questions in the affirmative since they argue for the ethics of responsibility without appealing to the normative power of divine revelation. They have done so as both committed Jews and as well-trained philosophers, although Levinas did not want to be known as a "Jewish philosopher." Trained in German universities, their ethical theories developed through a response to Western philosophy, especially Kantian philosophy.[3] Buber recognized natural entities as persons with whom one has a dialogical encounter and Levinas extended to Nature the status of the Absolute Other to which we are always already responsible. Both philosophers developed their ideas in conversation with Kantian ethics, especially the so-called "Formula of Humanity" of Kant's Categorical Imperative, but their relational or dialogical philosophy was also a critique of Kantian ethics.

Kant drew a sharp distinction between the moral status of human beings and all non-humans: only human beings are "persons," whereas all others are mere "things," because human beings are the only animals that are rational, autonomous (i.e., self-legislating), and free. For Kant, although animals are endowed with sensation and choice, they are "non-rational"—incapable of rational cognition—and lack free moral will. By virtue of their distinctive rationality, only human beings act in accordance with the universal moral law and only humans should be treated as ends-in-themselves rather than as means to an end. Therefore, human beings possess dignity that is absent in other animals or non-sentient beings. For Kant only beings with dignity can be obliged or oblige others, and only beings that fall under the rational universal moral law can be considered persons. Given this fundamental disparity between human and non-humans, humans do not have direct moral duties toward animals and cannot treat them as persons. Humans have a moral right to use animals (and Nature more generally) for their own benefit, but humans have an indirect moral duty to prevent "violent and cruel treatment of animals." Kant allows for the killing of animals, although he concedes that it should be quick and painless, and he agreed that animals ought not to be harmed without cause (not unlike the Jewish position). But even the indirect duties to animals are ultimately human-centered since they flow from "the human being's duty to himself as an animal being" (Metaphysics of Morals 6: 421). Animals, in short, are mere "means to an end. The end is man." Whether Kantian philosophy can sustain environmental ethics or whether Kant was deeply mistaken about his view on animals has been long debated (Krosgaard, 2011; Skidmore, 2001; Wood, 1998), but there is no doubt that Kant's Categorical Imperative influenced many environmental ethicists who argued for respect for Nature (Taylor, 2011 [1986]).

Martin Buber: Nature as a Moral Subject

Kantian philosophy reverberates in Buber's philosophy, although he moved beyond Kant to accord moral status to Nature. Buber was deeply rooted in the Jewish textual tradition, but he was not an observant Jew. While using God-language, Buber chose not to live an Orthodox life because he "could not accept the traditional and heteronomic belief in divine revelation of the Law" (Margolin, 2008, 235). Whether characterized as "religious secularism" (Moore, 1974) or "secular religiosity" (Margolin, 2008), Buber's philosophy could appeal to secular, non-observant, or progressive Jews and to non-Jews. If the rabbinic tradition understood the Covenant to be law-centered, Buber insisted that the covenantal relationship culminating in revelation means a direct, non-propositional encounter with the Divine Presence. According to Buber's famous formulation, humans relate to the world either directly and unconditionally ("I–Thou") or indirectly, conditionally, and functionally ("I–It"). The "I–Thou" modality means a direct encounter that encompasses all of one's personality and treats the other as an end rather than as a means. The "I–It" relationship has a purpose beyond the encounter itself, and involves only a fragment of the other, not the entire person. Between the I–It and I–Thou realms there is no sharp dualism, but rather a constant interplay as humans oscillate between the two postures or attitudes. Similar to Heidegger's notion of "standing reserve," the I–It relation is a lower mode of relating to others because we perceive others merely as an object whose value derives from their instrumental use to us. The I–It relation is, therefore, potentially exploitative and destructive. By contrast, the I–Thou relation (which echoes the Kantian notion of treating humans as ends rather than means) enables us to see the other as a moral subject with intrinsic worth that cannot be exhausted by the Self. In I–Thou relations we see the other as irreducible and inherently valuable, but also as utterly vulnerable.

Buber's ideas became very influential in environmental ethics because he extended the I–Thou relationship to an encounter with Nature. He was highly critical of the naturalism characteristic of modern philosophy and science precisely because it illustrates

I–It relations. Instead, he regarded plants and animals as subjects with which we have personal ethical relations. Buber described his encounter with a horse when he was a boy (Buber, 1970 [1923], 75) and extended the possibility of having such a relation with a tree (1970 [1923], 8). In treating Nature as a "Thou" rather than an "It," Buber personified natural phenomena and recognized not only the need of humans to communicate with natural objects, but also the inherent rights of Nature. Nature is a Thou, waiting to be addressed by the wholeness of our own being. I–Thou relations with animals are possible because animals can respond to us, in mutual, reciprocal relations. Relations with non-sentient natural entities such as trees or rocks are more difficult to characterize as reciprocal, but even these entities can reveal to us their Thou-ness, enabling us to understand them entirely as they are. What makes possible I–Thou relations with non-conscious Nature is God, the Eternal Thou, who is present everywhere and in everything. This panentheistic idea reflects Buber's indebtedness to Hasidism, whose cosmology and ontology were framed by Kabbalah.[4]

What does responsibility mean for Buber? Buber does not tell us what we must do in our relationships; his focus on direct encounter stands in contrast to rule-governed ethics. For Buber, an I–Thou relationship lacks prescriptive, normative content precisely because it is an authentic, non-objectifying encounter. But, with no reference to Jewish law, how do we know what we ought to do? The answer lies in the dynamics of the relationship between the two moral subjects, in the interpersonal dialogue between the moral persons. The relationship itself tells us what constitutes mistreatment and when we go wrong. Because we have the capacity to be in I–Thou relations, we are thus responsible for the quality of the dialogical relationship, of the encounter itself. As Maurice Friedman put it: "in Buber 'is' and 'ought' join" (Friedman, 2002, 236). The "ought" is not an abstract rule imposed on us from outside, but a response to the needs of the Other experienced in the actual "lived life" and in the context of the relationship itself. We are responsible by responding to the needs and wants of the Other with whom we are in relation. Buber's dialogical philosophy which sees Nature as a moral subject deeply influenced Christian eco-theologians such as Sally McFague and Paul Santmire. For McFague, Buber's subject–subject relations offers "a model that shows that, as incarnation insists, God is found in the depth and detail of life and the earth, not apart from it or in spite of it" (McFague, 1997, 102). For Santmire, Buber's relational philosophy makes it possible to speak about "a third type of relation, a construct that will make available a truly ecological and cosmic conceptuality, one that accounts for rich relationships between persons and nature that are not I—It relations" (Santmire, 2000, 68). Although Buber was not an environmental thinker, his dialogical philosophy exerted a significant influence on Christian environmental ethics.

Levinas: Nature as the Absolute Other to Whom I am Always Responsible

Another highly influential Jewish philosopher is Emmanuel Levinas, whose philosophy of alterity emerged from his experience as a prisoner of war in Fallingsbotel, a Nazi labor camp for Jewish French soldiers near Hanover, Germany where he was treated as an "unnatural being," a subhuman devoid of personhood and dignity. Indeed, in the

POW labor camp, as Levinas bitterly put it, Bobby the dog was the "last Kantian in Nazi Germany" (Levinas, 1990, 153).[5] As Levinas saw it, the dog revealed a Kantian respect for humanity lacking in the behavior of fellow humans. Remembering the loyalty of the dog, Levinas pondered "whether or not that animal was owed the responsibility that each prisoner owed the others" (Bloechl, 2000, 60). Levinas maintained that responsibility characterizes the entire life of the subject as a response to the appeal of the Other: the anxiety about the death of the Other is the source of the disinterested obedience (or disobedience) to the prohibition against murder of the Other. Indeed, Levinas saw responsibility as the core of the ethical as such. But Levinas further argued that responsibility comes first; each person is responsible for the one who faces him. Levinas argues for infinite individual responsibility: every person has an obligation to neighbors, expanding gradually to embrace all living humans. Levinas's ethics is decidedly human-centered and he repeatedly insisted that ethics is "against-nature, against the naturality of nature" (Levinas, 1998, 171). However, when the insights of Levinas's ethics are extended to Nature, as postmodernist environmental ethicists have done, they become a powerful reformulation of environmental ethics.

Levinas's ethics grounds the ethical in the account of the Other, namely, in alterity. Levinas spoke of two kinds of alterity: the Other (*l'autre*), whose meaning is constituted by consciousness, and the Absolute Other (*l'Autrui*), who signifies a meaning beyond all intentional horizon (Davis, 1996). The Other is what sustains me and what I transform through work, but the Other resists all attempts at assimilation or conceptualization. The Absolute Other cannot be thematized or conceptualized, but can only be encountered directly, similar to Buber's notion of I–Thou relations. The metaphor for the Other is the "face," which signifies the frailty and vulnerability of the one who needs you and who is relying on you. The face is the revelation of the Other. As Levinas explains, "[t]he face is not in front of me [*en face de moi*] but above me; it is the other before death, looking through and exposing death. Secondly, the face is the Other who asks me not to let him die alone, as if to do so were to become an accomplice in his death. Thus, the face says to me: "you shall not kill" (Levinas, 1986, 24). When we are "faced" by the Other, we are called to respond and as such we stand in a relation of ethical accountability, whether or not one is looking into the face of the Other. The Other's needs and suffering face us and make us responsible for it in a disruptive even somewhat violent way. In the ethical moment we are awakened to the precariousness of the Other.

Several postmodernist environmentalists (e.g., Atterton 2004; Edelglass, 2012; Llewelyn, 1991, 49–67) have found Levinas's phenomenological description of the "face" valuable to environmental ethics, giving rise to eco-phenomenology. If extended to Nature, the principles of Levinasian ethics could be aligned with several non-anthropocentric environmental philosophies while moving environmental discourse beyond traditional theories. But can Nature be identified with the Absolute Other? Is Nature "the persecuted one for whom I am responsible"? Do animals have ethical "faces"? On these questions the debate is still undecided: some interpreters argue that for Levinas ethical relations are limited to the inter-human realm: the Other pertains to the human Other to the exclusion of all others. Levinas's humanism is underscored by the fact that he repeatedly insists on the "irreducible dignity of humans, a belief in the efficacy and worth of human freedom and hence also of human responsibility" (Cohen, 2006, ix).

By contrast, some interpreters hold that for Levinas moral concern extends to the nonhuman realm: the facial status of animals derives analogically from the transference of human suffering to them. This interpretation is still anthropocentric rather than biocentric because in it Levinas extends ethical responsibility beyond the human life only in so far as he sees an analogy between human and animal suffering.

Indeed, Levinas's position is humanistic because he is more interested in the one who is responsible that he is in the Other for whom one is responsible. Nonetheless, as Diane Perpich puts it, Levinas suggests that "human ethics ... is the 'prototype' for an extension of obligation to animals" (Perpich, 2012, 91). In his famous interview with students at the University of Warwick in 1986, Levinas stated, "It is clear that, without considering animals as human beings, the ethical extends to all living beings" (Wright et al., 1988, 172). That is to say that because animals suffer, and humans know the torment of suffering, Levinas can say "we do not want to make an animal suffer needlessly and so on" (Wright et al., 1988). Not unlike Kant, he sees obligations to animals as purely negative duties of omission. However, since Levinas was deeply rooted in the Jewish tradition, we can surmise that he regarded the traditional prohibition against causing needless suffering to animals sufficient and did not see a need to elaborate the point. It is no coincidence that in Levinas's philosophy the paradigm of the Absolute Other is the orphan, the widow, and the stranger who are protected by biblical legislation of the sabbatical year. Jewish environmental legislation, therefore, provided Levinas with the deepest insight about infinite responsibility to the Other. For Levinas to be human is to be first and foremost responsible for the Other; responsibility defines human subjectivity. Like Buber, Levinas does not specify what we need to do about the environment but he enables us to see that the environmental crisis has made Nature a vulnerable and persecuted Other, toward whom we have infinite obligation.

Conclusion

As a normative tradition, Judaism specifies what one is expected to do in all aspects of life, including interaction with the natural world. Jews who define themselves in religious terms (e.g., Orthodox, Conservative, Reconstructionist, Reform, or Jewish Renewal) can find deep and rich insights within the Jewish tradition that support conservationist practices conducive to sustainability. In Jewish normative ethics there is a close connection between ethics and Nature: when human beings conduct themselves in accordance with God's will the Earth is fertile; when they sin against each other and against God, the Earth loses its fecundity and consequently human beings suffer and their life loses vitality. Framed within a religious narrative of covenantal theology, Jewish normative ethics is not anthropocentric but theocentric, because it claims that the world belongs first and foremost to God rather than to humans, while humans were given the task of caring for the created world. The human task is not understood as managerial "control and command," but rather as attentive "stewardship" or "caregiving," analogous to the loving work of the gardener. Although Jewish normative ethics is framed legally, in Jewish law there is no tension between duties and virtues: the divine commands that specify action also facilitate the cultivation of character traits conducive to the right action toward the environment. Jewish ecojustice (or Eco-Kosher) links right conduct toward humans with the appropriate treatment of the soil, vegetation, and animals. Finally, Jewish normative ethics does not exhibit the radical break between theory and practice because the Jewish sacred narrative shapes rules, attitudes, and acts in regard to a specific locale, the Land of Israel, and under very specific circumstances.

Buber and Levinas have offered philosophical interpretations of the imperative of responsibility. Long before the environmental crisis was recognized, Buber made it possible to think about Nature as a moral subject. By recognizing the possibility of personal (i.e., subject–subject) relations with Nature, Buber moved beyond the Kantian view of indirect duties toward Nature. Much more demanding than Buber was Levinas's radical understanding of responsibility according to which to be human is to be infinitely responsible to the vulnerable Other. When Levinas's ethics is applied to Nature, it offers an eco-phenomenology that makes each and every human being personally responsible. In its religious or secular forms, Jewish ethics of responsibility is a profound and compelling response to the environmental crisis.

Notes

1 For a critique of White's thesis, see Derr (1975); Passmore (1974); Santmire (1984).
2 For recent arguments in support of stewardship, see Attfield (2014, 30–35).
3 The overwhelming impact of Kant on modern Jewish philosophy is explained by the fact that first, Kant's philosophy dominated German universities precisely at the time that Jews started to enter universities after centuries of exclusion; and second, Kant's deontology was in full accord with the Jewish legal tradition's focus on duties. Jews who sought integration into European society and culture could render their religious belief into Kantian philosophical language. See Frank (2012).
4 Both Kabbalah and Hasidism viewed the physical world as a mirror of God, but neither strand was interested in the wellbeing of the natural world for its own sake. See Tirosh-Samuelson (2002).
5 This famous statement generated considerable literature. See Clark (1997).

References

Attfield, Robin. 2014. *Environmental Ethics: An Overview for the Twenty-First Century*. Cambridge: Polity Press.

Atterton, Peter. 2004. "Face-to-Face" with the Other Animal? (262–281). In Peter Atterton, Matthew Calarco, & Maurice S. Friedman (Eds.), *Levinas and Buber: Dialogue and Difference*. Pittsburgh, PA: Duquesne University Press.

Benstein, Jeremy. 2006. *The Way into Judaism and the Environment*. Woodstock, VT: Jewish Lights Publications.

Bleich, David J. 2001 [1999]. Judaism and Animals Experimentation. *Contemporary Halakhic Problems*, Vol. II. New York: Ktav and Yeshiva University Press. Reprinted in *Judaism and Environmental Ethics* (333–370). Ed. Martin D. Yaffe. Lanham, MD: Lexington Books.

Bloechl, Jeffrey. 2000. *Liturgy of the Neighbor: Emmanuel Levinas and the Religion of Responsibility*. Pittsburgh, PA: Duquesne University Press.

Buber, Martin. 1970 [1923]. *I and Thou*. New York: Scribners.

Chayne, Shmuel. 2010. Environment, Society, and Economics in the Philosophy of Rabbi Samson Raphael Hirsch and Dr. Isaac Breuer. PhD dissertation. Ramat Gan, Israel: Bar Ilan University.

Chapin III, F. Stuart, Kofinas, Gary P., & Folke, Carl (Eds.). 2009. *Principles of Ecosystem Stewardship: Resilience-Based Natural Resource Management in a Changing World*. Dordrecht: Springer.

Clark, David. 1997. On Being "The Last Kantian in Nazi Germany" Dwelling with Animals after Levinas (165–198). In Jennifer Ham & Matthew Senior (Eds.), *Animal Acts: Configuring the Human in Western History*. New York: Routledge.

Crutzen, Paul J. 2006. The Anthropocene (13–18). In Eckart Ehlers & Thomas Kraft (Eds.), *Earth System Science in the Anthropocene*. Berlin: Springer.

Cohen, Richard A. 2006. Introduction: Humanism and Anti-Humanism—Levinas, Cassirer and Heidegger (vii–xliv). In *Emanuel Levinas: Humanism of the Other*. Transl. Nidra Poller. Urbana and Chicago, IL: University of Illinois Press.

Davis, Colin. 1996. *Levinas: An Introduction*. Notre Dame, IN: University of Notre Dame Press.

Derr, Thomas Sieger. 1975. "Religion's Responsibility for the Ecological Crisis: An Argument Run Amock." *Worldview*, 18, no. 1, (1975): 39–45.

Edelglass, William, Hatley, James, & Diehem, Christian (Eds.). 2012. *Facing Nature: Levinas and Environmental Thought*. Pittsburgh, PA: Duquesne University Press.

Frank, Paul W. 2012 [2007]. "Jewish Philosophy after Kant: The Legacy of Solomon Maimon." In *The Cambridge Companion of Modern Jewish Philosophy*, ed. Michael L. Morgan and Peter Eli Gordon, pp. 53–79. Cambridge and New York: Cambridge University Press.

Friedman, Maurice S. 2002. *Martin Buber: The Life of Dialogue*. London and New York: Routledge.

Gottlieb, Roger S. (Ed.). 2006. *Oxford Handbook of Religion and Ecology*. Oxford and New York: Oxford University Press.

Grim John & Tucker, Mary Evelyn. 2014. *Ecology and Religion*. Washington, DC: Island Press.

Huber, Wolfgang. 1993. Toward an Ethics of Responsibility. *The Journal of Religion*, 73, 4, 573–591.

Hütterman, Aloys. 1999. *The Ecological Message of the Torah: Knowledge, Concepts and Laws which Made Survival in a Land of "Milk and Honey" Possible*. Atlanta, GA: Scholars Press.

Jamieson, Dale (Ed.). 2001. *A Companion to Environmental Philosophy*. Malden, MA: Blackwell.

Jamieson, Dale. 2008. *Ethics and the Environment: An Introduction*. Cambridge: Cambridge University Press.

Jenkins, Willis. 2008. *Ecologies of Grace: Environmental Ethics and Christian Theology*. New York and Oxford: Oxford University Press.

Krosgaard, Christine M. 2011. Interacting with Animals: A Kantian Account (91–118). In Tom L. Beauchamp & R.G. Frey (Eds.), *The Oxford Handbook of Animal Ethics*. New York: Oxford University Press.

Levinas, Emmanuel. 1986. Dialogue with Emmanuel Levinas (vii–xliv). In Richard A. Cohen (Ed.), *Face to Face with Levinas*. Albany, NY: SUNY Press.

Levinas, Emmanuel. 1990. The Name of a Dog, or Natural Rights (151–153). In *Difficult Freedom: Essays on Judaism*. Transl. Sean Hand. Baltimore, MD: Johns Hopkins University Press.

Levinas, Emmanuel. 1998. *Of God Who Comes to Mind*. Transl. Bettina Bergo. Stanford, CA: Stanford University Press.

Light, Andrew & Rolston III, Holmes (Eds.). 2003. *Environmental Ethics: An Anthology*. 2003. Malden, MA: Blackwell.

Llewelyn, John. 1991. *The Middle Voice of Ecological Conscience: A Chiasmic Reading of Responsibility in the Neighborhood of Levinas, Heidegger, and Others*. New York: St. Martin's Press.

Margolin, Ron. 2008. Hans Jonas and Secular Religiosity (231–258). In Hava Tirosh-Samuelson and Christian Wiese (Eds.), *The Legacy of Hans Jonas: Judaism and the Phenomenon of Life*. Leiden and Boston, MA: Brill.

McFague, Sally. 1997. *Super, Natural Christians: How We Should Love Nature*. Minneapolis, MN: Fortress Press.

Moore, Donald. 1974. *Martin Buber: Prophet of Religious Secularism*. Philadelphia, PA: Fordham University Press.

Oelschlaeger Max. 1994. *Caring for Creation: An Ecumenical Approach to the Environmental Crisis*. New Haven, CT: Yale University Press.

Riskin, Shlomo. 1974. Shemitta: A Sabbatical for the Land: "The Land Shall Rest and the People Shall Grow" (70–73). In Aubrey Rose (Ed.), *Judaism and Ecology*. London: Cassell.

Partridge, Ernest (Ed.). 1981. *Responsibilities toward Future Generations: Environmental Ethics*. Buffalo, NY: Prometheus Books.

Passmore, John. 1974. *Man's Responsibility for Nature: Ecological Problems and Western Traditions*. London: Duckworth.

Perpich, Diane. 2012. Scarce Resources? Levinas, Animals and the Environment (67–94). In William Edelglass, James Hatley, & Christina Diehm (Eds.), *Facing Nature: Levinas and the Environment*. Pittsburgh, PA: Duquesne University Press.

Sacks, Jonathan. 2005. *To Heal a Fractured World: The Ethics of Responsibility*. New York: Schocken Books.

Santmire, Paul H. 2000. *Nature Reborn: The Ecological and Cosmic Promise of Christian Theology*. Minneapolis, MN: Fortress Press.

______. 1984. "The Liberation of Nature: Lynn White's Challenge Anew." *The Christian Century* 102: 18: 530–33.

Schwartz, Eilon. 2001 [1997]. Bal Tashchit: A Jewish Environmental Precept. *Environmental Ethics*, 19, 355–374. Reprinted in *Judaism and Environmental Ethics* (230–249). Ed. Martin D. Yaffe. Lanham, MD: Lexington Books.

Shochet, Elijah Judah. 1984. *Animal Life in Jewish Tradition*. New York: Ktav.

Schorsch, Ismar. 1992. Learning to Live with Less (27–38). In Steven C. Rockefeller & John C. Elder (Eds.), *Spirit and Nature: Why the Environment is a Religious Issue*. Boston, MA: Beacon Press.

Seidenberg, David Mevorach. 2015. *Kabbalah and Ecology: God's Image in the More-Than-Human World*. Cambridge: Cambridge University Press.

Skidmore, J. 2001. Duties to Animals: The Failure of Kant's Moral Theory. *The Journal of Moral Inquiry*, 35, 4, 541–559.

Soloveitchik, Joseph B. 1964. The Lonely Man of Faith. *Tradition*, 6, 2, 5–29.

Taylor, Paul. 2011 [1986]. *Respect for Nature: A Theory for Environmental Ethics*. Princeton, NJ: Princeton University Press.

Tirosh-Samuelson, Hava (Ed.). 2002. *Judaism and Ecology: Created World and Revealed*. Cambridge, MA: Harvard University Press.

Tirosh-Samuelson, Hava. 2012. Jewish Environmentalism: Faith, Scholarship and Activism (1–53). In Daniel Lasker (Ed.), *Jewish Thought, Jewish Faith*. Beer Sheba: Ben Gurion University Press.

Tirosh-Samuelson, Hava. 2015. "Judaism and the Environment." *Oxford Bibliographies Online*. DOI: 10.1093/OBO/9780199840731-0118.

Troster, Lawrence. 2008. God Must Love Beetles: A Jewish View of Biodiversity and Extinction of Species. *Conservative Judaism*, 60, 3, 3–21.

Waskow, Arthur. 1996. What is Eco-Kosher? (297–300). In Roger S. Gottlieb (Ed.), *This Sacred Earth: Religion, Nature, Environment*. New York and London: Routledge.

White, Lynn Jr. 1967. The Historical Roots of our Ecologic Crisis. *Science*, 155, 153–157.

Wood, Allen. 1998. Kant on Duties Regarding Nonrational Nature: Allen W. Wood. *Aristotelian Society Supplementary Volume*, 72, 189–210.

Wright, Tamara, Hughes, Peter, & Ainley, Alison. 1988. The Paradox of Morality: An Interview with Emmanuel Levinas (168–180). In Robert Bernasconi & David Wood (Eds.), *The Provocation of Levinas: Rethinking the Other*. London and New York: Routledge.

Yaffe, Martin D. (Ed.). 2001. *Judaism and Environmental Ethics: A Reader*. Lanham, MD: Lexington Books.

Zalasiewicz, Jan, Williams, Mark, Steffen, Will, & Crutzen, Paul. 2010. The New World of the Anthropocene. *Environmental Science and Technology*, 44, 2228–2231.

Further Reading

Tirosh-Samuelson, Hava. 2005. Judaism (425–537). In Bron Taylor (Ed.), *Encyclopedia of Religion and Nature*. London: Continuum.

Tirosh-Samuelson, Hava. 2006. Judaism (25–64). In Roger S. Gottlieb (Ed.), *Oxford Handbook of Religion and Ecology*. Oxford: Oxford University Press.

Tirosh-Samuelson, Hava. 2011a. Judaism and the Care for God's Creation (286–319). In Tobias Winright (Ed.), *Green Discipleship: Catholic Theological Ethics and the Environment*. Winona, MN: Anselm Academic.

Tirosh-Samuelson, Hava. 2011b. Judaism and the Science of Ecology (345–355). In James Haag, Gregory R. Peterson, & Michael L. Spezio (Eds.), *Routledge Companion of Religion and Science*. New York and London: Routledge.

Tirosh-Samuelson, Hava, & Wiese, Christian (Eds.). 2008. *The Legacy of Hans Jonas: Judaism and the Phenomenon of Life*. Leiden and Boston, MA: Brill.

CHAPTER 15

Ecowomanism and Ecological Reparations

Melanie L. Harris

BlackLivesMatter is a global social justice movement initiated from within the African-American community in 2013 in response to brutal police killings of unarmed young Black men and women. Founded by three Black women and social organizers, Alicia Garza, Patrisse Cullors, and Opal Tometi, BlackLivesMatter organized a national and later international platform to protest unjust practices of police brutality as well as the devaluing of Black lives in an age of White supremacy. Calling on government leaders, politicians, teachers, and policy makers to analyze and dismantle the systemic racism woven into social culture, BlackLivesMatter protests grew from the development of the hashtag, #BlackLivesMatter on social media in 2013 to countless physical and highly publicized demonstrations in 2014 following the death of two African-American men, Michael Brown in Ferguson, Missouri, and Eric Garner in New York City, caused by police officers. Later, soldiers on the streets of Ferguson were equipped with tanks, guns, and artillery, sending a message of violent confrontation, intimidation, and terror to Black communities and neighborhoods.

Taking grassroots organizing lessons from the Civil Rights Movement, the Black Power movement, the 1980s Black feminist movement, Pan-Africanism, anti-Apartheid movement, Hip Hop, LGBTQ, and Occupy Wall Street community organizing, #BlackLivesMatter has sparked a commitment to justice by uncovering the brutality of multifaceted systemic oppression built on the paradigm of White supremacy.

Instructive for this chapter, the movement's overarching philosophy and embrace of intersectionality invites activist and scholarly reflection on the affirmation of all Black lives, including "the lives of black queer and trans folks, disabled folks, black undocumented folks, folks with records, women and all black lives along the gender spectrum" (#blacklivesmatter.com). Noting the embrace of intersectionality and Black feminist frameworks in the movement is especially important to the work of ecowomanism.

The Wiley Blackwell Companion to Religion and Ecology, First Edition. Edited by John Hart.

Ecowomanism is an approach to environmental justice that centers the voices, experiences, and perspectives of women of color and especially women of African descent on environmental justice. It examines the systemic nature of environmental health disparities between people and communities of color and White people, who often live in wealthier neighborhoods. Weaving attention to environmental care and justice into the concern for the liberation and true flourishing of Black lives, ecowomanist responses are influenced by the #BlackLivesMatter paradigm and approach to justice.

This chapter poses one primary question: in light of the significant contributions and templates for social justice organizing that have emerged from BlackLivesMatter, are there specific anti-racist reparations paradigms that can be translated into ecological reparations work? In order to answer the larger question, I focus here on explaining what ecological reparations is from an ecowomanist perspective.

Ecowomanism

Hava A. Tirosh-Samuelson's definition of ecowomanism is given elsewhere in this volume, but it needs to be expanded. Ecowomanism is a critical reflection on, and contemplation and praxis-oriented study of environmental justice from the perspectives of women of color, in particular women of African descent. It connects issues of social justice such as racism, classism, and sexism with issues of environmental concern. That is, through an ecowomanist lens we can examine the parallel oppressions that women of color have often survived when confronting racism, classism, sexism, heteropatriarchy, and like oppressions that the Earth is experiencing through environmental degradation. While anthropocentric in its focus, ecowomanism unashamedly takes the lives of these women of color as a starting point to reflect on climate justice, in part because of the historical and paradoxical connection that these women have with the Earth (Ruffin, 2010).

Conceptualizing the unique connections women have with the planet as mother, or the feminization of the planet, can serve as a connection point to the lives of women, but there is also a peculiar familiarity to the ongoing structural nature of the violence that the Earth has faced (eco-violence) and the structural forms of violence that Black women have faced historically. For example, as womanist theologian Delores Williams points out in her constructive essay "Sin, Nature and Black Women's Bodies" (Williams, 1993, 24–29), under slavery Black women's bodies were seen as property by White slave owners. Black women were not viewed as fully human. This is evident when we compare the structural violence that ravaged the lives and raped the wombs of Black women for the sake of a slave master's sexual gratification with the agricultural practice of "over"-producing cotton in the South prior to the development of the cotton gin, for the sake of a profit. This practice stripped the soil of nutrients in Mississippi and caused soil erosion in Alabama. The connection between violence against Black women and violence against the Earth is evident. In making these comparisons, an environmental justice paradigm, linking social justice to Earth justice, becomes central when crafting climate solutions and raising consciousness about ecological reparations.

Ecowomanism and Ecological Reparations

Ecowomanism

In entering this conversation, I am using an ecowomanist methodology that elevates the work, lives, and scholarship of Black women in the environmental justice movement. The method adopts a womanist race–class–gender intersectional analysis, featuring a seven-step process:

- Honoring womanist experience
- Reflecting on womanist experience
- Applying womanist intersectional analysis
- Critically examining African and African-American environmental religion, history, and tradition
- Engaging transformation
- Sharing dialogue
- Taking action for Earth justice

For the purposes of this chapter it is helpful to explain how the method opens up to a larger emphasis on the prophetic wisdom of ecowomanism. In keeping with a third-wave approach, I enter into this conversation rooted in a deep sense of justice and open to using interdisciplinary methodologies. Who are my conversation partners? Those in the wider field of environmental ethics, religion, gender, peace-building, and ecology; activists working everywhere to raise awareness about climate change; Brown and Black communities waking up to the realities of the impact of climate change on their bodies; and anti-racist activists and scholars wrestling with racial reconciliation. All or many of these partners point to faith-inspired ethics (Christian social ethics) that insist that repair and repentance are priorities in the work of justice. That is, it is not sufficient to simply dialogue our way out of racism and environmental racism. At some point, if true transformation is to take place, a genuine apology must be offered, a change must be made. And we must acknowledge that the greed and pride that is woven into our White supremacist, over-consuming society has caused historical pain—trauma; evidence of internalized oppressions; and, in too many instances, snuffed out the beauty of life with racial and ecological violence.

Ecological Reparations

Ecological reparations centers on repairing ecological violence and recognizing the logic of domination at work in ecocide and genocide—racial, gender, and sexual violence, and ecological violence. As Jenifer Harvey reminds us in *Dear White Christians*, there is something eerily familiar about the systematic ways in which White settlers justified stealing the lands of native peoples throughout North America based on European imperialist and colonialist claims, and the dominion biblical hermeneutic used to interpret God's direction in Genesis 1: 26 for some humans to "have dominion and subdue the earth." There is a connection, Harvey argues, between the White supremacy at work in the colonization of native peoples and the Christianity that allowed them to dehumanize people and objectify the Earth—all the while attending church and praising God. As native scholar Winona LaDuke in *All Our Relations: Native Struggles for Land and Life* stated, the colonizing of peoples is interwoven with a mindset that Earth herself—Mother Earth—can be commodified. In this line of thought, Harvey says, "ecocide and genocide go hand in hand" (Harvey, 2014, 175).

Ecological reparations faces this truth. It recognizes that to repair acts of violence against native peoples and enslaved (or free) African women, we must interrogate the White supremacist mindset and logic of domination found at the root of these structural forms of violence and see the impact that this logic of domination has on Earth.

In addition to pricking the conscience, ecological reparations dismantles White supremacy and colonial ecology. It reshapes the traditional theoretical frames used in the discourse by reasserting values of interconnectedness and interdependence. In the words of Robin Morris Collins and Robert Collins, ecological reparations recognizes that "the urgency of the need to repair the most impacted places on Earth is based not simply on claims for justice, but on recognition of the common dependence of all living things on heavily affected living systems" (Collins & Collins, 2005, 217). That is, in addition to recognizing the links between social justice and Earth justice, ecological reparations problematizes some of the frames of environmentalism, acknowledges the impact of colonial ecology, and replaces dualistic understandings that divide the Earth from the heavens. It provides a more fluid frame that values interconnectedness and interdependence.

Reimagining Theology: Ecowomanist Analysis and the Challenge of Reshaping Dualistic Theological Frames

According to an ecowomanist vision, the values of interconnectedness and interdependence that serve as a new base for shaping ecological reparations emerge by validating African, indigenous, and fourth-world cultural perspectives. In my previous work I have argued that by honoring the African cosmological frameworks embedded in many African-American approaches to ecological justice one can more clearly see a deep devotion to the Earth and justification for Earth care. However, it should not be assumed that a return to African cosmology is taking place in all African-American faith communities or lives in all the Black liberation theologies that are trying more deeply to commit themselves to environmental justice.

Challenges: Breaking the Addiction to Dualisms in Western Thought

While African cosmology suggest a fluid-like relationship between the human, Divine (Spirit), and natural (earthly) realms, it is important to note the dangerous hierarchical dualisms that function normatively in Christian and Western thought. These, which can often be found in Black Christian churches, separate the Earth from the Divine realm. In dualisms such as Heaven vs. Earth, Spirit vs. body, and male vs. female, we see that in place of an interconnection between the realms, a separation is made that sets one realm—Heaven—over the other. When engaging religion, gender, and Earth this kind of hierarchical dualism can be problematic. In theologies that discount the role of women in the church, for example, one often finds this kind of dualism (male vs. female) so that the man is placed in a hierarchal relationship over the woman. Tracing this logic from human-to-human relationships to human-to-non-human relationships, it is easy to see how the same logic of domination that suggests the feminine be devalued in women's own tradition suggests, too, that Earth be devalued. The challenge of hierarchal dualisms is taken up by many ecofeminist and ecowomanist scholars, who add to this discussion by noting that the relationship that women of African descent have with the Earth is paradoxical. They recognize that at the same time that women have been dehumanized and devalued, and in some cases theologically forbidden from having an equal voice in church and society, women's connection with the Earth is sacred. For example, a parallel is often drawn between an image of a woman as Creator (creative producer of ideas, thoughts, ethical systems, agency, communities, children, godchildren, adopted children, neighborhood children, space, food, etc.) and Earth as Mother who also creates.

An African cosmology integrated with the principle of interconnectedness counters Western Platonist dualistic views depicting the Earth and Nature as separate from the human realm. This is particularly important for ecowomanists to acknowledge because, as we have heard, this Platonist dualism functions as a conceptual root in the theologies of many spirituals, Blues, and hymns. Recall the lyrics of the spiritual "A City Called Heaven":

> I Am a Poor Pilgrim of Sorrow,
> I'm left in this whole wide world alone.
> I have no hope for tomorrow,
> but I'm trying to make heaven, My Home.
> Sometimes I am tossed and driven, Lord.
> Sometimes, I don't know which way to roam.
> But I heard of a city called Heaven,
> I'm striving to make Heaven, My home.

The theology woven into the lyrics of the song connotes a strong separation between the place called the world—a land of slavery, an onerous, laborious connection to the land, and sorrow—and the place called Heaven, in which a person has ultimate rest, peace, and freedom from oppression.

In place of Platonist dualism, African cosmologies present a more holistic religious perspective on the Earth, in which the realms of Nature (the Earth), humanity, divinity, and the Spirit are connected. Black religious ethicist Peter J. Paris describes this by naming each of the realms as "ontologically united and hence interdependent" (Paris, 1995).

The interdependence and interconnection that Paris elaborates as paramount in African cosmology and evident in some Black Liberation Theology also establishes a common moral discourse or ethical worldview about the importance of rationality among African diasporic peoples. Further, it undergirds the ethical imperative for Earth justice in many African-American communities of faith.

Honoring the Complexity

As important as it is to return to African cosmological roots, it is naïve to assume that an embrace of "the African nature" or "African cosmology" in these African-American religious traditions, whether they are influenced by Christianity, Yoruba, or Condomblee, is straightforward. As Edward Antonio reminds us in "Ecology as Experience in African Indigenous Religions," we must be wise enough to recognize the politics involved in colonial ecologies, and carefully problematize any move to assume that a return to the "African" will somehow save the planet. In fact, the political and social construction of what it means to be "African" or "indigenous" has to be examined in environmental studies. We must use postcolonial analysis even as we lift up African cosmologies as an important starting point for conversations about environmental justice. As Antonio explains, "I am suggesting here that ideas of nature are not always, if ever, politically innocent and that the claim that Africans are close to nature occurs in a historical context in which it cannot be exempted from the ideological ambiguities that have undermined its uses in the past" (2004, 156). The politics of colonial ecology must also be confronted in the work and vision of ecological reparations.

Ecological reparations constructs a reparative framework that recognizes links between inequalities, the reality of globalization, the push for justice, and the urgency of climate change. It recognizes that while Nature is not concerned with the politics of environmental policy, the reality is that mainstream environmentalism often masks its implicit bias against communities of color, all the while trying to protect the Earth and promote sustainability. An ecowomanist perspective helps us discern these connections, particularly in regard to how they can contribute new solutions to climate change, as well as be frank and honest about where we really are. It invites us to consider the words of Collins and Collins: "Racism is real and has consequences on the environment." In an age of police brutality against Black and Brown women and men, ecowomanism points out that what we are witnessing is a rise in racial violence, and that what the BlackLivesMatter movement is trying to shed light on is a rise in White anxiety about shifting global economics, changing racial demographics, and power. Collins and Collins explain the phenomenon: "Environmentalism masks an unconscious racism that threatens to replicate racist outcomes even without conscious intent" (2005, 209). From an ecowomanist perspective, this truth is acknowledged:

fear + white supremacy = racial and ecological violence.

As aptly noted by Dan Spencer, in response to an Emilie M. Townes presentation engaging "Race, Ferguson, and Democracy" at the American Academy of Religion 2015 annual meeting, there is a link between White anxiety about economic loss and displacement of power, and the present rise in racial violence against African-Americans, Latinos, and other peoples of color in the US. Almost echoing the disappointment that Martin Luther King Jr. expressed when reflecting on the slow movement of the White moderates, as recorded in his Letter from a Birmingham Jail, today ecowomanists and environmental activists from communities of color all over the world have pulled at the long coat tails of traditional environmentalists and asked

> What do you say about the connections between ecocide, and the genocide of Native and indigenous peoples? What say you about the legacy of slavery and the dehumanization of millions of people for the sake of building a base for a capitalistic society, and what do you say about these peoples' connectedness with Earth?

Conclusion: Ecological Reparations

Ecological reparations is multilayered, building on a "framework for a reparative, restorative environmental policy based on justice first, then sustainability" (Collins & Collins, 2005, 209). However, rather than stopping there, we must go further and engage movements like BlackLivesMatter, and the frameworks and templates that they and others are using, to engage both White supremacy and ecological reparations. Social justice is Earth justice.

References

Antonio, Edward P. 2004. Ecology as Experience in African Indigenous Religions (146–157). In Linda E. Thomas (Ed.), *Living Stones in the Household of God: The Legacy and Future of Black Theology.* Minneapolis, MN: Fortress Press.

Collins, Morris & Collins, Robin. 2005. Environmental Reparations (209–221). In Robert D. Bullard (Ed.), *The Quest for Environmental Justice: Human Rights and the Politics of Pollution.* San Francisco, CA: The Sierra Club.

Harvey, Jenifer. 2014. *Dear White Christians: For Those Still Longing for Racial Reconciliation.* Grand Rapids, MI: Wm. B. Eerdman.

Ruffin, Kimberly K. 2010. *Black on Earth: African American Ecoliterary Traditions.* Athens, GA: The University of Georgia Press.

Williams, Delores S. 1993. Sin, Nature and Black Women's Bodies (24–29). In Carol Adams (Ed.), *Ecofeminism and the Sacred.* New York: Continuum.

Further Reading

Cannon, Katie G. 1995. The Emergence of Black Feminist Consciousness (56). In *Katie's Canon: Womanism and the Soul of the Black Community.* New York: Continuum.

Harris, Melanie L. 2016. Ecowomanism. *Worldviews: Global Religions, Culture, and Ecology*, 20, 1, 5–14. doi:10.1163/15685357-02001002.

Jordan, Carl. 2013. *An Ecosystem Approach to Sustainable Agriculture: Energy Use Efficiency in the American South.* Athens, GA: Springer Press.

Moe-Lobeda, Cynthia. 2013. Structural Violence as Structural Evil (49–81). In *Resisting Structural Evil: Love as Ecological Economic Vocation*. Minneapolis, MN: Fortress Press.

Paris, Peter J. 1995. *The Spirituality of African Peoples: The Search for Common Moral Discourse*. Minneapolis, MN: Fortess Press.

CHAPTER 16

From Climate Debt to Climate Justice

God's Love Embodied in Garden Earth

Cynthia Moe-Lobeda

Climate change: it is an oddly inadequate term to express what may be the most extensive moral catastrophe in the history of this young and dangerous—yet precious and beloved—species called human. Climate change: a strangely neutral word for what could be our most deadly error. Climate crisis rings more real.

The moral quality of humankind's response to the climate crisis will shape the fate of life on Earth. That unprecedented challenge, however, is not the primary concern here. I am concerned with a less widely recognized moral issue in our response to the exploding climate crisis. It is the question of who has caused it in relationship to who suffers most from it. This haunting question is a foremost moral issue of the twenty-first century.

The moral problem has two layers. First, the people most vulnerable to the ravages of climate change are, in general, not those most responsible for it. The problem gets worse: climate-privileged societies and sectors may respond to climate change with policies and practices that enable them to survive with some degree of wellbeing under the limited conditions imposed by the planet's warming, while relegating others, the most climate-vulnerable, to death or a living death as a result of those conditions.[1]

The race and class dimensions of both layers are stark. Caused overwhelmingly by the world's high-consuming people, climate change is inflicting death and destruction first and foremost on impoverished people who are also, disproportionately, people of color. The island nations that will be rendered inhabitable by rising sea levels, subsistence farmers whose crops are blighted by climate change, and coastal peoples without resources to protect themselves against and recover from the fury of climate-related weather disasters are not the people largely responsible for greenhouse gas emissions. Nor are they, for the most part, White.[2]

The Wiley Blackwell Companion to Religion and Ecology, First Edition. Edited by John Hart.

Many voices of the Global South recognize this as climate debt or climate colonialism and see it as a continuation of the colonialism that enabled the Global North to enrich itself for five centuries at the expense of Africa, Latin America, Indigenous North America, and parts of Asia.[3] Climate debt theory posits that the costs of adapting to climate change and of mitigating it are the responsibility of the countries that created the crisis, the industrialized world.[4]

Within the US too, economically marginalized people, who are also disproportionately people of color, are most vulnerable to extreme suffering from the fierce storms, diseases, food insecurity, and drought brought on by climate change. Environmental racism and White privilege strike again in climate change. Elsewhere, drawing on structural violence theory, I propose climate violence as a concept to describe climate injustice and expose the structural factors at work in perpetuating it (Moe-Lobeda, 2016).

The dilemma and its legal and governance dimension are expressed in ethical terms by law professor Maxine Burkett (1983, 2), who writes that those who

> suffer most acutely are also those who are least responsible for the crisis to date. That irony introduces a great ethical dilemma, one that our systems of law and governance are ill-equipped to accommodate. Indeed attempts to right this imbalance between fault and consequence have resulted in a cacophony of political negotiation and legal action between and amongst various political scales that have yielded insufficient remedies.

In theological terms, "climate sin" identifies climate injustice or climate violence as a theological category. Climate violence is a "sin" not only because it transgresses God's call to love one's neighbor as oneself, but also because it defies the earliest vocation that God gave to the human creature: to "serve and preserve" (*shamar* and *abad*) God's garden (Gen. 2: 15). Climate change is a sin in yet another sense. Christians and Jews both hold that God created this Earth and then "saw that it was good" (Hebrew *tov*; Gen. 1). *Tov*, while commonly translated as "good," also implies "life-furthering." God said time and again that Creation was *tov*—a good that is life-furthering. Thus, the founding act of God—the Creation—is not merely to make a magnificent world. God creates a magnificently *life-furthering* world. The scandalous point is this. We are undoing that very *tov*, Earth's life-generating capacity. We—or rather, some of us—are "uncreating."

Where will we find the moral agency to resist ways of life that generate climate change and rebuild alternative lifeways that serve social justice and the Earth's wellbeing? In this chapter I pose that question and then pursue it by identifying obstacles to moral agency and identifying resources in Christian traditions for overcoming one of them.

Two methodological clarifications are in order. The first pertains to my use of the first-person plural. "Our," "we," and "us" are dangerous words. They require clarification. I grapple with the moral dilemma of a particular people of whom I am one. I speak of this people as "we," referring to the set of US citizens who are economically privileged,[5] and therefore are among the world's climate-privileged societies and sectors. At times I speak even more specifically to and about those of us who are White. The boundaries of economic privilege—and therefore the boundaries of "we" in this chapter—admittedly are not always clear. Many US citizens are economically privileged while also being exploited through inadequate wages, non-existent or sparse benefits, poor working conditions, wage theft, regressive taxation, exorbitant healthcare costs, and more. As a result, many live in poverty which renders them climate-vulnerable, or they are engaged in a ceaseless struggle to avoid it. These people are not the "we" of whom I speak, although much of what I say may pertain to them too.

Second, the reader will move from a voice of social analysis, used in the first two sections to describe an aspect of the climate crisis, to a particular kind of theological voice aimed at unfolding a response to that crisis in the third and fourth sections. Moving between these languages, and putting them in dialogue, inheres in the work of Christian ethics, my disciplinary lens. Presently, I address conundrums at play when theology speaks to and in a pluralistic public arena.

The Challenge of Moral Agency

In this condition of climate debt one thing is certain: our great enemy is the moral inertia of climate-privileged people; it is the compelling urge to resist change. The great task before us is to unearth and claim moral agency to reverse the magnetic pull of our death-dealing and fossil-fuel addictive way of life that parades as natural, normal, inevitable, and even divinely ordained. By moral agency I mean the capacity to move from "the way things are" to "the way that things ought to be."

What will enable that moral agency? What will generate the moral agency for a dramatic and rapid reversal, a turn to ways of living that the Earth can sustain and that foster economic and environmental equity? This is the crucial question facing climate-privileged sectors and societies at this moment in history.

Response requires posing a prior question: What is behind our moral inertia? What could possibly explain our willingness to carry on with ways of living that are destroying the Earth's life-systems? Why do we persist in this lethal nonsense?

Probing the question of moral inertia reveals two landscapes: one of denial or moral oblivion that bears many hiding places and one of despair. That is, one component of moral inertia is moral oblivion—not seeing but denying. And a second is hopelessness or despair. Both engender powerlessness. The great irony is that daring to exit the landscape of denial may catapult one quickly into the latter: a sense of hopelessness. Said differently, by seeing clearly, one ushers in despair.

Given these two landscapes, moral agency for radical change toward Earth-sustaining ways of life requires:[6]

- Seeing what we are doing, recognizing the magnitude of the disaster in the making in order to take moral responsibility for it, in particular demystifying what is masked from view by the blinders of privilege:[7] what we see and do not see, and how we see bear tremendous moral weight; perception is political; it may be matter of life and death
- Igniting and sustaining hope for radical change toward a more socially just and ecologically sustainable future

We need, then, an ethics for climate justice that is capable of naming reality for what it is and, in spite of that, instilling hope. I cannot overstate the crucial nature of both. The two must be held together because the former—seeing climate change clearly—is a fast and sure way to disable the latter—hope. This is a charge to ethics and to all people of goodwill at this point in human history. The survival of civilization in a relatively humane form may depend on it.

Our question unlocking moral agency has become more focused. What enables seeing the reality of what we are doing while also sowing hope? We turn to that question in the third section. This question, too, requires a prior query. Why do we fail to see? For a people with astounding access to information, what prevents our acknowledging the scale of the disaster at hand and our implication in it? That is the focus of the next section.

The Blinders of Climate Privilege[8]

Only by noting why we fail to see can we transform that oblivion into courageous moral vision. In previous work I have dissected moral oblivion, naming eight components to it, and possible paths to overcoming them (Moe-Lobeda, 2013). Here we note six more barriers to seeing what it is that we are doing as we carry on with public policies, corporate and institutional practices, and lifestyles that spew lethal greenhouse gases into the atmosphere. I refer to these barriers as blinders of climate privilege.

- For those of us who are White, our color feeds moral oblivion regarding climate change and its consequences. The links are many. As David Gushee notes, White privilege can lead White people to tacitly assume that things will work out for us. Many structures of Euro-Western society for at least five centuries have been set up to benefit White people while endangering others (e.g., the criminal "injustice" system, housing codes, hiring and firing norms, etc.)
- Enculturation from birth by White supremacy provides a second link between being White and climate oblivion. White people are shaped by a deeply ingrained but utterly denied societal presupposition that White lives matter more than other lives, and the lives of moneyed people matter more than the lives of economically destitute people. North American and European societies would respond very differently to climate disaster if we were experiencing that disaster as it is now experienced by Africans bearing the drought or island nations preparing to be submerged by rising seas. Privileged White folk in the US would respond differently to the fossil fuel orgy if we were living in the horrors of Shell Oil in the Niger Delta or Cancer Alley in the US. We would not deem a 1.9 °C climate increase bad but acceptable if it had the impact on us that it will have on sub-Saharan Africa, Southeast Asia and South Asia—death by starvation and water shortages[9]
- Seeing would mandate radical changes in how we live—changes that bear economic cost: "confronting climate change requires swearing off something that has been an extraordinary boon to humankind: cheap energy from fossil fuels" (Mann, 2014)[10]

- A privatized sense of morality obscures the moral dimension of our roles in social systems and the importance of engagement in social movements. Too easily we assume that morality in interpersonal relationships and lifestyle choices is adequate for moral being. That is, if I treat others with care, recycle, drive a hybrid or ride a bike, and take other steps to reduce my carbon footprint, I am morally good. Yet this does nothing to acknowledge that I continue as a player in an economic system that exploits the Earth and others to assure my present mode of living[11]
- The moral dimensions of climate change are monumentally complex. For example, the harm has been done over centuries and generations by people unaware of it and by people who may be both victims and perpetrators. Some of the harm is done through participation in systems from which many people cannot disentangle themselves without doing immediate harm to self or dependents. The harm is difficult to quantify.

  We do not have a picture of the good that we need; it is not clear what it means to be a moral person or to lead a good life in the context of climate debt. For the current human population to live sustainably and with relative environmental equity would be an unprecedented state of being
- We flee from the shame, guilt, and sense of impotence that seeing would evoke. The consequences of climate change as experienced by millions of people today are dire; the projected consequences, unless emissions are reduced much more rapidly than called for by current climate negotiations, are catastrophic, unimaginable. Moreover, the warming that has been set in motion cannot be reversed. The reality that our way of life is destroying the Earth's capacity to sustain life is too terrible to face; we flee to the comfort of ignorance, pretending that life can carry on as it is. We cannot bear for long the idea that we have generated so much suffering and death and that we are undoing the Earth's life-generating capacities. We cannot bear to see ourselves as so "bad." A sense of powerlessness merges with shame and guilt when we dare to acknowledge the power of the fossil fuel industry to influence public policy, and the extent to which every action of daily life depends on petroleum.

These are some of the attitudinal and perspectival reasons that we fail to see climate violence clearly.[12] The limitations of a brief chapter preclude addressing all these barriers. Thus, we turn now to address only one of them, the last in this list. Naming them all, despite not being able to address them signals the urgency of recognizing these components of moral oblivion so that subsequent work may chart the course of overcoming them.

A Resource in Christian Traditions for Moral Agency: A Subversive Liberative Perspective

What would disarm the power of shame, guilt, and powerlessness to immobilize us? What would enable facing the reality of what we are doing while also sowing moral agency and hope? To where shall we turn for the power to hold together fierce honesty about the destruction that our lives cause and fierce hope about our power for good?

Perhaps this is the responsibility of the world's religious traditions. Religion at its best has long been a wellspring of hope and moral agency for overcoming seemingly insurmountable odds and for acknowledging both the evil and the good that inhere in the human condition. Precisely here in the crucible of good and evil, the paradox of bondage to sin and freedom from it, religions are called for to plumb their depths for seeds of hope and moral power for the work of ecological healing. All fields of human knowledge are called on to bring their resources to the task of forging sustainable Earth–human relations marked by justice. Religion is one of those fields. If people faithful to particular religious traditions do not uncover and draw on the resources offered by their tradition, then those life-saving and life-sustaining resources remain dormant. The tremendous gifts of the power for life and for the good remain untapped.

In this chapter, I consider Christianity. But before proceeding, a word is in order about the use of theological discourse to address public moral matters. There are many forms of theological discourse. The one used here is to interpret the central Christian symbols (the Crucifixion, Resurrection, and Incarnation), suggesting that this interpretation holds morally empowering "truth." Four presuppositions about my use of religious truth claims undergird this move.

First, my interpretation is not the only valid one. Valid interpretations of the Crucifixion, Resurrection, and Incarnation are many and have been since the earliest days following Jesus's death. Second, my noting the power of Christian claims to serve the common good presupposes that other religious traditions also have that power; I make no claim that Christianity's moral wisdom is superior to that of other religious or spiritual traditions.[13] Third, I presuppose that spiritual and moral wisdom in religious traditions can benefit and enlighten people who do not identify with that tradition or share its belief systems. That is, religions exist not only for the benefit of their adherents but also for the sake of the world. Finally, I hold that the wisdom of each religious tradition is not adequate in itself and requires the insights of other religions. These four presuppositions are crucial to what follows, and I ask the reader to bear them in mind.

Christian traditions bring many profound resources to the work of climate justice. They span liturgical resources, hermeneutical approaches, theological claims, institutional networks, historical guides, value systems, spiritual practices, and more. The resource examined here is what I call a "liberative, subversive perception." It is a way of seeing the world and all of reality through three lenses at one time. They are a Crucifixion perspective, a Resurrection perspective, and an Incarnation perspective.

Christian faith offers to the work of dismantling the ecological and economic violence of climate change this threefold perception. What does this claim mean?

Crucifixion Lens

A Crucifixion perspective dares to acknowledge the magnitude of our participation in climate sin. This means not only acknowledging the catastrophic consequences of climate change, the magnitude of the forces lined up to maintain it, and our implication in this disaster, but also admitting what the North American public must avoid. That is the inverse relationship between who causes climate change and who suffers most from it. This is the core of the moral travesty. Yet, it is precisely what the dominant gaze of climate privilege obscures.

Climate debt and climate colonialism are terms coming from the Global South to describe the imbalance between nations and communities likely to suffer first and worst from climate change and those contributing most to it.[14] Why look at climate change in these terms? Why recognize this horror, why enter this abyss? Why not try to ignore it and simply focus on "being green?" Let us consider three reasons why a climate debt perspective is crucial.

First, what constitutes the morally right response to a moral dilemma depends on what the problem is understood to be. Inadequate analysis leads to inadequate diagnosis and remedies. To illustrate: when asked in the mid-1940s about the "Negro problem" in America, James Baldwin responded: "There isn't any Negro problem; there is only a White problem." The history of White racism in the US in housing, healthcare, law, education, exposure to toxic land use, and more would have been dramatically different had we addressed race as a "White problem" rather than as a Black problem.

Responses to the reality of climate change frequently are framed around the principle of sustainability. Climate change as a matter of sustainability calls for reducing carbon emissions through technological advances, energy efficiency and conservation, and replacing fossil fuels with renewable energy. The moves are crucial, to be supported. If climate change were not connected, historically and contemporarily, to the power imbalances that have rendered climate debt, then this response, together with assistance to victims of climate change, would be ethically adequate. It is, however, an inadequate and deceptive moral response for affluent societies and sectors if we are disproportionately responsible for climate change; could choose sustainability measures that have an adverse impact on impoverished people and peoples; are material beneficiaries of the fossil-fuel economies that generate the climate crisis; and have produced economic orders that impoverished vulnerable peoples, thus rendering them less able to survive climate change-related disasters. A response organized around sustainability alone allows the world's high-consumption societies and people to address climate change in ways that do not accept moral responsibility for these factors and for the disproportionate impact that climate change has on people of color and the economically impoverished.

If climate change, on the other hand, is seen also as a problem of climate debt, damage done by one group to another, or human rights abused, then more is required. Debt owed by the wealthy to the impoverished calls for compensation. Damage done or rights abused may call for reparations. If climate change is seen also as a matter of race and class-based climate privilege, then a moral response includes acknowledging and challenging that privilege.

The second reason for seeing climate change as climate debt is theological. It pertains to repentance. Christians profess that freedom from sin begins with repentance. When we do not repent, we remain in bondage to sin. Repentance, however, is possible only when sin is acknowledged. Climate violence is a powerful form of structural sin. If we do not see it, we cannot repent of it. Failing to repent, we remain captive to it.

The third reason, also theological in nature, is the transformative potential of lament. In a powerful sermon on the book of Joel, Christian womanist ethicist Emilie

Townes (2001, 24) claims that social healing begins with communal lament. Communal lament, she explains, is the assembly crying out in distress to the God in whom it trusts. It is a cry of sorrow by the people assembled, a cry of grief and repentance, and a plea for help in the midst of social affliction. Deep and sincere "communal lament ... names problems, seeks justice, and hopes for God's deliverance." "[W]hen Israel used lament as rite and worship on a regular basis, it kept the question of justice visible and legitimate." Perhaps for us too lament is integral to social restoration. Lament, like repentance, is not possible if we fail to see what we are called on to lament.

If repentance and lament are doorways to social healing, and if they depend on seeing the wrong that is done, then climate-privileged sectors and societies must open their eyes to the reality of climate debt and the catastrophic devastation and suffering that it will continue increasingly to spawn. The floodgates to guilt, shame, despair, and powerlessness fly open. How could we face unbearable truth?

Perhaps the Christian story offers power for that daring and seemingly damning vision precisely because of the Crucifixion linked to the Resurrection. On the one hand, Jesus's execution by the powers of imperial Rome as a threat to its hegemony forewarns us: the forces of brutality, empire, and self-serving power will go to all ends to maintain their interests, and seemingly innocent bystanders are complicit. Yet the Christian story holds the Crucifixion inseparably linked to forgiveness and Resurrection. God's grace—including both forgiveness and life arising from death—surpasses even the most heinous sin. We can see and confess the horror of climate sin because we trust that we do not stand condemned for it and because we know it is not the end of the story. The end of the story is Resurrection. It is to that second lens we now turn. But first a note is crucial. The promise of forgiveness and resurrection is not a free pass to continue in the ways of sin. To the contrary, trusting in these promises is a pathway to renouncing and resisting it.

Resurrection Lens

What does the Resurrection mean in the age of climate violence? I speak very personally. I am easily tempted to despair when I acknowledge the insidious nature of structural injustice and the projected consequences of climate change. A subtle but deep voice within me whispers that things will continue as they are despite our best efforts. However, the Resurrection defies that voice and promises something different.

I believe this with my whole being. In my late teens, I was filled with despair about structural injustice. Finding myself mired in hopelessness, I sought out a person whom I knew was deeply aware of the injustice that permeates our lives and yet who maintained a contagious and enduring sense of hope and joy. After spilling my pain to him, I asked him how it was that he could face those searing realities without giving up hope. "Cindy," he responded gently, "I know the end of the story." He meant that God's love for this world is more powerful than all forms of death and destruction, and ultimately will prevail. The power of God liberating Creation from the bonds of oppression and destruction is stronger than all the forces of evil. In the words of Douglas John Hall (1976, 149), God "will not allow our complicity in ... evil to defeat God's being for us and for the good of all creation." Soul-searing, life-shattering destruction and death are not the last word, in this moment or forever. In some fashion that we do not grasp, the last word is life raised up out of brutal death. In the midst of suffering and death—be it individual, social, or ecological—the promise given to the Earth community is that life in God will reign. So speaks the Resurrection.

I do not know what this promise means for us and for Earth's community of life. But it does not lessen our call to devote our lives to building a more just, compassionate, and sustainable world; it does not, that is, allow us to sit back and let God do the work. That conclusion would be absurd because, as biblical faith has insisted for millennia, God works through human beings and other parts of Creation. Nor does trust in the Resurrection ensure our survival as a species in the face of climate change. It does, however, promise that the radiant Good beyond comprehension that is above, beyond, under, and within all ultimately will bring all to the fullness of love and life. Resurrection from death-dealing ways of life is not only a possibility but a promise. We are to live trusting in it.

In an age of climate violence, a Resurrection perspective brings hope. But Resurrection, however, is not the end of the story. What it means to live the Resurrection is defined by God's continuing Incarnation in the world today. This is the third lens of a subversive liberative perspective.

Incarnation Lens

Incarnate love is the breathtaking centerpiece of Christian faith. The Incarnation story begins with God's infinite love. Creation unfolds embraced by a love that can be deterred by no force in Heaven or on Earth. This love, the love of God, is both intimately personal, for everyone without exception, embracing our very being, and expanding vastly beyond the person to envelop Creation as a whole. This love is more magnificent than we can imagine. We human creatures are created and called to recognize this gracious and indomitable love, receive it, relish it, revel in it, and trust it.

However, that is not all. Christian tradition holds that this spirit of love—the creating, liberating, healing, sustaining Source—is at play in the world. It is luring us and the entire Creation toward the reign of God, a world in which justice and compassion are lived in their fullness by all and in which all of Creation flourishes in the light of God. After receiving and trusting God's love, we are to embody it in the world. We are beckoned to be the body of God's justice-making, Earth-relishing love working through us, in us, and among us to bring healing from all forms of sin. That is, God's love is incarnate.

God's call to practice love as the guide and path of human life is declared by Jesus: "You shall love the Lord your God with all your heart and with all your soul and with all your mind. This is the first and the greatest commandment. And second is like it. You shall love your neighbor as yourself" (Matt. 22: 37–39). Jesus is calling on God's commandment expressed in the Hebrew scriptures, "to love the Lord your God"

(Deut. 6: 5)," and "to love your neighbor as yourself" (Lev. 19: 18). Similarly, Paul cites the Leviticus text in Galatians 5: 14: "For the whole law is fulfilled in one word, 'you shall love your neighbor as yourself.'"[15] Most important for our purposes, however, is the startling fact that Jesus's words are not only instruction; they are a declaration of what will be. The verb *agapao* is in the future indicative. This is the case in all three synoptic Gospels (Matt. 22: 37–39; Mark 12: 38–34; Luke 10: 25–28). Likewise in the Pauline epistles, "you shall love" is expressing, in the words of New Testament scholar Matthew Whitlock, "assurance in the fulfillment" of this declaration.[16] This assurance rests on the biblical claim that the actual love of God lives and loves within human beings. It is a profoundly hope-giving claim, particularly as heard by contemporary people caught in a web of structural injustice from which it is hard to imagine escape.

The understanding that God's love is incarnate in human beings produces the paradox inherent in Christian moral anthropology. The human creature—while implicated in horrific, systemic cruelty, including climate sin—is also the abode of the God whose passionate life-giving love is more powerful than any other force. Christian tradition has articulated the incarnate presence in humans in two ways.

The first is of Christ indwelling. Dietrich Bonhoeffer probed the ethical implications of God's love embodied in human communities. In his terms, Christ dwelling in the community of people who embody God's love "conforms" them to "the form of Jesus Christ."[17] That is, the form is God's overflowing love embodied as community that acts responsibly in the world on behalf of abundant life for all, especially on behalf of those who are persecuted or marginalized. This action requires recognizing structural evil, naming it, and "putting a spoke in the wheel" of earthly powers that demand disobedience to God. The power to resist structural evil, even when so doing is unbearably costly, is the actual love of Christ taking form in human community.[18] As revealed in the Cross and Resurrection, this love is indomitable even when it appears to be defeated.

The second expression of God's incarnate presence is the Holy Spirit. According to the first testament (i.e., the Old Testament), the ancient Hebrews experienced a power emanating from the One they called YHWH, reaching into their lives and into the entire created world awakening agency (or *being* agency) for maintaining and restoring relationships that cohere with God's will for life. These relationships might be interpersonal, societal, between humans and Earth, or between God and God's creation. They called this power *ruach*.

The second testament (the New Testament) describes a presence and power of God reaching into Jesus's life, speaking to him, leading or driving him, filling him, and empowering him for his work. The writers of these texts called that power *pneuma* (Spirit) or *pneuma* of God. Where the Spirit comes on, fills, speaks to, bids, drives, leads, or anoints Jesus, the result is tremendous power for remaining faithful to God in the face of temptation; for proclaiming the reign of God; and for liberating, healing, and giving sight.

After Jesus's Ascension his followers apparently understood themselves, as individuals and as a body, to be filled with (Rom. 8: 9) and led by the Holy Spirit, and to be empowered by and receive gifts from that Spirit for doing the will of God. God's will, in their estimation, included the commandment to love one's neighbor as oneself. This power too was called *pneuma* and was understood to be the *pneuma* of Jesus, the risen Christ. The coming of the Spirit was understood to be the coming of God's power and presence to "dwell in and among the people" (Karkkainen, 2002, 34).

Pneumatology from the first century to the twenty-first affirms that the Spirit enables people to act as God would have them act. In the words of theologian Yves Congar (2014, 4): "The Spirit-Breath is first and foremost what causes [humans] to act so that God's plan in history may be fulfilled." If living as God would have us live includes seeking sustainable Earth–human relations marked by social justice, the Spirit within and among us may enable that healing work.

Much is not clear. The implications of these findings for how contemporary people are to live and respond to the climate crisis are open to interpretation. It depends, of course, on how one understands God's will and what it means to love one's neighbor as oneself. Nevertheless, a few things pertaining to moral agency for embodiment of neighbor love may be said with some certainty. The relevant biblical texts, held together, testify that:

- The power and presence of God is immanent as well as transcendent
- This Spirit dwelling within communities and individuals brings moral power for neighbor love
- That love will be lived out with many mistakes, shortcomings, and other realities of human fallibility and finitude
- The presence of this Spirit at times has a transformative impact

Examining the incarnate Spirit in Christian sacred texts yields a disconcerting truth. Heeding the Spirit's bidding to follow God's ways may be dangerous. History confirms that following paths of neighbor love, especially amidst forces of systemic domination, often has been dangerous. It requires courage.

Herein may lie a key to the incarnate Spirit's power. The Holy Spirit renders courage. According to Luther (1992, 277), the most powerful courage known to humankind is generated by the Spirit living in the faithful. The Spirit brings into its human abode "true courage—boldness of heart" (275) "The Hebrew word for spirit," Luther preaches, "might well be rendered 'bold, undaunted courage'" (275) That "bold, dauntless courage ... will not be terrified by poverty, shame, sin, the devil, or death" (275–276). With courage comes hope.

A significant lacuna is presented here. We have discussed God's love incarnate in human beings, ignoring its presence in the rest of Creation. Significant streams of Christian tradition hold that Christ and Spirit abide within and among the creatures and elements of God's Earth, not only human creatures. This claim bears tremendous potential for moral agency. Here, bounded by the limits of a chapter, we have focused on God incarnate in the human, and for good reason: we are the problem.

Three Lenses Held Together

What do these three lenses held together reveal? If Christians are called to anything, it is to take seriously the Crucifixion, trust Resurrection, and practice the Incarnation. This is more than a calling: it is the reality within which life unfolds, to be recognized or not.

Incarnation as Resistance and Rebuilding

What then does it mean to practice incarnation in the face of climate reality? What does it mean to embody the love of God revealed in Jesus? What love is and requires is the great moral question permeating Christian history. For two millennia, people who follow Jesus have struggled to grasp what it means to claim that God's love takes on carnal form in the human creature. Just as God is both intimately knowable and infinitely beyond our knowing, so too is love; the nature of neighbor love flowing from divine love is beyond full comprehension. Yet seeking to the best of our ability to perceive what it means to embody God's love is at the heart of Christian faith.

What can be said is that the love of God, as known in the Hebrew Bible and Jesus, seeks to address suffering and dismantle the oppression and exploitation that cause suffering. Love, therefore, is contextual and asks different things of people based on their situations. Jesus bids us ask, "What does it mean in our here and now to love our neighbor as God loves us?" Theologian Daniel Day Williams (1968, 4–5) expresses this well: "Love ... changes form and brings new forms into being... God in his creativity and freedom reforms the modes of love's expression."

We must, then, ask what it means for climate-privileged peoples to practice incarnate love in the face of climate debt. What is love's bidding for those of us who are disproportionately responsible for climate change and owe our material wealth to the fossil-fuel economies that generated the climate crisis? Love, I submit, means faithfully seeking to dismantle the power structures and ways of life that undergird climate change. And, in the footsteps of Jesus, this calls for resistance and rebuilding.

Resistance and rebuilding are intertwining streams in the movement toward climate justice. One alone cannot begin to free us from our bondage to climate-catastrophic ways of living. "Resistance" means refusing to participate in some aspects of the global economic system that are fast destroying the Earth's atmosphere and countless communities and lives. Boycotting, divesting in fossil fuels, and withdrawing money from large corporate banking are examples. "Rebuilding" signifies supporting more socially just and ecologically healthy alternatives that are accountable to a "triple bottom line"—social, ecological, and financial. These alternatives pertain to all levels of social being: household/individual, corporate, institutions of civil society, and public policy. Examples include small-scale and local or regional business and banking, local sustainable agriculture, investing in and using renewable energy, and public policies that support these initiatives.[19]

Resistance and rebuilding are meant as a way of life, not merely as incidents in the midst of it. This duo is anchored in Christian theology as denouncing that which thwarts the in-breaking reign of God and announcing that which furthers it. Resistance and rebuilding—as an expression of love known in Jesus and his scriptures—takes fruitful form in a communal and ancestral mode.

Communal

To explore communal, the wrong question is helpful. "What does it mean for me to live as if risen from the dead and to live as if the Spirit of God is incarnate in my body, has made Her home in my being?" This is the wrong question. Incarnation in Christian tradition is not primarily a matter of I and me. Rather, incarnation is a communal reality.

We rise from and against death-dealing ways of life and embody God not primarily as individuals. Rather, we do this as woven into a body, a communion, a mystery beyond our understanding. John's story of Jesus with his terrified disciples after his Crucifixion illustrates this. When individual disciples address Jesus he responds in the plural: "Let not your hearts be troubled" (John 14: 1) refers to the community's heart. The "your" is plural. When the Spirit comes at Pentecost She comes to a body of people.

God, abiding within us, is calling forth a communion. It is a reality that even the disciples did not yet perceive. And nor do we, except in glimpses. In the imagery of Irenaeus of Lyons, it is a union and communion among those who hear God, and between them and Godself. In our communities of resistance and rebuilding, we are embodying the communion that God has given but that we only glimpse dimly, the communion we are called to embody in faithful resistance and rebuilding is our home.

Practicing incarnation means discovering evermore fully what it means to live in this already given union and communion with divine love, which ultimately will overcome all forms of death and destruction. This communion is not a present reality alone: it is a past, present, and future reality. It includes those who will come after us and those who came before, the ancestors.

Ancestral

Christians who seek justice in the face of climate debt stand in a heritage of resistance and rebuilding. The early Church told stories and believed that the community was shaped by an epic story in which they were players (Meeks, 1993, 189–210). They deemed it vital that the Church perceive itself within a heritage of resistance to whatever the powers-that-be demanded them to defy God's ways and will.

Contemporary faith communities embodying love by seeking climate justice and gardening Earth's renewal would be wise to highlight that heritage of resistance in sermon, song, and sacrament, to tell this sacred story in art and education, in prayer and celebration. What kinds of moral power will emerge if the practices of Christian communities teach our children that they walk in the footsteps of fiercely faithful, loving, Spirit-filled resisters whose words and deeds rejected ways of life that transgressed God's call to justice-making, Earth-serving love? This is the heritage of the Hebrew prophets, Jesus who refused to comply with the Roman empire, the early Church whose declaration that "Jesus is Lord" defied imperial Rome, the abolitionists, the "righteous gentiles" who defied Hitler's death machine, the Civil Rights Movement, and more. What if our youth learned that this is "the people" into whom they were baptized?

We will be more adept in the art of resistance and rebuilding if we locate ourselves in this rich heritage of resistance to dominant powers where they demand people to transgress ways of God's love. This ancestry is at the heart of Christian and Hebrew scriptures. Knowing it inspires courage and wisdom. When we honor it as our ancestral home, present in our present, we will be more fertile ground for incarnate love that resists climate violence and rebuilds Earth-honoring, neighbor-loving ways of living.

In Conclusion

US citizens of relative economic privilege have a sacred calling: it is to reverse a fiercely compelling trajectory of climate violence. That is, we are called to resist ways of life and power structures that generate climate change and its disproportionate impact on the world's already impoverished people and to rebuild Earth-serving, love-bearing ways of being human. Where we will find the moral agency for that massive shift is the question this chapter asks.

One clear factor in moral inertia is failure fully to acknowledge the depth of the crisis and in particular the extent to which those who "suffer most acutely [from climate change] are also those who are least responsible for the crisis" (Burkett, 1983, 2). We have noted the ingredients of that moral oblivion—"blinders of climate privilege"—and then have focused on one of them: the guilt, shame, and despair that may accompany daring to see more clearly.

Religious traditions offer resources for overcoming that hopelessness and other obstacles to moral agency. One resource offered by Christianity is a threefold lens for viewing life that may enable facing the climate crisis with hope, and thereby engender moral power for the seemingly impossible task of forging sustainable Earth–human relations marked by social justice. It is the lens of Crucifixion, Resurrection, and Incarnation. This means facing the brutality of climate debt and our implication in it, trusting that life will prevail over death and destruction, embodying God's love by resisting ways of life that generate climate change, and building alternatives. We will do so not as isolated individuals but as beings moving into communion with Earth's web of life and with its creating, liberating intimate Source, and as descendants of fallible yet courageous resisters. Our splendid charge is to repent and lament, and then to practice incarnate love through resistance and rebuilding. While we do not know where this path will lead us, we do know, according to central biblical claims, that nothing will separate us or this good garden Earth from the love of God made manifest in, but not only in, Jesus Christ (Rom. 8: 38–39).

Notes

1 Climate-vulnerable in the discourse of climate change refers to nations and sectors within them that are particularly vulnerable to the impacts of climate change, including drought, fierce storms, rising sea levels, disease, food shortages, and more. I use climate privilege to indicate nations and sectors most able to adapt to or minimize those impacts.

2 Another example is the 40% of the world's population whose lives depend on water from the seven rivers fed by rapidly receding Himalayan glaciers.

3 Climate debt theory derives from the more established body of theory pertaining to ecological debt. For more on ecological debt, see Peralta (2004), Simms (2005), and WCC Central Committee (2009). For the concept and its application to energy and climate policy, see Paredis et al. (2008).
4 UNFCCC, Article 3(1), addresses this responsibility by obliging the Global North to lead on efforts to combat climate change. Rees and Westra (2003) argue that "global society has a moral imperative" to "ensure that those responsible for making environmental demands assume the main responsibility for the consequences of their activity" and that "we will need no less than the strongest powers of international law" to do so (2003, 116). "Not acting to reduce or prevent eco-injustice," they continue, "would convert erstwhile blameless consumer choices into acts of aggression" (2003, 116). Taking a cue from Canadian national negligence law and the Criminal Code of Canada (s. 219), they argue that "lack of intent to harm is no defense if damage results from acts performed in careless disregard for others" (2003, 118). The issue of state or corporate legal liability for climate violence remains unresolved and is highly controversial. It is a key moral question of our day.
5 By economically privileged I mean people whose economic lives might be described in the following terms: their income is not totally dependent on wages or salaries. A severe recession probably would not place them in a position of having no home, inadequate food, or no access to healthcare, transportation, or other necessities. Perhaps more significant to this project, the economically privileged have enough economic resources that, without jeopardizing the basic ingredients of life for themselves and their dependents, they could make economic choices pertaining to consumption, investment, employment, and so on that would serve the cause of climate justice even if those choices were to diminish their own financial bottom line. They could choose, for example, to buy local, divest from fossil fuels, and reinvest in ecologically responsible investment funds, purchase a commuter bike, boycott products even if they are less expensive than the alternative, and so on. This category of economically privileged is porous.
6 These I refer to respectively as the descriptive task of ethics and the transformative task of ethics.
7 In Moe-Lobeda (2016), I propose four tools from Christian ethics for seeing what is going on in climate change.
8 Blinders are factors enabling those most responsible for climate change to ignore it and our responsibility for it.
9 See World Bank report: http://www.worldbank.org/en/news/feature/2013/06/19/what-climate-change-means-africa-asia-coastal-poor.
10 I would change humankind to parts of humankind.
11 See Moe-Lobeda (2013, 88–90, 117–130) for elaboration of this idea.
12 These factors are joined by social structural factors. See Moe-Lobeda (2002, ch. 2; 2013, 83–111).
13 While Christianity may not hold superior moral wisdom for the work of Earth-healing, it does bear a unique burden. Christianity, inseparably wound up in the philosophical and ideological assumptions of modernity, has contributed immeasurably to the Earth crisis. Having played this role, Christianity must offer its resources to the task of rebuilding Earth's health. I write out of this and a related assumption, a conviction that the damage wrought by Christianity is matched by its potential to help to build more equitable and ecologically regenerative ways of living.

14 More specifically, climate debt refers to the disproportionate per capita use of the atmospheric space for carbon sinks by industrialized countries in the past and present. The term climate debt was introduced into the international discourse by Latin American nongovernmental organizations (NGOs) at the 1992 UN Conference in Rio.
15 See also Romans 13: 10.
16 In conversation.
17 For Bonhoeffer, conformation with the form of Christ implies refusing to conform with ways of life that betray Christ. His use of *gestaltung* for "conformation" is a play on the word used by Hitler to mean conforming to fascism.
18 Bonhoeffer (1995, 55–56) writes: "The relation between the divine love and human love is wrongly understood if we say that the divine love [is] ... solely for the purpose of setting human love in motion... On the contrary ... the love with which [humans] love God and neighbor is the love of God and no other... [T]here is no love which is free or independent from the love of God."
19 Implications for public policy change are illustrated in Moe-Lobeda (2016). For more extensive accounts of policy implications, see Burkett (1983) and Gonzalez (2012).

References

Bonhoeffer, Dietrich. 1995. *Ethics*, Ed. Eberhard Bethge. New York: Simon & Schuster.

Burkett, Maxine. 1983. Climate Reparations. *Melbourne Journal of International Law*, 10.

Congar, Yves. 2014. *I Believe in the Holy Spirit*. Vol. 1, *The Holy Spirit in the "Economy."* London: Geoffrey Chapman and New York: Seabury.

Gonzalez, Carmen. 2012. Environmental Justice and International Environmental Law (77–95). In Shawkat Alam, Jahid Hossain Bhuiyan, Tareq M. R. Chowdhury & Erika Techara (Eds.), *Routledge Handbook of International Environmental Law*. London: Routledge.

Hall, Douglas John. 1976. *Lighten Our Darkness*. Philadelphia, PA: Westminster.

IPCC Working Group 2. 2001. *Third Assessment Report, Annex B: Glossary of Terms*. https://www.ipcc.ch/pdf/glossary/tar-ipcc-terms-en.pdf.

Karkkainen, Veli-Matti. 2002. *Pneumatology*. Ada, MI: Baker.

Luther, Martin. 1992. In *Sermons of Martin Luther*. Ed. John Nicholas Lenker, Ada, MI: Baker.

Mann, Charles C. 2014. How-to-talk-about-climate-change-so-people-will-listen. *Atlantic Monthly*. http://www.theatlantic.com/magazine/archive/2014/09/how-to-talk-about-climate-change-so-people-will-listen/375067/.

Meeks, Wayne. 1993. *The Origins of Christian Morality: The First Two Centuries*. New Haven, CT and London: Yale University Press.

Moe-Lobeda, Cynthia. 2002. *Healing a Broken World: Globalization and God*. Minneapolis, MN: Fortress Press.

Moe-Lobeda, Cynthia. 2013. *Resisting Structural Evil: Love as Ecological-Economic Vocation*. Minneapolis, MN: Fortress Press.

Moe-Lobeda, Cynthia. 2016. Climate Change as Climate Debt: Forging a Just Future. *Journal of the Society of Christian Ethics*, 36, 1.

Paredis, E. et al. 2008. *The Concept of Ecological Debt: Its Meaning and Applicability in Applicability in International Policy*. Ghent: Academia Press.

Peralta, Athena (Ed.). 2004. *Ecological Debt: The Peoples of the South are Creditors, Cases from Ecuador, Mozambique, Brazil and India*. Quezon City: WCC.

Rees, William & Westra, Laura. 2003. When Consumption Does Violence (99–124). In Julian Agyeman, Robert D. Bullard, & Bob Evans (Eds.), *Just Sustainabilities: Development in an Unequal World*. Cambridge, MA: MIT Press.

Simms, Andrew. 2005. *Ecological Debt: The Health of the Planet and the Wealth of Nations*. London: Pluto Press.

Townes, Emilie M. 2001. *Breaking the Fine Rain of Death*. New York: Continuum.

WCC Central Committee. 2009. Statement on Eco-justice and Ecological Debt. http://www.oikoumene.org/en/resources/documents/central-committee/2009/report-on-public-issues/statement-on-eco-justice-and-ecological-debt.

Williams, Daniel Day. 1968. *The Spirit and the Forms of Love*. New York: Harper & Row.

CHAPTER 17

The Vision of St. Maximus the Confessor

That Creation May All Be One

Elizabeth Theokritoff

With the resurgence of interest in the cosmological vision inherited from the Church Fathers, two phrases have become almost commonplace: "cosmic liturgy" and "microcosm and mediator." It is no coincidence that both are titles of early studies of St. Maximus the Confessor.

Maximus is increasingly regarded as the greatest and most profound of Byzantine theologians. He is also a figure in whom many strands of the Christian tradition coalesce. Born in 580, Maximus served in the imperial civil service before withdrawing to a monastery in his mid-30s. His early writings are concerned primarily with practical guidance in ascetic and spiritual life. Political instability caused him to flee Asia Minor in 626, settling eventually in North Africa. There he started to explore the theological and cosmological basis for his ascetic teaching in works such as the *Ambigua* ("Difficulties") and *Questions to Thalassius*—discussions of problem passages in the Church Fathers and scripture, respectively—and the *Mystagogy*. In Africa, too, he came under the influence of Sophronius, later Patriarch of Jerusalem, whose texts for the service for the Great Blessing of Waters are among the most remarkable expressions of cosmic theology. Maximus later became embroiled in theological controversy in defense of the human will in Christ, the principal subject of his later writings. His implacable opposition to the doctrinal compromise promoted by the emperor led eventually to his arrest, mutilation, and death in exile (662), before his christology was vindicated at the sixth Ecumenical Council (681).

Maximus' writings retain a profoundly monastic quality. Even when he is at his most philosophical, we are repeatedly reminded that he is striving to communicate a tradition of spiritual experience from "the Saints" or "the great Elder." The tradition includes the Cappadocian Fathers—Gregory of Nazianzus and Gregory of Nyssa, especially—and Evagrius, all profoundly influenced by Origen, as well as by Dionysius the

The Wiley Blackwell Companion to Religion and Ecology, First Edition. Edited by John Hart.

Areopagite, whose mystical theology weaves neo-platonist themes and structures into a Christian cosmology. All this and more Maximus integrates into a consummate synthesis of Orthodox theological and ascetic tradition.

Maximus' cosmological thought would later influence John Scotus Eriugena, who translated the *Ambigua* into Latin in the ninth century. It is probably no coincidence that Maximus was introduced to the West by an Irishman, for the early Irish tradition parallels his cosmic theology to a remarkable degree (Chrysostomos, 2013).

Maximus occupies an increasingly prominent place in environmental and cosmological thinking among Orthodox and others well versed in the patristic tradition. But there is still a pressing need to bring his thought into dialogue with the spiritual and eco-theological concerns of those unacquainted with Eastern Christianity, concerns that so often lead people to seek enlightenment anywhere but in the Christian tradition. One of today's most perceptive Maximus scholars, Andrew Louth, remarks on the Confessor's "sense of coherence of the whole," the loss of which, he suggests, "lies behind a host of modern fashions, from New Age religion, revival of paganism, alternative medicine, even ecological concerns" (Louth, 2004, 195; cf. Zakhos, 1998). This chapter is a contribution, however modest and sketchy, to the work that Louth describes as "thinking through Maximus' ideas again" in the light of our present problems and concerns. Much more work is required, but I suggest that it will be amply repaid.

The "coherence of the whole," for Maximus, lies in its orientation toward unity in Christ. We explore four aspects of this: the means of unification, in which the human role is crucial; the presence of the divine Word in the "words" (*logoi*) of all things; the patterns of distinction-in-unity recurring in the human, Creation as a whole, and scripture; and asceticism, as the way humans fulfill their role and reclaim the world as a path to unity in God.

The Blessed End of All Things: Unity in God

It might seem strange to begin with the end but, for Maximus and the Greek patristic tradition in general, it makes sense. The truth of things lies not in their present state or in their past, but in what they are ultimately called to become. The present relates to the future as shadow to truth, as type to archetype (Ambiguum 37, PG 91: 1296B).[1] It should be immediately apparent how important this perspective is for making sense of patristic thought today. There is a widespread assumption that the understanding of humans as created in God's image and the universe as a divinely ordered harmony has been rendered obsolete by scientific knowledge. But this dismissive attitude rests on an unquestioned assumption that the truth of things lies either in their outwardly perceptible present state, according to which the equilibrium in Nature is never more than relative, or in their beginnings, according to which humans are no more than animals. All this changes if "the essence of man[2] is not found in the matter from which he was created but in the archetype on the basis of which he was framed and *toward which he tends*" (Nellas, 1987, 33). What we constantly see in Maximus is that the Archetype, Christ, is the end-point not only for humans, but for the entire created order.

The "mystery of Christ," Maximus writes, is "the great and hidden mystery ... the blessed end for the sake of which everything came to be ... in which all things made by God are recapitulated in Him." Christ in His Incarnation "manifested the innermost depth of the Father's love, and showed in Himself the end for the sake of which created things clearly had their beginning" (*To Thalassius* 60, PG 90: 621AC). Here we have a summary of Maximus' worldview, in which "the mystery of the embodiment of the Word" is not only the key to all the riddles and types in Scripture, but also contains the knowledge of created things, both visible and intelligible (*Centuries on Theology* 1.66, PG 90: 1108AB).

If we are familiar with contemporary eco-theological discussions, two things may strike us here. First, the centrality of the Incarnation in Christian cosmology limits the usefulness of talking about a Judeo-Christian worldview; and second, this vision stands on its head the idea that an eschatological perspective devalues non-human Creation and encourages its abuse. It is not the physical end of the material universe that defines it; rather, it is "the ineffable power of the Resurrection," which reveals "the purpose for which God established everything in the first place" (*On Theology* I.66).

Maximus had good reason to emphasize the eschatological basis for the unity of all things. In terms reminiscent of some environmental thinkers today, he is sharply critical of "Hellenic doctrines" (Amb. 7, 1069A) that devalue material Creation in its variety and diversity: the belief that oneness and stability was the starting point for rational beings, who moved away from God and came into being as distinct embodied creatures, the world being created to accommodate them. This Origenist teaching has roots in neo-platonism (Constas 2014 v. I, 478). Maximus takes Origen's triad of stability, movement, and genesis, but transforms it so that coming into being naturally results in movement and stability in union with God is the ultimate goal. Maximus' rationale for the naturalness of movement is striking: everything that has come out of non-being must be in motion because it is carried *toward* some cause (Amb. 7, 1072BC). Such "motion" applies no less to inanimate objects: to be created is to be going somewhere. Maximus adopts the neo-platonist language of the *epistrophe* of creatures, but not its meaning of "return" to an original state (Tollefsen, 2008, 72). Rather, for Maximus *epistrophe* is a conversion, a turning toward a pole of attraction; it concerns the nature of the good and beautiful to draw all to itself. How this might apply to inanimate creatures is not clear. But Maximus' concept of movement toward a cause does open up a framework for thinking about a universe characterized by contingency, which yet responds at multiple levels to "attractors" and seems to "navigate" toward certain goals, if not with unerring precision, then certainly with an uncanny sense of direction (cf. Conway Morris, 2003).

The Workshop of Unity: The Human Being

For Maximus, the multiplicity and diversity of creatures is both intentional and real. Its unity has a dynamic quality: it is a divine work in progress; the workshop in which it takes place is the human being.

Maximus' "correction of Origen" relates to a passage where St. Gregory the Theologian speaks of the human as "a portion of God" that has "slipped down from above" (Amb. 7). Maximus pointedly refuses to interpret this in terms of a contrast between humans and the world. Rather, he interprets "portion of God" in terms of the destiny of all things, so that the composite nature of the human is revealed as a divine dispensation for the gathering in of the entire Creation. The bond between the human body and soul, Maximus says, means that as the soul acquires likeness to God, the body shares in immortality,

> so that what God is to the soul, the soul becomes to the body, and the one Creator of all is shown to enter into all things, proportionately to each, through humanity; and the many things that differ from one another by nature come into one, converging round the one human nature. And God Himself becomes all things in all, encompassing all things and causing them to subsist in Himself, because no entity will any longer possess a motion that is free-ranging and devoid of His presence. (Amb. 7, 1092C)

This illustrates with exceptional clarity both why the human is functionally "central" to God's purposes for Creation, and how little this has to do with anthropocentrism in most of the senses given to the term (cf. Bordeianu, 2009, 111–112; see further Fisher, 2010, 1–13). Fisher (2010, 165) suggests tentatively that "there is no necessary conflict between a humanly activated (in Christ) cosmic redemption and an understanding of humanity *with* rather than set over and apart *from* the rest of Creation." As far as Maximus is concerned, however, this misses the point. Cosmic redemption can be "humanly activated" only because humanity is "with"—consists of—the entire Creation.

The most detailed exposition of the connection between the Incarnation, God's ultimate purpose for all Creation, and the nature of man comes in a well-known passage in which Maximus speaks of all things as subject to five divisions: between uncreated and created, intelligible Creation and sensible Creation, Heaven and Earth, the Earth we live in and Paradise, and, finally, the division of human nature itself into male and female (Amb. 41; see further Thunberg, 1985, 80–91; Louth, 2004). The human is introduced into Creation last, "as a sort of natural bond mediating between the universal extremes through the parts of which it is composed, in itself bringing into one the multiplicity of things which are by nature widely separated" (1305BC). Being a "microcosm" makes the human creature a "most comprehensive workshop" in which divided things can be brought into one, to manifest "the great mystery of the divine purpose" which underlies the creation of divided beings (1305B). The human is to unite the "divisions," in reverse order, finally being united to God in love and "in its entirety co-inhering wholly in the whole of God" (1308B).

This was not, as we know, what happened. Man's task was to be centered on God, the one focus of unity. By focusing instead on the material things which he was appointed to "rule" (i.e., not be dominated by), he succeeded only in dividing what is united and risked the disintegration of his very being (1308C). One of Maximus' favorite images, of beings converging on God like the radii of a circle (e.g., Amb. 7, 1081C), illustrates why this is so: if we fail to converge, we remain at a level where things are separate or follow divergent trajectories into infinity. God therefore "moves" toward man, repositioning the focal point, in effect. He thus "recapitulates all things ... in Himself" (Eph 1: 10), revealing all Creation as one, "like another human being": the world as "human writ large" is the corollary of human as microcosm. All Creation, intelligible and sensible alike, is seen as united according to one universal principle—that it comes out of nothing (1312B). This might seem a slender basis for solidarity in creaturehood until we start to think of its implications. Everything that is not God is united in fragility, in its dependence on Him. Even the most transcendent of beings depends on God, while even the humblest of creatures has a relationship with the most exalted (1312BC).

It becomes apparent that "healing the divisions" does not mean eradicating differences, but removing their divisive potential: thus the division into male and female is to be overwhelmed by a full understanding of the principle of our common humanity. Even so, some aspects of Maximus' "divisions" may seem alien to the modern reader and hard to relate to our own picture of the universe. Others, however, have a more obvious contemporary relevance. The rift between Paradise and our world, for instance, might be said to encapsulate the problem of human relationship to the natural world. It clearly has nothing to do with the Garden of Eden conceived as a geographical location, but concerns the *way* we live in this world. It is perhaps what a contemporary ascetic Elder is describing when he speaks of day-to-day work in the monastic community as "a transfiguration of the world and of objects," "to make nature already now a partaker of the glory of the children of God, and allow it to sing praises with them" (Archimandrite Aemilianos, in Golitzin, 1996, 205).

Is there a contradiction between Maximus' account in Ambiguum 41 of the Incarnation "to save man who had strayed," and the "mystery of Christ" as the purpose for which everything is created? Maximus does give differing weights to the "remedial" purpose of the Incarnation, depending on context, but the fact remains that human nature has to be restored not simply for its own sake, but because Creation cannot be united with its Creator without it. In this sense, it would seem that "man exists for Creation," for the ultimate unity in God of the Creation which he encapsulates. There is a thorough mutual interdependence between humans and the rest of Creation such that Maximus can also speak of visible things having come into being "for the human" (Amb. 42). The argument here is that humans, as composite creatures, need the material world in order to exist; in the general resurrection, therefore, the world too will receive incorruption by grace (1349A).

This vision is undoubtedly "humanity *with* the rest of Creation." To ask whether it is humans as part of Nature, as some environmental thinkers would wish, is anachronistic. Patristic Greek has no terminology for "Nature" in the modern sense: humans form one of a myriad of created "natures," and indeed the human microcosm "contains" them all. Far from "deflect[ing] our attention from our evolutionary kinship with animals and our own dependence ... on other components of the biosphere" (Southgate, 2008, 106), "mediation" for Maximus depends absolutely on the sort of microcosmic solidarity that we might today express in the above terms. At issue is not whether we share the nature of the world about us, but what that shared nature means. In the materialist understanding, our "microcosmic" constitution defines us; in Maximus' understanding, the "components" that we share with other creatures determine not our nature but our vocation.

Finally, on the subject of the divisions, we note that Maximus is not talking in terms of an original state of perfection that needs to be reclaimed. He does sometimes speak of man having been created in an exalted spiritual state (e.g. Amb. 45, 1353CD); and he certainly connects our liability to the passions and the corruptibility and instability of matter with a human "fall," while entertaining the possibility that God made the world like this from the beginning in the foreknowledge *of* man's transgression (see Amb. 8, 1104B). But he also states more than once that man "fell"—inclined toward the world of the senses instead of God—"simultaneously with his coming into being" (Thal. 61, PG 90: 628A). This posits a conceptual distinction between the genesis of humanity and its fall, but not a temporal interval. The "divisions of being" give us another angle on the effects of the fall; the "divisions" reflect the way the universe is created, but humanity's deviation from its vocation means that they are solidified as rifts and oppositions, instead of becoming differences within a unity. But once it is accepted that the state in which all things are created is not their final perfection, how should the resultant "movement" manifest itself if not through fluidity and change? And what, we might wonder, is the "free-ranging" (*aphetos*: random?) movement which, as we have seen, is to cease when all things come to rest in God? Does this refer only to the wayward activity of volitional beings or to a level of real indeterminacy in the unfolding of the universe, which is in some way responsive to humans' orientation toward the divine source and goal of everything (cf. Osborne, 2008, 140–141, 157–172)?

How far does any of this help us with contemporary debates about the place of humans in Creation? For Maximus, our role is a dynamic one, in a process awaiting eschatological fulfillment. I have argued elsewhere (Theokritoff, 2005) that this vitiates any objection that human mediation diminishes the relationship of other creatures to their Creator. On the other hand, claims that the world needs to be transformed by direct human activity and "humanized" so as to be offered up to God (e.g., Staniloae, 1998, 4–5) seem to have a slender basis in Maximus' thought (cf. Jenkins, 2008, 196–201). Perhaps closer to Maximus' thinking is Nesteruk's idea (2004, 178–179) of a "cosmic liturgy of knowledge" in which humans "offer" the universe through their capacity to articulate not only the (mathematical) intelligibility of the visible universe, but the intelligibility of the whole in terms of God's purposes.

It is worth noting that the metaphors Maximus uses for the human's position are predominantly impersonal, focused more on Nature than on activity: the human is a "workshop," a "bond," or "link" that "mediates" (which does not have quite the force of the noun "mediator"). This suggests that everything we do affects all of Creation (cf. Bordeianu, 2009), but it gives little indication that this cosmic responsibility (which has already been taken on by Christ) correlates in any direct way with a "managerial" responsibility to transform the physical world by our own efforts, by creativity, or "Creation care." It undoubtedly does have practical implications for our behavior. (We return to this in the final section.) First, we look more closely at the structural ways in which all Creation is united, since these define our proper conduct as part of that Creation.

The Texture of All Things: The *Logoi* of Beings

Discussions of how we view the world and humans' place in it often come across as a sort of tug-of-war between the claims of humans and of "Nature." On one side is a seeming delight in cutting humanity down to size while extolling the power, inventiveness, and intricacy of natural processes; on the other, slightly petulant assertions of human dignity and depth, coupled with a pointed lack of interest in the wonder and depth of other creatures. Unfortunately, popular attempts to defend traditional Christian anthropology in this way tacitly accept that humanity and the rest of Creation are in competition, so that either one can be exalted only at the expense of the other: truly, an exercise in "dividing what is united."

Maximus shows us that the tug-of-war is a waste of effort. When he maintains that all things participate in God (Amb. 7), the key to participation lies in the notion of *Logos*, inadequately translated as "Word" in reference to Christ (John 1: 1) and "reason" in reference to the human constitution. Creation "in word (*Logos*) and wisdom" (Wisd. 9: 1–2) means that each thing is created according to its own principle (*logos*) of existence, which pre-exists in God in the divine Will (1084B). Maximus expresses this panentheism in strong terms: according to His creative and sustaining "procession" into the creature, the one [divine] *Logos* is many *logoi*; according to the providential process of the "conversion" of all things toward their point of origin, the many are one (Amb. 7, 1081BC). The very texture of the universe is thus God the Word in action; and in celebrating its wisdom, its rationality, its creativity, we celebrate our own archetype.

It is for this doctrine, if nothing else, that one might expect Maximus to be a household name in Christian eco-theology. The bond that he affirms between all Creation and its Creator, the cosmic reach of the doctrine of the Incarnation, is truly staggering. Indeed, Maximus warns us that the human mind will not be equal to understanding "how God who is in truth no one of the things that exist, and properly speaking *is everything and is beyond everything*, is in every *logos* of each thing separately, and in all the *logoi* of all things taken together" (Amb. 22 PG 91: 1257A). Maximus is not a pantheist. He is clear that God the Word never ceases to exist "without confusion" in His own person, even while being "multiplied" in the infinite variety of things (Amb. 7, 1077C). The Word is God, yet "He wills always and in all to accomplish the mystery of His embodiment" (Amb. 7, 1084CD). He is accordingly "thickened," as Maximus says, when He "conceals Himself in the *logoi* of beings" so as to be "signified, proportionately, through each visible thing, as if by letters" (Amb. 33, 1285D). This process of "thickening" parallels the "embodiment" of the Word in the words of scripture; it culminates in the Incarnation itself, which continues to be fulfilled in the deification of humans.

The *logoi* of beings, as Maximus understands them, cannot be reduced to platonic ideas or Stoic *logoi*, although his understanding clearly draws on both (Bradshaw, 2013). The doctrine of Creation through the *logoi* establishes the absolute freedom of the Creator, but perhaps also, in a certain sense, that of the creature. It means that God is the origin of all things, their intermediate state and their consummation (Thal. 1). But the providence that governs their "intermediate state" is the way God accompanies precisely the movement of created things, "holding the universe together and preserving it in accordance with its original *logoi*" (Amb. 10, 1133CD). It is a process of drawing beings toward God as their consummation:

> [Maximus] redefines the neo-platonist language of causality so that the principles (*logoi*) of beings are not simply formal causes and teleological finalities but are themselves grounded in the person of the *Logos* and identified as "divine wills" ... free, personal expressions of ... the divine passion to "love and be loved." (Constas, 2014, vol. I, xxiii)

Maximus speaks of the "attractive force" of deity in the context of beings capable of desire and love (*Amb.* 23, 1260C), but is it as clear where such a line is to be drawn? If it is possible to maintain that there is "mind inherent in every electron" and that "atoms in the laboratory act like active agents" (Freeman Dyson, in Frankenberry, 2008, 372, 381), could we then attribute to them something analogous to "desire"?

The *logoi* of being, together with those of judgment (i.e., distinction) and providence, could be said to "constitute the divine plan for the created cosmos" laying the basis for "cosmic conversion to God" (Tollefsen, 2008, 2), provided that "plan" does not suggest something external or bureaucratic. A closer, though still imperfect, image might be to see the *logoi* as something like spiritual DNA: the code of "letters" (note the coincidence of metaphors) that enables the creature to actualize itself. A *logos* cosmology effectively banishes God-as-watchmaker. Maximus will also use images such as "the artisan Word"; but, in conjunction with the language of *logoi*, such an image reminds us precisely that the "word" that expresses our deepest being is not simply a blueprint, but represents a personal labor of divine love.

There are vast differences between today's scientific understanding of the world and that of the seventh century, when the very idea of a "universe" in our sense would have been inconceivable (Louth, 2004, 193–194). So it is all the more remarkable how often attempts to make spiritual sense of the world described by the sciences come back to something very like Maximus' *logoi*. Sometimes this is explicit: physicist-theologian Christopher Knight draws extensively on Maximus in developing an understanding of divine action in the world which he calls "pan-sacramental" or "incarnational" naturalism:

> the presence of the divine *Logos* in all created things provides ... a kind of teleological dynamism that draws them toward their intended final goal, and this dynamism represents a mode of divine action that is neither the "special" nor the "general" one of Western thinking. The universe is ... neither a benignly designed machine nor something that needs to be acted on "from the outside." (Knight, 2007, 101)

Logoi also seem to lie behind the "holistic organizing principles" used to account for emerging levels of complexity "that can be understood neither through a vitalistic approach nor through an ontological reductionism" (Knight, 2007, 120).

Echoes of Maximus can be found far beyond those who draw on him explicitly, however. Particularly intriguing is the *logos*-like quality of the "morphogenic fields" postulated by Rupert Sheldrake (2012, 138–142), within which ends operate as "attractors." Sheldrake himself is wary of the idea of eternal natural laws dependent on a "mind-like realm beyond space and time," positing instead "a sort of memory inherent in nature" (2012, 85). According to Maximus' cosmology, one might expect to find both, reflecting the eternal *logoi* of things and the *mode of being* whereby conformity to their *logos* becomes habitual. Thus the sort of memory effect that Sheldrake calls "morphic resonance" would not shape the immutable *logos* of a creature's being; but it could suggest how the unity of creatures according to their *logoi* causes their behavior to influence each other. In particular, it might describe very well how habits cultivated by the human microcosm can affect the entire universe.

Any entity, for Maximus, is defined not only by its own *logos* of being, but also by the *logoi* of the things that make up its environment (Amb. 7, 1081B). Relationality is at the core of his cosmic vision: this resonates both with the dynamic and relational universe disclosed by modern physics (Zizioulas, 2010) and with the evermore complex web of interactions discovered in ecology. We see a similar "reading" of Creation in the insights of biologist Ursula Goodenough, as she rejects separations, such as physical versus spiritual, and "see[s] the whole enterprise, from bacteria to starfish to maples to humans, as operating on the same principles, as profoundly homologous" (in Frankenberry, 2008, 498), literally meaning, to labor the point, sharing the same *logos*.

A *logos* cosmology may set up many resonances, but is it compatible with the sort of evolving cosmos we now appear to inhabit? This important question has been answered in both the affirmative (e.g., Knight, 2007; Louth, 2004; Southgate, 2008) and the negative (e.g., Zakhos, 1998), and requires further exploration. Much depends on whether one focuses on Maximus' thought per se, or on the *logoi* of things as an intuition about the cosmos which Maximus necessarily works out in terms of the thought-world of his own times, in which "natures" are fixed and unchanging. Today, we might conclude that the *logoi* of things are the only fixed thing about them. Adam Cooper's remark (2005, 100) about deification in Maximus might therefore apply also to the very "being" of all things: "Material Creation, being inherently mutable and transient, cannot of itself possess any ontological stability ... Its ontological stability rests in God's will and purpose in creating it, and thus in its ordered relation to that will."

The Structure of All Things: Recurring Patterns

The texture of the world described by Maximus, then, is to be found in the creative "words" that define the distinctive character of each entity and at the same time its "participation in the One." It is hardly surprising, then, to find that the world is structured according to patterns of unity-without-confusion, mirroring each other but also pointing beyond themselves to the workings of God.

This vision is set out most explicitly in Maximus' *Mystagogy*. This is a commentary on the Divine Liturgy, but in the broadest imaginable perspective. The first third of this commentary (chapters 1–7, PG 91: 664–688) discusses how the Church, its liturgical action, and its ordering of space (i.e., the church building) attune us to a series of "echoing correspondences" (Louth, 1996, 77) among and within the three manifestations of the Word's "embodiment": Creation, scripture, and the human being.

First, the church provides the comprehensive image of God at work in Creation. As the church body brings disparate people together into one, like the radii of a circle again, so all things are gathered into a union without confusion: their identity is not dissolved, but all converge into one through the power of their relationship to God as their principle. Then the church building, with its sanctuary and its nave, corresponds to a whole set of syntheses: the world composed of visible and invisible, the sensible world composed of Heaven and Earth, the human being—the nave corresponds to the body, while the sanctuary (soul) contains the altar (spiritual intellect)—and the soul in itself, with its various faculties brought into unity. Maximus then further explores anthropic symbolism, of the senses in which scripture (composed of the Old Testament and New Testament, letter and spirit) is a symbolic of human being, as is the world composed of visible and invisible.

What are we to make of these symbolic images? It is initially somewhat dizzying, because the images are anything but a well-ordered set. They do not all face the same way, as it were; in most cases the symbolism is reciprocal. And they are also to some extent superimposed, because they exist on different levels. Thus the church images the world visible and invisible, as well as the visible world on its own; the human being, as well as the soul on its own. Most of the images are bipartite, encapsulating a synthesis whose parts are not equal, yet express and mirror each other, as do potentiality and actuality. The church images the human, however, in a tripartite symbolism: here nave and sanctuary image all things gathered for the consummation of their unity—"the mystery accomplished upon the altar," the union of the soul with God (681AC).

The symbolism points to an order that is hierarchical in the Areopagite's sense: a structure that unites disparate entities in indissoluble relationship to one another and movement toward God. Witness the "principle of unity" sown in the sensible and intelligible worlds so that beings "belong to each other more than to themselves," and their differences cannot overwhelm their "kinship of love" (*Mystagogy* 7, 685AB). In a parallel to the "mystery upon the altar," the unity of sensible and intelligible is fulfilled in the Resurrection, when "one divine power becomes a manifest and active presence in all, proportionately to each."

The relationship of the different levels means that they are mutually revelatory, too. In another remarkable passage, Maximus explains that not only do visible things symbolize intelligible things (cf. Rom. 1: 20), intelligible things also convey spiritual knowledge and understanding of visible things through contemplation of their *logoi* (*Mystagogy* 2). The presence of the sensible world within the intelligible, and vice versa, is likened to the wheel within a wheel of Ezekiel's vision (Ezek. 1: 16). In contemporary terms, the signature of the Word in the world has a holographic quality.

This observation is interesting in light of the parallels that have been drawn between the notion of implicate order and "holographic universe" advanced by physicist David Bohm and the "hierarchical" universe of Dionysius (Osborne, 1997), whose cosmic framework is especially evident in the *Mystagogy*. Maximus' vision and its christological basis anticipate Nicolas of Cusa (von Balthasar, 2003, 66), from whom the idea of implicate and explicit orders is drawn. The parallels suggest that the holographic approach to the physical world might fruitfully be developed further in the framework of a Christocentric cosmology, in which the reality imprinted on all Creation is the mystery of Christ, of divine embodiment.

The symbolic connections between Church, world, and human, and the fact that these are set out at such length in a commentary on the Divine Liturgy, have inspired characterizations of Maximus' vision,such as "cosmic liturgy" (von Balthasar, 2003) and "eucharistic ontology" (Loudovikos,2010). These formulations are illuminating if we remember that the Divine Liturgy is not the original archetype (cf. Myst. 24, 705A). The Eucharist encapsulates for us the pattern of God's working in His Creation "to deify all things" (Thal. 2), but does not exhaust that working. Maximus shows little inclination to fit his cosmological thinking into a single eucharistic metaphor in the way that is often done today, usually in conjunction with the idea of "man as priest of Creation." Certainly, the total cosmic movement is toward unity in God, and the human is the "natural bond" with which this is achieved; but it is surely significant that this movement cannot be captured in a linear set of images. For Maximus as for the Areopagite, it is not that "nature is ordered to man and man is ordered to God ... rather, all things are ordered to God, each in its own proper way" (Perl, 2013, 29). The movement toward ultimate unity is possible because all things, in their distinctive natures, bear the pattern of that movement.

The Reclamation of All Things: Asceticism and Transfiguration

To return to the question left hanging earlier: if we are meant to be the "workshop of unity" for a fragmented Creation, what does this entail in practice?

Any presentation of Maximus in relation to ecological thinking, selective as it will necessarily be, risks seriously distorting his thought. His is no sunny "Creation spirituality"; the dark, chaotic aspect of earthly existence, its impermanence and instability, are the daily reality of our life. Far from Creation being a "mere static hymn of praise" (cf. Southgate, 2008, 113), the words in which it speaks of God can be contemplated only in and through a process of transformation, of the world within us. This ceaseless exercise (*ascesis*) is "a micro-drama of the larger macro-drama of salvation," whereby we participate in the transfiguration of the cosmos and so "share actively in Christ's mediation of the new Creation" (Blowers, 2003, 38). The indivisible duality of ascetic struggle and cosmic transfiguration is general in Eastern Christian tradition; failure to hold the two constantly together leads to endless confusion.

Maximus has a strong sense of the impermanence and imperfections of our world, but he equally sees these very qualities as having, by God's providence, an educative value. A "manic" use of material things embroils us in confusion and turmoil, and this redirects our "irrational love for the things of this world into love for the natural object of desire" (Amb. 8, 1104C). An ascetic or "rational" use of the world—material things to cover material needs—is one that refrains from burdening the material world with demands that it cannot fulfill, be it ultimate satisfaction, happiness, or security.

Love—the proper direction of love—lies at the core of asceticism (Louth, 1996, 38–43). The problem with "irrational love" for things is that it is not really love for other created entities at all, but "self-love," an obsession with our own gratification—not just sensual gratification, but our desire for status, power, money, adulation. It is such desires, and the antipathies that attend them, that the ascetic tradition calls "passions."

Nothing created by God is intrinsically evil, as Maximus repeatedly emphasizes. When we see things in the light of our own passions, this spiritually is harmful, not least because it misrepresents the material world in its true essence. Life in this world is like crossing the Red Sea: beneath the turbulent waters of "appearances" which so confuse our senses, the true nature of things provides firm ground on which we may safely cross (Amb. 10, 1117A). And the rod that will part the waters is our capacity to behave "reasonably" and so bring all our faculties and senses into accord with our own *logos*. This refers to the first, "practical" stage of spiritual life: "purification through virtues". This is essential before we can attain "the illumination of knowledge" through contemplation of Nature, which in turn raises the soul to awareness of God (Amb. 40, 1301D–1304A). Purification renders the senses "rational" through a process Maximus discusses at some length (Amb. 21; see Bradshaw, 2013; Töronen, 2007, 157–162), so that our bodily senses become a spiritual asset, instructing the faculties of the soul and "activating them calmly through their perceptions of the *logoi* in things." Through these *logoi* we can now discern the word of God (Amb. 21, 1248AB) and even partake in communion with Him (Thal. 35, 377C).

Evagrius, one of great ascetic teachers on whom Maximus draws, speaks of the monk as one who is separate from all and united with all (On Prayer, 124). This could be applied to all created things: by attaining dispassion in his or her relationship to things, the Christian ascetic achieves the highest degree of openness to the world. Remarkably, even von Balthasar (2004, 282), despite his obsessive insistence on Maximus as a "Western" thinker, recognizes in the Confessor's ascetic theology a "mighty fusion" in which "the contemplative quest for freedom from desire characteristic of Buddhism and Gnosticism," the quest for nirvana and the pantheism of India and China, have found a "higher midpoint" in the saving love of Christ.

It is only through dispassion that we discover our proper "dominion" of the Earth: the power to use it as a guide to its Creator (Thal. 51, 477A–480A). This involves understanding the principles according to which things exist; but it also involves receiving the "laws" embedded in the nature of existent things as gifts, lessons in virtuous conduct to be imitated in our own lives. The examples that Maximus gives lean rather heavily on allegorical interpretations of the natural history of his day. But what he wants to express, I believe, is timeless: the "intuitive sense that the world should be built as it is; embedded in the universe are not only neurons but ... edicts" (Conway Morris, 2003, 315). This does not mean that Maximus' approach can simply be identified with the concept of "natural law" developed in the medieval West (cf. Knight, 2007, 79–85). Our fallen state has muddied the waters: that is precisely why discerning the "manners of virtue" embedded in the sensible Creation requires purification of the senses no less than does contemplation of the "spiritual principles of wisdom." Without the detachment that comes through ascetic preparation it is all too easy to "reap passions" from Nature instead of perceiving the inner *logoi* of things (Various Texts 2: 85).

The importance of the visible Creation to our spiritual life becomes clear when Maximus strikingly asserts that "virtues exist for the sake of the knowledge of created things" (On Love 3: 45). But at the same time this may make us wonder: if virtue is required in order to understand that created things teach us virtue, where does one start? Is Maximus saying that for those of us still far from purification, the visible world is simply a temptation to be avoided? This would be quite inconsistent with what we see in the Orthodox ascetic tradition. Besides, it would not make much sense: a right relationship to material things cannot be developed in isolation from them, but can be learned only by doing. The awareness that we inhabit a meaning-filled world intended to serve as our teacher and guide, rather than a pool of natural resources, is itself a powerful incentive to treat it "reasonably" and with restraint.

Such a reading of the world may also color our response to environmental problems. Consider the approach today called "biomimicry," which is described as taking "*nature as mentor*: based not on what we can *extract* from nature but on what we can *learn* from it" (Benyus, 1997; emphasis in original). We should note that this does not involve only technologies that are sustainable, but also a process of "quieting" and "listening" before "echoing" Nature in our actions. I am not suggesting that an environmental approach can take the place of an inner transformation in ourselves. But I am suggesting that the way we shape the world, the "large-scale human," affects the spiritual configuration of the (literal) human, as well as vice versa. It can either amplify the resonance of the Word in the world or generate interference. Using the world about us in a way that is synergistic rather than confrontational points us toward the intended synergy of humanity and the visible Creation, through which we reveal in our own lives "all the majesty of the divine wisdom which is invisibly present in existent things" (Thal. 51, 481C).

It is no coincidence at all that the passage (Amb. 10) where Maximus speaks at length of passing beyond matter and the "cloud" or "veil" of the flesh also contains some of his most remarkable evocations of the transfiguration of all things and the perception of the divine Word at their heart (which is the same thing). He uses the image of Moses: for each person, the path lies through the "wilderness," the long ascetic struggle to break the mind's attachment to things as perceived by the senses. And it leads to a theophany—to seeing and hearing with the mind "the ineffable and supranatural divine fire present in the essence of things as in a burning bush," namely "God the Word who in the last times shone forth from the burning bush of the holy Virgin" (Amb. 10, 1148CD). There is a paradox here: the ascetic is focused wholly on God, but what he receives in return is not God alone, but the Creator in and with all that He has made. If we climb the mountain of the Transfiguration, we shall see "the garments of the Word—the words of scripture and the visible elements of Creation—changed into radiance and glory, and through sublime contemplation rendered suitable for the divine Word ... And we shall know Him who is Himself the divine Word and God as *all things in all*" (Amb. 10, 1132CD).

Conclusion

It is widely held that, if environmental destruction has become systemic, this has much to do with humans' sense of alienation from other creatures. It is this alienation that Maximus totally and irrevocably destroys, not by declaring humans to be "merely" part of Nature, but through a vision in which no created thing is "mere" and differences serve unity rather than impeding it. All things at their core express the divine Will and purpose—the unifying web of the *logoi* of things pervades the physical universe no less than the spiritual, intellectual, and moral aspects of human life; and the social—far from being contrasted with cosmic unity, the solidarity in love that unites human beings is central to the movement toward Christ in which we bring with us all things. We have here an integrated vision that can inform the way we live our lives and frame our understanding of the physical systems on which our earthly life depends, and show us that these two are inseparable.

Notes

1 References are given to texts of Maximus in J.-P. Migne, *Patrologiae Cursus Completa, Series Graeca*, Paris, 1857–1866.
2 "Man" in the generic sense will be used periodically here to refer the human race as a corporate entity, summed up in Adam and destined to be recapitulated in Christ.

References

von Balthasar, Hans Urs. 2003. *Cosmic Liturgy: The Universe According to Maximus the Confessor*. San Francisco: Ignatius Press.

Benyus, Janine M. 1997. *Biomimicry: Innovation Inspired by Nature*. New York: William Morrow.

Blowers, Paul M., & Wilken, Robert Louis. 2003. *On the Cosmic Mystery of Jesus Christ: Selected Writings from St Maximus the Confessor*. Crestwood, KY: St Vladimir's Seminary Press.

Bordeianu, Radu. 2009. Maximus and Ecology: The Relevance of Maximus the Confessor's Theology of Creation for the Present Ecological Crisis. *Downside Review*, 127, 103–126. http://www.duq.edu/Documents/theology/_pdf/faculty-publications/art-mordeianu-max.pdf.

Bradshaw, David. 2013. The *Logoi* of Beings in Greek Patristic Thought (pp. 9–22). In John Chryssavgis & Bruce V. Foltz (Eds.). 2013. *Toward an Ecology of Transfiguration: Orthodox Christian Perspectives on Environment, Nature and Creation* New York: Fordham University Press.

Chrysostomos (Koutloumousianos). 2013. Natural and Supernatural Revelation in Early Irish and Greek Monastic Thought: A Comparative Approach (pp. 337–347). In John Chryssavgis & Bruce V. Foltz (Eds.). 2013. *Toward an Ecology of Transfiguration: Orthodox Christian Perspectives on Environment, Nature and Creation* New York: Fordham University Press.

Chryssavgis, John, & Foltz, Bruce V. (Eds.). 2013. *Toward an Ecology of Transfiguration: Orthodox Christian Perspectives on Environment, Nature and Creation*. New York: Fordham University Press.

Constas, Nicholas (Ed. and Transl.). 2014. *On Difficulties in the Church Fathers: The Ambigua: Maximus the Confessor*. Cambridge, MA and London: Harvard University Press.

Conway Morris, Simon. 2003. *Life's Solution: Inevitable Humans in a Lonely Universe*. Cambridge: Cambridge University Press.

Cooper, Adam G. 2005. *The Body in Maximus the Confessor*. Oxford: Oxford University Press.

Fisher, Christopher. 2010. *Human Significance in Theology and the Natural Sciences.* Eugene, OR: Wipf & Stock.

Frankenberry, Nancy. 2008. *The Faith of Scientists in their Own Words.* Princeton, NJ and Oxford: Princeton University Press.

Golitzin, Hieromonk Alexander. 1996. *The Living Witness of the Holy Mountain.* South Canaan, PA: St Tikhon's Press.

Jenkins, Willis. 2008. *Ecologies of Grace: Environmental Ethics and Christian Theology.* Oxford: Oxford University Press.

Loudovikos, Nikolaos. 2010. *A Eucharistic Ontology: Maximus the Confessor's Eschatological Ontology of Being as Dialogical Reciprocity.* Brookline, MA: Holy Cross Orthodox Press.

Louth, Andrew. 1996. *Maximus the Confessor.* London: Routledge.

Louth, Andrew. 2004. The Cosmic Vision of Saint Maximus the Confessor (pp. 184–196). In Philip Clayton &Arthur Peacocke (Eds.), *In Whom We Live and Move and Have Our Being: Panentheistic Reflections on God's Presence in a Scientific World.* Grand Rapids, MI and Cambridge: Eerdmans.

Nellas, Panayiotis. 1987. *Deification in Christ.* Crestwood, KY: St Vladimir's Seminary Press.

Nesteruk, Alexei. 2004. The Universe as Hypostatic Inherence in the Logos of God (pp. 169–183). In Philip Clayton &Arthur Peacocke (Eds.), *In Whom We Live and Move and Have Our Being: Panentheistic Reflections on God's Presence in a Scientific World.* Grand Rapids, MI and Cambridge: Eerdmans.

Osborne, Basil [then Bishop of Sergievo]. 1997. Beauty in the Divine and in Nature. *Sourozh*, 70, 28–37.

Osborne, Basil [then Bishop of Amphipolis]. 2008. *The Healing Word.* London: Darton, Longman & Todd.

Perl, Eric D. 2013. Hierarchy and Love in St. Dionysius the Areopagite (pp. 23–33). In John Chryssavgis & Bruce V. Foltz (Eds.). 2013. *Toward an Ecology of Transfiguration: Orthodox Christian Perspectives on Environment, Nature and Creation* New York: Fordham University Press.

Sheldrake, Rupert. 2012. *Science Set Free: 10 Paths to Discovery.* New York: Deepak Chopra Books.

Southgate, Christopher. 2008. *The Groaning of Creation. God, Evolution and the Problem of Evil.* Louisville, KY and London: Westminster/John Knox Press.

Staniloae, Dumitru. 1998. *The Experience of God: Orthodox Dogmatic Theology.* Vol. 1, *Revelation and Knowledge of the Triune God.* Brookline, MA: Holy Cross Orthodox Press.

Theokritoff, Elizabeth. 2005. Creation and Priesthood in Modern Orthodox Thinking. *Ecotheology*, 10, 3, 344–363.

Thunberg, Lars. 1985. *Man and the Cosmos: The Vision of St Maximus the Confessor*, Crestwood, KY: St Vladimir's Seminary Press.

Tollefsen, Torstein Theodor. 2008. *The Christocentric Cosmology of St Maximus the Confessor.* Oxford: Oxford University Press.

Töronen, Melchisedec. 2007. *Union and Distinction in the Thought of St Maximus the Confessor.* Oxford: Oxford University Press.

Zakhos, Konstantinos. 1998. *Lost Familiarity: The Ecological Crisis in the Light of the Thought of St Maximus the Confessor (in Greek).* Larisa: Ella.

Zizioulas, John. 2010. Relational Ontology: Insights from Patristic Thought (pp. 146–156). In John Polkinghorne (Ed.), *The Trinity and an Entangled World: Relativity in Physics and Theology.* Grand Rapids, MI and Cambridge: Eerdmans.

Further Reading

Blowers, Paul M., and Wilken, Robert Louis. 2003. *On the Cosmic Mystery of Jesus Christ: Selected Writings from St Maximus the Confessor*. Crestwood, KY: St Vladimir's Seminary Press. Readable if somewhat free translations of some key passages, with a useful introduction.

Bordeianu, Radu. 2009. Maximus and Ecology: The Relevance of Maximus the Confessor's Theology of Creation for the Present Ecological Crisis. *Downside Review*, 127, 103–126. http://www.duq.edu/Documents/theology/_pdf/faculty-publications/art-mordeianu-max.pdf. A valuable article focusing on how human spiritual life can affect the rest of material Creation and how ignorance of Maximus skews the debate about Christianity and ecology. It draws on the thought of Fr. Dumitru Staniloae, whose extensive commentaries on Maximus are not available in English.

Constas, Nicholas (Ed. and Transl.). 2014. *On Difficulties in the Church Fathers: The Ambigua: Maximus the Confessor*. Cambridge, MA and London: Harvard University Press. This well-annotated translation of the complete *Ambigua*, with parallel Greek text, achieves the seemingly impossible in being both beautifully lucid and meticulously faithful to the original text.

Loudovikos, Nikolaos. 2010. *A Eucharistic Ontology: Maximus the Confessor's Eschatological Ontology of Being as Dialogical Reciprocity*. Brookline, MA: Holy Cross Orthodox Press. Much more accessible than its title suggests, this detailed study engages with and sometimes challenges the classic Western Christian interpretations of Maximus.

Louth, Andrew. 1996. *Maximus the Confessor*. London: Routledge. Translations of some key texts, with an excellent, substantial introduction showing the coherence of various strands in Maximus' thought.

Louth, Andrew. 2004. The Cosmic Vision of Saint Maximus the Confessor (pp. 184–196). In Philip Clayton & Arthur Peacocke (Eds.), *In Whom We Live and Move and Have Our Being: Panentheistic Reflections on God's Presence in a Scientific World*. Grand Rapids, MI and Cambridge: Eerdmans. A thought-provoking and admirably clear discussion of Maximus' cosmic vision and how it might relate to modern problematics.

Osborne, Basil [then Bishop of Amphipolis]. 2008. An ecology of the Virtues: The Ecological Crisis and the Objectification of Nature (pp. 157-17). In Basil Osborne, *The Healing Word*. London: Darton, Longman & Todd. A profound yet accessible treatment of Maximus' ascetic theology in light of the philosophical background to the environmental crisis.

Paffhausen, Metropolitan Jonah. 2013. Natural Contemplation in St Maximus the Confessor and St Isaac the Syrian (pp. 46–58). In John Chryssavgis & Bruce V. Foltz (Eds.), *Toward an Ecology of Transfiguration: Orthodox Christian Perspectives on Environment, Nature and Creation*. New York: Fordham University Press. A profound discussion from within the monastic tradition of the way contemplation of Nature shapes our vision of the world.

Theokritoff, Elizabeth. 2012. The Book of the Word: Reading God's Creation (pp. 20–27). In *Caring for Creation (Christian Reflection), July*. Waco, TX: Center for Christian Ethics, Baylor University. A discussion on a popular rather than academic level of how we might "read" Creation as a pattern for our own conduct.

Töronen, Melchisedec. 2007. *Union and Distinction in the Thought of St Maximus the Confessor*. Oxford: Oxford University Press. Highly readable and engaging as well as scholarly, this study explores the nuances of "union" in Maximus and the way he uses his Christian and neo-platonist sources.

III. Ecological Commitment

Contextualization of Traditions in Diverse Contexts, Cultures, and Circumstances

CHAPTER 18

From Social Justice to Creation Justice in the Anthropocene

Larry L. Rasmussen

Our whole point is that this is a sacred universe. Cosmology without ecology is empty. Our future is at stake. Is there anything more important?

Mary Evelyn Tucker (2014)

On September 21, 2014, 350,000–400,00 people took to the streets of New York City for the Peoples' Climate March, held with a view to the UN Climate Summit of September 23–24. Self-identified faith communities were present and well represented. Many joined the evening multi-faith service of global religious and environmental leaders at the Cathedral of St. John the Divine. It was their conclusion to the Religions for the Earth Conference hosted by Union Theological Seminary.

In addition, the Aboriginal Indigenous Peoples' Council issued a declaration at the United Nations. In a statement of just over two pages the words "sacred," "sacredness," and "sanctity" appear 25 times, including in the title itself: Beyond Climate Change to Survival on Sacred Mother Earth (American Indian Institute, hereafter AII). Were "the sacred" or "sacredness" itself the subject, it might have been even more prominent. But it is not—getting beyond climate change to survival is the whole point. Much of the text is thus descriptive of changes to "Sacred Mother Earth" that follow on "modern living and all that it encompasses"; that is, changes that follow on the global reach of the Industrial Revolution and centuries of conquest, colonization, and "progress." "The Air is not the same anymore. The Water is not the same anymore. The Earth is not the same anymore. The Clouds are not the same anymore. The Rain is not the same anymore. The Trees, the Plants, the Animals, Birds, Fish, Insects and all the others are not the same anymore. All that is Sacred in Life is vanishing because of our actions" (AII, 1).[1]

"There is no more time for discussion on preventing 'Climate Change,'" the paragraph begins. "That opportunity has passed. 'Climate Change' is here" (AII, 1). "Not the same anymore" is both the consequence of the extractive global economy and the new normal.

The Wiley Blackwell Companion to Religion and Ecology, First Edition. Edited by John Hart.

This is not the declaration's first paragraph, however. That one sets the foundation and framework for what follows: "All Creation has a right to live and survive on this Sacred Earth and raise their Families where the Creator placed them to be" (AII, 1).

"Raise their Families" means the families of "all Creation." Insects, birds, fish, plants all have families. Citizens of Sacred Earth, all of them, are personal in the manner of family members. Members of the community of life, all of it, are the relatives. So are the primal elements—earth (soil), air, fire (energy), and water.

The declaration goes on to name changes to the planet beyond the ones cited above. There is no need to list them here, only the need to say what the document says. They all follow from the kind of economy that has ravaged Sacred Earth and its families; that has brought climate change and survival stakes in its wake; and that violates the sacred with its way of life.

The gravity and urgency the Indigenous People's Council seeks to convey is spelled out with the one sentence that it is in upper-case and bolded:

> **TO SURVIVE CLIMATE CHANGE AND SEE THE FUTURE WE MUST RESTORE THE SACRED IN OURSELVES AND INCLUDE THE SACREDNESS OF ALL LIFE IN OUR DISCUSSIONS, DECISIONS, AND ACTIONS.** (AII, 2)

A longer title for this essay would be: "Getting from Social Justice to Creation Justice: What Would it Take?" If the People's Climate March, the Religions for the Earth service at the Cathedral of St. John the Divine, and the statement of the Indigenous Peoples' Council are any measure, it would take a transformation of social justice to become creation justice. That likely entails a different cosmology from the one assumed by the Protestant social justice traditions I treat here, a cosmology in which all Creation, not human beings only, is sacred—a sacred universe.

What planetary developments make such justice compelling? Is social justice as we have known it insufficient, at least conceptually? Are there clues in the declaration that the air, water, earth, clouds, rain, trees, plants, animals, birds, fish, insects, and all the others "are not the same anymore?"

"Not the same anymore" introduces the Anthropocene, a prospective new geological epoch. The Anthropocene, if it is imminent, would be the successor to the epoch that has hosted all human civilizations to date, bar none: the late Holocene. Definitive word was expected in 2016 when the official keepers of geological time, after the International Commission on Stratigraphy (ICS) had voted whether or not to plant a new "golden spike." For the ICS "golden spikes" signal when geological epochs end and begin.

But does an official word matter? In 2012 the 34th International Geological Congress had declared that "For the first time in geostory [their word for Earth history] humans are the most powerful force shaping the face of the Earth."[2]

"The most powerful force shaping the face of the Earth"—thus "Anthropocene" from *anthropos*, Greek for "human" and so-named because of the "pervasive human influence throughout earth's systems" (Jenkins, 2013, 1). This *anthropos* has modified the flows of most rivers and changed the catchment areas of the world. This *anthropos* has re-engineered more rocks, soil, and landscapes in the last century than volcanoes, earthquakes, and glaciers have. The role of the carbon cycle in the acidification of the oceans and the re-regulation of solar radiation has fallen to this *anthropos* because this *anthropos* has taken it. This *anthropos* is now the main agent in the planet's nitrogen cycle. This *anthropos* now drives innocent species into extinction at an ever-quickening pace. This *anthropos*, in fact, seems to be bringing on a geological epoch whose tattoo is not like that of the Holocene—climate stability—but climate volatility and eco-social uncertainty. It is not a metaphorical creation that groans in travail, awaiting the redemption of this *anthropos*. It is the literal one (Rom. 8: 22–23).

The summary from climate science, in the words of Robert Stavins, one of the authors of three Intergovernmental Panel on Climate Change (IPCC) reports, is harrowing:

> The world is now on track to more than double current greenhouse gas concentrations in the atmosphere by the end of the century. This would push up average global temperatures by three to eight degrees Celsius and could mean the disappearance of glaciers, droughts in the mid-to-low latitudes, decreased crop productivity, increased sea levels and flooding, vanishing islands and coastal wetlands, greater storm frequency and intensity, the risk of species extinction and a significant spread of infectious disease. (Stavins, 2014, 6)

Elizabeth Kohlbert, calling species extinction at human hands "an unnatural history," captures the significance of the collective human impact well. In the last pages of *The Sixth Extinction*, she writes: "We are deciding, without meaning to, which evolutionary pathways will remain open, and which will forever be closed. No other creatures have ever managed this, and it will, unfortunately, be our most enduring legacy" (Kolbert, 2014, 268–269).

In sum, three epochal developments scramble the reality for social justice as we have known it. At the same time they create the mandate for Creation justice in an emerging epoch.

- *Humanity is now the single most decisive force of Nature itself.* Most systems of the natural world are currently embedded as part of human systems, or profoundly affected by human systems—the high atmosphere, the ocean depths, the polar regions. It was never thus but it is now, and for all foreseeable futures. Some "evolutionary pathways will remain open," others "will forever be closed" (Kolbert, 2014, 268)
- *Nature has changed course.* After graphing long-term trends in 24 areas, from the onset of the Industrial Revolution to the present, scientists of the International Geosphere-Biosphere Program concluded that "[e]vidence from several millennia shows that the magnitude and rates of human-driven changes to the global environment are in many cases unprecedented." "There is no previous analogue for the current operation of the Earth system" (Steffen et al., 2004, v). Industrial humanity has brought on a non-analogous moment, a unique epoch
- *In contrast to the climate stability of the Holocene, the mark of the Anthropocene is climate volatility and uncertainty.* The importance of this contrast can hardly be overstated, since it was the relative climate stability of the late Holocene that made possible the rise and spread of human civilizations from the Neolithic era (c. 10,000 BCE) to the present

What civilizational transitions are required if climate volatility and uncertainty belong to the new normal? More pointedly, what does this non-analogous time, with these three developments, mean for notions of justice? If our swollen powers are, to cite Willis Jenkins (2013, 1), now exercised "cumulatively across generational time, aggregately through ecological systems, and unintentionally over evolutionary futures," then the time and space dimensions of collective human agency and responsibility are stretched beyond anything we have known so far. If no natural terrain is left untouched by both human goodness and human molestation, then everything turns on our actions and choice, with consequences not only for present as well as future generations of humankind, but for the other relatives aboard the ark, together with the primal elements of earth, air, fire, and water.

Let me bare my soul: I find this burgeoning of human impact and responsibility frightening. While the new reality means the ascendency of ethics for our era, as an utterly practical affair, because everything turns on human choice and action, our canons and institutions of moral responsibility and justice do not begin to match the down-and-dirty consequences of actual human power. The neighbor we are to love as we love ourselves is no longer (only) the neighbor close at hand in time or space, but the neighbor in distant space and deep time. We will be the cause of unknown Jericho road victims generations hence, because we left them a changed, diminished, and dangerous planet.

Here, then, is the test for justice in the Anthropocene: What canons and practices of present love and justice reach across generational time to gather in the needs of future populations, human and other, and do so under the conditions of Nature on a different course? What canons and practices, for example, readily identify the following as violations of due justice? Shrinking habitat, disappearing species, eroding soils, modified gene pools, collapsing fisheries, souring seas, environment-related diseases, receding forests, melting glaciers, delta dead zones, migrating pests and diseases, rising sea levels, environmental refugees, biodiversity loss, vanishing wetlands and bleaching coral reefs, more greenhouse gases, surface temperature hikes, more intense storms and flooding, deeper droughts, and climate volatility. While all these are readily recognized as serious environmental "issues" or "problems," neither the present nor the future natural world seems to have, at least at present, sufficient standing in modern jurisprudence or modern morality to register these as justice claims, as claims for Nature's own regeneration and renewal on its own non-negotiable terms and time-lines. Despite the Earth-altering consequences of humankind's presence, the cosmology of official justice seems ecologically void. Nor does its cosmology "include *the sacredness of all life* in our discussions, decisions, and actions," to recall the Indigenous Peoples' UN Declaration (AII, 2, emphasis added). If anything has sacred standing, it is, at best, human life and not more.

That raises two questions. Why do most social justice traditions include so little of the natural world and do not deem it sacred? What would it take to alter both the content and status? If our best justice can barely imagine, much less construct, the new forms of responsibility needed for creatures with geophysical powers, and if we exercise all too real dominion via vast interlocking systems of great complexity, across extended time and space in a "non-analogous" era, how do we move to Creation justice for a new Earth Age? Can social justice be born again for a new vocation as Creation justice?

To begin to answer, I turn to the story of why modern Protestant social justice emerged in the first place. It was in response to what was identified early in the twentieth century as "the social question," or "the modern social problem." The phrases are those of Ernst Troeltsch in 1911. Troeltsch was a contemporary of Max Weber who, in 1904, published *The Protestant Ethic and the Spirit of Capitalism.* That book ends with the modern capitalist order pictured as an "iron cage" in which we have trapped ourselves. Bound to "the tremendous cosmos of the modern economic order," "the lives of all the individuals who are born into this mechanism [are determined] with irresistible force," Weber wrote. "Perhaps [this order] will so determine them until the last ton of fossilized coal is burnt," he added (Weber, 1904, 181). Troeltsch was responding to the consequences of the new economic cosmos of industrialized nature. His 1911 work includes the following:

> This social problem is vast and complicated. It includes the problem of the capitalist economic period and of the industrial proletariat created by it; and of the growth of militaristic and bureaucratic giant states; of the enormous increase in population, which affects colonial and world policy; of the mechanical technique, which produces enormous masses of materials and links up and mobilizes the whole world for purposes of trade, but which also treats men and labour like machines. (Troeltsch, 1981, II: 2010)

These were outcomes of the economy already made famous in Adam Smith's work of 1776, *An Inquiry into the Nature and Causes of the Wealth of Nations.* Smith had identified its engine, soon named "capitalism" by French philosophers, and it was already a world-shaping power. Not many years later, Karl Marx, shocked and awed by this capitalism, wrote:

> The bourgeoisie, during its rule of scarce one hundred years, has created more massive and more colossal productive forces than have all preceding generations together. Subjection of Nature's forces to man, machinery, application of chemistry to industry and agriculture, steam-navigation, railways, electric telegraph, clearing of whole continents for cultivation, canalization of rivers, whole populations conjured out of the ground—what earlier century had even a presentiment that such productive forces slumbered in the lap of social labor. (Marx, 1954, 23)

The year was 1848, more than a half-century before Weber and Troetsch. 1848 was barely on the cusp of the "application of chemistry to industry and agriculture ... clearing of whole continents for cultivation, canalization of rivers, whole populations conjured out of the ground." All those factors and more belong to our discussion that Nature's systems are now, 160 and more years later, embedded in human systems and profoundly influenced by them, air, water, and climate included. And while Marx was spectacularly wrong in his prediction that the proletariat would become the gravediggers of the bourgeoisie and that the coming socialist revolution would overturn capitalism, he was, like Troeltsch and, it should be added, Walter Rauschenbusch and the Social Gospel in the late 1800s and early 1900s, absolutely right about the atomization of society and the exploitative, alienating nature of industrial orders that nonetheless captivated people with the lure of enormous productivity and mounting material prosperity. Had all three, Rauschenbusch, Troeltsch, and Marx, been present in 2015, they would likely not have been surprised at the staying power of "the social question" or the fact it is now global. The assault on settled, intact communities attuned to intact places still defines our world. The gap between the rich and the rest widens while institutions of family, community, and nation-state still struggle to stave off atomization amid unleashed economic forces, shifting identities, and unsure local, regional, national, and global authority. This might have saddened or angered these students of early capitalism, but it probably would not have startled them.

The Social Gospel and other manifestations of Protestant-inspired justice soon responded to "the modern social problem" across a broad front and on innumerable issues. Social justice work included the right to unionize, a minimum wage, decent and safe working conditions, housing for workers that went beyond the hovels they knew all too well, the franchise, child labor laws, an eight-hour working day, legal recourse to discrimination in hiring and firing, protests against obscene wealth for the robber barons, but meager rewards for those receiving slave wages, and some provision for child care and healthcare.

Does our retrospective report notice anything else? Yes, but it went largely unnoticed by Weber, Rauschenbusch, and Troeltsch, but less so by Marx.

"The ecological question" joined "the social question." It, too, is the direct outcome and drawback of the organization, habits, and exacting requirements of modern industrial-technological society and its ever-expanding extractive economy. It manifests itself as the unending transformation of Nature, a parallel to the unending transformation of society, with both in pursuit of Mammon. We cited its warning signs earlier: shrinking habitats and disappearing species, eroding soils, modified gene pools, polar region and glacial melting, rising sea levels and stronger storm surges, drought and deluge, and so on. Like the social question, the ecological question has gone global.

Marx alone saw the social and ecological entwined. Yes, Weber worried that entrapment in the "iron cage" of capitalism might last until "the last ton of fossilized coal" had been burned. But he was less aware than Marx that the same economic logic productive of great material wealth for some populations was ruinous for the natural world. Well before factory farming and widespread mono-cropping became the norm, though not before what he called "the union of agriculture and industry," Marx offered his observations on "progress." Progress here is progress "in the art, not only of robbing the labourer, but of robbing the soil; all progress in increasing the fertility of the soil for a given time, is a progress towards ruining the lasting sources of that fertility." It saps "the original sources of all wealth—the soil and the labourer. The more a country starts its development on the foundation of modern industry, like the United States, for example, the more rapid is this process of destruction," Marx wrote in 1867 (Marx, 1967, 507).

I have trawled through this history so that we notice what has largely been overlooked in our conception of social justice; namely, the natural world as worthy of such reverence that it might make moral claims on us or itself be due justice. The People's Climate March in New York City, the global Religions for the Earth gathering, and the Indigenous Peoples' UN Declaration may well signal an important turning point. But historically, Protestant social justice has effectively affirmed the "tremendous [economic] cosmos" of the industrial paradigm, whether as industrial socialism or industrial capitalism. Its quest, and the glory of its achievement, was to render the benefits and burdens of the Industrial Revolution fairer in the lives of those determined by it. Yet this was justice captured by the very economy that was tone deaf to the deep needs of the natural world on which it depended, lock, stock, and (oil) barrel.

Look at it this way: life lived on certain economic and social assumptions created the "not-the-same-anymore" epoch that now overwhelms us. As I roll out these assumptions, ask not only whether they hold true for the industrial paradigm of modernity, but whether justice theory and practice have not also embraced them in its cosmology.

> Nature is a virtually limitless storehouse of resources for human use.
> Humanity has the commission to use and control nature.
> Nature is malleable and can be reconfigured for human ends.
> Humanity has the right, perhaps even the calling, to use nature's resources for an improvement in its material standard of living.
> The most effective means to raise material standards of living is ongoing economic growth.
> The quality of life is furthered by an economic system directed to ever-expanding material abundance.
> The future is open, systematic material progress for the whole human race is possible, and through the careful use of human powers humanity can make history turn out right.
> The things we create are under our control.
> The good life is one of productive labor and material well-being.
> The successful person is one who achieves and is on his or her own.
> Both social progress and individual interests are best served by achievement-oriented behavior in a competitive and entrepreneurial environment.
> A work ethic is essential to human satisfaction and social progress.
> The diligent, hardworking, risk-taking, and educated will attain their goals.
> There is freedom in material abundance.
> When people have more, their freedom of choice is expanded and they can and will *be* more. (Birch & Rasmussen, 1978, 44–45)[3]

Differently said, social justice as it emerged here, while admirably driven by fair play and a fair outcome for human communities (recall the list of Social Gospel issues) is justice shorn of any doctrine of Creation except Creation as the décor for the human and a storehouse of resources to be tapped for human benefit. The rest of the community of life and Nature's abiotic world have little presence in either the formation or execution of this justice. It is justice that assumes human wellbeing is primary even though human wellbeing is always derivative of something more basic—Nature's wellbeing. This is justice that assumes that the basic unit of human survival itself is human society, but it clearly is not; it is planetary creation comprehensively, with all the primal elements—earth (soil), air, fire (energy), water that is truly primary. The human good is not possible without the goods of the planetary commons.

Not only is the working understanding of justice inadequate here, the working understanding of Creation itself is unworthy. Even God seems to exist, for all practical purposes, only in relation to one late-arriving species perched on one branch of the great Tree of Life. Honey, we shrunk not only the kids; we shrunk the cosmos, its Creator and Sustainer. To return to our epigraph from Mary Evelyn Tucker, this is cosmology without ecology, and it is empty. Or put it this way: the natural world has no real standing in this cosmology, except as critical resources for human life, and some humans far more than others.

My criticism is not a criticism of what Christian social justice, Protestant and beyond, has included and accomplished. It has not only taken on the vital issues we mentioned. It has been right in eventually developing the means by which to do race, class, gender, and cultural analysis, thereby demonstrating in detail the gross injustice of severely inequitably distributed benefits and burdens. Liberation theologies refined these analytical tools and, like the Hebrew prophets, made the locus and play of power a centerpiece of theological and social ethical method itself. That focus on power, privilege, and the laying bare of injustice are precious gifts which now belong to social and environmental justice together. Yet the humanity/Nature dualism of most justice traditions, religious and secular, worked like blinders on a horse. Straight-ahead attention assigned to the sidelines the growing and unsustainable footprint of humanity in every natural domain that mattered—the carbon footprint, the water footprint, the biodiversity footprint, the ecological footprint (land and energy footprints), and the material footprint, meaning the measure of resources used.

Thus have we arrived, without much notice for justice theory, at the standoff described by Naomi Klein:

> [O]ur economic system and our planetary system are now at war. Or, more accurately, our economy is at war with many forms of life on earth, including human life. What the climate needs to avoid collapse is a contraction in humanity's use of resources; what our economic model demands to avoid collapse is unfettered expansion. Only one of these sets of rules can be changed, and it's not the laws of nature. (Klein, 2004, 21)

If the laws of Nature cannot be changed, then it is mandatory to reform or replace the economic model and exit Weber's "iron cage." Yet, those sturdy pillars of progress—the dominance of market logic, deregulated capitalism, and a global consumer ethic—continue to hinder the "grand project of mutual reinvention" (Klein, 2004, 23) that is needed. This is reinvention needed, above all, for comprehensive wellbeing, but it is also the reinvention needed to move from social justice to Creation justice. That reinvention is at least Wendell Berry's—a cultural, economic, social, and political transformation that nurtures the full community of life at home in any given place and lived according to the genius and constraints of that place, respecting the watershed, for example, or ocean biochemistry and coastal zone structure. Likewise, it is the reinvention set forth as "integral ecology" in the extraordinary papal encyclical *Laudato Si: On Care for Our Common Home* (June 18, 2015).

The transformation may also be Thomas Berry's—nothing less than the reinvention of the human at the species level. Who is this "weedy" species (Wake & Vredenburg, 2008, in Kolbert, 2014, 8) anyway? How do we fit in now, when humans have become the single most powerful force of Nature itself; and Nature, as a consequence, has changed course on a planet in jeopardy at human hands?

Short of this double reinvention, collapse—itself no stranger to human society or the rest of Nature in planetary history—is possible in the way that biblical prophecy and apocalypse warn (Diamond, 2005).

I highlight two outcomes of industrialized humanity's way of life and the notion of justice it carries. The first loops back to the call from the Indigenous Peoples' Council; the second probes more deeply into the history that has shaped the justice we know.

The cosmology of the industrial paradigm is one in which the sacred and numinous is leeched from all Nature except human nature, and its presence there is tenuous. (For European settlers in the Americas, those they named "Indians" were essentially "overburden," in the manner of mountaintop removal, not, as the "Indians" thought, peoples of the Earth living on sacred lands.) Only human life, or some human life, is valued as an end; all else is means only. Such is modernity's unqualifiedly utilitarian ethic. After all, "What good is a mountain just to have a mountain?" to quote Jason Bostic, Vice President of the West Virginia Coal Association (Klein, 2004, 337). Or, to cite ExxonMobil CEO Rex Tillerson's response in a shareholders' meeting to those who asked their company to stop using the atmosphere as a sewer: "What good is it to save the planet if humanity suffers?" (Gore, 2014, 11). The planet's standing here parallels that of Bostic's mountains. Both questions—Tillerson's and Bostic's—were meant to quash any further conversation by appealing to the plain common sense of industrialized humanity. Extra-human justice for the mountain or the planet does not fit in. Their value is limited to what is tellingly tagged "natural capital."

The second outcome includes the shock of recognition. The prevailing ethic is an ancient one made modern, namely, that of master–slave. I explored this in simplified fashion in *Earth-Honoring Faith*. In that account humans are masters, the rest of Nature is slave, in the continuing life of the industrial paradigm and the present global economy. Industrialized Nature "fits the classic understanding of the slave: living property to be bought, sold, and used in keeping with what is deemed necessary, desirable, and responsible on the part of the slaveholder—in this case, us" (Rasmussen, 2012, 100).

Domination of the rest of Nature is no equal opportunity affair across human ranks, however. Consequently *Earth-Honoring Faith* devotes pages describing the we/they, us/them play of power and privilege. Power and privilege vis-à-vis the rest of Nature are justified in a manner that parallels the domination of human races, classes, and genders. Still, that account of why "the injuries of nature delight" us (Rasmussen, 2012, 86–90) (to recall St. Ambrose) fails to draw the historical and ongoing connections between the past master–slave ethic and the present one. Allow further treatment.

James Cone opened his 1998 address, "Whose Earth Is It, Anyway?" with this: "The logic that led to slavery and segregation in the Americas, colonization and apartheid in Africa, and the rule of white supremacy throughout the world is the same one that leads to the exploitation of animals and the ravaging of nature. It is a mechanistic and instrumental logic that defines everything and everybody in terms of contribution to the development and defense of white world supremacy" (Cone, 2001, 23).

When I first heard that contention, I shrank from it. While I wholeheartedly agreed about the reigning "mechanistic and instrumental logic," my inclination was always to put "human interests" where Cone put "White world supremacy." I shrank from that contention a second time when Delores Williams argued in "Sin, Nature, and Black Women's Bodies" that the same logic of domination governing Black women's bodies in slavery holds for strip mining and human treatment of Earth. African enslaved women were forcibly raped and repeatedly impregnated to breed more slaves, some giving birth 20 and more times. The reason—always the reason for slavery everywhere and forever—was economic. Williams draws out the logic of an extractive economy built on the backs of slaves and argues that it continues as the domination of other Nature as well. Taking the license of the poet she is, she compares the treatment of the reproductive capacities of slave women and the productive/reproductive capacities of Appalachian mountains. Stripping and strip-mining, their violence and degradation, govern both (Williams, 1993, 24–29).[4] To recall Bostic: "What good is a mountain just to have a mountain?" (Klein, 2012, 337). What good is a slave woman if she doesn't do your economic and sexual bidding?

Are Cone and Williams right that slavery logic continues, with other than human nature the irreplaceable slave alongside exploited humans? Is Carl Anthony right that "Historic moments of excessive abuse—slave trade, colonization, genocide—developed in tandem with humanity's unsustainable relationship to the environment"? (2014).[5] Is the metaphorical truth of James Baldwin as he joined the Selma march correct? "I could not suppress the thought that this earth had acquired its color from the blood that had dripped down from these trees" (Schapiro, 2014, 109).[6] Are all four correct that historical slavery and industrialized Nature belong together in what Anthony calls "the old story" from which we need to be liberated in a reborn, abolitionist movement? Is the implication that, until we are rid of this "old story," we will not, perhaps cannot, imagine the "new story" of a sacred universe? Long-entrenched subject-to-object supremacy dies hard.

The point overall is that the extractivist economy of capitalism, marrying industrialization to conquest and colonization, is the "shared hinge on which these European–Indigenous–African relations swung" (Harvey, 2007, 14). The point as well is that this kind of economy has no sense whatsoever of the sacred, for the natural world or its peoples, unless it is the perverse sacredness of a joint mission—civilizing inferior peoples and "taming" the wilderness, both at the hands of Whites. Whether land or labor, whether Nature as natural resources and "overburden," whether people as chattel, capital, or inconvenient populations (Indians), a non-reciprocal logic of domination governs all. To understand how value is valued, then, follow the pursuit of possession, profits, and growth. And to unveil the assumed relationship that reigns throughout, consider subject-to-object. Some humans and the rest of Nature are object while other humans, tacitly superior, are subject. The reigning master image is the image of mastery itself, including the way mastery recounts its own history and tells its own story as a civilizing mission and as a good life in the service of the general welfare.

Social justice sought, again and again, to take the hard edge off the workings of this economy, just as it sought to distribute the benefits and share the burdens more fairly. It sought as well to elevate the standing of many human populations from "inferior" to "equal" as all are children of God. This was no mean achievement. Not least, social justice is, if anything, now more urgent than ever, since the new norm of climate change finds those who suffer most from it are those who contribute least to it.

Yet, as we have seen, social justice largely accepted the cosmology of industrialized Nature, whether socialist or capitalist. "The ecological question" was not part of "the social question" and vice versa, despite the alarming degree to which the same logic and agents of domination treated land and peoples in parallel fashion ("mechanistic and instrumental," to recall Cone).

So what would it take for social justice to conceive creation justice? One essential transformation rests in a simple contrast, the contrast of "personal" and "impersonal." Exactly that contrast is the contrast of sacred and slave.

A relationship with the sacred is always deeply personal. Orthodox theologian John Chryssavgis comments, "It has always been a source of great comfort to me that Orthodox spirituality retains a sacramental view of the world, proclaiming a world imbued by God and a God involved in the world—a sacrament of communion." He then goes on to say what the world as sacrament means: "We should respond to nature with the same delicacy, sensitivity, and tenderness with which we respond to a person in a relationship, and our failure to do so is the fundamental source of pollution" (Chryssavgis, 2014).[7] "The time has come," he says elsewhere, "to stop treating even things like things" (Chryssavgis, 1999, 15).

Differently said, in this relationship I experience a deep *feel* for the other in the gut, whether the other is animate or inanimate, a fellow creature, a mountain or river, a helpless newborn, or an emblazoned horizon at the day's onset or end. In Marilynne Robinson's *Gilead*, this is old Pastor Ames' sensation "of really knowing a creature, I mean really feeling its mysterious life and your own mysterious life at the same time" (Robinson, 2004, 23); a "sacrament of communion," in Chryssavgis' words (1999, 5); trying to "write down a baby's first cry," in John Rutter's (1985):

The gut feeling that accompanies the sacred is so deeply personal that any of the primary moral emotions—empathy, sympathy, compassion, awe, wonder, reverence and respect, a heartfelt loyalty to place and love of it—might well up. "The more I wonder, the more I love," is Alice Walker's version (1982).[8] Love, that most personal of all communal connections, is subject joined to subject in a common life. It might pertain to anything and all things, a mountain, a plain, a forest, a village, city, county, or life itself and the starry night sky. Of that which really counts, love may even be greater than faith and hope, as Paul thought (I Cor. 13: 13).

The impersonal, by contrast, is only instrumental. Its relationship is means-to-end, with no moral emotions or claims attached, other than all those pleasures of the consumer or the slave-master. The impersonal is the world as our oyster, the world in which we are "takers" but not "givers" or "leavers." As impersonal, Creation has no binding claims on us; we have claims on it. As subject to object, no genuine reciprocity exists either. It is the world as useful but without a soul, as commodities but not independent character with inherent worth. It parallels the personal and sacred in only one way; the impersonal, too, can pertain to anything and all things—that mountain, plain, forest, village, next door neighbor, or the stars.

Here is the surprise, at least for most Euro-Americans. The personal can be, and in the cosmology and practices of indigenous peoples classically has been, a relationship embracing both the animate and inanimate worlds. We are, by nature, soil people, or water people, or deer people, or forest people, or desert people, or mountain people.

We share a common energy, or spirit, with other natural entities. Our neighbor is "all that participates in being," or "being" as "companion," to remember both Marilynne Robinson (2014) and H. Richard Niebuhr (1956). We are companions to all that is. We're talking family here, all the "families of Creation," to recall the declaration of the Indigenous Peoples' Council at the UN (AII, 1).

"Person" ethics does not wipe away difference—birds, plants, insects, animals, winds, waters, and mountains are obviously distinguished from one another. Indeed, "person" heightens distinction and difference, since each knows uniqueness as an expression of evolving Creation's own processes and each carries value beyond "use." But this ethic grants a common citizenship to all. The universe is home to a communion of subjects (Berry).

Put it this way. "Things change according to the stance we adopt toward them, the type of attention we pay to them, the disposition we hold in relation to them" (McGilchrist, 2009, 4). Values arise with the relationships they express. It is little surprise, then, that different values belong to different relationships. If my relationship is instrumental and impersonal—at its working extreme, master to slave—values appropriate to a mechanistic and decontextualized world will rule. Everything except useful, "object-ive" service is alien. If Nature, including some humans, is without use, it is essentially overburden. But whether useful or overburden, its value is means-only in a world where any and all means are justified by ends and nothing more.

But if I belong "subject-ively" to living wholes of which I and the other are an integral part, intimate personal values of connection mark the relationship, rather than impersonal disconnected distance (psychological and moral). The same world is "out there" in both cases, personal or impersonal. How I take it in and lean into it makes all the difference. If I take it in as sacred, then some place, event, or natural phenomenon of that world appears in a different light, deeply personal and internal rather than extrinsic, at arm's length, and destined for some "useful purpose."

Of course, the sacred and the utilitarian might be, must be, joined, since use is essential to survival of any life at all. The matter at the moment, however, is first to see what prevails if the personal and sacred are more fundamental as the basic or prevailing relationship to the world "out there" than is the impersonal and utilitarian. And then to ask how different subject–object, master–slave utility is from current economic practice, practice that chases human and other natural resources around the globe in search of cheap labor and exploitable land. Neither labor nor land attains personhood in this ethic, just as neither possesses any value, save utility. Why should they be subjects with full moral standing? This is the legacy Cone, Williams, and Anthony identify as one that pits the global corporate economy against the planet's economy and many of its peoples, just as it did in an earlier era of overt imperial conquest, colonization, and the establishment of European and neo-European societies on every continent except Antarctica.

We close by sketching the transformations that would conceptually bring social justice to the threshold of Creation justice.

The first are principles for policy: principles that follow from the embeddedness of the social in the ecological and vice versa, and principles that acknowledge the primacy and priority of Creation. Behind these principles is Berry's maxim that "planetary health is primary and human well-being is derivative" (Berry, 2006). Or, to emphasize the point for Creation justice: planetary health is primary because human wellbeing is derivative. This makes the first law of economics "the preservation of the Earth economy" (Berry, 2002, 10). Economics and ecology merge to become "eco-nomics," with all human economic activity embedded in the ecological limits of Nature's economy.

A parallel exists for energy policy. Almost all justice attention to energy is about energy resources and use. Do we have enough to do what we want to do, namely, continue to grow the economy to meet human needs? Are we energy-independent and, if not, where will we go to secure that? How will energy be distributed fairly? These discussions all go on without first asking what sources and uses are mandated by the planet's climate–energy system, the way in which it regulates the incoming solar heat that keeps the Earth from being a sizeable frigid rock and nothing more. They assume that human energy use is primary, after that we will deal with the environmental effects. This is exactly seeing things backwards. The first law of energy is preservation of the planet's climate–energy system as conducive to life; human energy use is derivative of the planet's. This parallels Berry's maxim that the first law of the human economy is the preservation of Nature's economy.

We need not spell out the other principles that would follow—the primacy of the atmosphere's dynamics, or the hydrological system's, or eco-systemic requirements. All of them frame and permeate social justice with Nature's requirements for its own regeneration and renewal. Social justice is expanded and enhanced as Creation justice.

Yet getting economic and energy policy right, or water and clean air policy, vital though it be, is likely not sufficient for Creation justice. We will not escape the grip of the master–slave ethic of impersonal utility without a soul-deep, personal feel for the families of Creation, a gut connection that is profoundly personal, Earth-honoring, and Earth-healing. This subjective knowing of the other expresses a moral sense that nurtures ecological virtues, many of which have not been the coin of social justice traditions—wonder, awe, and reverence, for example, with all of "being" a companion and neighbor across time and space. These join virtues already found in social justice traditions—respect, empathy, and sympathy yoked to a passion for fairness and equality in lives that matter. In all events, the conviction that all Creation is sacred nurtures the formation of character and conduct in such a way that creation justice includes social justice and its ethos.

Is there more?

For religious devotees, especially those in theistic traditions, a sacred universe confesses God in all and all in God. But which God? To match what we now know about the universe, worthy "God-talk" would gather in all of Earth's voices to sing the hymn of Creation. God-talk that does not encompass all 13.8 billion years of the universe's pilgrimage to date and the immense wheeling of 100 billion galaxies, each swimming with billions of stars and who knows how many planets; God-talk that does not gather in all species come and gone, as well as those leaving as we speak; and God-talk that does not embrace the whole drama of life in all its misery and grandeur, is unworthy. In a sacred universe, worthy God-talk is about the mystery of matter and its drama—all of it, past, present, and future. It is an invitation to "sing with all the people of God and join in the hymn of all creation" (Lutheran Eucharist Liturgy, 1979, 88) so as to give voice, however partially and inadequately, to the carnal presence of the "uncontained God" (Levertov, 1984, 85). The uncontained God is the God of Creation justice.

A last critical element of Creation justice is an upgraded understanding of ourselves, an improved anthropology. Our present segregated sense of ourselves as a master-species is a miserably shrunken grasp of who we are in the scheme of things. From both a scientific and a religious point of view we are "fearfully and wonderfully made," in the phrase of the psalmist (Psalm 139). We are the handsome fruit of two wombs, our mother's and Mother Earth's. So the singer sings of God:

> For it was you who formed my inward parts;
> you knit me together in my mother's womb.
> I praise you, for I am fearfully and wonderfully made.
> Wonderful are your works; that I know very well.
> My frame was not hidden from you,
> when I was being made in secret,
> intricately woven in the depths of the earth.
> Your eyes beheld my unformed substance.
> In your book were written all the days that were formed for me,
> when none of them as yet existed. (Ps. 139: 13–16)

To be "fearfully and wonderfully made" across the stop-and-start eons of evolutionary life, to belong to life's drama and grandeur and have a perch of our own in the great Tree of Life, is our glory. To breathe the same air Jesus breathed and stand before the same waters Moses did, to share DNA with most of life and be composed of atoms 14 billion years old, that is enough. "I just try to act my age," quips Joanna Macy, "my atoms are 14 billion years old" (Macy, "Letters," www.joannamacy.net).[9] When justice is Creation justice, it takes on transcendence such as this.

These elements, composted with deep changes in policy that prioritize the requirements of life's generative elements and systems, transform social justice into Creation justice—Creation deemed sacred, character and conduct shaped by ecological virtues, God-talk worthy of the uncontained God, and a "fearfully and wonderfully made" understanding of ourselves. Here the "tremendous [economic] cosmos" of "the last ton of fossilized coal" (Weber) has more than met its match—the wonder of the real cosmos and its economy.

Notes

1 Beyond Climate Change to Survival on Sacred Mother Earth, made available in December 9, 2014, of the American Indian Institute Traditional Circle of Indian Elders and Youth, Bozeman, Montana.

2 Cited from the conclusions of the International Geological Congress of 2012, reported in *The New York Times*, August 15, 2012.

3 This is a modified version of the list Bruce Birch and I drew up for our volume, *The Predicament of the Prosperous* (Philadelphia: The Westminster Press, 1978), 44–45. This entire section on the history of social justice draws selectively from Rasmussen (2013, 46–50).

4 I am indebted to Melanie Harris and her remarks at Union Theological Seminary, New York, at the Religions of the Earth Conference, for this treatment.

5 Carl Anthony's remarks at the Living Cosmology Conference, November 7–9, 2014, Yale University Divinity School, as reported in the *National Catholic Reporter* by Jamie Manson, November 21, 2014. https://www.ncronline.org/blogs/grace-margins/yale-conference-continues-journey-universe.

6 Alabama soil, like much of the soil in the Deep South, is dark red. Reference to the trees is to their use as lynching trees.

7 Father John Chryssavgis, from comments at the Living Cosmology Conference, November 7–9, 2014, Yale University Divinity School, as reported in the *National Catholic Reporter* by Jamie Manson, November 21, 2014. Online at https://www.ncronline.org/blogs/grace-margins/yale-conference-continues-journey-universe.

8 The full quotation, in a letter from Celie, is: "I think us here to wonder, myself. To wonder. To ast. And that in wondering bout the big things and asting bout the big things, you learn about the little ones, almost by accident. But you never know nothing more about the big things than you start out with. The more I wonder, he say, the more I love."

9 There is a cautionary tale about the relationship of the sacred to justice that I feel compelled to include, even though it does not belong to the main discussion. The conquistadors and Franciscan priests colonizing the American Southwest where I live did *not* belong to the secular, utilitarian world of the later Industrial Revolution. On the contrary, theirs was a sacred (medieval) universe and their civilizing cause was a sacred mission. The universe was alive with the presence of the overflowing divine in all things. But it was also ordered as a Great Chain of Being that inscribed dominion and hierarchy, superiority and inferiority, with inferior peoples and cultures the unconsulted beneficiaries of a salvific gospel and way of life. When *any* cause or way of life bears sacred status, its potential for violence and abuse escalates. Its potential for non-violent love may escalate as well, but that does not negate the sacred as often a literal call to arms. Martyrs die and murderers kill for the sacred. A pact with the devil is a solemn, and wholly sacred, undertaking. Differently said, sacred status is no guarantee whatsoever of either social justice or creation justice. A moral plumb line must be brought to every sacred claim, to measure its rectitude. Indeed, that metaphor—the plumb line—belongs to a prophet, Amos. The passage in which it appears—7:7–9—is a passage in which God takes the measure of the Chosen People itself. This is the same God who, in 5:21 ff., rails: "I hate, I despise your festivals, and I take no delight in your solemn assemblies. Even though you offer me your burnt offerings and grain offerings, I will not accept them; and the offerings of well-being of your fatted animals I will not look upon. Take away from me the noise of your songs, I will not listen to the melody of your harps." Here sacred liturgy, with sacred sacrifice, is damned rather than praised because it lacks one thing. That one thing is made clear in the very next verse, a verse in which living water is the metaphor: "But let justice roll down like waters, and righteousness like an ever-flowing stream" (5: 24).

References

Berry, Thomas. 2002. Conditions for Entering the Ecozoic Era. *Ecozoic Reader*, 2, 2 (Winter).

Berry, Thomas. 2006. *Evening Thoughts: Reflecting on Earth as Sacred Community*. San Francisco, CA: Sierra Club.

Birch, Bruce & Rasmussen, L. 1978. *The Predicament of the Prosperous*. Philadelphia, PA: The Westminster Press.

Chryssavgis, John. 1999. *Beyond the Shattered Image*. Minneapolis, MN: Light and Life Publishing.

Diamond, Jared. 2005. *Collapse: How Societies Choose to Fail or Succeed.* New York: Viking.

Francis I, 2015. *Laudato Si. On Care for our Common Home*, June 18. http://w2.vatican.va/content/francesco/en/encyclicals/documents/papa-francesco_20150524_encyclical-laudato-si.html.

Gore, Al. 2014. The Turning Point: New Hope for the Climate. http://www.rollingstone.com/politics/news/the-turning-point-new-hope-for-the-climate-20140618?print=true.

H. Cone, James. 2001. Whose Earth Is It, Anyway? (23). In Dieter Hessel & Larry Rasmussen (Eds.), *Earth Habitat: Eco-Injustice and the Church's Response.* Minneapolis, MA: Fortress Press.

Harvey, Jennifer. 2007. *Whiteness and Morality: Pursuing Racial Justice through Reparations and Sovereignty.* Basingstoke: Palgrave Macmillan.

Jenkins, Willis. 2013. *The Future of Ethics: Sustainability, Social Justice, and Religious Creativity.* Washington, DC: Georgetown University Press.

Klein, Naomi. 2014. *This Changes Everything.* New York: Simon & Schuster.

Kolbert, Elizabeth. 2014. *The Sixth Extinction: An Unnatural History.* New York: Henry Holt.

Lavender, Paige & Hiar, Corbin. 2011. Blair Mountain: Protesters March to Save Historic Battlefield. *Huffington Post*, June 10.

Levertov, Denise. 1984. Annunciation. *The Door in the Hive.* New York: New Directions.

Lutheran Book of Worship. 1979. Minneapolis, MN: Augsburg.

Marx, Karl. 1954. *The Communist Manifesto.* New York: Henry Regnery.

Marx, Karl. 1967. *Capital: A Critique of Political Economy*, vol. 1. Transl. Samuel Moore and Edward Aveling. Ed. Frederick Engels. New York: International Publishers.

McGilchrist, Iain. 2009. *The Master and his Emissary: The Divided Brain and the Making of the Western World.* New Haven, CT: Yale University Press.

Niebuhr, H. Richard. 1956. *The Purpose of the Church and its Ministry: Reflections on the Aims of Theological Education.* New York: Harper & Row.

Rasmussen, Larry. 2013. *Earth-Honoring Faith: Religious Ethics in a New Key.* New York: Oxford University Press.

Robinson, Marilynne. 2004. *Gilead.* New York: Farrar, Straus & Giroux.

Robinson, Marilynne. 2014. Saying Grace. *The New York Times Magazine*, October 5, 27.

Rutter, John. 1985. *Candlelight Carol.* Hinshaw Music Inc., Oxford: Oxford University Press.

Schapiro, Steve. 2014. The Long Road. *The New Yorker*, December 22 and 29, 109.

Stavins, Robert N. 2014. Climate Realities, *The New York Times Sunday Review*, September 21, 6.

Steffen, W. L. et al. 2004. *Global Change and the Earth System.* Berlin and New York: Springer.

Troeltsch, Ernst. 1981. *The Social Teaching of the Christian Churches.* Chicago, IL: University of Chicago Press. First published in German, 1911.

Tucker, Mary Evelyn. 2014. In *National Catholic Reporter*, November 21. https://www.ncronline.org/blogs/grace-margins/yale-conference-continues-journey-universe.

Wake, David & Vredenburg, Vance. 2008. Are We in the Midst of the Sixth Mass Extinction? A View from the World of Amphibians, *Proceedings of the National Academy of Sciences*, n.p.

Walker, Alice. 1982. *The Color Purple.* New York: Pocket Books.

Weber, Max. 1958. *The Protestant Ethic and the Spirit of Capitalism*. New York: Charles Scribner's Sons. First published in German, 1904.

Williams, Delores S. 1993. Sin, Nature, and Black Women's Bodies (24–29). In Carol J. Adams (Ed.), *Ecofeminism and the Sacred*. New York: Continuum.

CHAPTER 19

Christianity, Ecofeminism, and Transformation

Heather Eaton

Introduction: Religion, Ecology, and Feminism

The ecological crisis is provoking a deep re-evaluation and transformation of religious traditions with respect to the natural world. This includes combinations of retrieval, re-evaluation, and reconstruction of texts and teachings, dogma, rituals and symbols, moral authority, soteriology, and ethics. It has led to an examination of universal claims and epistemological bases of, and critically assessing histories and dynamics among, religions, cultures, and their relation to the natural world. The ecological crisis is calling religions to reform these claims and revise these dynamics in order to promote constructive human–Earth relations. "Religion and ecology" are now a substantial theme in both academic study and religious practice.

It is important to note that a description or interpretation of any religion is ambiguous at best, given the multiple traditions, both historical and contemporary, the different conceptions of the relationships between religions and cultures, and the diverse emphases on history, texts, dogma, traditions, context, and current concerns. There is no "religion" outside of its countless historical forms, and the experiences and interpretations of adherents. The variations are limitless.

It is evident that religions, as worldviews and/or practices, include both life-affirming and life-negating attitudes, teachings, and cultural influences. Most religious traditions have otherworldly elements that need to be re-evaluated. Historical forms and activities are often fraught with bias, prejudice, limitations, and corruptions. The counterpoint is when religions reinforce movements of liberation, moral cohesiveness, and life-affirming orientations. Importantly, religions, in concepts and historical manifestations, are not static, and have been influenced, albeit unevenly, by diverse political ideologies, scientific findings, cultural combinations, and economic and political globalization. Many religions

The Wiley Blackwell Companion to Religion and Ecology, First Edition. Edited by John Hart.

have been challenged by feminism, ethnocentric critiques, postmodern hermeneutics, and postcolonial analyses. The feminist challenges to religions, combined with the ecological circumstances, are stirring an awakening that is new in human history.

Over the past 50 years, feminist analyses and critiques have examined and contested the patriarchal dimensions of religions. These include appraising texts, rituals, doctrines, ethics, leadership, and institutions. Religions have responded, in varying degrees, to these challenges. Feminist studies of religion have sought to extend places for women, to affirm that the religious ethos is supportive of women, to expose and invalidate patriarchal bases and biases, or to declare that religions are irretrievably oppressive to women.

The insights that developed from considering together feminism, religion, and ecology came from several pathways. One is from feminist analyses, which include what are now global movements for women's equity and autonomy, as well as innumerable modes of cultural scrutiny, inquiry, research methods, and scholarly contributions. Feminism represents a sea change in the role, value, and possibilities of women. Gender issues and studies, including LGBTQ studies, are now cross-cultural and multidisciplinary, and represent analyses and methods that are used by any and every discipline.

Feminist views on ecology (or the environment) are broad and deep, covering hundreds of topics from thousands of women and organizations, which, in turn, represent hundreds of thousands of women. There is agreement on some issues and not on others. There is a range of views, approaches, and strategies. Some put the emphasis on women's equity and rights, while others emphasize ecological integrity as foundational for a sustainable future. Given the diversity of peoples, cultures, and worldviews, and the complexity of issues, this is to be expected. All of this work indicates various ecology–feminist connections, using phrases such as feminist ecology, feminist social ecology, feminist green socialism, feminist environmentalism, feminist analyses of the environmental crisis (ecofeminist, ecowomanist, and feminist), and sustainability.

Feminism and Ecology: Historical Considerations

The connections between feminism and ecology first appeared in the 1970s, from two directions: women, environment, and development approaches, and ecofeminism. Each has a unique historical progression, which, at times, overlapped the other. Today they converge, and together represent a complex overlay of concerns, analyses, approaches, and strategies between feminism and ecology. Feminist and ecological approaches are influential when religious considerations are added, and for distinct reasons. These will be presented in the following sections.

Women, Environment, Development, and Sustainability

The women, environment, and development agenda was born of activists and analysts wanting a process of economic and social development geared to humans. However, after decades of a development agenda, it was evident that in many places women were not benefiting; and often their lives were made more difficult. Numerous organizations—Development Alternatives with Women for a New Era (DAWN), Association for Women's Rights in Development (AWID), and the Women, Environment, Development Organization (WEDO)—determined that many of the difficulties for women were rooted in a basic lack of equity, in the ideas and processes of development, and in capitalist and macroeconomic systems. The United Nation's Decade for Women: Equity, Development and Peace (1976–1985) culminated in a pivotal conference in Nairobi, where it was acknowledged that the development agenda had failed women. The United Nations then created a Development Fund for Women (UNIFEM). It has since evolved into UN Women with a larger and more comprehensive focus on gender equity. Development based on equity and equality requires access to economic and political power. It was evident that multiple issues intersected. The term "women and development" changed to "gender, equality, and development," expanding the focus to tackle the social and ideological causes of women's subordination, and the uneven power relations between women and men. Practically, this means that human rights include women's rights. Women need suffrage.

The global feminization of poverty had to be addressed. It enabled violence against women to be treated as a public policy issue rather than a private domestic problem. Women insisted that there can be no development in situations of women's systematic oppression. Any viable meaning to sustainability had to address economic, physical, and cultural violence against women.

Environmental issues surfaced on the global, development, and economic agendas and on the political landscape. The call for sustainable development opened the door for cooperation and consultation between global, national, and local partners, bridging government and civic society. Many of these initiatives did not include women; thus, women's organizations sprang up across the world adding environmental issues to their agendas (Dankelman & Davidson, 1988).

It became clear that environmental problems disproportionately affect women in most parts of the world. In 1989, the United Nations observed: "It is now a universally established fact that it is the woman who is the worst victim of environmental destruction. The poorer she is, the greater is her burden." The increased burdens women face result not only from environmental deterioration; a sexual division of labor found in most societies considers family sustenance to be women's work. As primary caregivers, women generally bear primary responsibility for the food and health of family members, but providing fuel, food, and water for their families becomes increasingly difficult with environmental degradation.

The amount of research and the number of activities, conferences, and publications from these interconnecting national and international agendas are astonishing. As environmental issues become more serious around the world, the need to remain vigilant on gender equality continues, because the underlying structures and ideologies that maintain gender inequities are not being dismantled. For example, life restrictions and injustices exist for women in virtually all countries.[1] The most acute is the systemic and persistent lack of basic human rights: food, water, safety, shelter, education, and healthcare. These are further exacerbated by intersectionality: structural inequalities or entrenched practices of domination reinforced through intersections of class, race, ethnicity, gender, sexuality, age, ability, and nationality. However, all women are at risk of physical and sexual violence.

The United Nations deems that the extent of violence against women is the most severe and pervasive human rights violation anywhere and everywhere in the world.[2] The World Health Organization (WHO) assesses that violence is the most significant health risk to women, and is a global public health problem that affects between one-third and two-thirds of women, depending on their culture.[3]

Today, many development organizations are engaging in systematic gender analysis, critiques, and collective visions and strategies for women, and especially for poor women (Lytte, 2011). There are thousands of non-governmental organizations (NGOs) addressing aspects of gender/feminism, development, environment, and sustainability. They deal with agriculture, biotechnology, fisheries, water, forests, or biodiversity. Other groups confront violence, global capitalism, militarism, and water piracy. Some are analytic, others activist. Some examine the dynamics of environmental ruin while others create local sustainable projects (Buechler & Hanson, 2015; Dankelman, 2010). They may deal with the theoretical or practical dimensions, or both. Large organizations like the United Nations, the World Bank, the Worldwatch Institute, and Amnesty International are addressing issues at the intersection of feminism and sustainability. Governments are encouraged to address these intersecting issues as well. This path—women, environment, and development—is an essential aspect to consider when adding religion or theology to the discussion.

Ecofeminism

A different set of voices and views on feminism and ecology were bringing forth distinct concerns with the term ecofeminism. Ecofeminism was used first by French feminist Françoise d'Eaubonne in *Le Féminisme ou la Mort* (1974), when she called on women to lead an ecological revolution to save the planet. Ecofeminism entered the scene in North America and Europe in the early 1970s. Broadly presented, ecofeminism is a convergence of ecological and feminist analyses and movements. It represents varieties of theoretical, practical, and critical efforts to understand and resist the interrelated dominations of women and Nature. It was an appealing and inspiring connection that quickly made sense to those developing various historical, ethical, and religious theories about the legacy and causes of women's oppression. Because it was such a flexible term, ecofeminism spawned countless research projects, conferences, publications, retreats, rituals, art, and political activism (Diamond & Orenstein, 1990; Gaard, 1998; Plant, 1998; Sturgeon, 1997). Over the years, ecofeminism represented activist and academic projects that explored critical connections between the domination of Nature and the exploitation of women. It was hailed by some as a third wave of feminism.

Ecofeminism, like ecology and feminism, is heterogeneous and has distinguishable themes and focuses. While ecofeminists share a basic awareness of the associations between women and the natural world, there are different entry points and distinct sets of concerns, orientations, and political goals. Ecofeminism stands for a diversity of approaches and perspectives. Over three decades it strengthened into versatile analyses enabling assessments of interconnections and layers of associations between women's oppression and the devaluing of the natural world. Most of ecofeminism comes from and speaks to Euro-Western cultures, although not exclusively so. It is, however, global in scope, which means that global issues and links are crucial to ecofeminist theories and actions. Not everyone who works on women and Nature or feminism and ecology uses the term ecofeminism.

The basic claim is that there are interconnections between cultural ideas about and social construction of women and Nature, the oppression of women, and the degradation of the natural world. These take specific forms in different cultures and contexts. Ecofeminism is a lens that allows one to see intersections that are usually obscured, and has developed into an interdisciplinary discourse within academia, a critique, and a vision. There are publications covering ecofeminist philosophy, theology, religious studies, spirituality, science, psychology, sociology, political thought and activism, economics, and animal rights (Kheel, 2008; Plant, 1989). Ecofeminists may be liberal, Marxist, socialist, cultural, radical, postmodernist, postcolonialist, or ecowomanist. They may advocate environmental resource management, deep ecology, social ecology, or evolutionary cosmology as an ecological framework. Much of ecofeminism has emerged in North America, yet a variety of regional, ethnic, and cultural ecofeminisms exists. There are ecofeminist reflections and activism from Latin America, Asia, India, and Africa. There are Buddhist, Native American, Goddess, Hindu, Muslim, Christian, Jewish, as well as thoroughly secular versions of ecofeminism (Adams, 1993).

Ecofeminists differ on foundational assumptions, on the nature of the relationship between women and the natural world, on ecological paradigms, on feminist approaches, on the roots of environmental crises, and on goals and the means of achieving them. Although ecofeminism represents this range of women–Nature and feminist–ecology interconnections, there are three main tenets: empirical evidence, epistemological privileges, and the most copious and relevant here, the conceptual/ideological or cultural/symbolic women–Nature nexus.

Empirical Evidence

As illustrated above, there is empirical evidence that environmental stress often disproportionately affects women (Shiva, 1989). Ecofeminists examine the sociopolitical and economic structures that restrict many women's lives to poverty, ecological deprivation, and economic powerlessness. This type of ecofeminism resonates with women, environment, and development work. Thus, the path to sustainability involves equity, justice, and economic and political power for women. It is not a sizable aspect of what usually is labeled ecofeminism.

Epistemological Privilege

A second theme within ecofeminism relates to epistemology, where women should be "epistemologically privileged." One version of this is a pragmatic claim. Since environmental problems affect women most directly, it may be that women possess greater knowledge and expertise in finding solutions to pressing environmental problems. For example, in many parts of the world women are the custodians of the land, are the primary subsistence farmers, and have greater agricultural knowledge than men. Thus, according to some ecofeminists, these women are in a good position to aid in creating new practical and intellectual ecological paradigms. Many organizations recognize that women's cultural formation and life experiences allow them to gain ecological and social knowledge that is extremely useful for sustainability ventures. This is often in the form of micro-financing projects that especially empower women. Most often this epistemological privilege is practical: women's expertise is needed to address local and global environmental problems.

Others make a different epistemological connection, that women and men have essential differences, which manifest as distinctive modes of knowing and being in the world. The separation of feminine and masculine embodied in women and men signifies essentialism. Some see women as "closer" to Nature/the Earth than men and possessing innate traits of caring, nurturing, cooperation, nonviolence, and Earth sensitivity. This "nature" of women allows for a particular knowledge based on individual biology. This type of women–Nature essentialism is found in some cultures and contexts. However, a cornerstone of patriarchal foundations is the precept of an essential difference between women and men, which translates into distinct life pathways where, for the most part, women are subordinate to men. Thus, most ecofeminists consider the connections between women and Nature to be based in cultural ideologies rather than in essence. Where women have expertise in agriculture or possess nurturing community-building traits, it is not due to their essential nature but to their life experiences.

Nonetheless, essentialism is intelligible in some contexts and cultures. It can be an unquestioned stance or a strategic tool, and essentialism can play a role in socio-ecological transformation in some, although few, circumstances. Both standpoints support an epistemological privileging of women's experiences, albeit for different reasons.

Women–Nature

The third and most prolific ecofeminist area is the study, largely in Euro-Western contexts, of how women and Nature have been and are connected ideologically, conceptually, and symbolically. Before delving into detail, it is important to grasp the meaning of ideology in this context. Many social theorists, such as Paul Ricoeur, understand that human action is oriented, mediated, structured, and integrated within symbolic systems related to ideologies (synonymous here with worldviews or social imaginaries) linked to power and politics (Ricoeur, 1986, 1991). Ideologies or worldviews function in the codification and substructure of a political society. Ideologies as worldviews are a system of interacting symbols that regulates and governs the actions of individuals and institutional frameworks. The primary purpose of these social ideologies is to ground a historical community, mediate and integrate human action at its public level, provide a social identity for the community, and prevent social upheaval by viewpoints that could destabilize the power and social structures. Ideologies function as a system of legitimacy and are a hidden phenomenon. They resist exposure because they are at times the unquestioned or unconscious belief systems of the society, or at least of those with power. Worldviews are ideologies that are an inverted image of reality, meaning that they function as an unquestioned belief system laden with values and thick with symbols. Ideologies/worldviews are, at their base, interpretations of reality taken to be descriptive. For example, patriarchy is an ideology or worldview replete with symbols, codifications, beliefs, and political structures to maintain a patriarchal social order.

The task to trace the ideological roots of the oppression of women is an ongoing feminist activity. The *eco*feminist addition was to grapple with the conceptual and mutually reinforcing linkages between the history of ideas about the inferiority of women and the devaluing of the natural world. The subsequent task was to understand how the cultural-symbolic level of the relationship between the oppression of women and ecological exploitation functions as the ideological substructure that directs and sanctions the social, economic, political, and religious order, and maintains the subjection of women and the domination of Nature. Each of these tasks exposes facets of the underlying worldview or ideology of Euro-Western civilization; that is, what is taken to be true about women and Nature. As Christianity deeply influenced this worldview, it includes interpretations of God's patriarchal vision for women, men, and the natural world.

Women / Nature, Feminism / Ecology, and Christian Theologies

Theologian Rosemary Radford Ruether writes:

> Women must see that there can be no liberation for them and no solution to the ecological crisis within a society whose fundamental model of relationships continues to be one of domination. They must unite the demands of the women's movement with those of the ecological movement to envision a radical reshaping of the basic socioeconomic relations and the underlying values of this society. (Ruether, 1975, 204)

Those studying the roots of ecological degradation repeatedly found that the devaluing of Nature and the unrestrained destruction of the natural world were deeply embedded in the history, worldview(s), and expansions of Euro-Western societies. The domination of Nature infiltrated the intellectual foundations, habits of thought, and cultural practices to the point that ecological deterioration was no longer offensive and was, and continues to be, often evaluated as progress.

Ecofeminists paralleled these theoretical developments by examining domination, especially that of women and of Nature. The inquiry into the Euro-Western woman–Nature construct has been prolific for ecofeminist theories, predominantly from philosophy and religion (Griffin, 1978; Primavesi, 1991; Ruether, 1975; Warren, 2000). The essential detection of ecofeminism is that the oppression of women and the natural world is ideologically built into the very mode of perceiving both.

Ecofeminists have discussed the origins of these modes of domination within the history of patriarchy. The conditions of domination and oppression have identifiable roots in the development of hierarchy, misogyny, agricultural mastery, slavery, anthropocentrism, androcentrism, and the conquest of reason over Nature. Both patriarchy and domination have long and complex histories in human communities, and little is certain. However, ecofeminists rightly expose that the history of the intertwined domination of women and Nature can help to resist the daily oppression of women and escalating ecological crises.

Ecofeminists claim there is sufficient evidence that women and the natural world are interlaced in a complex synthesis of hierarchical dualisms embedded in patriarchal worldviews and social structures. This claim is one of the bases for ecofeminist theology, because Christianity has been one of the chief proponents of a hierarchical dualistic worldview (Plumwood, 1993, 2001). Dualistic conceptual structures are those such as women/men, feminine/masculine, Earth/Heaven, Nature/culture, matter/spirit, demonic/divine, reproduction/production, body/mind, emotion/reason, intuition/thought, private/public, passive/active, natural/supernatural, and slave/master. The first half of each dualism is subordinate to the second. These dualisms are ideologically grouped together such that women are connected to the feminine, Earth, Nature, matter, demonic, reproduction, body, emotion, intuition, private, and slave; the other half of the grouping applies to men. These ideas, ideology, or worldview are defended as being the biological or ontological nature of reality, or as divine revelations of the correct scheme of things, or as indisputable truths, or with other arguments in favor of patriarchal ideologies. These hierarchical dualisms have been studied extensively by ecofeminists, and discovered throughout the religious, philosophical, social, political, and economic development of Euro-Western societies.

Ecofeminists show how this androcentric worldview sanctions that men have innate power over both women and Nature, and the dual domination of women and Nature is justified and appears "natural." They expose a logic of domination embedded in Euro-Western worldviews. Social patterns, including sexual norms, education, governance, and economic control reflect this logic of domination; it is entrenched in the worldview and thus obscured from view. Religion, philosophy, science, and cultural symbols reinforce this worldview. One outcome is the assurance that male power over both women and Nature appears normal, justified, and unquestioned. These dualisms were promoted, reinforced, and endorsed by precepts, philosophical and religious, chiefly Christian (Merchant, 1980; Plumwood, 1993). Thus, feminist and ecofeminism investigations excavated, exposed, and incriminated these themes within Christianity (Eaton, 2005).

Tertullian, for example, declared that women were the devil's gateway and were the cause of "man's" corruption: the devil enters the world through women, and women are closer to the Earth than are men.[4] For centuries Christian leaders taught that men were spiritual and women were bodily; that men, not women, were made in the image of God; that women were born of Nature and men were born of Spirit; that women were intellectually feeble and needed to be controlled, as does Nature. The majority of Christian theologians and philosophers, from the time of Augustine to the twentieth century, deemed that Nature was chaotic and unruly, and because women were closer to Nature, women were the same. Cornerstones of customary Christian theology became the feminizing of the natural world, the naturalizing of women, and the domination of both in theoretical, historical, and cultural webs.

Hierarchical dualisms are the framework of the Christian scaffold; to challenge them is to contest the theological edifice.Thus, the ecofeminist challenge to theology is profound and permeates all layers of theological reflection and praxis. It is undeniable that Christianity has played a role, perhaps even as a key player, in the domination of women, of the natural world, and of both together. Yet, to claim that Christianity is the only source of these dominations is too simplistic. While not minimizing the detrimental influences of Christian worldviews and practices, I would caution against a direct interpretation of cause and effect within enormously varied, convoluted, and perplexing historical processes.

A second troubling theme within Christianity is anthropocentrism. Ecofeminists, eco-theologians, and indeed most thinkers dealing with ecological issues must confront the blatant anthropocentrism that permeates much of Euro-Western worldviews. Anthropocentrism is taken for granted throughout these societies. Theologians exposed the Christian roots of anthropocentrism. One form of this human-centeredness is the claim of superiority and authority of humans over other animals and the natural world. Related to this is the idea that only humans are made in the image of God. Ecofeminists and eco-theologians have been compelled to deal with the Christian emphases on humanity's transcendence over the natural world and the thrust to desacralize nature. The Christian tradition constantly tries to "lift" humanity above the Earth and the limits it represents. Such a separation of humanity from the natural world, from evolution and Earth processes, has been questioned and found wanting. It is related to an inability to perceive a sacred dimension within the natural world, characteristic of many Christian-influenced cultures.

This has led to a re-evaluation, rejection even, of human transcendence. However, beliefs about human transcendence are interlocked in a scaffold or theological architecture with interpretations of sin, redemption, salvation, and an ultimate otherworldly resurrection. The difficulty is that the hegemonic Christian worldview is built on a scaffold based on dualisms and human transcendence; to undo one part weakens or dismantles the whole.

For ecofeminists Ivone Gebara and Rosemary Radford Ruether, the operative anthropocentric interpretations of Christology, sin, and salvation have created distortions at the level of foundational theological precepts. One such distortion throughout Christian history is the belief that the natural world is fallen, corrupt, sinful, imperfect, or incomplete. Death is the result. Humans must be saved, redeemed, or restored from "Nature" and death. Christianity promises eternal life, which is the next and improved life. Although each religious worldview has some perception that life does not end with death, the Christian tradition has fostered an otherworldly longing. This world, meaning the natural world and Earth community, is assumed to be insufficient and unacceptable, if not intolerable. People must be saved from the Earth community. This construal of salvation is operative across all Christian traditions. Ecofeminists challenge these theological worldviews and the presuppositions within them. Gebara, for example, re-examines the notion of sin. She suggests that the primal sin is not about a fall or evil intruding in Creation or in human life, or an inadequacy about Nature, which requires a salvation from the existential parameters. For ecofeminists, these are all problematic if not unacceptable beliefs. The primal sin in

Christianity has been to negate the non-negotiable existential circumstances of life: vulnerability, finitude, and mortality. When these actualities are denied, the consequences are escapist spiritualties, otherworldly ideations, and a fall into domination – of land, animals, and peoples. Domination becomes the mode of operation for those able to imagine they can supersede the inferior aspects of life. One such aspect would be our ultimate dependence on the natural world for survival. For Gebara, our salvation is found in returning to our embodied selves, refusing escapism and domination, and embracing with joy and sorrow the genuine limitations, richness, and struggles of life in community and of human solidarity with all life. Death is an inherent part of the human reality, not that from which we are to be saved. Gebara proposes a christology where Jesus is a salvific figure, prophet, model, and paradigm; unique but not exclusive, one among many who calls human communities back to authenticity. Her understandings of sin, redemption, revelation, Creation, Nature, humanity, and the Divine are a new scaffold for theology. Her proposal leaves room for deep inter-religious respect, supports liberation theologies, challenges otherworldly afterlife theologies, defies hierarchy, and confronts forms of christo-fascism. These counteract conventional theological interpretations.

The connecting of gender, theology, and ecology came, at times, from those with social, political, or liberation priorities. For example, as Christian liberation theologies expanded their use of (post-) Marxist analyses and/or critical theories, they became astute in understanding the nature of social oppression, confronting inequality, and advocating for social justice. The scrutiny of power and privilege in relation to social structures of race, ethnicity, class, gender, and culture became a forceful and critical medium for analyses and transformation. For a time these pursuits did not see ecological issues as directly pertinent. However, today attention to religions and ecojustice is worldwide.

Ecofeminist theologies, while always promoting gender justice, rarely worked from or explicitly promoted ecofeminist liberation theologies. Their intention was liberation, but not usually their method. Ecojustice expanded into a rubric to include gender/ecology approaches. However, the term ecojustice most often indicates an anthropocentric bias; that is, ecological decline becomes a further burden on those already suffering from the unequal distribution of benefits and burdens. Therefore, while ecofeminists always supported social transformation, the bulk of the theological work was research into the women–Nature nexus—the symbolic and historical associations and the theological impediments—to which they provided reformations and novel insights. It is important to recognize that liberation theologies are effective when they are within social movements. Feminist theologies are vibrant because there is a global women's agenda. Ecotheology is persuasive when in alliance with growing ecological awareness.

Several ecofeminist theologians are involved in dialogues between science and religion. They are engaging Christianity and ecofeminism in conversations with evolution, Earth sciences, and cosmology (Eaton, 2005; McFague, 1993; Primavesi, 2000; Ruether, 1992). One reason is that the evolutionary discourse of science puts into relief the religious beliefs and assumptions about Nature, challenges anthropocentrism, and raises questions about what it means to be human. As mentioned above, the hegemonic Christian worldview is a profoundly human-centered ideology. Without a dialogue with science it is effortless to develop anthropocentric ecological ethics that continue to see the Earth as a set of resources having no intrinsic value or sacred independence.

To see the Earth as primarily a whole and humanity as an integrated element is no easy task for many Christians. In fact, Primavesi writes that "the fears inspired by the loss of the theological anthropocentricity, or even the suspicion of its loss, explains why ecotheology seems to have lost its appeal for some theologians."[5] Theologian John Haught argues that much of the reluctance of theology to address ecological issues in depth stems from a prior reluctance to think about evolution and its relationship to God (Haught, 1993). The biblical-redemptive story rather than the Creation/evolution story has been chosen as the primary context for understanding and finding meaning in life. Because a sense of the Divine is derived extensively from biblical sources, an awareness of the revelation of the Divine in the natural world has been all but lost by many Euro-Western Christians. The excessive concern for the redemptive process has concealed the realization that the disintegration of the natural world is also the destruction of the primordial manifestation of the Divine (Berry, 1999).

Over the past few centuries, the Christian tradition has set aside Earth and its magnificence as the primary religious reality. At the core of the problem is a theological paradigm that radically separates humanity from the Earth. This separation permeates the entire theological tradition, including eschatology, teleology, anthropology, christology, and ethics. As Mary Grey writes, "An ecofeminist theology of creation demands a radical re-thinking of all our cosmic, cultural and vital reference points."[6] McFague suggests that a common Creation story could become the beginning of an evolutionary, ecological, theological anthropology that could transform our self-understanding and our responsibilities toward other people, other species, and our home, planet Earth (McFague, 1993). Some consider a cosmological horizon to be central to an ecological feminist theology (Ruether, 1992), while others study Gaia theories to develop a theology for an Earth community (Primavesi, 2000). To conceive of Christianity in light of an evolutionary cosmology requires a substantial re-evaluation of the self-understanding and foundational assertions of theology (Eaton, 2005, 2014).

Of the many potential approaches to religion in the light of evolution, the most consistent is one that integrates religion into an evolutionary framework, rather than the reverse. This means that the level and type of consciousness out of which religions have developed should be considered as a potential within the evolutionary processes. Religious sensibilities are a part of the evolutionary development of humans as a symbolic species: an emergent phenomenon within human consciousness, and a later cultural formation. Such an approach affirms that religions, and what they represent in terms of consciousness, are more, rather than less, inherent to humans as a species. It is not the particular religion that is ultimate; religions come and go. An evolutionary perspective requires that we think more about the nature of religion, of religious consciousness, and what experiences and knowledge are represented by religious sensibilities.

The natural world is revelatory. Relationships between religious experiences and the natural world are fundamental to most religions and many cultures. They are powerful, animating, orienting experiences. Classical approaches to religious experiences affirm these primal and formative states of awareness, often expressed as wonder and awe.

When we learn something of evolution, these sensibilities are engaged. What little we know of Earth's intricacies dazzles the human imagination. From the micro-biotic and genetic levels to the dinosaurs, the processes and life-forms are incredible. If we attend, even briefly, to the elegance of birds, the ingenuity of insect communication, and the emotions of mammals, how is it possible not to be thrilled and overwhelmed by the creativity, diversity, power, and beauty of the natural world (Eaton, 2007)?

Concentrating on and articulating the validity of such experiences, not only with respect to their power but also to their transformative capacity, would strengthen the field of religion and ecology. The aesthetic and emotional capacities of humans are more than adaptive. We do respond to life emotionally, intuitively, with revulsion and attraction, and with wonder and awe. We are moved by beauty and by ruin. These are not superfluous, but are foundational, functional energies. Earth life and processes have been, and are, a primary source of inspiration, aesthetics, ethics, and religious imagination (Eaton, 2011). To consider evolution and also cosmology opens up a larger horizon of understanding for the phenomena of religion, fosters a deeper meaning to religious imagination and experiences, and integrates the insights that we are emergent from and integral to a dynamic universe. The recent understandings of cosmological and evolutionary dynamics are revolutionary and are only beginning to be appreciated for the depth of transformations they elicit, especially for an ecological worldview.

In spite of the obvious religious and ecological implications, few ecofeminists venture far down this path, and for valid reasons. The daily struggles for women and issues of gender injustices can easily be lost in evolutionary or planetary perspectives. Power differentials are obscured, systematic oppression and violence against women seems extraneous, and the intractable and complex ideological systems that saturate cultures appear less critical. Regardless, both cosmological and evolutionary insights are invaluable to a viable future, and the oppressive gendered systems need to be resisted and abolished. The challenge is to find how these can mutually support each other.

Ecofeminist theologies are fundamentally different from the hegemonic classical discourse in method, attention to context, epistemological framework, and orientation toward liberatory praxis. The immense task of challenging foundational presuppositions and reshaping the infrastructure of theology remains substantive and difficult work. It is necessary to be explicit about the depth of challenge that ecology and feminism together pose to theological discourses. There are core problems that cannot be underestimated.

Ecofeminist theologians insist on the need to abolish the hierarchical dualisms because these have thwarted the possibilities of mutually enhancing relationships among humans and with the Earth community. From an ecofeminist perspective, spirit and matter, body and mind, reason and emotion, for example, are seen as interconnected rather than dualistic. The superiority of reason over emotion, culture over Nature, Spirit over matter, or objective over subjective, and all dualisms, are rejected outright.

As mentioned, one simply cannot add ecology and feminist to theology. Many questions emerge as to the meaning of theological terms within Christian paradigms. For example, in much of ecofeminism and eco-theology, the Divine and the human are seen as embedded within the natural world and within natural processes. The Earth community is revelatory, a "divine milieu." This can be supported by recent work in connecting ecology, feminism, theology, and the new materialism. Noting that ecological thinking requires a fundamental shift of perspective, any understanding of materiality constitutes not only humans but also the Earth and cosmos. As a way of situating feminist theological discourses and experiences ecologically, some see this "shared materiality as a basis for reframing human being, dwelling, agency, and labour, in terms of co-being, habitat, co-agency, and more-than-human labour" (Elvey, 2015). Theological categories are shifting to see that the immanence of the Divine is imprinted in the evolution of the Earth. Here spirit and matter are intimately and indistinguishably bound together in a life-process.

It seems that those who take the magnitude of the ecological crisis seriously tend to scrutinize Christianity itself in more radical ways than those who are either defending Christianity or principally retrieving resources. Although there are both continuities and discontinuities with classical methodologies and interpretations, there are some cherished notions that will need to be abandoned or rejected. There is a tension between how far a tradition can be stretched and reinterpreted and the need for new religious sensitivities that can respond to the socio-ecological plight. To some extent, this tension mirrors the feminist ambivalence with patriarchal religions.

Challenges to Ecofeminist Theologies

Ecofeminist analyses developed in a multidisciplinary manner. Theologians were partners in the expansion and elaboration of the many layers that became ecofeminism. Over the years, in-depth ecofeminist research revealed the extent to which Euro-Western cultures were rooted in ideologies of domination, a central one being the interconnected domination of women and Nature. While this work exposed the ideological substructure of the problem, it was not straightforward to know how to change it. A tension existed between those developing ecofeminist theories, usually from affluent countries, and those working for political change in social movements, usually from the Global South. This women, environment, and development work seemed separated from the ecofeminist theoretical work. Some ecofeminists seemed to be more interested in the historical and symbolic connections between women and Nature, or sophisticated theories of how the world should be, than the actual suffering of women and ecosystems. Others perceived the greatest need to be in addressing economic and material realities, and concrete issues of women's poverty and ecological stress. Spirituality or religion were central to some and for others irrelevant, hopelessly idealistic, or suspect. Some found the diversity unmanageable, while others rejoiced in the multitude of voices. The benefit was that it forced ecofeminist theologians to be clear about the dialectic of religion and culture, to be clear about how their work contributed to other issues, and to work in multidisciplinary arenas.

Multi-religious voices were often a part of the ecofeminist conversation. They provided a reality check for ecofeminist theologies in several ways. First, they often made concrete connections between theory and praxis, North and South, affluent and poor, and the actual life-and-death struggles of the many women of the world (Ress, 2006;

Ruether, 1996, 2005). Voices from the impoverished South or North brought an awareness of the daily relationship between many women and the natural world: issues of toxins in the air, water, and soil, garbage dumps where people live, economic exploitation from globalization, and stories of resistance and celebration. Second, they reminded all that "religion" is religions—multiple, distinct, and dissimilar (Eaton, 2006). The world is full of religions, each religion is internally multiple, and the exchanges are innumerable. Theologians need to take seriously religious pluralism and to be cognizant of theories of religions. Religious analyses can no longer be self-referencing, isolated, or imperialist. Third, they showed that concepts such as ecofeminism cannot be transported everywhere. While ideological connections between women and Nature are found in all religions and cultures, they vary on how they were constructed and sustained, and how they contribute to ecological ruin and the subjugation of women. After years of researching, developing, and disseminating these analyses, it became evident that the connections between women and Nature are distinct in terms of culture, religion, context, and social norms. A dialogue between predominantly conceptual categories and case studies became essential (Eaton & Lorentzen, 2003). Fourth, they revealed that the ecological crisis is generating profound levels of analysis and effecting a thorough rethinking of religions and their cultural roles. Many of the attitudes toward the natural world have been shaped by religious worldviews. This challenges each tradition to revisit its presuppositions, discover its particular strengths and lacunae, and find resources that encourage benevolent human–Earth relations.

It took time and effort for activists and academics to work together and to comprehend complex relationships between the ideological analysis of the cultural-symbolic levels and social, economic, political, and material difficulties. A willingness to collaborate and mutually to challenge developed, strengthening the work among feminism, ecology, and religion. The term ecofeminism was initially popular, then faded from view, although is now reappearing (Adams & Gruen, 2014; Elvey, 2015). Lively debates continue on every topic: transcultural or context-specific approaches, theory and social transformation, and international conversations about democracy, globalization, what sustainability means, and specific issues of climate change, water protection, agriculture, and ecojustice.

Larger Horizons

The insistence that women gain equity and autonomy has reverberated globally. Albeit dissimilar, there are micro-women's movements around the world, primarily using ethics as leverage. Stepping back from the myriad issues the impulse for gender justice is more than a social political movement and an ethical transformation. From a larger horizon this "movement" is a planetary change of human consciousness about women's and men's equality, dignity, and rights. This further signals a massive transformation of human social structures, ideologies, and symbolic systems. The women's movement is arguably the largest shift of consciousness humanity has made since the Neolithic revolution. Patriarchy has been the ruling social, ideological, and symbolic organization and governance for between 3,000 and 8,000 years, globally. Classical religions all developed with the rise of patriarchy. From this vantage point, the task of displacing patriarchy is substantial and is in its early days.

What is occurring is an awakening of consciousness regarding human social organization. Domination as a mode of social interaction is objectionable. Patriarchal reference points of hierarchies, supremacies, and male dominance are contested. Feminism represents a transformation of consciousness that offers an amplified, intensified, and strengthened appreciation of humanity and a radically new perception of human capacity. Women are entering human consciousness as full planetary participants. As a consequence, the subjectivity, diversity, and elegance of the human as a species are expanded and enhanced.

The need for gender analyses of the relationships between religion and ecology has spawned countless approaches, critiques, and reconstructions: from textual methods to cosmological horizons, from limits and negation to vision and activism. The theoretical inquiries and contributions from ecofeminism pushed the field of religion and ecology to consider the ubiquitous nexus of women and Nature, and feminism, gender, and ecology. From a larger horizon, it also is clear that something innovative is happening at the intersection of religion, spirituality, and ecology. One can glean a growing consensus that the boundaries of religions or spiritualties are porous. New visions are emerging and are untethered from conventional religious forms, beliefs, institutions, or leadership, emphasizing transformation, equity, and inclusion. Awakening, consciousness transformation, socially engaged spirituality, and reconnecting with Nature are common aspirations. Many express an emerging, holistic worldview, with images of one planet. They envision Earth democracy, global ecological citizenship, bio-spheric egalitarianism, global bio-democracy, planetary civilization, or consciousness of integral creation (Eaton, 2014).

The alliance of religion and ecology has become a multifaceted and global agenda. To speak of religion and ecology is to note the multiplicity of initiatives and to understand that these represent a transformation of consciousness, not only about ecological issues, but also about the nature of religion and religious epistemologies, sensibilities, orientation, and sources. Taken together, the efforts of religion and ecology represent a significant development in both areas, and the emergence of a new spiritual paradigm. It is a new phase of human understanding about planetary dynamics, as well as a reassessment of the human presence within a larger Earth community. Ecological worldviews integrated with the need for gender justice are two revolutions of consciousness. Together, they too are invoking transformations in religions. If they are combined, then gender, religion, and ecology are potent forces for an ecological civilization that includes equality and human rights, and hopes of a sustainable future.

Notes

1 UN Women: The United Nations Entity for Gender Equity and the Empowerment of Women. http://www.unwomen.org/.

2 United Nations Humans Rights: Office of the High Commission for Human Rights. http://www.ohchr.org/EN/NewsEvents/Pages/ViolenceAgainstWomen.aspx.

3 *Global and Regional Estimates of Violence Against Women: Prevalence and Health Effects of Intimate Partner Violence and Non-Partner Sexual Violence.* 2013. Geneva: World Health Organization. http://www.who.int/reproductivehealth/publications/violence/9789241564625/en/.
4 See Tertullian, *Des Cultu Feminarim*, quoted in O'Faolain & Martines (1973. 132–133).
5 Anne Primavesi. 2000. Ecology's Appeal to Theology. *The Way*, 40, January, 63.
6 Mary Grey. 2000. Ecofeminism and Christian Theology. *The Furrow*, 51, September, 486.

References

Adams, Carol (Ed.). 1993. *Ecofeminism and the Sacred*. New York: Continuum.

Adams, Carol J. & Gruen, Lori (Eds.). 2014. *Ecofeminism: Feminist Intersections with Other Animals and the Earth*. New York and London: Bloomsbury.

Berry, Thomas. 1999. *The Great Work*. New York: Bell Tower.

Buechler, Stephanie & Hanson, Anne-Marie S. (Eds.). 2015. *A Political Ecology of Women, Water, and Global Environmental Change*. New York: Routledge.

Dankelman, Irene. 2010. *Gender and Climate Change: An Introduction*. New York: Routledge.

Dankelman, Irene & Davidson, Joan. 1988. *Women and Environment in the Third World*. London: Earthscan.

Diamond, Irene & Orenstein, Gloria Feman (Eds.). 1990. *Reweaving the World: The Emergence of Ecofeminism*. San Francisco, CA: Sierra Club Books.

Eaton, Heather. 2000. Ecofeminist Contributions to an Ecojustice Hermeneutics (54–57). In Norman Habel (Ed.), *The Earth Bible*. London: Sheffield Press.

Eaton, Heather. 2005. *Introducing Ecofeminist Theologies*. London: T&T Clark International.

Eaton, Heather. 2006. Ecotheology. Theme: *Gender, Religion and Ecology*, 11, 4, December.

Eaton, Heather. 2007. The Revolution of Evolution. *Worldviews: Environment, Culture, Religion*, 11, 1, Spring, 6–31.

Eaton, Heather. 2011. An Ecological Imaginary: Evolution and Religion in an Ecological Era (7–23). In Sigurd Bergmann and Heather Eaton (Eds.), *Ecological Awareness: Exploring Religion, Ethics and Aesthetics*. Studies in Religion and the Environment, Vol. 3 [Studien zur Religion und Umwelt, Bd. 3]. Berlin: LIT Press.

Eaton, Heather (Ed.). 2014. *The Intellectual Journey of Thomas Berry: Imagining the Earth Community*. Lanham, MD: Lexington Press.

Eaton, Heather & Lorentzen, Lois Ann (Eds.). 2003. *Ecofeminism and Globalization: Exploring Religion, Culture and Context*. Lanham, MD: Rowman & Littlefield.

d'Eaubonne, Françoise. 1974. *Le Féminisme ou la Mort*. Paris: Pierre Horay.

Elvey, Anne. 2015. Matter, Freedom and the Future: Reframing Feminist Theologies Through an Ecological Materialist Lens. *Feminist Theology*, 23, 2, 186–204.

Gaard, Greta. 1998. *Ecofeminist Politics: Ecofeminists and the Greens*. Philadelphia, PA: Temple University Press.

Gebara, Ivone. 1999. *Longing for Running Water: Ecofeminism and Liberation*. Minneapolis, MN: Fortress Press.

Grey, Mary. 2000. Ecofeminism and Christian Theology. *The Furrow*, 51.

Griffin, Susan. 1978. *Woman and Nature: The Roaring Inside Her*. London: Women's Press.

Haught, John. 1993. *The Promise of Nature: Ecology and Cosmic Purpose*. New York: Paulist.

Kheel, Marti. 2008. *Nature Ethics: An Ecofeminist Perspective*. Lanham, MD: Rowman & Littlefield.

McFague, Sallie. 1993. *The Body of God: An Ecological Theology*. Minneapolis, MN: Fortress Press.

Merchant, Carolyn. 1980. *The Death of Nature: Women, Ecology, and the Scientific Revolution*. London: Wildwood House.

O'Faolain, Julia & Martines, Lauro (Eds.). 1973. *Not in God's Image: Women in History from the Greeks to the Victorians*. New York: HarperCollins.

Plant, Judith. 1989. *Healing the Wounds: The Promise of Ecofeminism*. Philadelphia, PA: New Society.

Plumwood, Val. 1993. *Feminism and the Mastery of Nature*. London: Routledge.

Plumwood, Val. 2001. *Environmental Culture: The Ecological Crisis of Reason*. London: Routledge.

Primavesi, Anne. 1991. *From Apocalypse to Genesis: Ecology, Feminism and Christianity*. Minneapolis, MN: Fortress Press.

Primavesi, Anne. 2000. *Sacred Gaia: Holistic Theology and Earth Systems Science*. New York: Routledge.

Primavesi, Anne. 2000. Ecology's Appeal to Theology. *The Way*, 40, January.

Ress, Mary Judith. 2006. *Ecofeminism in Latin America: Women from the Margins*. Maryknoll, NY: Orbis Books.

Ricoeur, Paul. 1986. *Lectures on Ideology and Utopia*. New York: Columbia University Press.

Ricoeur, Paul. 1991. *From Text to Action: Essays in Hermeneutics*. Evanston, IL: Northwestern University Press.

Ruether, Rosemary Radford. 1975. *New Woman/New Earth: Sexist Ideologies and Human Liberation*. New York: Seabury Press.

Ruether, Rosemary Radford. 1992. *Gaia and God: An Ecofeminist Theology of Earth Healing*. San Francisco, CA: Harper.

Ruether, Rosemary Radford. (Ed.). 1996. *Women Healing Earth: Third World Women on Ecology, Feminism, and Religion*. Maryknoll, NY: Orbis Books.

Ruether, Rosemary Radford. (Ed.). 2005. *Integrating Ecofeminism, Globalization, and World Religions*. Lanham, MD: Rowman & Littlefield.

Shiva, Vandana. 1989. *Staying Alive: Women, Ecology and Development*. London: Zed Books.

Sturgeon, Noel. 1997. *Ecofeminist Natures: Race, Gender, Feminist Theory and Political Action*. New York and London: Routledge.

Warren, Karen J. 2000. *Ecofeminist Philosophy: A Western Perspective on What it is and Why it Matters*. Lanham, MD: Rowman & Littlefield.

Further Reading

Eaton, Heather. 2014. Global Visions and Common Ground: Biodemocracy, Postmodern Pressures and the Earth Charter. *Zygon: Journal of Religion and Science*, 49, 4, December, 917–937.

Mies, Maria & Vandana, Shiva. 1993. *Ecofeminism*. London: Zed Books.

Nhanenge, Jytte. 2011. *Ecofeminism: Towards Integrating the Concerns of Women, Poor People, and Nature into Development*. Lanham, MD: University Press of America.

CHAPTER 20

The Face of God in the World

Insights from the Orthodox Christian Tradition

John Chryssavgis

Conservation and Conversion

In recent years, issues such as climate change, flora and fauna extinction, soil erosion and forest clearance, noise, and air pollution have received prominence globally. Indeed, they have assumed a progressive sense of urgency. Nonetheless, the intensity with which they are handled and resolved is far less impressive or intense. With the emphasis in the twentieth century on the individual and individual rights, who would have predicted that the exploitation and violation of Nature would become more important than, even equivalent to, fear for the survival of the human race? No matter how carefully modern man has sought to foster material prosperity and self-sufficiency, it is clear today that certain "cracks" have appeared on the face of the Earth. Consequently, despite actions in the past that sought to contain or constrain the world, we are now facing a global problem that affects everyone, regardless of ecological awareness, geographical location, or social class. Nature, we now know, waits like an enraged animal in a cage and it is only a matter of time before it takes revenge. Indeed, we are already feeling the rumblings. The rupture has been initiated; ecological justice will follow sooner or later, with mathematical precision.

Green perspectives, political lobbies, philosophical attitudes, theology (usually as a last resort), all endeavor to grapple with the problem. Yet, we seem so often to be dealing only with the symptoms rather than with their causes. People are increasingly demonstrating commitment, but they seem unconvinced about their responsibility to convert to a lifestyle that might hold the answer to the ecological crisis, a challenge that threatens the existence—not simply the wellbeing—of humanity, as well as the very heart of Creation. Nonetheless, before we can deal with the ecological problem effectively—and our aim surely is to do something—our goal is ultimately to practice what conservatives

The Wiley Blackwell Companion to Religion and Ecology, First Edition. Edited by John Hart.

and preservationists have faithfully claimed but failed to do: we must first change our self-image and our worldview. After all, Creation itself awaits with eager longing such a revelation from the children of God (Rom. 8.19).

Not that the global community has been lacking in recent years in admirable individual or collective efforts to restore a balance in the ecosystem. However, the urgent intention is to question the way in which we appreciate and interpret the world around and inside us. And we must admit that, on that level, we remain dominated by certain assumptions and presumptions: we still tend to present and promote the world as an objective reality to be examined, experimented on, and exploited, rather than as a sacred presence to be loved, transformed, and venerated. In so doing, we overlook the dignity that is fitting to the world and the grace with which it is endowed.

Of course, most people appreciate that the world should not be regarded as a mere necessity or means. We admit that we need to live in harmony with Nature and not in audacious supremacy over it. We may even accept that the world must be respected as being created in love by a Divine Creator, who calls everyone and everything into an intimate interrelationship. Yet in our efforts to express or expose the environmental crisis, we remain trapped in our individual desires and our need for self-preservation. Some people may, for instance, consider the human person to be exclusively apart from and above the rest of Creation (a gross form of anthropocentrism); others may prefer to contain the human person as part of and within Creation (a more subtle kind of anthropocentrism). The perspective, though, always remains that of subjecting the world to our own selfish needs and self-centered concerns. In this regard, the human being is persistently seen as the heart of what surrounds humanity, the center of the environment. The consequences are tragic.

In the final analysis, awareness of the cosmic problem is due primarily to the threat that it poses to our own cozy life. This is why the message for environmental awareness has, at least in the past, been based on individual fear, even though while fear is a proven inhibitor it not a good motivator. With all the alarming data that are available about the issues posed by global warming and ecological destruction, the coherence of the world is rapidly being lost. The problem, then, becomes one of failing to relate properly toward the cosmos. This failure in turn harms both parties in the relationship: not only do humans suffer, there is total disharmony and global disruption too.

Ecology and the Church

To a large extent, the Christian Church has also opted for this narcissistic worldview. Proof of this is that the 1.5 billion followers of Jesus, "who had no place to lay his head," now control two-thirds of the Earth's resources and, on average, are three times better off than their non-Christian neighbors. Indeed, "the life-style and consumption patterns of many people in first world countries are way beyond what the earth can support."[1]

Ironically, it is in those so-called developed countries and among those same followers of Jesus that our deep ecology thinking is taking place. By the same token, it seems to be the same Christians who condemn oppressive systems of government and economy, while condoning political, and especially economic, disparity in their own society, and do so with the greatest of ease and the least sense of guilt. This is why it is a theology of the created world, as seen, for example, through the theology and spirituality of the early classics of Christian thought, which holds out the most hope for an endangered environment. However, this chapter is not meant as an apologetic defense of church life and classic practice, but simply an endeavor to articulate some personal insights into traditional theology.

In our world, an unfortunate shift in emphasis has undoubtedly occurred: from God to man, from Heaven to Earth, and from liturgical symbolism to mathematical analysis. However, the distinct accent in the Orthodox Christian tradition has always been on the importance of cosmic transfiguration, which is especially evident in the liturgical texts for the Feast of Theophany, the celebration of Christ's Baptism commemorated each year on January 6. There, as the hymns proclaim, "the nature of the waters is sanctified ... the Earth itself is blessed ... and the heavens are enlightened." The reason for this is, as the prayer of the Great Blessing of the Waters that is read on the day concludes: "So that by the elements of Creation, and by the angels, and by human beings, by things visible and invisible, God's most holy name may be glorified."

Cosmic Liturgy

So, the Orthodox Church has retained a more "eucharistic" and, in the end, a more balanced view of Nature and the environment, proclaiming a world imbued by God and a God involved in the whole world. Indeed, Orthodox liturgy offers more tangible and truly concrete (we might even describe these as incarnate) answers to the ultimate questions about salvation from corruptibility and death, teaching that our original sin lies in turning away from God, manifested in the refusal to view life—and essentially the life of the world—as a matter of interpersonal communication and a sacrament of communion with the Divinity. God is the Lord of the Dance of Creation, which is perceived as a voluntary overflowing of divine gratuitousness and grace. A seventh-century writer, Maximus the Confessor, describes the divine event of the Incarnation as a divine act of re-creation wherein "God is emptied and descends without change to the last extremities of nature."[2]

In a sense, the only duty of humanity is through theology and doxology to recognize and respond to the reality that the human person is a liturgical celebrant of this innate joy and mystery in the world, before comprising a social or individual being, beyond constituting a political or rational animal. This dimension of liturgy, of joyful praise in Creation, is God's gift to the world independent of any environmental effort or awareness. Augustine long ago acknowledged this truth: "Through the mouth of the good, all the lands make a joyful noise to the Lord... No words are needed to make this joy heard ... overflowing with joy ... above the level of discourse."[3]

So, unless we willingly entertain and joyfully enter into this interdependence of all persons and things, which Maximus describes as a "cosmic liturgy,"[4] we certainly cannot hope to resolve issues of economy and ecology or politics and preservation, for we should respond to Nature with the same delicacy, the same sensitivity, and the same tenderness with which we respond to a human being in a relationship. Our failure to do so is the fundamental source of our pollution and passion, a consequence of our inability to relate with care and compassion to the created world.

The way in which we behave toward Creation also reflects the manner in which we relate to the poor. The term ecojustice was originally coined in religious/ecumenical circles because all ecological activities, like all economic programs, and even all theological principles (Matt. 25.31 f.), are measured and finally judged by their effect on human beings, and most especially the poor.

Cosmic Image

The interdependence between ourselves and the world is eloquently portrayed by the contemporary American farmer and writer Wendell Berry, who touches in a prophetic and even healing manner on the deeper implications of our global crisis:

> The earth is what we all have in common, that is what we are made of and what we live from, and we therefore cannot damage it without damaging those with whom we share it. But I believe it goes further and deeper than that. There is an uncanny resemblance between our behavior toward each other and our behavior toward the earth. Between our relation to our own sexuality and our relation to the re-productivity of the earth, for instance, the resemblance is plain and strong and apparently inescapable. By some connection that we do not recognize, the willingness to exploit one becomes the willingness to exploit the other. The conditions and the means of exploitation are likewise similar.[5]

In fact, not only are we members one of another (cf. Eph. 5.19), but, to carry Berry's image further and create an identity of this interdependence, we could say that there is an uncanny resemblance between our body and the Earth. If the Earth is our very flesh, then it becomes inseparable from our story, our destiny, and our God. After all, as St. Paul writes, no one hates one's own flesh (Eph. 5.29). This attitude echoes the later thought of Origen of Alexandria (c. 185–254), for whom "The world is like our bodies. It, too, is formed of many limbs and directed by a single soul. Yes, the world is an immense being directed by the power and the word of God, who is, so to say, its soul."[6]

However, we may choose or endeavor to disguise our autonomous regard for created matter as a service to humanity and contribution to its progress. We finally need to unmask the illusion and become aware of the fact that our individual destiny and sacred purpose are profoundly interconnected and identified with those of our world, just as we are all susceptible to each other's influence. There is no autonomy, just a distinction between a sense of responsibility and a lack thereof.

Now, in order to understand how our world and humanity are intertwined, and by extension together intimately connected with God, we must learn to see all things in

God and God in all things. This is the fundamental difference between the secular worldview and the sacred vision:

> The person with a secular mentality feels himself to be the center of the universe. Yet he is likely to suffer from a sense of meaninglessness and insignificance because he knows he's but one human among five billion others—all feeling themselves to be the center of things – scratching out an existence on the surface of a medium-sized planet circling a small star among countless galaxies.
>
> The person with a sacred mentality, on the other hand, does not feel herself to be the center of the universe. She considers the center to be elsewhere and other. Yet she is unlikely to feel lost or insignificant precisely because she draws her significance and meaning from relationship, her connection, with that center, that other.[7]

For St. Paul, the "difference" lies in the face of Christ. He describes Christ as the image of the invisible God, observing that all things were created through Him and for Him. He is before all things, and in Him all things hold together (Col. 1.15–20, esp. 16–17).

Cosmic Vision

Paul's words are echoed in seventh-century monastic literature by Isaac the Syrian, who asks: "What is a merciful heart? It is a heart that burns with love for the whole of creation: for humans, for birds, for beasts, for demons – for all God's creatures."[8] The tradition is ages-old and universal, transcending time, culture, and disciplines. Hence, it is hardly surprising to discover it in Dostoevsky's *The Brothers Karamazov*, where the exhortation of Fr. Zossima is to "Love all God's creation, the whole of it and every grain of sand. Love every leaf, every ray of God's light. Love the animals, love the plants, love everything. If you love everything, you will perceive the divine mystery in things."[9]

Toward the end of his life, the elder Zossima was characterized by an all-embracing love, which included his whole body, all of humanity, and the entire world. Such a love for Creation shatters the self-centered, secular worldview and suggests a sense of an enlarged existence. In this perspective, we gain access to other dimensions of life and are empowered to move beyond our own lives in order to see others and the world around us both as part of us and distinct from us, for we constitute a part of Creation and should never be considered apart from it; much less should we dare to set ourselves over or against Creation. The vision and boundaries of the world are always far broader than the limited space and life of any human being. The kaleidoscope of Creation reveals a variegated splendor of perception and a rich diversity of beauty, both of which reflect the dignity of God. Indeed, as St. Gregory the Theologian intimates, this depth and breadth provide a glimpse into the grandeur of divinity: "Study the enormous number of different kinds of birds, the variety of their shapes and colors ... It gives me joy to speak of these things because they unfold to us the greatness of God."[10]

Thus, we come to comprehend that we can never exhaust the essence of even the smallest flower. For when we look at a flower, we do not perceive its intrinsic nature as a reflection in this flower of the intrinsic nature of our own consciousness in relation to the flower. Similarly, a bee can only perceive the nectar of the flower; a snake will perceive the same flower as an infrared object; a bat perceives the flower as an echo of ultrasound. In this way, the essential reality of the flower always remains unknown and unobjectifiable, beyond our narrow interest or individual indulgence. Centuries ago, Cappadocian theologians such as Basil the Great and Gregory Nazianzus were well aware that the essence of the smallest flower and the slightest blade of grass evades human knowledge: "We cannot understand the nature of these things. Much less are we likely to be able to understand the nature of the first being, the unique being, who is the fullness of everything."[11] Such is the breadth and depth of the Orthodox Christian cosmic vision, one that is much larger than that of any one individual. I may be the center of this vision or theophany, but I become aware that I am also but a minute—albeit neither insignificant nor negligible—detail of the world. Indeed, the world ceases to be something that I observe objectively and instead becomes something of which I am a part personally and actively. No longer do I feel like a stranger, whether threatened or threatening, but as a friend in and of the world, both caring for and concerned about it. How sadly Christians have misinterpreted the words of Christ that we are "in the world" but "not of the world" (cf. John 17.14, 16). These two phrases should never be detached, still less are they to be divorced, from the middle verse which serves as a clarification of Christ's prayer: "I am not asking you to take them out of the world, but I ask you to protect them from evil" (John 17.15), for whenever we fail to seek the cosmic vision, we narrow life to ourselves, our concerns and our desires, neglecting the vocation to which we are called to transform the Creation of God. At the same time, whenever we reduce religious life to ourselves, our concerns, and our desires, we forget the calling of the Church to implore God, always and everywhere, to renew the whole polluted cosmos.

In this respect, the Church becomes a unique symbol, a term that I understand not so much as a way of perceiving reality, but as a profound way of realizing and reconciling (the literal translation of the Greek *sym-bolon* is bringing together) distinct, though not unrelated realities: divinity and Creation, grace and Nature, God and world. The Church brings the world to God, for the life of which God gave his only Son (John 3.16); and the Church also brings God to the world, which God so loved (John 3.16). This reconciliation is the essential function of the Church, which in turn means that the direct opposite of a symbolic worldview is a diabolical outlook. And the diabolical (Greek *dia-bolos*, the one who disperses) heresy of the ecological crisis is the exclusion from this world of the reality of the Kingdom of Heaven, the disconnection between this world and the next. By contrast, the symbolic worldview contains the intuition that everything is a unique manifestation and making of that Kingdom.

The Seed of God

It is a tragedy that, in spite of the destruction caused and the suffering inflicted on our planet, we have not yet learned our lesson. We are still far from any balanced perspective of Creation as deriving from, dependent on, and deified by God. The world remains for us a human-centered reality; indeed, we are not even embarrassed to conceive the world even more narrowly as a man-centered reality. We are preoccupied at all times with ourselves, with our problems, our destructiveness, even our perseverance. Yet, this is precisely what led us to this fateful predicament, where priority is given to humanity (in fact, more particularly and more specifically, to human reason) as the center of all Creation. The result is that human reason examines and exploits Nature and matter; human reason decides the relatedness and determines the relevance of the individual parts of the world; and human reason uses, or perhaps more accurately abuses Creation through manipulation and domination.

Contemporary deep ecology emphasizes the fact that the correct perspective and relationship between humanity and Creation has been distorted, almost destroyed. Yet, little significance is attached to the reality that all things are coherent not just in their interrelatedness and interdependence, but also in their relation to and dependence on God. In fact, to be estranged from God is to lose touch with created reality and with what really matters in this world. It is to be enslaved in the vicious cycle of pollution and corruption, death and destruction. Symeon the New Theologian expressed this mystically and poetically in tenth-century Constantinople: "What is more painful than to be separated from life?... For it also means to miss out on all good things. The person that moves away from God loses all that is good."[12] According to Gregory Nazianzus, a fourth-century poet and theologian of the same city: "All things dwell in God alone; to God all things throng in haste. For God is the end of all things."[13]

The Ancient Greeks had a similar worldview, discerning the presence of the Divine in all things. Thales exclaimed: "Everything is full of God."[14] In fact, in the cosmology of classical Greek literature, the transcendence of God was perceived as a characteristic that rendered divinity more accessible and more familiar. The slightest detail of Creation was regarded as bearing some mark or trace of the Creator:

> Look at a stone, and notice that even a stone carries some mark of the creator. It is the same with an ant, a bee, a mosquito. The wisdom of the creator is revealed in the smallest creatures. It is he who has spread out the heavens and laid out the immensity of the seas. It is he also who has made the tiny hollow shaft of the bee's sting. All the objects in the world are an invitation to faith, rather than to unbelief.[15]

The same theological truth is expressed outside of traditional theology and established poetry. The twentieth-century Greek writer Nikos Kazantzakis experienced a tumultuous life and his works caused uproar among pious leaders and believers. They clearly misunderstood him, for he has a powerful religious worldview of the seed of God in the world. This helps in understanding the theological notion of the connection between the divine *Logos* and the *logoi* in Creation. For seed requires soil, the appropriate earth on which to be sown and in which to grow (see Matt. 13). Moreover, seed requires an almost cosmic passion for its cultivation. The image resembles Antoine de Saint-Exupéry's Little Prince, who knows that "Seeds are invisible. They sleep deep in the heart of the earth's darkness, until someone among them is seized with the desire to awaken."[16] This is the kind of passion displayed and described by Kazantzakis. In *Ascetic Exercises* he describes compellingly this very relationship among God, the world, and us:

> Everything is an egg, and within it lies the seed of God, calmlessly and sleeplessly active... Within the light of my mind and the fire of my heart, I beset God's watch—searching, testing, knocking to open the door in the stronghold of matter, and to create in that stronghold of matter, the door of God's heroic exodus... For we are not simply freeing God in struggling with and ordering the visible world around us; we are actually creating God. Open your eyes, God is crying; I want to see! Be alert; I want to hear! Move ahead; you are my head!... For to save something [a rock or a seed] is to liberate the God within it... Every person has a particular circle of things, of trees, of animals, of people, of ideas—and the aim is to save that circle. No one else can do that. And if one doesn't save, one cannot be saved... The seeds are calling out from inside the earth; God is calling out from inside the seeds. Set him free. A field awaits liberation from you, and a machine awaits its soul from you. And you can no longer be saved, if you don't save them... The value of this transient world is immense and immeasurable: it is from this world that God hangs on in order to reach us; it is in this world that God is nurtured and increased... Matter is the bride of my God: together they struggle, they laugh and mourn, crying through the nuptial chamber of the flesh.[17]

The Distinction between Essence and Energies

Scripture and the Christian classics reflect the same worldview, refusing to divide grace and Nature, Spirit and matter. The fundamental dichotomy in Judeo-Christian literature is not so much between Nature and grace as between two levels within human Nature itself: the fallen and unfallen, the sinful and the redeemed. Created Nature is the only premise and promise for salvation or destruction; Creation is not a finished product, but a moving ground, a process of continuous self-transcendence and transformation.

Contemporary Western theology no longer espouses God as an eternal substance, a concept proposed by classical Greek philosophy and characteristic of medieval scholasticism. The Eastern Christian tradition modified this Hellenistic concept of God as immobile essence, though not to the point of embracing its opposite—a God who is conceived as becoming. A systematic examination of the notion of God in scripture, liturgy, and spirituality reveals a God who ceaselessly moves between these two poles.

In its attempt to reconcile the immutability or stability of God with divine becoming or historicity—namely, God's involvement in human hearts and history—Eastern theology is inevitably directed toward the "difference/unity" model. Tracing back at least as far as Gregory Palamas in the fourteenth century, this model relates the immutable essence to the uncreated energies of God. The latter manifest the infinite possibilities of the inexhaustible richness in the former, as well as the diverse acts expressing these possibilities. The energies of God—what the Hebrew scriptures refer to as God's "glory"—charge the created world with reality and transparency, allowing it to reveal and conceal the mystery of God. Therefore, the Christian God transcends all opposition and contradiction; the Christian God dwells in the dialectic of grace and in the paradox of love.

This distinction between divine essence and divine energies defines the relationship between God and Creation. In other words, nothing lies outside the embrace of God. Everything is immediately related to God and integrally dependent on God inasmuch as it is a reflection of the divinity. At the same time, God's essence remains fully transcendent and undetermined. This paradox is prescribed and preserved in the teaching of St. Gregory Palamas, but it is also apparent in the earlier Christian tradition.[18] Palamas writes:

> On the one hand, the divine super-essentiality is never called multiple; on the other hand, the divine and uncreated grace and energy of God is, being indivisibly divided, like the sun's ray, which warms and lightens and vivifies and increases its own splendor in what it enlightens, and shines forth in the eyes of the beholders; in the way, then, of this faint image the divine energy of God is called not one, but multiple, by the theologians; and thus Basil the Great declares: "What are the energies of the Spirit? Their extent cannot be told, and they are numberless. How can we comprehend what is beyond the ages? What are the energies of that which precedes the intelligible creation?" For before the intelligible creation and prior to the ages (for the ages themselves are intelligible creations), no one has ever said, or considered, that there is anything created. Therefore, the powers and energies of the divine spirit, which are, according to the theologians, multiple, are uncreated, indivisibly distinguished from the entire Essence of the undivided Spirit.[19]

The same paradox of divine transcendence and divine immanence was saliently formulated in more recent years by Philip Sherrard, translator of the mystical texts of the *Philokalia* and pioneer theologian of the sacredness of Creation:

> For if only the total transcendence of God is affirmed, then all created things, all that is in change and visible, must be regarded as without any real roots in the divine, and hence as entirely negative and "illusory" in character; while if only the total immanence of God is affirmed, then creation must be looked upon as real in its own right, instead of as real only because it derives from and participates in the Divine; and the result must be a pantheism, and a worship of creation rather than of the creator, which must ultimately lead to the notion that God is superfluous, and hence to an entirely materialistic conception of things. The full Christian understanding demands, thus, the simultaneous recognition of both the total transcendence and the total immanence of the divine, the affirmation of the one at the expense of the other being the negation of this understanding and the supreme doctrinal error; and it was for this recognition that Christian theologians had to find an adequate doctrinal expression.[20]

God and the World

The universe, then, is never totally external to God but is entirely within God, revealing yet another interpretation of the phrases "not of the world" and "in the world." At the same time, the limitations of such terms as "essence" and "energies" must be acknowledged when it comes to understanding God; there are no sacred or sweeping conceptions of the Divine. On the other hand, the essence/energies distinction allows for the transcendence of God as well as for divine, free-willed activity in the world.

Process theologians have made overtures toward this medieval essence/energies doctrine in their distinction between the "primordial" and "consequential" nature of God. In response, Orthodox theologians would insist that the personal distinction of the Trinity in God should never be compromised, while the distinction between the primordial and consequential aspects in God must not be reduced to a philosophical exercise. For the Orthodox, the essence/energies distinction remains real at all times, even when it comes to the state of deification and the life beyond. At the same time, process theology has in recent years revived the concept of panentheism—the notion that God includes or incorporates the world, while not being exhausted in or effaced by the world. The inherent danger of panentheism is that God, being almost identified with Creation, may cease to evoke adoration and wonder. Yet, no scientific theory or philosophical knowledge can ever detract from our surprise at the beauty of God's Creation. On the contrary, we are always called to perpetual wonder.

Thus, the Orthodox doctrine of the divine essence and the divine energies has much to say and offer in an age when the relationship or reconciliation between God and the cosmos must constantly be reaffirmed and fundamentally honored. For the essence/energies distinction takes seriously both human responsibility for the whole of Creation and divine redemption or transfiguration of the whole world.

The God contemplated by Christian mystics in the Middle Ages was a God elusive yet familiar, both transcendent and immanent; a God who was distant and at the same time at hand (Jer. 22.23). This God is worshiped in Heaven and also venerated on Earth. Above and beyond our vocation to stand as scientists before a telescope or a microscope, and above and beyond our responsibility to respond as economists and stewards to the current ecological threat, we are called to serve as priests at the altar of the universe.

The Shattered Image

An image that does not bear on reality is a meaningless dream; a reality lacking the insight of an image is senseless drudgery. Heaven and Earth are full of God's glory; the world is a burning bush of divine energy, steeped in the divine Presence. Such is the way we received Creation as a gift from our Creator, and such is the way mystics in the past perceived Creation as an image of God. It remains for us to recognize this gift or image for what it is. After all, Creation itself has clearly understood, long before any human interest or anxiety, the vocation and obligation to restore this reality: "From the beginning till now the entire Creation, as we know, has been groaning in pain" (Rom. 8.22).

Restoring this reality is less a matter of deconstruction or reconstruction for any philosophical ideologies as it is an urgent question of reorientation to and rediscovery of ways of thinking that are familiar to early mysticism, aboriginal spirituality, and indigenous mythology. An image, even if shattered, when combined with a realistic task can transform the world. For there is a beauty in our planet and universe that is beyond the shattered image, an ancient beauty that merely requires reconstruction.[21] We need urgently to heal our relationship with Creation and establish a proper attitude within the order of things.

There is, nevertheless, one important parenthetical remark that should be added here. The shattered image of Creation is not a problem only of Western Christianity or Western civilization. No single era, faith, or culture can be held entirely responsible for the contemporary disastrous deterioration of our planet. It would be naïve to suppose that early theology and Orthodox spirituality automatically have the answers where others have failed.

Clearly, Western civilization represents a particular worldview and attitude, but it is arrogant and erroneous to explain away or justify the contemporary ecological crisis in terms of deviation on the part of Western philosophy and theology. So much fine literature has described this crisis as a process that emerged in the late Middle Ages, matured in the Reformation and Counter-Reformation, and produced the more recent Enlightenment and modern technology. Instead, everyone—of Western or Eastern background alike—should respond to the godless anthropocentrism that colors our world and jeopardizes the natural environment.

While technology may inspire humanity with a dangerous inclination toward autonomy and a perilous temptation toward self-adoration and self-destruction, one must never forget that the supreme goal of humankind is to progress in the sight of the Creator within a continually renewed covenant of Creation. Today's immense technical and technological progress only renders humanity more responsible. Consequently, the Church's relationship with and responsibility toward the world oblige it to exercise clear and candid prophetic criticism within highly technological and rapidly changing cultures.

There can never be a fixed formula; there will never be a definitive solution. Nonetheless, defensive or apologetic attitudes certainly should be abandoned. We must enter into a radical, albeit responsible, criticism of our civilization and of the fundamental presuppositions of economic life as we know and practice them. Surely it is presumptuous, if not audacious, to suppose that the Orthodox worldview presents the essence of Christianity—that would once have been labeled the mortal sin of pride—but it is important for Orthodox Christianity to rethink its calling and contribution to our present world. With regard to Creation, Orthodox theology has certainly preserved an unrivalled dynamism and unqualified optimism; it has also reserved an unprecedented affirmation of every particle of Creation. Nonetheless, it must translate these into tangible virtues and disciplines for a contemporary ecological lifestyle.

It is a paradox that Orthodox spirituality has often been identified as a mystical religion or conviction in the sense of presenting an otherworldly perspective and promoting an almost unworldly attitude. Yet in its most powerful criticism of the destruction wrought on God's wonderful Creation and the shattered image of our world, Orthodox theology emphasizes precisely the significance of Creation as the incarnation of God in the widest and deepest sense. One needs, however, to learn how to rediscover the penetrating insights offered by the Orthodox worldview, not so much to impose a particular vision, but to awaken a presence, to reveal an image beyond the world around us:

> The fact is that God is at work in the world, the same God who infuses into Creation the power needed for it to continue stable throughout all time... Through the things that are seen let us be led toward the things that are not seen. To do this there is no need to travel far. Only faith is required, because only through faith can we behold him.[22]

Thankfully, we have progressed to the point where we know better than to treat people like things. It is now time that we learn no longer to treat even things like mere things, although this will only come from a fundamentally altered perspective and a radically converted heart. St. John of Kronstadt described the same paradox in the early nineteenth century when he claimed that we have arrived at the original, primeval state where "We see flesh and matter in everything; and yet nowhere, nor at any time, is God before our eyes."[23]

We do not need to travel far to discern the divine image in the shattered image. The dynamic presence of Christ's countenance is a reality perceived through the eyes of faith in every corner of the world. This is the conviction of the Orthodox tradition of spirituality. In this regard, the words of the Psalms are more pertinent today than ever before: "I discerned before me [the face of] my Lord in everything" (Psalm 16.8). For, "all things look to [His] face ... which renews the face of the earth" (Ps. 104.30).

Notes

1 S. McDonagh (1986, 5 and 8).
2 *Ambigua* 253, in PG 91.1385.
3 *On Psalm 99*, in PL 37.1271.
4 *Mystagogy* 2, in PG 91.669.
5 Berry (1991, 48–49).
6 *On First Principles* II, i, 2–3, in PG 11.183.
7 See M. Scott Peck. 1993. *A World Waiting to be Born*. London: Bantam Books, 46.
8 *Homily* 48, in his *Mystic Treatises*. Wiesbaden, 1986, 30.
9 Dostoyevsky (1982, 375).
10 *Oration* 28, 23–5, in PG 36.57–60.
11 Gregory, *Oration* 28, 25, in PG 36.60.
12 *Hymn* 1, in *Sources Chrétiennes* 156, Paris, 1969, 164.
13 *Dogmatic Poems* 29, in PG 37.508.
14 *Fragment* 22.
15 Basil of Caesarea, *On Psalm 32*, 3, in PG 29.329.
16 Saint-Exupéry (1971, 16–17).
17 Athens, 1971 (5th ed.), 85–89.
18 See J. Chryssavgis, *Phronema* 5, Sydney, 1990, 15–31.
19 Translated in Sherrard (1992, 37–38).
20 Sherrard (1992, 36).

21 See hymns of the Orthodox funeral service that speak of restoring and reconstructing the distorted and shattered image in humanity and the world.
22 Theodoret of Cyrus, *The Cure of Pagan Diseases* IV, 60, in *Sources Chrétiennes*, 221.
23 John of Kronstadt (1977, 143).

References

Berry, Wendell. 1991. *Standing on Earth: Selected Essays*. Ashuelot, NH: Golgonooza Press.

Dostoevsky, Fyodor. 1982. *The Brothers Karamazov*. Harmondsworth: Penguin.

John of Kronstadt. 1977. *My Life in Christ*. Jordanville, NY: Holy Trinity Publications.

McDonagh, Sean. 1986. *To Care for the Earth*. London: Chapman.

Saint-Exupéry, Antoine de. 1971. *The Little Prince*. New York: Harcourt, Brace.

Sherrard, Philip. 1992. *The Greek East and the Latin West*. Newport Beach, CA: D. Harvey & Co.

CHAPTER 21

Climate Change and Christian Ethics

Michael S. Northcott

The Christian Roots of and Responses to the Ecological Crisis

Christian ethics is a discipline of sustained rational inquiry into the practical implications of Christian faith and doctrine for the ethos, lives, and practices of Christians, individually or in households, as members of local churches, and as citizens within nations. Christian theological ethics has had a major role in the formation of the familial, legal, moral, and political ethos of Western nations. It is a key source of European ideas and practices concerning education, the family, human freedom, the distinctiveness of and duties owed to persons, the rule of law, and moral virtues, including charity, hope, justice, mercy, and peace. Christian virtues are distinct from classical virtues, or virtues in Islam and other faith traditions, and their shaping influence in Western societies can be seen, among other places, in laws to protect and support the disabled and unemployed, the practices of universal education and healthcare, gender equality, and the proscription of slavery.

As Western law, polity, and economics spread beyond the Mediterranean region, Christian influence shaped the laws and practices of many nations. This is due not least to the spread of Western trade and colonialism, which inflicted forms of rule, including at times slavery, on other peoples, subjugating them and their territories to Western economic imperatives while not offering them the full status of free persons. But more positively, the pre- and postcolonial spread of Western law reflects the enduring influence of Christian ethics on the moral and political philosophy of the European Enlightenment. The philosophy of Immanuel Kant, in particular his rational account of the Christian concept of the intrinsic value of persons, and of the moral law as innate to the consciousness and conscience of each individual, has been particularly influential. Kant also envisaged the extension of the self-governance of the moral law from

The Wiley Blackwell Companion to Religion and Ecology, First Edition. Edited by John Hart.

rational persons to rule-governed nations, and by extension to relations between nations. He was the first to envisage a world-governing body along the lines of the United Nations (Kant, 1991).

Another central and globally shaping aspect of the Christian theological and ethical inheritance is the concept of a law-governed universe. This gave rise in the Middle Ages to a series of remarkable technological innovations, including the mechanical clock and the deep plow. It also fostered the modern scientific method, double-entry book keeping (thereby paving the way for the emergence of capitalism), and hence the scientific and industrial revolutions. Since the eighteenth century, and in particular the invention of the condensing steam engine, human technological powers in both scope and scale have begun to change and reorder Earth habitats not only locally but globally, at the level of what James Hutton in the eighteenth century first called the Earth System. In particular, the extensive burning of carbon in the form of fossil fuels and widespread deforestation are changing the energy balance of the Earth. They are also reducing the number of species with which humans share the Earth.

Christianity was the first of the world religions to develop a set of formal positions on climate change and the ecological crisis more broadly. The first evidence for this is in the reports and statements of the World Council of Churches, beginning with a speech made by Charles Birch to the General Assembly in Nairobi in 1975. In it he warned that the increased reliance on science and technology and the growth in human population could threaten human survival, and called for the churches to lead in the development of a "sustainable society" that took up the Genesis 1 mandate to replenish Creation, and not only to dominate it (Birch, 1976). The speech drew the constituent communions of the WCC, principally mainstream Protestant and Orthodox churches, "to acknowledge and take up their responsibility for creation" (Robra, 1997). Later, the WCC adopted the discourse of sustainability and called on all peoples to develop societies which are "just, participatory and sustainable." In the 1980s the Anglican, Lutheran, Orthodox, Methodist, and Presbyterian churches began to envisage ecological sustainability, or care for Creation, as a dimension of the Church's worship and witness. Pressure for this came not only from the WCC but from churches in global communions located in the developing world, where signs of ecological crisis were visibly reducing the quality of life opportunities for economic and personal development of poorer Christians.

In this earliest use of the concept of sustainability, the WCC emphasized that there were limits to economic growth on one Earth and that growth in the North, or in developed countries, had often been resourced by the stripping of resources and oppression in the South, in developing countries (Cobb, 1992). However, when the discourse of sustainability was taken up more widely, after the publication of the report of the United Nations Commission on Sustainable Development, otherwise known as the Brundtland Commission, it increasingly meant sustainable *economic* development. Recognition of the duty to preserve the Earth for future generations in subsequent international economic discourse was merged with the claim that economic growth is essential for the wellbeing of all peoples, in both developed and developing nations. Sustainable development came to mean not that there are limits to growth, but that the ecological impacts of ever more economic activities need to be restrained. This is illustrated in relation to climate change, where international negotiations have focused on reducing the carbon intensity and hence greenhouse gas emissions associated with economic growth, rather than on restraining the destructive activities, in particular fossil fuel extraction, cement making, and deforestation, which are the principal drivers of both economic growth and climate pollution.

That there are earthly limits to growth in economic activities in every nation is more clearly revealed by climate change than by any other feature of the ecological crisis. This is because economic growth has mostly occurred on the basis of the energetic flow from historic subterranean carbon to atmospheric carbon which fuels industrial and transportation machinery, and is the feedstock for artificial fertilizers, pesticides, and plastics. The transition of carbon, stored by plants and shellfish over millennia in the Earth's crust, into the atmosphere threatens to take the Earth back to an earlier geological state when it was dominated by reptiles, and *Homo sapiens* had not yet evolved. The WCC was one of the first global bodies, along with the World Meteorological Organization, to highlight the planetary emergency represented by global warming (what is now called more often "climate change"), and to call for the establishment of a global treaty process to reduce human impact on the climate. Both bodies accepted the emerging scientific evidence that the burning of fossil fuels and other human-generated greenhouse gases were causing temperatures to rise and melting the three permanent cryospheres: the Arctic, Antarctic, and Himalayas. In response, in 1988 the United Nations inaugurated the Framework Convention on Climate Change (UNFCCC) with the express aim to "prevent dangerous climate change"; virtually all the member nations of the United Nations are signatories. The establishment of the UNFCCC led to annual Conferences of the Parties, at which the WCC has been a regular participant and which, in 2015, led to a new and ongoing agreement by all signatory nations, known as the Paris Agreement, to limit greenhouse gas emissions to a quantity consistent with constraining global warming to 2 °C of the Earth's pre-industrial average.

Fossil fuel extraction and burning, deforestation, damming of rivers, deep ocean fishing, cement and concrete manufacture, mining of precious metals, plastics production and waste disposal, agriculture-related soil erosion, and production of nitrogen from oil and air, have been conducted on such a scale since 1950 that industrial humanity has become a geological force. Human interventions in the atmosphere, chemistry, rocks, soils, species distributions, and the waters of the Earth are so extensive that soil samples reveal a new, human-influenced geological stratum in the Earth's crust. Consequently, geologists and stratigraphers claim that industrial humanity has inaugurated a new geological epoch in which humans have become the dominant force on the evolution of life. They name this epoch the Anthropocene. In this epoch, the central moral dilemma is that while human powers over Creation have grown immensely through science and technology, and been applied on an unsustainable industrial scale to the transformation of Nature, human moral capacities to use these powers wisely have not grown in tandem to limit irreparable damage to ecosystems and the Earth System. This is evidenced in the continuing failure of the nations to act to stem greenhouse gas emissions or to reduce habitat destruction and associated species extinctions.

The Growth of Human Technological Power and the Theologies of Crisis

Through the twentieth century Christian theologians developed a range of responses to the rise of the new powers of industrial humanity. The most influential of these was the "theology of crisis" associated with neo-orthodox Protestant theologians including Reinhold Niebuhr, Dietrich Bonhoeffer, Karl Barth, and Jacques Ellul. For Barth, and for theologians influenced by him, secular scientific reason and the subjection of Christianity to science are resisted by the assertion of the world-shattering and revolutionary implications for all times, cultures, and histories of the revelation of the Divine Word, Jesus Christ. Barth developed this doctrine of revelation in response to the dominant world-shaping crises of the twentieth century, including two world wars, the Holocaust, the nuclear arms race, and the Cold War. These events took their rise not only from increased human powers over the Earth but from increased human powers over other humans, and in particular the strength of German and other forms of totalitarian power. For Barth, the subjection of scripture to scientific inquiry in nineteenth-century German liberal theology was the key root of German totalitarianism since it permitted the state to claim superiority over scripture and the Church. By subjecting Christian revelation and witness to scientific investigation, theologians had subverted the distinctive witness of the Church to the origin and dependence of political authority on God. They produced a theology closer to German Romanticism than to the teachings of the Reformers, and the witnesses of the scriptures and the Church Fathers.

Barth's theology of crisis, first announced in his groundbreaking commentary on Paul's Epistle to the Romans, was designed to resist this scientific subversion by declaring a moment of crisis, a confessional crisis for Christian theology (Barth, 1933). The theologians of crisis, as they became known, called for the bold reassertion of the intellectual distinctiveness of Christian confessional doctrines and the cultural distinctiveness of Christian moral and worshiping practices in the face of the crises of the twentieth century. For the theologians of crisis, modern Western culture represented a secular scientific and technological subversion of Christian doctrine and ethics. The most poisonous fruits of this subversion were two world wars and the Holocaust.

Although today Europe is again engulfed in a migration and refugee crisis reminiscent of the last days of World War II, and the Middle East is engulfed in a geopolitical crisis related to extreme drought, this has not driven efforts to restrain climate pollution higher on the political agenda. In 2015, when this chapter was written, the UK government reversed the pollution reduction commitments of predecessor governments, while the European Commission was strenuously pursuing an international trade treaty with the US government—the Transatlantic Trade and Investment Partnership—which would undermine democratic and lawful efforts to restrain climate and other kinds of pollution, and habitat destruction. India was planning a new generation of coal-fired power stations. The United States and Canada were extracting large quantities of shale oil and gas for both domestic and international energy markets, and in the process damaging domestic water supplies and the atmosphere.

Barth's theology of crisis identified the combination of the rise of the nation-state (especially Germany) and the powers of science and technology as the root of the crises that threatened the collapse of the legal, moral, and political order in the twentieth century. In response to these crises Barth attempted to trump the German Enlightenment's confinement of theology and religion to the realm of inner experience or feeling by resituating the datum of theology in the objective scientific sphere, in which he located the graced revelation of the Divine Word of the Incarnate Christ. However, in so doing Barth did not challenge, but rather underwrote, the Kantian epistemological divide between scientific (theoretical) and practical (ethical and experiential) reason. Hence he also failed to critique the Enlightenment distinction between Nature and culture. I argue that it is this distinction, rather than nationalism, which is at the core of the failure of the nations to respond to the ecological and climate crises (Northcott, 2013).

The Global Economy and the Refusal of Terrestrial Limits to Growth

The dominant culture of late modernity is that of a global, technologically enabled market economy which enables the nations, and multinational corporations mostly owned by developed nations, to pollute other nations' skies and waterways to produce the consumer goods of an increasingly throwaway culture, even as environmental regulations reduce pollution of air and water in developed countries. The core problem here is not so much with nationalism as it is with the global, borderless character of the modern market economy and the economic theory that legitimates it. Present levels of consumption of water, soil, minerals, meat, fertilizers, fossil fuels, fish, and consumer goods such as clothing, electronic machinery, and other artefacts are occurring annually at approximately four times the replacement capacity of the living systems of the Earth. Put another way, humans are consuming and polluting in the first three months of each year what the Earth can sustainably provide without being systematically degraded for future generations. The remaining nine months of consumption would require three planets the size of the Earth to sustain indefinitely. Hence 90% of the fish in the ocean have disappeared due to industrial scale fishing since 1950 and 70% of tropical forests have been destroyed or significantly degraded in the same period. Groundwater is being systematically depleted beneath the croplands of the mid-western United States, the Middle East, Southern Africa, and north India. And the climate is becoming polluted with excess carbon. This is increasing the heat-retaining properties of the atmosphere and, at the same time, acidifying the oceans, so reducing the capacity of shellfish, coral, and other species to draw down carbon into the oceans, and ultimately the seabed, through photosynthesis. But economists and financiers do not accept that there are terrestrial limits to the scale of the capture and re-engineering of the Earth's life systems for human industrial production and wealth accumulation. Hence, the money supply that underwrites the production system has grown exponentially in the last three decades and without regard for the ecological or social limits to growth.

Climate change science reveals that industrial humanity, despite having invented the most productive and technologically advanced economy in history, in which globally average levels of personal comfort, longevity, medical services, and nutrition have never been higher, is living in ways that reduce the comfort, health, longevity, and nutrition of future generations, and increasingly of some people today. Climate science reveals that the human economy is not only a cultural artefact driven by shareholder value, consumer choice, and corporate investments. It is also an earthbound economy because there is only one planet humans can call and experience as home. If the Earth and its ecosystems limit the capacity of the wealthy to accumulate more through industrial activities and investments, this means that the wealthy need to be restrained if others, both now and in the future, are to live well or live at all. But the neoliberal tenor of much economic thinking and policy making has eroded the willingness of national governments to restrain wealth accumulation by the richest through financial regulation, or to redistribute the fruits of wealth creation through taxation.

In parallel with the rise of neoliberalism as a governing ideology, in the last four decades rich individuals, business corporations, and financial institutions have moved more than a third of existing monies in the global economy into tax havens, which are in effect extraterrestrial economic zones where neither redistributive nor regulative projects by national, earthbound governments have much purchase. It is because climate science conflicts with this desire for an economy free of ecological, legal, and social restraint that it is resisted by businesses, economists, governments, investors, and politicians. Climate science is a politics and not only a science. Hence the Enlightenment distinction between Nature and culture, facts and values, is challenged and rejected by climate science. Climate science reveals that the cosmos is again, as it was for the Ancients, a source of value and revelation, a living being with which human beings are in a living relationship, involving exchange and negotiation. The cosmos is not merely a fixed material and mechanistic backdrop for human affairs.

The refusal of fossil fuel corporations and governments to reduce climate impacts by reducing the extraction and use of coal, oil, and gas, and by restraining deforestation, cement making, and harmful consumption and waste, is at root about economics and not science. Few in government challenge climate science, but given the very great wealth derived from fossil fuels, no government whose terrain has supplies of them has yet shown a willingness to legally restrain licensing of their extraction and use. All governments adopted emissions targets in the "Intended Nationally Determined Contributions" (INDCs) of the 2015 Paris Agreement, but these targets are easily avoided by importing carbon-intense goods and services from other domains. And INDCs do not include fossil fuel production (Helm, 2012). The availability of substitute technologies for fossil fuel use, including renewable power, building insulation, and heat pumps, presents industrial civilization with choices to make about investment in infrastructure and energy production. But decisions on these technologies are still largely made by short-term cost considerations and not future climate instability.

Caring for the Earth as Spirit-Infused Divine Creation

Science and technology were crucially implicated in the twentieth-century theology of crisis, as they are in the climate crisis. The use by Germany and the Allies of the technologies of war, including chemical weapons and aerial bombing, took the violence and ecological destructiveness of war to unprecedented heights, so much so that the Vatican significantly revised Roman Catholic Just War doctrine subsequent to World War II (Northcott, 2007b). In his theological reflections on Genesis 1–3, which originated as lectures in 1932 in the context of the rise of the Third Reich, Bonhoeffer argued that a scientific and technologically advanced form of civilization carries particular threats to human beings and to life on Earth more broadly because its people refuse to recognize the Earth as a divine creation. Consequently, "the earth is no longer our earth, and then we become strangers on earth," and from strangers we finally become the Earth's subjects: through the power of technology "the earth grips man and subdues him" (Bonhoeffer, 2004).

Cooperative international action to mitigate climate change is corrupted by greed and acquisitiveness. National representatives at climate negotiations claim to be doing their duty when they pursue their perceived national self-interest by resisting restraints on climate-damaging activities. In so doing they mirror the sinful tendencies of individuals to refuse their original relatedness to the divine Creator. They refuse to acknowledge that life itself, and the Creation that pollution is destabilizing, is a divine gift and not merely a stable material background for human life. Hence they refuse to see that their interests coincide with the interests of other created beings. They deny other creatures their legitimate being when this refusal results in the destruction of a stable climate or other ecological conditions essential to their wellbeing.

Christian moral and ecological theologians have argued, like Bonhoeffer, that central to the Christian response to the climate crisis, and the ecological crisis more broadly, is the acknowledgment that the Earth is not only a unique set of habitats and species that have evolved through four billion years of planetary and evolutionary history, but also a divine creation. As a divine creation the present ordering of Creation, including the great diversity of species and the stability of the climate, ought to exercise moral and material restraint on the ways in which humans dwell on and transform the Earth. This acknowledgment carries with it the implication that the Earth is a continuing creation in which the divine Creator Spirit continues to undergird and bring forth life even in the midst of ecological destruction.

This concept of a continuing creation that is still indwelt by the divine Spirit counteracts the tendency of eighteenth- and nineteenth-century theologians and scientists to conceptualize the Earth as a mechanical sphere set amidst other mechanical spheres, whose interactions are governed by fixed laws, which humanity cannot alter; in this approach God is external to the life-forces which continue to evolve on Earth. Modern philosophers also tend to think of the Earth as a fixed mechanical backdrop to human history and values. The Kantian ethical imperative and the Utilitarian ethics that underwrite modern economic thinking resist the concept of a relational divine creation in which reverence for and sensitivity to other life, not only to and for persons, is required of human beings. Both Kant and John Stuart Mill attempted to delineate a cultural arena for human values apart from the industrial, science-informed transformation of Nature that has been central to the direction of civilization since the Enlightenment. However, as the ecological crisis becomes a crisis in the Earth System, it is evident that marking off the personal from the rest of life has merely underwritten scientistic and economistic tendencies to disregard the needs and sensitivities of other life, even when this disregard threatens human welfare.

Philosophical and Theological Approaches to Ecological Ethics

The principal strategy in philosophical ethics for responding to the ecological crisis has been to extend the Kantian account of the intrinsic ethical value of persons and the Utilitarian account of the overriding duty to relieve suffering from humans to other kind and to habitats. This extension, through the conservation and setting aside from industrial use of landscapes of great beauty, and through efforts to reduce the suffering of animals, has helped to reduce damage to local ecosystems and habitats in those nations that have passed laws to protect endangered species and areas of outstanding natural beauty, and to regulate for clean air and water. But these local regulations have not changed the multi-scalar and systemic impacts of industrial activities on the Earth System as a whole. Nor have these approaches changed the technological imperative that drives the subjection of all species and habitats to human engineering and production. Humans are now in charge of the carbon and nitrogen cycles of the planet as a whole; they actively manage more than 70% of the Earth's land area; they fish and drill for oil throughout all seven oceans; they fill orbital space with junk from the legacy of 60 years of space exploration; they are changing the formation and structure of life from the cell upwards at the microbial sphere where synthetic chemicals are now widespread; and they are intentionally re-engineering cells in the form of genetically modified plants and other species, which alter the DNA of other life they come into contact with.

Christian ethics has taken a different route to philosophical ethics in response to the ecological and climate crisis. The priority among Christian moral theologians has been to recognize that the Earth does not belong to human beings but to God. When its origin as gift in the creative work of God is recognized, its destiny to be part of the divine redemptive work, as focused in the Incarnation of God in Christ, is also recognized. The first theologian in the twentieth century to emphasize the ethical implications of divine redemption for all creatures and for Creation as a whole was Albert Schweitzer. Schweitzer argued that human experiences of wonder and delight in the elemental beauty of the Earth, such as delight in falling snow, are evidence for the existence of a foundational attitude in all people of reverence for life; ignorant egoism and materialistic concerns for property and possessions tend to suppress it. He argued that reverence for life is the connective logic of the Christian commands to love God and to love people: "reason discovers the connecting link between love for God and love for man: love for all creatures, reverence for all being, a compassionate sharing of experiences with all of life, no matter how externally dissimilar to our own" (Schweitzer, 1988, 11). Reverence for life is deeply commended in the biblical texts, most seminally in the accounts of Adam naming the animals as they are first presented to him by the Creator in the Garden of Eden, and again in the injunction to Noah to save other species from the primeval flood. Barth also commended reverence for life since life cannot be owned but only lived and received as a gift from God. But Barth resisted the implication that humans were therefore required to organize their societies and economic activities in ways that reduced their impacts on other kind. As Rowan Williams comments, against Barth, "Genesis tells us that when we are called to relationship with our creator, we are in the same moment summoned to responsibility for the non-human world" (Williams,

2014, 198). It is therefore intrinsic to what it is to be human, a person made in the divine image, to care for life, to seek to sustain biodiversity, and to enhance the beauty, fecundity, and future wellbeing of the planet and its habitats. Living irreverently in relation to other kinds, in ways that destroy their habitats and threaten their extinction, as well as to the quality of life of other persons, is to live in ways that deform our humanness.

The Christian Discovery of Environmental (In)Justice

If the first move in ecological theology was to recognize reverence for life as a fundamental feature of Christian ethics, the second was to recognize that ongoing ecological destruction harms not only other kinds but other people, especially the poor in developing countries. Impoverished communities in Africa, Asia, Latin America, and small island states in the Indian and Pacific Oceans are already suffering from worsening weather extremes and rising seas which threaten their ability to grow food and find potable water. The majority of the Earth's poor rely directly on the capacity of the Earth to grow food, and of coastal waters to harbor fish, for their survival. What Alliez called the "environmentalism of the poor" represents an important rebalancing of the argument that environmentalism is a feature of late modern societies which, having achieved security in material circumstances through industrial development, are enabled to turn their attention to conserving "post-material" resources, such as clean air and water, and recreational and wilderness parks (Martinez-Alier, 2002).

Against the claim that environmental conservation is a romantic invention, and a luxury that only wealthy nations and communities can afford, climate pollution, deforestation, groundwater depletion, local air and water pollution, soil erosion, and industrial overfishing of coastal waters are all forms of environmental damage that directly impact the livelihoods and health of the poor. In the developed world, and in developing world cities, it is the poor who are most likely to be forced to breathe dangerously polluted air since it is the poor who live close to landfill and toxic waste dumps, chemical factories, mines, heavily trafficked roads, and coal-fired power stations, and who lack access to water uncontaminated by industrial pollution or human or animal wastes. A United Church of Christ Commission for Racial Justice report first revealed the geographical proximity of toxic waste dumps to people of color in the United States, where the phrase "environmental justice" was first coined (UCCCRJ, 1987). Subsequently, Ruether and Northcott argued that environmental justice has biblical roots, especially in the Old Testament narration of the Exile of the people of God from the land of Israel. Millennia ago the Hebrew prophets, in their interpretation of the meaning of Exile, argued that the reason the Hebrews lost the land, and the land was losing its fertility, was that they had worshiped idols instead of God who had given them the land. And in neglecting God they turned against the covenantal terms on which they received the land, which required them to share it equitably, and not permit debt bondage to alienate families from their biblical land inheritance across the generations (Ruether, 1992). The prophets also indicted their failure to give the land and its non-human inhabitants their own Sabbaths by leaving the land fallow periodically and by making space for wild animals, as the law had commanded (Northcott, 1996). When Aldo Leopold (1949) argued that the Abrahamic faiths had not included the land in their ethic, he had not read or studied the Old Testament.

From environmental justice it is not a large leap to the concept of climate justice and to its elaboration in relation to the intergenerational as well as international inequities of the climate change conundrum (Northcott, 2007a). Church leaders have mobilized the concept of climate justice in calling for serious and rapid mitigation of climate pollution by national governments and corporations in the developed world. They are influenced in this respect by meeting their counterpart leaders in the churches of the South whose members are already suffering climate damage. For the same reason, churches in Sweden, Germany, and England have begun withdrawing their pension fund investments from fossil fuel companies. Churches are also investing in renewable power generation, as witnessed in particular in the network of Interfaith Power and Light organizations across the United States, begun by the Episcopal priest Sally Bingham. In Europe networks of "eco-congregations" and "green churches" have developed curricula to train their congregations in Creation care, and in the environmental practices of recycling, reuse, and repair. Hundreds of local congregations in Europe, North America, and Australia have installed solar panels on the south-facing roofs of their church buildings. Pope Benedict did the same with the roof of the papal audience hall in the Vatican.

The connection between climate care and Creation care has not been hard to make in the churches; they are an alternative form of global communion to that of the global market. In Scotland, where the present author resides, a number of congregations belonging to a network of "eco-congregations" are taking action to conserve their environment because they have links with congregations in Malawi through which they have come to know of communities for whom drought and famine are daily realities. In the international networks of Christians across continents climate change becomes real and personal and not merely a set of scientific predictions about future apocalyptic events.

In addition to the global communion of Christians and the tradition of support to Christians between nations, first begun by St. Paul's collection for the victims of the Judean famine as indicated in the first letter to the Corinthians, there is also in the Christian tradition a concept of the communion of souls which links Christians across the generations, including the unborn and the unconceived as well as those who have died in the faith. The idea of the communion of souls, or saints, is particularly associated with Christian worship since the idea was first proposed by the writer of the Letter to the Hebrews who wrote of a "great cloud of witnesses" who are present when Christians break bread and share the Divine Word with one another in worship. This idea is a source of intergenerational connection between past, present, and future generations and a potential spiritual source of resistance to the short-termism of contemporary economics and consumer culture (Northcott, 2011).

It has proven less easy for secular economic and political theorists to convincingly weigh the life-chances of future people on a rapidly warming planet against the consumption and production preferences of present people. Some philosophers even argue that since future people do not exist, morally and economically they cannot be said to have a claim on present people (Parfitt, 1984). Similarly, it has proven difficult to find political leaders and legislators prepared to restrain the profits and consumer preferences of their corporations and citizens for the sake of the needs of future generations or of poor communities in the developing world suffering from degradation of their natural environment. A fundamental reason why the intergenerational inequity of climate change is not being properly articulated and addressed in the secular social sciences is the dominance in modern economies of debt-based banking and money-creation. The Bible clearly proscribes the lending of money at interest and this proscription was observed in Christian circles until after the Reformation. The moral constraints on usury were gradually removed in early modern Europe banking systems. They developed where debt (money lent at interest to finance factories, houses, cars, and even consumer products) had become the principal means by which money was created. The interest rate on debt generates a closely related discount rate in the calculation of the relative benefits and costs of investments. Whereas benefits are counted in full as consequences of investment (e.g., in a coal-fired power station or a new airport) the climate costs to future generations of increased greenhouse gas emissions are discounted, typically at the real rate of interest, which is bank rate less inflation. This means that with a typical discount rate of 5%, costs from an investment 20 years hence are calculated at zero. The additional justification for future cost discounting is the assumption that future generations will have greater economic wealth, along with technological advancements, to draw on relative to the environmental legacy costs they inherit from previous generations. Climate costs to future generations, therefore, do not enter significantly into the balance sheets of nations, corporations, or households.

Natural Law and the Ways of the Earth

If the second move in Christian ethics in relation to climate change has centered on the idea and practice of environmental and climate justice, the third and perhaps most radical move concerns the idea that the Earth is itself a source of guidance and law for the ways in which humans are to dwell on it, and to produce goods and sustenance for themselves (Northcott, 1996). Humans are intrinsically makers, and not only gardeners and tenders of the soil and crops. This is affirmed more strongly in the Christian tradition than in classical or Eastern philosophies because the founder of Christianity was a maker for most of his earthly life, and a philosopher, preacher, and healer for only a few years of it. Christ was born to a builder and joiner, and tradition has it that he worked in Joseph's workshop until he embarked on his career as a religious teacher at the age of 30.

The Apostle Paul was also a maker and through much of his apostleship practiced the craft of tent-making to support his apostolic ministry. Craftsmanship and making acquired a hallowed status in Christian tradition because of these seminal makers. It is, therefore, unsurprising that Christian ascetics over the generations developed strong traditions of craft making in the monasteries they established. Benedict in his *Rule* argued that manual work was an intrinsic part of the calling of a monk. Over time, having so many highly intelligent and reflective people, which many monks were and are, engaged in manual labor—tilling fields, tending gardens and vines, sawing wood, brewing beer, grinding grain, keeping sheep, making cheese, and weaving cloth—meant that they applied their brains to the tasks in hand and, in the process, developed novel technologies to undertake these tasks in more time-efficient and productive ways. The mechanical clock, the watermill, the deep plow, the domestication of sheep, and myriad other inventions and practices emerged in Europe from the monasteries in the late Middle Ages. These inventions and practices also underwrote the emergence of craft guilds in medieval cities, in which so many young men escaped serfdom to become apprenticed craftsmen.

As experimental craft techniques developed into the scientific method in the course of the Renaissance and the Enlightenment, scientists developed new technologies which, unlike the medieval technologies, increasingly worked against the grain of the natural order. Fossil fuels were a crucial source of this change since the synthetic chemicals they made possible gave rise to whole new industries, eventually including the plastics industry, whose products are among the most commonly thrown away. They remain durable in the environment hundreds of years after the product has broken down and been disposed of. Plastic pollution is among the most ubiquitous forms of industrial pollution and is increasingly affecting waterways and oceans with long-term consequences for aquatic life that are still not fully understood.

Making and economic production are principal sources of climate and other kinds of toxic pollution. It is therefore vital, if such pollution is to be mitigated, that human beings find ways to make and transform the natural order—in the making of food, clothing, buildings, artefacts, and technological devices—that follow the laws of Nature rather than countermand them. Among the most fundamental of Nature's laws is that Nature does not waste. A forest is a perfect example of this since leaves from the canopy replenish the forest floor. This regenerates and protects the soil from erosion, enabling the soil to absorb more moisture from rain and to sustain a large volume of insects, which in turn feed birds, small mammals, and other forest inhabitants. The productivity of a wild forest in producing timber is far greater than plantation forests precisely because of the natural ways in which forests function to conserve biodiversity, photosynthesis, and microclimates suitable for forest-dwelling life. When scientific forestry was introduced it was envisaged that plantations would produce more lumber than natural forests, but this was not the case. The key feature of plantations was not productivity but control and accountability; the planted forest was so arranged that it could be reliably predicted to produce so many feet of lumber per year.

If "Nature does not do waste" is one law around which the human economy of making needs to be redesigned, another is that natural systems promote maximal biodiversity. Human agriculture, especially in its industrial form, has tended in the opposite direction. But again it is becoming clear that the monocrop field is far less productive than imagined because the inputs of fertilizers, machinery, pesticides, and water, and the soil erosion involved in annual plowing, together represent a cost that is far greater in relation to the end product—food for human consumption—than methods of farming involving more diverse planting and greater human manual tending of plants, species, and soils.

It is possible with existing technologies to design buildings, energy systems, manufacturing systems, and agricultural systems that do not require climate-damaging inputs of fossil fuels, do not produce irresolvable long-term toxic wastes, and do not systemically erode soils or destroy whole classes of insects, and hence up the food chain reduce birdlife, small mammals, and so on. But what is lacking is the widespread belief that Nature knows best, that the ways of Earth are ways that humans ought to respect. Industrial humans disregard these ways at the peril of the future habitability of the planet and its myriad diverse species, as well as of future people. Absent the theological belief that these natural laws originate in the wisdom of a divine Creator and are imbued into the continuing unfolding and evolution of created order, industrial societies have proven resistant to the idea that respect for Nature's ways ought to be a dominant feature of human making.

Eschatology and Ecclesia

The fourth and final feature I will treat here of a Christian ecological ethics that is highlighted by the climate crisis concerns the future destiny of life on Earth. Teilhard de Chardin was the first modern theologian to note the extent to which humanity was changing and adapting life on Earth. He argued in eschatological vein that this transformation was indicative of the merging of mind, matter, and spirit—the destined fruit of the emergence of the human mind into planetary dominance. The merging of mind and matter was producing a new Earth, a noosphere, in which mind and spirit add a conscious dimension to matter. Unconscious cellular life and the progressive merging of the human spirit with material and organic life was already presaged in the Incarnation of Jesus Christ who is "alpha and omega." For Teilhard the noosphere is progressively moving toward the "omega point," when all life will find its ultimate fulfillment and perfection in union with the divine Trinity (Teilhard, 1958). Berry analogously argued that humanity is entering a new era in the twenty-first century, an era that he called the ecozoic. In this era, when human influence over the Earth is increasingly all-pervasive, humanity will need to awake to a new ecological consciousness and become more sensitive to the needs of all other kind. Berry argued for a close alignment between the Christian future, the mission of the Church on Earth, and the care of Creation. Recognizing that Western industrial civilization, while a deviation from Christian theology and ethics, is nonetheless rooted in Christianity means that Christians have a unique responsibility to turn their rituals, ethics, and beliefs toward a greater sensitivity to the planet, and the care and stewardship of Earth's future:

> The Church could be a powerful force in bringing about the healing of a distraught Earth. The Church could provide an integrating reinterpretation of our new story of the universe. In this manner it could renew religion in its primary expression as celebration, as ecstatic delight in existence. This, I propose, is the Great Work to which Christianity is called in these times. (Berry, 2014, 110)

In similar vein Orthodox theologian Tamara Grdzelidze argues that the Church "was founded by Christ himself for the salvation of the created order following the broken covenant between God and human beings" (Grdzelidze, 2014). In this perspective the human Fall and exile from Paradise affected the whole created order and in this respect climate change is an atmospheric illustration of a pre-existing cosmic condition. This situation accentuates the Church's salvific role as mediator of divine grace to Creation. The Church carries the destiny of the cosmos declared in the divine promise to "make all things new" (Rev. 21.5). The Church is therefore required by this vocation to witness, liturgically and in her own life, to human creaturely relations which symbolize the graced destiny of Creation in Christ. This witness finds moral force when Christians reduce their consumption of climate-damaging goods and services and seek to live more lightly on the Earth. This witness also has economic and political implications for secular power, particularly in relation to the excess consumption and greed which are implicated in the refusal of rich and powerful nations and corporations to limit fossil fuel extraction and other sources of greenhouse gas emissions.

For Orthodox theologians such as Grdzelidze, as for Berry and Teilhard, the sacramental life of the Church participates in the life-giving and life-sustaining power of the Creator Spirit. It reconciles in the performative nature of the liturgy the reconciliation of created and uncreated life begun in the revelation of the Incarnate Christ as the divine *Logos*. The *Logos* is also crucial to understanding the human vocation, in making and transforming creation for human sustenance and livelihood, to draw the cosmos toward its destiny to participate, alongside humanity, in the life of God. Hence the divine image in humanity places humanity, and more especially the Church as the "new creation," in a priestly relation to Creation in which the Church represents the Creation as Offering to the Creator. Climate change more than any of the other crises that have beset the modern world therefore calls forth the Church as a mediating institution in drawing political leaders, policy makers, and citizens toward the solutions that are already in the hands of ecologically enlightened designers and makers, and willing citizens. This made all the more timely and significant the papal intervention in international debates in the form of the encyclical *Laudate Sí*, in the run-up to the crucial climate summit in Paris in 2015. Regardless of the eventual outcome of the UNFCCC process, the Christian hope remains for the transformation of Creation into the beauty, compassion, and peace which were the marks of the character of Christ in His ministry on Earth. As the climate emergency gathers pace with melting ice, rising seas, and strengthening storms, Christians and the secular world may find that the Church's affirmation and practice of charity, hopefulness, and peace is needed more than ever in the rest of the present century.

References

Barth, Karl. 1933. *The Epistle to the Romans*. Transl. E. C. Hoskyns. London: Oxford University Press.

Berry, Thomas. 2014. *Thomas Berry: Selected Writings on the Earth Community*. Eds. Mary Evelyn Tucker & John Grim. Maryknoll, NY: Orbis Books.

Birch, Charles. 1976. Creation, Technology, and Human Survival: Called to Replenish the Earth. *The Ecumenical Review*, 28, 66–79.

Bonhoeffer, Dietrich. 2004. *Creation and Fall: A Theological Exposition of Genesis* 1–3. Minneapolis, MN: Fortress Press.

Cobb, John B. 1992. *Sustainability: Economics, Ecology and Justice*. Maryknoll, NY: Orbis Books.

Grdzelidze, Tamara. 2014. 9: The Church (141–156). In Michael S. Northcott & Peter M. Scott (Eds.), *Systematic*

Theology and Climate Change: Ecumenical Perspectives. London: Routledge.

Helm, Dieter. 2012. *The Carbon Crunch: How We're Getting Climate Change Wrong and How to Fix It*. New Haven, CT: Yale University Press.

Kant, Immanuel. 1991. Idea for a Universal History with a Cosmopolitan Purpose. In H. S. Reiss (Ed.), *Kant: Political Writings*. Transl. H. B. Nisbet. Cambridge: Cambridge University Press.

Leopold, Aldo. 1949. *A Sand County Almanac and Sketches Here and There*. Oxford: Oxford University Press.

Martinez-Alier, Joan. 2002. *The Environmentalism of the Poor: A Study of Ecological Conflicts and Valuation*. Ann Arbor, MI: University of Michigan Press.

Northcott, Michael S. 1996. *The Environment and Christian Ethics*. Cambridge: Cambridge University Press.

Northcott, Michael S. 2007a. *A Moral Climate: The Ethics of Global Warming*. London: Darton, Longman & Todd.

Northcott, Michael S. 2007b. The Weakness of Power and the Power of Weakness: The Ethics of War in a Time of Terror. *Studies in Christian Ethics*, 20, 88–101.

Northcott, Michael S. 2011. Anthropogenic Climate Change, Political Liberalism and the Communion of Saints. *Studies in Christian Ethics*, 24, 34–49.

Northcott, Michael S. 2013. *A Political Theology of Climate Change*. Grand Rapids, MI: Eerdmans.

Parfitt, Derek. 1984. *Reasons and Persons*. Oxford: Oxford University Press.

Robra, Martin. 1997. Foreword (ix–xiii). In L. C. Birch & Lukas Vischer, *Living with the Animals: The Community of God's Creatures*. Geneva: WCC Publications.

Ruether, Rosemary Radford. 1992. *Gaia and God: The Ecofeminist Theology of Earth Healing*. London: SCM Press.

Schweitzer, Albert. 1988. *A Place for Revelation: Sermons on Reverence for Life*. Transl. D. L. Holland. New York: Macmillan.

Teilhard de Chardin. Pierre. 1958. *The Phenomenon of Man*. Transl. Bernard Wall. New York: HarperPerennial.

United Church of Christ Commission for Racial Justice. 1987. *Toxic Wastes and Race in the United States: A National Report on the Racial and Socio-Economic Characteristics of Communities with Hazardous Waste Sites*. New York: UCCCRJ.

Williams, Rowan. 2014. *Faith in the Public Square*. London: Bloomsbury.

CHAPTER 22

Islamic Environmental Teachings

Compatible with Ecofeminism?

Nawal H. Ammar and Allison Gray

Introduction

It is hard to imagine that the violent public behaviors exhibited by a minority of Muslims in 25 years could be based on any religious tradition which has the least focus on preservation, equity, or justice toward anything. The reality is that Islamic texts, history, and traditions contain guidelines on how to treat all things created by God responsibly and justly, including the environment (ecology) and women. Given the diversity and history of the Muslim community it is unrealistic to assume that there is a monolithic understanding of Islam. Nevertheless, this chapter presents a perspective on two questions: Do Islamic thought and ecofeminism have any commonalities? And if so, what are they?

The chapter is presented in four sections: the first describes the main ideas of the ecofeminist perspective; the second a perspective on Islam's view of environmental ethics; the third explores the relationship between the ideas of ecofeminism and Islamic views of the environment; and the fourth offers a critique of the patriarchal interpretations of Islam's view of the environment and women. A brief conclusion looks to future explorations of ecofeminism and Islam.

Ecofeminism

The term ecofeminism was coined by Françoise d'Eaubonne in 1974. She argued that the link between women and ecology is special as women are more involved in ecological questions due to their ability to give life; thus they have a greater concern for future generations (d'Eaubonne, 1999a; Moore, 2008). In this perspective most, if not all,

The Wiley Blackwell Companion to Religion and Ecology, First Edition. Edited by John Hart.

sociopolitical problems are connected to the problematic system of patriarchal capitalism and its (direct) treatment of the ecological context and women with forms of domination, inequality, and competition (d'Eaubonne, 1999b). For ecofeminists, a society and culture founded on the ideas of ecofeminism is the only way to save both humanity (women in particular) and the environment from their common exploitation by men (Merchant, 1980). Academic ecofeminists incorporate a range of issues and explanations about the degradation of the environment. They theorize the co-positioning of Nature and women through a multidimensional view of their intersectionality (Twine, 2010). A key intersectional observation is the acknowledgment of various forms of differential victimization (Heckenberg, 2011) and environmental racism (Cole & Foster, 2001), where vulnerable populations, including women and people who are members of cultural, racial, and religious minorities, lower socioeconomic classes, and so on, are significantly, disproportionately, and negatively impacted by structural events such as climate change, food shortages, pollution, and natural disasters (Parikh, 2007). It is important, however, that while adhering to an intersectionality approach, an ecofeminist perspective seeks to avoid hierarchies by broadening analysis to relationships involving the more-than-human (Twine, 2010). Essentially, ecofeminism seeks to politicize ecological issues.

An Islamic View of the Environment: Relational View

Most Muslims agree that the Qur'an is the absolute source of Islam, along with the Prophet's sayings (*hadith*), actions (*sunnah*), and the juristic decisions (*Sharī'ah*). All three sources have guidelines on the importance of protecting the environment, while not dominating or abusing it, as a religious duty. One can argue that the Islamic view of the environment is not biocentric, but relational, behavioral, and action-oriented. This view is multi-leveled and is founded on the idea of *Tawhid*, the monotheistic principle of Islam in which God the Creator is a unique and different entity from all other creations. This Oneness of God is a strict monotheism; God has no anthropomorphic characteristics. He stands in a dual relationship with all His Creation, who are dependent on Him as the Absolute and Almighty Creator (Ammar, 2000, 195). The Qur'an states, "Allah, [who is] One, Allah, the Eternal Refuge. He neither begets nor is born, nor is there to Him any equivalent" (Al Ikhlas, 1-4).[1]

In the Islamic view of the environment, the first relational level is one of dependence on and reverence of the One and only Creator and his Creation. This duality renders everything created by God divine because it is a manifestation of the Almighty's power and not because it is sacred (Ammar, 1995, 2003). To respect God means one has to respect and glorify all Creation, including the environment.

The second relational level in the Islamic environmental view is that of "oneness among the created." The *Tawhid* view of the Creator and the created "renders the latter a unified class of God's creation" (Ammar, 2000, 196). The created are equal in their relationship with God (Chishti, 2003) and entitled to use the Earth equally without discrimination, corruption, abuse, or coercion (Ammar, 2000, 129). All creatures (e.g., humans, birds, trees, mountains, seas) are alike in a number of other ways, including their common origin of life in water (Qur'an-Al Anbiya 21: 30), their social structure as communities (Qur'an-Al Anam 6: 38), and their obedience to God (Qur'an-Al Hajj 22: 18).

For humans this respect of God's Creation is more than ritualistic worship (Saniotis, 2012); it is a devotional practice exercised on a daily basis. Humans are the custodians of the Earth, the *Khala'if* (sing. *Khalifah*),[2] vice-regents on Earth who are responsible not only for maintaining its order and harmony for God, but improving it as well (Qur'an-Ali Imran, 6: 165; Ammar, 1995, 2000, 2005; Chichti, 2003; Khalid & O'Brien, 1992). Humans are *Khalifah* not because they are a "greater creation" (Qur'an Ghafir, 40: 57), or as a punishment for falling from Heaven (Qur'an-Al Baqarah 2: 35), but because humans possess special qualities (Qur'an-Sad 38: 72). Ali (1989, 1081) says that "Allah breathed something of His own spirit into humans ... [giving humans the ability to choose] between good and evil, and ... [capable] of Forbearance, Love, and Mercy." But also, humans were entrusted with the responsibility of *Khalifa* because God (Qur'an-Al Ahzab 33: 72) offered the Trust to "the Heavens, the Earth and the Mountains," but they "refused to shoulder the responsibility out of fear," and humans "assumed it," and accepted it when they bore witness to God in their covenant of *Tawhid* and became Muslims. Fulfilling this trust of caring for God's Creation is part of the devotional duties of Muslims and they will be held accountable on the Day of Judgment if they do not fulfill this responsibility (Ammar, 2005).

Human Devotional Dimension of the Islamic Environmental View

For humans, these relations of dependence on the One God and interdependence with all God's Creation have both a devotional dimension of worshiping the One Almighty by glorifying His Creation through ritual and reverence, and a behavioral/action dimension toward God's creations as vice-regent. This behavioral/action dimension is complicated because Islam is not an aesthetic religion requiring abstinence from worldly pleasures. To the contrary, the Qur'an (Qur'an-Luqman 31: 20, Qur'an-Al Mulk 67: 15, Qur'an-Al Khahf 18: 46) encourages the use, acquisition, and enjoyment of the bounties provided by God. To some scholars this dual role of vice-regent on Earth as custodian and protector of God's Creation and at the same time one who uses the Earth is the moral imperative of humanity in Islam (Al Faruqi & Al Faruqi, 1986; Ammar, 2005; Nasr, 1998). The Qur'anic verse notes this: "We made you successors [*Khalifah*] on the Earth, after them, to see how you would act" (Qur'an-Younus 10: 14).

Knowledge and Activism in the Islamic Environmental View

This moral imperative is guided by two ideas in Islamic theology. The first is the ability of humans to learn and know right from wrong. There are numerous verses in the Qur'an on the idea of learning and knowing generally, and in turn knowing right from wrong: knowing as wisdom (Qur'an- Al Baqarah 2: 269), knowing as understanding (Qur'an- Al Baqarah 2: 114; Qur'an-Ali Imran 3: 190–191), and knowing as learning (Qur'an- Al Jumar 39: 9, Qur'an- Al Mujadilah 58:11).[3] The responsibility of humans to balance their needs against the needs of other creatures created by God relies on

Muslims understanding the consequences of their actions (Chishti, 2003, 76). This knowledge includes also knowing how to maintain a balance between utilizing the bounty of God's Creation and protecting and improving it.

The second idea guiding the moral imperative of using and protecting the Earth incorporates an action/activism component. The action component requires humans to utilize knowledge not only in their ritualistic worship and daily life, but also in protecting all God's creatures and creations as His vice-regents on Earth. The Qur'an says, "[God is] the one who created life and death to test you, which of you is best in action" (Qur'an- Al Mulk 67: 2). This action for humans is clearly prescribed in Islamic texts. In the Qur'an it is about not "exceeding the balance" (Khalid, 1992, 316). The Qur'anic verse says, "In order that you may not transgress [due] balance" (Al Rahmaan, 55: 8). In the Prophet's *hadith* the more engagement the action has, the higher its value. The Prophet Muhammad's famous saying clearly underscores this: "Anyone who witnesses evil should remonstrate upon it by his hand, his mouth or his heart, the last is the weakest of faith" (Sahih Al-Bukahri, 1998).

The Islamic Environmental View and Ecofeminism

Islamic texts and teachings view the environment as God's Creation, where the focus is not only on ritualistic worship and reverence of the Creator and created, but also on human relational dimensions among the created. This relational dimension requires humans, as God's vice-regents, to utilize the bounties of the universe and to be kind, respectful, responsible not wasteful, fair, and just in treating God's creations as part of their overall devotion. The following Qur'anic verse exemplifies such teachings:

> It is not *Al-Birr* [righteousness, piety, and virtue] that you turn towards the East or the West [in prayer], but the righteousness to believe in Allah and the Last Day, in the Angels, in the Books and in the Prophets. To spend of your substance, out of love from Him, for your kin, for orphans, for the needy, for the wayfarer, for those who ask and, for the ransom to set slaves free. To be steadfast in prayer, practice regular charity, fulfill promises made. And be firm and patient in pain or suffering and adversity and throughout all periods of panic. Those are the truthful and mindful of God. (Al-Baqarah 2: 177)

However, the current situation in Muslim countries shows a wide gap between Islamic teachings and reality today. While a society's religion is one of the many intersecting variables contributing to maldevelopment and environmental degradation, the record of the Muslim world shows a disregard for God's Creation even when other structural impediments are absent. The following are examples:

- The excessive deforestation taking place in Indonesia (the loss of 3.9 million hectares of forest) in the years between 1990 and 2005 (Food and Agriculture Organization of the United Nations, 2010, 11)
- The water stress registered in every country in the Middle East (except Iraq) since 2003 (United Nations Development Program, 2009, 4)

- In 2015, the death of more than 500 people in the northern Sharqia Governorate of Egypt after drinking Nile water polluted by a ship that had capsized in the southern stretches of the river, spilling phosphate and other toxic substances (World Bulletin, 2015)
- A calculated increase in flooding over the next 30 years, and a sharp reduction in the water supply in Pakistan, India, and Bangladesh due to an increase in the melt rate of the Himalayan glaciers (Wihbey, 2012)
- In 2015 the country with the highest level of pollution was the United Arab Emirates (World Bank Group, 2015)
- Sixteen of the 30 world conflicts in 2015 were in the Muslim world (Geopol Intelligence, 2015)
- Muslims are the least willing to pay more to support efforts to improve the environment (Pew Global Attitudes, 2010)

Islam's response to Muslims' disregard of the environment closely parallels the intersectionality of the ecofeminist view. Ecofeminists note that the degradation and domination of the environment by humans is "directly connected to a set of cultural, psychological and economic factors that create hierarchies, which in turn oppress women and other vulnerable segments of society" (Ammar, 2003, 1). A draft of a declaration on climate change, launched officially at a major Islamic symposium in Istanbul in August 2015, underscores this similarity; it notes:

> Their [rich countries'] reluctance to share in the burden they have imposed on the rest of the human community by their own profligacy is noted with great concern... Wealthy oil-producing countries must refocus their concerns from profit to the environment and to the poor of the world. (Cooke, 2015)

The ecofeminist perspective parallels Islam's environmental response in that both see a multitude of cultural and behavioral factors as contributing to the corruption of the environment and humanity. These include, but are not limited to, excessive consumption of goods and services, increased violence against children, anti-intellectualism and opposition to science and scientific knowledge, and maintaining women's lesser status.

Excessive Consumption of Goods and Services

While Muslims are not the only group that has indulged in excessive consumerism in the last half-century, and are not uniform in their consumption patterns, excessive consumption among oil-rich Muslims is evident. Even during the most spiritual month of Ramadan binge-eating and wastage by Muslims throughout the world has been reported. An article published by *Al Bawaba Business* (July 4, 2014) notes that, "In Qatar, it has become an annual occurrence for people to be hospitalized from eating too much at *iftar* [sunset meal] and *suhoor* [pre-dawn meal]. While in Dubai landfill sites see an increase of 20% of food during Ramadan alone." The same article notes that consumption is said to increase by 30% in the Arabian Gulf countries during this period. Such behavior unnecessarily burdens the agricultural production system and creates significant pollution, while enabling a discourse of ignorance and continued environmental exploitation—uncharacteristic actions and omissions of vice-regents.

Increasing Neglect of and Violence against Children

While data about child abuse in the Muslim world is almost non-existent, there are various phenomena that reflect the increasing disrespect for children in Muslim countries. Gohir (2010, 1) writes about the *bacha bazi* (toy boy) custom in which boys are dressed in women's clothes and are made to entertain a male audience by dancing before they are "carted away by men for sex." Khaled Hosseini's (2003) famous novel *The Kite Runner* describes this custom in detail when one of the main characters is captured by the Taliban and becomes involved in this. Gohir (2010) notes that the custom has been revived in two Muslim majority countries that adopt the Islamic *Shar'iah*: Afghanistan and Pakistan.

Another example of child abuse is the phenomenon of street children—often the outcome of physical or sexual abuse in the home (Ammar, 2007). Research has shown, for example, that in Pakistan in 2014 there were more than 1.5 million street children (Karim, 2014), and in Indonesia in 2013 there were 4.5 million (Rikin and Ludji, 2013). The Scorecard of the Save the Children Report on the State of Mothers (2015, 5) found that out of the 11 countries where the urban child survival gaps are largest, seven (64%) are either Muslim majority countries or have a large Muslim population (Bangladesh, Ghana, India, Kenya, Madagascar, Nigeria, and Zimbabwe). The report indicates that "In these countries, poor urban children are 3 to 5 times as likely to die as their most affluent peers" (2015, 5).

In contrast to these realities, the religious texts are full of examples of how to be kind to all creatures, including children. The following saying from the Prophet exemplifies this. A man by the name Al-Aqra' said to the Prophet that he "has ten children and have never kissed one of them." The Prophet's response was "whoever is not merciful to others will not be treated mercifully" (Sahih Al-Bukhari, n.d., 1224).

Anti-intellectualism and Opposition to Science

The state of knowledge production in the Muslim world is another problem that contributes to the degradation of the environment and other creations of God. Many Muslims and Muslim countries have become suspicious of intellectualism and science. Hence, the level of knowledge has deteriorated to the point that myths and ideology direct the course of many human affairs in Muslim countries. While there is variation, it is no exaggeration to argue that most of the educational curriculum in Muslim countries depends on rote memorization and includes little space for the development of critical or independent thinking (Ammar, 2003). Hoodbhoy (2007, 5) shows the level of scientific and intellectual productivity in the Muslim world by noting that in 2007 the "seven most productive Muslim countries combined produced fewer scientific papers than did India by itself." Similarly, a US Patent and Trademark Office Report (2009, 3) shows that in the years between 1963 and 2009, the 57 countries of the Organization of the Islamic Conference (OIC) "obtained half of the patents awarded to Norway ... [constituting] less than 0.06% of the patents ... granted worldwide over the same period." Today, only one Muslim country invests more than 1% of its GDP in research and development: Tunisia (Sherani, 2013). This is the educational achievement and scientific productivity of an Islamic world that was once a pioneer in scientific knowledge, architecture, and art (Bakar, 1999). This is a community that has many religious commands on learning and knowledge which the following Qur'anic verse exemplifies: "My Lord! Enrich me with Knowledge" (Qur'an-Taha 20: 114).

Ecofeminism, Islamic Environmental Ethics, and Women's Status

There is no doubt that an Islamic environmental ethics perspective sees a direct relationship between the mistreatment of women and the degradation of the environment. This relationship is apparent in ideas on respecting all God's creatures. The Qur'an and the Prophet's sayings and traditions speak to women's rights and responsibilities very clearly. Islam denies the concept of women as seductresses, responsible for original sin and the Fall (Shahroor, 2000). Islam sees males and females as equal, as is evident in many chapters of the Qur'an (Qur'an-Al Hujirat, Qur'an-49: 13, Qur'an-Al Shura 42: 11). This reflects the grace of God, as the Qur'an says, "And Allah [has] made for you from yourselves spouses, and has made for you from your spouse's children and grandchildren and has provided for you from the good things. Then in falsehood do they believe, and in the Favor of Allah they disbelieve?" (Qur'an-Al Nahl 14: 72). However, the Qur'an is a complex book containing a number of metaphoric and abstract meanings that have been interpreted in ways to discriminate against women. Suffice it to use Wadud's (1999, 16) argument that the "complete meaning of allegorical verses [the revelation] describes itself as allegorical, (Qur'an-Ali Imran, 3: 7) cannot be empirically determined ... my discussion then is primarily a discussion of language." It is the patriarchal and other conditions, including insufficient knowledge of the Qur'anic language or any Arabic, that have led to such prejudicial and misogynist interpretations.

A number of scholars have in recent decades provided alternative/corrective egalitarian interpretations. They include Abou Fadle (2014), Ahmed (1992), Barlas (2002), Mernissi (1987, 1997, 2009), Stowasser (1998), and Waddud (1999). Such interpretations are in step with ecofeminist ideas about the relationship between the domination of women and the domination of Nature. For example, in the Qur'an the role of *Khalifah* was given to humans—both men and women. The Qur'anic verse says,

> And when your Lord said to the angels: I am making a Khalifah on the Earth. They said: Are You making therein one who corrupts it and sheds blood, while we hymn Your praise and sanctify You? He said: Surely I know that which you do not know. (Al-Baqara, 2: 30)

However, patriarchal interpretations, such as Al-Tabri's and Al-Qurtubi's, have emphasized that God made Adam his successor (Saliba, 1985). Barlas (2002), in her book about the unreading of patriarchal interpretations in the Qur'an, notes that the attempt to make the *Khalifah* only Adam anthropomorphizes God by making him masculine, something that contradicts the strict Islamic dictum of God's Oneness and Difference. In support of the argument that an interpretation that effaces women as *Khalifah* from the Qur'anic verse is a patriarchal imposition one can look at the Al Baqarah Qur'anic chapter, vv. 30 and 31. Verse 30 uses the word *Khalifah* in reference to humans as vice-regents when it says, "Behold, thy Lord said to the Angels: 'I will create a vice-regent (*Khalifah*) on earth.'" However, verse 31 uses the word "Adam" when comparing the angel's knowledge to Adam's. If God's revelation wanted to single out Adam, the male, as the only vice-regent, then why is it that verse 30 uses *Khalifah*, if not to include both females and males?

These patriarchal readings of the Qur'an, and other informational sources about Islam, have gone hand-in-hand with the degradation of the environment, as well as other oppressions, such as religious discrimination, inequality, and authoritarianism in Muslim majority countries. Today, Muslim women's status as a group leaves a lot to be desired. The Global Gender Gap Index 2014 ranks countries according to their proximity to gender equality, rather than to women's empowerment. Out of 142 countries, the five countries with the largest gender gaps were Muslim majority countries (The World Economic Forum, 2014).[4] Similarly, Arab countries—making up less than one-third of Muslims in the world, are all (with the exception of Lebanon) considered majority Muslim countries[5]—have the world's lowest levels of female participation in the labor force and in parliament (Economic and Social Commission for Western Asia [ESCWA], 2015). In a number of Arab countries women earn less than men for the same job. According to an ESCWA report, in "Egypt, Jordan, Palestine and Syria, women's wages in manufacturing as a share of men are 66%, 68%, 50% and 79% respectively" (Economic and Social Commission for Western Asia, 2015, 12). In Indonesia, the country with the largest Muslim population, discriminatory local laws against women more than doubled from 154 to 334 between 2009 and 2013, the rate of unemployment for women is high (47%), and more women than men are employed in the informal sector (UN Women, 2012). In Nigeria, one of the larger Muslim countries, 60–80% of the rural workforce, the lowest paid sector, are women (British Council, 2012).

The inconsistencies in the conditions and non-religious factors influencing Muslim majority countries make it hard to present a generalized picture of the status of women as solely influenced by Islam. Regardless, the data presented here illustrate how the patriarchal interpretations of Islam have contributed to the decline in the status of women and the environment. In reality, these conditions are an outcome of humans not following the moral imperative of Islam: to protect, be kind, just, and merciful to God's Creation. As both are creations of the Almighty God, the wellbeing of women and the environment is crucial in Islamic devotion. Thus, in line with an ecofeminist perspective, it is the patriarchal culture, influenced by the capitalist/free market global system, which enables a discourse of Islam filled with inequality, domination, and exploitation.

Patriarchal Interpretation of the Islamic Perspective on the Environment and Women

For ecofeminists, the degradation of the environment is not a biospheric issue but an ecological one of domination of the environment and women, as well as vulnerable species. This interrelated view of domination and corruption on Earth resulting in the degradation of the environment is consistent with the Islamic message of the seventh century CE. This corruption is mentioned 19 times in the Qur'an; the following verse exemplifies the warnings against it:

> And remember when He made you successors after the 'Aad and settled you in the land, [and] you take for yourselves palaces from its plains and carve from the mountains, homes. Then remember the favors of Allah and do not commit abuse on the earth, spreading corruption. (Qur'an-Al Araf 7: 74)

There are various reasons for the current patriarchal domination, some of which are not of the making of the Muslim population, such as [post]colonialism and global hierarchies, while others are associated with Muslims' (lack of) responsibility, both those living in Muslim majority countries and as minorities elsewhere. An example of the latter is the continued and increased patriarchal and aggressive interpretations of Islamic texts. These are not a new phenomenon, but the consequences, such as global pollution and its disproportionate impact on the vulnerable, including women, now extend beyond the Islamic world. While there is a long history of corrective interpretative traditions in Islamic history, they have largely been thwarted by strong opposition, exemplifying the systemic power of tradition and the case of Muslims' very rigid patriarchy.

Nevertheless, more recently some "patriarchal unreadings" (borrowing from Barlas, 2002) of Islamic texts have emerged and are widespread. However, when these "unreadings" have taken place in Muslim majority countries there have been attempts to suppress them (e.g., Fatima Mernissi's work has been banned in Morocco many times). The mushrooming "patriarchal unreadings" scholarship of Islamic texts has been mostly conducted in the West. While this has advanced a number of ideas, availability is limited to those who can read European languages, as there have been very few attempts to translate them into languages that are understood by people in Muslim majority countries (Indonesia may be the exception). Such perspectives are also significantly subject to ideological critiques accusing the authors of projecting "Orientalism," "blasphemy," or "stereotyping" Muslim women and Muslim societies.

This "unreading" faces another longstanding difficulty that is becoming more and more entrenched among Muslim masses who are semi-literate or, if educated, are more credentialed than learned. This difficulty is the elevation of the Prophet's sayings to a holy status, sometimes overriding the Qur'anic text (*nasikha al Quran*). A good case in point here is the practice of stoning. This is not mentioned in the Qur'an, but there has been a school of interpreters that see the Prophet's sayings as having the theological ability to "abrogate" the Qur'an (Kusha & Ammar, 2014).

There are some religious leaders who have even resorted to unacceptable interpretations by claiming that God revealed a verse on stoning to the Prophet, but it was stored in a place where wild birds destroyed it (Kusha & Ammar, 2014). There are a number of problems in accepting this practice. First, it contradicts theologically the strict monotheism and reverence required in Islam, that God alone is the Almighty. He created everything in balance (Qur'an Al-Ala, 87: 1–5, Qur'an-Al-Baqarah, 2: 29) and perfected everything He created, that is to say, He does not make mistakes, including in the revelation (Qur'an-As-Sajdah, 32: 7). The Prophet, while a respected and beloved messenger, was human. The Prophet's words and sayings are subject to human conditions and cannot revoke God's revelations. Shahroor (2000) notes that, in an attempt to impose unenlightened interpretations, some scholars go as far as ignoring the most elemental ideas in Islam. In addition to the theological problem of elevating the Prophet's sayings to the status of the Qur'anic scripture there is a sociopolitical issue in the use of fabricated sayings. The fabrication of the Prophet's sayings has been one such issue since the eighth century and has resulted in the development of a science of *hadith* (*Ilm alhadith*). This classifies the Prophet's sayings as *sahih* (authentic), *hasan* (good), and *dai'f* (weak) (Ammar, 1980). Today, six collections of *hadiths* (Bukhari, Muslim, Tirmidi, Nasa'i, Ibn Majah, and Abu Da'wod) are the most respected (Ammar, 1995). The problem today is that often misogynist weak *hadiths* are being repeated in communal mosques, neighborhood religious gatherings, or even in Qur'anic schools with very little opposition and often in direct contradiction to the words and spirit of the Qur'an. Various media, both traditional (television, radio, and newspapers) and social (especially the internet, but also Twitter and phone apps), have supported the elevation of such weak *hadiths*, entrenching religious myths that are far from Islamic in spirit. These weak *hadiths* are often used to justify oppression and patriarchal attitudes toward women, other vulnerable groups, and the environment.

Conclusion

While the environment is meant to be treated with ecological stewardship according to Islamic environmental ethics, this has been devastatingly overshadowed by sociohistorical conditions that have rendered it marginal in Muslims' devotional duties. While engaging with environmentally damaging behaviors such as wanton waste, wars, industrial pollution, and indifference to ecological protection, the Muslim community cannot effectively practice the custodial duty entrusted to it by God. The same argument extends to the wellbeing, status, and treatment of women, for both the environment and women are considered as part of Creation and should be treated responsibly and with respect and equity. This Islamic environmental view overlaps with ecofeminism's argument that women and the environment must be treated similarly—that is, free from exploitation.

It is thus essential for scholars to continue their work on "unreaping" patriarchy in Islamic texts. Nasr, the pioneer scholar in Islamic environmental thought, observes that "[t]he Islamic view of the natural order of the environment, as everything else that is Islamic, has its roots in the Qur'an, the very Word of Allah, which is the central theophany of Islam" (Nasr, 1998, 119). It is important to retrieve this central religious component of Islam. One way is to conduct research on the spread of the Islamic message at the local level. Such research could contribute to a better understanding of how a religious tradition about mercy, justice, and protection of God's Creation is paradoxically leading to environmental depletion and other corruptions on Earth. It is possible, necessary, and desirable that diverse discrete perspectives be bridged in order to conceptualize the realities of the world today.

Notes

1 God is neither male nor female, and the imposition of the male pronoun is a linguistic framing following Arabic grammar and mistranslation.
2 Qur'anic verse in the *Fater* (Chapter 35) verse 30 uses the plural *Khali'f*, which is different from the standard Arabic plural *Khulafah*, He is Who has made you successors (caliphs) on the Earth. So he who disbelieves, his disbelief will be on him (He will bear the consequences) (*Fater*, 35: 39).
3 [Qur'an- 2: 269] "He [Allah] grants *wisdom* to whom He pleases; and the one to whom wisdom is granted indeed receives a benefit overflowing. But none will grasp the Message except men of understanding. [Qur'an-2: 114] But say, 'O my Sustainer! Increase my *knowledge* [Qur'an-3: 190–191]. Verily in the creation of the heavens and the earth, and the alternation of night and day there are indeed signs for humans of *understanding* [Qur'an-39: 9]. Say, are those who know equal to those who know not? [Qur'an-58: 11] ... Allah will raise up to [suitable] ranks [and degrees] those of you who believe and who have been granted *knowledge*."
4 These countries are Yemen, Pakistan, Chad, Syria, and Mali.
5 The Arab Middle East–North Africa region while associated with Islam does not have the largest population of Muslims; Indonesia does. However, the region has the highest concentration of Muslims relative to any region of the world: 93% of its approximately 341 million inhabitants are Muslim, compared with 30% in sub-Saharan Africa and 24% in the Asia-Pacific region (DeSilver, 2013).

References

Ahmed, L. 1992. *Women and Gender in Islam: Historical Roots of a Modern Debate*. New Haven, CT: Yale University Press.

Al Bawaba Business. 2014. The Economics of Ramadan: from Piety to Commercialization and Excessive Consumption. July 14. SyndiGate.info. http://www.albawaba.com/business/ramadan-islam-commercialization-588028.

Al-Faruqi, I. R. & Al Faruqi, L. I. 1986. *Cultural Atlas of Islam*. London: Macmillan.

Ali, A. Y. 1994. *The Holy Qur'an: Text and Translation*. Kuala Lumpur: Islamic Book Trust.

Ammar, Nawal. 1980. Islam: Religion and way of life. (Unpublished Honours Dissertation). Salford University, Salford, United Kingdom.

Ammar, N. H. 1995. "Islam, Population, and the Environment: A Textual and Jurisdiction View." In Harold Coward, *Population, Consumption, and the Environment: Religious and Secular Responses*, Albany: SUNY Press, 123–36.

Ammar, N. 2000. An Islamic Response to the Manifest Ecological Crisis: Issues of Justice (230–226). In H. Coward & D. Maguire (Eds.). *Visions of a New Earth: New Vision on Population, Consumption and Ecology*. New York: SUNY Press.

Ammar, N. 2003. Islam, Justice and Deep Ecology (285–300). In R. Gottlieb (Ed.), *Liberating Faith: Religious Voices for Justice, Peace, and Ecological Wisdom*. Evanston, IL: Rowman & Littlefield.

Ammar, N. 2005. *Islam and Eco-justice. Environmental Ethics and Encyclopedia of Religion and Nature*. Ed. Bron R. Taylor. London: Thoemmes/Continuum, pp. 862–866.

Ammar, N. H. 2007. Wife Battery in Islam: A Comprehensive Understanding of Interpretations. *Violence against Women*, 13, 516–526.

Bakar, O. 1999. *The History and Philosophy of Islamic Science*. Philosophical Research Online. https://philpapers.org/rec/BAKTHA.

Barlas, A. 2002. *Believing Women in Islam: Unreading Patriarchal Interpretations of the Qur'an*. Karachi: SAMA Editorial & Publishing Services, pp. 361–368.

British Council. 2012. *Gender in Nigeria Report 2012: Improving the Lives of Girls and Women in Nigeria*. London: British Council. https://www.gov.uk/government/uploads/system/uploads/attachment_data/file/67333/Gender-Nigeria2012.pdf.

Bosworth, C. E., Van Donzel, E., Lewis, B., & Pellat, C. 1986. *Encyclopaedia of Islam*, Vol. 5 (Khe-Mahi). Brill Archive.

Chishti, S. K. K. 2003. Fitra: An Islamic Model for Humans and the Environment (67–84). In Richard C. Foltz, Frederick M. Denny, & Azizan Baharuddin (Eds.), *Islam and Ecology: A Bestowed Trust*. Cambridge, MA: Harvard University Press.

Cole, L. & Foster, S. 2001. *From the Ground Up: Environmental Racism and the Rise of the Environmental Justice Movement*. New York: New York University Press.

Cooke, K. 2015. Muslim Scholars Say Climate Change Poses Dire Threat. *Climate News Network*. July 15. https://www.climatenewsnetwork.net/muslim-scholars-say-climate-change-poses-dire-threat/.

d'Eaubonne, F. (1999a). Feminism—Ecology: Revolution or Mutation? *Ethics and the Environment*, 4, 175–177.

d'Eaubonne, F. 1999b. What Could an Ecofeminist Society Be? *Ethics and the Environment*, 4, 179–184.

DeSilver, D. 2013. World's Muslim Population More Widespread than You Might Think. Pew Research Center, June 7. http://www.pewresearch.org/fact-tank/2017/01/31/worlds-muslim-population-more-widespread-than-you-might-think/.

Economic and Social Commission for Western Asia. 2015. Access to Justice for Women and Girls in the Arab Region: From Ratification to Implementation of International Instruments. https://www.unescwa.org/publications/access-justice-women-arab-region-2015.

El Fadle, K. A. 2014. *Speaking in God's Name: Islamic Law, Authority and Women*. London: Oneworld Publications.

Food and Agriculture Organization of the United Nations. 2010. *Global Forest Resources Assessment: Main Report*. http://www.fao.org/docrep/013/i1757e.

Geopol Intelligence. 2005. *Global Conflict Tracker—Interactive Guide to the World's Conflict Zones*. http://www.geopolintelligence.com/global-conflict-tracker-interactive-guide-to-the-worlds-conflict-zones/.

Gohir, S. 2010. The Hypocrisy of Child Abuse in Many Muslim Countries. *The Guardian*.

April 24. http://www.theguardian.com/commentisfree/2010/apr/25/middle-east-child-abuse-pederasty.

Heckenberg, D. 2011. Studying Environmental Crime (9–23). *Environmental Crime: A Reader*. Portland, OR: Willan.

Hoodbhoy, P. A. 2007. Science and the Islamic World: The Quest for Rapprochement. *Physics Today*, 60, 49–55.

Hosseini, K. 2003. *The Kite Runner*. New York: Riverhead Books.

Karim, S. 2014. Pakistan's Street Children: Concrete Dreams. *The Express Tribune*. June 1. https://tribune.com.pk/story/714378/pakistans-street-children-concrete-dreams/.

Khalid, F. M. & O'Brien, J. 1992. *Islam and Ecology*. London: Burns & Oates.

Kusha, H. R., & Ammar, N. H. (2014). Stoning Women in the Islamic Republic of Iran: Is it Holy Law or Gender Violence? *Arts and Social Sciences Journal*.

Merchant, C. 1980. *The Death of Nature: Women, Ecology, and the Scientific Revolution: A Feminist Reappraisal of the Scientific Revolution*. New York: Doubleday/Anchor.

Mernissi, F. 1987. *Beyond the Veil: Male–Female Dynamics in Modern Muslim Society* (Vol. 423). Bloomington, IN: Indiana University Press.

Mernissi, F. 1997. *The Forgotten Queens of Islam*. Minneapolis, MN: University of Minnesota Press.

Mernissi, F. 2009. *Islam and Democracy: Fear of the Modern World*. New York: Basic Books.

Moore, N. 2008. Eco/Feminism, Non-Violence and the Future of Feminism. *International Feminist Journal of Politics*, 10, 282–298.

Nasr, S. H. 1998. Sacred Science and the Environmental Crisis: An Islamic Perspective. *Islam and the Environment*, 118–137.

Parikh, J. 2007. *Gender and Climate Change: Framework for Analysis, Policy and Action*. United Nations Development Program in India. https://www.gdnonline.org/resources/UNDP_Gender_and_Climate_Change.pdf.

Pew Research Center: Global Attitudes & Trends. 2010. *Environmental Issues*. http://www.pewglobal.org/2010/06/17/chapter-8-environmental-issues-2/.

Rikin, A. & Ludji, R. 2013. Indonesia Sets 2014 Target For Pulling Children Off Streets. *Jakarata Globe*. July 22. http://thejakartaglobe.beritasatu.com/news/indonesia-sets-2014-target-for-pulling-children-off-streets/.

Sahih Al-Bukhari. 1998. *Sunnah.Com*. https://sunnah.com/bukhari.

Saliba, G. 1985. *The History of Al-Tabarī: Ta'rīkh Al-rusul Wa'l-mulūk* (Vol. XXXVIII). New York: SUNY Press.

Saniotis, A. 2012. Muslims and Ecology: Fostering Islamic Environmental Ethics. *Contemporary Islam*, 6, 155–171.

Save the Children. 2015. *The Urban Disadvantage: State Of The World's Mothers 2015*. Fairfield, CT. http://www.savethechildren.org/atf/cf/%7B9def2ebe-10ae-432c-9bd0-df91d2eba74a%7D/SOWM_2015.PDF.

Shahroor, M. 2000. Applying the Concept of "Limits" to the Rights of Muslim Women. *Islam and Human Rights*.

Sherani, S. 2013. Economies of the Ummah. *Dawn*, August 12. http://www.dawn.com/news/1035026.

Stowasser, B. 1998. Gender Issues and Contemporary Quran Interpretation. *Islam, Gender, and Social Change*, 30, 44.

Twine, R. 2010. Intersectional Disgust? Animals and (Eco)Feminism. *Feminism and Psychology*, 20, 397–406.

UN Women. 2012. *Indonesia*. http://asiapacific.unwomen.org/en/countries/indonesia.

Wadud, A. 1999. *Qur'an and Woman: Rereading the Sacred Text from a Woman's Perspective*. London: Oxford University Press.

Wihbey, J. 2012. "Green Muslims," Eco-Islam and Evolving Climate Change Consciousness. *Yale Climate Connections*. http://www.yaleclimateconnections.org/2012/04/green-muslims-eco-islam-and-evolving-climate-change-consciousness/.

World Bank Group. 2015. *The Little Green Data Book 2015*. Washington, DC: International Bank for Reconstruction and Development/ The World Bank. https://openknowledge.worldbank.org/bitstream/handle/10986/22025/9781464805608.pdf.

World Bulletin. 2015. Egypt: 586 People Hospitalised over Water Poisoning. April 25. http://www.worldbulletin.net/middle-east/158319/egypt-586-people-hospitalised-over-water-poisoning.

World Economic Forum. 2014. *The Global Gender Gap Report 2014*. http://reports.weforum.org/global-gender-gap-report-2014/.

CHAPTER 23

The Divine Environment (*al-Muhit*) and the Body of God

Seyyed Hossein Nasr and Sallie McFague Resacralize Nature

Ian S. Mevorach

Introduction

Christianity and Islam are the two largest and fastest growing religions on Earth. According to the latest report from the Pew Research Center (2015), by 2050 just over 60% of the global population will be either Muslim or Christian. In the face of our planetary ecological crisis, as well as the related crises of economic inequality and hyper-militarization, the need for dialogue and cooperation between Christians and Muslims is evident. This dialogue has just begun. It has yet to bear fruit in intentional cooperation for Earth's healing.

Seyyed Hossein Nasr, a respected Muslim philosopher, sought to initiate a Muslim–Christian dialogue on the ecological crisis in 1966 with his four Rockefeller Lectures at the University of Chicago Divinity School. They were published in 1968 as *Man and Nature: The Spiritual Crisis in Modern Man* (Nasr, 1968a). In this work, Nasr expresses hope that Christians will find, in dialogue with Islam (especially the mystical insights of Sufism), an occasion to recover their own spiritual vision of Nature as exemplified by Christian mystics such as Francis of Assisi, Hildegard of Bingen, and Julian of Norwich. In Nasr's historical and philosophical analysis, the ecological crisis has its genesis mainly in the secularism and scientism of the Western world, where the desacralization of Nature originated and from which it has since spread around the globe. However, Christianity's neglect of its own spiritual vision of Nature, and corresponding metaphysical cosmology, set the stage for this desacralization. Therefore, the recovery of Christianity's spiritual vision of Nature is essential to the global process of resacralizing Nature.

Unfortunately, Nasr's call has not been heard by contemporary Christian eco-theologians, who have virtually ignored Islam as a potential dialogue partner. One notable exception is John Hart, who briefly summarizes Nasr's views in *Cosmic Commons*

The Wiley Blackwell Companion to Religion and Ecology, First Edition. Edited by John Hart.

(Hart, 2013, 37–41) and compares them with Alister McGrath's *The Reenchantment of Nature* (2002). Hart notes the similarities of their visions: "They call for a religious recovery of traditional attitudes toward and actions upon Earth, so that Nature might be 'resacralized' (Nasr) and 'reenchanted' (McGrath)" (47). This juxtaposition of Nasr's and McGrath's views serves as an enticement to a Christian–Muslim dialogue on the ecological crisis: there is potential to find common ground.

This chapter explores a dialogical pairing of Nasr with a different thinker, Christian ecofeminist theologian Sallie McFague. In 1990, during the Spirit and Nature Symposium at Middlebury College, Vermont, Nasr and McFague engaged in dialogue in the context of a broader interfaith panel, including the Dalai Lama and leaders from other world religions (Rockefeller & Elder, 1992). Nasr and McFague, committed to the healing of the Earth, had come to the table of dialogue in order to build interfaith understanding and solidarity in face of the ecological crisis. However, they were unable to recognize their common ground. In tension with Nasr's traditionalist prescription for Christianity to restore its spiritual vision of Nature by recovering a medieval cosmology and mysticism, McFague's postmodern eco-theology calls for the deconstruction and reconstruction of the Christian tradition. This methodological divide led to two key differences that effectively blocked their dialogue.

To begin with, McFague and Nasr disagree about the use of traditional male language for God: McFague is committed to the deconstruction of patriarchal images of God; Nasr is committed to their preservation. Their other major disagreement concerns the relationship of theology and evolutionary thought. Nasr rejects evolutionary theory and secular science in general as a theological source, whereas McFague accepts and integrates the theory of evolution and insights from the postmodern sciences into her theological vision. These specific dialogue obstacles are not particular to Christians and Muslims. The debate about evolution has occupied Christians since the Fundamentalist–Modernist Controversy of the early twentieth century; the debate about gendered language for God has been active since the 1970s. Among Christians, conservatives generally prefer male language, while liberals favor balanced or gender-neutral language; conservatives often reject or marginalize evolutionary thought in their theologies, while liberals tend to accept and integrate evolutionary thought and other contemporary scientific theories into their theologies. The conflicts that are particular to Christians and Muslims are more profound and have far deeper historical roots. In an intentional and sustained Muslim–Christian dialogue, traumatic memories of violent conflicts going back to the Crusades and polemical misunderstandings of each other's beliefs going back to the seventh century would inevitably be raised. An empathetic and thorough dialogue on these subjects might help to heal and re-establish the relationship of Christianity and Islam as one of cooperation rather than competition. Working through the differences between Nasr and McFague is important groundwork for Muslim–Christian dialogue, though only a beginning.

It should be recognized and celebrated that there have been groundbreaking Muslim–Christian dialogues in recent years, especially those prompted by "A Common Word" (2007), an open letter inviting dialogue with Christians, which has been signed by hundreds of influential Muslim sheiks and scholars, including Seyyed Hossein Nasr, who played an important role in the drafting process. This letter has inspired numerous constructive responses, including two national Baptist–Muslim dialogues in which I participated. These dialogues, held at Andover Newton Theological School in Newton, Massachusetts, were based on the two principles for Muslim–Christian unity that "A Common Word" puts forth: love of God and love of neighbor. I saw firsthand in these dialogues how the crisis of religiously polarized war and the need to make peace has inspired significant willingness among Christians and Muslims to work through long-standing conflicts and misunderstandings in order to find common ground.

Taking the ecological crisis as a starting place opens a new dialogical space for Christians and Muslims. The central epiphany of ecological consciousness—that human beings and all beings are interdependent parts of the same web of life—can serve as its centering theme. Rather than seeing religious differences as signs of separateness or incompatibility, we can celebrate religio-diversity (which is akin to biodiversity) as a sign of health and life. We can embrace synergistic, win–win relationships as we work together to heal the Earth and establish a life-sustaining society.

The dialogue between the ideas of Nasr and McFague presented here will, of necessity, proceed in a hypothetical, imaginative mode. Nasr and McFague did not achieve a fruitful exchange of ideas. Yet beneath a veneer of obvious disagreement and incompatibility, the spiritual visions of Nature that McFague and Nasr articulate throughout their works resonate harmoniously. Their theological responses to the common problem of the ecological crisis are complementary and mutually reinforcing. Despite consistent ideological differences, there is a mystical unity at the heart of their perspectives that may inspire Christians and Muslims alike to turn from a desacralized view of the world as a lifeless machine for human beings to use, toward a vision of the Earth as a living body inbreathed by the Spirit of God.

Dialoguing Through Differences

Beginning with the Problem

The common ground of Nasr and McFague begins with their similar understandings that the ecological crisis is rooted in a spiritual crisis—modern humanity's loss of a spiritual vision of Nature. Both regard the rise of modernity as a "fall" from pre-modern ways of appreciating Nature's sacred value. In this fall, Earth—which people throughout the world have traditionally viewed as a sacred body of which human beings are a part—came to be viewed as a machine-like object to be controlled and exploited for the exclusive benefit of human beings.

In this fall, modern humanity lost the spiritual knowledge that "the very stuff of the Universe" is sacred and "the very structure of the cosmos contains a spiritual message for man and is thereby a revelation coming from the same source as religion itself" (Nasr, 1968a, 21). Nasr attributes this fall mainly to the influence of the secularizing forces of Renaissance and Enlightenment science (64–74), but also notes that Christianity's God/world and sacred/secular dualism, anti-naturalism, and remote God-concept laid the groundwork for this (55–57). For Nasr the desacralization of Nature is characterized primarily by the loss of the symbolic meaning of Nature in regard to "other orders of reality" (21). Nature as symbol points beyond itself: it both veils and reveals higher orders of spiritual reality. Yet for modern humanity, Nature is opaque and meaningless, a veil not recognized as a veil but seen as the totality of reality. Modern human beings, without a higher spiritual and ethical reference point beyond their earthly existence, perceive Nature as having merely an instrumental value in meeting human needs.

As in Nasr's version of the modern fall, in McFague's version the ecological crisis grows out of the Cartesian objectification and Newtonian mechanization of Nature; it is rooted in an inability to recognize the sacredness of Nature and humanity's interconnection with Nature. But McFague tells the story differently because she does not believe that recovery of a medieval worldview is possible or desirable. McFague argues that "The Great Chain of Being at the heart of the medieval picture, with God at the top as the transcendent Determiner of Destiny and all creatures arranged in descending order—angels, men, women, children, animals, plants, matter—is antithetical to an ecological and feminist perspective." She takes issue with the medieval model because of its extreme transcendent definition of God as king of a hierarchically arranged universe; this imagery, she argues, supports an unjust social hierarchy, also known as patriarchy. Therefore, McFague is "by no means suggesting it as a picture to which we can return ... rather, what it suggests is that we must do *for our time* what that picture did for its time—namely, work out a functional cosmology" (McFague, 1997, 53).

McFague and Nasr agree that the spiritual crisis underlying the ecological crisis begs the question of cosmology and demands the revival of our spiritual vision of Nature; but they differ sharply regarding hierarchical cosmology. For Nasr, in order to "see the cosmos as theophany and not veil, it is necessary to return again and again to the truth that reality is hierarchic, that the cosmos is not exhausted by its physical aspect alone" (Nasr, 1981, 197). At issue theologically is Nasr's insistence that any true cosmology must include a transcendent spiritual dimension of reality beyond the physical world. At least in her initial eco-theology in *The Body of God*, McFague (1993) does not speak of God being beyond the world. However, as her eco-theology develops, especially after her fourth conversion—an awakening to God as love and reality, described in *Life Abundant* (2001, 8–9)—McFague unapologetically affirms God's existence beyond the world while still eschewing patriarchal and hierarchical images for God. Over their careers, the doctrines of the God–world relationship that Nasr and McFague espouse move closer as McFague strengthens her concept of God's transcendence beyond the world and Nasr strengthens his concept of God's immanence in the world. While retaining their distinctiveness, their functional cosmologies become increasingly compatible.

The World as God's Body

The major move of McFague's new model of the God–world relationship, which she proposes as a replacement for the model of God as king of the world (the prevalent model in Christian theology), is to see both God's immanence and God's transcendence as connected to the world. If God is "the inspirited body of the whole universe," then both God's transcendent dimension—the Spirit—and God's immanent dimension—the body—are intimately connected to the natural world in which we live. McFague argues that when people image God as above and apart from the world they also envision themselves as separate from and in control of the world. By bringing God closer to the world, so that we identify the world quite fully with God and vice versa, McFague hopes that we will be moved to identify with and love the world.

In *Religion and the Order of Nature* (1996), Nasr's engagement with McFague's theology centers on a passionate defense of the traditional concept of God as king of the world, which McFague deconstructs (Nasr, 1996, 196, 215). As if unwilling to proceed beyond McFague's act of theological deconstruction, Nasr does not seriously consider McFague's alternative model, the world as God's body. Nasr affirms that God is king for many reasons: it is one of God's names revealed in the Qur'an and shared by other major religious traditions; it is in accord with his political preference for monarchy rather than democracy (Nasr was aligned with the Iranian royal family and has been in exile since the last Shah—Muhammad Reza Pahlavi—was deposed in 1979); it affirms the hierarchy of the universe and majesty of God. However, this is not the model of the God–world relationship that he emphasizes in response to the ecological crisis. In fact, the Qur'anic descriptions of God that Nasr finds particularly relevant to the ecological crisis resonate with McFague's model. Because Nasr and McFague share a common mission of resacralizing Nature, their theologies find common ground despite their conflicting theological methods and ideological concerns.

McFague's and Nasr's Unity of Purpose

In *Man and Nature* (1968a) Nasr cites Hildegard of Bingen as "an eminent example of the Christian contemplative vision of Nature":

> In her vision she is addressed by the Spirit in these remarkable words:
>
> "I am that supreme and fiery force that sends forth all the sparks of life. Death hath no part in me, yet do I allot it, wherefore I am girt about with wisdom as with wings. I am that living and fiery essence of the divine substance that flows in the beauty of the fields. I shine in the water, I burn in the sun and the moon and the stars. Mine is the mysterious force of the invisible wind. I sustain the breath of all living. I breathe in the verdure, and in the flowers, and when the waters flow like living things, it is I. I founded those columns that support the whole earth ... I am the force that lies hid in the winds, from me they take their source, and as a man may move because he breathes, so doth a fire burn but by my blast. All these live because I am in them and am of their life. I am wisdom. Mine is the blast of the thundered word by which all things were made. I permeate all things that they may not die. I am life."

Directly after quoting this passage, Nasr remarks approvingly: "Here is a vision of Nature still sacred and spiritual before it became profane" (Nasr, 1968a, 102–103). This contemplative vision of Nature, especially its doctrine of God as Spirit, bears a striking resemblance to McFague's doctrine of God as the transcendently-immanent, inspirited-body of the universe.

Hildegard's presentation of her spiritual vision of Nature as a direct communication of the Spirit is vastly different from McFague's (1993) presentation of her theology of the universe as God's body, given as a reasonable, academic argument. McFague does not claim direct inspiration, but rather "suggest[s] ... that we think of God metaphorically as the spirit that is the breath, the life, of the universe, a universe that comes from God and could be seen as the body of God" (McFague, 1993, 144). Yet McFague draws her concept of God as the spirit of the universe from the "deepest traditions of Christian thought," which apparently include Hildegard of Bingen:

> That tradition is of God as spirit—not Holy Ghost, which suggests the unearthly and the disembodied, nor initially the Holy Spirit, which has been focused largely on human beings and especially the followers of Christ, but the spirit of God, the divine wind that "swept over the face of the waters" prior to creation, the life-giving breath given to all creatures, and the dynamic movement that creates, recreates, and transcreates throughout the universe. (McFague, 1993, 144)

At the heart of McFague's theology, what she calls "the prime analogy of this essay," is the affirmation that "the dust of the universe [is] enlivened by the breath of God." In language like the striking prose of Hildegard, McFague declares:

> Each of us, and each and every other part of the body as well, owes our existence, breath by breath as we inhale and exhale, to God. We "live and move and have our being" in God (Acts 17:28). Indeed we do. That is, perhaps, the most basic confession that can be made: I owe my existence at its most fundamental level—the gift of my next breath—to God. God is my creator and recreator, the One who gives and renews my life, moment by moment, at its most basic, physical level. And so does everything else in creation also live, moment by moment, by the breath of God, says our model. (McFague, 1993, 144)

McFague would be even closer to Hildegard if she ended with "says the Spirit" instead of "says our model," but the contents of their visions are profoundly in concert, both flowing from one current of biblical nature mysticism.

In light of the fall of modernity, Nasr challenges Christian theologians and philosophers to mine their tradition in order to contribute to the resacralization of Nature in human perception.

> The long tradition of the spiritual vision of Nature, with the metaphysical doctrines upon which it is based, must again be brought to life within Christianity if the encounter of man and Nature is not to result in complete disaster. Theologians and philosophers have been for the most part responsible, or at least have contributed during the past few centuries to making Nature profane, thus setting the stage for its becoming profaned through the industrial revolution and the unending applications of modern sciences. They are responsible also for reinstating a more wholesome and integral attitude toward Nature. Too many modern religious thinkers and theologians have put aside the question of Nature and considered man's salvation with a total disregard for the rest of God's creation. (Nasr, 1968a, 105–106)

McFague really does respond to Nasr's call—not his call per se, but the challenges he identifies. As much as Nasr opposes her deconstruction of the model of God as king, McFague deconstructs it precisely because she believes it has, in Nasr's words, "contributed during the past few centuries to making Nature profane." Furthermore, her theological construction of the world as God's body is in the interest, again in Nasr's words, of "reinstating a more wholesome and integral attitude toward Nature." Her theology is explicitly consistent with what Nasr calls "the long tradition of the spiritual vision of Nature" within Christianity. Her theology also transcends what Nasr laments, a singular concern with human salvation, and moves the whole Earth to the center of theological attention. McFague's eco-theology flows from her acceptance of the task of correcting what Christian theologians have done in the last few centuries to make Nature more profane. For example, McFague's new model contradicts Karl Barth's hyper-transcendent vision of God that explicitly relegates the whole realm of Nature and human experience to the realm of the "No-God," where if one tries to find or name God, one is guilty of setting up an idol (Barth, 1975 [1933], 50). Despite their differences, McFague and Nasr occupy profound common ground in how they define the Western Christian theological task regarding the ecological crisis.

God as Al-Muhit (the Divine Environment)

In *Man and Nature* (1968a), Nasr calls attention to the spiritual crisis underlying the ecological crisis, but does not advance an Islamic environmental theology per se. He argues, in broad terms, that traditional Islamic theology participates in what he calls the symbolist spirit that sees the spiritual quality of Nature, and not only its physical quantity, that does not divide people from Nature or the natural from the supernatural, and that views Nature as a sacred source of revelation on a par with the Qur'an. In "Islam and the Environmental Crisis" (1992) Nasr presents a specific proposal for an Islamic doctrine of God that is especially pertinent to the ecological crisis: God as *al-Muhit*. Here is Nasr's discourse on God as *al-Muhit* in its entirety:

> It is of the utmost significance that in the Quran God is said to be the All-Encompassing (*Muhit*), as in the verse, "But to God belong all things in the heavens and on the earth: And He it is who encompasseth (*muhit*) all things" (IV: 126); and that the term *muhit* also means environment. In reality, humans are immersed in the Divine *Muhit* and are only unaware of it because of their own forgetfulness and negligence (*ghaflah*), which is the underlying sin of the soul to be overcome by remembrance (*dhikr*). To remember God is to see Him everywhere and to experience His reality as *al-Muhit*. The environmental crisis may in fact be said to have been caused by the human refusal to see God as the real "environment" which surrounds us and nourishes our life. The destruction of the environment is the result of the modern attempt to view the natural environment as an ontologically independent order of reality, divorced from the Divine Environment without whose liberating grace it becomes stifled and dies. To remember God as *al-Muhit* is to remain aware of the sacred quality of Nature, the reality of natural phenomena as signs (*ayat*) of God and the presence of the natural environment as an ambience permeated by the Divine Presence of that Reality which alone is the ultimate "environment" from which we issue and to which we return. (Nasr, 1992, 89)

Remembering God as *al-Muhit* allows people to recognize that the natural environment is surrounded by the Divine Environment and permeated by the Divine Presence. By lifting up the divine name *al-Muhit* Nasr resacralizes Nature by remembering its intimate connection with God.

The model of God as *al-Muhit* is much closer to McFague's model of the world or environment as the inspirited body of God than it is to the idea she deconstructs—God as a distant king ruling the world. *Al-Muhit* is not patriarchal, nor does it suggest that God is apart from or over the world. Like the world as God's body, God as *al-Muhit* pictures the God–world relationship in a way that the sacredness of the world cannot be missed because of its integral connection with God. God as *al-Muhit* permeates and surrounds Nature, which is what the transcendent dimension of God's body, that is, the Spirit, does in McFague's theology. And yet, the models are certainly different. A clue to this is that Nasr does not call the natural environment God's body.

For Nasr there is a transcendent hierarchy of bodies and it is only at the top of this hierarchy that it is proper to speak of the Divine Body:

> Not only are we endowed with a physical body, but also a subtle body, an imaginal body, and even "bodies" on higher planes reaching the Divine Order itself in which it is possible to speak of the Divine Body. We possess bodies situated in a hierarchic fashion and corresponding to the various levels of the cosmic and meta-cosmic hierarchy. (Nasr, 1996, 260)

Nasr's exposition of God as *al-Muhit* explicitly includes this doctrine of transcendence, which is the most substantial area of disagreement between Nasr's thought and McFague's early eco-theology. For Nasr, God as Spirit permeating Nature is immanent, whereas for McFague the Spirit is the transcendently immanent dimension of God. For Nasr the transcendent Nature of God corresponds to higher orders of reality which go beyond the visible world altogether:

> The visible or manifested world is not an independent order of reality but a manifestation of a vastly greater world which transcends it and from which it issues. The visible world is like what one can observe around a campfire during a dark desert night. The visible gradually recedes into the vast invisible which surrounds it and for which the invisible is the veritable environment. Not only is the invisible an infinite ocean compared to which the visible is like a speck of dust, but the invisible permeates the visible itself. It is in this way that the Divine Environment, the Spirit, permeates the world of Nature and of normal humanity, nourishing and sustaining them, being at once the origin (*al-mabda'*) and entelechy or end (*al-ma'ad*) of the manifested order. (Nasr, 1992, 90–91)

Nasr's concept of God as "the Divine Environment, the Spirit" is close to McFague's. They are both panentheistic visions of God that resacralize Nature. Yet Nasr's and McFague's concepts of God diverge because of their basic cosmological differences.

Diverging and Converging Theological Cosmologies

McFague's starting point of contemporary science limits her world to the visible, and thus limits the way she envisages God, especially in God's transcendent dimension: "the 'world' in question, the world in which to understand both God and human beings, is the contemporary scientific picture of the earth, its history, and our place in it that is emerging from astrophysics and biology" (McFague, 1992, 50). For Nasr, this world of contemporary science is like a campfire flickering in a dark desert night—it is minuscule compared with the invisible world. From Nasr's perspective McFague's theology does not adequately include the dimension of God's transcendence that corresponds cosmologically to "Heaven" or the unmanifested transcendent—orders of reality beyond the earthly world of sense experience. In answer to McFague's suggestion that religion accept the contemporary scientific picture of the world, Nasr writes: "It seems that having surrendered the world of Nature to modern science, religion is now asked, in the name of the environment, to also surrender God to this science and allow a quantitative science of Nature to determine for us who have created such a science the way to understand God" (Nasr, 1996, 226, n. 25). For Nasr, the problem is not only that McFague denies the hierarchical nature of the cosmos; she also reverses the proper hierarchy between religion and science.

For Nasr, science should operate within the limits set by metaphysics, the ultimate science (Nasr, 1993). He is concerned that placing religion under the authority of a secularized science will lead to the desacralization of religion itself. As a traditionalist, he believes that religious forms are sacred revelations rather than human constructions, and hence not subject to rational or scientific criticism. As a feminist, McFague does not envision the ideal relationship between religion and science in hierarchical terms, in which one discipline's truth claims would dominate and control the other's; as in all her interdisciplinary work, McFague hopes for Christian theology to find power with, rather than power over, contemporary science. Nasr's theology of science corresponds with his doctrine of God insofar as he envisions metaphysics resacralizing science by surrounding and permeating it in an "all-encompassing" way; metaphysics should also control and have power over science, like its king. It should be noted that Nasr accepts current climate science and other contemporary scientific descriptions of the ecological crisis; for example, Rachel Carson's *Silent Spring* (1962) has been a major inspiration for his eco-theology. Nasr cannot be placed with American Christian fundamentalists whose rejection of evolutionary theory goes hand in hand with climate-change denial. In fact, Nasr's efforts to preserve the integrity of the body of the world go hand in hand with his efforts to preserve the integrity of the bodies of religious traditions.

As McFague's perspective becomes more mystical and theocentric, especially after her fourth conversion, her cosmological tensions with Nasr lessen and their common ground grows. In *Life Abundant* McFague comes to recognize that the natural world is not ontologically independent of God, who is reality (McFague, 2001). In *A New Climate for Theology*, she clearly defines this new insight in panentheistic terms: "So, to say that God is reality is not to say that God contains or includes all that is in a pantheistic fashion.

Rather, it is to say that God is that from which all else derives its being, its reality" (McFague, 2008, 164). She also makes a metaphorical addition to her model of the world as God's body which more adequately describes God's transcendence: "first, as we are to our bodies, so God is to the world (the body infused, enlivened by mind/soul/spirit); and second, the world is in God as a baby is in the womb" (McFague, 2008, 115). McFague remains true to her concerns about the distance and indifference of God as king of the world by imaging God's transcendence in a way that conveys God's intimacy with and care for the world; of course, the picture of God carrying the world like a child in the womb is anything but patriarchal. Even while critiquing McFague in *Religion and the Order of Nature* (1996), Nasr's theology of the God–world relationship comes closer to McFague's by strengthening its emphasis on God's immanence. Here he recognizes that the world is, in a certain sense, God's body or God incarnate. Nasr writes, "[O]ne can say that the order of Nature is nothing but the Divine Reality manifesting itself on the plane of phenomenal existence" (62). And again, "The order of Nature is not only created by God through His Will, but derives from the Divine Substance" (63). Nasr's philosophical description of Nature as a self-manifestation of God that "derives from the Divine Substance" comes quite close to McFague's metaphysical claim that "God is that from which all else derives its being, its reality." And her metaphor that "the world is in God like a baby in the womb" mirrors Nasr's idea of God as the Divine Environment encompassing the natural environment. To synthesize these insights on God and the world: the natural environment derives its being from the Divine Environment, the Spirit, as if it were a baby in the womb.

The Mysticism of the Body: Universal Self and Universal Man

Another area of common ground for Nasr and McFague is their appreciation of the mystical union of the human body and the body of the world. As Nasr writes: "[I]n the deepest sense the body of the cosmos is *our* body" (Nasr, 1996, 63). For him, the union of humanity and Nature is spiritually substantive, insofar as the Spirit of God animates all bodies:

> Our intimate contact with the forms of Nature around us as well as attraction to the beauty of the stars issues not from simple sentimentality but from an inner *sympatheia*, which relates us to all things, a union of essences of "inner breath" to which Rumi refers as *hamdami* and which joins us, in our mind and body bi-unity, to the world about us and finally to the entire cosmos. (Nasr, 1996, 260)

Because the Spirit within the human being is the same Spirit that inbreathes all created bodies, humans can come alive to our interconnection and deep unity with all life through our bodies. The most direct affirmation of this experience is the insight that "the world is *our* body," an insight that McFague shares, verbatim, with Nasr.

In *Blessed Are the Consumers* (2013), McFague lays out her concept of "the universal self," which she fleshes out through her readings of the lives of saints such as John

Woolman, Dorothy Day, Martin Luther King, Jr., Simone Weil, and Gandhi. They all go through a process of self-emptying or *kenosis*: "relinquishing material and emotional possessions (voluntary poverty) and diverting attention from the self to others" (111). They emerge from this process with a new sense of self that goes beyond the limits of the ego-bound individual:

> This new view could be called the "universal" self. Its signature characteristic is that it has no boundaries: the understanding of the self here does not stop with one's own body, or the bodies of one's loved ones, or the bodies of similar people, or the bodies of human beings, or even the bodies of other animals, or amazingly even all bodies, for it includes the systems that keep bodies flourishing (water, land, climate, air). (McFague, 2013, 111)

For McFague, this new experience of "the world becom[ing] my body" (202) is a natural outgrowth of love and empathy for others. She declares: "The world is your body; you are a universal self, and hence to love others as yourself means the extension of the same feelings of empathy, attention to basic needs, and concern for recognition of intrinsic value that one 'naturally' has for oneself" (115). The process of awakening to the universal self is grounded in an ethical commitment to love our neighbors, but also involves the mystical experience of the death of the ego. John Woolman, for example, had a dream in which he heard a voice say, "'John Woolman is dead'" (190). This marked his realization of the universal self. McFague suggests that the self-emptying that leads to the universal self is central "to other wisdom traditions" besides Christianity, though she is "not equipped to substantiate that claim" (154). This feeling is confirmed by a parallel theme in Nasr's work, the universal man (*al-insan al-kamil*), a concept deeply rooted in the Sufi tradition.

Nasr's use of "man" in translating this concept from Arabic (where a gender-neutral term like person is more accurate) encodes that ideological difference between Nasr, who insists on traditional male language for God and humanity, and McFague, who would never use the term "man" to speak of humanity in general or "He" to speak of God. We need to push through this significant difference regarding gender, recognizing it but not trying to resolve it here.

Nasr first describes his concept of the universal man in *Science and Civilization in Islam*: "Since the universe is the 'body' of the *Logos*, and since the *Logos* also manifests itself microcosmically in man, the gnostic gains greater intimacy with the universe the more he becomes integrated into the luminous source of his own being" (1968b, 339). Nasr states that in the Sufi tradition, "the Prophet is the Universal Man par excellence" who most fully manifests the *Logos* at the center of human nature. He also affirms that prophets and great saints of other faiths have achieved the status of universal man. While all people have the potential to manifest the universal man by virtue of our "central position in the cosmos ... higher states of being remain latent for the majority of men, and become fully realized only in the person of the gnostic, or the perfect Sufi, who has reached 'the end of the path'" (340).

Nasr also comments on this in *Man and Nature* (1968a), asserting that the goal of human existence is to become the universal man: "The purpose of man's appearance in this world is, according to Islam, in order to gain total knowledge of things, to become the Universal Man (*al-insan al-kamil*), the mirror reflecting all the Divine Names and Qualities." In Islamic mysticism humanity's reason for being in the world is reciprocal with God's reason for creating the world: "The purpose and aim of creation is in fact for God to come 'to know' Himself through His perfect instrument of knowledge that is the Universal Man" (96).

Nasr does not speak of the process of becoming the universal man primarily in ethical terms, but rather in spiritual and ontological terms: "Man sees in Nature what he is himself and penetrates into the inner meaning of Nature only on the condition of being able to delve into the depths of his own being and to cease to lie merely on the periphery of his being" (Nasr, 1968a, 96). He describes a process of awakening that begins by turning within. By getting in touch with the center of one's being one becomes aware of the intrinsic connection between one's true self and the true self of the world. Although McFague's concept of the universal self is formally based on the ethical dimension of the lives of the saints she mentions in *Life Abundant* (2001), her mystical interpretation of these lives would not have been possible without the awakening to God as love and reality that she experienced through spiritual direction and practice of daily meditation and prayer. By the same token, Nasr could also have described the robust ethical dimensions of the lives of Sufi saints whom he recognizes as embodiments of the universal man.

Nasr is convinced that human beings, especially the universal man, play an essential role in the health of the cosmos: "In fact man is the channel of grace for Nature; through his active participation in the spiritual world he casts light into the world of Nature. He is the mouth through which Nature breathes and lives... Were there to be no more contemplatives and saints, Nature would become deprived of the light that illuminates it and the air which keeps it alive" (Nasr, 1968a, 96). McFague also affirms this view of human beings as channels of grace: "When we become aware of God, who is the Alpha and Omega, as the source and goal of everything and of all life, love, and power, then we become channels for these realities both in our own lives and for others. We become available to be 'saved' (restored to health and happiness) and to help 'save' others" (McFague, 2001, 12).

Nasr's and McFague's visions of universal persons who bring grace and healing to the world beg the question of whether such persons can also bring new life to Muslim–Christian relations. The unity of the body of the world is fulfilled by the universal person, who consciously inhabits this unified body. So too, the unity of world religions requires actualization by the universal person, who recognizes the universal Spirit in the biodiversity of Creation as well as in the spiritual diversity of human cultures, religions, and spiritual understandings. The potentiality for interfaith collaboration regarding the ecological crisis cannot be fulfilled by merely outlining a method for dialogue or demonstrating that there is common ground to be discovered. Such conceptualizations are helpful guides, but they need to be fulfilled in experience by twenty-first-century ecological saints who know and feel their spiritual interconnection with persons of all beliefs.These universal persons are able to dialogue and find common ground with each other and recognize each other's "universal" connection to the Spirit that permeates all

Creation; by their example, they illuminate this unity in religio-diversity in the sight of their constituencies and make space for them to cooperate for Earth's healing.

Conclusion: Revisioning the Dialogue

In *Blessed Are the Consumers*, McFague's latest book, she gives elegant voice to the virtue of theological humility. She is more convinced than ever of the relevance and vitality of her organic model. Yet, her increasing conviction is matched by increasing humility:

> Thus what we see emerging from these reflections is a modest, relative, qualified—indeed, humble—mode of operation in which we are moved by a vision for a better world, but not in an absolute way. Utopias are important: imagining another way is critical to actually moving toward the new vision, but again, it is not up to us, the few privileged ones who can set the stage for what should happen and then control others so that our vision will dominate. We have seen many instances of totalitarian thinking—people who are certain that their vision of the way things should be is the only right way, and if not their way, no way! This mind-set is entirely alien to kenosis. (McFague, 2012, 213)

McFague is certain that her vision is a right way, but not the only right way.

In *Man and Nature*, when Nasr first opens a conversation with a Western Christian audience regarding the ecological crisis, he hopes Christians will sincerely listen to the wisdom of his tradition:

> If a day were to come when Christianity, rather than trying to convert the followers of Oriental religions, should also try to understand them and enter into an intellectual dialogue with them then Oriental metaphysics, which is also in its essence the *philosophia perennis*, as well as the cosmological doctrines of the Oriental traditions (which could also be referred to as *cosmologia perennis*), could act as a cause and occasion for recollection of elements forgotten in the Christian tradition. They could aid in restoring a spiritual vision of Nature that would be able to provide the background for the sciences. (Nasr, 1968a, 99)

Implicit in this call is Nasr's hope for mutual appreciation between Christianity and Oriental traditions, including Islam. He hopes they can engage in a dialogue that does not posit the superiority of one tradition over another, but one that is mutually enriching.

McFague and Nasr acknowledge that their theological perspectives are not absolute and exclusive, but only "relatively absolute" (Nasr 1981, 284) or a "relative absolute" (McFague, 2000, 33). Yet despite their wariness of absolutism and their openness to other perspectives, both absolutize an element of their theologies—not the Christian or Islamic element but the "postmodern" for McFague and the "traditional" for Nasr. If McFague and Nasr were religious absolutists and believed in the superiority of their religions as such, they probably would not have attempted an interfaith dialogue with one another. However, because of their methodological absolutism, they were unable to dialogue successfully.

Methodological Absolutism

Nasr considers "the real battle of the future as not being between Islam and the West, but between tradition and modernism/postmodernism in both Islam and the West and in fact throughout the world" (Nasr, 2010, 277). Beginning in *Man and Nature*, he uncompromisingly presents traditionalism as the only way for Western Christians to overcome the ecological crisis. Only through the recovery of a pre-modern cosmology, including the traditional hierarchy of Heaven over Earth, can an ecological balance be restored in the West. In *Religion and the Order of Nature* Nasr reiterates his argument that the resacralization of Nature can only be achieved through a recovery of traditional religion. Clearly, his method itself has been absolutized into an only way that invalidates postmodern Christianity and other forms of postmodern spirituality.

McFague's theological method of deconstruction and reconstruction might sound, to Nasr, as much like a battle cry as his traditional method of recovery might to her:

> We live within the models we create, and when they control our actions in ways that are diminishing and destructive, we have the responsibility to suggest alternative models. This is, I believe, action of the highest order and the greatest importance; to refuse this task is to refuse the role of human beings on the planet. We are fast destroying the planet by our actions taken within a false model, and we owe it to our earth and to each other to imagine and to embody a different vision, a different model. (McFague, 2013, 214)

Does McFague's "we" include Nasr and the Muslim world in general? Is this a cry to deconstruct the traditional Muslim conception of God or invalidate the Qur'an? No, not directly. McFague's audience is a North American Christian one. However, her argument that the model of God as king needs to be deconstructed, even if directed to a North American Christian audience, alienates Nasr and other traditional Muslims. In a traditional Muslim perspective God as king is not a humanly constructed model that one can choose to reject, but an invariable truth revealed by God in the Qur'an.

Revisions

In order to enable pathways to dialogue between Nasr and McFague (and others like them) to be opened, revision of their methodological premises is required. Nasr claims that it is only possible to restore humanity's spiritual vision of Nature by returning to pre-modern traditions. In direct contradiction, McFague argues that it is not possible to return to a pre-modern worldview. However, they agree that a shift is needed so that we see the world as a living body animated by God's Spirit rather than an inanimate machine that is ontologically independent of God. The needed revision is to remove the element of exclusivity or absoluteness from the theological methods each author proposes. Nasr's strategy of recovering a pre-modern cosmology is not the only way to restore "our" spiritual vision of Nature. If this "our" refers to all those seeking to restore a spiritual vision of Nature, rather than a select audience of traditionalists, this strategy must be seen as one of many. Likewise, McFague's postmodern construction of an organic model of the world does not require the premise that Nasr's type of recovery strategy is impossible. With a few linguistically minor but conceptually major changes, Nasr and McFague could restate their strategies for recovering a spiritual vision of Nature in ways that do not drive each other from "we" to "they."

McFague and Nasr describe ways of seeing the natural world that correct the reduction and objectification of Nature in the modern worldview. McFague speaks of viewing Nature with a "loving eye" (1997) and Nasr speaks of viewing Nature with the "eye of the heart" (1996). This empathetic way of seeing is also essential to interfaith dialogue. The arrogant eye, the ego, identifies the differences in another person's perspective as threats that could undermine one's own perspective. The loving eye, or eye of the heart, appreciates how these differences make sense from the other's perspective.

In *A New Climate for Theology*, McFague stretches in this direction of greater unity during her discussion of the doctrine of *kenosis*: "Giving space is a basic Christian doctrine, but it is also deep at the center of most religions—and it is felt in the hearts of all people, whether religious or not, who know that 'love is the discovery of reality,' the realization that something besides oneself is real" (McFague, 2008, 138). The same process of *kenosis* that is so essential to fashioning a sustainable way of life on Earth is also essential to interfaith dialogue. In order for interfaith dialogue (or dialogue between religion and science) to be successful, we need to make space for each other. When we make exclusive or absolute claims about our perspectives, we crowd others out and there is no room to stand together on common ground. The art of interfaith dialogue is humbly and empathetically to make room for others' perspectives as possibilities alongside one's own, as indeed they are.

References

Barth, Karl. 1975 [1933]. *The Epistle to the Romans*. Transl. Edwyn C. Hoskyns. Oxford: Oxford University Press, p. 50.

Carson, Rachel. 1962. *Silent Spring*. Boston: Houghton Mifflin.

Hart, John. 2013. *Cosmic Commons: Spirit, Science, and Space*. Eugene, OR: Wipf & Stock.

McFague, Sallie. 1992. A Square in the Quilt, 39–58. In Stephen C. Rockefeller & John C. Elder (Eds.), *Spirit and Nature*. Boston, MA: Beacon Press.

McFague, Sallie. 1993. *The Body of God: An Ecological Theology*. Minneapolis, MN: Fortress Press.

McFague, Sallie. 1997. *Super, Natural Christians: How We Should Love Nature*. Minneapolis, MN: Fortress Press.

McFague, Sallie. 2001. *Life Abundant: Rethinking Theology and Economy for a Planet in Peril*. Minneapolis, MN: Fortress Press.

McFague, Sallie. 2008. *A New Climate for Theology: God, the World, and Global Warming*. Minneapolis, MN: Fortress Press.

McFague, Sallie. 2013. *Blessed Are the Consumers: Climate Change and the Practice of Restraint*. Minneapolis, MN: Fortress Press.

McGrath, Alister. 2002. *The Reenchantment of Nature: The Denial of Religion and the Ecological Crisis*. New York: Doubleday.

Nasr, Seyyed Hossein. 1968a. *Man and Nature: The Spiritual Crisis of Modern Man*. Chicago, IL: ABC International Group.

Nasr, Seyyed Hossein. 1968b. *Science and Civilization in Islam*. Cambridge, MA: Harvard University Press.

Nasr, Seyyed Hossein. 1981. *Knowledge and the Sacred*. New York: Crossroad.

Nasr, Seyyed Hossein. 1992. Islam and the Environmental Crisis, 83–108. In Steven Rockefeller & John Elder (Eds.), *Spirit and Nature: Why the Environment is a Religious Issue*. Boston, MA: Beacon Press.

Nasr, Seyyed Hossein. 1993. *The Need for a Sacred Science*. Albany, NY: SUNY Press.

Nasr, Seyyed Hossein. 1996. *Religion and the Order of Nature*. New York: Oxford University Press.

Nasr, Seyyed Hossein. 2010. *Islam in the Modern World: Challenged by the West, Threatened by Fundamentalism, Keeping Faith with Tradition*. New York: HarperOne.

Pew Research Center. 2015. *The Future of World Religions: Population Growth Projections, 2010–2050*. http://www.pewforum.org/2015/04/02/religious-projections-2010-2050/.

Rockefeller, Steven C. 1992. Keeping Faith with Life, 173–192. In Steven Rockefeller& John Elder (Eds.), *Spirit and Nature: Why the Environment is a Religious Issue*. Boston, MA: Beacon Press.

Rockefeller, Stephen C. & John C. Elder (Eds.). 1992. *Spirit and Nature*. Boston, MA: Beacon Press.

CHAPTER 24

Chondogyo and a Sacramental Commons

Korean Indigenous Religion and Christianity on Common Ground

Yongbum Park

Western Civilization, the Ecological Crisis, and Their Influence on Korean Society

Environmental pollution and the destruction of the ecosystem foretell the impending demise of all living beings if critical steps are not taken to reverse current trends and mitigate the impacts of human conduct on Earth. Desertification is progressing at an alarmingly rate in many parts of the world, and disasters such as floods, typhoons, tsunamis, extreme heat waves, and cold spells have killed thousands of people and other living creatures. If climate change continues to worsen, biota's—living beings'—survival will become exceptionally challenging, if not impossible, for the vast majority of species. Biota extinctions are already evident: species of plants, animals, birds, and even insects have declined and become endangered and, in some cases, are now extinct (Hart, 2006, 107–109)[1] owing to human conduct. While in the case of evolutionary processes species naturally become extinct, today humans are superseding natural processes and causing extinctions.

In the face of this crisis, doubt is escalating about the values, economic structures, and practices of Western civilization, the pioneer of modernity.

Economic globalization has converted the entire planet into a commercial common ground. Economic access enables individuals and organizations to exploit distant resources and shirk responsibility for the consequences to a greater extent than is the case when the Earth commons is regional or local. The global commons is unmanaged ecologically and even economically when development ignores humankind's responsibility to its own future generations and those of other species. A widely accepted proposition is that it is impossible to do something to one species or part of an ecosystem in isolation from other things. In reality, the consequences can be far-reaching.

The Wiley Blackwell Companion to Religion and Ecology, First Edition. Edited by John Hart.

Sustainable use of the planet requires that humankind do nothing that seriously depletes and/or damages natural capital and ecosystem services. In an uncrowded world, a sustainability ethic would be less pressing globally and nationally. But humankind lives in a crowded world where leaving a habitable planet for future generations is increasingly problematic.

The problems we are currently experiencing are not limited to certain areas or regions, but are global and general, so it is imperative that we search for an alternative for the sake of all Nature, humanity, and human society. James Lovelock states that many have asserted that we need to view these three as a single organic, living entity. He notes the value of treating each of these as parts of a single body in the making of a new mode of life (Lovelock, 1979, 9–10).

The human-centered, dominant, minority-controlled industrial culture of the Western world which pioneers scientific technology has dominated, conquered, and exploited the relatively weak nations, peoples, and biota. Its underlying perspective and practice has dichotomized all living beings and understood them to be in conflictive and competitive relationships. It has ignored or rejected precious spiritual values, which cannot be reduced to material values, and has continued to destroy the natural world and annihilate life in the name of development and progress. Consequently, as Edward O. Wilson points out, Western anthropocentric ideologies are now rejected in many parts of the world and novel discourses have emerged to establish a new value system and seek alternatives (Wilson, 2006, 6–8).

The global scale of the ecological crisis, therefore, requires the united measures and efforts of East and West to establish a common ground to address them. An ecological problem is global not only because it endangers the entire world, but also because its solution depends on substantial efforts from all peoples on the planet. The problem is a challenge to humankind and to every organism affected by human conduct. We need to awaken a sense of unity with Nature and all humankind, and consciously participate—directly or indirectly—in everything that transpires.

Ecological destruction cannot be solved simply with technology or money. This chapter emphasizes the source of our ecological problems to be as fundamental as our perspectives on or consciousness about Nature and the value of life. Determining our life values and attitudes is crucial. Socioecological movement and conduct require a more basic approach, in addition to concrete practices, to deal with our immediate problems. By this I mean a critical modification of how we think and live.

If an ethics is intended to be ecologically relevant, it has to have its own voice regarding sociopolitical situations. For example, in Korean contexts where the ethics and practice of the churches have been separate from the actual lives of society and politics, ethics needs to be reconstructed relative to the areas in which it embodies its own practical meaning in terms of the issues with which people are struggling. This constructive work is planned as a proposal for socioecological ethics (Hart, 2013)[2] for members of churches as well as other religious people who are sincerely concerned about Nature on the Korean peninsula. In fact, the ecological crisis has been one of the most serious concerns for the Korean people. In response, they are called to participate in efforts to protect and preserve their country from ecological destruction.

In Korea ecological concerns have hardly penetrated the consciousness of modern religions, including Christianity. The project of socioecological spiritual reconfiguration has not been considered seriously in the actual circumstances of Korean daily life. The new global ecological challenge, however, calls us far beyond recycling, a few prayers for Earth in worship services, turning the church grounds into a bird sanctuary, or discussing from time to time a relational ethic that includes the planet. If we take the challenge seriously, it will penetrate the roots of our religious consciousness and conduct. Specifically, it will ask how Korean Christianity can become a more Nature-conscious, Nature-related, and Nature-integrated religion.

Can socio-ethical reflection discover in Korean indigenous religion and Christian teachings on sacramentality a common place for dedicated ecological action? This question is one of Christian social ethics' most important challenges in Korean contexts, especially in view of accusations that Christianity is itself responsible for our ecological oversight. Such a serious indictment forces us to ask whether Christian social ethics can demonstrate an essential connection between *Chondogyo* and Christian sacramental commons.

Chondogyo (天道教, 천도교, the heavenly way) is the first Korean indigenous religion mainly focused on socio-religious movement. It was initiated against fierce competition and foreign encroachment in the 1860s, when it was known as *Donghak* (東學, 동학, Eastern learning) in contrast to *Seohak* (西學, 서학, Western learning). Following a name change in 1905, the religion continued to gain converts, spearheading the March First Independence Movement of 1919 against the Japanese occupation.

Donghak was founded by Je-Woo Choi (pen name, Su-woon) in 1860 and had an enormous impact in the final days of the Chosun Dynasty (1392–1910) and the dawn of modern Korea. While spending his adult life searching for truth through Confucianism, Buddhism, Daoism, and Catholicism, Su-woon[3] could not find a way to reach the ultimate religious authority. His personal religious experience convinced him that none of the religions was sufficient to find the truth or salvation. Su-woon's conversations with *Hanulnim* (한울님, God) were revolutionary for a Confucian scholar, since they enabled him to ignore the established channels of existing religions and make direct contact with the "ultimate authority." He came to believe that *Hanulnim* is immediately accessible to all humans, and that every human being is immediately in touch with *Hanulnim*.

How can Christian faith provide a vision that can move us to a firm and permanent commitment to ecological responsibility in Korean society? This kind of ethical question complements the ecological inquiry and spirituality of *Shi Chonju* (侍天主, 시천주);[4] that is the main idea of the *Donghak* philosophy and movement. I understand this concept to be closely related to Christian sacramental commons.

Chondogyo sees the source of ecological catastrophe as a crisis of consciousness and conduct, as does the concept of a sacramental commons. As No-bin Yun claims (1989, 139), the second sage of *Chondogyo*, Si-Hyung Choi (pen name, Haewol), elaborated *Chondogyo* thought and organized the *Donghak* movement systematically. Most importantly, Haewol furthered the core idea of the relation between God and human in *Chondogyo*, *Innaechon* (人乃天, 인내천, God is in humans). He introduced the concept of *Samkyong* (三敬, 삼경, Honor God, humans, and Nature as a whole), which means that every human and all of Nature have God's original energy within them and should be respected or revered (Mun-hwan Oh, 1996, 125–130). Integrating the *Chondogyo* and sacramental commons perspectives will contribute to formulating innovative ecological principles and practices in contemporary Korean contexts. The concept of sacramental commons plays a role as a critical hermeneutical tool for the project because the idea of *Chondogyo* needs to be re-contextualized in this social and cultural location.

Historical Background and Development of the *Chondogyo* Tradition

New scientific thought emerging in the West urges a fundamental change in our view of the Earth. Lovelock (1979, 40–43) argues that the Earth is "Gaia," a gigantic body of life (or at least a planet that appears to act as if it were a living being) where all forms of life are connected in an intricate web. This organic worldview, whether understood literally or analogously, demands a shift in our understanding of the Earth, from viewing it as simply the physical "environment" in which humans live, to having an ecological perspective that acknowledges that the Earth is an abiotic context shared by members of the biotic community. During this extraordinary period of cultural and social transition, McFague states, the world has begun to pay attention to the value of life in terms of "coexistence," "symbiosis," "communal life," and "interrelatedness," and there has been a surge of interest in spirituality and spiritual lifestyles that foster a connection with the essence of life (McFague, 2008, 34). This interest as the foundation of human life has led to an increased interest in the religions of the East.

Since ancient times, Korean philosophies have thought of *Chon* (天, 천, heaven), *Ji* (地, 지, land), and *In* (人, 인, human) as the fundamental elements of the universe. The traditional Korean idea of *Chon-Ji-In* (天地人, 천지인) expresses an integral, circular interrelationship among God, human beings, and Nature. This holistic harmony in Korean thought has its origins in the Dan-gun myth, Korea's founding story. According to the myth, both God and Nature are concerned with how to participate in the human world. Hwan-in, a god in the myth, contemplated *Hong-ik-in-gan* (弘益人間, 홍익인간), an all-encompassing blessing on the human world. He allowed Hwan-woong, one of his sons who always wanted to go to the human world, to serve humanity.

Three assistants who controlled the wind, rain, and clouds helped him to supervise 360 areas of human life, including food, longevity, illness, punishment, and good and evil. At that time, a bear and a tiger that wanted to become human implored their help. Hwan-woong told them to avoid sunlight for 100 days and gave them only garlic and wormwood to eat. Only the bear survived, and became a woman. She was married to Hwan-woong and they gave birth to a son, Dan-gun. When he grew up, he built a nation. This was considered the beginning of the Korean nation.

Since Dan-gun mythology contains a sense of worldliness, holistic inclusiveness, and symbiotic harmony, the thought of Korean *Chon* (天, 천) has been not only substantiated with Heaven but also with God living with humanity. The origin of the concept of *Chon* in *Chondogyo* can be found in the Dan-gun myth, and *Chondogyo* represents it in its modern expression. *Chondogyo* appeared when the Cho-sun feudalistic society was deeply troubled sociopolitically. The feudal dynasty together with foreign, especially

Japanese, colonial aggressors inspired revolutionary thoughts that contributed to the construction of a new paradigm. The 1894 Peasant Revolution, which was sparked by the *Donghak* movement, is considered to be the beginning of the most significant historical epoch and marks the beginning of modern Korea.

The national belief systems of that time could not give the people revolutionary energy because of their internal contradictions. The ideology of the Cho-sun dynasty, Confucianism, cared little for the common people. Buddhism itself was rejected from the beginning. Daoism was widely connected to people's beliefs but never succeeded in becoming dominant. *Seohak* (서학, literally Western learning or Western Christianity) was a novel approach, but its colonial aggression and individualism, based on dichotomous thought, did not prove attractive. *Chondogyo* evolved in the midst of all this (Cumings, 2005, 115). In the distinctive liberated administration zones—*Jip-gang-so*—of the peasants, the *Donghak* leadership set up a system of self-government and practiced revolutionary policies. These included the emancipation of slaves, women's liberation, and land reform. Their new and alternative paradigm was the world of *Hu-chon-gae-byeok* (後天開闢, 후천개벽, opening a new world).

Chondogyo is composed of the most representative characteristics of Confucianism, Buddhism, Daoism, and Christianity in terms of life based on the traditional thought of the indigenous common people of Korea. Other Eastern systems tend to consider impersonal concepts: *Chon* (천, heaven) in Confucianism, *Gong* (공, emptiness) in Buddhism, and *Mu* (무, nothingness) in Daoism. In contrast, the Korean people had Han (한) thought, a philosophy unique to native Korean culture. Han means "large," "high," or "whole." Ancient Korean people planted their philosophical roots deep in what has come to be known as Han thought. It has contributed to the building of a Korean traditional philosophy, ethic, paradigm, theory and, eventually, practice. Korea's ancient people attempted to learn what was most essential and meaningful in life. Han thought embraces complete harmony within wholeness. It encompasses everything in the universe. According to Han thought, all things are related in harmony, not in conflict, and so excludes both disruption and confrontation, bringing all things into a large oneness. Sang-yil Kim claims that the principles of Han thought also emphasize love of peace (Sang-yil Kim, 1989, 3–6). Extreme individualism and egoism are excluded in Han thought. Han thought provides a humanistic and ethical foundation for Korean socio-ecological ethics. It has been a valuable philosophy for Korean religions to explore, leading toward development of the discipline in Korea.

This traditional Korean way of thinking involves reconciliation, harmony, and symbiotic holism. The Han way is represented in all aspects of Korean life: history, culture, and ideas. This made it possible to accept aspects of Christianity, such as the idea of a personal God, which was previously unknown to the Koreans. The Korean common people's Han thought, Confucianism (respecting Heaven), Buddhism (being present), Daoism (caring for other beings), and acceptance of elements of Christianity have been fused into *Chondogyo*.

Through the concepts of *Shi-Chonju* (侍天主, 시천주, all human beings and other living beings in our universe bear God within) and *Hon-won-il-gi* (混元一氣, 혼원일기, a single sacred energy that works in various ways on a variety of levels), Su-woon maintained the existence of a sacred spirit that connects each individual with *Hanulnim*,

Nature, other human beings, and even with the entire universe. In other words, as Cumings points out, Su-woon believed that *Hanulnim* interacts with every single entity in the universe through this sacred energy (Cumings, 2005, 114–116).

Founded on this philosophy, Su-woon offered a new paradigm with which to overcome the anthropocentric worldview of the modern Western world. He spoke of the beginning of a new world (개벽, *gae-byeok*) to usher in a new civilization and construct a different framework for human life. In a contemporary Korean Christian ecological spirituality that overcomes the limitations of modern Western civilization, it is necessary to illuminate the implications of *Chondogyo* as an alternative worldview and examine its potential to assist in formulating proposals to renew Nature.

Christian Sacramental Tradition

The theological resources for an ecological renewal of faith can be found not only in biblical texts and doctrinal tradition, but also in the "sacramental" character of Nature itself. In this understanding, Nature in all its beauty and diversity reveals the divine mystery—not just to Christians, but to people of all traditions. When people of faith have no *sacramental* understanding, as Hart explains, an alternative complementary (but not congruent) term would be *sacred* (Hart, 2013, 181). The ecological implications of sacramentality have been expressed by several Christian ethicists, including James Nash in *Loving Nature: Ecological Integrity and Christian Responsibility*, Sallie McFague in *The Body of God: An Ecological Theology*, Larry Rasmussen in *Earth Community Earth Ethics*, and John Hart in *Sacramental Commons: Christian Ecological Ethics*. Their common idea is that since Christian faith teaches that the world reveals God and is the locus of God's engagement with humanity, Christians should be cautious about their impact on the world and treat natural systems with respect. Nash describes this well:

> Nature is sacred by association, as the bearer of the sacred. We are standing perpetually on holy ground, because God is present not only in the burning bush but in the nurturing soil and atmosphere, indeed, sharing the joys and agonies of all creatures. The sacramental presence of the Spirit endows all of creation with a sacred value and dignity. (Nash, 1991, 115)

The natural world is important, in part because it provides access to the God who created it. Ecological degradation is sinful. When people degrade the Earth, they abandon their place in Creation and set themselves against God's creative work. The nonhuman world should be preserved: it is a sign of God's presence and provides a means of moving closer to God.

Sacramentality extends beyond particular material substances and rituals to emphasize that the incarnation of God on Earth in Jesus Christ signifies something about the relationship between Creator and created. If we want an ethic capable of responding to the full dimensions of the ecological crisis, we must learn once more to revere the natural world for showing us the sacred reality that underlies it (Thomas Berry, 1988, 81).

We cannot do this without the help of science and cosmology. Our spirituality has become so obsessed with themes of history and human freedom, so concerned with interpreting written texts, that it has lost touch with the sacramentality of Nature. It is now time to resacramentalize ethics.

Sacramental Universe and Sacramental Commons

In *Sacramental Commons: Christian Ecological Ethics*, Hart affirms that sacramental moments are experiences of the loving and creative presence of the Spirit. Creation flows from the divine vision and is the locus of the human experience of the divine Presence. For him, people perceive signs of the Spirit in Creation, signs that might or might not be acknowledged, but which nonetheless link innermost human being with Divine Being (Hart, 2006, xiv). People have moments of engagement with the Spirit when they are open to the loving and creative presence of the Spirit in Creation.

In Christian churches, Hart explains, sacraments traditionally have been religious rituals, mediated by a member of the clergy in a dedicated, human-constructed sacred space. They are visible signs or symbols of an invisible experience of God's grace in significant life moments (Hart, 2006, xiv). In the twentieth century and into the present time, a new understanding has emerged, an extension of "sacrament" into non-ecclesial spheres: the *sacramental universe*. In this perspective, Hart declares:

> The universe is *sacramental*. It is a revelation of the Spirit's ongoing creativity and a place of interaction and relationship between the human and the divine. The holistic universe and its local places are sacramental. The cosmos as an integrated whole and in each of its parts can be a sign and experience of divine creativity and a revelation of Spirit's presence; an occasion of grace and a conveyor of blessing; and a bearer of sacred creatures, all called "very good" by their Creator. (Hart, 2006, 12)

For some Christians, Earth places have come to be viewed as sacramental because they reveal the Spirit's loving creativity in their biodiversity, textured topography, and provision of food, water, and shelter for the community of life (Hart, 2006, 62). Hart states that the idea of a sacramental universe elaborated by Christian leaders and scholars becomes a sacramental commons on the common ground of Creation that people experience:

> The sacramental universe is localized in the *sacramental commons*... The sacramental commons is a revelatory *locus*, the place of Spirit–spirit engagement and relation... A sacramental commons is a place ... which at special moments is revelatory of God-immanent, and in every moment is the sign of a divine intention that natural goods[5] be shared among members of the biotic community for their sustenance... A sacramental commons is transparent to the eyes of faith. It mediates and reveals the immanent presence of the engaged Spirit. (Hart, 2006, 61)

The understandings of *sacramental universe* and *sacramental commons* are complementary and mutually reinforcing:

> The terms *sacramental universe* and *sacramental commons*, which express a profound sense of divine immanence in, and divine engagement with, creation and creatures, articulate the special relationship of Creator and creation, as well as acknowledge awareness of the ongoing loving presence of the creative Word in all creation. (Hart 2006, 16)

As a socioecological ethicist, Hart suggests that for some Christians, ethical conduct and ecological consequences are stimulated by and flow from sacramental understandings of cosmos and commons. Christians who acknowledge the creative, communicating, and community-creating immanence of the Spirit in Creation, recognizing thereby the revelatory power of Creation as a whole and of the biotic community within it, treat the Earth and its inhabitants with reverence and respect. In understanding that the Spirit intends that the Earth's goods meet the needs of all the Earth's creatures, and acting accordingly, they avoid consumerism and exploitation. In viewing Creation holistically, they act responsibly toward strangers in space, time, and species—not solely human "neighbors" who have the most obvious claims on their concern, but also other-kind and pristine Nature that comprise the variant forms of the community of Creation ever-emerging from the creative power and loving presence of the Spirit. Within this consciousness, Hart asserts, "generational and intergenerational responsibility are fostered, the limits on Earth's livable space, productive places, and available goods are respected, and space, places, and goods are shared equitably" (2006, 77).

Furthermore, Hart's idea of sacramental commons represents an achievement of innovative integration. His "creation-centric consciousness" blends contemporary science, environmental philosophy, biblical and historical theology, Native American Indian spirituality, and sociopolitical-economic analysis. He explores the commonality of Nature as a locus for spiritual experience across world religions and spiritual traditions. He notes that some form of responsibility for Creation has also been practiced in diverse traditions, as *Chondogyo* has done in Korea. On a practical level, Hart's approach establishes a deep, interreligious moral pull that can be used for the comparative interpretation of Christianity and *Chondogyo*.

Theological bases for understanding a "sacramental commons" were developed by Hart in his first published work, *The Spirit of the Earth: A Theology of the Land*. He declares that "the earth and all in, on and around the earth are the Creator's... God became enfleshed on the earth, and experienced first-hand the relation of the creature for its Creator... God contains the finite earth within infinite Being, and so God's Spirit permeates the earth" (Hart, 1984, 155). Hart observes further that "the Spirit of the earth is God, the Great Spirit, the transcendent yet immanent One who created the world, restored its relation to its Creator, and continually renews that relation" (1984, 158). The interrelatedness of humans and Nature and God in Catholic teachings is similar to *Chondogyo*'s concept of *Shi-Chonju* as "all creatures in the universe bear God within."

Comparative Constructs: Sacramental Commons and *Chondogyo*

A comparative approach is a meaningful method of ethics that constructs balanced moral views and practical approaches. Social, economic, and ecological circumstances have been integrated in comparative ecological ethics as empirical data and diverse cultural backgrounds have correlated. Since all societies have unique ethical traditions and practices, comparative studies have explored similarities and differences between the ethical theories and practices of diverse peoples. As a socioecological comparison between the West and the East, this section analyzes and connects sacramental commons and *Chondogyo*.

Western religious tradition has unnecessarily subordinated Creation—and by implication sacramentalism—to redemption. According to Matthew Fox, the Christian tradition has focused too strongly on Fall/redemption theology. He disapproves of this dualistic approach and points out that "to teach original sin and never to teach original blessing creates pessimism and cynicism" (Fox, 1983, 11). He further criticizes the focus on original sin as being a key in separating humans from the rest of Creation and Creator (1983, 11). Similarly, Berry notes that a recovery of the sense of the sacred in the natural world as a "primary revelation of the divine" would rightly "diminish our emphasis on redemption experience in favor of a greater emphasis on creation processes" (1988, 81).

An exclusive emphasis on redemption has led Christian theology to exaggerate the Fall not only of humankind but also of the natural world. The assumption has been that redemption would be a momentous event only in proportion to the abysmal depths of a primordial Fall. By overemphasizing the Fall "in the beginning," Nature has been made at times to seem perverse and therefore undeserving of our care. By exaggerating the Fall of Nature we have too easily lost sight of the original goodness of the entire Creation which God declared to be "very good." At the same time, an undue focus on human need for redemption from evil has distracted us from the travail of the whole of Creation, which also "groans" for radical renewal (Rom. 8: 22). The renewal of Nature to which Christian faith alludes need not be postponed until the "last day"; it can begin to become a reality here and now.

The sacramental commons approach emphasizes the present renewal of Nature when it interprets "sin" to mean more than just our human separation from God or from each other. Sin also affects the current alienation of Nature from humanity and stands in the way of Nature's creative possibilities as envisaged by God from the outset of Creation. Consequently, "redemption" and "reconciliation" must mean not only the restoration of the Divine–human relationship, but also human responsibility for God's world as evident in human action to heal the entire Earth community and indeed renew the whole of Creation.

Moreover, the sacramental commons approach is a powerful idea and experience because it both draws on deep traditions in Christian faith and responds to the current and urgent issues of ecological devastation. Ecological ethicists frequently stress that this approach has deep roots, a faithful communication of the Christian tradition that has long expressed an immanent, incarnational, and sacramental presence of God in the world (Hart, 2006, 109). The sacramental commons approach does not call us as believers to change the object of our worship or to reimagine God, but rather to recognize the importance of the natural world in the faith we inherit.

Along these lines Larry Rasmussen is careful to distinguish Nature from the Divine in his discussion of sacramentality: "To identify something earthly as holy and sacred is not to say it *is* God. Rather it is *of* God; God is present in its presence" (1996, 239). John Haught is even more cautious and limited in his use of language, emphasizing that seeing the world as sacramental is fundamentally different from seeing it as sacred: "Nature is worth saving not because it is sacred, but because it is sacramental, capable of mediating to our religious awareness the otherwise hidden mystery of the divine" (Haught, 1993, 78). While these thinkers define "sacred" in different ways, both stress that sacramentality is a faithful strand of Christianity, calling believers to see the natural world as a bearer of God but not as God. This concept is very similar to *Shi Chonju* of *Donghak*. This approach about valuing, respecting, and appreciating the natural world is much more important, vital, and faithful to the Christian tradition than worshiping Nature.

Since it is a faithful inheritance of tradition, sacramentality is a powerful response to critics who argue that Christianity is too otherworldly and Heaven-obsessed to respond to the crisis of ecological degradation. The biologist Edward O. Wilson writes: "The most dangerous of devotions, in my opinion, is the one endemic to Christianity: *I was not born to be of this world*" (1999, 245). This is a familiar critique, one that fairly indicts some parts of the Christian tradition that are dangerously focused on ideas of Heaven and the afterlife to the exclusion of this world. Sacramentality, however, is a deeply rooted tradition of the faith that moves in the opposite direction, emphasizing God's presence in the world and thereby demonstrating that Christianity is not exclusively about a transcendent, otherworldly God. This approach is proof that otherworldliness is not endemic to Christianity, or at least not necessarily so.

Hart's work is explicit about this, highlighting the sacramental tradition as a corrective to Christianity's overemphasis "on a heavenly afterlife," an emphasis that should never take precedence over "present 'earthly' concerns, occupations, and preoccupations" (Hart, 2006, 34). McFague embraces Christian sacramentality for the same reason, appreciative of its potential as "one of the few traditions within Christianity that ... has included nature as a concern of God and a way to God" (1993, 184). Contemporary sacramental thinkers emphasize the presence of God immanent in the Earth and the importance of human life on Earth, a vital corrective to those who believe Christianity celebrates Heaven to the exclusion of this world. Consequently, sacramentality calls us to commit to God's world rather than turn away from it.

Emphasizing the importance of sacramentality for contemporary ecological thinking, Hart offers an extended reflection of "sacramental universe" and then works to localize it. While stressing that the presence and revelation of the Creator throughout the whole of the Creation is important, the complementary notion of a "sacramental commons" focuses on "a moment and locus of human participation in the interactive presence and caring compassion of the Spirit who is immanent and participates in a complex cosmic dance of energies, elements, entities, and events" (2006, xviii). The commons exists on a smaller scale, implying that God is revealed and present in *this* community at *this* time. While the sacramental universe makes a claim about the eternal nature of Creation, the sacramental commons approach refers to a more localized, particular, and individual or communal social experience. It attends to more distinct spaces and times in finer detail. Hart explains that the sacramental commons approach is an important localization of the sacramental universe because people can often recognize God's presence and mystery in the world when their attention shifts "from the macro to the micro, from the cosmos to the commons" (2006, 61).

In addition, the sacramental commons approach adds indispensable ingredients to the larger project of formulating a socioecological ethics. Today, Christian ethics in particular needs to retrieve a sacramental sense of the cosmos. The ancient Christian intuition of the revelatory character of the universe is a significant ethical and ecological contribution to this approach. It enables Christians to recognize the intrinsic relation between religious faith and contemporary ecological concern. The sacramental commons approach helps us to realize that without the freshness of air, the purity of water, and the fertility of soil, the power of Christians' most enduring symbols of God is diminished or lost. The integrity of Nature is inseparable from the flourishing of religion and ethics. If people lose Nature, as Berry points out, they will lose God also (Berry, 1999, 9).

The sacramental commons approach, however, is unable to give us a fully integrated ecological ethics if we do not embrace its complementary understandings of "relational consciousness" and "relational community." Hart states,

> The relational consciousness and the relational community together express a sense of communion among member individuals and species of biokind, between biokind and Earth, and between biokind and the Spirit. They express the meaning of the "reign of God" advocated by Jesus. The evolving social reality of Spirit–Earth–spirit engagement is the creation commons community, with its creation-centered consciousness. (2006, 200)

An incomplete understanding of what a sacramental commons means can easily allow us to overlook the pivotal motif of ecological relationality that underscores particularity and universality, similarity and difference, and unity and diversity between Divine Being and Nature.

Mystical Unity of *Bul-yon-Ki-yon* in *Chondogyo*

The emergence of *Chondogyo* out of crisis in the 1860s Korean context was inescapably related to Su-woon's experiences of wandering and misery, poverty and social discrimination. Above all, his experience of *Hanulnim* out of his miserable social reality was the most crucial motivation for the rise of *Chondogyo*.

Su-woon's spiritual experience is indispensable to the rise of *Chondogyo*. Especially, the significance of Su-woon's experience of *O-sim-chuk-Yo-sim* ("my mind is also your mind") lies in its relation to social, historical, and ethical dimensions. His spiritual experience did not occur only at the personal and metaphysical levels. It was a result of seeking the Truth for about two decades as he sought a way to deliver the people and nation from total crisis. Su-woon's personal and spiritual vision was never separated from his social vision.

If Su-woon's spiritual experience of the mystical unity of himself and *Hanulnim* is the basis of the rise of *Chondogyo*, how is this experience possible? How is *Chondogyo*'s notion of the Divine, *Hanulnim*, so inclusive and so relational of very different divine characteristics?

Su-woon described his evolutionary view of reality, from which he explained the way of perceiving, experiencing, and embodying the world in *Bul-yon-Ki-yon* (不然其然, 불연기연). The term *Bul-yon* literally means "it is not," while the term *Ki-yon* means "it is." The two terms have opposite meanings and thus seem to lie in a contradictory relationship. "It is not" never coexists with "it is." This is the law of contradiction; there should be either "it is not" or "it is." This is the law of the excluded middle (Chi-ha Kim, 2003, 169). Instead of being based on the logic of the dominating relationship, Su-woon stated, the logic of *Bul-yon-Ki-yon* is rooted in all aspects of life by grasping the interdependent and relational nature of consciousness in the world. According to his logic, reality is composed of seemingly opposite categories and principles. One aspect of reality is well grasped from one category and principle. The other aspect of the same reality is well obtained from its opposite. They seem contradictory, but are just different perspectives from which to look at the same reality.

Su-woon relates *Bul-yon*, the origin, the energy or principle of life, with *Ki-yon*, the concrete phenomenon and appearance of *Bul-yon*. He locates *Bul-yon* in *Ki-yon*, the infinite in the finite, the mystery in the ordinary, the one in the many, and the sacred in the worldly (Mun-hwan Oh, 1996, 33). Many ecological ethicists, though they may differ in their emphasis on the analysis of ecological problems and alternatives, hold in common their attempt to restore ecological relationality to a dynamic unity of the Divine and the earthly, the infinite and the finite, transcendence and immanence, universality and particularity, and individuality and diversity (Mun-hwan Oh, 1996, 35). For his part Hart, in his concept of a relational consciousness in Nature, attempts to integrate the transcendent and the immanent. He affirms that "people who link the transcendent and the immanent in their lives experience sacramental moments" (2006, xxii). Sacramental commons "focuses on Earth as a place on which and in which all life in its personal and communal manifestations strives to find its place and meet its needs, while interacting in integrated ecosystems with other individuals and species" (2006, xxiii).

A comparison of the themes of "relational consciousness," "relational community," and "interconnectedness" in sacramental commons with *Chondogyo* will reveal not only how these approaches overlap, or are at least complementary, but also how the interrelatedness between the Divine, humans, and Nature is possible without becoming a meaningless fusion and rootless separation.

Creation Consciousness as a Common Socioecological Vision

Showing fundamental human vulnerabilities to Creation, ecojustice points to a theological strategy that narrates grace within an embodied human intimacy with Creation. By pointing to disembodiments of the self from social community and from the Earth, ecojustice summons re-embodiments of self, Earth, and God (Baker-Fletcher, 1998, 8). The response, says Baker-Fletcher, means "to become part of the body of God," redemptively re-embodying an interrelational human self through creative political actions that "participate in God's creation of a new heaven and a new earth" (1998, 57), which is remarkably similar to the notion of *Chondogyo*'s *Hu-chon-Gae-byeok* (後天開闢).

If we do not move beyond strategies that treat humanity and Nature separately, says Osage Indian thinker George Tinker, "we have not yet begun to deal with ecojustice, let alone ethno-ecojustice and racism, as a systemic whole, as a system of oppression rooted in structures of power that touch every part of our lives" (1996, 180). The ecojustice movement traces ecological disruptions in human dignity and contrasts them with non-dualist, non-individualist, ecologically-relational concepts of human personhood (1996, 183). Womanist theologian Emilie Townes writes complementarily that "The yoking of civil and environmental rights is crucial to ontological wholeness," because they counter serially related lynching with a spirituality of socioecological wholeness (1995, 60).

Ecojustice does not, therefore, produce an anthropocentric version of the strategy; rather, its human concern serves a different pastoral strategy altogether, in which the structure of human personhood illuminates ecological problems and guides Christian responses to them. By theologically qualifying that association, ecojustice advocates treat Creation's integrity and human dignity as essentially related moral concerns and noncompetitive moral interests (1995, 72). That practical strategy discloses similarities to creation consciousness in *Chondogyo* and sacramental commons, which otherwise might seem socially and ideologically distant.

Creation Spirituality and Consciousness

Creation spirituality sometimes presents itself as a "liberation theology for the so-called 'First-World' peoples" (Fox, 1983, xi). Reconceptualizing subjectivity and spirituality within a cosmic story, Creation spirituality reclaims Nature for alienated human individuals. Humans discover their earthly place by first rediscovering their own inward cosmic consciousness and inner mysteries of the cosmos itself. Hence Berry says that "we bear the universe in our beings as the universe bears us in its being. The two have a total presence to each other and to that deeper mystery out of which both the universe and ourselves have emerged" (1988, 130). This notion is comparable to *Chondogyo*'s idea of *Shi-Chonju* ("bearing God within") and *O-sim-chuk-Yo-sim* ("my mind is just your mind"). Moreover, it links to Hart's concept that "a creation-centered consciousness is a holistic understanding that the Creator, abiotic creation, and the biotic community are interrelated" (2006, 17).

Creation consciousness, therefore, refuses to begin from Nature or human practice in prior isolation, and instead addresses their alienation within human personhood as the root of ecological problems. The common Creation story and the story of Jesus reveal the same sacred reality: human persons are a living cosmology, active manifestations of the world's communion. "In creation spirituality God has been speaking the truth since the beginning of time... We're just the lucky ones who have come along now in a moment of time to bring it to consciousness, to give a word to it: Jesus" (Rohr, 1994, 153).

Discovering in the cosmic Christ "the interconnectivity of all things and ... the power of the human mind and spirit to experience personally this common glue," humans find themselves at once in solidarity with all things and uniquely empowered to creatively realize that relationality (Fox, 1988, 133).

Chondogyo also stresses the "organic interdependence" of the body; this is far from reductionist and mechanistic ideas (Suk-san Yun, 2009, 216). The realization of the importance of the organic body makes possible the creative spiritual understanding of *Shi Chonju*. Some religious teachings advise followers to abandon fellow human beings for the sake of God or kill them in the name of God. Such extreme teachings arise from a lack of a conscious understanding of the interdependence between human beings and God. This falsehood never occurs in *Chondogyo* thanks to its concept of the body. Moreover, the concept of the interdependence of the body develops into consciousness of the suffering of other lives and so affirms human dignity, social ethics, and ecojustice, as well as reverence for the cosmos.

Developing Su-woon's *Shi Chonju* concept, Haewol introduced the idea of "Three Respects": respect for God, respect for Nature, and respect for humanity (Chi-ha Kim, 2003, 221). In this we can see a definite expansion from a God–human relationship to a God–Nature–human relationship. Haewol developed the concept of *Shi Chonju* and expanded it to a cosmo-socioecological dimension. The result, inherited in Uiam's *In-Nae-Chon* (人乃天, "Human is *Hanulnim*"), is clearly revealed in *Chondogyo*'s Creation spirituality and consciousness.

The concept of *In-Nae-Chon*, as Chi-ha Kim points out, implies trinitarian spirituality: egalitarian humanism, socioecological consciousness, and faith in God. These three support one another (Chi-ha Kim, 2003, 157). That is, egalitarian humanism never degenerated into anthropocentrism because of socioecological consciousness. We have observed such a deterioration in the past in Western traditions, whether they are theistic or atheistic. Although faith in God assures human egalitarianism, it often fails to extend its justice to Nature. The contemporary ecological crisis is the proof of this failing. The modern atheistic tradition also celebrates humanitarianism. However, its sense of socioecological consciousness is scarce. In *Chondogyo* spirituality, humanitarian justice does not exclude ecojustice since its understanding suggests the organic interrelatedness of human beings and the world. This comprehensive spirituality is possible because of its panentheistic[6] perspective, which is a major difference from some Eastern religious thought (Chi-ha Kim, 2003, 159). In fact, the concept of *Chondogyo* supposes that theism buttresses ethics. The trinitarian spirituality is of great value and applicability to socioecological ethics in Korean contexts.

Chondogyo's spirituality is supported not only by its philosophical teachings but also by its quest for religious discipline. *Chondogyo* regards humans as respectful beings; however, the respectful state is not warranted in itself. *Su-sim-jung-ki* (修心正氣, 수심정기, "keeping mind and having right energy") is encouraged. Su-woon stresses religious discipline at various points in his writings. Suk-san Yun explains that the idea of *Shi Chonju* (bearing God) is not merely a philosophical understanding but implies spiritual training: "*Sung* (誠, 성, sincerity), *Kyung* (敬, 경, respect), and *Shin* (信, 신, faith)" (2009, 321–323). Su-woon borrows the Confucian virtues (sincerity and respect) and completes them by adding his own religious experience.

For Su-woon, the virtues of sincerity and respect derive from Confucianism; however, they do not refer to goodness, achieved by ethical self-realization. Rather, they are based on "faith in God." As in trinitarian spirituality, the three virtues are interdependent, yet faith plays a dominant role. Starting from Su-woon's creative religious experience, *Chondogyo* expanded to provide a solid socio-ethical background to promote an ecological spirituality (Chi-ha Kim, 2003, 226). *Chondogyo* presents both a respectable spiritual idea that is highly viable in the current socioecological debates and a balanced consciousness useful in the formation of an ethic to overcome the contemporary ecological crisis. Its consciousness and spirituality are essentially joined so that it succeeds in offering the potential to build a common moral vision in Korean contexts.

Notes

1 During evolution, species become extinct through natural processes when they no longer have an ecological niche. Humankind, however, actively exterminates species irresponsibly, knowingly, or unknowingly.

2 Hart, *Cosmic Commons*, 30, n. 2; 184–189. Hart coined the term to express the integration, in context, of justice within and among human communities and the ecological wellbeing of the Earth and all living beings.

3 Biographies of Su-woon include Paul Beirne. 2009. *Su-un and His World of Symbols: The Founder of Korea's First Indigenous Religion*. Burlington, VT: Ashgate; Charles Allen Clark. 1981. *Religions of Old Korea*. New York: Garland; James Huntley Grayson. 2002. *Korea: A Religious History* (rev. ed.). London: Routledge. His principal ideas are elaborated in Mun-hwan Oh. 1996. *Sarami Hanulida* [Humanity is Heaven]. Seoul: Sol; Won Park. 2002. *Traditional Korean Thought*. Inchon, Republic of Korea: Inha University Press; Se-myong Pack. 1956. *Donghak Thought and Chondokyo*, Seoul: Donghaksa; Suk-san Yun. 2009. *Joohae Donghak Kyongjeon* [Annotations of Donghak Scripture]. Seoul: Donghak-sa.

4 *Shi Chonju* is composed of *Shi* (a predicate), which literally means "to bear" or "to serve," and *Chonju* (an object), which means the Heavenly Lord as the Catholic term for God in Korea. See Kyong-jae Kim. 1989. *Donghak Sasang kwa Donghak Hyongmyong* [Donghak Thought and Donghak Revolution]. Seoul: Chong-a Publishers; Jang-Hwa Hong, 1990. *Chondogyo Gyori wa Sasang* [Chondogyo Doctrine and Thought]. Seoul: Chondogyo Jung-ang Chongbu; Don Hwa Lee. 1969. *Chondogyo Changgun-sa* [History of Chondogyo Foundation]. Seoul: Kyoungin Munhwa-sa; and Chi-ha Kim. 1994. *Donghak Iyagi* [The Story of Donghak]. Seoul: Sol.

5 Hart prefers *natural goods* to *resources*.

6 According to *The Stanford Encyclopedia of Philosophy*, "panentheism considers God and the world to be interrelated with the world being in God and God being in the world. It offers an increasingly popular alternative to both traditional theism and pantheism. Panentheism seeks to avoid either isolating God from the world as traditional theism often does or identifying God with the world as pantheism does. Traditional theistic systems emphasize the difference between God and the world while panentheism stresses God's active presence in the world. Pantheism emphasizes God's presence in the world but panentheism maintains the identity and significance of the non-divine." John Culp. 2015. Panentheism. In Edward N. Zalta (Ed.), *The Stanford Encyclopedia of Philosophy* (Summer ed.): https://plato.stanford.edu/archives/sum2015/entries/panentheism.

References

Baker-Fletcher, Karen. 1998. *Sisters of Spirit, Sisters of Dust: Womanist Wordings on God and Creation*. Minneapolis, MN: Fortress Press.

Berry, Thomas. 1988. *The Dream of the Earth*. San Francisco, CA: Sierra Club Books.

Berry, Thomas. 1999. *The Great Work: Our Way into the Future*. New York: Bell Tower.

Cumings, Bruce. 2005. *Korea's Place in the Sun: A Modern History*. New York: W.W. Norton.

Fox, Matthew. 1983. *Original Blessing*. Santa Fe, NM: Bear & Co.

Fox, Matthew. 1988. *The Coming of the Cosmic Christ*. San Francisco, CA: Harper & Row.

Hart, John. 1984. *The Spirit of the Earth: A Theology of the Land*. Mahwah, NJ: Paulist Press,

Hart, John. 2006. *Sacramental Commons: Christian Ecological Ethics*. Lanham, MD: Rowman & Littlefield.

Hart, John. 2013. *Cosmic Commons: Spirit, Science, and Space*. Eugene, OR: Cascade Books.

Haught, John F. 1993. *The Promise of Nature: Ecology and Cosmic Purpose*. New York: Paulist Press.

Kim, Chi-ha. 2003. *Saengmyonghak [Life Thought]*. Seoul: Hwanam.

Kim, Sang-yil. 1989. *Segae Chulhak-goa Han* (Global Philosophy and Han). Seoul: Jeonmangsa.

Lovelock, James E. 1979. *Gaia: A New Look at Life on Earth*. Oxford: Oxford University Press.

McFague, Sallie. 1993. *The Body of God: An Ecological Theology*. Minneapolis, MN: Fortress Press.

McFague, Sallie. 2008. *A New Climate for Theology: God, the World, and Global Warming*. Minneapolis, MN: Fortress Press.

Nash, James A. 1991. *Loving Nature: Ecological Integrity and Christian Responsibility*. Nashville, TN: Abingdon.

Oh, Mun-hwan. 1996. *Sarami Hanulida [Humanity is Heaven]*. Seoul: Sol.

Rasmussen, Larry L. 1996. *Earth Community Earth Ethics*. Maryknoll, NY: Orbis Books.

Rohr, Richard. 1994. "Christianity and the Creation." In Albert LaChance and John E. Carrol, eds., Embracing Earth, 129–155. Maryknoll, NY: Orbis Books.

Tinker, George. 1996. "Spirituality, Native American Personhood, Sovereignty, and Solidarity." in Treat, James. Native and Christian: Indigenous Voices on Religious Identity in the United States and Canada 115–131. New York and London: Routledge.

Townes, Emilie. 1995. *In a Blaze of Glory: Womanist Spirituality as Social Witness*. Nashville, TN: Abingdon.

Wilson, Edward O. 1999. *Consilience: The Unity of Knowledge*. New York: Vintage Books,

Wilson, Edward O. 2006. *The Creation: A Plea to Save Life on Earth*. New York: W.W. Norton.

Yun, No-Bin. 1989. *Dongkhak Sasang kwa Donghak Hyongmyong [Donghak Thought and Donghak Revolution]*. Seoul: Chong-a Publishers.

Yun, Suk-san. 2009. *Joohae Donghak Kyongjeon [Annotations of Donghak Scripture]*. Seoul: Donghak-sa.

Further Reading

Boff, Leonardo. 1997. *Cry of the Earth, Cry of the Poor*. Maryknoll, NY: Orbis Books. This book strongly emphasizes ecojustice. It links well the theology of liberation and ecological deterioration.

Carroll, John E. & LaChance, Albert (Eds.). 1994. *Embracing Earth: Catholic Approaches to Ecology*. Maryknoll, NY: Orbis Books.

Hart, John. 2004. *What Are They Saying About ... Environmental Theology?* Mahwah, NJ: Paulist Press.

Hessel, Dieter T. 1996. *Theology for Earth Community: A Field Guide*. Maryknoll, NY: Orbis Books.

Hessel, Dieter T. & Rasmussen, Larry (Eds.) 2001. *Earth Habitat: Eco-Injustice and the Church's Response*. Minneapolis, MN: Fortress Press. Provides a dynamic framework for thought and action that fosters ecological integrity and the struggle for social and economic justice, especially in Christian churches.

Hessel, Dieter T. & Ruether, Rosemary Radford (Eds.). 2000. *Christianity and Ecology: Seeking the Well-being of Earth and Humans*. Cambridge, MA: Harvard University Center for the Study of World Religions/Harvard University Press. Expresses constructive human responses that serve environmental health and social equity together.

Moltmann, Jürgen. 1985. *God in Creation: A New Theology of Creation and the Spirit of God*. Transl. Margaret Kohl. San Francisco, CA: Harper & Row. In this book Moltmann rediscovers the Creator's immanence in Creation, a teaching that is also embedded in the *Chondogyo* tradition.

CHAPTER 25

The Religious Politics of Scientific Doubt

Evangelical Christians and Environmentalism in the United States

Myrna Perez Sheldon and Naomi Oreskes

On August 18, 2011, Republican Party primary presidential candidate John Huntsman tweeted, "I believe in evolution and trust scientists on global warming. Call me crazy." And in fact, the former Governor of Utah's proclamation of confidence in the scientific community was widely considered to be out of step with the rest of the Republican Party. Throughout that fall many other Republican candidates issued public statements expressing their doubts about the scientific validity of evolution and climate change. For instance, when primary candidate Michele Bachman was asked about climate change, she replied, "I think all these issues have to be settled on the base of real science, not manufactured science." Candidate Rick Perry made a similar claim, "I think there are a substantial number of scientists who have manipulated data so that they will have dollars rolling into their projects. I think we're seeing it almost weekly or even daily, scientists who are coming forward and questioning the original idea that man-made global warming is what is causing the climate to change." These politicians wove together a distrust of the scientific consensus on these issues, while also claiming to champion "real science." Moreover, this rhetoric of doubt toward professional science was understood to be part of the same broad political world that included pro-life stances on abortion, opposition to same-sex marriage, and abstinence-only education. In other words, raising doubts on the scientific consensus on climate change was one way for these Republican presidential candidates to signal their allegiance to a bloc of conservative evangelical Christian voters (Dade, 2011).

This chapter unfolds the history of how a specific political tactic—distrust of climate-change science—came to be associated with the cultural values of American evangelical Christianity. Historians of US politics have shown great interest in the story of evangelical Christianity in recent decades, largely to understand the influence of this

The Wiley Blackwell Companion to Religion and Ecology, First Edition. Edited by John Hart.

form of religiosity on American styles of governance, culture wars, economic development, and foreign relations. The role that evangelical leaders played to secure the prominence of socially conservative values in the Republican Party platform beginning in the 1980s has been well documented (Brown, 2002; Diamond, 2000; Lambert, 2010; Sutton, 2014; Williams, 2012). What has been less thoroughly explored, however, is the effect that evangelicalism played on the public perception of scientific expertise and authority from the early 1980s onward (Jewett, 2012, 365). In this chapter, we contend that the same period that reframed evangelical political identity also witnessed a series of well-organized evangelical advocacy movements against the authority of professional scientific expertise. Thus, we trace the development of distrust toward professional science from the Creation-science movement in the early 1980s, through the Intelligent Design movement in the 1990s and 2000s, and subsequently into the cultural debates around climate-change science in recent years. In doing so, we argue that the religious inflection of contemporary debates over climate-change science is best understood in light of the longer history of evangelicalism in the American context.

Although it has been tempting for many contemporary political pundits to assume that the distrust of science is an essential feature of evangelical Christianity or even of religion, empirically the situation is far more complicated. Attitudes toward professional scientific expertise vary widely among American religious groups, including communities that self-identify as evangelicals (Ecklund & Scheitle, 2014; Jones et al., 2014; Rosen, 2004; Shapiro, 2013). Despite this complexity, there has arisen a persistent connection between the conservative Christian Right and tactics of scientific distrust. By uncovering the history of this connection, we argue against the assumption that religion, broadly speaking, must necessarily oppose scientific consensus, environmental protection, or government regulation. Further, we suggest that setting aside this assumption makes it possible not only to imagine, but also encourage, a different public conversation about the role and responsibility of evangelical Christian communities with regard to the environment.

The rhetoric of doubt over climate-change science is only a single node in a larger story of the relationships between religion, governance, and civic identity in the United States. It would be possible, for instance, to focus an analysis of religiously inflected debates over environmental protection in terms of views on government regulation. Indeed, a key feature of evangelical political identity throughout the twentieth century was fervent opposition to communism and the championing of capitalism as an essential feature of American global exceptionalism (Moreton, 2009). Anti-communism resulted in a distaste among many evangelicals for government regulatory practices, including those aimed at environmental protection. As Oreskes (2010) has documented elsewhere, public confusion on a number of scientific issues (e.g., the link between smoking and cancer, and the environmental science of acid rain and of climate change) was a political strategy executed by well-funded right-wing think tanks. The increasing political association between evangelicalism and pro-business, anti-government, right-wing politics was an important foundation for the conservative Christian antipathy to environmental protection. However, because our interest in this chapter is the rhetorical structures that frame distrust of science, we have chosen to center our analysis on the development and deployment of scientific doubt within communities of evangelicals. Beginning in the early 1980s, the expanding cultural reach of the Creation-science movement brought debates over scientific authority into national political dialogue. Beginning our story about climate-change skepticism in these crucial years of Creation-science allows us to see most clearly the entanglement of evangelical identity and the politics of scientific doubt.

We begin with the history of evangelical and fundamentalist Christianity in the US during the twentieth century. Scholars have variously characterized these communities according to their institutional histories, their relationship to sacred texts, and their influence on US political alignments. Our own framework for "evangelicalism" will be to consider it as a cultural and political identity that was crucially reframed by the rise of the Christian Right in the early 1980s. Next, we consider how these transitions in evangelicalism were manifested in different political actions toward professional scientific expertise. We trace these developments through the Creation-science and Intelligent Design movements, and then follow the deployment of this rhetoric by opponents to climate-change science in the early twenty-first century. We conclude by moving from this history to suggest a new framework for evangelical communities to engage with environmental protection.

Throughout the chapter, we make a baseline assumption that environmental protection and concern is a positive, and we recognize that this is a normative claim. However, we do not propose specific policy directives or complete acquiescence of cultural authority to professional scientific expertise. After all, scholars involved in the social scientific and humanistic study of science have urged scholars and the public to take seriously the social context of scientific knowledge. Thus, our interest is not to set up science—whether evolutionary, climate, or otherwise—outside the purview of public criticism and critique. The power of science, in its technological innovations, self-information, and transformative power, make scientific self-reflectivity and thoughtful criticism, from all parts of its cultural context, paramount. Thus, our hope is not to recuse a pure science from the political machinations of a caricatured religion. Rather, we suggest a historically informed, pragmatic approach to environmental ethics that reimagines the political influence of these religious communities in favor of environmental concern.

Evangelicalism and Science in the Twentieth Century

During the late nineteenth and early twentieth centuries, the term "evangelical" was adopted by Anglo-American Protestants in the Reformed and Wesleyan traditions who emphasized the "centrality of the Bible, the death and resurrection of Jesus, the necessity of individual conversion, and the spreading of the faith through missions" (Sutton, 2014, x). By the early decades of the twentieth century the term "fundamentalism" was used to describe a distinctive movement within the broader evangelical tradition. Partly in reaction to modernist theological movements, fundamentalists emphasized a plain-sense adherence to the Bible, mission, and individualistic piety. However, early twentieth-century fundamentalism did not attempt to discredit natural science on the national stage, set up alternative scientific institutions, or offer alternative scientific theories, not even during the most famous interaction between fundamentalism and modern science: the 1925 Scopes monkey trial. Orchestrated by the American Civil Liberties Union (ACLU), the Scopes trial was an effort by Northern progressives and theological modernists to defend the teaching of evolution in public school classrooms (Shapiro, 2013). Seizing an opportunity in Dayton, Tennessee, the ACLU persuaded a high school teacher, John Scopes, to incur a fine for teaching evolution in his classroom. The hope was that the trial would become a test case bringing the defense of evolution before the US Supreme Court, wherein the Court would overturn any law banning the teaching of evolution at the state level.[1]

During the trial, fundamentalists rejected evolution, viewing it as a harbinger of cultural modernism, secularism, and northern progressive values. The teaching of evolution in schools was associated with the new civic values of the urban, northern, progressive movement, while fundamentalism was based in the traditional values of the rural regions of the American South and Southwest (Larson, 1997; Numbers, 1998; Shapiro, 2013). Officials in Tennessee defended the law as an appropriate exercise of the right of states to establish school curricula, but they did not propose or attempt to teach alternatives to evolution, nor did they organize political action against professional scientific institutions.

The Scopes trial has loomed large in the history of early twentieth-century Christian reactions to modern science; much less has been written about conservative Christian views on environmental protection in the same period, despite the fact that the environmental movement of that time saw itself as secular, progressive, and science-based. Indeed, American environmentalism during the Progressive era drew on a set of cultural values that were strongly at odds with fundamentalism, including advocacy for centralized control and scientific management of natural resources (Appfel-Marglin & Marglin, 1996, 115). It was an ethos that melded well with the mainline Protestant Social Gospel which championed social reform, in the form of the temperance, sanitation, and education movements, as the primary work of the church in American culture. Conservationist activists, such as Theodore Roosevelt, who sought to protect the American wilderness, looked to the churches of the urbanized Northeast for support, not to fundamentalists in the rural American South (Rosen, 2004). Fundamentalism, though not overtly hostile to environmentalism, was simply not a participant in the political dialogue around it in the early part of the twentieth century.

Early historical work on fundamentalism argued that this community retreated from the national mainstream after their defeat at the Scopes trial.[2] But since the 1980s, American historians have focused on the greater continuities between the fundamentalists of the early part of the century and later evangelicals. Despite a persistent caricature of fundamentalism and anti-evolutionism as a rural phenomenon, historians have stressed that the leaders of these movements often came from Northern urban areas (Sandeen, 1970; Szasz, 1982). Recent historical work has continued to nuance the regional movement of fundamentalism, in order to more carefully account for the influx of national attention to evangelicalism in the early 1980s. Darren Dochuck (2011), for instance, has argued that the character of earlier evangelical "plain folk" religion was transferred and transformed after the Depression with massive migrations from states such as Texas, Arkansas, Oklahoma, and Tennessee to southern California. Transformed in the southern California suburban landscape, evangelical religious culture moved from communities in the north- and southeast to the mainstream of southern California life during the 1950s and 1960s. Sutton (2014), in a study of the apocalyptic narratives within evangelicalism, argues that these communities infused local, state, and finally national politics with a moral agenda that was focused on the end times. By the later decades of the century, these transformations enabled evangelicals to occupy the main stage of national politics.

But although historians have documented a persistent desire by evangelicals for political engagement, it was not until the 1980 presidential election that this occurred, when evangelicalism was taken on by Ronald Reagan and conservative Republicans, who installed partisan politics into an apocalyptic narrative of good versus evil (Williams, 2012, 2). The 1980s represented the "first time [conservative Christians] began to think they could use their own political power to take the nation back from the 'secular humanists'" (Williams, 2012, 160). Leading up to the election, a number of key Christian leaders succeeded in rallying evangelicals to the Republican Party over a number of significant issues; these included abortion, gay rights, and the tax-exempt status of Christian institutions.[3] Evangelical leaders, including Jerry Falwell, believing that the Republican Party under Ronald Reagan's leadership was the most promising place for evangelical influence, encouraged their followers to align themselves accordingly. This was a somewhat surprising decision, insofar as President Jimmy Carter was an avowed evangelical and Ronald Reagan was not. However, sexual morality was such a crucially defining aspect of political evangelicalism that evangelical leaders abandoned Carter when he supported aspects of the gay rights movement and refused to back evangelical pro-life campaigns. Reagan did not fulfill many of the hopes of the evangelical Right, but its leaders continued to support him and the Republican Party through the 1980s, and by the end of the twentieth century, evangelicalism was inextricably associated with the Republican Party and its platform.

Anthropologist T. M. Luhrmann's recent ethnography of the evangelical Association of Vineyard Churches highlights the significance of this shift in conservative Christian spiritual culture. She argues that "the God [evangelicals] seek is more personally intimate, and more intensely experienced, then the God most Americans grew up with" (Luhrmann, 2012, xv). Luhrman points to the influence of the hippie culture on fringe elements of Christianity during this period as one origin for an evangelical spirituality that earlier generations of Americans would have "regarded as vulgar, emotional, or even psychotic" (Luhrmann, 2012, xv). Another crucial source for this energetic spirituality was the rise of Pentecostalism during the twentieth century. Broadly speaking, Pentecostalism was a renewal movement within evangelicalism which stressed personal experience of God through the baptism of the Holy Spirit (Hollenweger, 2005). By the 1970s, these influences helped to transform conservative Christianity into something more than a theological perspective. Being an evangelical was an all-encompassing spiritual identity, one that called its followers into increasing visible action on the national scene.

Evangelicalism and Science

During the critical years around 1980, when evangelical Christianity became synonymous with the Christian Right, the Creation-science movement laid the foundation for a politics of doubt that questioned the scientific consensus on Darwinian evolution. These strategies continued their life in the early 1990s in the Intelligent Design movement and were subsequently deployed in the next decade during public debates on climate change. The evangelical relationship to environmental protection was mediated by more than just associative politics. It had a foundation in a strategy of public doubt about science that became a marker of right-wing politics and conservative Christian values in this period.

The 1980s evangelical political platform included a reinvigorated opposition to Darwinian evolution, now organized around the idea of offering a scientific alternative to the theory of evolution by natural selection (Larson, 1985). The spearhead for this can be found in the work of Henry Morris, a civil engineer, and John C. Whitcomb Jr., a theologian. Together, they were two of the key founders of young-earth creationism in the United States. In their 1961 book *The Genesis Flood*, Morris and Whitcomb argued that a literalist interpretation of Genesis could and should be supported by modern geological evidence. The marriage between literalist biblical interpretations and this flood geology soon became known as Creation-science, and Morris became one of the co-founders of the Institute for Creation Research (ICR) in El Cajon, California.

As the institutional heart of Creation-science, the ICR published a wealth of material touting scientific evidence that supports biblical literalist accounts of Earth's geological history. These materials were circulated through networks of churches and were regularly endorsed by leading evangelicals such as Charles C. Ryrie, Josh McDowell, Jerry Falwell, and Tim LaHaye (Numbers, 2006, 316). By the end of the twentieth century, the influence of creationism within evangelicalism was profound, reinforcing a conservative Christian suspicion of Darwinian evolution. Rather than argue, as their fundamentalist precursors had done, that communities had the right to reject evolution and teach concepts that were consistent with community values, creationists took on science directly, arguing that evolutionary theory was a "theory in crisis." Essentially, they argued that academic scientists were unwilling to consider the evidence that might support creationism, and that Creation-science offered an alternative to evolution with a theory that was consonant with the biblical account of Creation.[4]

During the 1970s and 1980s, Morris and the ICR played a crucial role in the entanglement between evangelical identity and public suspicion of mainstream scientific consensus. Although the ICR represented itself as a scientific research institute, its time and resources were primarily given to strategic activities to promote Creation-science to the wider public. In this, Morris and the ICR were occupied with the legal battle to introduce Creation-science into public science classrooms. Morris's 1974 book *Scientific Creationism* was intended to convince public school teachers that Darwinian evolution was faulty science and to provide teachers with a manual for teaching Creation-science as a legitimate scientific alternative. These efforts culminated in a highly publicized court case in 1981: *McLean v. Arkansas*. Creation-science efforts had succeeded in pushing a bill through the Arkansas state legislature that mandated "balanced treatment for Creation-science and evolution-science" in Arkansas' public school classrooms. The ACLU helped to bring a suit against the state, arguing that the bill represented an incursion of religion into public schools, violating the establishment clause of the first amendment.

Convincing the court to strike down the equal-time ideal required that the plaintiffs prove that Creation-science was not science, but was in fact religion, and that teaching it would violate the establishment clause of the first amendment. The plaintiff's strategy was twofold. First, they demonstrated that Creation-science had religious motivations; this was relatively straightforward because, although the Arkansas bill was stripped of religious language, the rest of the Creation-science literature (including Morris's work) was replete with biblical references. (This helped set the precedent for the 1987 US Supreme Court Case, *Edwards v. Aguilard*, which ended the Creation-science bid for equal time in public schools.) But the second aspect of the plaintiff's argument was perhaps more important in terms of the cultural impact of the trial. Plaintiffs maintained that Creation-science, irrespective of its religious motivations, did not meet the necessary criteria to be defined as a science. This argument was developed by the use of expert testimony from academic historians and philosophers of science.

The presiding judge, William Overton, drew heavily on expert testimony in crafting his decision (reprinted in *Science* and at least three evolution advocacy books). He quoted philosopher of science Michael Ruse that Creation-science did not meet the philosophical definition of science, which Ruse defined by five criteria. It was: (1) guided by natural law, (2) explanatory by reference to natural law, (3) testable against the empirical world, (4) its conclusions are tentative, and (5) it is falsifiable. Most histories of the trial (including, not surprisingly, Ruse's own) have focused on Overton's use of these traditional philosophical demarcation criteria (Pennock & Ruse, 2008; Ruse, 2013). But Overton also drew on the testimony of a sociologist of science, Dorothy Nelkin. During the trial, when asked "what constitutes science?" Nelkin replied that science was "a body of knowledge and a set of procedures that are widely accepted by the scientific community at a given time" (*McLean v. Arkansas*, 529 F. Supp.155) (E.D. Ark. 1982). Overton drew on this testimony as well, noting that a descriptive definition was said to be that science is what is "accepted by the scientific community" and is "what scientists do."[5] Overton concluded that Creation-science not only did not operate as a science, methodologically, it failed the more general criteria of "what scientists think" and "what scientists do." He continued:

> The scientific community consists of individuals and groups, nationally and internationally, who work independently in such varied fields as biology, paleontology, geology, and astronomy. Their work is published and subject to review and testing by their peers. The journals for publication are both numerous and varied. There is, however, not one recognized scientific journal which has published an article espousing the creation science theory described in Section 4(a). Some of the State's witnesses suggested that the scientific community was "close-minded" on the subject of creationism and that explained the lack of acceptance of the creation science arguments. Yet no witness produced a scientific article for which publication has been refused. Perhaps some members of the scientific community are resistant to new ideas. It is, however, inconceivable that such a loose knit group of independent thinkers in all the varied fields of science could, or would, so effectively censor new scientific thought.

Creation-science was not a science because it was not done by professionally credentialed scientists in the recognized venues for academic scientific research (Overton, 1983, 60–62).

The plaintiff's arguments and Overton's decision during *McLean* were, in a real sense, the other side of the Creation-science coin. Both Creation-scientists and their opponents worked with a definition of science that was defined by the boundaries of the scientific community.[6] Unlike the plaintiffs in the *Mclean* case, though, the ICR wished to contest the credibility of that community. Throughout the 1970s and 1980s, Morris and the ICR worked tirelessly to debate the empirical evidence for Darwinian evolution and to secure young-age interpretations of Genesis among evangelicals. First, they argued that the scientific community's refusal to accept Creation-science was nothing more than a dogmatic dismissal of an alternative, legitimate scientific perspective. To this end, the ICR sponsored public debates with evolutionists, believing that debates would give voice to Creation-science within academic science and help to portray the scientific consensus on Darwinian evolution as a hegemonic dogma, one that inhibited the true spirit of science as an open dialogue, not only tolerant but encouraging of dissenting views. The second tactic was to focus on disagreements between professionally credentialed evolutionists to argue that the scientific consensus was not as complete as scientists insisted it was. They concentrated particularly on the work of Harvard evolutionary biologist Stephen Jay Gould, who put forward a series of unorthodox theoretical perspectives on Darwinian evolution during the 1980s. Gould was certainly no creationist, but Morris trumpeted Gould's disagreements with other evolutionists (Morris, 1985, vii–viii).

These two strategies might seem contradictory, for, on the one hand, the ICR argued that the professional scientific community was dogmatically wedded to their beliefs in Darwinian evolution, but on the other, highlighted dissent among scientists. But these two tactics represented the same argumentative logic: that the consensus on Darwinian evolution was only forged through scientific dogmatism and that the cracks in this intellectual hegemony could and should be exposed to cast doubt on the science of evolution and, indeed, to suggest that creationists were truer to the spirit of science than mainstream biologists were.

While this argument failed in the law court, it achieved considerable success in the court of public opinion, particularly evangelical opinion. The close association between the ICR and key evangelical church leaders was enough to connect these political tactics against evolutionary science with the broader goals of the conservative wing of the evangelical movement. In the shifting culture wars of the 1980s, creationism became one on a long list of issues that redefined the American political spectrum as the Moral Majority came to dominate right-wing politics. Leftists responded with a growing anxiety about the political alliance between evangelicals and the Republican Party—a concern that was captured by the 1982 publication of a collection of essays titled *Speak out against the New Right* (Vetter, 1982). Essays by leading liberal lights such as Gloria Steinem and John F. Kennedy, Jr. implored readers to recognize the Right's reactionary political agenda which targeted social welfare programs, sex education in schools, and abortion rights. The contributors believed that creationism was one brick in the New Right's political platform, which they characterized in the opening of the volume to be:

> Ban godless books from our libraries and schools.
> Get women back home and out of the job market
> Make the Bible the foundation of our government and laws
> Become the dominant power in the Congress, the courts, and the White House
> Help fund religious schools through government vouchers
> Oppose both contraception and abortion
> Write creationism into science textbooks.
>
> (Vetter, 1982, xv)

The Leftist objection to creationism was represented by Gould's essay "Evolution as Fact and Theory." Gould denounced Creation-science as "politics, pure and simple; it represents one issue and by no means the major concern of the resurgent evangelical right" (Gould, 1981, 34–37, reprinted in Vetter, 1982, 197–202). These words, from evolution's most overtly Leftist figure, helped evangelical Christians to define the defense of academic science as a Leftist value (Perez, 2013). Defending the professional scientific consensus now became a left-wing value.

This point is worth dwelling on, since it is not at all obvious that it would necessarily have come about. After all, during the 1960s and 1970s, the Left had been the home of radical activism against the scientific establishment (Beckwith, 1986; Moore, 1996). During the Cold War, academic science was often criticized by Leftist activists for its association with the military-industrial complex which funded and set agendas for scientific research. The anti-nuclear and environmental movements of the 1960s and 1970s pitted themselves against the twin evils of scientific overreach and hawkish military agendas. During the sociobiology controversy of the 1970s, feminists and other New Left activists criticized evolutionary biology for its attempts to provide biological explanations for American social gender roles (Jumonville, 2002; Perez, 2013). Through the 1990s during the so-called "Science Wars," feminists and others on the academic Left were associated with the most elaborated and damaging critiques of the objectivity and reliability of science (Gross & Levitt, 1997). But the creationist controversy severely complicated the Left's ability to criticize the academic scientific establishment. Wary of being associated with the reactionary politics of conservative Christianity, Leftist critics of science were forced to defend the ability of the scientific community to define the boundary between credible science and illegitimate pseudoscience (Sheldon, 2014).

Creation-science was dealt a fatal blow by the 1987 US Supreme Court case *Edwards v. Aguillard*, which held that it was a form of religion and therefore its teaching in public schools violated the establishment clause. With this, scientists and scientific advocacy groups believed that the creationist movement had been defeated. But this conclusion proved premature, and confidence was quickly set aside when pro-evolution activists received word of the activities of a new type of creationism, called Intelligent Design. In response to *Edwards v. Aguillard*, which ensured that creationism was forever tainted by its religious associations, the Intelligent Design movement promoted a new creationist agenda that sought to develop theories that would look more like science, as defined in the *Overton* decision.

The new approach used the language of "design" rather than "Creation." Although some of the foundational texts of the Intelligent Design movement put forward biochemical arguments for the role of design in the origin of life, most of its key texts still focused on attacking the consensus on Darwinian evolution (Behe, 1996; Denton, 1986). For instance, Phillip Johnson's 1991 book *Darwin on Trial*, focused on the theoretical differences among prominent evolutionary biologists. Johnson attempted to portray Darwinism as a frayed consensus—a theory held together only by the stubborn dogmatism of evolutionary biologists who refused to acknowledge their own disagreements (Johnson, 1991). This strategy of framing evolution as a "theory in crisis" was also the mandate for the Center for Science and Culture (CSC), a project of the non-profit Discovery Institute. Founded in 1996 as the institutional heart of Intelligent Design, the CSC put together a series of campaigns, which argued for the teaching of Intelligent Design as a scientific alternative to Darwinian evolution in public schools. The Discovery Institute's desire to use Intelligent Design as a "wedge" with which to reform American culture according to Protestant Christian values was made public when the famous (or infamous) "wedge document" outlining this strategy was published on their website in 1997 (Center for the Renewal of Science and Culture, 1997). The Discovery Institute had now cast academic science as its explicit foe in a war over values in American culture.

In this brief consideration of the politics of the Creation-science and Intelligent Design movements, we have suggested that a hostile suspicion of the consensus of the scientific community was engendered by these movements. And because of the close association between evangelicalism and the Republican Party, distrusting scientific authority on these issues became a way for conservative politicians to signal their allegiance to an entire set of religio-political values. The association among evangelical Christianity, conservative politics, and distrust of academic science had been deepened in the decades since Morris's early work with Creation-science. And this association meant that organizations such as the Discovery Institute were poised to encourage a "theory-in-crisis" rhetoric on the science of climate change.

From Evolution to Climate Change

In the Winter of 2009, the Republican senator from Pennsylvania, Rick Santorum, penned an op-ed in the *Philadelphia Inquirer*: "The Elephant in the Room: Challenging Scientific Dogma." In it, Santorum claimed "as with evolution, the 'consensus' on climate change has become an ideology." Santorum, who had been a significant proponent of Intelligent Design (in 2001 he had introduced an Intelligent Design amendment to the "No Child Left Behind" education bill), described the science of climate change as the same kind of dogma as Darwinian evolution (Numbers, 2006, 389). Santorum outlined what he believed were the true features of science, "Questioning the scientific consensus in pursuit of the truth is an important part of how science had advanced through the centuries. But what happens when the scientific consensus becomes an ideology that trumps the pursuit of truth? Answer:

those making legitimate inquiries are ostracized, the careers of dissenters are destroyed, and debate is stifled." Santorum was clear which scientific topic he had in mind. Continuing the comparisons between Darwinism and climate change, he declared: "it is one thing for ideologically driven science to indoctrinate children in classrooms. It is another for politicians to use science to destroy national economies and redistribute global wealth. I refer, of course, to the latest scientific non-controversy, man-made global warming." He continued, "Climate Change's Pharisees reassure us the global-warming science is still settled... Never mind the legitimate questions that climate-change skeptics have been asking for some time. There's nothing to see here; move along" (Santorum, 2009).

Santorum's editorial captured in a nutshell the links that had been forged among climate-change science opponents, the Republican Party, and evangelical Christianity during the years of the George W. Bush presidency. Bush, a self-identified evangelical Christian, led a Republican Party whose platform cemented the connections among conservative social values, anti-regulatory free enterprise, and America's Christian identity. In the last section, we described the rhetorical strategy that the Discovery Institute and other Intelligent Design advocates developed to unpick the scientific consensus over evolution. These rhetorical strategies were subsequently deployed in the politics of climate change skepticism. Journalists picked up on this smooth transition. In 2010 the *New York Times* noted that "[c]ritics of the teaching of evolution in the nation's classrooms are gaining ground in some states by linking the issue to global warming, arguing that dissenting views on both scientific subjects should be taught in public schools" (Kaufmann, 2010). In the same article John West, an executive at the Discovery Institute, told the *New York Times* that the Institute believed that "There is a lot of similar dogmatism on this issue, with scientists being persecuted for findings that are not in keeping with the orthodoxy. We think analyzing and evaluating scientific evidence is a good thing, whether that is about global warming or evolution" (Lebo, 2010). Indeed, taking on climate change helped the Discovery Institute to claim that it was not an "anti-evolution" organization, but an "anti-scientific dogma" one (Lebo, 2010).

During the Creation-science era, evolutionary activists—that is, evolutionary scientists who acted as witnesses in cases such as *McLean v. Arkansas*, and supported the pro-evolutionary non-profit National Center for Science Education—had argued against Creation-science on the basis that it was not professionally credentialed science. Thus, a critical part of the argument against Creation-science was the view that "science is what scientsts do and that a scientific community exists, marked by its own rules" (Herlihy, 1983). This defining of science by the boundaries of the scientific community continued through the era of Intelligent Design. But this definition by professional scientists and science activists had a curious effect on the arguments for Intelligent Design or against climate change. The Discovery Institute and conservative politicians now argued that their skepticism about climate change was based on a championship of true scientific values, and not religion or politics. By framing the mainstream scientific consensus on climate change as a dogma, the Discovery Institute portrayed itself as the light of healthy scientific skepticism. As John West, vice president of the Institute, expressed it in 2007,

> Unfortunately, a growing chorus urges that public policy be dictated by the majority of scientific experts without input from anyone else. This bold assertion is made not just with regard to evolution, but concerning a host of other controversial issues such as sex education, euthanasia, embryonic stem-cell research, cloning and global warming. Any dissent from the orthodoxy of "experts" on these issues allegedly represents a "war on science." But that's just not the case. (West, 2007, 362)

Just as the Intelligent Design movement had framed evolutionary science as a dogma, the Discovery Institute attempted to portray climate-change science in the same light. This tactic had an interesting effect. Many of the most public arguments that defended climate-change science focused on the overwhelming scientific consensus on the anthropomorphic origin of climate change; since the Discovery Institute depicted this consensus as a hallmark of the close-mindedness of the scientific establishment, touting the agreement of the scientific community may have actually had an adverse effect on the cultural perception of climate change, at least among evangelicals. The louder that scientists proclaimed their agreement, the more this appeared to be at least dogma, if not an actual liberal conspiracy, to conservative Christian audiences. During the Bush era, denying climate change became an issue that Republican politicians could use to signal their allegiance to the platform of traditional American values that were so dear to evangelical audiences.

The linkages between climate change and the Christian Right continued into the next decade. As recently as January 2015, lawmakers in South Dakota were "pushing a bill that would allow teachers to address the supposed 'weaknesses' in the scientific theories of evolution and global warming." The measure proposed in South Dakota "does not advance intelligent design or creationism, but it would allow teachers to question accepted scientific theories." The Discovery Institute, which helped draft the bill, clarified that "the bill would not protect teachers who present creationism to students," but that the "group's model legislation simply offers a shield for teachers who question the science of evolution or climate change" (Gettys, 2015).

The activities of the Discovery Institute had a political and cultural impact that now reached far beyond their specific complaints about evolutionary theory. Through the "theory in crisis" rhetoric developed by the organization, the Discovery Institute helped to fuel the Right's approach to undermining any science that conflicted with its political aims. And the Institute's connections with networks of evangelical churches and organizations helped to deepen the connection between American Christian identity and the politics of scientific doubt.

Evangelical Environmentalism

We have offered a narrative of historical developments that undergird the current hostility among some parts of the conservative Christian community toward environmental protection. By arguing that this antipathy to the environmental movement is the result of associative politics, we do not claim that these intertwined political, social, and intellectual movements have somehow violated essential features of Protestant Christianity. But we do argue that they are not rooted in essential features of that religious tradition. Moreover, by highlighting this history, we hope that it becomes possible and necessary to imagine other political, social, and theological configurations within evangelicalism that might embrace environmental protection. The strongest argument for these possibilities lies in two already existing evangelical environmental movements: environmental protection as social justice and the Creation care movement.

Broadly speaking, the liberal secular arguments for environmental regulation have focused on caring for the planet as a duty of the human species. This duty is given greater weight by the urgent alarms raised by the environmental science community. In contrast, evangelical environmentalists frame their position in theological terms, describing care of the planet as a calling to love God and to love others. Both movements have begun to gain traction in evangelical circles, even amidst its most conservative leaders. Given this, it is perhaps unnecessary (or inadvisable) to argue for conservative Christian support for environmental activism on the basis of scientific consensus. Rather, we suggest that evangelical environmentalism can be situated within the moral framework that is already present in evangelical theology.

Beginning in the late 1990s, a number of evangelical environmentalists began to use the term "Creation care" to describe their activism. The term was an explicit attempt to distance their work from secular environmental movements and to claim a biblical basis for Christian environmentalism. For instance, Creation care activists argued that the verses in Genesis 1 that had traditionally been interpreted as a mandate for humanity's "rule" over the Earth were in fact a call for humanity to be "stewards" of Creation (Wilkinson, 2012). These activists also called Christians into a deep wonder and love of God's handiwork in Creation, arguing that it was the duty of Christian to preserve and protect God's creative work.

Although it began in the 1990s, the Creation care movement drew on natural theology, a theological framework that dates to the earliest periods of Christian history. Broadly speaking, natural theology advocates that the natural world can reveal the character of God, and it is to be explored, studied, and revered for this reason (Berkel & Vanderjagt, 2005, 2006). Natural theology holds that there are in effect two books of revelation, God's word and God's work. The natural world is the second of these books, to be read and revered alongside the first, the revelation of scripture. Historians of science, particularly of the early modern era, have argued that this framework undergirded the rationale for many investigations of Nature in the so-called scientific revolution of the sixteenth and seventeenth centuries.[7] This theological thread was woven into the institutionalization of science, especially in Anglo-American contexts, as natural theology provided the rationale for the study of natural history into the early part of the nineteenth century (Outram, 1996; O'Connor, 2008, 40–43; Rudwick, 2008). Much of scientific investigation itself therefore depended on the framework of natural theology. Importantly, much of the historical consideration of the impact of Darwinian evolution has been over whether, and to what extent, Darwinian evolution overturned the logic of natural theology. Darwin's mechanism of natural selection argued that the apparent order and harmony of the world was not the work of a benevolent God, but was the epiphenomenon of selfish actors.[8] Indeed, one way of understanding the epistemological impulse of the Intelligent Design movement was the desire to revive the arguments from design from early nineteenth-century natural theology (Shapiro, 2009).

Natural theology, however, was not only an argument about modes of scientific investigation; it was also a perspective about the quality and character of the world. In the late twentieth century, the natural theology of Creation care pushed evangelical environmentalists to focus on the conservation of wild spaces in the United States and abroad (Abbate, 2012; Liederbach & Bible, 2012). During this period a number of evangelical Christian organizations that embraced wilderness protection proliferated around the country. Nature camps, which blended vacation Bible schools, outdoor skills, and field biology, sprung up in the Great Lakes, Puget Sound, and parts of the Sierra Nevada. These institutions were primarily targeted at K-12 students, aiming to instill a love of the natural world and an environmental ethic in young evangelicals. One notable organization, the Au Sable Institute, was founded in 1979 as an institute in field biology for undergraduate students at partnering evangelical Christian colleges; the Institute currently has campuses in the Midwest, Costa Rica, the West Coast, and Florida. Its mission promises prospective students that they "will encounter both the wonders of God's world and the challenges of caring for creation" (Au Sable, 2015).

These organizations come close to embodying the vision that Wilson hoped to inspire in his 2004 book *The Creation: An Appeal to Save Life on Earth.* Wilson, a Pulitzer Prize recipient, internationally famous evolutionary biologist, environmental activist, and self-proclaimed secular humanist, wrote the book as an appeal to an imagined Protestant Christian pastor (Wilson, 2006). In it he entreated this hypothetical pastor to work with him to set aside their different worldviews in order to embark on the common task of caring for the natural world. Wilson believed it was irrelevant that he cared for the Earth as an evolutionist, and the pastor saw Nature as the creation of God. In the opening of the book he declared, "I suggest we set aside our differences in order to save the Creation. The defense of living Nature is a universal value. It doesn't rise from, nor does it promote, any religious or ideological dogma. Rather, it serves without discrimination the interests of all humanity" (2006, 4).

The vision of Wilson and the Creation care movement had a significant appeal to some evangelical circles, particularly those associated with the nationwide network of evangelical Christian colleges. However, the movement has had limits for two primary reasons. First, it has focused on the preservation of wild spaces, which has made it difficult to translate into environmental regulations, such as those that might be used to control greenhouse gases or pollution more generally. Second, it relies on convincing evangelicals that valuing the wilderness is a core Christian value, and this has not always resonated in urban and suburban evangelical churches which have primarily urban and ethnically diverse congregations. Thus the "wilderness encounter" has so far proven to be an important, but as yet narrow, foundation for evangelical environmentalism.

In contrast, evangelicals who have argued for environmental activism as an issue of social justice have had a broader impact. Characterized first in the work of Jim Wallis, the most prominent voice of progressive evangelicalism, evangelicals have begun to argue for environmental regulation as a way to combat global poverty (Wallis, 2005). In 2006, 86 evangelical churches launched the Evangelical Climate Initiative, which called for the reduction of carbon dioxide emissions. Initially backed by evangelical progressives (including the presidents of a number of evangelical colleges and Wallis), the initiative eventually received the support of the largest evangelical organization, the National Association of Evangelicals (NAE) (Goodstein, 2006; NAE, 2006). This climate initiative acknowledged the scientific community's consensus on the reality of anthropogenic climate change and argued that Christians had a moral duty to combat climate change as an obligation to the global poor:

> Poor nations and poor individuals have fewer resources available to cope with major challenges and threats. The consequences of global warming will therefore hit the poor the hardest, in part because those areas likely to be significantly affected first are in the poorest regions of the world. Millions of people could die in this century because of climate change, most of them our poorest global neighbors. (NAE, 2006)

This argument for environmentalism as social justice is now the centerpiece of evangelical climate change advocacy. One particularly prominent voice is Katherine Hayhoe's, an atmospheric scientist at Texas Tech University and outspoken evangelical environmentalist. Hayhoe tours the country arguing for the reality of climate change and for the moral duty of Christians to combat it. Among other things, she claims that environmental activism that has focused on "saving the polar bear" has not persuaded most Americans (Hayhoe & Farley, 2009).

This direct connection between caring for people and environmentalism appears to have gained purchase among evangelicals; even some very conservative voices have adopted this social justice rhetoric. Baptist pastor and author John Piper, for example, one of the most outspoken evangelicals against feminism and gay rights, has adopted this language. He states in regard to environmentalism, "I think the best argument for environmental concern is love for people, not love for mother earth. Who cares about mother earth as a mother? The earth is the Lord's and the fullness thereof. It's his and he meant it to serve people. He put us here to enjoy it. So, if we mess it up we are hurting people" (Piper, 2010). Piper's politics may be antithetical to many of those in the secular environmental movement, and his theology is by no means representative of all evangelicals, or all Christians, much less all American religious communities. However, if even Piper, a figurehead in the conservative corner of the Religious Right, can articulate an ethic of environmental activism, it suggests that the contingent historic linkages that aligned American evangelicals with anti-environmental thinking may now be shifting.

Conclusion

Rather than seeing recent clashes between scientific and religious communities as examples of a timeless conflict between irreconcilable worldviews, we have described these clashes as particular features of American political alignments over the last several decades. In doing so, we have not meant to portray these debates as "only" or "merely" political. Politics are not simply superficial debates among social groups, although they may feel this way in contemporary contexts. The conflicts between social conservatives and secular environmentalists were ones of associative politics, but also revealed deeply divergent perspectives on the role of the state, the nature of the citizenry, and the sources for effective social and cultural change. In other words, by understanding these controversies not as conflicts between abstract instantiations of "science" and "religion," we do not claim to have solved the debates by seeing them as being primarily political.

As we have discussed, the evangelical movement and American partisan politics were tightly stitched together from the 1980s onward. Crucially, this weaving together of evangelicalism and American politics effected a kind of historical erasure—even as the movement became more overtly political, leaders in the movement framed political issues as indispensable Christian values. What historians of evangelicalism have accomplished, therefore, is to describe the contingent history that underlies this rhetoric. By opening up the historical intertwining of evangelical identity, conservative politics, and climate change skepticism, we have worked to disprove that evangelicals in particular or Christians in general are necessarily anti-science or anti-environmental protection. Combined with a reflection on environmental protection movements within the evangelical community, this history provides a potential argument for a broad and inclusive foundation of environmental protection in the US.

Notes

1 Importantly, the ACLU was unsuccessful in this aim. The trial was thrown out by the state supreme court over a technicality in sentencing and was therefore ineligible for appeal to a higher court.

2 In his review of the "legends" of the trial, Numbers stresses the historiographic disagreements that persisted as a reflection of the cultural importance that the trial holds for historians and the American public alike (Numbers, 1998). Here we refer to the historiographic impulse in the 1990s that interpreted the Scopes trial as the cause of the fundamentalist retreat from the national mainstream (Carpenter, 1997; Marsden, 1991). More recent work has sought to complicate this narrative and stressed that evangelical religious communities sought political engagement throughout the twentieth century (Dochuk, 2011; Sutton, 2014).

3 A number of historians located the origins of the Christian Right in the "culture wars" of the 1970s, pointing to various issues as the source for this new political entity (Brown, 2002; Heineman, 1998). Williams (2012) makes a strong case that the 1980s did not represent a new desire for political action on the part of evangelicals, but rather a new tactic of political engagement one that focused evangelical efforts exclusively within the structures of the Republican Party.

4 An important nuance to this point is the different attitudes by young earth creationists to micro- versus macro-evolution. The distinction between the processes was brought into English-speaking contexts by one of the architects of the evolutionary synthesis, Theodosius Dobzhansky (1937). In this usage, micro-evolution refers to the changing frequency of alleles in a population over time due to the action of mutation, genetic drift, gene flow, and natural selection. Macro-evolution is a description of the change of populations or species across geological time. For the most part, young earth creationists accepted the action of

natural selection in micro-evolution but not in macro-evolution, as they believed it only reflects the natural development within species, not the origin of new species (Numbers, 2006, 245).

5 Historians will recognize this as similar to Daniel J. Kevles argument of the same era, in a debate with Paul Forman over the impact of military funding of physics: "physics is what physicists do" (Kevles, 1978).

6 Importantly, a significant shift had occurred since the 1920s, when anti-evolutionists attempted to argue that evolution lay outside the boundaries of science. Here anti-evolutionists argued that creationism was within science (Larson & Numbers, 2012).

7 This was not uniformly the case, and there were important differences between natural historians' and natural philosophers' use of the notion that the natural world was a mode of understanding the character of God (Shapin, 2008, 156–158).

8 The interpretation that Darwin's theory of natural selection had replaced designed order with the apparent order obtained by selfish actors was prominent during the early 1980s in theoretical evolutionary theory, particularly in the early applications of game theory in evolutionary theory (Allen, 1983; Gould, 1977; Smith, 1982). For historical perspectives on the relationship between natural theology and Darwinian evolution, see Peterfreund (2012) and Robinson (2012).

References

Abbate, Michael. 2009. *Gardening Eden: How Creation Care Will Change Your Faith, Your Life, and Our World.* New York: Crown Religion Publishing.

Allen, Gar. 1983. The Several Faces of Darwinism: Materialism in Nineteenth and Twentieth Century Evolutionary Theory, 81–102. In D. S. Bendall (Ed.), *Evolution: From Molecules to Men.* Cambridge: Cambridge University Press.

Apffel-Marglin, Frédérique & Marglin, Stephen A. 1996. *Decolonizing Knowledge: From Development to Dialogue.* Oxford: Oxford University Press.

Au Sable. 2016. About. *Au Sable Institute.* ausable.org/about.

Beckwith, Jonathan. 1986. The Radical Science Movement in the United States. *Monthly Review*, August.

Behe, Michael J. 1996. *Darwin's Black Box: The Biochemical Challenge to Evolution.* New York: Simon & Schuster.

Berkel, K. van & Vanderjagt, Arjo. 2005. *The Book of Nature in Antiquity and the Middle Ages.* Dudley: Peeters.

Berkel, Klaas van & Vanderjagt, Arie Johan. 2006. *The Book of Nature in Early Modern and Modern History.* Dudley: Peeters Publishers.

Brown, Ruth Murray. 2002. *For a Christian America: A History of the Religious Right.* Amherst, NY: Prometheus Books.

Carpenter, Joel A. 1997. *Revive Us Again: The Reawakening of American Fundamentalism: The Reawakening of American Fundamentalism.* Oxford: Oxford University Press.

Center for the Renewal of Science and Culture. 1997. The Wedge. www.antievolution.org.

Dade, Corey. 2011. In Their Own Words: GOP Candidates and Science. *NPR News*, September 7.

Denton, Michael. 1986. *Evolution: A Theory in Crisis.* Bethesda, MD: Adler & Adler.

Diamond, Sara. 2000. *Not by Politics Alone: The Enduring Influence of the Christian Right.* New York: Guilford Press.

Dobzhansky, Theodosius. 1937. *Genetics and the Origin of Species.* New York: Columbia University Press.

Dochuk, Darren. 2011. *From Bible Belt to Sunbelt: Plain-Folk Religion, Grassroots*

Politics, and the Rise of Evangelical Conservatism. New York: W. W. Norton.

Ecklund, Elaine Howard & Scheitle, Christopher. 2014. Religious Communities, Science, Scientists, and Perceptions: A Comprehensive Survey. Presentation at Annual Meetings of the American Association for the Advancement of Science.

Gettys, Travis. 2015. South Dakota Bill Would Allow Teachers to Question Evolution and Climate Change. *Raw Story*, January 29.

Goodstein, Laurie. 2006. Evangelical Leaders Join Global Warming Initiative. *New York Times*, February 8.

Gould, Stephen Jay. 1977. *Ever since Darwin: Reflections in Natural History*. New York: W. W. Norton.

Gould, Stephen Jay. 1981. Evolution as Fact and Theory. *Discover Magazine*, May.

Gross, Paul R., & Norman Levitt. 1997. *Higher Superstition: The Academic Left and Its Quarrels with Science*. Baltimore, MD: Johns Hopkins University Press.

Hayhoe, Katharine & Farley, Andrew. 2009. *A Climate for Change: Global Warming Facts for Faith-Based Decisions*. New York: FaithWords.

Heineman, Kenneth J. 1998. *God is a Conservative: Religion, Politics and Morality in Christian America*. New York: New York University Press.

Herlihy, Mark E. 1983. Scientific Disputes and Legal Strategies, 97–103. In Marcel Chotkowski LaFollette (Ed.), *Creationism, Science, and the Law*. Cambridge, MA: MIT Press.

Hollenweger, Walter J. 2005. *Pentecostalism: Origins and Developments Worldwide*. Peabody, MA: Baker Academic.

Jewett, Andrew. 2012. *Science, Democracy, and the American University: From the Civil War to the Cold War*. Cambridge: Cambridge University Press.

Johnson, Phillip E. 1991. *Darwin on Trial*. Downers Grove, IL: InterVarsity Press.

Jones, Robert, Cox, Daniel, & Navarro-Rivera, Juhem. 2014. Believers, Sympathizers, & Skeptics: Why Americans are Conflicted about Climate Change, Environmental Policy and Science. Findings from the PRRI/AAR Religion, Values and Climate Change Survey.

Jumonville, Neil. 2002. The Cultural Politics of the Sociobiology Debate. *Journal of the History of Biology*, 35, 3, 569–593.

Kaufmann, Lesli. 2010. Darwin Foes Adding Warming to Targets. *New York Times*, March 3.

Kevles, Daniel J. 1978. *The Physicists: The History of a Scientific Community in Modern America*. New York: Knopf: Distributed by Random House.

LaFollette, Marcel Chotkowski. 1983. *Creationism, Science, and the Law: The Arkansas Case*. Cambridge, MA: MIT Press.

Lambert, Frank. 2010. *Religion in American Politics: A Short History*. Princeton, NJ: Princeton University Press.

Larson, Edward J. & Numbers, Ronald L. 2012. Creation, Evolution, and the Boundaries of Science: The Debate in the United States. *Almagest*, 3, 1, 4–24.

Larson, Edward John. 1985. *Trial and Error: The American Controversy over Creation and Evolution*. Oxford: Oxford University Press.

———. 1997. *Summer for the Gods: The Scopes Trial and America's Continuing Debate over Science and Religion*. New York: BasicBooks.

Lebo, Lauri. 2010. Global Warming Denialists the New Creationists? *Religion Dispatches*, March 9.

Liederbach, Mark & Bible, Seth. 2012. *True North: Christ, the Gospel, and Creation Care*. Nashville, TN: B&H Publishing Group.

Luhrmann, T. M. 2012. *When God Talks Back: Understanding the American Evangelical Relationship with God*. New York: Random House.

Marsden, George. 1991. *Understanding Fundamentalism and Evangelicalism*. Grand Rapids, MI: Eerdmans.

Martin, William. 2005. *With God on Our Side: The Rise of the Religious Right in America*. New York: Random House.

Maynard Smith, John. 1982. "The Evolution of Behavior." *Scientific American*, 176–192.

Moore, Kelly. 1996. Organizing Integrity: American Science and the Creation of Public Interest Organizations, 1955–1975. *American Journal of Sociology*, 101, 6.

Moreton, Bethany. 2009. *To Serve God and Wal-Mart: The Making of Christian Free Enterprise*. Cambridge, MA: Harvard University Press.

Morris, Henry Madison. 1985. *Scientific Creationism*. Green Forest, AR: New Leaf Publishing Group.

Morris, Henry M. (Henry Madison) & Whitcomb, John Clement. 1961. *The Genesis Flood: The Biblical Record and Its Scientific Implications*. Philadelphia, PA: Presbyterian and Reformed Pub. Co.

National Association of Evangelicals (NAE). 2006. "Climate Change: An Evangelical Call to Action." *Evangelical Climate Initiative*. http://christiansandclimate.org/learn/call-to-action/signatories/.

Numbers, Ronald L. 1998. *Darwinism Comes to America*. Cambridge, MA: Harvard University Press.

Numbers, Ronald L. 2006. *The Creationists: From Scientific Creationism to Intelligent Design*. 2nd ed. Berkeley: University of California Press.

O'Connor, Ralph. 2008. *The Earth on Show: Fossils and the Poetics of Popular Science, 1802–1856*. Chicago, IL: University of Chicago Press.

Oreskes, Naomi, & Erik M. Conway. 2010. *Merchants of Doubt: How a Handful of Scientists Obscured the Truth on Issues from Tobacco Smoke to Global Warming*. New York: Bloomsbury Press.

Outram, Dorinda. 1996. New Spaces in Natural History, 249–265. In Nicholas Jardine & Emma Spary (Eds.), *Cultures of Natural History*. Cambridge: Cambridge University Press.

Overton, William R. 1983. *McLean v. Arkansas* Opinion, District Judge, Eastern District of Arkansas, Western Division. In Marcel Chotkowski LaFollette (Ed.), *Creationism, Science, and the Law: The Arkansas Case*. Cambridge, MA: MIT Press.

Pennock, Robert T. & Ruse, Michael (Eds.). 2008. *But is it Science? The Philosophical Question in the Creation/Evolution Controversy* (updated ed.). Amherst, NY: Prometheus Books.

Perez, Myrna. 2013. Evolutionary Activism: Stephen Jay Gould, the New Left and Sociobiology. *Endeavour*, 37, 2, 104–111.

Peterfreund, Stuart. 2012. *Turning Points in Natural Theology from Bacon to Darwin: The Way of the Argument from Design*. New York: Palgrave Macmillan.

Piper, John. 2010. Reformed Theology and Environmentalism. *Caffeinated Thoughts*. July. http://caffeinatedthoughts.com/2010/07/john-piper-reformed-theology-and-environmentalism/.

Robinson, Andrew. 2012. *Darwinism and Natural Theology: Evolving Perspectives*. Cambridge: Cambridge Scholars Publishing.

Rosen, Christine. 2004. *Preaching Eugenics: Religious Leaders and the American Eugenics Movement*. Oxford and New York: Oxford University Press.

Rudwick, Martin J. S. 2008. *The Meaning of Fossils: Episodes in the History of Paleontology*. Chicago, IL: University of Chicago Press.

Ruse, Michael. 2013. From Pseudoscience to Popular Science, from Popular Science to Professional Science, 225–244. In Massimo Pigliucci & Maarten Boudry (Eds.), *Philosophy of Pseudoscience: Reconsidering the Demarcation Problem*. Chicago, IL: University of Chicago Press.

Sandeen, Ernest R. 1970. *The Roots of Fundamentalism: British and American Millenarianism, 1800–1930*. Chicago, IL: University Of Chicago Press.

Santorum, Rick. 2009. The Elephant in the Room: Challenging Science Dogma. *Philadelphia Inquirer*, December 17.

Shapin, Steven. 2008. *The Scientific Revolution*. Chicago, IL: University of Chicago Press.

Shapiro, Adam R. 2013. *Trying Biology: The Scopes Trial, Textbooks, and the Antievolution Movement in American Schools*. Chicago: University of Chicago Press.

———. 2009. "William Paley's Lost 'intelligent Design'." *History and Philosophy of the Life Sciences*, 31, 1, 55–77.

Sutton, Matthew Avery. 2014. *American Apocalypse: A History of Modern Evangelicalism*. Cambridge, MA: Harvard University Press.

Szasz, Ferenc Morton. 1982. *The Divided Mind of Protestant America, 1880–1930*. Tuscaloosa, Alabama: The University of Alabama Press.

Vetter, Herbert F. (Ed.). 1982. *Speak Out against the New Right*. Boston, MA: Beacon Press.

Wallis, Jim. 2005. *God's Politics*. San Francisco, CA: Harper.

West, John G. 2007. *Darwin Day In America: How Our Politics and Culture Have Been Dehumanized in the Name of Science*. Wilmington, DE: Intercollegiate Studies Institute.

Wilkinson, Katharine K. 2012. *Between God and Green: How Evangelicals Are Cultivating a Middle Ground on Climate Change*. New York: Oxford University Press.

Williams, Daniel K. 2012. *God's Own Party: The Making of the Christian Right*. Oxford: Oxford University Press.

Wilson, Edward O. 2006. *The Creation: An Appeal to Save Life on Earth*. New York and London: W. W. Norton.

CHAPTER 26

The Covenant of Reciprocity

Robin Wall Kimmerer

We are showered every day with the gifts of the Earth, gifts we have neither earned nor paid for. When we woke this morning and put our feet on Mother Earth we were met with air to breathe, nurturing rain, black soil, berries, and honeybees, the tree that became this page, a bag of rice, and the exuberance of a field of goldenrod and asters in full bloom.

Many people in the society in which we live speak of these everyday miracles as "natural resources," as if they were our property, waiting to be transformed. In the ecological sciences we call them "ecosystem services" as if they were the inevitable outcomes of the function of the ecological machine. But to me, simply as a person filling my basket with berries and my belly with pie, they feel like gifts, bestowed by the beings whose lives surround us.

Though we live in a world made of gifts, we find ourselves harnessed to institutions and an economy that relentlessly asks, "What more can we take from the Earth?" This worldview of unbridled exploitation is, to my mind, the greatest threat to the life that surrounds us. Even our well-worn definitions of sustainability, such as "to ensure that the benefits of the use to present generations does not diminish the capacity to meet the needs and aspirations of future generations," revolve around trying to find a formula by which we can keep on taking, far into the future. Isn't the question we need, "What can we give in response for all we've been given, for all we have taken?"(Kimmerer, 2014).

It seems to me that for the past couple of centuries—just an eye blink in the lifetime of our species—we have been performing an unintended experiment, an experiment based in philosophy, but with very tangible manifestations. We have unwittingly asked, what would happen if we believed in human exceptionalism? What if a single species, out of the millions which inhabit the planet, was somehow more deserving of the richness of the Earth than any other? And not only that, in this experiment all the

The Wiley Blackwell Companion to Religion and Ecology, First Edition. Edited by John Hart.

ecological laws which constrain growth and consumption do not apply to us, and the laws of thermodynamics had been repealed on our behalf. What happens if we continue to take without giving in return? This poorly conceived experiment tests the hypothesis of what would happen if we behaved as if the Earth were nothing more than "stuff"—a strictly materialist, utilitarian view of the Earth—and, moreover, that all this stuff belonged to us?

After several centuries of data collection, the results of that experiment are in. We face natural goods ("resources") depletion, massive loss of biodiversity, accelerating climate change, inequity, and the systematic extinction of land-based cultures whose members question the very premise of this experiment. We find ourselves teetering on the edge of a precipice of climate chaos, entering what evolutionary biologists are calling the Age of the Sixth Extinction, in which we are losing 200 species every day.

How do we repair the harm we have done to the Earth? It is imperative that we do so, but first we should remember that it is not the Earth that is broken but our relationship with the Earth. The great thinker and botanist Gary Nabhan (1991) said that what we need is not only restoration, but "re-storyation," a healing new narrative for our relationship with the Earth.

The scientific worldview that has dominated our landscape for the past 500 years has undoubtedly yielded tremendous gains in the quality of human life. Science by its very nature seeks to generate knowledge which is free of the influence of human values and there is an important role for that attempted objectivity. However, the problems that our societies face today lie at the intersection of Nature and culture, in values and priorities. Science has brought us huge advances in knowledge, but it is not more knowledge that we now need; it is wisdom. And generating wisdom is not within the purview of science alone. For that we need a new kind of science, one that engages all the human faculties, not just the intellect, but also the mind, body, emotion, and spirit; one that includes not only *p*-values, the common scientific measure of statistical significance, but also human values.

Yet, much of our environmental discourse is about changing the type of lightbulbs we use. While new technologies are an important part of our response, as a scientist, I do not think that it is necessarily new technology, more data, or more money that are needed. If we are to survive, and if our more-than-human relatives are to survive as well, we need a change of heart, a change of worldview.

We are living in an era of profound error, which by virtue of our historical shortsightedness we have come to accept as "normal" when it is, in fact, an anomaly. If we set aside the post-Columbus era, we recognize that for much of humans' time on this planet we lived in cultures of balanced reciprocity with the land that sustains us. For much of our human history we understood ourselves not as "masters of the universe," but as "the younger brothers of Creation" as many indigenous cultures think of us.

The contemporary industrialized worldview understands the meaning of land primarily from a fourfold, materialist perspective. Land is recognized first, as property and its associated exclusionary rights, second, as capital, third, as a source of natural resources, and, more recently, fourth, as the provider of "ecosystem services" (soil fertility, oxygen, habitat and water purification). Humans' relationships with the land are many and diverse, but collapsed to these commonly used definitions land is understood metaphorically as a "machine," with humans playing the role of mechanic and beneficiary of the machine's production. Across the globe, this worldview has been imposed through colonialism, in an effort to replace a more ancient view which understands the land as a web of relationships which are simultaneously spiritual and material. In the indigenous worldview, these meanings include: land as sustainer, as the dwelling place of non-human relatives, as a source of knowledge, as a pharmacy, as the intergenerational home of both ancestors and descendants. The land is the place where our moral responsibility to life is enacted, land is home, land is inspirited, and land is sacred. Land and life are mutually sustaining when the worldview is based on responsibility *for* land rather than on rights *to* land. Is the land merely a source of belongings or is it also the source of our sense of belonging? We can choose the lens through which we view the world.

Our current adversarial relationship with the rest of the living world is not all that we are as a species. We can learn from the global mistakes we are making. We have stories to help us remember a different past and imaginations to help us find the new path. We are a species that can adapt.

This time we live in—of great change and great choices—has been spoken of by our ancestors in the teachings of the "Prophecies of the Seventh Fire," a long and important history, of which I will share just a fragment (Benton-Banai, 1988). It is the history of the migration of our Anishinaabe people. Each fire represents an historical era beginning with our migration from the East, where we lived among our Wabanaki relatives on the Atlantic shore. It is said that a prophet arose among the people warning of great changes to come and cautioning the people to divide and move to the West to safeguard the sacred fire. The history unfolds as our people moved through the generations to "where the food grows on the water," the wild rice lands of the Great Lakes. At each fire, or historical stopping place, teachers once again emerged to guide the people through the coming changes, including the upheaval caused by the arrival of the newcomers. It was foretold that the people would become alienated from their lands and from each other, that their language would be lost, that the black robes with their black book would seek to replace the ancient spiritual traditions, that the knowledge of the elders would be all but lost. This we know has come to pass. After all the losses of land, of language, of sacred ways, of each other, it is said that the people will find themselves in a time when we can no longer fill a cup from the streams and drink, when the air is too thick to breathe, and when the plants and animals begin to turn away from us. In the time of climate chaos and the Age of the Sixth Extinction, we know that this too has come to pass. It is said that in the time of the Seventh Fire, all the world's peoples, newcomers and original peoples, will stand together at a fork in the road, and have a choice to make. In my imagination, one of the paths is soft, green, spangled with dew—you could walk barefoot there. The other path is black and burnt, made of cinders that would cut your feet. Prophecy has become history, for at this time, when the world as we know it hangs in the balance, we know we have reached that fork.

The prophecy tells us that we must make a choice between the path of materialism and greed that will destroy Earth, or the spiritual path of care and compassion, of *mno bmaadiziwin*, the good life. We know which path we want, but we are told that we cannot simply walk forward. Instead, the people of the Seventh Fire must walk back and pick up what was left for us along the ancestors' path: fragments of land and shreds of story; to retrieve our language, ceremonies, and spiritual ways; to pick up our relatives, the other species who have been harmed and cast aside. Only when we have reclaimed what was lost and put it in our bundles can we walk down the green path of life together, all the world's people, immigrants and indigenous, for the same Earth sustains us all. This teaching is not for a return to a romanticized past, but to recover spiritual, cultural, and relational elements of that past so we can go forward.

What do we love too much to lose, such that we will carry it through the straits of climate change, safely to the other side? For there is another side. The prophecy foretells that the People of the Seventh Fire will need great courage, creativity, and wisdom to do the work of healing the world, but that in doing so they will lead us to the lighting of the Eighth Fire, of kinship and life. Our elders have said that we are living in the time of the Seventh Fire. In this moment, at the cusp of undoing, we are the ones who must bend to the task of putting things back together. We are the people of the Seventh Fire, and the wisdom that we reclaim will enable us to renew the world.

We know that we stand today at a crossroads. We need to look for the stories, left along the ancestors' path, that will heal us and bring us back in balance. I have been told that my Potawatomi ancestors taught that the job of every human is to learn the answer to the question, "What can I give in return for the gifts of the Earth?" This is so fundamental to our worldview that it holds a place in the mythic Creation story of our people, a story shared by the peoples of the Great Lakes:

> In the beginning, there was the Skyworld, where people lived much as they do on Earth, alongside the great Tree of Life, on whose branches grew seeds and fruits and medicines, all the gifts of the plants on a single tree. One day a great wind felled the tree, and a hole opened where its roots had been. When a beautiful young woman, called in our language, Gizhkokwe (Skywoman), ventured to the edge to look down, she lost her footing. When she reached out to the tree to stop her fall, a branch broke off in her hand.
>
> She fell like a maple seed pirouetting on an autumn breeze. A column of light streamed from a hole in the Skyworld, marking her path where only darkness had been before. But in that emptiness there were many, gazing up at the sudden shaft of light. They saw there a small object, a mere dust mote in the beam. As it grew closer, they could see that it was a woman, arms outstretched, long black hair billowing behind as she spiraled toward them.
>
> The geese nodded at one another and rose as one from the water, in a wave of goose music. She felt the beat of their wings as they flew beneath and broke her fall. Far from the only home she'd ever known, she caught her breath at the warm embrace of soft feathers. And so it began. From the beginning of time, we are told that the very first encounter between humans and other beings of the Earth was marked by care and responsibility, borne on the strong wings of geese.
>
> The world at that time was covered entirely by water. The geese could not hold the woman much longer, so they called a council of all the beings to decide what to do. As Turtle floated in the watery gathering, he offered to let her rest upon his back. The others understood that she needed land. The deep divers among them had heard of mud at the bottom of the water and agreed to retrieve some. One by one, the animals offered their help: the otter, the loon, and the beaver. But the depth, the darkness, and the pressures were too great for even these strongest of swimmers, who came up gasping. Only the little muskrat

> was left, the weakest diver of all. He volunteered to go while the others looked on doubtfully. His small legs flailed as he worked his way downward. He was gone a very long time. They waited and waited, fearing the worst for their relative. A stream of bubbles rose and the small limp body of muskrat floated upward. But the others noticed that his paw was tightly clenched, and when they pried it open, there was a small handful of mud. Turtle said, "Here, spread this mud on my back and I will hold it."
>
> Skywoman did as Turtle asked and then began to sing her gratitude and then to dance. As her feet caressed the Earth, the land grew and grew from the dab of mud on Turtle's back. From the branch in her hand, she seeded the earth with green. And so, the Earth was made. Not by one alone, but from the alchemy of two essential elements of gratitude and reciprocity. Together they created what we know today as Turtle Island. Our oldest teachings remind us that gratitude and reciprocity are the threads that bind us together. The other species were her life raft at the beginning of the world, and now, so much closer to the end, we must be theirs. (Kimmerer, 2013)

The Earth was new then, when it welcomed the first human. It is old now and some suspect that we have overstayed our welcome. The stories of reciprocity have faded in our memory. How can we translate from the stories at the world's beginning to this hour which is so much closer to its end? Can we understand the Skywoman story not as a relic from the past, but as instructions for the future? In return for the gift of the world on Turtle's back, what will we give in return?

How do cultures engage in reciprocity with the more-than-human world? As the Skywoman story and millennia of lived experience attest, this was a central question for our ancestors, as it is for us today. Traditional knowledge is replete with teachings about how to reciprocate. The imperative of reciprocity is explored in what have been called our "Original Instructions" (Nelson, 2008), which are the ethical systems that govern relations with the human and the more-than-human world. Reciprocity can take many forms, just a few of which are explored here.

What Can We Give?

Gratitude

Native environmental philosophy acknowledges that our human lives are utterly dependent on the lives of other beings and thus our first responsibility is for gratitude. As the Skywoman story suggests, recognition of the world as a gift is an invitation to give thanks; indeed, many indigenous cultures have been characterized as "cultures of gratitude."

For much of humans' time on the planet, before the great delusion, we lived in cultures that understood the covenant of reciprocity—that for the Earth to stay in balance, for the gifts to continue to flow, we must give back in equal measure. The most powerful offering we possess is gratitude. Gratitude may seem weak given the desperate challenges that lie before us, but it is powerful, much more than a simple thank you. Giving thanks implies recognition not only of the gift, but of the giver.

When I eat an apple, my gratitude is directed to the forces of Creation and to that wide-armed tree whose tart fruit is now in my mouth, whose life has become my own. Gratitude is founded on the deep knowing that our very existence relies on the gifts of other beings.

The evolutionary advantage for cultures of gratitude is compelling. This human emotion has adaptive value because it engenders practical outcomes for sustainability. The practice of gratitude can, in a very real sense, lead to the practice of self-restraint, of taking only what you need. Naming and appreciation of the gifts that surround us create satisfaction, a feeling of "enough-ness" that is an antidote to the societal messages that drill into our spirits, telling us we must have more. Practicing contentment is a radical act in a consumption-driven society.

Indigenous story traditions are full of cautionary tales about the failure of gratitude. When people forget to honor the gift, the consequences are always material as well as spiritual. The spring dries up, the corn crop fails, the animals do not return, and the legions of offended plants, animals, and rivers rise up against the ones who neglected gratitude. The Western story-telling tradition is strangely silent on this, so we find ourselves in an era when centuries of overconsumption have depleted natural goods (resources) and left human societies materially and culturally impoverished by a deep alienation from the living world.

We humans have protocols for gratitude; we apply them formally to one another. We say "thank you." We understand that receiving a gift incurs a responsibility to give a gift in return. Gratitude is our first, but not our only gift. We are storytellers, music-makers, and devisers of ingenious machines, healers, scientists, and lovers of an Earth that asks that we give our gifts on behalf of life. The next step in our cultural evolution, if we are to persist as a species on this beautiful planet, is to expand our protocols for gratitude to the living Earth.

Gratitude is most powerful as a response to the Earth because it provides an opening to reciprocity, to the act of giving back, to living in a way that the Earth will be grateful for us.

Ceremony

Among the treasures we can pick up along that path of traditional knowledge are the ceremonies. Ceremonies are a potent cultural expression of reciprocity which renews bonds between the land and people and focuses intention, attention, and action on behalf of the natural world, which is inclusive of the spiritual world. From the First Salmon ceremonies of the Northwest to the great Thanksgiving Address of the Haudenosaunee, ceremony represents a ritual gift of spiritual energy, power, and beauty that is offered in reciprocity for the gifts we have received and contributes to a balance between humans and the more-than-human world. Plants and animals, of course, often play vital roles in ceremony, as ritual foods and objects, and as vehicles for interface with the sacred. Consuming feast foods in ceremony reinforces our appreciation of the way that plants and animals offer their bodies to feed our own, in a sacred transaction of life for life (Kimmerer, 2016).

It is important to remember that spiritual ceremonies, in addition to their power in unseen dimensions, may also have important immediate, direct effects on the physical world and thus constitute a form of "practical reverence." For example, the traditional four-day ceremony to honor the ripening of wild rice includes a ban on gathering during that ritual period. Abstaining from the harvest during ceremony yields pragmatic consequences for the flourishing of the rice, which benefits from four days of seed-drop to reseed the rice beds before people come to gather. Likewise, Salmon ceremonies, which permit the salmon to run upriver without impediment during the ceremony that welcomes them back to their natal waters, ensure that an adequate number of fish return to the spawning grounds.

Attention

Every one of us is endowed with the singular gift of paying attention, that remarkable focused convergence of our senses, our intellect, and our feeling. It is so appropriate that we call it *paying* attention, for it is perhaps a near-universal form of currency—it is exchangeable, valuable, and it incurs an expense on the part of the payer. For attention, we all know well, is a limited resource. Science is a powerful tool for paying attention to the Earth, as are art and religion.

What should be our response to the generosity of the more-than-human world? In a world that gives us maple syrup, spotted salamanders, and sand hill cranes, should we not at least pay attention? Paying attention is an ongoing act of reciprocity, the gift that keeps on giving, in which attention generates wonder, which in turn generates more attention, more joy. Paying attention to the more-than-human world does not lead only to amazement; it leads also to acknowledgment of pain. Open and attentive, we see and feel equally the beauty and the wounds, the old growth and the clear-cut, the mountain and the mine. Paying attention to suffering sharpens our ability to respond, to be responsible. This too, is a gift, for when we love the living world, we cannot be bystanders of its destruction. Attention becomes intention, which coalesces itself to action.

Deep attention calls us inevitably into a deep relationship, as information and energy are exchanged between the observer and the observed, and neither partner in the exchange can be anonymous. They are known; they have names. There was a time, not so long ago, when to be human meant knowing the names of the beings with whom we cohabit the world. Knowing a name is the way humans build relationship. It is a sign of respect to call a being by its name, and a sign of disrespect to ignore it.

Ethnobiologists tell us that our great-grandparents spoke fluent natural history. They knew the names and personalities of dozens of birds and hundreds of plants. Today, a typical American schoolchild can recognize more than 100 corporate logos but fewer than ten plants. We have lost an entire vocabulary, of speech, of experience, and of relationship. Our fundamental currency of relationship, our highly evolved capacity for paying attention to those species that sustain us, has been subverted in an intellectual hijacking. How can we care for them, monitor their wellbeing, and fight for their existence if we do not even know their names?

The way that we name these beings both reflects and grows from our worldview. For example, in Western scientific ways of knowing, we honor Linnaeus as the father of taxonomy, the inventor of binomial nomenclature. Linnaeus was charged with giving standardized names and systematic clarity to the world's flora and fauna, at a time when discovery was rapidly accelerating the lists of biodiversity. He stamped each species with a universal Latin binomial, based on its morphological characteristics, becoming the "great namer" of plants which he may have known from only a herbarium sheet, as if they did not already have names. In contrast, let us consider another "great namer" from the indigenous tradition, Nanabozho, the cultural hero of my Anishinaabe people. It is said that when Nanabozho, the original man, was placed on the Earth, he was filled with wonder at its beauty. The Creator had instructed him to travel to the Four Directions as a humble student, learning all that he could from the others who were already living there in harmony with one another. He was given the responsibility of speaking with every kind of being and learning from them what gifts they had to share with the people who would be coming. Every plant he encountered taught him of its worth, the way its roots could be eaten, the medicines it made, how its bark was ready to become lodges, its branches baskets, its berries food to sweeten life. As Nanabozho came to know and respect each plant, he also came to know their names. His way of being was not to impose foreign names on them, but to humbly learn their own. The way that we name can create relationships of dominance and distance, or relationships of relatedness and respect. But whether the names are Linnaean, indigenous, or English, the sad truth is that we know very few. For many in industrial societies, the living world has become an inanimate collection of objects.

We have enabled a state of nameless anonymity, bringing human people to a condition of isolation and disconnection, which philosophers call "species loneliness." "Species loneliness," a deep, unnamed sadness, is the cost of estrangement from the rest of Creation, from the loss of relationship. Our Potawatomi stories relate that a long time ago, when Turtle Island was young, the people and all the plants and animals spoke the same language and conversed freely with one another. But no more. As our dominance has grown, we have become more isolated, more lonely on the planet, and can no longer call our neighbors by their real names. If we are to manifest the values of the Skywoman story, we have to once again call each other by name.

Knowing the beings with which we share the world is also the pathway to recognition of the world as gift. The world seems less like a shopping bag of commodities and more like a gift when you know the one who gives you the aspirin for your headache. Her name is Willow; she lives up by the pond. She is a neighbor of Maple, who offers you the gift of syrup. Paying attention is a pathway to gratitude.

Respectful relationship

In her poem "When Earth becomes an It," Cherokee poet Marilou Awiakta (1993) considers the consequences of naming:

> When the people call the Earth "Mother,"
> They take with love

And with love give back
So that all may live.

When the people call Earth "it,"
They use her
Consume her strength. Then the people die.

Already the sun is hot
Out of season.
Our Mother's breast
Is going dry.
She is taking all green
Into her heart
And will not turn back
Until we call her
By her name.

In the absence of names, it all comes down to pronouns. Grammar is how we chart relationships in language and, as it happens, our relationship with the land. When you look closely at the English language, is it any wonder our worldview objectifies Nature as property? In English, a being is either a human or an "it." The language gives us no choice—it imprisons our ideas.

Imagine seeing your grandmother standing at the stove and then saying, "Look, it is making soup. It has gray hair." We might snicker at such a mistake, but recoil from it also. In English, we never refer to a member of our family, or indeed any other person, as "it." That would be a profound act of disrespect. "It" robs a person of selfhood and kinship, reducing a person to a mere "thing." And yet in the English language, we speak of our beloved grandmother Earth in exactly that way. But in Potawatomi and many other indigenous languages, it is impossible to speak of a tree or a fish or a bird as an "it." We use the same grammar to address the living world as we do our family, because they are our family.

Speaking of and understanding other beings as objects, as mere "its," opens the door to exploitation. Linguistics codes our relationships with the world, delineating the boundaries for our circle of respect and compassion. When Maple is an "it," we can take up the chainsaw. When Maple is a "her," we think twice.

If we are to survive here—and if our neighbors are to survive, too—we need to learn to speak the grammar of animacy. Language has always been adaptive, we lose words we no longer need and coin new ones. We do not need a worldview of Earth beings as objects; that has led us down the blackened path. We need a new language for our journey on the green path (Kimmerer, 2015b). And so, as people of the Seventh Fire, can we undo linguistic imperialism with linguistic biomimicry from the Anishinaabe language?

In our Anishinaabe language, the word for "land" is a small word with a big meaning. It is more than terrain, than soil, than area—it is the living land, the inspirited, animate land. That small word is *aki*, the Earth that sustains us.

Just a small thing: let us replace the word "it," the pronoun we use for non-human beings, with a new pronoun: not "he" or "she," but "ki," from *aki*, to signify animate, being of the Earth. So that when we speak of the sugar maple, we say "Oh, that beautiful tree, ki is giving us sap again this spring."

And we'll need a plural pronoun, too. Let us make it "kin," those Earth beings. And so we can now refer to "them" not as things, but as our earthly relatives. On a crisp October morning we can look up and say, "Look at the geese, kin are flying south for the winter. Come back soon."

Words have power. Let us speak of the beings of the Earth as "kin" and leave "it" for tables, bulldozers, and paperclips. Every time we say *ki* let our language reaffirm our respect and our kinship with the more-than-human world. Let us speak of the beings of Earth as the "kin" they are.

Recognition of Personhood

The Skywoman story is grounded in the fundamental ethical tenet that the other beings with whom we share the planet—the ones who sustain us—are persons too: non-human persons with their own ways of being, their own intentions, their own contributions to the world, their own rights to life. Science and spirituality both demonstrate the fundamental nature of our relatedness with all living beings: we are more similar than we are different. We are governed by the same ecological and evolutionary rules.

Reciprocity is rooted in the understanding that we are not alone, that Earth is populated by non-human persons. How different our world would be if we extended the same respect, compassion, and agency to other species that we do to human people. We tolerate governance that grants legal personhood and free speech to non-living corporations, but denies that respect to voiceless salamanders and sugar maples.

Reserving personhood for a single species, in language and in ways of living, perpetuates the fallacy of human exceptionalism, that we are fundamentally different and somehow better, more deserving of the wealth and services of the Earth than other species. Recognition of the personhood of other beings asks that we relinquish our perceived role as dominators and celebrate our essential role as an equal member in the democracy of all species.

Paying attention to other beings, recognizing their incredible gifts of photosynthesis, nitrogen fixation, migration, metamorphosis, and communication across miles is humbling and leads inescapably to an understanding that we are surrounded by intelligences other than our own, by beings who evolved here long before we did, and who have adapted innovative, remarkable ways of being that we might emulate, through intellectual biomimicry, for sustainability. We are surrounded by teachers and mentors who come dressed in foliage, fur, and feathers. There is comfort in their presence and guidance in their lessons.

Not only are other beings understood as sovereign persons, but many are regarded as our teachers. A fundamental tenet of traditional plant knowledge is that the plants are understood, not as mere objects or lower life-forms as the Western "pyramid of being" might suggest, but as persons, non-human persons, with their own knowledge, intentions, and spirits, to whom we owe our respect. Not only are plants acknowledged as persons, but they are also recognized as our oldest teachers. It is said that the plants have been here far longer than we have, they know how to make food and medicine out of light and air, and then give it away. They unite Earth and sky and exemplify the virtues of generosity; they heal the land and feed all the others in Creation. No wonder they are revered as teachers by humans who are learning how to live on the Earth.

Granting personhood to all beings can be an economic and political construct, as well as an ethical stance. Recognition of personhood for all beings opens the way to ecological justice. Our laws are about governing our rights to the land. We need to include the rights of the land, the rights to be whole and healthy, the right to exist. We can follow the lead of indigenous nations: the Maori, who granted personhood to a river; the Ecuadorians, whose constitution enshrines the rights of Nature herself in the law of the land; and the Bolivians, who brought to the United Nations the *Declaration on the Rights of Mother Nature.*

Land Care

Reciprocity can also manifest through the exercise of traditional resource management or "land care" practices embedded in traditional ecological knowledge (TEK). This large body of knowledge is beyond the scope of this chapter, but represents a significant manifestation of reciprocity, in which humans invest their knowledge and tools on behalf of mutual flourishing, manifesting the understanding that "what is good for the land is good for the people." There is a substantial and growing academic literature which demonstrates the diversity and sophistication of the methods used by indigenous peoples to enhance the productivity and biodiversity of their landscapes (Anderson, 2005; Becker & Ghimire, 2003; Berkes, 2004, 2008; Drew & Henne, 2006; Kimmerer, 2000, 2003, 2013b; Kimmerer & Lake, 2001).

Acknowledgment of the dependence of human life on gifts—the lives of other beings—sets up a tension between the necessity of taking other lives and simultaneously honoring those lives. This contradiction, implicit in our heterotrophic biology, is resolved in indigenous philosophy by the practice of reciprocity, by giving back in return for the gift of the lives that sustain us. It is understood that we humans must take other lives in order to sustain our own, so the manner in which they are taken becomes very important: to take in such a way that the life received is honored.

In the context of the Western worldview, which regards plants primarily as objects, they are seen as either "wild," and therefore free for the taking, or "property," which can be bought and sold. From this perspective of plants as "natural resources," harvesting protocols are typically oriented toward efficiency and lie strictly in the secular realm. However, when plants and animals are viewed as respected persons, relatives, and teachers, harvesting moves from the secular to the sacred. Additional protocols arise as part of traditional harvesting practices. The Honorable Harvest is a set of unwritten guidelines, both ethical and practical, which govern human consumption. They represent acts of reciprocity in return for the gift of life. The Honorable Harvest guidelines are embedded in the indigenous worldview which recognizes the personhood of all beings, in which plants are treated with the same respect and responsibility as human persons. These ancient practices have resonance today in prescribing an alternative to the dominant consumptive materialist worldview, in which humans are understood solely as consumers, and not as active participants in the wellbeing of other organisms.

Collectively, the Honorable Harvest guidelines are "rules" of sorts that govern our taking, so that the world is as rich for the seventh generation as it is for us. These rules are simultaneously biophysical and spiritual; in the indigenous worldview the realms are mutually reinforcing, not mutually exclusive.

The guidelines for the Honorable Harvest (Kimmerer, 2013a, 2015a) were taught to me by generous teachers, in picking medicines and how to gather berries, but they apply to every exchange between people and the Earth. Although the protocol for the Honorable Harvest is not written down, if it were it, it would look something like this:

- Never take the first plant you see. Never taking the first, means you'll never take the last. This is a prescription which has inherent conservation value, through the practice of self-restraint
- Ask permission. I've been taught to address that plant, to introduce myself, to explain why I need those berries or roots. If you are going to take a life, you have to be personally accountable
- Listen to the answer. You can listen in different ways: look around and see whether the plants are numerous and healthy, whether they have enough to share. And if the answer is no, go home. Remember that they do not belong to us, taking without permission is also known as stealing
- If you are granted permission, take only what you need and no more
- Take in such a way that does the least harm and in a way that benefits the growth of the plant. Don't use a shovel if a digging stick suffices
- Use everything you take. It is disrespectful of the life that is given to waste it
- Be grateful. Give thanks for what you have received
- Share the gift with others, human and non-human alike. Earth has shared generously with you, so emulate that behavior in return. A culture of sharing is a culture of resilience
- Reciprocate the gift. We know that in order for balance to be achieved, we cannot take without giving back. Plant gatherers often leave a spiritual gift, but also a material gift, through the act of weeding, scattering seeds, helping the plants to move and flourish

Can we extend the concept of the Honorable Harvest to address the environmental dilemmas that we face today? We need acts of restoration, and not only for polluted waters and degraded lands; we need a restoration of honor for the way we live. The reward is not just a feel-good sense of responsibility; it may save our lives. Our economies and institutions enmesh us all in a profoundly dishonorable harvest. Collectively, by assent or by inaction, we have chosen the policies we live by. But we can choose again—we can choose reciprocity to sustain the ones who sustain us.

What Can We Give in Return for the Gifts of the Earth?

I think that the teaching that we most need to reclaim, to carry in our Seventh Fire bundles to the future, is the teaching of reciprocity. To heal our relationship with the land we must reclaim our roles as givers to the Earth.

It may be hard to know what our responsibilities are, especially in uncertain times, so I find it helpful to remember that gifts and responsibilities are two sides of the same coin. Asking "What is my responsibility?" is also asking "What is my gift?" Birds were given the gift of song, so it is their responsibility to greet the day. Stars were given the gift of sparkling, and therefore the duty to guide our way at night. What are our gifts as human people? We cannot fly, we cannot breathe underwater, and we cannot photosynthesize. What we have is the gift of choice, of story, of gratitude, of love. We can put our hands into the soil, restoring the damage that we have done, healing the land the way the plants have shown us to do it. It is not the land which is broken, but our relationship to it. We can heal that.

Ceremony is a powerful expression of reciprocity. An old ceremony of Anishinaabe people is known as the giveaway, *minidewak*, meaning they give from the heart. In the outside world, a person celebrating life-events may be the recipient of gifts in their honor. But, in the Anishinaabe way this is reversed. The honored one is the giver, enacting reciprocity by sharing gifts in return for their good fortune. I do not know the origin of the ceremony, but I think we learned it from the berry plants, who generously offer up their gifts wrapped in red and blue. In fact, at the heart of the word *minidewak* is the word *min*, which is the root word for both berry and gift. Might the ceremony be a reminder to us to be like the berries?

In closing, let us imagine a different kind of *minidewak*. We are bound by a covenant of reciprocity: plant breath for animal breath, winter and summer, predator and prey, grass and fire, night and day, living and dying. Water knows this, clouds know this. Soil and rocks know they are dancing in a continuous giveaway of making, unmaking, and making the Earth again.

We live in a moral landscape. The land is reading us law over and over, but we forget to listen. Our elders say that ceremony is the way we can "remember to remember." In the dance of the giveaway, remember that the Earth is a gift that we must pass on, just as it came to us. We forget this at our peril. When we forget, the dances we will need will be for mourning, for the passing of polar bears, the silence of cranes, the memory of snow.

When I close my eyes and wait for my heartbeat to match the drum, I envision people recognizing, for perhaps the first time, the dazzling gifts of the world, seeing them with new eyes, just as they teeter on the cusp of undoing. Maybe just in time; maybe too late. Spread on the grass, they will see at last the giveaway that Mother Earth has prepared. Blankets of moss, robes of feathers, baskets of corn, vials of healing herbs, silver salmon, sand dunes, thunderheads and snowdrifts, cords of wood and herds of elk, tulips, potatoes, luna moths and snow geese, and berries. More than anything, I want to hear a great song of thanks rise on the wind. I think that song might save us.

Then, as the drumbeat begins, we will dance, wearing regalia in celebration of the living Earth: a waving fringe of tall grass prairies, a whirl of butterfly shawls with nodding egret plumes, bejeweled with the glitter of a phosphorescent wave. When the song pauses for the honor beats, we will hold high our gift and ululate our praise for a glittering fish, a branch of blossom, and a starlit night. The moral covenant of reciprocity calls us to honor our responsibilities for all we have been given, for all we have taken. It is our turn now, and it is long overdue. Let us hold a giveaway for Mother Earth, spread our blankets out for her and pile them high with gifts of our own making. Imagine the books, paintings, poems, ingenious machines, compassionate acts, transcendent ideas, perfect tools. A fierce defense of all that has been given: gifts of mind, hands, heart, voice, and vision all offered up on behalf of the Earth. Whatever our gift, we are called to give it and to dance for the renewal of the world in return for berries, in return for birds, in return for the privilege of breath (Kimmerer, 2010).

References

Anderson, M. K. 2005. *Tending the Wild: Native American Knowledge and the Management of California's Natural Resources*. Berkeley, CA: University of California Press.

Awiakta, Marilou, 1993. *Selu: Seeking the Corn Mothers Wisdom*. Golden, CO: Fulcrum.

Becker, C.D. & Ghimire, K. 2003. Synergy between traditional ecological knowledge and conservation science supports forest preservation in Ecuador. *Conservation Ecology*, 8(1): 1. http://www.consecol.org/vol8/iss1/art1/.

Benton-Banai, E. 1988. *The Mishomis Book: The Voice of the Ojibway*. New York: Red School House.

Berkes, F. 2004. Rethinking Community-Based Conservation. *Conservation Biology*, 18, 3, 621–630.

Berkes, F. 2008. *Sacred Ecology* (2nd ed.). New York: Routledge.

Drew, J. A. & Henne, A. P. 2006. Conservation Biology and Traditional Ecological Knowledge: Integrating Academic Disciplines for Better Conservation Practice. *Ecology and Society*, 11, 2.

Kimmerer, R. W. 2000. Native Knowledge for Native Ecosystems. *Journal for Forestry*, 98, 8, 4–9.

Kimmerer R. W. 2002. Weaving Traditional Ecological Knowledge into Biological Education: A Call to Action. *Bioscience*, 52, 5, 432–438.

Kimmerer R. W. 2010. The Giveaway, 141–145. In K. Moore K & M. Nelson (Eds.), *Moral Ground: Ethical Action for a Planet in Peril*. San Antonio, TX: Trinity University Press.

Kimmerer R. W. 2012. Searching for Synergy: Integrating Traditional and Scientific Ecological Knowledge. *Environmental Science Education. Journal of Environmental Studies and Sciences*, 2, 4, 317–223.

Kimmerer R. 2013a. Braiding Sweetgrass: Indigenous Wisdom, Scientific Knowledge and the Teachings of Plants. Minneapolis, MN: Milkweed Editions.

Kimmerer, R. 2013b. The Fortress, the River and the Garden. Eds. A. Kulnieks, D. Longboat, & K. Young. Rotterdam: Sense Publishers.

Kimmerer, R. W. 2014. Returning the Gift. *Minding Nature*, 8, 1. Center for Humans and Nature.

Kimmerer, R. W. 2015a. The Honorable Harvest. *Yes! Magazine*, December.

Kimmerer, R. W. 2015b. Nature Needs a New Pronoun. *Yes! Magazine*, Spring.

Kimmerer, R. W. 2017. Mishkos Kenomagwen: Lessons of Grass, Restoring Reciprocity with The Good Green Earth. In M. K. Nelson & D. B. Schilling (Eds.), *Keepers of the Green World*: Cambridge University Press. (In press).

Kimmerer, R. W. & Lake, F. K. 2001. The Role of Indigenous Burning in Land Management. *Journal of Forestry*, 99, 11, 36–40.

Nabhan, G. P. 1991. Restoring and Re-storying the Landscape. *Ecological Restoration*, 9, 1, 3–4.

Nelson, M. K. 2008. *Original Instructions: Indigenous Teachings for a Sustainable Future*. Rochester, VT: Inner Traditions/Bear & Co.

IV. Visions for the Present and Future Earth

The Earth Transformed: Altered Consciousness and Conduct on Common Ground

CHAPTER 27

Prayer as if Earth Really Matters

Arthur Waskow

Increasingly, religious communities are bringing their prayers and practice to bear on the ultimate religious and spiritual question: current dangers to the web of human and more-than-human life forms on planet Earth. There are two aspects of what is beginning to happen in relating prayer to the present crisis. One is exploring how Earth-awareness can enter more deeply into our formal prayer services; the other is exploring how public action intended to affect public and corporate policy toward the Earth can become prayerful.

Earth-Awareness in Formal Prayer

> Prayer is meaningless unless it is subversive.
>
> Rabbi Abraham J. Heschel

One powerful way to enhance Earth-awareness in the formal prayer of many religious traditions would be to introduce new symbols and rituals. An extraordinarily powerful effort along these lines was undertaken at the Interfaith Summit on the Climate Crisis called in 2008 by the Church of Sweden and chaired by its Archbishop in Uppsala. The initial service in the Cathedral was in many ways a conventional, interfaith service: a *shofar* (ram's horn) blown by Jews, a bell rung by Buddhists, etc. The most moving aspect of the initial service was the rolling of a large green moss globe down the central aisle of the Cathedral—the symbol of no one religious community and a possible symbol for them all.

A version of this practice has been introduced since then into a number of multi-religious services focusing on the climate crisis, especially several held by Interfaith Moral Action on Climate (IMAC) in Washington, DC, at the White House fence and Lafayette

The Wiley Blackwell Companion to Religion and Ecology, First Edition. Edited by John Hart.

Park in 2012 and 2013. At those events, the participants passed an inflatable globe from hand to hand, singing:

> We have the whole world in our hands,
> We have the rain and the forests in our hands,
> We have the wind and the clouds in our hands,
> WE HAVE THE WHOLE WORLD IN OUR HANDS!
>
> We have the rivers and the mountains in our hands,
> We have the lakes and the oceans in our hands
> We have you and me in our hands,
> WE HAVE THE WHOLE WORLD IN OUR HANDS.
>
> We have trees and tigers in our hands,
> We have our sisters and our brothers in our hands,
> We have our children and *their* children in our hands,
> WE HAVE THE WHOLE WORLD IN OUR HANDS!

It is notable both factually and theologically that this liturgy transformed an older hymn in which the refrain was "***He*** has the whole world in ***His*** hands." That assertion—***He*** is in charge of the world—is closely related to an important traditional metaphor in most Jewish, Christian, and Muslim prayer. In that metaphor, God is King, Lord, Judge above and beyond the human beings who are praying. In regard to the Earth, this metaphor topped a series of hierarchies: the Great Chain of Being is a hierarchy from rocks and rivers up to vegetation, thence to animals, then to human beings, and finally to the Divine King and Lord.

Today, we know that the relationship between the human species and the Earth is ill described by these metaphors of hierarchy. Not only do we now know that what we breathe in depends on what the trees and grasses exhale; we know, too, that within our own guts are myriads of microscopic creatures that occasionally make us sick but far more often keep us alive and healthy. There is no "environment" in the sense of an "environs" that is "out there" and is not us. There are fringes, not fences, between us and other life, and sometimes not even fringes at our edges but in our very innards.

Though now we know that the human species has great power to shape and damage the web of life on Earth, we also know that we are part of that web—a strand within it—not above and beyond it. What we may do to the web with our power also has an impact on us. The more we act as if we are in full control, the closer we come to "totaling" the whole intricate process to use a phrase that—perhaps not accidentally—comes from the world of automobiles.

So, those metaphors of ordered hierarchy are no longer truthful, viable, or useful as tools of spiritual enlightenment. If we are to seek spiritual depth and height, the whole framework of prayer must be transformed.

How can we do this while drawing on the rich experience of prayer that spiritually enlightened many in the generations that came before us? If we look deep into the Torah tradition, we find accounts that hint at a very different metaphor and therefore a very different path of prayer. When Moses heard a voice speaking from the Burning Bush, the voice gave him two new names by which to understand the universe and God, and by which to lead the liberation of the Israelites from their slavery to the Pharaoh.

One of those new names is in Hebrew—Ehyeh Asher Ehyeh—that is, "I will be who I will be." The world, we understand, is always becoming, not simply being. In such a world, slaves can be freed; a rabble of runaways can become a community. The other name was/is, in the Western alphabet, YHWH. Much later in biblical understanding, we were taught this name must not be spoken. In its place the Hebrew word *Adonai*, meaning Lord, should be used. This practice greatly affected Christian prayer and practice, as Adonai became Kyrie, then Dominus, and later Lord.

But if we try to pronounce YHWH without any vowels as it was written in the original Hebrew Bible, which was written without vowels (these were added later), what we sound and hear is not quite a pronunciation but a breath, a breath that occurs not only in Hebrew, Sanskrit, Latin, Swahili, Greek, English, and Chinese but in every human language. And it appears not only in human languages but in every life-form. No living creature on our planet breathes within a little bubble. We breathe each other into being, into living. What we breathe in is what the trees breathe out. What the trees breathe in is what we breathe out.

The metaphor that God is the Interbreathing of all life is far closer to the truth than the metaphor that God is King and Lord. It brings together spiritual truth and scientific fact. It has only been about 250 years since human beings discovered that the great exchange of carbon dioxide and oxygen between plants and animals is what keeps our planet alive. Yet this scientific fact echoes the ancient sense that we are all interwoven as we are interbreathing.

Even to say the word "spiritual" is to teach the importance of this interbreathing. For just as the Latin word *spiritus* means "breath" and "wind" as well as what we call "spirit," so too the Hebrew word *ruach* means "breath," "wind," and "spirit." Much the same sense is expressed in many other languages.

What would it mean, then, to reframe our forms of prayer around the metaphor of God as interbreathing? I will speak here from my own roots in Jewish prayer, but the basic question should arise in the prayers of all cultures. Let us start with what many consider the central affirmation of Jewish prayer, the Shema. Drawing on our new metaphor, we might hear the Shema saying "Hush and listen, you God wrestlers! Our God is the Interbreathing of all life, and the interbreathing is ONE."

In the traditional Jewish prayer book, the Shema is followed by three paragraphs of explication and affirmation. The second paragraph is devoted to the relationship between human beings and the Earth. It asserts that if human beings follow the sacred teachings that the Divine is One, then the rivers will flow, the rains will fall, the heavens will bless the Earth, and the Earth will be plentiful in feeding human beings, in making the harvest abundant, and in making the land flourish. But, the paragraph continues, if we venerate false gods, if we carve the world into parts, and worship not the One Breath of life but a piece of the world we have carved out, then the rivers will not run, the rain will not fall, and the heavens will turn against us. We will perish from the good Earth that the one breath of life, our God, has given us.

In the last half-century, that second paragraph has been excised from many Jewish prayer books. The argument for removing it has been that it teaches a false notion of a certain reward coming from good actions and punishment coming from bad actions. But that excision came before we understood how interwoven, how fragile was our relationship with the

Earth, and how we might act with such strength and arrogance as to wound even the rain and the rivers. So, as a way of understanding the Shema so that the Earth really matters, I offer this translation of the three paragraphs; it can be chanted quite easily in English:

The Sh'ma, a Jewish invocation of the unity: An interpretation for the twenty-first century

Sh'sh'sh'ma Yisra'el—
Hush'sh'sh and Listen, You Godwrestlers—
Pause from your wrestling and hush'sh'sh
To hear—
YHWH/Yahhhhhh.
Hear in the stillness the still silent voice,
The silent breathing that intertwines life;

YHWH/Yahhhh elohenu
Breath of life is our God,
What unites all the varied
forces creating
all worlds into oneness,
Each breath unique,
And all unified;

Listen, You Godwrestlers—
No one people alone
owns this Unify-force;
YHWH/Yahh is One.

So at the gates of your cities,
where your own culture ends,
and another begins,
And you halt there in fear—
"Here we speak the same language
"But out there is barbaric,
"They may kill without speaking"—
Then pause in the gateway to write on its walls
And to chant in its passage:
"Each gate is unique in the world that is One."
If you hush'sh'sh and then listen,
yes hush'sh'sh and then listen
to the teachings of YHWH/Yahh,
the One Breath of Life,
that the world is one,
all its parts intertwined,
then the rains will fall
Time by time, time by time;
The rivers will run,
the heavens will smile,
the good Earth will fruitfully feed you.

But if you chop the world into parts
and choose parts to worship —
gods of race or of nation
gods of wealth and of power,
gods of greed and addiction
If you Do and you Make,
and Produce without pausing;
If you Do without Being—

Then the rain will not fall—
or will turn to sharp acid—
The rivers won't run—
Or, flood homes and cities;
The heavens themselves
will take arms against you:
the ozone will fail you,
the oil that you burn
will scorch your whole planet—
and from the good Earth
that the Breath of Life gives you,
you will vanish—yes, perish.

So on the edges of your Self,
On the corners of your clothing,
take care to weave fringes—
threads of connection.
So you end not with sharpness,
A fence or a wall,
But with sacred mixing
of cloth and of air—
A fringe that is fuzzy,
part yours and part God's:
They bind us together,
Make One from our oneness.
Good fringes/good neighbors.

Now let us go to an earlier part of the traditional Jewish service which precedes the Shema. There are three passages there in which the Hebrew word *neshama* (breath) is central. The first begins "*Elohai neshama sheh'natatah bi t'horah hi* (My God, the breath You have placed within me is pure); the second "*Nishmat kol chai tivarekh et-shimcha YHWH elohenu*" (The breath of all life blesses Your Name, our God); and the third "*Kol hameshama t'hallel YAH: Hallelu Yah*" (Every breath praises Yah, the breath of life).

In order to pray so that the Earth really matters, we might breathe these three passages in three ways. For the first, we might experience the breath entering our nose, mouth, and throat, descending into our lungs to be picked up in our bloodstream, to transport oxygen to our brain, our arms, our heart and legs, our genitals and skin, to all our organs which, in their diversity, make each of us into a One. This is *my* breath, and it comes from *my* God.

The second passage invites us to see the breath of all life, praising the name of *our* God—no longer *my* God. For this passage, we might begin by experiencing how our breath—now mostly carbon dioxide—leaves our mouth and nose, moves into the air and atmosphere of all God's creatures, then is inhaled by trees and grasses; how they absorb the carbon to make new leaves, new wood—then breathe out oxygen into the world, so that we can breathe it in.

We might chant the passage thus:

Nishmat

You Whose very Name—
YyyyHhhhWwwwHhhh—
Is the Breath of Life,
The breathing of all life
Gives joy and blessing to Your Name.
As lovers lie within each other's arms,
Whispering each the other's name
Into the other's ear,
So we lie in Your arms,
Breathing with each breath
Your Name, Your Truth, Your Unity.
You alone,
Your Breath of Life alone,
Guides us, Frees us, Transforms us,
Heals us,
Nurtures us,
Teaches us,
First, last,
Future, past,
Inward, outward,
Beyond, between.
You are the breathing that gives life to all the worlds.
And we do the breathing that gives life to all the worlds.
As we breathe out what the trees breathe in,
And the trees breathe out what we breathe in,
So we breathe each other into life,
We and You.
YyyyHhhhWwwwHhhh.

Finally, the third passage comes from the last phrase of Psalm 150, the last psalm. It affirms that every breath praises, blesses, the God who is the breath of life. It uses one of the ancient names of God—*Yah* (as in *Hallelu Yah*)—the name that has the initial Y and the ending H of YHWH. We might say "Yah" is the pet name of YHWH.

The exercise I have described is a way to teach and remind the community that we are part of the Earth, interwoven with the Earth, and not its ruler nor the viceroy of a king still higher and more royal.

With this new relationship with the Earth in mind, we move to the moment in the Jewish service that affirms there is a *minyan*, a community, a quorum for prayer, in the room. Traditionally, this required ten male Jews at least 13 years and 1 day old. Today, ten adult Jews of any gender would, in many Jewish circles, make a minyan.

As we pause to say a welcoming affirmation—*Let us praise that holy breath of life which is indeed to be well praised*—we might in our new mode look from face to face around the room, pausing at each phase to say to ourselves, "This is the face of God. And this, so different, is the face of God. And this, and this, and this." We affirm that each face—so different not only in its physical shape and look but in its history and future—is the face of God, not despite their differences but precisely because of their diversity. For the infinite can only be expressed in the world through the many facets of diversity.

With the Earth in mind, we might then turn to see the green faces of God, especially if the prayer space has been so shaped that there are windows to see the trees and grasses. (For this kind of prayer, it would be important for the spaces of our congregations to include exactly these windows like this.) Someone might say, "We invite into our minyan these green faces of the holy breath of life, for no minyan could live and breathe if these green faces of the Holy One were not breathing into us what we need to live."

There are many other moments in the service when this new metaphor takes on a fuller meaning as it seems more accurate in our prayers than do "King," or "Lord." For example, as we celebrate the way in which the wind parted the Red Sea for the Israelites to walk through and into freedom, the action of a great wind, the wind of change, seems a truer metaphor for that force than the metaphor of King. In the Alenu prayer, when traditionally we bow and bend before the Royal Majesty, we can bow and bend and let our bodies sway and move in the great wind of change.

Finally, the Kaddish that bridges sections of Jewish prayer, addresses God as *shmei rabbah* (the Great Name). One way to understand the Great Name is that it is the name that includes all the names of all the beings in the world: all species, all mountains, rocks, and rivers (just as the 55,000 names on the Vietnam War Memorial in Washington together make one "great name"). Asking people to envision and mention one of these names would help the whole community to begin weaving these names into the Great Name, and thus heighten awareness of how all of the Earth is interwoven.

Making Public Advocacy Actions Prayerful

I felt as if my legs were praying.

Rabbi Abraham Joshua Heschel, returning from the great Selma, Alabama, march for equal justice in voting rights

The intertwined religious stories of Passover and Holy Week speak in powerful ways to the danger facing the Earth; and, although in Islam there is no analogous festival, the

Exodus story and the story of Jesus are major features in the Qur'an. So interfaith and multi-religious groups have drawn on this tradition in these ways:

- Recalling that the arrogance and stubbornness of the Pharaoh brought plagues to the Earth—all of them ecological catastrophes—as well as oppression to the human community
- Understanding the annual gatherings of a million people in ancient Jerusalem on Passover itself and the march of protest against the Roman Empire led by Jesus at Passover on the first Palm Sunday, as protests against oppression by the Pharaohs and Caesars of every generation
- Holding public religious gatherings to raise the symbols of Passover and Palm Sunday—matzah and palms—in calls to act against the plagues of global scorching brought on by the modern Pharaohs (Big Coal and Oil)
- Marking the matzah as a call to urgent action—what Martin Luther King called "the fierce urgency of Now"—and the palms as witnesses of green life renewed
- Carrying these religious celebrations into the city streets with marches interspersed with vigils at local centers of "pyramidal power"
- Welcoming arrests at the White House to demand urgent action against tar sands pipelines, coal plant CO_2 emissions, and so on

Eco-Jewish activists have in similar ways reconfigured many Jewish festivals as direct actions to protect and heal the Earth:

- Reshaping Tu B'Shvat, the ReBirthday of the Trees, as a time for protests and civil disobedience to protect ancient redwoods and the Everglades from corporate depredation
- Drawing on the tradition of Hanukkah as celebrating the miraculous fulfillment of one day's supply of sacred oil to meet eight days' needs, as a spur to energy conservation
- Celebrating Hoshana Rabbah—the seventh day of the harvest festival of Sukkot, a day traditionally set aside for invoking rain, honoring the seven days of Creation, and praying for salvation from insect swarms, droughts, and other natural disasters—as a day of protest against the corporate poisoning of the Hudson River with polychlorinated biphenyls (PCBs)
- Observing the laments of Tisha B'Av over the destruction of the Holy Temples in Jerusalem by defining the Earth as the universal Temple of today, and gathering at the Capitol to lament the ongoing destruction of Temple Earth and demand action to save it

The reframing of Jewish fasts and festivals in this way has been especially attractive because the Jewish festival cycle is closely linked to the dance of the Sun, Moon, and Earth. Many of the festivals, therefore, can be understood as universal at heart, though clothed in Jewish history and culture. Probably for that reason, these actions drawing on uniquely Jewish ceremonies and practices have often attracted members of other faith traditions and secular eco-activists to take part.

As the experience of religious communities grows in exploring this whole area of reframing festivals as forms of public action, there has begun to emerge a pattern of spiritual practice in each event: first, public celebration of the Earth; then mourning the Earth's wounds and dangers; and finally, declaring a commitment and covenant to act on the Earth's behalf and challenge whatever power centers are deepening its wounds.

This threefold pattern echoes many powerful evocations of spiritual depth: the prosperity of ancient Israel in Egypt, slavery, and Exodus; the Promised Land, Exile, and Return; Celebration, Crucifixion, Resurrection; Gautama's life of royal luxury, discovery of suffering, Enlightenment.

This process of reframing festival observances as actions to protect the Earth has only just begun. It is likely that much additional richness of spiritual imagination and political adeptness will be brought to bear as religious and spiritual communities continue to face the planetary crisis.

Further Reading

Waskow, Arthur. 2013. Jewish Environmental Ethics: *Adam* and *Adamah*. In Elliot N. Dorff & Jonathan K. Cran (Eds.), *Oxford Handbook of Jewish Ethics and Morality*. Oxford: Oxford University Press.

CHAPTER 28

The Evolutionary and Ecological Perspectives of Pierre Teilhard de Chardin and Thomas Berry

Mary Evelyn Tucker and John Grim

Introduction

French Jesuit and paleontologist Pierre Teilhard de Chardin (1881–1955) and passionist priest and cultural historian Thomas Berry (1914–2009) grappled with the critical question of the significance of traditional religions and their cosmologies in light of the scientific story of an evolving universe. Their thought extends into current discussions regarding the relationship of religion and science, religion and evolution, religion and ecology, and environmental humanities.

During the last century many thinkers pondered the relationship between human consciousness and matter. From the standpoint of the empirical sciences, life and consciousness appear as anomalies that arose from the inert matter that composes the known universe. For religious thinkers, consciousness is imaged as extending from the divine realm to the human. Teilhard and Berry took a different approach from either of these predominantly modern scientific or traditional religious positions. They each offered a holistic vision by situating consciousness as integral to the evolving universe. This chapter traces their positions as articulated over the twentieth century.

The Spirit of the Earth

Teilhard proposed that the increasing complexity and consciousness of the evolution of the universe and Earth is manifested in the appearance of self-reflective humans out of this developmental process. However, he asserts that our capacity for self-reflection is not dropped into the process from the outside but emerges from within.

The Wiley Blackwell Companion to Religion and Ecology, First Edition. Edited by John Hart.

Unwilling to separate matter and spirit, he understood these linked spheres as differentiated yet interrelated dynamics operative within reality. Thus complexity-consciousness, for Teilhard, is an inherent property of matter from the beginning of the universe.

Consequently, the diverse matter of the universe in the process of evolutionary change is ultimately pulled forward by the unifying dynamics of spirit. This eventually becomes "the spirit of the Earth," where the quantum of matter successively evolves into the spheres encircling the planet: the lithosphere of rock, the hydrosphere of water, and the biosphere of life. This "spirit of the Earth" subsequently evolves into the consciousness humankind now displays in the thought sphere or noosphere surrounding the globe.

Teilhard dedicated his life-work to fostering an active realization by humans of their evolutionary roles in relation to matter-spirit. This he framed as the challenge of seeing. To assist this Teilhard articulated a phenomenology of the involution of matter, a metaphysics of union with spirit, and a mysticism of centration of persons (Teilhard, 1974, 205), We explore these areas as Teilhard defined them and then discuss some of the contributions and limitations of his thought.

Teilhard's Life Quest: Seeing

Born in southern France, Teilhard entered the Jesuit religious order where he was encouraged to study paleontology. He spent two decades in China doing paleontological work and traveled to Africa, India, and Indonesia in search of fossil evidence. It is not surprising that these studies brought him to question the Genesis Creation story. The challenge, as Teilhard saw it, was to bring Christianity and evolution into dialogue with one another. The path to this rapport was first to awaken to the deep dimensions of time that evolution opens up: "For our age, to have become conscious of evolution means something very different from and much more than having discovered one further fact ... It means (as happens with a child when he acquires the sense of perspective) that we have become alive to a new dimension" (Teilhard, 1968a, 193).

Teilhard struggled to extend contemporary science beyond an analytical, demystifying investigation of the world toward a means of seeing the spiritual dimensions of space and time in the evolutionary process. For Teilhard evolution was a unific movement. Thus, he identified the perceived separation of matter and spirit as a central problem in comprehending the unity of evolution. This was evident, he observed, in mechanistic, Cartesian science that viewed matter as dead and inert. Moreover, a split was also evident in dualistic religious worldviews that saw God as transcendent and apart from created matter. He sought to unite his scientific affirmation of the world of matter with his faith in the Divine. In one of his most striking statements, Teilhard presents his personal belief that proclaims his faith in the world:

> If, as the result of some interior revolution, I were to lose in succession my faith in Christ, my faith in a personal God, and my faith in spirit, I feel that I should continue to believe invincibly in the world. The world (its value, its infallibility and its goodness)—that, when all is said and done, is the first, the last, and the only thing in which I believe. It is by this faith that I live. (Teilhard, 1971b, 99)

As Henri de Lubac noted, Teilhard is addressing secular scientists here (de Lubac 1967, 129–143). However, Teilhard also argued that the scientific investigation of evolution would actually lead to a profound sense of the cosmic Christ in the universe. Teilhard saw evolution as drawing toward a greater personalization and deepening of the spirit. He coined the term "christic" as an expression of his experience of the cosmic Christ of evolution: the "omnipresence of transformation" in evolution centrated in complexity-consciousness that draws matter forward (Teilhard, 1979, 94).

As evolutionary science since Darwin has observed, the universe is cosmogenesis, namely, a state of continual development over time. This is in stark contrast to two major cosmological positions in Western religion and philosophy—the one-time creation of all existence as presented in Genesis; and the degeneration from a once perfected cosmos as in classical neo-Platonism. Evolution displays dynamic, self-organizing processes from small-scale atomic structures to large-scale galactic structures. Thus, a new cosmology was emerging in the twentieth century, which described the emergence of galaxies and solar systems and eventually the rise of the first cells that evolved into multicellular organisms and complex life-forms. This is the process over which Teilhard puzzled when he noted that with greater complexity of life comes greater consciousness until self-reflection emerges in humans.

Phenomenology: The Significance of Complexity-Consciousness

Teilhard presents his fullest telling of the story of evolutionary processes in *The Human Phenomenon*, completed in 1940. This comprehensive synthesis first appeared in English in 1959 and an updated translation was published 40 years later, in 1999. Here, and throughout his writings, Teilhard describes evolution as both a physical and psychic process; matter has its within and its without. His justification for such a view of inwardness lies in inductive observation. In this sense, human consciousness is not situated as an aberration or addendum, but as arising from the evolutionary process:

> Indisputably, deep within ourselves, through a rent or tear, an "interior" appears at the heart of beings. This is enough to establish the existence of this interior in some degree or other everywhere forever in Nature. Since the stuff of the universe has an internal face at one point in itself, its structure is necessarily bifacial; that is, in every region of time and space, as well, for example, as being granular, coextensive with its outside, everything has an inside. (Teilhard, 1999, 24)

Teilhard describes two kinds of energy as involved in evolution, namely, the tangential and the radial. Tangential energy is "that which links an element with all others of the same order as itself in the universe." Radial energy is that which draws the element "toward ever greater complexity and centricity in other words, forwards" (Teilhard, 1999,

30). Teilhard observes that there are self-organizing principles or tendencies evident in matter that result in more intricate systems:

> Left long enough to itself, under the prolonged and universal play of chance, matter manifests the property of arranging itself in more and more complex groupings and at the same time, in ever deepening layers of consciousness; this double and combined movement of physical unfolding and psychic interiorisation (or centration) once started, continuing, accelerating and growing to its utmost extent. (Teilhard, 1965, 139)

The thresholds of the evolutionary process as outlined by Teilhard are first, cosmogenesis in the sense of origin, namely, the emergence of the atomic and inorganic world; second, biogenesis in which organic life appears; and third, anthropogenesis marked by an increase in cephalization (the development of a more complex nervous system) and cerebration (a more complex brain). This third phase implies the birth of thought in humans and, for the first time, evolution is able to reflect on itself. Humans become heirs of the evolutionary process capable of determining its further progression or retrogression. This is an awesome responsibility and much of Teilhard's later work explicates how humans can most effectively participate in the creativity of evolutionary processes.

Teilhard summarizes the implications of his phenomenology for human action as follows:

> The essential phenomenon in the material world is life (because life is interiorized).
>
> The essential phenomenon in the living world is the human (because humans are reflective)...
>
> The essential phenomenon of humans is gradual totalization of humankind (in which individuals super-reflect upon themselves). (Teilhard, 1975, 175)

Teilhard realized that the collective human consciousness emerging in the noosphere has enormous potential for creating a planetary community, such as we are witnessing today. Thus, Teilhard saw a need for increased unification, centration, and spiritualization. By unification, he meant the need to overcome the divisive limits of political, economic, and cultural boundaries. By centration, he meant the intensification of reflexive consciousness, namely, a knowing embrace of our place in the unfolding universe. By spiritualization he meant an increase in the intensifying impulse of evolutionary processes that create a zest for life in the human. In all of this he saw the vital importance of the activation of human energy so as to participate more fully in the creative dynamics of evolution. Human creativity, for Teilhard, derives from a passionate dedication to meaningful work and productive research informed by the renewing dimensions of the arts and cultural life.

As humans currently make themselves felt in every part of the globe the challenge now is to enter appropriately into the planetary dimensions of the universe story. As Thomas Berry has suggested in drawing Teilhard's thought forward, this requires new ecological and social roles for the human—roles that enhance human–Earth relations rather than contribute to the deterioration of the life-systems of the planet (Berry, 2003a, 77–80). Because humans are increasingly taking over the biological factors that determine their growth as a species, they are capable of modifying or creating themselves. The full range of ethical issues in such a progress-oriented view of human cultural evolution were not considered by Teilhard. His contributions, however, do lead to a greater realization that as we become a planetary species by our physical presence and environmental impact, we need also to become a planetary species by our expansion of comprehensive compassion to all life-forms.

Metaphysics: The Dynamics of Union

Teilhard realized that his speculations regarding the inherent nature of the universe were preliminary (Teilhard, 1975, 192). Yet, what he sought was a "universe-of-thought" that would increasingly build toward a unified center of coherence and convergence. Thought, as a form of animated movement, carries forth complexity-consciousness.

Such an animating and alluring center, Teilhard recognized, may not be directly apprehensible to humans, but its existence can be postulated from three points. First, the irreversibility of the evolutionary process—once put into motion, it cannot be halted. Furthermore, there must be a supreme focus toward which all is moving, or else a collapse would occur. Second, polarity. This implies that a movement forward necessitates a stabilizing center influencing the heart of the evolutionary vortex. This center is independent but active enough to cause a complex centering of the various cosmic layers. Third, unanimity. Here, he suggests that there exists an energy of sympathy or love that draws things together, center to center. However, the existence of such a love would be lost if focused on an impersonal collective. Thus, there must exist a personalizing focus: "If love is to be born and to become firmly established, it must have an individualized heart and an individualized face" (Teilhard, 1975, 187).

Teilhard calls this the "metaphysics of union" for he claims that the most primordial notion of being suggests a union (Teilhard, 1975, 193). He describes the active form of being as uniting oneself or uniting with others in friendship, marriage, or collaboration. The passive form he sees as the state of being united, or unified by, another. "To create is to unite," thus by the very act of Creation the Divine becomes immersed in the multiple. This implies for a Christian that the scope of the Incarnation extends through all Creation. Teilhard regards his metaphysics as being linked with the essential Christian mysteries, such as the Trinity. That is, "There is no God without creature union. There is no creation without incarnational immersion. There is no incarnation without redemption" (Teilhard, 1975, 198). Interestingly, Teilhard presents here a formidable challenge to the traditional anthropocentric Christian emphasis on redemption exclusively for humans by extending redemption into the cosmological context.

Mysticism: The Centering of Person in Evolution

Traditional mysticism in the world's religions is often understood as an interior experience that demands a de-materialization and a transcendent leap into the Divine. Teilhard, however, realized a radical re-conceptualization of the mystical journey as an entry into evolution, discovering there an immanental sense of the Divine.

As a stretcher-bearer during World War I, he had intuited this inherent direction when he wrote, "There is a communion with God, and a communion with the Earth, and a communion with God through the Earth" (Teilhard, 1968b, 14). Eventually, Teilhard came to realize that human participation in this communion led into the depths of mystery. The process of communion is for Teilhard the centration and convergence of cosmic, planetary, and divine energies in the human. We are centered in the whole, which, for Teilhard, is the divine milieu within which we live, breathe, and have our becoming. Thus, Teilhard sees the mysticism that is needed for the future as the synthesis of two powerful currents—evolution and human love. To love evolution is to be involved in a process in which one's particular love is universalized, becomes dynamic, and is synthesized.

This view embodies not simply an anthropocentric or human-centered love, but a love for the world at large. Teilhard's mysticism is activated, for example, in scientific investigation and social commitment to research, as well as in a comprehensive compassion for all life. Mysticism is something other than simply passively enjoying the fruits of contemplation of a transcendent or abstract divinity. For Teilhard, love is always synthesized in the personal. Here lies the point of convergence of the world for Teilhard, the center in which all spiritual energy lies. By means of this personalizing force at the heart of the universe and of the individual, all human activities become an expression of love. It is in this sense Teilhard conjectures that, "every activity is amorized" (Teilhard, 1968a, 171).

Contributions and Limitations in Teilhard's Thought

Teilhard's legacy includes a vastly deepened sense of an evolutionary universe that can be understood as not simply a cosmos but a cosmogenesis. This dynamic emergent universe can now be viewed as one that is intricately connected, both unified and diversified (Swimme & Tucker, 2011). This interconnectivity changes forever the role of the human. We can no longer see ourselves as an addendum or something "created" that is apart from the whole. We are, rather, that being in whom the universe reflects back on itself in conscious self-awareness. The deepening of interiority in the mind and heart gives us cause for celebration and participation in the all-embracing processes of universe emergence. The implications for a greatly enlarged planetary consciousness and commitment to ecological awareness are clear.

Such a perspective leads to a subtle but pervasive sense for Teilhard that the universe is threaded throughout with mystery and meaning. This is in distinct contrast with those who would suggest (often dogmatically) that the universe is essentially meaningless, that evolution is a random process, and that human emergence is a result of pure chance; it is in contrast too with the beliefs of advocates of creationism and their proposals for Intelligent Design. Teilhard would not describe the evolving universe as coming into existence due to Intelligent Design. Rather, evolution for him is dependent on an intricate blending of the forces of natural selection and chance mutation, on the one hand, and increasing complexity and consciousness, on the other. This does not lead automatically to a teleological universe, but one nonetheless that holds out to the human a larger sense of both purpose and promise.

This promise at the heart of an innately self-organizing evolutionary process is also the lure toward which the process is drawn (Haught, 2002). With this insight Teilhard provides a context for situating human action. This context of hope is indispensable for humans to participate with a larger sense of meaning in society, politics, and economics, as well as in education, research, and the arts. A primary concern for Teilhard is the activation of human energy that results in a zest for life. The existentialist despair that pervaded Europe between the two world wars was something he wished to avoid. For Teilhard, the spirit of the human needed to be brought together with the spirit of the Earth for the flourishing of both humans and the planet.

Thomas Berry identified some limitations in Teilhard's thought along with his contributions (Berry, 2003b, 57–73). Berry observes that Teilhard inherited a modern faith in progress. This accounts for his optimism with regard to humans' ability to "build the Earth" and his emphasis on technological achievements. Teilhard's laudatory reflections on scientific research and technology did not always account for its potential implications for disrupting Earth processes, as when he wrote about the marvels of nuclear power and genetic engineering (Teilhard, 1968a).

Like most people of his time, Teilhard was also limited by his understanding of the world's religions. For example, he discussed Hinduism through the lens of Upanishad/Vedantic monism. This emphasis on one phase of Indian thought did not consider the other, equally significant varieties of philosophical or devotional Hinduism, such as yoga or bhakti. In addition, Teilhard had little textual or anthropological understanding of Confucianism, Daoism, or Chinese Buddhism even though he spent several decades living in China. This is no doubt because so few texts from these traditions had been translated into Western languages. Finally, he had a stereotypical Western view of indigenous traditions as "static and exhausted" (Teilhard, 1971a, 25). Teilhard, on the other hand, privileged Christianity as a major axis of evolution rather than affirming it as his entry into reflection on evolution.

Despite these limitations, what emerges in any consideration of the life and thought of Teilhard is an appreciation of his grace under pressure, his steadfast commitment to a vision that challenged many of his deepest values, and his efforts to align a life of science with his religious journey. He has provided us with one of the few intellectual and affective syntheses that draw on science and religion in such profound and novel ways. His vision of universe emergence and of the role of the human in that emergence stands as one of the lasting testimonies of twentieth-century thought.

Thomas Berry's Life Quest: A New Story

Thomas Berry (1914–2009) was born in Greensboro, North Carolina and attended high school and college at St. Mary's in Maryland. He entered the Passionist Order and received his doctorate from the Catholic University. He eventually taught the history of religions at St. John's University, Long Island, and then Fordham University in the Bronx. He established the Riverdale Center for Religious Research alongside the Hudson River where he hosted many talks and gatherings for nearly two decades. Berry spent the last 14 years of his life in Greensboro with family and friends. From his studies of world religions he expanded his life quest to articulate an engaging evolutionary narrative, a "new story" that would respond effectively to the overwhelming ecological crisis facing the planet.

To fully understand this quest it is helpful to highlight some of the major intellectual influences on his life and thinking. In this way we can more fully appreciate the nature and significance of evolution seen as a story. Here we first discuss Berry's studies of Western history, Asian traditions, and indigenous religions. We then describe the important influence of Teilhard on Berry's thought. Finally, we outline some of the major features of the new story as Berry has described it.

Berry's Intellectual Journey from Human History to Earth History

It is significant to see Berry's contributions initially as a cultural historian whose interests spanned Europe and Asia. He undertook his graduate studies in Western history and spent several years in Germany after World War II. In addition, he read extensively in the field of Asian religions and history. He lived in China the year before Mao came to power and published two books on Asian religions, *Buddhism* and *Religions of India*. He also studied the traditions of indigenous peoples and met with native peoples in North America and the Philippines.

From this beginning as a cultural and intellectual historian Berry moved to become a historian of the Earth. Berry thus came to describe himself not as a theologian but as a "geologian." The movement from human history to cosmological history was a necessary progression. He witnessed in his own lifetime the emergence of a multicultural planetary civilization as cultures have come in contact around the globe, often for the first time. But he wanted to explore this even further back in Earth history and the evolution of the universe. This is what led to his signature essay in 1978 on "The New Story." Expanding on Teilhard's evolutionary perspective, he moved toward evolution as an epic narrative, one that can inspire human action. Thus, in 1992 he published *The Universe Story* with Brian Swimme.

Historian of Western Intellectual History

Berry began his academic career as a historian of Western history. His thesis at Catholic University on Giambattista Vico's philosophy of history was published in 1951. Vico outlined his philosophy in *The New Science of the Nature of the Nations*, which was first published in 1725 after some 20 years' research. Vico was trying to establish a science of the study of nations comparable to what others had done for the study of Nature. Thus, he hoped to make the study of history more "scientific" by focusing on the world of human institutions and causation.

Vico's thought was seminal for Berry as he developed a constructive critique of our own period. Berry draws on Vico in several respects: the sweeping periodization of history, the notion of the barbarism of reflection, and the poetic wisdom and creative imagination needed to sustain civilizations. With regard to periodization, Berry defined four major ages in human history: the tribal shamanic, the traditional civilizational, the scientific technological, and the ecological or ecozoic. He observed that we are currently moving into the ecozoic era, which he felt will be characterized by a new understanding of human–Earth relations. Nonetheless, he acknowledged that we are in a period of severe cultural pathology with regard to our blind yet sophisticated technological assault on the Earth. In other words, we are in a time of a "barbarism of reflection," a period of over-refinement of a civilizational age at the same time as we have lost Earth wisdom.

To extract ourselves from this cultural pathology of alienation from one another and destruction of the Earth, Berry eventually called for a new story of the universe. By evoking such an epic and poetic vision he felt we might be able to create a sustainable future. It took some three decades for him to articulate this vision after being inspired by Vico.

Historian of Asian Thought and Religions

In 1948, after completing his doctorate, Berry set out for China intending to study language and Chinese philosophy. On the boat leaving from San Francisco he met Wm. Theodore de Bary, who later became one of the premier scholars in Asian studies. Their time in China, while fruitful, was cut short by Mao's Communist victory in 1949. After they returned to the United States they worked together to found the Asian Thought and Religion Seminar at Columbia University. De Bary helped to establish one of the nation's premier programs in Asian studies at Columbia and they remained friends for 60 years.

Berry began his teaching of Asian religions at Seton Hall (1956–1960) and St. John's University (1960–1966). He eventually moved to Fordham University (1966–1979) where he founded a graduate program in the history of religions. What was distinctive about Berry's teaching was his effort not only to discuss the historical unfolding of the traditions being studied, but also to articulate their spiritual dynamics and ecological significance. Well before interreligious dialogue emerged, Berry was studying the texts and traditions of the world's religions, often in the original languages. During this process, he examined their cosmologies and Creation stories to imagine a more comprehensive and inclusive cosmology for our times.

In this respect, the most seminal Asian tradition for Berry's thinking was Confucianism. For Berry, Confucianism is significant because of its cosmological concerns, its interest in self-cultivation and education, and its commitment to improving the social and political order. In Confucian cosmology Berry identified the key understanding of the human as a microcosm of the cosmos. Essential to this cosmology is a "continuity of being" and thus a communion between various levels of reality: cosmic, Earth, and human. This is similar to Teilhard's ideas, as well as those of Alfred North Whitehead and other contemporary process thinkers.

Confucianism remained for Berry a dynamic, vitalistic tradition with important implications for current environmental philosophy. Berry noted, however, that there is a disparity between theory and practice in the case of China. He recognized that China, like many countries, has been responsible for deforestation and desertification over the centuries. Furthermore, the contemporary record of China on the environment remains far from ideal. Nonetheless, he felt the comprehensive cosmological framework of Confucian thought is a valuable intellectual resource in reformulating a contemporary ecological cosmology with implications for environmental ethics. Indeed, this is what is occurring in China today with the effort to formulate an "ecological civilization," drawing particularly on Confucian perspectives.

Indigenous Religious Traditions

In addition to a remarkable ability to appreciate the diversity and uniqueness of Asian and Western religions, Berry had a lively interest in and empathy for indigenous peoples and their cultural life-ways. He taught courses at both Fordham and Columbia on American Indian religions and published articles on the topic. He encouraged his graduate students to write dissertations in this field; several of these have now been published. Various native groups warmly received him, including tribes on the Northern Plains, the northwest coast, and the Cree and Inuit peoples in northeastern Canada who have struggled against the massive James Bay hydroelectric project. Overseas, he has spent time with the Tboli people in the southern Philippines. He encouraged them to touch lightly into the current industrial-technological period and move more fully into the ecozoic era.

In addition to his own research, writing, and teaching in the field of Native American religions, Berry's appreciation for native traditions and for the richness of their mythic, symbolic, and ritual life was enhanced by his encounters with the ideas of Carl Jung and Mircea Eliade. Within this larger framework of interpretive categories Berry was able to articulate the special feeling in native traditions for the sacredness of the land, the seasons, and the animal, bird, and fish life. He understood how native peoples respect Creation because they respect the Creator; how they have a deep reverence for the gift of all life and for humans' dependence on Nature to sustain life. He studied the ancient techniques of shamanism, including ritual fasting and prayer, to call on the powers in Nature for personal healing and communal strength.

Berry recognized that native peoples have cultivated an ability to use resources without abusing them and to recognize the importance of living lightly on the Earth. However, he did not assume that native peoples were the ideal ecologists. As in the Chinese case, abuses certainly have occurred. However, for Berry these two traditions—Confucian and Native American—remained central to the creation of a new cosmological understanding and ecological spirituality for our times. They also have affinities with a sense of the Earth as a dynamic, unfolding force that inspired the new story.

Teilhard's Influence on the New Story

In formulating his idea of a new story Berry was also indebted to the thought of Pierre Teilhard de Chardin. He began reading Teilhard during the 1960s after the publication of *The Phenomenon of Man* in 1959 (republished in 1999 with the title *The Human Phenomenon*). In particular, Berry gained from Teilhard an appreciation for developmental time. As Berry wrote, since the publication of Charles Darwin's *On the Origin of Species* we have become aware of the universe not simply as a static cosmos but as an unfolding cosmogenesis. The theory of evolution provides a distinctive realization of change and development in the universe that resituates us in an encompassing sweep of geological time. For Berry the new story is a primary context for understanding the immensity of cosmogenesis.

From Teilhard, Berry also derived an understanding of the psychic-physical character of the unfolding universe. As we have noted, this implies that if there is consciousness in the human and if humans have evolved from the Earth, then from the beginning some form of consciousness or interiority is present in the process of evolution. Matter for both Teilhard and Berry is not dead or inert, but a numinous reality possessing both a physical and spiritual dimension. Consciousness, then, is an intrinsic part of reality and is the thread that links all life-forms. There are various forms of consciousness and, in the human, self-consciousness or reflective thought arises.

Berry also obtained from Teilhard an appreciation for his law of complexity-consciousness. This suggests that as things evolve from simpler to more complex organisms, so consciousness increases. Ultimately, self-consciousness or reflection emerges in the human order. The human as a highly complex mammal is distinguished by this capacity for reflection. This gives humans a special role in the evolutionary process. We are part of, not apart from, the Earth.

For Teilhard and for Berry, evolution provides the most comprehensive context for understanding the human phenomenon in relation to other life-forms. This implies for Berry that we are one species among others, and as self-reflective beings we need to understand our particular responsibility for the continuation of the evolutionary process. We have reached a juncture where we are realizing that we will determine which species survive and which will become extinct. We have become co-creators as we have become conscious of our role in this extraordinary, irreversible development of the emergence of life-forms. This is what Berry called the Great Work, what humans can do to enhance human–Earth relations.

As we have noted, Berry critiqued Teilhard's over-optimistic view of progress and his apparent lack of concern for the devastating effect that industrial processes were having on fragile ecosystems. He pointed out that Teilhard was heir to a Western mode of thinking which saw the human as capable of controlling the natural world, usually through science and technology.

In addition, Berry noted Teilhard's lack of appreciation for Asian religions despite his long residence and extensive travels in Asia. His attachment to the unique revelation of Christianity is reflective of the Catholic theology of his time, which did not recognize truth in other religions. It may also be explained as the absence of the opportunity for communication with Chinese scholars of traditional Chinese religions while he resided in Beijing. This may have been due to a language barrier, wartime constraints, or lack of time or interest due to other scholarly commitments.

Berry's approach has been much more inclusive in terms of cultural history and religion, while Teilhard was focused on geology and paleontology. These two approaches came together in Berry's book written with mathematical cosmologist Brian Swimme, *The Universe Story* (1992). Here for the first time is the narration of the story of the evolution of the solar system and the Earth, along with the story of the evolution of the human and of human societies and cultures. While not claiming to be definitive or exhaustive *The Universe Story* presents a model for telling a common Creation story. It marks a new era of self-reflection for humans, one that Berry described as the "ecological age" or the beginning of the "ecozoic age." Brian Swimme and Mary Evelyn Tucker extended this perspective in their multimedia project, *Journey of the Universe*, a film, book, and conversation series.

In telling the story of evolution Berry also tried not to keep his language exclusively Christocentric as Teilhard did. His intention was to appeal not only to the Christian community but beyond it too. He was aware of the barriers theological language sometimes creates in the secular world, particularly among environmentalists and people of different faith commitments. He hoped to appeal to a wide variety of individuals who are responsive to the paradigm shift in worldviews that is beginning to take shape in human consciousness. It is a shift that transcends religious or national boundaries and helps to create the common grounds for the emergence of an Earth community.

The Origin and Significance of the New Story

Berry spent some 20 years studying the world's religions starting in 1948, and during the 1960s immersed himself in Teilhard's thought. In the 1970s Berry's ideas on the new story began to take shape as he pondered the magnitude of the social, political, and economic problems the human community was facing. Berry saw this as a comprehensive basis for nurturing reciprocity between humans and for fostering reverence in humans for the Earth in a period of increasing assault on the Earth's ecosystems.

The idea of a new story or a functional cosmology, then, arose not as an abstract idea, but as a response to the sufferings of humans in a universe where they saw themselves as deeply alienated. This alienation was, no doubt, a particular experience of the West during the postwar years as expressed in existentialist philosophy, the death of God theology, and the theater of the absurd. Nonetheless, the spirit of disaffection, ennui, and alienation spread to other parts of the world in the wake of Western cultural influences and the rise of unfettered materialism. Berry's new story provided an important antidote to disillusionment and despair, especially regarding our destruction of the environment. It created, above all, a new context for connection, for purpose, for action because it provided a comprehensive perspective for activating the human energy needed for positive social, political, and economic change.

Berry first published the "New Story" (subtitled "Comments on the Origin, Identification and Transmission of Values") in 1978 as the initial essay of the *Teilhard*

Studies series. It was republished nearly a decade later in the journal *Cross Currents* and revised for publication in *The Dream of the Earth* in 1988.

From Old Story to New Story

Berry opens his essay by observing: "We are in between stories." He notes how the old story was functional because "It shaped our emotional attitudes, provided us with life purpose, energized action. It consecrated suffering and integrated knowledge" (Berry, 2003a, 77). The context of meaning provided by the old story is no longer relevant. People are turning to New Age solipsism, technological utopias, or religious fundamentalism for their orientation. However, for Berry none of these directions could ultimately be satisfying. He recognized dysfunctionalism in both religious and scientific communities and proposed a new story of how things came to be, where we are now, and how the human future can be given meaningful direction. In losing our direction we have lost our values and orientation. This is what he felt the new story could provide, bringing science and the humanities back together.

The Historical Split between Religious and Scientific Communities

Berry cites the Black Death of the fourteenth and fifteenth centuries as a watershed moment in Western thought when religion and science began to divide. On the one hand, there arose the religious redemption community, while on the other, there emerged the scientific secular community. The religious community embraced redemption out of this world, while the scientific community fostered empirical study of an objectified world.

With the spread of the Black Death in Europe the need arose to have the intervention of supernatural forces to mitigate the awesome power of death. Because of the vast numbers of people who died, Christianity held to a strong redemption-oriented theology. To be redeemed and saved out of this world of suffering was the hope held up for all believers. To be assisted in this redemption from suffering by the power of Christ's suffering and death was the aim of the Christian message.

As Berry observed, something was lost in this exclusive focus on redemption. Creation theology was subsumed in redemption soteriology: "The primary doctrine of the Christian creed, belief in a personal creative principle, became increasingly less important in its functional role. Cosmology was not of any particular significance." Berry (2003a, 78) claims that the Christian story lost its cosmological import.

Increasingly, scientific secular communities sought to remedy the terror of natural events by studying the processes of the Earth itself rather than seeking supernatural intervention. The heavens and the Earth were studied with the aid of the telescope and microscope. Scientific empiricism was paralleled by the eighteenth-century Enlightenment philosophers' celebration of Reason and the sociologists' articulation of progress in human societies. The biological understanding of developmental time, which began in the nineteenth century, was a significant addition to this. In the twentieth century it was enhanced by astrophysicists' explorations of the expanding universe.

The divide between science and religion has remained strong to the present day. In fact, in our own time the split between the religious creationists and the scientific evolutionists has been quite heated. On the other hand, a new dialogue is also emerging between science and religion, which is attempting to overcome the dichotomy that was exacerbated by the Copernican and Darwinian revolutions.

Earth Unfolding in Space and Time: Cosmogenesis

Copernicus's discoveries changed our sense of human spatial orientation in the universe. No longer was the Earth considered the center of reality. In a similar manner, the Darwinian revolution altered our sense of time. Human consciousness is awakening to the realization that the Earth is part of an irreversible developmental sequence of time. Life has evolved from less complex to more complex forms. In other words, "the Earth in all its parts, especially in its life forms, was in a state of continuing transformation" (Berry, 2003a, 80). This is a key implication of the new story. We live not simply in a cosmos but in a cosmogenesis. This reflects the influence of Teilhard on Berry's thinking. However, developmental time is still being absorbed by the human community while being resisted by Christian creationists.

Subjectivity

A radical new realization of the subjective communion of the human with the Earth is now beginning to be understood. As Berry expresses it, "The human being emerges not only as an earthling, but also as a worldling. Human persons bear the universe in their being as the universe bears them in its being. The two have a total presence to each other" (2003a, 78). This subjective presence of things to one another is one of the most distinctive features of Berry's thought and reflects Teilhard's influence. In *The Divine Milieu* Teilhard writes of this interior attraction of things: "In the Divine Milieu all the elements of the universe touch each other by that which is most inward and ultimate in them" (1960, 92). Berry has suggested that the importance of the awareness of the subjective dimension of the universe story cannot be underestimated. Indeed, he writes: "the reality and value of the interior subjective numinous aspect of the entire cosmic order are being appreciated as the basic condition in which the story makes any sense at all" (Berry, 2003a, 86).

Values: Differentiation, Subjectivity, Communion

Berry states that to communicate values in this new frame of the Earth story requires identifying the basic principles of the universe process itself. For Berry these are the primordial tendencies of the universe toward differentiation, subjectivity, and communion. Differentiation refers to the extraordinary variety and distinctiveness of everything in the universe. No two things are completely alike. Subjectivity is the interior numinous component present in all reality, also called consciousness. Communion is the ability to relate to other people and things due to the presence of subjectivity and difference. They create the grounds for the inner attraction of things for one another. Berry felt these three principles could become the basis of a more comprehensive ecological and social ethics that understands how the human community is dependent on and interactive with the Earth community.

Confidence in the Future

For Berry such a perspective is crucial for the survival of both humans and the Earth. As he has stated, humans and the Earth will go into the future as a single, multiform event or we will not go into the future at all. Berry closes "The New Story" with a powerful passage evoking his confidence in the future despite the tragedies of the present:

> If the dynamics of the universe from the beginning shaped the course of the heavens, lighted the sun and formed the Earth, if this same dynamism brought forth the continents and seas and atmosphere, if it awakened life in the primordial cell and then brought into being the unnumbered variety of living beings, and finally brought us into being and guided us safely through the turbulent centuries, there is reason to believe that this same guiding process is precisely what has awakened in us our present understanding of ourselves and our relation to this stupendous process. Sensitized to such guidance from the very structure and functioning of the universe, we can have confidence in the future that awaits the human venture. (Berry, 2003a, 88)

This is Berry's life-journey, born of his intellectual formation as a cultural historian of the West, turning toward Asian religions, examining indigenous traditions, and finally culminating in the study of the scientific story of the universe itself. It is a story of personal evolution against the background of cosmic evolution. It is the story of one person's intellectual history in relation to Earth history. It is the story of all our histories in conjunction with planetary history. As Berry noted it, is a story awaiting multiple tellings and an ever-deeper confidence in the beauty and mystery of its unfolding.

Conclusion

It is out of these kinds of concern for the future direction of human–Earth relations that Teilhard wrote *The Human Phenomenon* and Berry developed the "New Story." Both Teilhard's and Berry's aim was to evoke the psychic and spiritual resources to establish a reciprocity of humans with Earth and of humans with one another. They believed that with a comprehensive perspective regarding our place in this extraordinary unfolding of the universe and Earth history there would emerge a renewed awareness of our relation to and responsibility in evolutionary processes at this crucial point in history.

References

Berry, Thomas. 2003a. The New Story (77–88). In Arthur Fabel & Donald St John (Eds.), *Teilhard in the 21st Century*. Maryknoll, NY: Orbis Books.

Berry, Thomas. 2003b. Teihard in the Ecological Age (57–73). In Arthur Fabel & Donald St John (Eds.), *Teilhard in the 21st Century*. Maryknoll, NY: Orbis Books.

Berry, Thomas. 2015. *The Dream of the Earth*. Berkeley, CA: Counterpoint. (Originally published by Sierra Club Books, 1988.)

de Lubac, Henri. 1967. *Teilhard de Chardin: The Man and His Meaning*. New York: New American Library.

Haught, John. 2002. In Search of a God of Evolution: Paul Tillich and Pierre Teihard de Chardin. *Teilhard Studies*, 45. American Teilhard Association.

Swimme, Brian & Berry, Thomas. 1992. *The Universe Story*. San Francisco, CA: Harper.

Swimme, Brian Thomas & Tucker, Mary Evelyn. 2011. *Journey of the Universe*. New Haven, CT: Yale University Press.

Teilhard de Chardin, Pierre. 1960. *The Divine Milieu*. New York: Harper & Row.

Teilhard de Chardin, Pierre. 1965. *The Appearance of Man*. New York: Harper & Row.

Teilhard de Chardin, Pierre. 1968a. *Science and Christ*. New York: Harper & Row.

Teilhard de Chardin, Pierre. 1968b. *Writings in Time of War*. New York: Harper & Row.

Teilhard de Chardin, Pierre. 1971a. *Human Energy*. New York: Harcourt Brace Jovanovich.

Teilhard de Chardin, Pierre. 1971b. *How I Believe. Christianity and Evolution*. New York: Harcourt Brace Jovanovich.

Teilhard de Chardin, Pierre. 1975. *My Fundamental Vision. Toward the Future*. New York: Harcourt Brace Jovanovich.

Teilhard de Chardin, Pierre. 1979. *The Christic. The Heart of Matter*. New York: Harcourt Brace Jovanovich.

Teilhard de Chardin, Pierre. 1999. *The Human Phenomenon*. New transl. Sarah Appleton Weber. Bristol: Sussex Academic Press. (Originally titled *The Phenomenon of Man*.)

Further Reading

Berry, Thomas. 1999. *The Great Work*. New York: Random House.

Berry, Thomas. 2006. *Evening Thoughts: Reflecting on Earth as Sacred Community*. Ed. Mary Evelyn Tucker. San Francisco, CA: Sierra Club Books.

Berry, Thomas. 2009. *The Christian Future and the Fate of Earth*. Eds. Mary Evelyn Tucker & John Grim. Maryknoll, NY: Orbis Books.

Berry, Thomas. 2009. *The Sacred Universe: Earth, Spirituality, and Religion in the Twenty-First Century*. Ed. Mary Evelyn Tucker. New York: Columbia University Press.

Berry, Thomas. 2014. *Selected Writings on the Earth Community*. Eds. Mary Evelyn Tucker & John Grim. Maryknoll, NY: Orbis Books.

Eaton, Heather. 2014. *The Intellectual Journey of Thomas Berry*. Lanham, MD: Lexington Press.

Teilhard de Chardin, Pierre. 1979. *Let Me Explain*. New York: Harper & Row.

CHAPTER 29

Earth as Community Garden

The Bounty, Healing, and Justice of Holy Permaculture

Tallessyn Zawn Grenfell-Lee

Introduction: The Burden of More

The socio-ecological crisis is truly daunting. Humanity has unleashed an overlapping chain reaction in population expansion, growth economics, ecosystem degradation, and the planet's climate, with the worst consequences reverberating through the most vulnerable communities. Organizations from every part of the world scramble to find strategies and resources with which to respond. Yet, despite decades of research, activism and political collaboration, the pace of destruction still seems to accelerate faster than our efforts to stem and reverse the damage. Somehow, no matter what we do, it seems as if we never have enough political will, enough resources, or enough hands on the ground to meet the defining challenge of our time. No matter what we do, we always need more.

Maybe our endless quest for more is the problem itself. For example, many once believed we needed more food to address hunger, so scientists created chemical fertilizers as part of an industrial agricultural model designed to help feed the world. The resulting "more"—crop surpluses, pollution, and a population explosion—has destabilized economies, destroyed ecosystems, and damaged health across the globe. These combined forces also drive global urbanization, which leads to additional socio-ecological harm. Today's burgeoning mega-cities not only struggle with unemployment, pollution, and violence, but also, ironically, unhealthy food. Surplus crops flood cities with processed calories and cheap alcohol, such that more and more urban communities now contend with obesity and alcoholism. And as city dwellers continue to move away from Nature, they spend more time indoors by themselves. With life-threatening health consequences, today's overcrowded populations are lonely.

The Wiley Blackwell Companion to Religion and Ecology, First Edition. Edited by John Hart.

"More" seemed like such a good idea; and the progress has not been all bad. When economics and politics align, global transport allows us to get emergency food to needy communities quickly. Yet somehow, we remain trapped in a worldview of scarcity without regard for either the real causes of brokenness or the healing potential all around us. How can it be that we choke on abundant food while we simultaneously waste away? Surrounded by more and more people, why are we more isolated than ever? In a world abounding in grace, how did so many of us end up sick and alone, diseased and filled with despair? How can we reclaim our communities away from desolation and death, and toward life and hope?

A key path to rebirth lies in reclaiming our broken relationship with food. This daily, elemental part of our human existence—its source, growth, and consumption—plays a foundational, transformational role in the disease or health of a community, both as an ecosystem and for individuals. Sustainable agriculture, and permaculture in particular, reorients food to the limits of what an ecosystem can bear. It addresses the diverse needs and wounds of our communities all over the world. We need to banish the fears of scarcity that trap us in cycles of "more," so that the whole community can survive and flourish together. As we rediscover a covenantal relationship with our food, we simultaneously bring abundant healing and justice to our bodies, our communities, and our precious, holy lands.

Industrial Farming and Relentless Growth

A driving force behind the myriad facets of the socio-ecological crisis leads back to a simple invention: chemical fertilizers. Eager to grow crops more efficiently, scientists sought to capture atmospheric nitrogen in order to bypass Nature's slower cycles of soil replenishment. In the early 1900s, widespread synthetic nitrogen fertilizer use led to an agricultural boom which enabled the human population to quadruple. In the developed world, the sudden overabundance of world grains drove local prices down and small farmers out of business. These surpluses also fed cattle for a surging meat industry. Fertilizer, along with livestock waste, started to release increasing quantities of greenhouse gases into the atmosphere. Huge swaths of grasslands lost over a quarter of their biodiversity. Nitrogen leached into the world's rivers and ocean deltas, contaminating drinking water and killing the fish. Nitrogen-related air pollution increased the incidence of human diseases such as cancer (Townsend & Howarth, 2010).

The chemists had good intentions, but they neglected to consider that hunger stems from broken politics, not from a lack of food. Corporate subsidies and trade agreements leave small farmers vulnerable to surpluses, price fluctuations, and unreliable markets; consolidated farming corporations continue to dump excess grains on the global market, which destabilizes the economies and political systems of developing nations and drives small farmers out of business. Despite decades of international attention, food insecurity continues to impact nearly 800 million people, particularly women and young children in rural areas of the developing world (WFP, 2015). In the wake of industrialized agriculture, the vulnerable communities in the developing world have suffered the most.

In addition to the economic challenges, the forces of population growth, natural disasters, and conflicts continually drive these communities onto smaller, less arable lands. Ever-growing populations increase pressure on farmland and fisheries as well. Rural subsistence farmers and herders can no longer rotate fallow and productive lands to allow ecosystems to recover, and large fishing corporations deplete fish stocks without regard for local fishers. As a result, over-intensive farming, herding, and fishing have jeopardized the livelihoods of the billions of people who depend on them to survive (Townsend & Howarth, 2010). Over a billion people are still trying to hold on to what remains of the livelihoods of their ancestors—farming, herding, fishing—until their depleted homelands can no longer feed or protect them. Then, in desperation, they seek refuge and hope in cities.

City Earth

In 2007, for the first time in human history, more people resided in cities and their surrounding suburbs than in rural areas. Unless national governments have strong protective policies, rural and fishing communities—and women in particular—become victims of global economics and politics that favor free trade and widen the gap between wealthy and impoverished peoples. Eventually, these families abandon their fields or boats and migrate to urban areas (FAO, 2015). As a result, a rapidly growing number of food-insecure communities now live in shantytowns on the outskirts of the burgeoning cities of the Global South (WFP, 2015). Rapid urbanization can surpass a city's ability to absorb newcomers into its housing, education, healthcare, and labor force (DESA, 2014). "Turbo-urbanization" (Muggah, 2015) leads to destabilization, hazardous health conditions, unemployment, and violent crimes.

Ironically, some of the same economic forces that drive mass urban migration also leave urban populations vulnerable to food shortages. Modern cities rely almost entirely on petroleum-based supply chains to provide industrially farmed food and other essential goods, and these global transport chains fluctuate in response to economics, supply, and natural disasters. Large agricultural conglomerates secure lucrative trade deals with these urban markets, with which small, local farms cannot compete (DESA, 2013); and due to "just-in-time" delivery systems, a city likely has only enough food to feed its citizens for three days (Cockrall-King, 2012, 107–109). In some cases, what looks like "more" really means "less."

The problems with this kind of food economy go beyond food security. Agricultural surpluses have flooded urban areas with cheap, grain-based alcoholic beverages and foods packed with processed grains, sweeteners, and fats. Alcoholism is rampant among urban adults and street children alike; and inexpensive industrial food has led to another great irony, in which millions of well-fed people in both the developing and the developed world now suffer simultaneously from obesity and malnutrition. For the first time in human history, large swaths of the population suffer from over-nutrition—people over-consume food and nutrients, which leads to a variety of health risks, such as morbid obesity. According to the World Health Organization (WHO), over 65% of the world now live in areas where over-nutrition causes more death than hunger (WHO, 2013, 1). In fact, these non-communicable diseases kill more people today than all other causes of death combined: two-thirds of all deaths are now the result of alcoholism, obesity, coronary disease, diabetes, and cancer (Alwan, 2010). Obesity endangers human health as much as smoking does, and urban malnutrition poses a critical threat, particularly to pregnant women, young children, and elders (Fernández, 2011; OECD, 2014). Across the board, this phenomenon hits poorest communities hardest; during economic stress, households replace fresh food with subsidized industrial foods. Even worse, transnational corporate food giants pack their representatives into the international programs designed to address these issues, and then block efforts to reform safety, health, or trade policies (Chopra, Galbraith, & Darnton-Hill, 2002). In the meantime, we are poisoning ourselves and sabotaging our future with the abundant crops we thought we so desperately needed.

Hunger, Poverty, and Politics

It turns out we focused on hunger when we should have been targeting poverty. In order to feed the world, we must understand the global political and economic forces that drive the widening disparities of wealth. Strategies that focus on large, monoculture cash crops, support global free trade, and rely on safety nets to address poverty occasionally do reduce hunger, but they also tend to create widely divided upper and lower economic classes and few opportunities for poor communities to establish economic resilience and independence. Conversely, strategies that successfully address poverty, hunger, and gender integrate the wellbeing of both urban and rural communities (DESA, 2013, 2014). These programs include local, sustainable agriculture as well as political and economic reforms that empower women and support local economies (FAO, 2015).

The processes that link politics, poverty, and agriculture should come as no surprise. Social scientists have known for decades that world hunger persists irrespective of abundant industrial food surpluses. Despite this, the powerful economic forces driving industrial agriculture continue to promote a narrative that disparages sustainable farming and insists poor communities need to industrialize in order to produce enough food to feed the world (Halweil, 2006). In recent years, however, the prominent narrative has started to shift. A 2013 UN report not only urged an immediate, global transition to sustainable, small farms, but also pointedly criticized governments that continue to prioritize corporate profits over the welfare of vulnerable communities:

> hunger and malnutrition are not phenomena of insufficient physical supply, but results of prevailing poverty, and above all problems of access to food. Enabling these people to become food self-sufficient or earn an appropriate income through agriculture to buy food needs to take center stage in future agriculture transformation... One does neither see the necessary level of urgency nor the political willingness, from the international community, for drastic changes. Priority remains heavily focused on increasing production (mostly under the slogan "more with less"). The currently pursued approach is still very much biased towards expansion of "somewhat-less-polluting" industrial agriculture, rather than more sustainable and affordable production methods. It is still not recognized that a paradigm shift is required. (UNCTAD, 2013)

Today's sustainable farms differ greatly from the subsistence agriculture methods practiced by displaced rural farmers and refugee communities in the developing world. In fact, modern sustainable farms use a variety of new and old technologies to build drought and flood resistance, enhance soil nutrition and stability, and increase crop yields. According to a detailed United Nations (UN) analysis of farming options for refugee communities, "modern" or "science-based" agriculture produces high yields only in combination with good soil, plentiful water, chemical fertilizers, and pesticide inputs; even then, its benefits do not reach poor communities, except in their "adverse environmental and social effects," such as pesticide poisoning and aquatic "dead zones." In contrast, "sustainable agriculture" incorporates farming innovations and adapts to local resources and knowledge, distributes benefits more equitably, and works "within the constraints of climate, soils, and water availability to ensure sustainability of production, resources, and livelihoods." The report goes on to point out the far-reaching value of "permaculture," which goes further than sustainable and organic farming by focusing on the relationships among animals, plants, and the soil in order to increase crop yields and discourage pests. Permaculture prevents problems before they begin, by understanding an ecosystem and working with the land to plan a logical farm based on what various land "zones" need and can feasibly produce (UNHCR, 2002).

Relationships among creatures? Listening to the land? Permaculture sounds more like a New Age spiritual pilgrimage than a practical guide to farming. But maybe this humble approach does have something to offer. The report also pointed out other ingredients required for self-sufficient farming communities; in particular, it urged approaches that look to local knowledge and expertise, networking among local institutions, and building relationships of trust. After decades of research, analysts believe that "External experts ... seldom know all the facts, and cannot understand the implications of the many factors that influence people's decisions and actions"; moreover, "the best way to get people committed to an idea or process is to help them work out a problem or issue, and then help them develop their own responses" (UNHCR, 2002). Short-term emergencies may still require top-down "training and extension systems"; but in the long term, community-based approaches enable the people involved to express their needs and provide settings in which people can exchange ideas and find practical solutions.

The strengths of these community-based models rely on the same fundamental ideas of permaculture: to focus on the relationships, strengths, and needs of the community, and to involve and empower local peoples. Aid organizations have learned the lessons of humility and mutuality, and they have begun to apply these ideas to land management. The philosophical parallels between community-based aid extension and permaculture farming reveal why these approaches yield similarly longstanding success. The land, the aid organizations, and the local communities form a three-way covenant in which they steer one another toward solutions that build on the strengths and address the needs of all members of their ecosystems. Given the multifaceted, far-reaching benefits, it is no wonder that the UN described these programs as "the most suitable strategic approaches for dealing holistically with the inter-related problems of hunger and poverty, climate change, economic, social and gender inequity, poor health and nutrition, and environmental sustainability" (UNCTAD, 2013).[1] Apparently, we do not need more food or even more aid; to heal our world, we need to liberate the abundant resources already present in the ecosystems. If humanity is to find liberation from social injustice, ecological devastation, and the toil of the soil, we need to bend our long agrarian journey toward permaculture.

Permaculture as Ecocentric Liberation

The current surge in community-based agriculture represents more than past movements, which tended to focus on narrower goals. The wider, ecocentric "Food Revolution" incorporates all the interrelated issues that encompass justice, healing, and liberation (Robbins, 2010). Humanity is remembering that we need both wholeness and righteousness in order to flourish. Just as physical intimacy does not necessarily heal loneliness, time spent in Nature alone cannot address poverty and oppression. At least 21 million people now endure forced labor, many of them in agriculture, fishing, and the sex trade (ILO, 2012). For the world's most vulnerable communities, a human–Nature "connection" without justice readily devolves into slavery.

It turns out that redemption is hard work. We know from history that social justice movements wax and wane; so, even given its momentum, the current revolution has a long way to go to bring about embedded societal transformation. Leaders acknowledge the challenge:

> For those who have been working in urban agriculture for many years (and in a few cases, many decades), they know that the excitement level is high right now, but they also have a realistic view of what it will actually take to change our habits, behaviors, and expectations of how we will live if we want to truly address sustainability in our lifestyles... Any type of sustainable living takes time. (Cockrall-King, 2012, 309)

These leaders do not romanticize their work; they know well the time, energy, and raw labor needed to have a lasting impact. Like the UN, local leaders increasingly look to the maverick approach found in permaculture.

The holistic elements of permaculture that take it beyond simple organic or sustainable farming also give it a greater chance as a permanent solution. Its basic techniques were practiced by many ancient societies (and subsequently lost during industrialization), such as edible forests and layered growth levels; and over a billion people, including many indigenous peoples, still rely primarily on forest ecosystems. Yet beyond immediate food needs, permaculture examines all human needs in the context of the other elements of a given ecosystem, including water, energy, and shelter. Its practitioners coax the land into producing food in self-regenerative systems that imitate healthy natural ecosystems. They study the characteristics of each plot of land and create a closed cycle of nutrients and energy that requires little or no external inputs. Permaculture requires wildlife corridors for conservation, biodiversity, and pest management. Over time, the system can produce a succession of harvests and a wide variety of foods as it simultaneously builds topsoil, drought and flood resistance, and pest immunity (Doel, 2013).

Perhaps most compellingly, permaculture acknowledges that modern life and sustainability need to find a practical meeting point in order to work for the majority of people. Although it can at times appear wild or unkempt, it produces abundant food with a fraction of the effort of traditional approaches; some call it "reaping what you do not sow" (Cockrall-King, 2012, 309–311). Permaculture combines the best of the past with innovations of today in a system that adapts to any region or community. Practically speaking, some analysts predict that many communities will first move to agro-ecological agriculture, a compromise that seeks ecosystem-specific, immediate, and less polluting solutions. In the meantime, permaculturists continue to develop techniques that agro-ecology can subsequently incorporate. And, as more of our communities move toward permaculture, we discover the paradoxical, joyful abundance found in embracing our limits.

Permaculture Ethics

Wild berry patches laden with fruit need no fertilizer or pesticides. Likewise, Creation left alone finds balance and fecundity. Permaculture requires great humility and respect for the land and all its creatures; it incorporates care of the Earth and care of the people, which includes equitable sharing and distribution of natural goods ("resources"). It includes sacrifice: humanity must give up some luxuries and surpluses so that everyone has enough. Humans have a unique role as shepherds to tend the fragile land so that all Creation can flourish. These ideas may sound new because they have been found anew; in fact, they are ancient.

Given the brokenness of industrial agriculture, ethicists have explored agrarian alternatives at length. Norman Wirzba argues that plow-based agriculture, while providing ample food, also enabled much of humanity to take a significant step away from the rhythms of Nature that had long informed their understanding of finitude. Wirzba argues further that a Nature connection—falling in love with the Creation again—will help us rediscover this lost rhythm. Gardening in particular brings us to our knees in the soil, to interact with the Earth with patience and humility, reliant on the cycles of the seasons. Tending the Earth will help us release our fear of finitude and death, because it enables us to experience death as part of our connection to all life and to the Divine (Wirzba, 2003, 33–41, 73–74, 114–122).

Ellen Davis agrees that humanity is called to tend the garden of Creation as our primary vocation. Davis examines the similarities between agrarian scriptural themes and contemporary writers such as Wendell Berry (Davis, 2009). She explores the role of the Creation as a third member in the covenant between humanity and the Divine; it has moral agency, and as a holy member of this covenant, it can never be truly privatized. In particular, the Creation poem in Genesis 1 reveals that the Creation expresses divinity through its permanent, self-perpetuating abundance, which disappears only when humanity violates the covenant. Thus, our foundational identity involves eating and tending, or shepherding, the Creation.[2] Faithfulness involves fulfilling our divine purpose as humble gardeners who tend the self-seeding abundance that the divinely wrought Creation provides (Davis, 2009, 32–34, 40, 51–58, 60–62). In other words, we are called to holy permaculture.

In an eerie reflection on today's food economy, biblical authors distinguish between food as empire or commodity and food as covenant and justice. Like Berry, biblical authors do not romanticize the struggles of agrarian life; in the face of fierce physical and political challenges, they promote an unsentimental pastoralism, in which food expresses divine sovereignty rather than human power. Biblical stories of Egypt and empire point to Israel's own abuses of power, hoarded surplus grain, and gluttonous luxury foods for the wealthy. The Hebrew slaves built silos for imperial grains as they sat by fleshpots of which they could not partake. Those silos represent a surplus economy, grown for trade and profit and based on oppression and the denial of limits:

> The ban on hoarding and manna that spoils overnight are symbols that touch us closely, living as we do in a culture of unprecedented hoarding, consumption, and waste. Our take is unlimited—the destruction already accomplished is staggering... Forty percent of the world's population lives in countries suffering from serious freshwater shortages, and irrigated agriculture accounts for a staggering 70 percent of water usage ... thus endangering the food supply over the long term. We have incurred damage on a scale that bewilders us, that we cannot repair, and even worse, our currently dominant economies implicitly mandate that the damage continue. The manna story attests to the inherent difficulty of living with restrictions we do not wholly understand. (Davis, 2009, 75)

In fact, food economics reveals the health or disease of a given nation. The Torah contrasts communal living with exploitative living, which commodifies the land, workers, and women's bodies: cultures that concentrate land and its wealth force others into desperation, slavery, and prostitution. Davis applies this biblical critique to the "bioserfs" of today, who continue to farm the land they have lost to large corporate farms and who suffer a significantly higher incidence of suicide, depression, mental illness, substance abuse, and domestic violence. At the same time, wealthy businessmen from the developed world fly into the same countries their economies devastate in order to enjoy "sex tourism," which the daughters of these impoverished farmers provide, farmers who cannot make ends meet or who have lost their lands. To possess the land in the Bible means to care for it; in fact, possession requires care, but exploitation leads to war and exile (Davis, 2009, 91–92, 105–107).

Manna and Eden symbolize the pastoral alternative: abundant economies of permanence, which humanity achieves through Sabbath restraint and the integration of human needs within the limits of Creation's ecosystems, or what Thomas Berry calls "the Great Economy" (Davis, 2009, 78). Applying Davis's analysis to the New Testament reveals similarly subversive themes: Luke 12 directly contrasts storing surplus crops with the lilies of the field and the ravens, which "neither sow nor reap" and "have neither storehouse nor barn, and yet God feeds them" (NRSV). In this text, Jesus not only admonishes individual hoarding, he also critiques the Roman imperial agricultural system. The prayer for our "daily bread" likewise acquires specifically liberating agrarian undertones. Luke's birth narratives emphasize manna bread as well, with the movement to Bethlehem, the "house of bread," and Jesus's place in the eating trough—a small, humble space that can nonetheless nourish the whole Earth. In fact, the word "frugality" comes from the Latin word for fruitfulness: frugal living affirms the abundant life we discover when we limit overconsumption so that all may flourish together (Nash, 1995, 152). Humanity bears a special responsibility in the covenant, not as an imperial ruler or a fellow creature, but as a shepherd-gardener.

Shepherds of the Creation

This perspective reveals how even the biblical shepherds subverted the imperial food economy. Ancient corruption and greed similarly led to agricultural and population pressures, which reduced the available pastureland, which in turn led to poverty, overgrazing, and destruction of the fragile ecosystem that supported the community (e.g., Ez. 34). Ancient communities blended farming with herding livestock in order to create greater resilience in the face not only of crop fluctuations but also political instability and agricultural exploitation. Women and youth also served as shepherds and goatherds (e.g., Gen. 29: 6), and stood up to violent theft and predation. Pastoral life generally requires common lands for grazing, and "guerrilla pastoralists" throughout history frequently ignored private property claims. Still today, herding communities the world over avoid global economic pressures by pursuing a livelihood that provides alternate sources of food, clothing, tools, and other goods. In other words, shepherds, too, represent divine liberation from the behemoth of empire.

Shepherds also understand permaculture. They must manage the size and activity of their flocks to prevent overgrazing and soil erosion. In return, ruminants fertilize and build up the soil and protect ecosystem biodiversity. True pastoralists both reflect and integrate into the agrarian rhythms and humility articulated by Wirzba. So much so, in fact, that modern conservationists have begun to promote increased herding as an effective permaculture technique to increase farming yields, sequester atmospheric carbon, and restore vast areas of the world's prairies (FAO, 2012). As these humble ruminants patiently chew the cud, their "slow food movement" nourishes not just humanity but the soil, insects, grasses, birds, and even the air we breathe. Is it any wonder that the Hebrew word for shepherd also means to feed?

Thus, in Luke's narrative of Jesus's birth, the lowly and despised shepherd families are the first to recognize and give witness to the rebirth of the Divine. They reflect the outdoor birth in their own open-air vocation, where they keep watch for the new life found in the eternal cycles of Creation's seasons. The shepherds do not just testify to the Divine come to Earth; they embody it. Shepherds' flocks provide milk in a manner complementary to the way in which farmers' grapes and figs provide the honey of the Promised Land (King & Stager, 2001, 101–114).[3] The Divine Shepherd-Gardener gives us a fecund Creation of seed-bearing plants and animals with breasts full of nourishing milk. Shepherds intimately and tenderly suckle the Earth. These metaphors mirror many other ancient images of the Divine, as in the form of a woman whose large and sometimes multiple breasts provide both spiritual and bodily nourishment (AKL, 2006: Pathak, 2013, 132). In the covenant with the Divine and the Creation, the people are called to sustain, nurture, liberate, and protect the precious and vulnerable parts within us, in one another, and in the land itself (Boff, 1997, 104–114). When we fulfill this role faithfully, the Creation showers us with abundant blessings, even in cities.

Healing Through Urban Agriculture

All the farms and gardens around the planet arise ultimately from the basic human need to eat in order to survive; yet the historical ebb and flow of small-scale community farms and gardens also reflect specific economic trends or communal needs. In the developed world, these cultivated plots flourish during times of crisis, including in war and economic downturns, as well as in response to local issues—violence, unemployment, at-risk youth, and the need for urban green spaces. Community gardens have often sought to provide benefits beyond fresh food, such as a connection with Nature, education, employment, and community building, but these programs frequently wither away once the crisis has passed or a specific need has been met. In contrast, the current global food-growing movement recognizes the long-term communal benefits of permanent food production and seeks to incorporate sustainable farms and gardens into communities permanently (Lawson, 2005).

Local food offers obvious benefits to a community, such as nutrition, employment, and training; in fact, garden-based programs boost fruit and vegetable consumption more than nutrition education alone (Morris & Zidenberg-Cherr, 2002). These farms and gardens also provide less obvious benefits. Schools utilizing gardens report more effective general instruction and better overall learning (Graham et al., 2005; Robinson-O'Brien, Story, & Heim, 2009). Increases in local, sustainable land management build resilient ecosystems at the same time that they help mitigate climate change (UNCTAD, 2013, 7). Community gardens also stabilize neighborhoods, reduce crime, increase property values, and contribute to a resilient local economy. Organizations now incorporate food-growing into programs in rehabilitation, homelessness stabilization, recidivism reduction, race relations, and peacebuilding (Lautenschlager & Smith, 2007). By becoming involved in these programs, people unite with one another and with many other plants and creatures, and form bonds of respect, care, and commitment. Gardens grow more than food; they grow companionship, which means, literally, "to share bread." As people nurture plants and soil and share the food, they experience the togetherness of communion.

This kind of Creation communion, in which people connect with one another, their physical bodies, and the rest of the natural world, helps heal the growing, toxic burden of loneliness. Amid unprecedented global population numbers, urban dwellers are lonely. Studies reveal alarming increases in loneliness in the past few decades, to over half of some populations surveyed (Wilson & Moulton, 2010; Yue et al., 2011). Urban crowding in particular leads to chronic loneliness; loneliness spreads like a contagion through communities, exacerbated by its own symptoms (Miller, 2011). The more crowded we are, the lonelier we become; and the lonelier we are, the lonelier we become. This epidemic not only carries social stigma; it also endangers mental and physical health.

New research reveals why loneliness poses such a health risk. Humanity has evolved to fear social isolation and rejection as a mortal threat that activates the same neurological centers as physical danger and pain do. This protective psychological response sometimes leads to pro-social behaviors, which prompt us to seek out new relationships with increased openness and friendliness; however, it often has reverse (and self-reinforcing) anti-social effects: less empathy and self-awareness, and increased defensiveness, aggression, and apathy (Pond, Brey, & DeWall, 2011, 109–112). Loneliness then spreads, exacerbated not only by urban overcrowding or decay, but also by upward trends in consumerism, living alone, stay-at-home parenting, and internet use (Pieters, 2013; Yue et al., 2011). Prolonged loneliness leaves people at high risk for an alarming array of health problems, including depression, addiction, suicide, eating disorders, and a variety of life-threatening physical illnesses (VanDerHeide, 2012, 369); according to a meta-analysis, "social isolation increases the risk of death about as much as smoking cigarettes and more than either physical inactivity or obesity" (Holt-Lunstad, 2010; Miller, 2011). Recent studies even link chronic social isolation and loneliness to violent and sexually violent crimes (Blake & Gannon, 2011).

We do not need these data to understand that human beings need companionship. We are starting to understand just how much people also need relationships with the rest of the natural world. Increases in the incidence of loneliness and its accompanying mental and physical illnesses correlate to less time spent out of doors or in natural settings. Industrialized societies, particularly in urban areas, have moved steadily away from interactions with wildlife that were taken for granted only a generation ago; and eco-psychologists believe this change impairs our ability as individuals and societies to develop healthy empathy and a sense of identity (Glendinning, 1995, 50–53; Shepard, 1995, 23–27). Studies from the past several decades have confirmed the profound value of various forms of Nature connection for both mental and physical health. Nature connection programs successfully address the same array of symptoms and disorders associated with chronic loneliness: research shows that time interacting with non-human Nature reduces stress, depression, blood pressure, blood cholesterol, dementia, obesity, substance abuse, and aggression, and increases self-esteem, healing rates, mental focus, self-discipline, energy, and a general sense of peace and wellbeing (Frumkin, 2012, 142–154). Perhaps not surprisingly, we need Creation companionship as much as we need human companionship.

Yet some communities have limited access to woods, wilderness areas, or even green spaces; for many people, food has become the last consistent, physical interaction with non-human Creation. Could Nature connection through the local agriculture movement simultaneously heal our isolation from one another, our relationship with food, and our alienation from the Creation? Practitioners in the rapidly expanding field of therapeutic horticulture insist on this. While some projects in this movement achieve their goals more effectively than others, as a whole, local farms and gardens confer a particular and potent kind of Nature-based community and connection. Horticultural therapy eases loneliness through physical and psychological bonding. In addition, the healing potential of working with the soil, animals, and plants confers tranquility and mental focus, and reduces pain, anxiety, fatigue, aggression, violence, and crime (Frumkin, 2012, 146–148). In fact, lonely people relate to non-human creatures as human-like companions (Epley et al., 2008). As the seeds of our rooted relations sprout and grow, they give us hope even in the midst of despair. Nurturing a plant can become a lifeline.

Gardening as Liberation

Some such unlikely seedlings sprouted at the US detention center in Guantanamo Bay. In the post-9/11 War on Terror, the United States captured and imprisoned hundreds of civilians; because no country would take them, these people remained in this desolate place, separated from their families, year after year. In 2007, it was revealed that one such detainee, Saddiq Ahmed Turkistani, had worked with a few other prisoners to plant a rebel garden. Although some of them had requested permission, the authorities refused; the prison forbids even flower bouquets. Yet these men did not give up hope:

> With their bare hands and the most basic of tools, [they] have fashioned a secret garden where they have grown plants from seeds recovered from their meals. Mr. Turkistani said he and other prisoners ... softened the ground with water overnight and then used the spoons to dig. Every day they managed to loosen more soil until they had enough for a bed for planting... Using water to soften soil baked hard by the Caribbean sun and then scratching away with plastic spoons ... [they] produced sufficient earth to grow watermelon, peppers, garlic, cantaloupe and even a tiny lemon plant, no more than two inches high. (Buncombe, 2006)

This small garden brought comfort, connection, and purpose to the detainees, and inspired their legal allies: "I could not believe it," stated one lawyer; "I knew they had no tools... The look on his face as he told me ... was something wonderful." According to another legal advocate, these seedlings represent David against Goliath, the indomitable strength of the human spirit in the face of overwhelming oppression:

> The massive might of the US military is intent on holding prisoners in an environment that is stripped of comfort, humanity, beauty and even law. Yet the prisoners held there have overcome this with a plastic spoon and a lemon seed. (Buncombe, 2006)

Something about growing the plants gave these men more than just a hobby, more than a way to pass the time. As they commune with one another and the Creation, they find hope and healing; they find liberation. These men had unknowingly joined a revolution; they had become guerrilla gardeners.

Guerrilla gardeners (also called "garden pirates" or "Farmers Feeding Families") remind us how subversive and liberating it can be to grow food. They call into question a basic capitalistic assumption: "whether a nonoccupying owner who [holds] a legal claim to a piece of land really should triumph over productive occupants providing a demonstrable social good" (Cockrall-King, 2012, 152). According to the guerrilla gardeners, humans must ultimately choose between two fundamental human occupations: gardening and war. This premise recognizes the struggle against adversity in both options; and the choice to plant and build also involves some uprooting and tearing down. These growers refuse to accept the inequitable distribution of land as a financial asset instead of a human right. They claim a third possibility, that "society need not choose between dense cities and garden cities," and anyone has the right—perhaps even a moral duty—to utilize neglected and "orphaned" spaces (Reynolds, 2008, 13–14, 44–49). They deride the idea that cities lack space for crops or natural beauty; they plant rooftops, abandoned lots, balconies, and even potholes. In short, guerrilla gardeners show us that we do not need more land; we simply need to claim the right to tend what there is.

The revolution is taking hold. Civil authorities are giving permission for "outlaw chickens," replacing ornamental trees with fruit groves, and incorporating more and more school and community gardens and farms. Green rooftops creep across urban skylines. Urban and suburban neighborhoods hum with beehives. Diverse groups come together to rebuild their communities and the way our planet feeds itself. From the parched soils of Guantanamo Bay, to poor rural communities, gray, paved urban spaces, and mile upon mile of suburban lawns, more and more people are moving out of the prisons of isolation, alienation, and despair, and reclaiming kinship with the Creation.

Tendrils of Hope

The Church at its best mirrors the strengths of the movements for Nature connection and the liberation of food. In an age lacking political cooperation, these movements bring together throngs of people from otherwise politically disparate groups over shared goals. They seek freedom and healing for the whole Earth community. Traditional hunting and fishing communities join environmentalists, nature skills practitioners, and academic scientists to save our forests and waters. Struggling, conservative farming families join poor urban neighborhoods and gourmet chefs to promote local gardens and farms. Just like our churches, these movements bring people from all walks of life together, because they focus on the essence of our deep need for physical, communal, and spiritual succor. They connect us to the source of our being and they bring us salvation.

The People of the Divine experience seasons of death and rebirth. Faithfulness to our vocation and covenant means we must recognize and acknowledge the practices that poison us, and we must put them in the compost bin and let the Spirit turn them into rich and fertile soil for new growth. A theology of permaculture embraces not ossified tradition but permanent regeneration and resurrection. The manifestations of the Spirit shift and transform, but a body of people will always seek healing and justice in the Earth. Thus, the Church endures; however, it is ever-changing.

Indeed, congregations offer a unique permacultural intersection between the permanence and continual rebirth of human communities. Our spirituality continues in diverse and evolving manifestations over time. Communities of faith gather to observe the death and resurrection that we all experience, and they join the resources of each member to meet the many needs of the community. In true permaculture fashion, they even leave room for wilderness, the unpredictable and uncontrollable workings of the Spirit that connects us all eternally. Simply put, communities of faith are holy permaculture gardens.

This deep integration of communal spiritual life with sacred agrarian life reveals our covenantal vocation within the Creation to be more than a metaphor. Alienation from the covenantal rhythms of the Earth has trapped us and made us ill; kinship is beginning to heal us and set us free. More and more houses of worship are joining forces with the global momentum of Creation ministry, with powerful results. As religious leaders continue to call for ecological healing and justice, congregations increasingly incorporate Creation care into their ministries and missions, from race relations to feeding the hungry (Langlands, 2014). It turns out that ministry works better when we empower the voices of both marginalized communities and marginalized Creation. Again and again, communities of faith discover unforeseen abundance when they step outside into the wilderness and encounter the Divine.

Today's prophets have spoken. The path of hoarding and consumption leads to death. The Food Revolution is surging ahead, leading to life. Our choice is before us. A lackluster response will not suffice: our land is holy *because* it is fragile and it is up to us to care for it. Whatever the obstacles, communities of faith are meant to shepherd us through the turmoil of rebirth and resurrection. We do not need to fear; we need only to open our hearts to the abundant, nourishing grace all around and within us. We need to reach out to one another, to our local communities, and to the whole of Creation in support and compassion. And we need to plant a seed.

Notes

1 This report uses the term "agro-ecology" to describe permanent and sustainable agricultural models that address the specific needs of given communities in the community-based approach described above.
2 Davis points out the important and often missed role of satire in scripture; she argues that verses that suggest humanity should conquer or subdue the Earth point out to an exiled Israel that such efforts did not work out well for them.
3 In ancient Israel, the word honey referred to agricultural juices and syrups made from grapes, figs, and dates, as well as bees.

References

AKL. 2006. *Images of the Divine Feminine.* http://yourworldreligions.blogspot.ch/2009/10/images-of-divine-feminine-western.html.

Alwan, Ala. 2010. *Global Status Report on Noncommunicable Diseases 2010.* Geneva: World Health Organization.

Blake, Emily & Gannon, Theresa A. 2011. Loneliness in Sexual Offenders (49–68). In Sarah J. Bevinn, *Psychology of Loneliness.* Hauppauge, NY: Nova.

Boff, Leonardo. 1997. *Cry of the Earth, Cry of the Poor: Ecology and Justice.* Maryknoll, NY: Orbis Books.

Buncombe, Andrew. 2006. Guantanamo Bay Prisoners Plant Seeds of Hope in Secret Garden. *The Independent*, 40. http://www.independent.co.uk/news/world/americas/guantanamo-bay-prisoners-plant-seeds-of-hope-in-secret-garden-476011.html.

Chopra, Mickey, Galbraith, Sarah, & Darnton-Hill, Ian. 2002. A Global Response to a Global Problem: The Epidemic of Overnutrition. *Bulletin of the World Health Organization*, 80, 952–958.

Cockrall-King, Jennifer. 2012. *Food and the City: Urban Agriculture and the New Food*

Revolution. Amherst, NY: Prometheus Books.

Davis, Ellen F. 2009. *Scripture, Culture, and Agriculture: An Agrarian Reading of the Bible*. New York: Cambridge University Press.

DESA. 2013. *Sustainable Development Challenges*. New York: United Nations Department of Economic and Social Affairs.

DESA. 2014. *World Urbanization Prospects: The 2014 Revision, Highlights*. New York: United Nations.

Doel, Gary. 2013. Permaculture Design Principles. *Simply Green*, 182–185.

Epley, Nicholas, Akalis, Scott, Waytz, Adam, & Cacioppo, John T. 2008. Creating Social Connection through Inferential Reproduction: Loneliness and Perceived Agency in Gadgets, Gods, and Greyhounds. *Psychological Science*, 19, 114–120.

FAO. 2012. *Livestock and the Environment: Finding a Balance*. Rome: Food and Agriculture Organization of the United Nations.

FAO. 2015. *The State of Food Insecurity in the World 2015: Meeting the 2015 international Hunger Targets: Taking Stock of Uneven Progress*. Rome: United Nations (Food and Agriculture Organization, International Fund for Agricultural Development, and World Food Programme).

Fernández, Laura. 2011. *Time to Recognise Malnutrition in Europe*. Brussels: European Food Information Council.

Frumkin, Howard. 2012. Building the Science Base: Ecopsychology Meets Clinical Epidemiology (142–172). In Peter H. Kahn & Patricia H. Hasbach (Eds.), *Ecopsychology: Science, Totems, and the Technological Species*. Cambridge, MA: MIT Press.

Glendinning, Chellis. 1995. Technology, Trauma, and the Wild (41–54). In Theodore Roszak, Mary E. Gomes, & Allen D. Kanner (Eds.), *Ecopsychology*. San Francisco, CA: Sierra Club Books.

Graham, Heather, Lane Beall, Deborah, Lussier, Mary, McLaughlin, Peggy, & Zidenberg-Cherr, Sheri. 2005. Use of School Gardens in Academic Instruction. *Journal of Nutrition Education and Behavior*, 37, 147–151.

Halweil, Brian. 2006. Can Organic Farming Feed Us All? *Worldwatch Magazine*, 19, 3, 18–24.

Holt-Lunstad, Julianne. 2010. Social Relationships and Mortality Risk: A Meta-analytic Review. *PLoS Medicine*, 7, 2–20.

ILO. 2012. *21 Million People are Now Victims of Forced Labour, ILO Says*. Geneva: ILO.

King, Philip A., and Lawrence E. Stager. 2001. *Life in Biblical Israel*. In the series "Library of Ancient Israel," edited by Douglas A. Knight. Louisville: Westminster John Knox Press.

Langlands, Bryan K. 2014. *Cultivating Neighborhoods: Identifying Best Practices for Launching a Christ-Centered Community Garden*. Eugene, OR: Resource Publications.

Lautenschlager, Lauren & Smith, Chery. 2007. Beliefs, Knowledge, and Values Held by Inner-City Youth About Gardening, Nutrition, and Cooking. *Agriculture Human Values*, 24, 2, 245–258.

Lawson, Laura J. 2005. *City Bountiful: A Century of Community Gardening in America*. Berkeley, Los Angeles, CA, and London: University of California Press.

Miller, Greg. 2011. Why Loneliness Is Hazardous to Your Health. *Science*, 331, 6014, 138–140.

Morris, J. L. & Zidenberg-Cherr, S. 2002. Garden-Enhanced Nutrition Curriculum Improves Fourth-Grade School Children's Knowledge of Nutrition and Preferences for Some Vegetables. *Journal of the American Dietetic Association*, 102, 91–93.

Muggah, Robert. 2015. Fixing Fragile Cities. *Foreign Affairs*. https://www.foreignaffairs.

com/articles/africa/2015-01-15/fixing-fragile-cities.

Nash, James. 1995. Toward the Revival and Reform of the Subversive Virtue—Frugality. *Annual of the Society of Christian Ethics; Annual of the Society of Christian Ethics*, 137–160.

OECD. 2014. *Obesity Update*. Paris: OECD Directorate for Employment, Labour and Social Affairs.

Pathak, Shubha. 2013. *Figuring Religions: Comparing Ideas, Images, and Activities*. Albany, NY: SUNY Press.

Pieters, Rik. 2013. Bidirectional Dynamics of Materialism and Loneliness: Not Just a Vicious Cycle. *Journal of Consumer Research*, 40, 4 (December), 615–631.

Pond, Richard S., Jr., Brey, Joseph, & DeWall, C. Nathan. 2011. Denying the Need to Belong: How Social Exclusion Impairs Human Functioning and How People Can Protect Against It (107–122). In Sarah J. Bevinn (Ed.), *Psychology of Loneliness*. Hauppauge, NY: Nova.

Reynolds, Richard. 2008. *On Guerrilla Gardening: A Hand Book for Gardening Without Boundaries*. London: Bloomsbury.

Robbins, John. 2010. *The Food Revolution: How Your Diet Can Help Save Your Life and Our World*. San Francisco, CA: Conari Press.

Robinson-O'Brien, Ramona, Mary Story, & Heim, Stephanie. 2009. Impact of Garden-Based Youth Nutrition Intervention Programs: A Review. *Journal of the American Dietetic Association*, 198, 273–280.

Shepard, Paul. 1995. Nature and Madness (21–40). In Theodore Roszak, Mary E. Gomes, & Allen D. Kanner (Eds.), *Ecopsychology: Restoring the Earth, Healing the Mind*. San Francisco, CA: Sierra Club Books.

Townsend, A. & Howarth, R. W. 2010. Fixing the Global Nitrogen Problem. *Scientific American*, 302, 2, 64–71.

UNCTAD. 2013. *Wake up Before it is Too Late: Make Agriculture Truly Sustainable Now for Food Security in a Changing Climate*. New York: United Nations Conference on Trade and Development.

UNHCR. 2002. *Livelihood Options in Refugee Situation: A Handbook for Promoting Sound Agricultural Practices*. Geneva: United Nations High Commissioner for Refugees; CARE International.

VanDerHeide, N. 2012. Can You Hear Me Now? Twinship Failure and Chronic Loneliness. *International Journal of Self Psychology*, 7(3), 369–390.

WFP. 2015. *Who Are the Hungry?* New York: WFP.

WHO. 2013. *Global Action Plan for the Prevention and Control of Noncommunicable Diseases 2013–2020*. Geneva: World Health Organization.

Wilson, C. & Moulton, B. 2010. *Loneliness among Older Adults: A National Survey of Adults 45+*. Washington, DC: AARP.

Wirzba, Norman. 2003. *The Paradise of God: Renewing Religion in an Ecological Age*. New York: Oxford University Press.

Yue, Zhenzhu, Feng, Cong, Zhou, Xinyue, & Gao, Ding-Guo. 2011. Being Lonely in a Crowd: Population Density Contributes to Perceived Loneliness in China (137–149). In Sarah J. Bevinn (Ed.), *Psychology of Loneliness*. Hauppauge, NY: Nova.

Further Reading

Cockrall-King, Jennifer. 2012. *Food and the City: Urban Agriculture and the New Food Revolution*. Amherst, NY: Prometheus Books. An honest assessment of the history, challenges, and promise of the exploding urban agriculture movement.

Davis, Ellen F. 2009. *Scripture, Culture, and Agriculture: An Agrarian Reading of the*

Bible. New York: Cambridge University Press. Davis elegantly reveals the biblical basis for a foundational human vocation in sustainable agrarian life and its integration into cities and other communities through systems that respect limits and promote justice.

Reynolds, Richard. 2014. *On Guerrilla Gardening: A Hand Book for Gardening without Boundaries*. London: Bloomsbury. Reynolds demonstrates that anyone can grow a garden, anywhere, and that these gardens inspire health, hope, and liberation in an increasingly privatized, paved-over world.

Robbins, John. 2010. *The Food Revolution: How Your Diet Can Help Save Your Life and Our World*. San Francisco, CA: Conari Press. In the midst of the overwhelming power of industrial agriculture, Robbins manages not only to expose its horrific consequences but also leave us filled with energy, motivation, hope, and redemption.

UNCTAD. 2013. *Wake Up Before It Is Too Late: Make Agriculture Truly Sustainable Now for Food Security in a Changing Climate*. New York: United Nations Conference on Trade and Development. This report carefully researches the current status of global food and agriculture and makes detailed recommendations for political, economic, and structural reforms that greatly help vulnerable human populations and restore ecosystems for future generations.

Wirzba, Norman. 2003. *The Paradise of God: Renewing Religion in an Ecological Age*. New York: Oxford University Press. This book describes the beauty and strength of biblical agrarian theology and how we must reclaim it today in order to find truly ethical relationships with one another and the land.

CHAPTER 30

Theo-Forming Earth Community

Meaning-Full Creations[1]

Whitney A. Bauman

Ludwig Feuerbach's (1989) insight that all theology is anthropology is not a demotion of God-talk or religion. Rather, it is an attempt to understand the importance and power of religion from within a more immanent and materialist framework. If we are meaning-making creatures within a larger planetary community, then theology really matters in both meanings of that word. Our values, ethics, ideas, and beliefs take shape in the world. In a play on the word terra-forming, in which scientists and science fiction writers imagine transforming other planets to be Earth-like, we might call this mattering of meaning, "theo-forming."[2] Theo-forming in itself is not good or bad; rather, it is, like the dog's bark is to the dog, or the bird's flight is to the bird—just something that we do. However, if we can imagine a spectrum of meaning-making practices and the ways in which they take shape in the world, at one end of the spectrum there might be immanent notions of meaning and value and, at the other end, transcendent notions. Eco-theology, like religion and ecology more broadly, has in many ways been an attempt to relocate value and meaning on the immanent side of the spectrum. This chapter begins by outlining some of the perilous ways in which ideas of transcendent value help to create an anthropocentric theo-formation of the world that turns the world into a "standing reserve" for human ends (Heidegger, 1977). Next, I describe some of the ways in which various eco-religious thinkers in the field of religion and ecology have reimagined meaning-making practices within a more immanent framework. Finally, I suggest an experimental approach to theo-forming for the planet's future—an approach that understands meaning-making in its larger ecological context.

Before beginning, I should offer a cautionary note. I do not think that transcendent notions of meaning are inherently bad or that immanent notions are inherently good. Indeed, certain types of transcendence help us to be revolutionary and iconoclastic. Ruether (1992) argues that we need both immanent and transcendent models of

The Wiley Blackwell Companion to Religion and Ecology, First Edition. Edited by John Hart.

meaning-making, both Gaia and God. This can be good, for example, when meaning-making becomes too attached to nationalism or to a specific order in the world. Without some sort of transcendence, we collapse into confusing our understanding of the world with the way that the world actually is. Furthermore, immanence is not always good: some versions of deep ecology, to note one example, are misanthropic and tend to undermine the political and ethical responsibility of what it means to be human (e.g., Plumwood, 2002, 196–214). To imagine the dissolving of one's consciousness into the whole, or to "think like a mountain," as Leopold (1949) suggested, is to deny our unique, specific, particular embodiment and role in the planetary community. In a sense, either end of the spectrum leads to an a-contextuality, which, I argue, is part of the problem. Too transcendent a notion of value and meaning implies that the planetary community might not matter in itself, and too immanent a notion of value and meaning might lead to dissolving differences within the planetary community.

Transcendent Theo-Formations

Understandings of God, truth, ultimate value, and reality tend to oscillate between transcendence and immanence. The basic question in many meaning-making traditions is whether the world we experience—a world of evolution, decay, change, and constant process—is really real, or whether there is something beyond the world we experience as real, grounding all that seems to be in flux in a more permanent reality. In Ancient Greece Parmenides argued for the reality of permanence and Heraclitus for that of change; the Buddha argued that the fixed reality we experience as real is in fact impermanent; laws of karma which form the background of many Vedic traditions try to strike a balance between the impermanence of reality and something really real beyond the flux that determines the fate of individuals; the God Incarnate of the Christian tradition like the "God with us" of Judaism meets a radically transcendent God in Islam; and the cyclical lifecycles of many indigenous traditions find endurance in the ancestors and future generations which seems to transcend present realities. As many scholars of religious studies have pointed out, this seems to be one of the shaping phenomena of meaning-making creatures (Eliade, 1957).

The balance between transcendence and immanence matters in and to the world. For the most part, over the past 2,000 years a radical transcendence has helped to create conditions for "human exceptionalism" (Peterson, 2001). This, supported by what feminist and queer theorists call "patriarchy" and "heteronormative patriarchy," understands the cosmos to be ordered by a hierarchy of diminishing value with God (often male) at the top, followed by (elite) men, then (elite) women, slaves, and "others"; finally, animals, other life, and the inanimate Earth are ordered in a descending hierarchy of value. Such a patriarchal theo-anthropology is so widely understood and described that I shall not pursue it here; rather, I discuss how this type of theological anthropology takes shape in the world. Put another way, I want to examine the ecological implications of such a theo-anthropology.

As Moltmann, among others, has noted, such a powerful vision of the special place of humanity was probably once quite necessary and advantageous in a world without modern medicines and agriculture, when humans were subject to the whim of natural cycles of disease, famine, and weather patterns (Moltmann, 2003, 137–139). This type of theo-anthropology helped secure hope in the face of adversity. However, it became too successful. Through the processes known as the scientific revolution, colonization, the Industrial Revolution, and on into the present, human beings have remade themselves in this image of transcendence and have attempted to live as if they are separate from the rest of the natural world. Many now argue we have ushered in a new era: the Anthropocene (e.g., Jenkins, 2013). The ecological implications of a transcendent notion of humanity based on being made in the image of a transcendent God may very well be exemplified in today's environmental crises despite all the medical, ecological, and other benefits that have accompanied this understanding.

This is not merely Lynn White's (1967) infamous argument that "dominion" in the book of Genesis is the problem. Rather, it is a broader and more complex understanding of this insight which suggests humans inevitably perform their identities by materializing their own and other bodies according to their beliefs about the world. This is precisely the insight that Butler (1993) comes to, regarding the ways in which identities are performative and materializing processes rather than something essential and immutable. If we live by the idea that our humanity is transcendent, then we begin to use all of our economic, political, and other powers to create worlds that help to reinforce the belief that we are radically distinct from the rest of the natural world. As such, we begin to "background" our embeddedness and interrelatedness with the rest of the natural world and to believe that we are just below God and above animals and the Earth (Plumwood, 2002, 99). The more economic and political power we have, the more we can enforce and act out this transcendent identity. In other words, not all humans experience the world in the same way; nor do we experience the ecological and social consequences of this fossil-fueled understanding of transcendence and power in the same way (Nixon, 2013).

If this millennia-old problem of human exceptionalism found in many meaning-making traditions is part of the problem, then no shift can occur overnight through a conceptual attempt to restore us to the rest of the natural world. The way in which the Copernican and Darwinian revolutions "decentered" humans and returned us to the rest of the natural world did nothing to rid us of anthropocentrism. Even though one story from each of these conceptual shifts could suggest that humans are not at the center of the universe but have evolved along with the rest of life on the planet, this is not necessarily the story of science that is highlighted. On the contrary, a large part of the truth known as modern science has been using our embeddedness in Nature to create or theo-form the world toward ultimate human ends (Merchant, 1980, 2004). Though the evolutionary, cosmological, and ecological stories may suggest that we emerged from and are part of the natural world, anthropocentrism persists as a strong tradition in modern science. The fact of our interrelatedness has not been equaled by an obvious ethical turn toward kinship and equality, but rather has been used instrumentally to make the rest of the world a "standing reserve" for (some) human ends (Heidegger, 1977). I would argue that this is in part due to the old hierarchy of value that places ultimate value, and humans as the ultimately valued creature, outside this world.

Finally, human exceptionalism depends in part on the speed of fossil-fueled time, or what some are calling "social acceleration" (Nixon, 2013; Rosa, 2013). The acceleration of time which results from fossil-fueled forms of communication, transportation, and production, enables us to get carried into linear understandings of time that are not of this world. Ideas about progress, development, and even individuation enable us to place ourselves linearly in a timescale that ignores the geographies of our theo-formations. If I am concerned with progressing toward a transcendent point that has not yet arrived, and this is coupled with an understanding of individualism and human exceptionalism, then efficient causality and instrumental reason become the quickest way to get from the present to the goal. Efficient causality and instrumental reason are encouraged by the space–time crunch, in which one takes advantage of the technologies of speed or is left behind. But these rapid technologies create unequal geographies of violence and are outstripping the regenerative capacity of humans, animals, and the Earth (Brennan, 2003).

Eco-Religious Responses: Theo-Forming in an Immanent Frame

As we have seen, there is no escape from theo-forming. As human beings, or meaning-making creatures, we find ourselves making meaning out of any situation. We wake up in the morning and tell ourselves a story so that we get out of bed; we place the quotidian within a wider context of meaning so that we can carry on throughout the day; we hope and tell ourselves that things will work out. Even nihilists are constantly in the process of theo-forming, though they impose meaninglessness on the world around them. Wherever we find ourselves on a sliding spectrum from meaning to despair, we are making meaning out of the world around us.

In the preceding section, I argued that theo-forming based on notions of value and meaning leads to re-creating the entire world as a "standing reserve" for human beings. In this section I argue that theo-forming from an immanent frame of value and meaning might help to re-situate humans, meaning, and value in the context of a geography of meaning (Nixon, 2013), or help us develop what Tweed (2008) calls a spiritual cartography. A geography of meaning investigates how our ideas, values, and meaning-making practices affect bodies around us differently. Religion and ecology, the study of religion and Nature, and more broadly the academic field known as environmental history, have all brought our meaning-making practices back down to Earth.[3] There are more examples than I can list here to show how these fields have helped ground religion over the past four decades. So, I look at just three ways in which these fields have understood meaning in a more immanent frame: rethinking the Divine as an immanent reality; rethinking the human as one creature among many; and rethinking hopes and dreams for the future as this-worldly.

According to Feuerbach, all theology is anthropology. Thus, if one has a transcendent notion of the Divine, one has an exalted understanding of humanity. This has been true in many religious traditions and thought systems throughout human history. Humans have written themselves outside the rest of the natural world in an attempt to become like the gods in which they believed, whether a monotheistic god, the Buddhist concept of Nirvana, or science's beloved Reason. If this is the case, then one way to begin to make immanent our meaning-making practices is to reconceive God or value as immanent. After all, even within monotheistic traditions there are strands of thinking of God as "with us," or as incarnate, or as embodied in the world.

Spinoza considered some of these more immanent strands of thinking about God and developed a full-blown pantheism. From within this pantheism, God and Nature became one and were also in part identified with the ongoing process of "naturing" (Spinoza, 1994). Later, Bergson (1944) picked up on this immanent process of divine creativity with his notion of the *élan vital*. Teilhard de Chardin's (1959) attempt to rethink theology in light of evolution also made God spatially, though not temporally, immanent. What Teilhard was to evolution, North Whitehead (1978) was to "new physics," with his construction of a panentheistic god based on his understanding of the quantum world. In this model Nature is God, but God is greater than the whole of Nature, analogous to the way that our brains are necessary for our minds, but minds are not reduced to brains. There is "always something more from nothing," as the emergent theorists would later claim (e.g., Goodenough & Deacon, 2006). My aim in going down this more philosophical detour is to suggest that these shifts toward immanent thinking were shifts that took place in many disciplines in light of evolution theory, ecology, physics, and cosmology. It was not just religious thought that made humans transcendent creatures, but also philosophical and scientific thought. From the Copernican revolution onward, such thinking began to be challenged in ways that we are still trying to make sense of today.

Out of this background and in response to the problems brought about by the Industrial Revolution and the threat of a nuclear disaster, the beginnings of sustained reflections on religion and ecology were forged. Sittler, Cobb, and Santmire were among the many early eco-theologians to sound the alarm that Creation was under threat. The first recorded meeting of a religion and ecology consultation at the American Academy of Religion was in 1974, just a few years after the first Earth Day. Many of these early attempts were geared toward getting theology and religion in general to pay attention to the rest of the natural world. As Tucker (2003) suggests, this was the beginning phase of the world's religions becoming aware not just that all humans matter, but that all life matters. This shift in consciousness over time fundamentally altered the *topoi* of religion. In a sense there is a dialectic process to theo-forming: meaning shapes and changes bodies, but bodies also shape and change meaning. This is what Butler (1993) had in mind when she declared that bodies matter. A frightening Nature might lead to a theology of transcendence, and then the theo-forming of that omni-god in such a way that humans live as if they are exceptions to the rest of the natural world, made in the image of that omni-god. Similarly, the uncertainties brought about by global climate change and environmental responses to anthropocentric theo-formations now result in a shifting of theo-forming toward a more immanent frame. One such shift is represented by the process- and feminist-influenced theology of Sallie McFague.

In *Body of God* (1993) McFague refashions *theos* in what she calls an "organic model." Earth and even the universe become the body of God. We are all, then, parts of God, yet God is greater than any single part. Indeed, for McFague God is not equated with the whole of all bodies but is greater than the sum of all the parts: hence her panentheism. For this writer, however, the important point is that she takes an incarnational theology seriously and understands in a radical new way that God is with and in all things. This means that all suffering bodies are also the suffering body of God. Many since McFague have reconceived God as immanent, including ecofeminist thinker Ivone Gebara (1999), and some have gone as far as to suggest that we no longer need to talk about God, but rather about the universe or Nature (Berry & Tucker, 2009; Goodenough, 1998; Taylor, 2009). Wherever one is on this spectrum, the point is that the making immanent of theos begins to change the anthropos as well. If theology is in the end anthropology, then such a radical shift is bound to help return humans to the rest of the natural world.

Whereas McFague and others working in religion and ecology focus on making the Divine immanent, others begin with the hope of decentering and regrounding the human being. These two are clearly intertwined. However, I should note here an environmental ethic can still be derived from a theology of transcendence: namely, stewardship. If humans are "above" Nature and responsible for all of Nature, as stewardship models assume, then we ought to be the best managers of Earth we can be. The problem with this model is that it does nothing to decenter the place of humans within Creation; this, I argue, is at the root of most problematic theo-formations.

Among the models of eco-anthropology which have been helpful in rethinking the human are Hefner's "created co-creator," Merchant's "partnership" model, and the "plain citizen" model of the land ethic (Hefner, 1993; Leopold, 1949; Merchant, 2004). The created co-creator both places humans as created along with the rest of Creation and suggests that the special role of humans is that the human being also helps co-create the rest of the natural world. This model, for all its benefits in making sure the context for the human being is the wider context of Creation, still places humans in a privileged space, perhaps rightly so. If humans do play a special role in co-creating the world, then we ought to acknowledge that context.

A model I prefer is the partnership model. As Merchant points out, partnerships can imply varying degrees of power and responsibility between the parties involved. Furthermore, partnerships can be between men, men and women, women, or between humans and other animals. By extension, the idea of partnership suggests that our relationship with the rest of the world cannot be just one in which humans create the world around them randomly, as if out of nothing. Rather, humans must work with the rest of the natural world as partners, in creating a future planetary community.

Yet another model that has had some traction among scholars of religion and ecology is Leopold's model of human beings as simple citizens of the land community. In this model, which is similar to Macy's council of all beings (Macy & Brown, 1998), humans become one voice, vote, or citizen among many in the overall "land community." There is a lot of overlap between Leopold's model and Latour's idea of the collective, where scientists become spokespersons for various aspects of the rest of the natural world, and the whole collective of beings in a given time/place decide how the collective becomes (Latour, 2004). In this way, humans become immanent to the process of ongoing Creation, rather than sole managers of the process.

Numerous others propose models for returning humans to the ongoing process of Creation, including those who are beginning to articulate the agency and actions of other animals (Hobgood-Oster, 2014) or forests (Kohn, 2013). These are very important for creating a planetary community in which humans are but one participant. Though space prevents me from detailing every attempt to return humans and their meaning-making to the rest of the natural world, there is one more area of theo-forming that I want to bring down to Earth before moving on to rethinking hopes and dreams for the future.

Whereas it may be easier to imagine an immanent understanding of the Divine and an immanent understanding of humanity, surely hopes and dreams are by their very nature transcendent. Hopes and dreams reject the present state of affairs and suggest that there is another way in which the world might become. Does not such iconoclasm or a deconstructive element in religious and philosophical thinking require a certain amount of transcendence? I would argue that transcendent forms of hopes and dreams emerge from transcendent forms of theology and theo-anthropology, and that these hopes and dreams can be destructive on a planetary scale. Nixon has recently asked, "What can we really hope for?" In *Slow Violence*, he asks if our dreams and visions of what is possible in and for the world might not themselves be fossil-fueled dreams that literally take us "out of this world," and even into space (Nixon, 2013, 68–100). The problem is that the hopes and dreams of fossil-fueled realities enable many to live as if they are outside the cyclical, regenerative cycles of the planet. In other words, we theo-form a linear understanding of time on the planet which moves from the present to a more developed or progressed future. Brennan (2003) argued that this "tunnel of time" is literally outstripping the reproductive capacities of the planet. Nixon argues that this linear notion of time covers over the geographies of violence that result in our everyday interactions with the world. As anyone who has filled out an ecological footprint knows, our actions are connected to many locales around the globe on a daily basis. Yet, those who can afford it, "background" these relations so that we can imagine the continuation of our individual narratives of development and progress (Plumwood, 2002).

This analysis has implications for what we can hope for in a transformed present and our envisioned future, interrelated with the rest of the evolving planetary community. In a sense, this analysis urges us to return hope to its original meaning, within the context of uncertainty. The opposite of hope is certainty, as Bloch pointed out over a century ago (Bloch, 1986). Whatever else religious hope means, it cannot mean any sort of certainty that eventually things will be all right. Rather, it must be a critical aspiration for the entire planetary community, not just for humanity. After all, if we are emergent from and part of an evolving community, then will humanity not eventually evolve beyond itself? Projecting hope for a reified humanity into the future may be part of the problem of making the world instrumental toward human ends (Bauman, 2014). This is why I argue that meaning-making ought to become a more experimental practice.

Ecology of Experimental Meaning-Making

If one understands meaning-making from within an immanent frame, then there is no Archimedean standpoint from which to form the world around us. In other words, we are part of the very theo-formations that we are constantly enacting. What better way to understand religion and meaning-making as ecological than to allow for ecological experiments within our meaning-making structures? We might then be able to speak of an ecology of meaning-making. Before I venture too far down this path, I should note that I am not advocating a form of scientism or for turning religion into a scientific enterprise. Such reductionism is part of the very problem leading to ecological crises. Rather, what I am arguing for are thought experiments that take bodies seriously. If the Divine or ultimate reality is immanent, humans are a part of the planetary community, and our hopes and dreams are for the future of the entire planetary community, then perhaps we ought to start looking at how bodies are affected by different ways of making meaning. In order to do so, I propose a three-part experimental meaning-making method which begins by articulating multiple possibilities for becoming; then identifying how these possibilities affect Earth bodies in a geography of meaning; and finally, negotiating technologies that help us move toward certain possibilities over others.

Too often we proffer solutions to our problems that fail to work, not because of faulty technology or logic, but because the solution does not capture the imagination of enough people. This is another way of putting the insight that we have the tools to feed the world and deal with our ecological problems, but do not have the political will, desire, or imagination to do so. Part of any ecology of meaning-making, then, should involve a healthy period of commentary in which people can articulate "multiple lines of flight" toward the future becoming of the planetary community (Deleuze & Guattari,1987). It is at least plausible that solutions to our current and future problems are not yet imagined; thus, we need to begin a creative, imaginative process for thinking about who we might want to become and how we might want to live. Furthermore, attempting to project solutions from outmoded ways of meaning-making and thinking about problems may be a theo-forming/terra-forming that does not account for ways in which the planetary community might become. Enforcing sameness onto the becoming planet can itself be problematic. Dealing with such ambiguity is a large part of dealing with "wicked" environmental problems (Crosby, 2008; Hogue, 2008). Finally, we must develop ways of thinking about the future that make eco-social ways of being and becoming persuasive and "sexy." Rather than focusing on all that we must give up or on returning to a romanticized past, we ought to think about viable partnerships with the planetary community. As many have pointed out, it is during crises in evolutionary and cultural history that creative possibilities emerge that could not have been imagined until the point at which they open up (DeFries, 2014). Some will be more persuasive than others.

The second step in experimental meaning-making is to identify how Earth bodies are affected by different possibilities for becoming. This requires developing criteria by which we can judge ways of becoming that are better or worse than others. This system of classification is not so much about identifying what is ultimately good, true, and beautiful as it is about identifying criteria for what types of behaviors and actions toward and with Earth others foster the type of worlds that we want to help co-create. This involves the articulation of a set of virtues for which to strive. These contextual virtues provide common grounds for evaluating visions for the future of life on the planet (Keller & Kearns, 2007). We might agree, for example, that we should eliminate gross economic inequality, gross inequality in sharing the eco-social benefits and ills that result from our ways of becoming, extinction of species, mass deforestation, cruelty to animals by factory farming, and the continued use of fossil-fueled energy that is leading to all sorts of ecological problems when we have access to the technologies that would enable us to survive and thrive on renewable and more democratic forms of energy. The extent to which we eliminate or at least mitigate such harms by developing and enacting co-creating partners' ideals will provide benchmarks with which we can judge the ways in which various possibilities for planetary becoming are better or worse. These ideals must be contextual, that is, they may not be the same for all places and all peoples (an arctic culture and environment will surely call for different common ground from a tropical or a desert culture and environment). Whatever our criteria are, we must begin to analyze how various Earth bodies (ecosystems, humans, organisms, other animals, plants, etc.) might be affected when we transition to such realities. Some of this can be done with software, which can generate possible outcomes based on the confluence of multiple factors.[4] But the real test will only come as we begin to implement technologies. We must not necessarily begin to look to what futures these experimental ways of becoming might lead us, but rather toward the geography of effects caused by each transition. If it turns out that carbon credits lead to mass inequities in the distribution of greenhouse gases and other pollutants based on demographics such as race, gender, or class, then we shall have to revise that practice and technology. If it turns out that foods genetically modified to be grown with less water have positive effects on the Earth bodies of the bioregions in which such technologies are utilized, and that it leads to water conservation for future Earth bodies, then we may have to see genetically modified organisms as part of promoting a healthy planetary future. This point brings us to the third and final point of an experimental meaning-making practice: technology transfer.

Once we begin to identify criteria by which we can judge one way of becoming over another as better or worse, and we begin to perform a geographical analysis of the effects of these possibilities on Earth bodies, then we have to think about the technologies that will move us in the directions we want to move in. By technologies I do not mean only tools and machines such as windmills, solar cell streets, and biochemical technologies that arise from bio-mimicry. While these are helpful and necessary, I mean that we must think about technologies for all Earth bodies: for example, what technologies does a river system need to thrive, or a forest, or a mangrove, or even polar bears, in light of the types of planetary futures we hope to move toward and create with other life on the planet? Finally, I also mean technology in the broadest (ancient) sense that encompasses language, concepts, values, and meaning. It is one thing to articulate the vision of the world we want to help co-create, and then to articulate criteria by which we can judge whether we are moving in the right direction; it is another thing to transform these ideas, hopes, dreams, and imaginings into things we hold to be self-evident. We need a technology transfer that creates the desire and will to transform the world. Some exist already, among them the ecological footprint, toxic tours, and the transformation of religious traditions to be more Earth-friendly. But other technologies need to be developed as the technologies cited have not been sufficient. Perhaps exercises that help us overcome our "Nature–deficit disorder" will be helpful (Worthy, 2013), or various forms of animal therapy, or keeping track of the daily amount of "natural goods" one's food requires (Hart, 2013). Better yet, and as I have argued elsewhere (Bauman, 2014), perhaps free education and healthcare might release the creative energy of younger generations to think about education for a critical, creative consciousness, to find meaning in our world for ourselves and others, rather than to think about how to use education solely to get a job, have healthcare, and repay student loans. After worrying about how to get a job to maintain a household, there is little creative energy left to think about different ways of becoming in the world and changing it. Might these be technologies necessary for freeing up the creative and imaginative human resources needed to change the world around us rather than to live merely according to the ways that have been bequeathed to us? Regardless of what these technologies are, there needs to be far more dialogue between the environmental humanities and environmental sciences so that new ways of becoming can be tested.

This experimental meaning-making method might help to restore both scientific and religious components of meaning-making to a political and experimental process of co-construction (Stenmark, 2013). Currently, both religion and science tend to act as "conversation-stoppers," whether as dogma or expert authority (Rorty, 1999). This slows or halts the process of reflecting together, from our pluralistic and multi-perspectival contexts, about how together we might strive toward a better planetary future in which more and more Earth voices are active participants in deciding which futures we want to pursue.

Notes

1 My thanks to Lisa Stenmark for comments on an earlier draft of this chapter.
2 My thanks to John Hart for suggesting this term.
3 There is a vast literature for each of these areas, but for a good introduction I point the reader to three websites: The Forum on Religion and Ecology: http://fore.research.yale.edu; The International Society for the Study of Religion, Nature, and Culture: http://www.religionandnature.com/society; and the American Society for Environmental History: http://aseh.net.
4 For instance, one such software that allows multifactor analysis is Mental Modeler: http://www.mentalmodeler.org.

References

Bauman, Whitney. 2014. *Religion and Ecology: Developing a Planetary Ethic*. New York: Columbia University Press.
Bergson, Henri. 1944. *Creative Evolution*. New York: Modern Library.
Berry, Thomas & Tucker, Mary Evelyn. 2009. *The Sacred Universe: Earth, Spirituality and Religion in the 21st Century*. New York: Columbia University Press.
Bloch, Ernst. 1986. *The Principle of Hope*, 3 vols. Cambridge, MA: MIT Press.
Brennan, Teresa. 2003. *Globalization and its Terrors: Daily Life in the West*. New York: Routledge.
Butler, Judith. 1993. *Bodies that Matter: On the Discursive Limits of Sex*. New York: Routledge.

Crosby, Donald. 2008. *Living with Ambiguity: Religious Naturalism and the Menace of Evil*. Albany, NY: SUNY Press.

DeFries, Ruth. 2014. *The Big Ratchet: How Humanity Thrives in the Face of Natural Crisis*. New York: Basic Books.

Deleuze, Gilles & Guattari, Felix. 1987. *A Thousand Plateaus: Capitalism and Schizophrenia*. Minneapolis, MN: University of Minnesota Press.

Eliade, Mircea. 1957. *The Sacred and the Profane: The Nature of Religion*. New York: Harcourt.

Feuerbach, Ludwig. 1989. *The Essence of Christianity*. Amherst, NY: Prometheus.

Hogue, Michael. 2008. *The Tangled Bank: Toward and Ecotheological Ethics of Responsible Participation*. Eugene, OR: Pickwick.

Gebara, Ivone. 1999. *Longing for Running Water: Ecofeminism and Liberation*. Minneapolis, MN: Augsburg Press.

Goodenough, Ursula. 1998. *The Sacred Depths of Nature*. New York: Oxford University Press.

Goodenough, Ursula & Deacon, Terrence. 2006. The Sacred Emergence of Nature (853–871). In Philip Clayton (Ed.), *The Oxford Handbook of Religion and Science*. New York: Oxford University Press.

Hart, John. 2013. *Cosmic Commons: Spirit, Science and Space*. Eugene, OR: Wipf & Stock.

Hefner, Philip. 1993. *The Human Factor: Evolution, Culture, and Religion*. Minneapolis, MN: Augsburg Press.

Heidegger, Martin. 1977. *Questions Concerning Technology and Other Essays*. New York: Harper & Row.

Hobgood-Oster, Laura. 2014. *A Dog's History of the World: Canines and the Domestication of Humans*. Waco, TX: Baylor University Press.

Jenkins, Willis. 2013. *The Future of Ethics: Sustainability, Social Justice, and Religious Creativity*. Washington, DC: Georgetown University Press.

Keller, Catherine, & Kearns, Laurel. 2007. Grounding Theory: Earth in Religion and Philosophy (1–20). In Catherine Keller & Laurel Kearns (Eds.), *EcoSpirit: Religions and Philosophies for the Earth*. New York: Fordham University Press.

Kohn, Eduardo. 2013. *How Forests Think: Toward an Anthropology Beyond the Human*. Berkeley, CA: University of California Press.

Latour, Bruno. 2004. *The Politics of Nature: How to Bring the Sciences into Democracy*. Cambridge, MA: Harvard University Press.

Macy, Joanna & Young Brown, Molly. 1998. *Coming Back to Life: Practices to Reconnect our Lives, Our World*. Gabriola Island, BC: New Society Publishers.

McFague, Sallie. 1993. *The Body of God: An Ecological Theology*. Minneapolis, MN: Fortress Press.

Merchant, Carolyn. 1980. *The Death of Nature: Women, Ecology and the Scientific Revolution*. New York: HarperCollins.

________________. 2004. *Reinventing Eden: The Fate of Nature in Western Culture*. New York: Routledge.

Moltmann, Jürgen. 2003. *Science and Wisdom*. Minneapolis, MN: Fortress Press.

Leopold, Aldo. 1949. *A Sand County Almanac: Outdoor Essays and Reflections*. Oxford: Oxford University Press.

Nixon, Rob. 2013. *Slow Violence and the Environmentalism of the Poor*. Cambridge, MA: Harvard University Press.

Peterson, Anna. 2001. *Being Human: Ethics, Environment and Our Place in the World*. Berkeley, CA: University of California Press.

Plumwood, Val. 2002. *Environmental Culture: The Ecological Crisis of Reason*. New York: Routledge.

Rorty, Richard. 1999. *Philosophy and Social Hope*. New York: Penguin.

Rosa, Hartmut. 2013. *Social Acceleration: A New Theory of Modernity*. New York: Columbia University Press.

Ruether, Rosemary Radford. 1992. *Gaia and God: An Ecofeminist Theology of Earth Healing*. New York: HarperCollins.

Spinoza, Bendedict de [Baruch]. 1994. *Ethics*. New York: Penguin.

Stenmark, Lisa. 2013. *Religion, Science and Democracy: A Disputational Friendship*. Lanham, MD: Rowman & Littlefield.

Taylor, Bron. 2009. *Dark Green Religion: Nature Spirituality and the Planetary Future*. Berkeley, CA: University of California Press.

Teilhard de Chardin, Pierre. 1959. *The Phenomenon of Man*. New York: Harper & Row.

Tucker, Mary Evelyn. 2003. *Worldly Wonder: Religions Enter Their Ecological Phase*. Peru, IL: Open Court Press.

Tweed, Thomas. 2008. *Crossing and Dwelling: A Theory of Religion*. Cambridge, MA: Harvard University Press.

White, Lynn. 1967. The Historical Roots of Our Ecological Crisis. *Science*, 155, 3767, 1203–1207.

Whitehead, Alfred North. 1978. *Process and Reality*. New York: Free Press.

Worthy, Kenneth. 2013. *Invisible Nature: Healing the Destructive Divide between People and the Environment*. Amherst, NY: Prometheus Books.

Further Reading

Barad, Karen. 2007. *Meeting the Universe Halfway: Quantum Physics and the Entanglement of Matter and Meaning*. Durham, NC: Duke University Press.

Bennett, Jane. 2010. *Vibrant Matter: A Political Ecology of Things*. Durham, NC: Duke University Press.

Keller, Catherine & Kearns, Laurel (Eds.). 2007. *EcoSpirit: Religions and Philosophies for the Earth*. New York: Fordham University Press.

Mickey, Sam. 2014. *On the Verge of a Planetary Civilization: A Philosophy of Integral Ecology*. Lanham, MD: Rowman & Littlefield.

CHAPTER 31

Religious Environmentalism and Environmental Activism

Roger S. Gottlieb

When unethical harvesting of trees is infringing on the health of the land, on sacred mountains, then we have to protect it.

Earl Tulley, Diné (Navajo) Committee against Ruining the Environment, October 1994. (Atencio, 1994)

Global climate change, rampant species extinction, water and air pollution, babies born with countless toxins in their bloodstream, deforestation, acidifying oceans—the dimensions and intensity of our global environmental crisis are real, frightening, and in the view of many the most daunting challenge our civilization has ever faced. While there is typically more bad news about the environment than good, one optimistic development of the last three decades is the emergence of a specifically *religious* environmentalism. This chapter first defines religious environmentalism and then shows its connection to secular environmental activism, raising questions about it as a phenomenon that is simultaneously religious, environmental, and political.

Religious Environmentalism Defined

At the core of religious environmentalism is the belief that non-human Nature has value, moral standing, and spiritual significance—apart, that is, from the way it can be used to meet human needs and desires. Religious environmentalism is now found in almost all current forms of religious life. In varying expressions and with varying degrees of intensity it has been expressed by theologians and institutional authorities of all the major religions: Judaism, Christianity, Islam, Buddhism, Hinduism, Taoism, Sikhism, Bahai; and by native traditions from Africa, the Americas, and Asia. There is as well an active environmental presence in the non-denominational spiritual community.

The Wiley Blackwell Companion to Religion and Ecology, First Edition. Edited by John Hart.

Given this range of sources, it is not surprising that religious environmentalists assert Nature's value in a wide variety of forms. At on one end of the spectrum there is a belief that as a gift from God, Nature partakes of God's bounty and love for people. At the other end there is the idea that Nature itself expresses or contains a kind of divinity. Virtually throughout, there is recognition that human likeness to and dependence on the non-human demands that we change our current mode of living to one much more shaped by respect and care. What we do to Nature matters not just instrumentally, in terms of how it does or does not meet human goals. Rather, just as theft, murder, and exploitation are wrong because of what they do to people, so wanton, uncontrolled, and thoughtless environmental activity is wrong because of what it does to beings that are not people.

A second aspect of religious environmentalism concerns how our treatment of Nature both shapes and reflects our moral connections to other people. To poison rivers, overfish the oceans, or destroy the rainforest is not only to hurt the non-human but to inflict illness, poverty, and cultural genocide on other people. While seeing the harm to other people as a central concern for religious ethics is nothing new, seeing how central our environmental practices are to moral life is. Pollution is now understood to be a long-distance, slow-motion assault—or worse, manslaughter. It is, in the words of the patriarch of the world's 300 million Orthodox Christians, "a sin" (Gottlieb, 2006, 83–94).

Environmental Activism Defined

Environmental activism is the organized response to the environmental crisis: the attempt to make a fundamental change in the way people relate to Nature and, through Nature, to each other. There are countless forms of this activism, but they can be roughly classified on two dimensions. The first is that of the intensity of the action. At one end we have public "speaking," which, in the broad sense, includes such things as books, magazines, internet posts, teaching, public lectures, and the like. At the other end is violence: physically resisting polluting "development" projects that threaten land and people, breaking equipment that constructs roads through the wilderness, and freeing experimental animals from laboratories. In between we have mass demonstrations, engaged projects to protect or restore particular ecosystems, lobbying government, research on particular environmental problems, organizing a neighborhood or community for a crucial vote, and supporting "green" political candidates.

The other dimension concerns the scope of the environmental demand advocated by any particular instance of activism. Is it to eliminate one dangerous chemical or protect one particular species (whales, the great apes) or ecosystem (a river, a forest)? Is it to change a significant aspect of economic or industrial policy: reduce fossil fuel use or make it much harder to introduce chemicals into the environment by making corporations prove their safety before they are used? Is it a challenge to central cultural values, such as promoting veganism or opposing consumerism? Or is it the idea that we must make an even larger transformation if we are to adequately address the environmental threat, for instance, by ending capitalism or overcoming patriarchy?

We should note that intensity and scope can vary both directly and inversely. Environmental activists (e.g., Earth First) have been physically violent in defense of a particular landscape. Alternatively, there are writers who in peaceful and often highly intellectual terms advocate the abolition of capitalism.

What's the Connection?

Why do theological recognition of Nature's inherent value and the moral criticism of poisoning people with toxic wastes necessarily lead religious environmentalists to political activism? Because the "political" is the realm in which we determine the bulk of our collective behavior. It is where power, privilege, production, consumption, distribution, sanctioned violence, and law are shaped. And while the environmental crisis certainly has an individual aspect (Do I eat meat? Do I recycle? Do I drive less and buy organic cotton clothes?) it is the central features of our legal and economic system that allow highly polluting and monstrously cruel factory farms, the wholesale production of toxins, and mountaintop removal mining.

In turning to environmentalism, religions necessarily turn to the political in the modern sense of large-scale movements of citizens to transform their societies in the direction of freedom, equality, justice, and reason. For a variety of reasons, one simply cannot be moral in the modern world without assessing and critically engaging with political reality. For people of faith, this is so for several reasons.

First, widely shared religious moral values of respect, care, compassion, and love are violated by environmental practices that cause global damage. Religious ethicists can no more legitimately turn a blind eye to the human suffering caused by environmental abuse than they can legitimately turn a blind eye to vast income inequality, slavery, aggressive wars, or sexual trafficking.

Second, and perhaps even more pressingly, while theologians and religious authorities might criticize political systems that allow or support militarism, racism, or misogyny, they might well not participate at all, or not very much, in such collective evils. Yet at this point religious leaders, like virtually everyone living above the poverty line in developed societies, and the upper classes in less developed ones, are part of the problem no matter how much they would also like to be part of the solution. The bishop, the rabbi, and the imam all plug in computers, drive cars, fly to international conferences—even those conferences such as the environmentally oriented ones regularly hosted by the head of Orthodox Christianity whose goal is environmental awareness and reform.

Finally, environmental ethics necessarily leads to political activism because our environmental practices are so deeply rooted in complex, interdependent social relationships that can only be adequately addressed by confronting the basic norms of law, economics, education, transportation, and agriculture (for a start). How does one go about changing from a fossil fuel to a renewable, non-polluting energy economy? What legal restraints could limit corporations from causing the distribution of toxic chemicals? What fundamental social changes would lead to pollution being more equally distributed among different races, ethnic groups, and economic classes? Answering these questions requires that whoever asks them, religious or secular, addresses the connections between the end-point conditions (e.g., pollution and climate change) and the social institutions most responsible for them. Put more simply: it is a good thing if a church stops using carcinogenic pesticides on its lawn, yet it has little social significance unless that church publicly announces its decision and the reasons for it, taking a public stand on the need for vastly more restrictive environmental regulations. It is with this morally necessary public commitment that religions enter the political realm of environmental activism.

Is the Political World Any Place for Religion?

Modern, pluralistic, democratic societies have typically marginalized religion. Faith is thought to be a private matter, properly removed from both rationality and social policy. Should we therefore relegate all religion and all religious environmentalism to the sidelines? Such a position rests, I believe, on the mistaken belief that mass societies can organize themselves on the basis of a disinterested concept of scientific reason and on the "neutral" values of freedom and equality. In fact, while the techniques of science and a deep respect for human rights are essential, they are not nearly enough. Complex social policies—whether or not to develop a wetland, what we owe to future generations, how we should balance the demand for economic growth with the need for non-toxic environmental products—require the application of large-scale norms and values that tell us what is most important, meaningful, and valuable (Gottlieb, 2002).

These views may be derived from the Bible or Karl Marx or Ayn Rand, from Thomas Jefferson or the Qur'an. The democratic element of our society means that we decide collectively which principles will guide us. The element of equality means that all citizens have equal access to that decision. But public discussion will almost always include some broadly religious (or philosophical) principles: that, for instance, we are all made in the image of God, that Creation is a gift, that all sentient beings should be aided in reaching enlightenment, that the world is a very good place, that a culture of life forbids the destruction of ecosystems, that all animals form communities similar to the communities formed by humans, that we can learn essential spiritual lessons from non-human Nature. Such values, invoked by religious environmentalists of Jewish, Christian, Buddhist, Islamic, or indigenous traditions, are at least as rational, and surely have as much of a place in social debate as the idea that people are essentially consumers whose goal is maximizing satisfaction, that he who dies with the most toys wins, that the most powerful should rule, or that everything outside of the human realm is simply raw materials for human satisfaction.

Some Examples

Here are some brief, initial examples, the purpose of which is not to delve into any particular action in detail, but rather to give the reader an idea of the range of religious environmental activism. Listed on the website of the National Religious Partnership for the Environment, a US-based interfaith environmental group that serves as a source of information, coordination, and shared action, we find:

- The Catholic Diocese of Houma-Thibodaux, LA has worked to prevent erosion of fertile wetlands and loss of marine livelihood to overdevelopment
- Members of the Social Action Committee of Temple Beth El, East Amherst, NY organized legislative meetings in support of a pesticide registry to reduce the incidence of breast cancer
- Holman United Methodist Church, Culver City, CA worked to prevent the dumping of radioactive waste at a Native American burial ground in the Mohave Desert
- Volunteers from First Presbyterian Church, Kirkwood, MO hold clean-ups of storm water creeks, beautifying the waters, improving wildlife habitat, and promoting public health
- The Church of the Intercession, Harlem, New York led a struggle to provide buses with cleaner emissions in communities with high asthma rates

It might be thought that the people involved in actions of this kind are always the "usual suspects" of liberal Protestants (Methodists, Presbyterians), progressive Catholics, and Reform Jews. While such groups have been highly active, political and theological liberalism is not the only source of religious environmentalism. Consider, for example, the Evangelical Environmental Network (2015), a loosely affiliated group of American evangelicals, generally among the most religiously and socially conservative groups in the United States. The Network has spoken out about toxic pollution and climate change in a wide variety of settings, for example, advocating for reduction in mercury emissions because of mercury's effect on fetuses and children. In 2004 it sponsored the "What Would Jesus Drive?" campaign which confronted US automakers about fuel efficiency and cavalcaded across the American South demanding that Christians apply the Golden Rule to transportation choices.

Statements on the religious aspect of environmental responsibility from the Network included those from deans of seminaries, well-known ministers, and editors of major evangelical publications. Similar high-ranking faith leaders from other traditions have legitimated the religious commitment to environmentalism. Such action is politically significant for many reasons, but perhaps especially because of the common (and generally mistaken) notion that environmentalism is a "group" interest limited to upper-class secular liberals.

Such a distorted image is hard to maintain in the face of a succession of popes (from John Paul II to the present pope, Francis I) and national bishops' groups who have made highly visible statements about the need to value Creation, respect Nature, learn from environmentalists, subject economic development to a rational plan, and protect children from environmental poisons. Institutionally powerful religious groups (e.g., the World Council of Churches) and highly visible religious individuals (e.g., the Dalai Lama) have made comparable statements.

A Historic Shift

Yet, for a time there was some truth in the image of environmentalism as the preserve of upper-class Whites more interested in polar bears and redwoods than in the fate of suffering human beings. Interestingly, the United Church of Christ (UCC) in the US played a key role in changing that image and transforming secular environmentalism.

The story begins in the mid-1980s, as the residents of Warren County, North Carolina—the county with the highest proportion of African-Americans in the state—were resisting the placement of yet another toxic waste facility there (Gottlieb, 2006, 134–138). The UCC took an active role in the struggle, which involved demonstrations and the arrest (among others) of noted civil rights veteran and Congressman John Lewis. As a response to what seemed to be a racially motivated siting of toxic facilities, the UCC sponsored the first systematic study comparing toxic waste facilities to the racial makeup of every county in the US (Commission for Racial Justice, 1987). The results confirmed their belief in the existence of environmental racism—the vastly disproportionate distribution of pollution on racial minorities. In 1991 the UCC sponsored a conference of people of color environmental activists, who created the now well-known Principles of Environmental Justice (Gottlieb, 2003a, 729–730).

This historic document codified the connections among race, class, ethnicity, and human suffering from environmental causes. "Environmental racism" and "environmental justice" became essential concepts for the global environmental movement, secular or religious. A formally organized religious group was at the center of this critically important transformation.

Half a world away we find religious values appealed to in very different national and cultural settings. Also viewing issues of justice as part of an environmental perspective, Mongolian Prime Minister Nambaryn Enkhbayar, the country's first leader after liberation from Soviet domination, appealed to Buddhist values in a call for "a pollution free way of living, ability to adapt quickly to the new environment in a broad sense, mobility, a more or less harmonious relationship with the environment, and readiness to give up the demands or things which turn into a burden" (Enkhbayar, 2014).

Similar challenges to development at all and any costs in models of modernization can be found in the Sri Lankan group Sarvodaya (which means "everyone stands up"; Bond, 2004). Instead of export agriculture which displaces peasant communities, and mega-dam projects which encourage consumerism in the cities while leaving local people with no electricity, Sarvodaya advocated moderate consumption, the eradication of extreme poverty, the centrality of close community ties, and women's education—all this in the framework of an essentially Buddhist understanding of the importance of spiritual values such as self-knowledge and compassion and a critical attitude toward the thoughtless adoption of technology and material goods.

When Religions Turn Green

Cooperation

As a global threat of unprecedented significance, the environmental crisis has provoked deep and wide-ranging shifts in religious life. Yet the advent of religious environmentalism does not simply alter our understanding of the environment or lead to demands for solar power. It changes the conduct and self-understanding of religion itself in at least three crucial ways.

First, there is the way religious environmentalism encourages—some would say requires—a new and highly important level of interfaith cooperation. There has been a proliferation of organizations such as Interfaith Power and Light (cooperating on raising awareness of energy use and the greening of religious buildings; Interfaith Power and Light, 2015) and of important projects such as the reforestation and conservation efforts undertaken in Zimbabwe by a coalition of African Christians and indigenous spirit-worshiping groups (Daneel, 2001). The ecological values and knowledge of native traditions are now spoken of by leaders of the world's dominant faiths with respect and appreciation—a far cry from centuries in which adherents were typically dismissed as pagan and forcibly converted. Even within the struggle between Israel and Palestine there has been a religious dimension to cooperation over the fate of the sadly depleted Jordan River.

Such cooperation also extends to working with explicitly non-religious environmental organizations. There has been public cooperation between the Sierra Club and the National Council of Churches. John Paul II ordained St. Francis as the patron saint of all those, Catholic or not, who work for the environment. The National Resources Defense Council features self-identified religious members as part of their human resource base.

It is perhaps not surprising that a universal threat to the very continuity of religious institutions might help bridge the gap between different doctrines and rituals. Yet given both the history of religious conflict and the seemingly inescapable tendencies of human beings to focus on difference rather than connection, it is a welcome development nevertheless.

Science as Ally

The rise of modern science in the sixteenth century provoked serious conflict with many religious thinkers and authorities. The new astronomy directly contradicted the then dominant Christian view of the structure of the universe. Further, the scientific method's effective approach to posing and settling questions offered a stark contrast to religion's appeal to faith over empirical evidence. Perhaps most significantly, the rise of Darwinian models of evolution seemed to remove the unique moral and spiritual status of human beings. For science, humans were just a tiny, accidental part of an unthinkingly large, and essentially meaningless, universe.

Accordingly, there has been a marked trend within religious settings to contradict scientific claims head on. This continues today in Intelligent Design movements, which argue against the reigning theories of cosmology and evolution. Alternatively, theologians proclaimed that there were different realms of knowledge, belief, and mastery. Science properly ruled in the restricted area of the behavior of physical objects and processes. But religion was—and would always be—the unerring guide to meaning, morality, and spiritual development.

Under the sway of religious environmentalism the situation has changed dramatically. Instead of relentless opposition or avoidance, there is comradely respect and use.

As with interfaith cooperation, this is perhaps inevitable. How else would religious authorities know that an environmental crisis exists—that the world is warming, newborns have pesticides in their bloodstream, and oceans are acidifying—if not for the information provided by scientific authorities? To whatever extent the modern marriage of science and technology has created the environmental crisis, it is obvious to theologians and religious leaders that science and technology are essential to diagnosing and (to whatever extent is possible) solving it. As a result, virtually all major religious statements on environmental issues include long references to scientific findings about major environmental issues.

In a related and fascinating development, the desire to cooperate does not move in one direction only. In the early 1990s a group of prestigious scientists sent an open letter to the religious community, asking for cooperation on environmental issues, acknowledging the importance of religion's social standing and important moral voice (Gottlieb, 2003a, 735–737). Since then, there have been joint letters to political leaders, joint press conferences, and continuing cooperation. All in all, another remarkable and hopeful change.

To the Left

Religions have always had a pronounced tendency toward social conservatism. One can think of the resistance to women's equality, turning a blind eye to slavery, and supporting class inequality in the form of India's caste system or the vast privileges of Europe's aristocracy. There is also a tendency to claim that spiritual development requires dedication to faith, religious practice, and obedience to religious strictures, not involvement with politics. The aim of life, we are told, is Heaven or enlightenment, not political liberation or progress.

At the same time, religion also has a tendency, perhaps not as powerful or widely expressed as its social conservatism, toward conservatism's opposite: in support of social justice, fairness, equality of respect and rights, and universal compassion (Gottlieb, 2003b).

It is not surprising, therefore, that since the advent of modern political movements aimed at national freedom from colonialism, democratic politics, expanding rights to include the whole population, and protecting the economic interests of workers, religions often have been on both sides of the resulting struggles.

In the context of environmental activism we have already seen how the United Church of Christ helped to establish the link between racism and environmental concerns. Among many in the religious environmentalist community this developed into a broadly defined concern with ecojustice—the belief that human treatment of Nature is directly connected with forms of social organization, and that environmental sanity and respect of the non-human require a comprehensive respect for social justice and human wellbeing. From an ecojustice perspective there is ultimately no conflict between caring for people and caring for Nature. Both are essential moral tasks and each requires the other to be successful (Gibson, 2004).

More broadly, as is the case with almost all environmental activists, religious groups have to confront the global effects of environmentally damaging corporate practices. The reality is that enormously powerful capitalist corporations dominate the fossil fuel economy, transportation choices, the highly polluting extraction of minerals, the development and distribution of toxic chemicals, the production of highly polluting war materials, and the decimation of natural goods ("resources"), such as forests and fish stocks. Corporations also use their vast economic power to influence governmental regulatory bodies in damaging ways, and their power over the media fuels a consumerist mentality that is at odds with any rational economic planning or restraint (or rationality!) in consumption.

Thus, most environmental groups, religious or not, sooner or later arrive at a position critical of the power of corporations and call for political change to increase collective social control over them. Among the clearest examples of this are statements that came from the leadership of the World Council of Churches (WCC), an umbrella organization representing some 400 million Protestants. In 2003, in preparation for a meeting with the World Bank, WCC general secretary Konrad Raiser questioned "the allegedly irrefutable logic of the prevailing economic paradigm." Simultaneously, representatives of 70 member churches signed a document stating that "nothing less than a fundamental shift in political-economic paradigms is necessary" (Gottlieb, 2006, 107). WCC's criticism of globalization is based on an ecojustice perspective. This critique sees the widespread growth of poverty, the privatization of natural resources, the encouragement of national debt, and vastly unequal distribution of wealth as directly connected to worldwide environmental problems.

In Sarvodaya's critique of globalization, in Thailand's Buddhist critique of consumerism (a critique for a time made illegal by the Thai government), in campaigns against Home Depot's sale of wood from ancient forests, or McDonald's buying beef from rainforest-destroying Brazilian cattle farms—in all these case religious environmentalists have challenged capitalist prerogatives. They have made it clear that if corporations are not the enemy, at least in many instances corporate behavior is.

Dilemmas of Religious Environmentalism

What about Capitalism?

Environmental activism, like any other kind, is necessarily defined as much by what it is against as by what it is for. To the extent that it is oriented toward more than an immediate issue—stop the outflows from one factory, protect a single wetland, get church members to carpool to services—the movement must ask: What are the major sources of the environmental crisis? In simplistic, but not totally inaccurate terms: What (or who) is the enemy? What fundamental social structures, cultural norms, or forms of self-understanding require transformation if environmentalism is to be seriously effective?

In raising these questions religious environmentalists associate themselves with the many and diverse movements that have defined liberal, radical, progressive, or revolutionary politics since the late eighteenth century. Those movements have called for democracy, human rights, political equality for subordinated groups, and decent living conditions for workers and the poor. And they identified what they needed to overcome: the inherited privilege of the aristocracy, racial and gender discrimination based on unjust assumptions of racial or gender privilege, and the irrational and immoral power wielded by the economic elite.

As religious environmentalists confront global environmental problems they too must ask: What are the ultimate causes which must be discarded if we are to make things fundamentally better?

The first candidate—and the only one I discuss here—is capitalism. This system is based on private ownership of the forces of production, relentless competition leading to unending technological innovations, and a corresponding need to expand production. It possesses an inescapable tendency toward the concentration of wealth and the creation of mammoth transnational corporations. Further, it gives such corporations the ability to undermine both democracy and rationality through their influence in the realms of politics, media, education, and culture.

While the ultimate coexistence of capitalism and stable ecosystems may be highly doubtful, religious environmentalists face a dispiriting reality: no workable and effective alternative to capitalism has been devised. Heavy-handed and undemocratic, Soviet-style central planning led to extreme economic inefficiency and environmental disasters the equal of any capitalist economy. The Chinese have combined dictatorial, one-party rule with economic freedom for a rising class of private owners, creating massive environmental problems along the way. What seems possible, given the failures of the anti-capitalist left democratic nations, is only a range of degrees of government control over environmental issues, an attempt, that is, to make ecological damage a visible cost of production rather than an "externality," the cost of which is borne by society, while producers and consumers reap the benefits.

While many religious environmentalists critique particular corporate policies and the unfortunate influence of corporations on government policy, and while there may be an occasional lament over the power of the market, few religious voices actively call for anything like socialism. This may be partly because of the historical antagonism between religions and socialist or communist regimes; because the vast majority of the faithful are not committed leftists; or because of the recognition that, given the state of ordinary citizens throughout the world, collectivizing the forces of production would not lead to their rational use for the world community but simply the creation of a new social elite, one rooted in governmental power rather than economic ownership.

Religious environmentalists are not alone in these dilemmas; they are faced by political progressives throughout the world. The system as it now stands is unworkable and destructive, but the political will and maturity of the population to change it are lacking. Without deep change any particular reform can easily be overthrown later. But deep change does not seem possible.

At least for the unforeseen future, I suspect, religious environmentalism will have to settle for a comparatively agnostic position on capitalism: whether or not it can be reformed to be compatible with a sustainable environmental practices, and whether or not the current population is capable of reforming it. At best religious environmentalists can, like other progressive groups, seek to arouse the general population to form a mass, activist interest group that will compel the government—under the threat of massive loss of legitimacy—to constrain corporate behavior in the direction of environmental responsibility. Given the power of corporations to influence public opinion, buy politicians' allegiance, and cause economic downturns by their refusal to invest, this is a strategy with obvious limitations. But it may be all we have.

Political Boundaries and Limits

We have seen how environmental activism leads religious actors to interfaith cooperation and joint efforts with scientists and secular political groups. Yet other questions of cooperation arise in the context of political work, namely, significant differences that are political or moral rather than explicitly religious in nature.

Consider the Interfaith Moral Action on Climate (Interfaith Moral Action on Climate, 2015), a recent group whose origins lie in demonstrations about climate change in Washington, DC in 2011. The group has a variety of religious sources of support and participation, and announces its goals as a fundamental and equitable transformation of energy policy away from fossil fuels and toward renewable sources, with the change accompanied by concern for which segments of the population bear the brunt of the new policy.

As admirable as these goals and the use of religious reasons in support of them are, the group makes no explicit reference to the disastrous consequences of factory meat farming (indeed all meat farming has negative climate effects, but factory farming causes the vast majority), such as high water consumption, groundwater pollution, methane from pigs and cows, and high consumption of fossil fuels.

Could it be that Interfaith Moral Action avoids criticism of meat production because of a desire to avoid conflict with a culture that is typically centered on meat-eating? Or because it wants to avoid association with people concerned about animal cruelty in agriculture and simply to focus on the wider (though perhaps not wide enough) issue of global warming?

This, to be clear, is a strategic political decision on the group's part since the unfortunate role of factory farming in global warming, by producing as much as 18% of greenhouse gas emissions, is well known. But what about stating the full truth from the outset? And what about the associated moral issue, one mentioned in passing by many religious authorities, of cruelty to animals? How a group defines itself, what it sees as essential and what as distracting or insignificant, is a key part of its political identity, as is the line it draws about the kinds of differences with other groups that make it possible or impossible to cooperate.

Consider another difficult area. Virtually all religions have lay leaders, people distinguished by a combination of commitment to the faith and an ability to make significant monetary contributions. Yet no matter how large the contribution, it is doubtful if a religious group would be eager to have a publicly known pornographer or drug dealer on its board of trustees. The values of the church in question would be too much at odds with the aspiring lay leader.

But what about a person who owns a polluting factory or lobbies to dilute environmental regulations? On the one hand, the damage done by a polluter might outweigh that of a drug dealer. At the same time, however, while the local priest might not use drugs or consume pornography, it is likely that he contributes to global warming by driving and by using common products that pollute. As far as I know few religious voices have discussed this problem. I imagine many will in the future and it will be fascinating to see what results.

Violence

Many would say that advocating violence in pursuit of political change is unviable, especially for religious people. Religions, after all, preach love rather than hate, compassion rather than conflict. The great religious social activists—King, Gandhi, Ang San Suu Kyy—achieved their results through nonviolence, civil disobedience, and preaching respect for opponents despite the terrible sufferings inflicted by the authorities and groups of ordinary citizens they sought to change.

As well, many of a religious or spiritual persuasion will argue that violence does no good: it breeds more violence, providing only the most temporary of victories. It leaves people with lingering despair, hate, and the desire for revenge. Finally, violence is almost always non-selective in its application. Terrorists kill members of their own religious or ethnic group by accident; smart bombs obliterate wedding parties; actions to stop wars kill innocent bystanders.

On the other hand, however, there is a militant strain in many religious traditions. The Israelites were instructed to conquer the Promised Land, often by killing all the men there and enslaving the women and children. The Catholic Church was the religious dimension of the highly militant Holy Roman Empire and has long taught that under certain circumstances a "just war" might be worthy of fighting. Hinduism, which in certain variants renounces violence completely, has in one of its central religious texts, the *Bhagavad Gita*, a justification for fulfilling one's social role as a warrior.

Even more, the extremes of modern conflict would seem to create contexts in which violence makes moral sense. Jews in the Nazi-controlled ghettos or concentrations camps or women responding to organized rape by ethnic militias are two examples which might well challenge the presumption that in virtually any circumstance the proper religious response is nonviolence.

A question arises: Of the wide variety of environmental contexts, do some morally warrant violence? And in such contexts, is violence effective? I will not try to offer anything like a comprehensive answer here, on an issue which I believe has not been fully examined by any thinker. Rather, I will simply offer two contrasting examples.

First, consider the long-distance, slow-motion assault of toxic chemicals. Such poisons are responsible, many experts tell us, for at the very least tens of thousands and more likely millions of deaths. One calculation puts deaths in the US from air pollutants from coal-fired power plants alone at more than 7,000 a year. If we add to that environmentally caused cancer, immune system deficits, and birth defects the scale of damage rises dramatically, especially for children (Shabecoff & Shabecoff, 2010).

What is the proper political response to this kind of socially sanctioned, economically legitimated, but morally heinous violence? Vigilante attacks on corporate polluters? Political assassination of executives? Just raising such possibilities reveals, I believe, how futile they would be, for polluting industries are an essential part of our entire economic and cultural structure. We need to change fundamental energy policy, models of consumption, regulations on the introduction of new chemicals, and our preferences in food and entertainment. Such changes, in turn, require a significant reorientation of power relations, widely held beliefs, and social priorities. This long, difficult task of transformation violence is likely to be counterproductive or at best irrelevant.

In a very different situation, consider, for example, the Nigerian Ogoni peninsula region, where oil development has destroyed villages by life-threatening air, water, and soil pollution. Violent conflict has erupted a number of times as locals sought to curtail or stop oil production. Oil companies backed by the Nigerian government and hired thugs responded with brutality.

If my village was being destroyed, and my sources of water and the air my children were breathing were under assault, I might well take up arms. And I'm not sure it would be the place of local religious leaders to do anything but approve of my action or fight by my side.

Religion? Politics? Both?

For most of the last 10,000 years the concept of religion as a culturally and institutionally separate aspect of human existence did not exist. What in modernity we call specifically religious belief, practice, and authority were woven into so much of everyday life that a concept of religion as distinct from politics, philosophy, or art, for example, would have been hard to understand.

With the rise of an enlightenment mentality the place of religion in many (clearly not all) parts of the world shifted. In democratic practice political authority was sharply insulated from religious authority. Science was now the source of reliable information about the natural world. With the advent of pluralistic societies, social mobility, and personal freedom individuals were able to adopt, reject, or modify religious traditions according to personal desires. It was largely accepted that religious forms of reasoning and institutional relationships were separate from government and law.

At the same time, however, the last century has witnessed some historically significant social movements in which religion and politics are intimately intertwined. Interestingly, such movements—Gandhian nonviolence in India, the American Civil Rights Movement, religious anti-war groups during the Vietnam War—arose as progressive or radical alternatives to the social and political status quo. Unlike religions which typically legitimated existing relations of social and political domination, they vigorously opposed colonial power, racial discrimination, and an imperialist war, at times, capitalism and patriarchy alike.

There have also been intensely politically conservative religious movements. Generally, however, these have been limited to single issues (abortion, gay marriage) or to the general "culture wars" concerns. At least in the West, they have not called for wholesale social transformation of political and economic life.

In this both fascinating and confusing conceptual context, what are we to make of religious environmentalism? Is it political or religious or both? A fusion of the two shaping a new social form entirely?

Consider the following examples, which speak to a number of issues raised in this chapter.

In 1997, on the Jewish holiday of Tu B'Shvat (a late winter celebration of vegetation and the yearly natural cycle), in a grove of northern California redwood trees under a cutting order by owner Maxaam Corporation, a group of self-identified Jews, many of them ordained rabbis, violated court orders and planted redwood seedlings in a denuded stream bank. Over the preceding 18 months three local rabbis had pursued Maxaam CEO Charles Hurwitz, a leading member of the Houston Jewish community. His willingness to despoil the area, they argued, violated Jewish ethics. The group, called in the press the Redwood Rabbis, had observed that of the original 2 million acres of redwoods fewer than 100,000 remained. Many of the protesters wore traditional Jewish prayer shawls and had been careful to inform Maxaam and the police beforehand of their plans. The authorities allowed the civil disobedience to proceed without arrest. "At a place where demonstrators before have been met with billy clubs, nightsticks, and arrests, we are now walking freely," said a local environmental activist who had been struggling to protect the areas for years, "It reminds me of the parting of the Red Sea" (Zuckerman, 1998).

In 2002, The Rev. Henry Simmons, board chair, Justice and Witness Ministries of the United Church of Christ, addressed a rally protesting plans to incinerate nerve gas in East St. Louis. "We come here as multi-racial and multi-cultural witnesses to shed light on long-term health consequences associated with toxic waste... We are here to name the sin of environmental racism and to renew our call for real and lasting environmental justice in order that the burden of toxic waste will be shared by all—and not just some" (Gottlieb, 2006, 111).

On May 18, 2001 a letter, signed by 39 heads of denominations and senior leaders of major American faith groups, was sent to then-US President George W. Bush. In part it read: "By depleting energy sources, causing global warming, fouling the air with pollution, and poisoning the land with radioactive waste, a policy of increased reliance on fossil fuels and nuclear power jeopardizes health and well-being for life on Earth" (Energy Conservation and God's Creation, 2001).

Two weeks earlier, in part attempting to apply lessons from Gandhi and King, and seeking to demand that religious groups move from greener theology to political action, 22 members (including Christians, Jews, Buddhists, and Muslims) of the Interfaith group Religious Witness for the Earth had been arrested in Washington, DC protesting the government's energy policy. Responding to what he termed the administration's "drill and burn" policy, the group's co-chair, Rev. Fred Small, had declared, "Despoiling the earth is sacrilege, and exhausting its resources is theft from our own children" (Gottlieb, 2006, 112).

In these instances, and the many more which could be cited, we see a seamless movement from theology, to ethics, to political action. A theological perspective identifies the natural world as having its own moral value. An ethical imperative to love and care for that which has value—Nature and human beings alike—necessitates political challenges to governmental policy and economic prerogatives—and, of course, to personal behavior. But it is public, collective, social demands that make religious environmentalism specifically political. A theological language of sin joins a political challenge to existing social authorities and norms. It is just because of the fully integrated character of this progression that conventional distinctions between "religion" and "politics" may not be adequate to this phenomenon.

Religion's Political Gifts

At their best (i.e., at their most authentically religious), activists from Religious Witness for the Earth or the interfaith reforestation efforts in Zimbabwe do not simply lend their energy to secular environmental groups or commonly agreed environmental goals. Rather, from what might be called the "culture" of religion they have at their disposal certain values and practices that are capable of making distinct and significant contributions to the movement as a whole. While at least some of these values and practices are theoretically accessible from secular culture, they have historically been much more likely to emerge from a religious source. For example, there is the perspective of non-violence. While there have been secular adherents of this model of political activism, the most significant—Gandhi, King, Ang Sang Suu Kyi, Bishop Tutu—rejected violence for explicitly religious reasons. And this rejection was not simply on the pragmatic grounds that their movements faced more powerful adversaries. Rather, it was based on certain religious values of moral humility, self-criticism, and universal love; and in religious perspectives that violence always damages the self that engages in it, or that we are all—even those we energetically opposed—made "in the image of God" (Smith, 2004).

The appropriateness of this perspective to the vast majority of environmental struggles (though, as I have argued, not necessarily all) resides in the fact that large parts of society must be won over to accept the likely inconveniences and significant sacrifices environmental rationality requires. As well, attitudes of moral superiority, arrogance, and disrespect for those not on the "right" side are a notoriously poor basis for organizing those who remain unconvinced, in the middle, leading toward your side and also leaning away. As dire as the situation is, King's vision of a "beloved community" (Garrow, 1986) is likely to be more appealing to climate change skeptics than the widespread secular political image of oppressor and oppressed, villains and good guys. Since we are literally all in this together, an attitude of respect and mutuality is both better politics and more morally accurate.

Another example is religious culture's ability to offer examples of non-commodity, non-consumerist human fulfillment. Religions, as opposed to the dominant forces of capitalist culture, teach that community, compassion, connection, and simple enjoyment are the paths to human fulfillment. The Sabbath is, after all, a time of rest and appreciation, not shopping. The fellowship of prayer depends on comparatively little energy use. The peace of meditation might require a new meditation cushion every five years or so, but not much else. Further, virtually every tradition teaches an imperative to gratitude, to enjoying, valuing, and accepting what one has, rather than compulsively desiring more (Lerner, 2002).

All these perspectives on human fulfillment are at odds with a civilization geared toward domination, control, and additive consumption. If they have not always, or even for the most part, been essential to the conduct of religious people, they have sometimes, and they remain invaluable if the global shift in political structures and personal attitudes demanded by the environmental crisis has a chance at success.

Conclusion

Not unlike a student of mechanical engineering researching the *Titanic* or a Jew studying the history of anti-Semitism in Nazi Germany, all of us who investigate the nature of the environmental crisis and the human response to it are personally implicated in what we read and write. To pretend otherwise is to ignore the reality in a most non-objective, unscholarly fashion. It is therefore appropriate, I believe, to conclude by observing that even a cursory examination of this day's, week's, or year's environmental news gives me scant hope.

Yet it is another one of religious environmentalism's gifts to political activism to offer the culturally religious idea that we cannot think only of the rationally calculable results of our actions. Even if we do not succeed in achieving the goal, it is incumbent on us to pursue it. Even if we cannot complete the task, control the outcome, or have any confidence in success, we will live this way just because by some mysterious cosmic calculus it is the right thing to do and has some kind of beneficial effect: on our own souls for doing it, and on the world of life where we can save and love whatever we can.

In our current world this is the best we can do and it will have to be enough.

References

Atencio, E. 1994. After a Heavy Harvest and a Death, Navajo Forestry Realigns with Culture. *Western Roundup*, October 31.

Bond, George D. 2004. *Buddhism at Work: Community Development, Social Empowerment, and the Sarvodaya Movement*. Bloomfield, CT: Kumarian Press.

Commission for Racial Justice. 1987. *Toxic Wastes and Race in the United States*. New York: United Church of Christ.

Daneel, Martinus L. 2001. *African Earthkeepers: Wholistic Interfaith Mission*. Maryknoll, NY: Orbis Books.

Energy Conservation and God's Creation. 2001. http://earthjustice.org/news/press/2001/energy-conservation-and-god-s-creation.

Enkhbayar, Nambaryn. 2014. Some Thoughts on Buddhist Philosophy and Economics, Alliance for Religions and Conservation. http://www.arcworld.org/projects.asp?projectID=186.

Evangelical Environmental Network. 2015. http://www.creationcare.org/.

Garrow, David J. 1986. *Bearing the Cross: Martin Luther King, Jr., and the Southern Christian Leadership Conference*. New York: Quill.

Gibson, William E. (Ed.). 2004. *Eco-Justice: The Unfinished Journey*. Albany, NY: SUNY Press.

Gottlieb, Roger S. 2002. *Joining Hands: Politics and Religion Together for Social Change*. Cambridge, MA: Westview.

Gottlieb, Roger S. (Ed.). 2003a. *This Sacred Earth: Religion, Nature, Environment* (2nd ed.). New York. Routledge.

Gottlieb, Roger S. (Ed.). 2003b. *Liberating Faith: Religious Voices for Peace, Justice, and Ecological Wisdom*. Lanham, MD: Rowman & Littlefield.

Gottlieb, Roger S. 2006. *A Greener Faith: Religious Environmentalism and our Planet's Future*. New York: Oxford University Press.

Interfaith Moral Action on Climate. 2015. http://www.interfaithmoralactiononclimate.org/.

Interfaith Power and Light 2015. http://www.interfaithpowerandlight.org/.

Lerner, Michael. 2002. *Spirit Matters*. Charlottesville, VA: Hampton Roads Publishing.

National Religious Partnership for the Environment. 2015. http://www.nrpe.org/.

Shabecoff, Philip & Shabecoff, Alice. 2010. *Poisoned for Profit: How Toxins Are Making Our Children Chronically Ill*. White River Junction, VT: Chelsea Green Publishing.

Smith, Gordon (Ed.). 2004. *Religion and Peacebuilding*. Albany, NY: SUNY Press.

Zuckerman, Seth. 1998. Redwood Rabbis. *Sierra Magazine*, 62–63, 82–83.

Websites

Alliance of Religions and Conservation. http://www.arcworld.org/.

Forum on Religion and Ecology. http://hds.harvard.edu/links/forum-religion-and-ecology.

Indigenous Environmental Network. http://www.ienearth.org.

Religion and Nature. http://www.religionandnature.com.

Further Reading

Boff, Leonardo. 1997. *Cry of the Earth, Cry of the Poor*. Transl. Philip Berryman. Maryknoll, NY: Orbis Books. Environmental justice from a radical Catholic perspective.

Bond, George D. 2004. *Buddhism at Work: Community Development, Social Empowerment, and the Sarvodaya Movement*. Bloomfield, CT: Kumarian Press. Activist, environmentalist Buddhism in Sri Lanka.

Daly, Herman E. & Cobb, Jr. John B. 1994. *For the Common Good: Redirecting the Economy toward Community, the Environment, and a Sustainable Future* (2nd ed.). Boston, MA: Beacon Press. Economic and social goals from a sustainable, religious perspective.

Gebara, Ivone. 1999. *Longing for Running Water: Ecofeminism and Liberation*. Minneapolis, MN: Fortress Press. Catholic environmentalist liberation theology from a feminist perspective.

Gottlieb, Roger. S. 2006a. *A Greener Faith: Religious Environmentalism and Our Planet's Future*. New York: Oxford University Press. The first comprehensive overview of religious environmentalism.

Gottlieb, Roger S. 2006b. *The Oxford Handbook of Religion and Ecology*. New York: Oxford University Press. Essays on theology and activism from leading scholars.

Grim, John & Tucker, Mary Evelyn. 2014. *Ecology and Religion*. Washington, DC: Island Press. An overview of history and recent developments.

Kaza, Stephanie. 2005. *Hooked! Buddhist Writings on Greed, Desire, and the Urge to Consume*. Boston, MA: Shambhala. Buddhist values analyzing and opposing consumerism.

Laduke, Winona. 1999. *All Our Relations: Native Struggles for Land and Life*. Boston, MA: South End Press. Native American values and environmental struggles.

Rasmussen, Larry. 2012. *Earth-Honoring Faith: Religious Ethics in a New Key*. New York: Oxford University Press. Theology, political critique, and social vision by a long-standing scholar in this area.

Taylor, Bron (Ed.) 2005. *Encyclopedia of Religion and Nature*. New York: Continuum. Vast and comprehensive on theory and practice in this field.

CHAPTER 32

Global Heating, Pope Francis, and the Promise of *Laudato Sí*

Bill McKibben

The heating of the planet is such a large issue that it demands theological reflection, and indeed innovation. That is to say, humans have never done anything larger and with greater impacts and challenges on the Earth than climate change. In effect, we are busily supplanting the traditional deities as the defining force on the planet. Those events we have always turned to as definitions of the power of the Almighty—hurricanes, floods, withering droughts, blizzards—are now increasingly viewed as the result of the actions of human beings. What even the insurance companies continue to call "acts of God" are now clearly the acts of people. Where God once could turn to Job and ask if he set the boundaries of the ocean and told the proud waves where to break—and receive only silence in return—now we are able to answer back.

Some, suspicious that faith is a quieting force, may view this is as a small, salutary development in the otherwise grim tide of effects of climate change; at least it ends the idea of a large, controlling, external force as being responsible and imposes a sense of isolation on our species. Others will view it as one of the best possible moments for a new theology of human solidarity. It strikes me that this is the greatest import of Pope Francis's groundbreaking encyclical *Laudato Sí*, issued in May 2015, to date the hottest year that humans have ever recorded and with the prospect of more to come.

Yes, the encyclical includes some fairly straightforward paragraphs explaining climate science, condemning its denial, and calling for the kind of actions scientists have long suggested: the switch, for instance, to renewable energy. But the pope devotes far more effort to a much grander project: defining a useful way for human beings to relate to the physical world and to each other in a straitened age. "A certain way of understanding human life and activity has gone awry, to the serious detriment of the world around us," he maintains (101). We have succumbed to a "technocratic paradigm," which leads us to believe that "every increase in power means an increase

The Wiley Blackwell Companion to Religion and Ecology, First Edition. Edited by John Hart.

in progress itself ... as if reality, goodness and truth automatically flow from technological and economic power as such" (105). This paradigm "exalts the concept of a subject who, using logical and rational procedures, approaches and gains control over an external object" (106). Men and women, he writes, have from the start "intervened in nature, but for a long time this meant being in tune with and respecting the possibilities offered by the things themselves. It was a matter of receiving what nature itself allowed, as if from its own hands." In our world, however, "human beings and material objects no longer extend a friendly hand to one another; the relationship has become confrontational." With the great power that technology has afforded us, it has become "easy to accept the idea of infinite or unlimited growth, which proves so attractive to economists, financiers, and experts in technology. It is based on the lie that there is an infinite supply of the earth's goods, and this leads to the planet being squeezed dry beyond every limit." This understanding—that human beings have stretched the physical capacity of the planet beyond its breaking point—is joined by another thought, this one more political. It's not "human beings" in general that have managed this task, but specific groups of human beings: the richer ones. And just as they have pushed the planet too hard, so have they pushed their brothers and sisters. Automation, for instance: "the orientation of the economy has favored a kind of technological process in which the costs of production are reduced by laying off workers and replacing them with machines," which is a sadness since "work is a necessity, part of the meaning of life on this earth, a path to growth" (the type of "growth" needs more elaboration; see *Deep Economy* [McKibben, 2008]) or genetic modification of plants, to be feared less because of the threat of so-called frankenfood than because "following the introduction of these crops, productive land is concentrated in the hands of a few owners" who can afford the new technologies. Just as these forces have reduced biodiversity and ushered in a new age of extinction, so too have they had a "leveling effect on cultures," diminishing the "immense variety which is the heritage of all humanity." (Coming from the throne which most enthusiastically embraced the idea of reducing cultural distinctiveness in the name of universal belief, this is a striking position.)

The pope's prescription is the substitution of ethical limits on our behavior for the now-absent physical limitations that once constrained us. He calls on us to keep "the poor of the future in mind and also today's poor, whose life on this earth is brief and who cannot keep on waiting." Think for a minute of the limits such a doctrine would actually impose. Were we to take it seriously we would have, for instance, to put off-limits almost all the remaining stores of carbon fuel on our planet, for the science indicates quite clearly that if we burn them, the sea will rise 200 feet over the next millennium, enough to constrain life for all who follow (on climate heating, see McKibben, 2006 and 2012 for a century's worth of voices on climate change). Instead, we would need to move with a forced step toward renewable energy, with whatever limitations on our power that would imply. We would need to quickly adapt our diets, so that meat became the smaller portion of our sustenance. We would need to move toward public transport and away from the private car—indeed, increasingly away from the private world that consumerism has allowed us to inhabit.

Francis maintains that we would become more fully ourselves were we to follow such a course, and I believe there is evidence that he is right. But that is the argument that religious leaders have been making back to the time of the Buddha, and we have paid little attention to it: it has always been countercultural, not cultural. What has changed is the context. In a world where we are literally building our own hellfire—where more of the US burned this past hot summer than any year on record—the pope's ethical choices also become physical imperatives. God is no longer larger than we are, which means that we need to rein ourselves in. Religion, going forward, will largely be a question of whether that is possible and, if so, how.

References

Francis I, 2015. Laudato Sí. http://w2.vatican.va/content/francesco/en/encyclicals/documents/papa-francesco_20150524_enciclica-laudato-si.html.

McKibben, Bill. 2006. *The End of Nature*. New York: Random House.

McKibben, Bill. 2008. *Deep Economy: The Wealth of Communities and the Durable Future*. New York: St. Martin's Griffin.

McKibben, Bill (Ed.). 2012. *The Global Warming Reader: A Century of Writing About Climate Change*. New York: Penguin.

CHAPTER 33

Respect for Mother Earth

Original Instructions and Indigenous Traditional Knowledge

Tom B. K. Goldtooth

> Wherever forests have not been mowed down, wherever the animal is recessed in their quiet protection, wherever the earth is not bereft of four-legged life—that to the white man is an "unbroken wilderness." But for us there was no wilderness, nature was not dangerous but hospitable, not forbidding but friendly. Our faith sought the harmony of man with his surroundings; the other sought the dominance of surroundings. For us, the world was full of beauty; for the other, it was a place to be endured until he went to another world. But we were wise. We knew that man's heart, away from nature, becomes hard.
>
> Chief Luther Standing Bear (1868–1939)

The Indigenous Environmental Network (IEN), based in Minnesota, was established in 1990. It was formed by community-based indigenous peoples, including youth and elders, to promote a rights-based approach to environmental and economic justice in North America—Turtle Island. I am its executive director.

Working for environmental and economic justice is spiritual work, it reaffirms our human relationship with and our responsibility to protect the sacredness of Mother Earth and to honor Father Sky. One of the goals of this work is to secure a healthy and safe environment for all people and all future generations, with no disparities of treatment where some are more and others are less protected.

Humanity must re-evaluate its relationship to the sacredness of Mother Earth. In our IEN work, our network firmly supports the right that all people have, in civil society in North America and throughout the world, to speak out for Nature and our Mother Earth.

Indigenous peoples, within our traditions and in the teachings of our many indigenous (tribal) nations of the North and South, understand our responsibilities to live within the natural order that is sacred to all life on Earth and on, in, and above the Earth, the soil that nurtures the seeds of all plants that provide life for all life.

The Wiley Blackwell Companion to Religion and Ecology, First Edition. Edited by John Hart.

Consistent with indigenous prophecies, a reawakening to our true human nature is sweeping across both indigenous and non-indigenous societies. For millennia, the wisdom keepers of indigenous societies kept alive the deep wisdom of our traditional indigenous worldview, our understanding of the Original Instructions given to us by the Creator and passed on from generation to generation.

Our network has been working to build indigenous and non-indigenous alliances for developing a common vision of a new paradigm in this world: living in peace with each other and with Mother Earth to ensure harmony with Creation. In order for this to happen, the economy needs to be redefined and reorganized to recognize the ecological limits and vital natural lifecycles of water, air, soil, all of Nature, and all life. The modern world cannot achieve economic sustainability without environmental and economic justice and without a strong environmental ethic that recognizes the human relationship and responsibility to protect the sacredness and integrity of Mother Earth. The future of humankind depends on a new economic and environmental paradigm that recognizes the rights of Mother Earth.

Indigenous peoples are confronting many challenges: dangerous changes in the environment, pollution, extreme weather events, massive energy development, the continued push of economic globalization, and a continuation of Western forms of extracting industrial development, despite the portents of financial collapse and the depletion of species and Mother Earth's natural goods ("resources") around the world.

Fossil fuel development within indigenous territories—land, fresh water, and seas—is increasing. It is business as usual. The petroleum industry and private corporations, with the help of governments and financial institutions, are expanding exploration to find more unconventional fossil fuels and thereby further societies' energy addiction and high consumption levels.

The survival of our indigenous cultures, languages, and communities continues to be threatened and affected by a modern industrialized world that lacks awareness of and respect for the sacredness of Mother Earth. As guardians and caretakers of Mother Earth, we acknowledge and accept our responsibility as indigenous peoples to protect the natural environment, to generate awareness of indigenous traditional ecological knowledge, and to promote models for sustainable development based on our spiritual values.

Climate Change

Rachael Smoker said that "Climate change has provided the perfect disaster capitalism storm: an excuse for expanding corporate ownership and control over the commons."

Indigenous peoples participating in the United Nations Framework Convention on Climate Change (UNFCCC) negotiations and in other UN meetings such as the UN Convention on Biological Diversity understand well her comment. We are in the frontline confronting a power structure that trivializes the importance of indigenous cosmologies, philosophies, and worldviews. Oppressive power structures reside within UN processes. They prop up inequalities found in industrialized countries, the more developed of the developing countries, and the World Bank and other financial institutions.

These powerful actors have economic systems that objectify, commodify, and put a monetary value on land, water, forests, and air that is contrary to indigenous understanding. Indigenous peoples, North and South, are forced into the world market with nothing to negotiate with except the natural goods of Mother Earth that we rely on for our survival.

Historically, numerous attempts have been made to commodify land, food, labor, forests, water, genes, and even ideas (e.g., through the privatization of our traditional knowledge). Carbon trading follows in the footsteps of this history. It turns the sacredness of our Mother Earth's carbon-cycling capacity into property to be bought and sold in a global market. Through this process of creating a new commodity—carbon—Mother Earth's ability and capacity to support a climate conducive to life and human societies is now being seized by or passing into the same corporate hands that are destroying the climate. Carbon trading and carbon offset regimes will not contribute to achieving protection of the Earth's climate. These false solutions entrench and magnify social inequalities in many ways, and do not cut emissions at their source. They promote violation of the sacred, plain and simple.

In June 2012 at the Earth Summit (Rio + 20) the push for a "green economy" was widely promoted as the key to our planet's survival; it became the new buzzword for sustainable development. However, the green economy is nothing more than capitalism of Nature; a perverse attempt by corporations, extractive industries, and governments to cash in on Creation by privatizing, commodifying, and selling the sacred, all forms of life, and land, water, and sky—including the air we breathe, the water we drink, and all the genes, plants, traditional seeds, trees, animals, fish, biological and cultural diversity, ecosystems, and traditional knowledge that make life on Mother Earth possible and enjoyable.

We feel the pain of disharmony when we witness the dishonor of the natural order of Creation and the continued economic colonization and degradation of Mother Earth and all life on her.

The value conflicts between indigenous peoples and the dominant society, and in their respective relationships to the natural world, lie in their differing Creation stories, from which relationships in Creation are learned and experienced. What are known as indigenous Original Instructions are the instructions given by the Creator to our people at the time of Creation. This is woven into our teachings from infancy to youth to adulthood. Original Instructions consist of two components; first, how people are to treat each other; and second, how they are to interact with the rest of Creation.

Respectful Relations, Not Dominating and Destructive Dominion

The basis for what I call the industrialized mindset in the dominant Western society is the Judeo-Christian tradition of "dominion over all things." This means that the world was created for the use of people and that people are to have final say in how it is used. Although it is my understanding that this was not spelled out in the Bible, over time this has come to be interpreted to mean the objectification of the natural world. (I have mentioned this objectification before; further discussion of it is critical for this chapter.)

This colonial industrialized mindset believes that Mother Earth is to be controlled; Nature is to be managed for the comfort of humans. "Mother Earth" becomes depersonalized, humanized into a vague concept of an abstract "Nature." In indigenous peoples' understanding, we are related to the Earth, our Mother, to each other, and to all our relations, all beings: the two-legged people, the four-legged people, the winged people, the finned people, the rooted people.

To provide some context to altering this mindset and promoting care for and living respectfully and relationally within the Creator's creativity, I must talk about the sacred elements of water.

Water: Consciousness, Intelligence, Spirit, and Sacredness

In the Creation stories of indigenous peoples, water plays an integral role. Water has consciousness and intelligence, and should be treated appropriately with this in mind. Water has spirit, and should be engaged spiritually as well as in its physical form.

In direct opposition to the objectification of the natural world in the Western mind, in our indigenous mind water is inexpressibly sacred. The reverence we hold for it is difficult to discuss because of the reticence that indigenous peoples have to exhibit to the world at large our most fundamental and sacred teachings. We have good reason for this caution. We are aware that we are presenting our most precious ways of thinking while we are faced by a power structure that has no respect for any of this and in fact ridicules and minimizes the importance of indigenous cosmologies, philosophies, and worldviews.

In the indigenous view, the Earth is our true mother who gives birth to us and maintains our life through hers. She is the mother of all living things. She is the Mother Earth. Water, her life blood, courses through her body and maintains all life. Our first environment is water. We live in water throughout gestation inside our mother's womb, and our mother then gives birth through water. She maintains our life through her own body, through the milk and water from her own body. From this understanding comes our reverence for water. It is from this comprehension of the totality of Creation that our political positions about water are informed and based. It is impossible to act on one part of Creation without impacting the rest.

Any way of thinking and acting that objectifies, commodifies, or puts a monetary value on land, air, and water is antithetical to indigenous understanding. Yet we are forced into the world market with nothing to negotiate with except our "natural resources." The imposition of these alien values changes the way in which we relate to the environment in which we live. In the United States and Canada, governments and churches have deliberately disrupted the transmission of traditional knowledge from one generation to the next. We often find ourselves in the untenable and impossible position of being financially dependent on our own cultural self-destruction.

Within the indigenous languages lay the full capacity to grasp the minutiae of the science of Creation. Our Creation stories begin with the Creator's origin, awakening, and awareness. We liken this to our own birth, in which water is present at the very beginning. Water is the medium which carries us from the spirit world to the physical world. Mother Earth and our own natural mother have carried the sacred vessel of water from which we come.

Without water, nothing could have come together. Matter could not have come together without moisture. Every part of Creation took part in the creation of physical life. Life could not have come together without water and without spiritual motivation.

Indigenous Traditional Knowledge Confronts Alien Colonial Consciousness

The dynamics of colonialism, which have been internalized by indigenous peoples, unfortunately demand that we accept that as indigenous peoples we are not entitled to our own thinking. All indigenous thought and ways of being were militarized and criminalized, and so many of us are hesitant to share our high consciousness with a society that cannot and will not comprehend it.

Another threatened element of our culture is Indigenous Traditional Knowledge (ITK), developed on Turtle Island on-site. It emerged in context, informed by direct experience of the Creator's interactive presence and Mother Earth's living engagement with indigenous peoples. ITK must be protected from foreign invaders, who are aliens to and "pilgrims" on our territories. Disregarding the teachings of the Creator and Mother Earth, they exploit ITK and manipulate it for purposes other than those for which it was given to us.

From native peoples' "view from the shore" on Turtle Island, when the European invaders came to indigenous lands and territories they brought with them a cosmology so different from our own that we could not comprehend them and they could not comprehend us. The most destructive value that the European invaders imposed is the quantification and objectification of the natural world, expressed by imposing a monetary value on sacred things, replacing communal consciousness and sharing with private property ideology, practices, and laws, all the while committing physical and cultural genocide against indigenous peoples who resisted. They brought with them, too, an assumption that any open land is there for the taking: all they have to do is erect a fence to own it. Soon after they landed, built their colonies, and imposed their governmental structures, they sent out surveyors to all corners of America to plot out every inch of land. Eventually, this led to private and governmental ownership of all lands and waters, justified by colonial laws regulating property rights. The colonizers also dumped their garbage into the water, contaminating the very force that holds and nurtures life.

What does this mean for our relationship with water, Nature, and Mother Earth? The discussion about water translates into the colonial progression that transforms the elements of life into so-called "natural resources," rather than recognize that they are "natural goods" provided by the Creator and Mother Earth to benefit all of us, not some of us, and all living beings. This transformation is at its core about the commodification, the objectification, and the dehumanization of all of our ways of understanding.

For indigenous peoples, the suffering caused by this history is beyond human. One of the residual problems is that now we are in a period when we are just distant enough from the trauma to begin to talk about our own experience.

If the suffering of our indigenous peoples is caused by the disruption and destruction of all that is ours, then it would seem that the way to a strong position in any national or global negotiations about natural goods or the provisions of Nature (erroneously called "resources," as if they were there solely to be extracted and exploited by humankind) would be to strengthen and revitalize our cultural and spiritual identity. No one can claim our traditional knowledge and give permission to others to use it except us. Before we share, we must become clear about it ourselves, and secure within our own knowledge. Before we give anyone else permission to use our knowledge we must claim it first as our own. Ignorance of our sacred teachings about water and Nature, about Creation, is not natural, but a consequence of the Western culture's colonization of our consciousness. That is why many of our communities and nations in the North are prioritizing the revitalization of language and culture as being vital to indigenous thought.

The authority of colonization with the implementation of the Doctrines of Discovery is based on an insane idea of racist superiority. It allows for all lands and territories and all things indigenous to be fair game for the taking. And take they do. This ideology of racial superiority, progress, and entitlement enables a deliberate disregard for the outcome of shortsighted and destructive policies. The indigenous high intelligence of the "Seven Generations" concept, meaning that every decision we make is with the consciousness of how that decision will impact our world and peoples seven generations from now, is absent from the environment, energy, water, social justice, and land policies of the current dominant and dominating "dominion" societies. The precautionary principles developed by science are similar to these indigenous principles about the Seven Generations.

The indigenous worldview recognizes that all Creation is alive and imbued with the intelligence of the Creator, who has put all knowledge of the science of Creation in every single individuated part. Although every atom and particle is individuated, we are all part of an integrated whole. This assumes a caring and loving Creation where all parts of Creation care for all of the other parts. No part is superior. No part has "dominion" over any other part. We were not here to be "stewards" of anything. Rather, we were all created to live in a harmonious, conscious, loving, and intelligent relationship with all other aspects of Creation.

If we are to negotiate from a position of strength, we must start from a position of self-knowledge. Currently, all terms are defined not by indigenous peoples, but by systems that disregard our interests. It is an imbalanced power structure, in which we are always on the defensive.

It is time to change. With the protocols established for indigenous peoples' engagement, and our understanding of our processes for healing from the colonial historical trauma whose impacts continue today, we are at a juncture for sharing our knowledge with the world toward re-evaluating its sacred relationship with Mother Earth. This inseparable relationship between humans and Mother Earth, inherent to indigenous peoples, must be learnt, embraced, and respected by all people for the sake of all of our future generations and all of humanity. Within our environmental and climate justice campaigns, our indigenous network urges humanity to join with us in transforming the social structures, institutions, and power relations that underpin the conditions of oppression and exploitation.

The response to global warming is global democracy for life and for Mother Earth. We need responsible action for humanity: we should not be carbon colonialists who sell the air we breathe and privatize the Earth and sky.

The UNFCCC, Environmental Safeguards, and Human Rights

I participated in the 21st session of the Conference of the Parties (COP 21) of the UN Framework Convention on Climate Change (UNFCCC) in Paris, in December 2015. Marked by the heavy influence of the fossil fuel industry and other corporations, the Paris Agreement did not mention the need to curb extractive energy and set real goals far below those needed to avert a global catastrophe. The Agreement, signed by 196 countries, does acknowledge the global urgency of the climate crisis but ignores the roots of the crisis.

In our IEN critique of the Paris Agreement, a critique shared by the US-based organizations Grassroots for Global Justice and the Climate Justice Alliance, five core concerns are described:

1. The Agreement relies on voluntary rather than mandatory emission cuts; these voluntary cuts do not meet the targets scientists say are necessary to avoid climate catastrophe
2. The Agreement advances pollution-trading mechanisms that allow polluters to purchase offsets and continue to emit extremely dangerous levels of pollution
3. The Agreement relies on false promises and dirty energies that include hydraulic fracturing, nuclear power, agro-fuels, carbon capture and sequestration, and other technological proposals that pose serious ecological and human rights risks
4. The operating text of the Agreement omits any mention of human rights or the rights of indigenous peoples and women
5. The Agreement weakens or strips the rights of reparations owed to the Global South by the Global North

The Paris Agreement fails to address the impending climate crisis. It allows countries to claim reductions through pollution trading schemes; these are written in the Agreement as "results-based payments," rather than requiring actual reductions of pollution emissions at their source. The underlying approach is to create a market for emission credits that allows polluters to continue releasing greenhouse gases if they can produce a certificate attesting that they have contributed toward preventing a similar volume of emissions elsewhere. Thus, they avoid taking action against burning fossil fuels.

The Perils of Reducing Emissions from Deforestation and (Forest) Degradation

The green economy regime puts a monetary price on Nature and creates new derivative markets that will only increase inequality and increase the destruction of Mother Earth. We cannot put the future of Nature and humanity in the hands of financial institutions' speculative mechanisms, such as using forests and agriculture as carbon offsets, which they call Reducing Emissions from Deforestation and (Forest) Degradation (REDD); other market systems of conservation and biodiversity offsets; and payment for environmental and ecological services.

In California, there is growing opposition to the state's Global Warming Solutions Act, AB 32, and its cap-and-trade—carbon offset provisions that would implement a California REDD initiative. Through REDD, the state would use forests in Mesoamerica, the Amazon, Africa, and other subnational "partner jurisdictions" as "sponges" for the carbon pollution of polluting industries such as Chevron and Shell. For communities such as Richmond, California, this only furthers environmental justice issues for people living close to the Chevron refineries who have to endure more pollution in their communities. The refineries cause long-term health problems, including asthma, birth defects, cancer, and depression. REDD prolongs these impacts by making offsets available to these polluting companies, allowing them to avoid reducing their emissions at source. REDD-type and carbon offset projects are already causing human rights violations, land grabs, and environmental destruction. If REDD is implemented worldwide, it may open the floodgates to the biggest land grab of the last 500 years.

Just as historically the Doctrine of Discovery[1] was used to justify the first wave of colonialism by alleging that indigenous peoples did not have souls and that our territories were *terra nullius* (no one's land), now carbon trading and REDD are formulating equally dishonest premises to justify a new wave of colonialization and the privatization of Nature.

Mother Earth is the source of life. She needs to be protected, not regarded and used as a resource to be exploited and commodified as "natural capital." In the words of Herman Daly, father of ecological economics, "There is something fundamentally wrong in treating the Earth as if it were a business in liquidation."

The REDD mechanism provides an example of what is being traded. Within climate negotiations, deforestation has become a global issue. Living forests provide vast areas of carbon sinks that absorb carbon which would otherwise be released into the air and contribute to global warming. When forests are burned or otherwise destroyed, they emit CO_2. The loss of these forests, especially in the Global South, is a major force driving climate change, accounting for roughly a fifth of global greenhouse gas (GHG) emissions. The Paris Agreement approves REDD for implementation despite continued debates on how to make forests fit into a financial carbon market regime. REDD provides no guarantees that it would advance the reduction of the underlying causes and impacts of the loss of forests. These carbon market regimes allow for the privatization of the carbon in the forests. Tree plantations, wetlands, agriculture, and soils are supposed to be used as sponges for mitigating GHGs, but such provisions allow governments and polluting corporations to offset their carbon and other GHGs to meet emission reduction targets rather than cut emissions at their source.

Offsets and pollution trading have a double-edged impact. In the Global North, they give polluters in the industrialized countries cover so they can continue to poison the air and water in the communities living alongside refineries, coal mines, and fracking wells. In the Global South, including Mexico, these projects fail to secure the rights of forest-dependent communities, peasants, and indigenous peoples to their lands. Even if land titles are recognized on paper, implementation of REDD projects that generate carbon credits is likely to lead to these people losing control of their lands, land evictions, and restrictions on entering forested areas. Current safeguard mechanisms, as developed, have no guarantees of being implemented at the national or subnational areas of developing countries.

Tradable REDD credits are a form of property rights, property title—privatization. Those owning the credit do not need to own the land or the trees, but they do own the right to decide how that land will be used. They also usually have the contractual right to monitor what is taking place on the land and request access to the territory whenever they choose as long as they own the carbon credit.

With the Paris Agreement linked to the free-market economy, carbon trading and other market mechanisms will allow polluters to profit, and the impacts of climate change will worsen. The Paris Agreement will be a crime against humanity and Mother Earth. It will allow business-as-usual: the continued extraction, production, and combustion of fossil fuels, and the continued exploitation of "natural resources": land, agricultural products, genetically engineered (GE) trees, and aquatic resources. If the Paris COP21 talks had seriously addressed climate change, there would have been a discussion about how to keep fossil fuels underground. This would have protected and upheld indigenous rights, and peoples' territorial rights would be respected now and in the future. Instead, the hegemonic and colonial powers continue to harm the people who are the least responsible for current and historical pollution levels and who suffer the most from the impacts of pollution.

> The Paris Agreement is a trade agreement, nothing more. It promises to privatize, commodify and sell forested lands as carbon offsets in fraudulent schemes such as REDD+ projects. These offset schemes provide financial laundering mechanisms for developed countries to launder their carbon pollution on the backs of the Global South. Case-in-point, the United States' climate change plan includes 250 million megatons to be absorbed by oceans and forest offset markets. Essentially, those responsible for the climate crisis not only get to buy their way out of compliance but they also get to profit from it as well. (Alberto Saldamando, human and indigenous rights expert and attorney)

The mechanisms cited have given way to a "financialization of Nature" process. This separates and quantifies the Earth's cycles and functions (carbon, water, biodiversity), turning them into "units" to be sold in financial and speculative markets. When governments establish legal frameworks to set these markets in place, they also provide the financial infrastructure for negotiating financial instruments, by using derivatives, hedge and equity funds, among others. While financial markets have a growing influence over economic policies, the financialization of Nature goes further than privatization—it empowers financial markets run by bankers, intermediaries, and others far removed from the effects on the ground: their priority is profit-making, not the wellbeing of Mother Earth, indigenous peoples, humankind in general, and all living beings.

The Paris Agreement expands free-market (free for whom?) logic into all cycles and functions of the Earth. This includes the further financialization of Mother Earth, a process that is advancing rapidly. Banks, conservationist non-governmental organizations

(NGOs), the World Bank, and transnational corporations stand to gain more rights and power over Nature and Mother Earth. However, the architecture behind the process is cloaked in secrecy, difficult to research, and complex to understand. Many of these decisions are made behind closed doors in boardrooms to which indigenous peoples and other frontline communities are not invited. The complexities that are being built must be exposed in order to unmask the architecture of the financialization of Nature and provide the knowledge needed to give people the power to dismantle the structure.

Consistent with indigenous prophecies, a reawakening to our true human nature is sweeping through both indigenous and non-indigenous societies. For millennia, the wisdom-keepers of indigenous societies kept alive, and in some areas revitalized, the deep wisdom of our traditional indigenous worldview, passed down by our understanding of the Original Instructions.

Many concepts and proposals already available contain the key elements needed to build systemic alternatives. Examples include Buen Vivir (living well), recognition of indigenous peoples' territories, indigenous peoples' tenure of and title to land, the rights of Mother Earth and Nature, food sovereignty, rights to water, prosperity without growth, deglobalization, and duties to and the rights of future generations.

This inseparable relationship between humans and the Earth must be respected for the sake of all life, future generations, and the people of the world. We urge all humanity to join with us in transforming the social structures, institutions, and power relations that underpin our deprivation, oppression, and exploitation.

Long-term solutions require us to turn away from current paradigms and insidious ideologies centered on pursuing economic growth, corporate profits, and personal wealth accumulation as the primary engines of social wellbeing. The transitions will inevitably be toward societies that can equitably adjust to reduced levels of production and consumption, and increasingly localized systems of economic organization that recognize, honor, and are bounded by the limits of Nature, and support the Universal Declaration on the Rights of Mother Earth.

Industrialized countries must focus on new economies that are governed by the limits and boundaries of ecological sustainability, focused on the carrying capacities of our sacred Mother Earth.

To restore the Earth's balance, we need to shift from a philosophy of dominion over Nature to a relationship of understanding Mother Earth, respect for natural laws, and love for the beauty of the creative female energy of Mother Earth.

Earth jurisprudence recognizes that we have only one Mother Earth. We must stand together, in solidarity, to protect her.

Note

1 Papal bulls of the fifteenth century gave Christian explorers the right to claim lands they "discovered" and lay claim to those lands for their Christian monarchs. Any land that was not inhabited by Christians was available to be "discovered," claimed, and exploited. If the "pagan" inhabitants could be converted, they might be spared. If not, they could be enslaved. The Discovery Doctrine is a concept of public international law expounded by the US Supreme

Court in a series of decisions, first laid down in *Johnson v. M'Intosh* (1823). The Doctrine was Chief Justice John Marshall's explanation of the way in which colonial powers laid claim to newly discovered lands during the Age of Discovery. Under it, title to newly discovered lands lay with the government whose subjects discovered new territory. The Doctrine has been primarily used to support decisions invalidating or ignoring aboriginal possession of land in favor of colonial or postcolonial governments (http://www.doctrineofdiscovery.org).

CHAPTER 34

Common Commons

Social and Sacred Space

John Hart

Introduction

Consciousness exists in a dynamic cosmos. In this universe, the consciousness of living beings is present in an evolving world. The Creating Spirit envisioned and brought into being in seminal form all biota (living beings) and abiota (non-living beings), with freedom to develop in responsible relationship with each other. Human consciousness on Earth developed once humankind had evolved from its primate ancestors over millennia, after more than three billion years of geological history.

In the Earth commons within the cosmos commons humanity was entrusted with a particular responsibility to care respectfully for living beings and for the non-living context of their existence. Humans were not gifted with the Earth, or placed above and over the Earth and Earth's creatures. The Creator's trustees were not to be lords over Creation or stewards—managers—of Creation. Creation "worked" well for billions of years before humans evolved and came on the scene, and continued to do so when and where humankind did not interfere with its processes; it did not need to be controlled or managed.

Select segments of humanity did not act like "images of God" as they were instructed in the Genesis narratives. In the first Creation story, God looked at everything God had made, not just humankind, and saw that it was "very good." Human beings, as God's "images," were supposed to see as God did that all Creation is "very good." Instead, many violated the trust they were given. They exploited and devastated God's Earth, divided the Earth into nations and private property, and competed with each other to acquire the Earth's land, water, air, and natural goods that had been created for their and other living beings' use, not abuse, to meet their respective needs. Some communities, in particular indigenous communities, did retain their sense of responsibility for

The Wiley Blackwell Companion to Religion and Ecology, First Edition. Edited by John Hart.

Mother Earth, lived communally, and shared the goods they found so that they could meet the needs of each and all.

One select group, the exploiters, often elevated greed to a virtue with their ideology of individualism become selfishness and acquisitiveness, as expressed today especially in capitalism. The other group, the caretakers, who sometimes saw themselves as relatives of other life and children of Mother Earth, had the primary virtues of compassion and sharing. Few individuals fitted exclusively into either group. Some among the exploiters had a change of consciousness and conduct to become, at least in part, caretakers; some among the caretakers were drawn from their customary communities to become, at least in part, exploiters. The tension between the groups continues today.

A pressing question of our time is, "Will humankind acknowledge, accept, and act on our responsibilities in the common Earth commons that is our home?" An affirmative response would mean that the Earth's land, water, and all natural goods would be shared equitably so that everyone's needs were met, all biota respected and given sufficient habitat for their survival and wellbeing, and the Earth would be restored to health once again. A negative response would mean completion of an imperiled Earth's ecological destruction and environmental devastation; a desolate Earth; and life driven into extinction.

Humankind needs to undergo socioeconomic and socioecological conversion for its own survival and wellbeing, as well as the survival and wellbeing of the Earth and the entire community of living beings. It is still possible. and especially possible if leaders in religion, science, and social sciences, and government officials, politicians, and business people, work together on common ground—philosophical and physical—to make it so. The likelihood of this depends on the extent to which a core, committed community accepts and acts as if all life exists in a common commons composed of communal sacred and social space.

Sacred Space, Sacred Commons

The creative and creating *Logos*, the living Word, is the alpha and omega by and through which the dynamic and evolving cosmos as a whole—and all the stars, planets, asteroids, and other cosmic entities—came into being and toward which all being is invited, guided, and led by the divine Spirit. The biotic beings of the cosmos have come into being and gradually evolved through cooperation and competition, during the 13.8 billion years estimated to be the lifespan of the cosmos. Stars, planets, and whole galaxies have coalesced, evolved, and disappeared during that time. The stellar cycle of being continues in space and time in an autopoietic (self-organizing) mode since the singular beginning of the universe. At that moment, divine creativity set parameters of and fixed characteristics and physical laws for being. (These were later discerned by scientists: in the Enlightenment, some said that they were "thinking God's thoughts after Him.") Entities and energies were provided freedom to dynamically interact and for life to evolve when it emerged.

The stellar birth-to-death process is replicated time and again as new stars form and are born in stellar "nurseries" visible through powerful telescopes. The evolution process, too, involves the birth of new species when a world's environment can accept and nurture them. Over long or short periods, species may gradually lose their niche and become extinct, or be deprived of their niche or killed *en masse* by humankind, and made extinct by human actions. Alternatively, species may adapt and readapt, either where they live or by migration.

The cosmos emanates from and is immanented by the creating Spirit: it is *creatio ex Deo* or *creatio ex divinitate* (not *creatio ex nihilo*, Creation from nothing). Therefore, it is *sacred space*. The cosmos—the universe—is a sacred commons, a social space for all biota, known and unknown. It is sacred space in the panentheistic reality of all integral being immanented by the Creator Spirit. The cosmos is a sacred commons because it is a divine creation, permeated by divine being, and ever-engaged with divine being in integrated, interdependent, and interrelational integral being, the origin and totality of all being-becoming.

The Earth is a commons. It is shared in common by all members of the community of life (the biotic community), who live as part of a relational community of the Earth and all biota, in which abiota provide the material setting for biotic existents.

The Earth is a sacred commons. As a sacred space, the Earth emerged from the seeds of divine creativity; it came into existence some 4.5 billion years ago, almost 10 billion years after the singular primordial explosion from which the cosmos began. After another billion years or so, life emerged on Earth. (During the billions of years of the existence of the cosmos, which is more than three times as old as the Earth, life may have begun and evolved elsewhere in the universe—even to become intelligent life.)

The Earth is a shared sacred space, and a social space, as the shared home of all biota, a place of ongoing interactions between biota and abiota, living and non-living being.

Earth is a common commons, a world whose wellbeing requires that it be shared equitably by its biota living in balance, all of whom are members of an interdependent, integrated, evolving relational community.

Living Temples: Biota and Earth

A temple is a place in which the divine Being in whom the whole cosmos exists is particularly present and accessible. In the belief and minds of the individual believer and the community of the faithful who worship in a temple building, this is especially true or solely true in their holy place. Here, worship of and gratitude to the Spirit are often expressed in culture-specific rituals and place-specific symbols and religious artefacts; a representative of the clergy ordinarily presides. Dialogic engagement between the Spirit and the temple faithful occurs.

Temples are holy places; in a temple building people experience a special sense of divine Presence. Temple buildings are set apart to provide a dedicated sacred space that temporarily separates worshipers from the hustle and bustle and distractions of everyday life at home or work, so that they can focus on spirituality and the Spirit. The faithful pray, often in a focused, formal way, in temples; some worshipers experience then or thereafter what they understand to be a response to their prayers.

Before dedicated temples were built, people worshiped on mountains, in forests, by lakes, and at other outdoor sites, often without designated spiritual leaders. When building a temple in Jerusalem was discussed, some people objected: they thought that people would lose their wilderness association with and experiences of God. But King Solomon and others who wanted to have a special place prevailed. Later, at the dedication of the temple Solomon acknowledged people's concerns and fears about the Most High being viewed as contained in a single space. He declared: "But will God indeed dwell on the earth? Even heaven and the highest heaven cannot contain you, much less this house that I have built!" (1 Kings 8: 27). Eventually, though, the people's fears proved justified as temple-dedicated clergy, prophets, and the common people eradicated the shrines and abandoned most other worship sites in Nature outside of Jerusalem, and had formal religious ceremonies only in the temple in Jerusalem.

When related to the temple conflicts and construction, Jesus's words to the woman in Samaria are particularly intriguing. When she said that the Samaritans and the Jews have their respective places of worship, Jesus replied, "The hour is coming, and is now here, when the true worshipers will worship the Father in spirit and truth, for the Father seeks such as these to worship him. God is spirit, and those who worship him must worship in spirit and truth" (John 4: 23–24).

In the Christian Scriptures, Paul's first letter to the people of Corinth states that people are temples of God in whom God lives: "Do you not know that you are God's temple and that God's Spirit God dwells in you?" (1 Cor. 3: 16, NRSV).

All living beings are, to some extent, temples. They are immanented by the divine Presence and can inspire prayerful appreciation for the gifts and goods they provide for each other and for humankind. The heavens and Earth and all beings on the Earth proclaim the glory and creativity of God. The beauty of flowers, the flight of an eagle, a spectacular sunset can impact people in this way.

In an extension of Paul's teaching, it could be said that people are mobile temples and carry potential awareness of and access to the divine Presence wherever they are and go. Their words and actions can inspire people to be faithful to the Spirit. Consequently, temple and faithful could relate responsibly to other people, the Earth, and all living beings. The Hindu word *Namasté* expresses this well: "The Spirit in me greets the Spirit in you; the Spirit in me greets the spirit in you; my spirit greets your spirit; the Spirit in you greets the Spirit in me; the Spirit in you greets the spirit in me; your spirit greets my spirit." A spontaneous spiritual bond is activated in the spiritual dimension of being in which we both share. This overcomes religious, cultural, ethnic, class, gender, and any other characteristics that might otherwise cause friction or distrust between us.

In Revelation, the last book in the Christian Scriptures, the visionary says that in the "new heaven and the new earth" there are no buildings in which to worship: "I saw no temple in the city, for its temple is the Lord God the Almighty and the Lamb" (Rev. 21: 22). In the holy city, the new Jerusalem, God is the Temple.

The Earth is God's Temple; God's Spirit is immanent in God's Earth Temple. The Earth temple cannot contain God, but can mediate and be revelatory of the divine Presence.

The Earth has been described in terms of a human construct, a temple building in which the Spirit dwells. It is perhaps more appropriate to consider temple Earth as a divine construct, the micro-reality of the sacred Earth in the macro-reality of the sacred cosmos. The human-constructed temple building, then, is understood to be a reflection and appropriation of the divine-created sacred Earth temple.

A human-constructed temple is the Earth understood in human terms through human eyes conditioned by urban life, formal, institutional religion, and human architecture. This combination of factors can generate the design of a building constructed and viewed as a sacred space, and formally dedicated as such through a human-originating ceremony. Church liturgies might be regarded as reflections of, and foster participation in, the divine liturgy that continually *takes place* (literally) on Earth.

When the temple–Earth perspective is shifted, a temple is like the Earth. The Earth is immanented by and mediates the Creator Spirit and is a locus of focused engagement with the Spirit, expressing the divine–human relation and engagement in the open air outside of human constructs. A forest is not "like a cathedral"; rather, a cathedral is like a forest. The first and universal divine–human/Spirit–spirit engagement occurs in Nature, not in buildings. The Earth is the first place of worship, a place presenced by the Spirit billions of years prior to the evolution of humankind and the eventual development of buildings, including temples. The Earth is the first temple. In it all creatures praise God, as noted in Ps. 148 and in the Canticle of Creation of St. Francis which rephrases and complements that psalm.

When the places of worship of diverse religions are viewed as representations of the Earth, the ultimate mediation of the Spirit, it becomes possible for people of all religions to worship together: a temple is like the Earth, a mosque is like the Earth, a synagogue is like the Earth, a church is like the Earth. People from diverse traditions can worship together ecumenically, meaningfully, and spiritually outside of buildings. On Earth, the first place of worship, social space and sacred space are one.

Sacred Place in the Sacred Commons

A decade ago, I began to explore the concept and meaning of sacred place. I came to realize that "a *sacred* place is a place made holy by an active and relational divine Presence. Creation is sacred because it is the dynamic realization of divine imagination and the locus of divine immanence" (Hart, 2006, xiii). Further,

> All places are sacred because all creation is present in and to the Creator. Since the transcendent-immanent Spirit simultaneously is in creation and is not limited by space or time, every place is a sacred place. But the sacrality of a place is visible only to those who use their physical and spiritual eyes to see beyond the immediately apparent. Then they participate in all of reality in its spiritual, social, and personal dimensions. Spiritual vision enables people to experience the sacred presence of the immanent-transcendent Spirit who permeates Earth and the cosmos at large. Creation mediates the Creator... While creation mediates—reveals—the Creator in different dimensions of reality, spiritual vision provides a deeper encounter with the Spirit than what eyes perceive.

Currently, people take little time—having eyes they do not see, having ears they do not hear—to be immersed in the Earth and thereby in the Spirit. Cell phones, head phones, and mobile CD players distract them from the beauty of the being in which they are immersed and deprive them of the experience of the deep community that surrounds them.

Social Commons

In some educational institutions, a "commons" is the dining hall where students and faculty gather to eat together. This communal partaking of food for nourishment is an apt image for acknowledging that the Earth as a whole and in its bioregions provide the necessities of life for all life. Dining hall food symbolizes all plants growing wild in Nature's fields, agricultural crops cultivated by farmers, and people-prepared products available in supermarkets.

The "commons" dining room replicates indoors agricultural fields outdoors which provide crops for food and nourishment.

Commonize and Communalize the Commons

The commons, in order best to become a common commons, should be commonized (or communized; see "communize" in Hart, 2006, 191–194), communalized, or both. Extensive private property in land is a major cause of widespread poverty and oppression around the world. Conversion of private property in land to commonly shared property would reduce and even eliminate poverty and oppression.

Regarding communized or commonized land,

> To commonize the commons would be to complement the biblical idea of a periodic redistribution of land [which was supposed to happen in the Jubilee Year, every 50 years] with a just, ongoing redistribution of the land into cooperative holdings, along with associated water sources and water rights, to benefit the common good. This would require a reevaluation of patterns and practices of land ownership and laws and policies related to them, in light of the common good and the needs of the commons. (Hart, 2006, 192)

A commons that is commonized is a place that is shared in common by a local or regional community, all of whom have equal access to it and to the natural goods it has available. Commonized agricultural land might be worked as one farm for which all the shareholders have responsibilities for its operation and receive a share of what it produces. Or commonized agricultural land might be worked in individual shares of the commonly held land. In both cases the land is common property, the property of a specific community, not private or privatized property.

A commons that is communalized is a place that is shared in common and worked in common, whose type of production and harvest products are decided by consensus at shareholder gatherings in a local or regional community. It, too, is common property owned by a specific community.

In both cases, shareholders determine acquisition of new common property or disposition of existing common property.

Commonize means to make common or share in common; communalize means that and more the common property is owned by a commune, or by a community that is part of a community of communities, or the community of communities as a whole. Shareholders—community members—jointly share equitably in the commonized commons.

In order to bring about commonization or communalization:

> Individual and corporate land ownership could be redistributed into cooperative holdings through a progressive land tax [advocated by, among others, Thomas Jefferson] and progressive inheritance laws, and provision of low-interest loans to actual and potential owner-operators of family farms who want to form a single cooperative from their individual properties. Naturally occurring essential goods ("resources") such as oil would become public property; their extraction would be licensed to responsible, locally owned corporations and cooperatives so that the community, and not a handful of outside investors, would benefit from the profits that are currently accruing to energy corporations and set just rates for residential, commercial and industrial consumers. Agricultural, industrial, and commercial cooperatives would be initiated and maintained. Water, a natural right, human right, and common good, would be publicly owned, and conserved and retained for the common good. National, state, and local community parks, forests, and waterways would be retained in the public domain for public use and as reminders of ongoing divine presence, power, and providence. People who prioritize private property over community needs and social responsibility object to the commonization of Earth's land. (cf. Hart, 2006, 192)

The commonization and communalization of land benefits communities and individuals as members of communities. Initiating and implementing the process would shift properties, priorities, and perspectives from current selfish individualism to self- and community-benefiting practices.

> Humans are part of the natural world and are responsible to God and to community to care for it and use it wisely and sparingly. Humans may use Earth's land and goods to meet their needs, but may not abuse Earth's land and goods to satisfy their wants; sufficiency should have primacy over satiety. Private property is a civil good that must be integrated with public property as a common good. Common needs take precedence over individual wants, and property holdings—whether in land, water, or any of Earth's goods, including energy sources—are all part of divine creation and are intended to meet community needs before their individual appropriation. (Hart, 2006, 193)

Over the centuries, major historical figures have advocated greater sharing of property—in both land and goods—so that the needs of all could be met. The biblical Jubilee Year required the redistribution of agricultural lands that had been sold since the last Jubilee to their original owners or their descendants (see Lev. 25; Hart, 2006, 181–198). Later representatives of this type of thinking include Thomas Aquinas in the thirteenth century, Thomas Jefferson and Thomas Paine, American revolutionaries and revolutionary thinkers in the eighteenth century, and José María Arizmendiarrieta, founder of the highly successful Mondragón Cooperative Movement in the Basque Country, who serves here as a representative of other advocates of cooperatives in the twentieth century.

In his *Summa Theologica* discussion of the Seventh Commandment prohibiting theft, Aquinas states that by the natural law, a reflection of divine law, all property is in common. People developed the practice of private property for social stability; it became part of positive law or civil law. In times when and places where people lack the necessities of life, all property reverts to common property; the natural law takes precedence over positive law. So, for example, a malnourished peasant whose basic needs are not provided by the lord of the manor might go quietly at night to the lord's barns to find food. This is not theft, Aquinas says: since the property needed (in this case, food) is now common property because of need, the peasant is not taking the lord's property, he is taking his own. Similarly, if the peasant cannot provide what a hungry neighbor needs, he might take food from the barn for that purpose. In Aquinas's thought, taking needed goods is prioritized over respecting private property.

In 1776, two starkly contrasting documents emerged on opposite sides of the Atlantic: the *Declaration of Independence* from the 13 British colonies in the Americas and *The Wealth of Nations* by philosopher and economic thinker Adam Smith. Jefferson wrote the *Declaration* and was a leading proponent of its message. He urged secession from England to benefit the common people of the colonies. He urged too, when independence was achieved, taxation to promote a nation of small farmers, whom he considered the backbone of democracy. Smith, by contrast, advocated for protection of the wealthy and rejected government policies that taxed the wealthy and business owners to help the poor. He declared that an "invisible hand" would help the poor. However, in the more than three centuries since Smith's claim, the poor have not experienced such compassionate concern from the wealthy.

Paine, for his part, advocated progressive taxation to redistribute land. In *The Rights of Man, Part Second* (1792) he decried poverty, said that there should be a limit to property, and declared that the wealth of vast estates is a "prohibitable luxury" if it exceeds what is necessary to support a family. In *Agrarian Justice* (1796) he stated that the Earth was originally "common property," that humans did not make the Earth, and that the one who did, the "Creator of the earth," did not open a land office from which to issue deeds of title.[1]

José María Arizmendiarrieta founded the Mondragón Cooperative Movement in Spain's Basque Country. He sought to put into practice papal social teaching on social justice, particularly as expressed by Leo XIII in *Rerum Novarum* (1891), the first social encyclical, and Pius XI in *Quadressimo Anno* (1941). Mondragón was highly successful in developing more than 100 cooperatives. It presents a fine example of cooperatives, which are extant around the world; they are, to some extent, the "best of both worlds" of competing economic systems: they are owned by their workers, a form of private property (as in capitalism), but their benefits are equitably distributed among all members (as in socialism).[2]

Native peoples who lived in the Americas had no concept of private property before the arrival of European explorers and European settlements. In their tradition, Mother Earth could not be owned. She provided land and natural goods for people's use. She was to be respected. Only what was needed was to be taken from her bounty. The voices of traditional Indians in the Americas have been heard since the late twentieth century through groups such as the American Indian Movement, the International Indian Treaty Council (the first native peoples' organization recognized and accredited to the United Nations as a non-governmental organization, it initiated discussions of and participated in the development and dissemination of the United Nations *Declaration on the Rights of Indigenous Peoples*, 2007),[3] and the Indigenous Environmental Network. The US Constitution is based in part on the governance of the Haudenosaunee (the "people of the longhouse") in what is now the US northeast (other people call them the Six Nations). Scholars such as William Cronon, in *Changes in the Land: Indians, Colonists, and the Ecology of New England*, and the various authors in Chief Oren Lyons and John Mohawk, *Exiled in the Land of the Free*, document this well.

These highly abbreviated examples are provided to plant the seeds of and a foundation for efforts to communalize the commons, to break up large landholdings and redistribute them to a multitude of responsible new owner-operators, and to democratize into public ownership for public benefit oil, gas, and other natural goods.

Space as Sacred Commons

Poets through the ages have expressed and stimulated insights into humans' present and potential cosmic consciousness. Their ideas can be helpful not only in exploring the cosmos and expanding consciousness, but also in exploring the Earth and expanding cultural consciousness, appreciation, and acceptance. Among the latter is Phillis Wheatley. Her poem "Imagination" (1773) is an inspiration for daring to think beyond cultural and spatial (geographic or planetary) limitations and become consciously engaged with other worlds.

Wheatley celebrated the role of the imagination in our lives as she imagined traveling to new places on a mental, not physical, journey. Addressing a personified Imagination, She observed:

> We on thy pinions can surpass the wind,
> And leave the rolling universe behind;
> From star to star the mental optics rove,
> Measure the skies, and range the realms above.
> There in one view we grasp the mighty whole,
> Or with new worlds amaze th' unbounded soul.[4]

Wheatley wrote "Imagination" five years before she became a freed slave. She was rare among slaves: she had been secretly and illegally taught to read and write by her owners when they realized that she was an exceptional child. She became a creative, insightful poet whose works were published by, among others, her contemporary admirer Thomas Paine.

Today, more than two centuries after Wheatley's (ethereal, in multiple material and symbolic ways) imaginative poem was written, the universe is perceived and pondered in very different ways. While she imagined a mental journey leaving the universe to travel among distant stars, people in the twenty-first century can project, plan for, and participate in an actual physical journey in spacecraft among Exo-Earth worlds. In a complementary journey, people can similarly leave their culturally and geographically defined place: mentally, through books and films and television travel documentaries; materially, through moving elsewhere for professional or personal reasons; and meta-materially, by creatively thinking and courageously activating their thoughts and dreams by daring to explore another culture or cultures, and to dwell, at least temporarily if not permanently, among diverse people(s), and engage their thinking.

In terms of twenty-first-century travel throughout the universe,

> Humankind expects to roam the cosmos not only in imagination, through "mental optics." This we do still, but now our minds are capable of going beyond just imagining roaming the cosmos, since our eyes enable us to roam in actuality in what we see through optical telescopes, for example, the Hubble, Kepler, and forthcoming Webb telescopes, and hear through radio telescopes, such as the Allen array in California. Their technologically engineered and enhanced optics take us where no one on Earth has ever gone before. We "range" in our imagination today stimulated by scientific data and theory, and by literary works that include imaginative science fiction. As our technology has progressed so, too, have our abilities to see farther and journey further. While currently we travel only to the moon as exploring humans and to Mars through human-manufactured machines, we expect to go beyond, at first through robots but then in person as a species: to space outside the solar system's chaotic boundary bubble, where Voyager vehicles now traverse places billions of Earth miles from our solar center. We surmount the pull of gravity and surpass the winds of Earth, and envision—and begin to experience through telescopes and technology—leaving behind the "rolling universe." We dream of—and construct craft to—rove "from star to star." In aspiring to such journeys, we begin to develop new modes of interplanetary and interstellar travel no longer bound by previously known or theorized laws of physics.
>
> Wheatley writes reflectively that we might "grasp the mighty whole" in our imagination; current science provides ways to understand the integral being of the cosmos in all its complexity and yet its current incomprehensibility, in greater depth and with greater clarity than we can imaginatively conceive. Future science will carry such exploration further and deeper. We recognize as we travel in both our mental and material exploratory journeys that the "whole" might not ever be understood completely because of cosmic complexity, distance, and time. (cf. Hart, 2013, 404)

When we experience different Earth cultures and exo-Earth worlds, our "unbounded soul" will continue to be "amazed" by the new worlds, once only imagined, that we find—conceptually and concretely, imaginatively and materially, speculatively and actually—on Earth and in the heavens.

In cultural and geographical explorations people can see the humanity that they share with all other peoples, celebrate cultural and geographical diversity and differences, and become accustomed to adapting to or from distinct peoples, and sharing with them the culture and persona they carry with them on their journey.

When the Earth's diverse human communities and individuals come together conscientiously and compassionately, and collaborate as one, the resulting interrelated human Earth community can communally envision and "grasp the mighty whole" of all human life and thought. This will provide human community consciousness common ground, not only to unify humankind on Earth, but to take up residence in distinct places on cosmic common ground, perhaps relating to other intelligent species. To be a "good neighbor" elsewhere in the universe, humankind on Earth must first put its own house in order—develop the consciousness and conduct needed to conserve and care for its Earth home—and take into unimaginable space its newly acquired and lived attitudes and actions. Then, humanity will experience in breadth and depth its "unbounded soul" when it encounters, experiences, and is enlightened by the wonders of Exo-Earth environments (cf. Hart, 2013, 405).

Social Space, Social Commons

Earth is a social space, a shared commons, a shared place. It cannot long endure if endless conflicts exist between the haves and the have-nots. There is a sufficiency of natural goods (but not a sufficiency of "resources") to meet every human's needs, but not the greed of a dominant few. Nor is the social space sufficient to meet the needs of other living beings if it is satisfying the unlimited claims and greed of humankind alone. Just as in biological interactions a balance develops in predator–prey relationships, in competition over limited earth space on Earth a balance should be fostered to counter the natural goods acquisition and consolidation of a small segment of humanity, such that all people's and all biota's needs are met. The social commons is shared space, a biota reserve rather than a human preserve: "The *Earth commons* is Earth as a whole, in which ecosystems are globally related and integrated. Earth has integrity in itself, in the integrated workings of its basic elements and events, and Earth is a commons for others as it nourishes all peoples and all living creatures" (Hart, 2006, xvii).

Earth is a social commons because humans are social beings. This is well expressed in the African concept of *Ubuntu*, "I am because we are," elaborated by Archbishop Desmond Tutu, Nobel Peace laureate.

Other species are social beings, too. The social lives of whales, elephants, gorillas, wolves, eagles, and ants, among other species, have been studied in depth for decades. Scientists have established, from direct observation in the field, that species other than humankind are intelligent, compassionate, self-reflective, and family-oriented; and species live in communities, feel pain, make moral judgments, and use tools, all of which were once supposed to be exclusively human traits.

Interpersonal Social Relations

Existential philosopher, Jewish thinker, and mystic Martin Buber (1878–1965), in his classic *I–Thou* on interpersonal encounters between subjects (I–Thou) or between subject–object (I–It), describes contrasting modes of interacting with and relating to others.

The I–Thou and I–it relations are not only person-to-person; they are also person-to-other living beings, and person-to-God. The I–Thou intersubjectivity should be extended to the relation of person–Earth. Most people see the Earth as an "it," not as a "thou." It is understood to have only instrumental value as if it exists solely to be a background for human lives and events, and provides only for human needs and wants—and not even all humans' needs. The Earth's intrinsic being, from which as a planet it provides natural goods to meet the needs of all living beings, is rejected or ignored. Indigenous peoples' Mother Earth becomes Western individuals' and communities' earth, lower case e instead of upper case, making the planet share its name with the word for soil trodden underfoot. Humankind must come to understand the Earth as subject, not object, and strive to live on and with the Earth in an I–Thou relation. Inter- and intra-biota relations might be pondered in a similar manner.

Injustices in the human community might be understood, and rightly so, to result from humans' relating to other humans as "it." The current Western economic system justifies individualism and acquisitiveness based on personal and corporate greed, which harms both individuals and communities. In *Paths in Utopia*, Buber discusses the types of social arrangements that would be most conducive to human well-being. He favors "a rebirth of the commune... An organic commonwealth ... will never build itself up out of individuals but only out of small and ever smaller communities: a nation is a community to the degree that it is a community of communities ... By the new communes—they might equally well be called the new Co-operatives—I mean the subjects of a changed economy... The era of advanced Capitalism has broken down the structure of society..." The social structure in a consociation of communities "is based on one of society's eternal human needs ... the need of man to feel his own house as a room in some greater, all embracing structure" (Buber, 1958, 139–140).

Humankind in Space

Dialogic relationships are possible between the Earth's cultures and other worlds' contexts through trans-contextual and trans-temporal contacts between places, and through space and time. The question might rightly arise here, "Why think about and be concerned about exo-Earth matters at this moment in history, when racism is rampant, Earth is in danger of ecological catastrophe, the poor are getting poorer, species are being extincted, and indigenous peoples are targeted to be victims of physical and cultural genocide?" Precisely because people say, in acknowledging how humankind has caused social and ecological destruction and devastation on Earth, they "will do better in space than they have done on Earth," it begs the question: "Why wait until some nebulous future time and place to do what should be done now and here?" Envisioning responsible human consciousness and conduct could—should—cause people to similarly envision the Earth no longer being drastically harmed by humankind, but continually being dramatically helped by humankind to recover from prior excesses. Earth as "Thou" would be cared for, not cursed by, human actions. Conscientious consideration of the present state of the planet would catalyze a consciousness and stimulate creative and creating conduct that brings responsible care home to the Earth in the present from its projected space-based future provision of care for the Earth, care for all biota, and care for human communities.

The recent achievements in space theory and technology, and the construction of space satellites, planetary rovers, and spacecraft, catalyzed awareness that we might be on the brink of startling discoveries. These might prompt psychological, social, spiritual, and ideological crises, and challenge prevailing ethical, economic, ecological, and ecclesial ideas and practice. Alternatively, they might stimulate profound thinking and creativity. A dialogic relationship might be prompted between present and distant places and present and future time. People might consider, for example, how their awareness that humankind is destroying its home planet by ecological devastation could lead them, rather than to say, "We'll do better in a future world discovered in space," to theorize a better home in space, and then consider: "Why wait for a future time and place? Why is it, or why is it not, possible to work in the present to make the idealized place a reality?" Envisioning how this might be done and what steps might or must be taken to make this a reality would improve current socioecological awareness and action, thereby mitigating harm and providing insights and tools to construct and conserve a new home.

We are thinking stardust. We are the cosmos become reflective in an Earth locus, 13.8 billion years after the Day without Yesterday (in Georges LeMaître's words), the "Big Bang" from which the universe as we know it came into being. We aspire to travel round our solar system and then beyond. (Concurrently, some people's curiosity might stimulate them to consider if there are other intelligent beings—extraterrestrial intelligent life—exploring space.)

As we think about what we might find, and project into space what we know about the Earth, we might do what poet William Blake suggests in "Auguries of Innocence": "To see a world in a grain of sand/And a heaven in a wild flower,/Hold infinity in the palm of your hand/And eternity in an hour."[5] In "Auguries," Blake prompts people, in this oft-quoted verse, to understand the world and experience time in a way that goes well beyond ordinary ways of perception and thoughtful consideration. Seeing a world in a grain of sand suggests pondering the possible origins of the grain and, in seeking its past, come to see it in its present with all its relationality, and thereby being able to project future possibilities for and paths to a new Earth commons. Seeking such an understanding and experience in travel around the globe among diverse cultures, and into space among diverse worlds, could provoke and provide a profound passage from material reality to meta-material reality. Materiality would be viewed with different eyes and temporality would be extended into different realms of being, and on into infinity.

We share with all beings interrelated in the integral being of our universe a common origin from which we have evolved respectively in different ways, places, and cosmic time, the "stardust" that burst forth in seminal form from the Singularity, from whose primordial explosion and expansion we have all emerged in space and time.

Common Commons

Emeritus Harvard biologist and Pulitzer Prize recipient Edward O. Wilson proposes, in *Half-Earth: Our Planet's Fight for Life* (2016), that half of the Earth's surface be dedicated to, reserved for, and conserved by practices that bring about a newly restored pristine Nature to the extent that "pristine" is possible in a biologically and meteorologically linked and altered planet. This is an intriguing, insightful, and "inciteful" suggestion. It complements his earlier work, *The Creation: An Appeal to Save Life on Earth*, in which Wilson states that religion and science, meeting "on the near side of metaphysics" and working together, provide the greatest possibility for saving species. In *Half-Earth* he proposes a concrete solution for saving the Earth's biota directly: limit human actions that endanger and extinct them, and provide an adequate habitat for their survival and eventual wellbeing. Related to this is the practical ecological necessity that humankind limit its currently geometrically progressive population growth. The latter devastates the Earth while causing privation of necessities for the "least of these"—humans, other biota, and the Earth—and imperiling humanity along with other biota. The Earth has limited natural goods of available land for agriculture and homes, and available fresh water necessary for all life. Farms are being paved over for suburban residential development and shopping malls, and underground aquifers are being drained to assist gas extraction by fracking (rightly called energy source exploitation). Wilson's proposal is insightful for its presentation of factors that are endangering all species' survival, let alone wellbeing; it is inciteful for its provocative (for some) statement that human population and consumption will have to be cut significantly to benefit one and all.

Wilson's proposal supplements other projects and places, focused on restoring large tracts of land for natural processes and a diversity of life unhindered by human interference, such as the vast African plains, notably the Serengeti; forests in India, several of which are now protected by the women's Chipko ("tree hugger") movement; national parks and reserves throughout the world, in numerous nations; and several US states' contiguous Buffalo Commons.

Wilson's concept of "half-Earth" complements the proposal discussed above to "commonize the commons." His focus is on saving species—including the human species—and species habitats. The commonize proposal is to effect a just distribution of Earth goods to all people; this would be the case whether or not a "half-Earth" becomes a reality. It would, in fact, expedite that process. If people share the natural goods of land and energy sources, and greed is constrained by progressive taxation on property and income, then humans' financial security and consumer restraint will help to promote the Earth's wellbeing.

Envision and Effect a New Earth

Although people discuss and debate "renewing the Earth," "renewal" has become ecologically impossible, given the devastation that has been wrought by harmful industrial technologies embodied in machines. By contrast, the benefits that have been engendered by appropriate, intermediate technologies not only enhance the lives of humankind and other biota, but conserve energy and aid agriculture. Humankind must work from the positive lessons and beneficial aspects of current reality, not from the facts and dreams of the past which can no longer be romanticized.

Earth's religions have an important role to play vis-à-vis ecology: to imagine today and actualize toward tomorrow the new Earth that is envisioned in and by a community of communities. Social justice and ecology, the interdependent wellbeing of humankind and the wellbeing of Earth and all living beings, are integrally interrelated and intertwined. Wars, preparations for war, and rumors of wars will continue until all people have at least the necessities of life, including food, clothing, shelter, healthcare, rest, education, and meaningful employment at a living wage, and are secure in having them available and accessible in the present and into the future. A common commons, in thought and practice, in theory and in reality, will enable this. All people's needs will have been prioritized over a wealthy minority's greed.

As we continually enrich our consciousness and enhance our conduct while evaluating conditions on Earth and in the heavens, we should bear in mind the dialogic intergenerational and intertemporal relationship between entities existing in space, places, and time:

The past is the mother of the present:

- The decisions and actions of our ancestors over millennia have influenced the development of our spatial, social, and spiritual contexts in our present historical moment

The present is the mother of the future:

- Our own decisions and actions in the present, even more than in the past because of developments in communications and means of travel, are based on greater interaction between diverse cultures, ethnicities, social systems, fields of knowledge, and beliefs. We will be, collectively, the mother of the future
- What we do today will give birth to the social world of our descendants and the Earth we bequeath to them to live in and care for responsibly

The future is the mother of the present:

- Our cultures today evidence understanding of possible impacts—positive and negative—that might result from what we have been or are doing on Earth. This view of possible futures will—or should—influence, give birth to, what we think and do in the present
- What we envision today for the future will give birth to what we do today in the present to conserve planet Earth, promote social justice, and ensure the wellbeing of all living beings, far into the future.

Complementary Views from Earth and Space

People would come to realize as they journey among and land on distant worlds an enhanced version of what the psalmist experienced gazing at the heavens from a place situated on just one planet of one solar system in one galaxy: "The heavens speak of the Presence of divine Being, and the skies proclaim the Spirit's creativity" (cf. Ps. 19). People would realize, too, as they journey around the world—actually or imaginatively—what astronauts noted from space: that Earth is one beautiful world, precious and precarious in the vastness of the heavens.

In a common commons, the complementary views and perspectives become one: humankind realizes that it incorporates diverse ethnic cultures and that conceptual formulations within one human family relate to all biota and abiotic Earth settings. People of diverse faith systems might on some occasions, as individuals and in communities, transcend the structured institutions and rituals of formal religion that separate them (without rejecting or abandoning the older traditions if they choose not to), and experience communally moments of a common spirituality on common spiritual ground. The sacred commons and the social commons become an integral commons and common commons in such moments, and effect the wellbeing of all being.

Notes

1 A deeper comparative discussion of Aquinas, Smith, and Paine is presented in Hart (2013, 43–52).
2 An extensive discussion of Arizmendiarrieta and Mondragón is presented in Hart (1997).
3 I have worked with the IITC for almost 40 years, have been a member of the delegation of the IITC to the UN International Human Rights Commission, Geneva, 1987 and 1990, and invited to testify at the UN Consultation on the *Declaration on the Right of Indigenous Peoples*, held at Sinte Gleska University, Rosebud Reservation, South Dakota.
4 Phillis Wheatley (1753–1784), "On Imagination," verse 2. http://archive.vcu.edu/english/engweb/webtexts/Wheatley/phil.htm. The section on Wheatley has been revised and adapted from Hart (2013, 403–405).
5 William Blake (1757–1827). Available at: http://www.blakearchive.org/. The section on Blake has been revised and adapted from Hart (2013, 399–400).

References

Buber, Martin, 1958. *I and Thou* (2nd ed.). Transl. Ronald Gregor Smith. Postscript Buber. New York: Charles Scribner's Sons.

Buber, Martin, 1958. *Paths in Utopia*. Transl. R. E. C. Hull. Boston, MA: Beacon Press.

Cronon, William, 1983. *Changes in the Land: Indians, Colonists, and the Ecology of New England*. New York: Hill & Wang.

Foner, Philip S. (Ed.). 1974. *The Life and Major Writings of Thomas Paine*. Secaucus, NJ: Citadel Press.

Hart, John. 1997. *Ethics and Technology: Innovation and Transformation in Community Contexts*. Cleveland, OH: Pilgrim Press.

Hart, John. 2006. *Sacramental Commons: Christian Ecological Ethics*. Foreword Leonardo Boff, Afterword Thomas Berry. In Roger Gottlieb (Ed.), *Nature's Meaning* series. Lanham, MD: Rowman & Littlefield.

Hart, John. 2013. *Cosmic Commons: Spirit, Science, and Space*. Eugene, OR: Wipf & Stock, Cascade Books.

Lyons, Oren, Chief & Mohawk, John (Eds.). 1992. *Exiled in the Land of the Free: Democracy, Indian Nations, and the U.S. Constitution*. Foreword Peter Matthiessen. Preface Senator Daniel K. Inouye. Santa Fe, NM: Clear Light Publishers.

Wilson, Edward O. 2016. *Half-Earth—Our Planet's Fight for Life*. New York: Liveright Publishing.

Wilson, Edward O. 2006. *The Creation: An Appeal to Save Life on Earth*. New York: W.W. Norton.

CHAPTER 35

A New *Partzuf* for a New Paradigm

Living Earth—An Icon for Our Age

Rabbi Zalman Schachter-Shalomi, and in Conversation with John Hart[1]

In recent decades the movement for spiritual renewal in Judaism has prompted individuals and communities to explore more deeply how they are interrelated not only each to the other, but also with the Earth and all living beings. Judaism is being transformed despite the resistance of primarily Orthodox Jews, and, however reluctantly, members of other Jewish traditions, approaches to Jewish spirituality, or ways of thinking acknowledge and adapt to it. This movement has taken into consideration, in context, Judaism's engagement with the environmental and social crises that today confront all humanity and our living Earth.

In this time of a change in our consciousness within a shifting social and ecological setting, the best of Jewish traditions are being reviewed, reinforced, and renewed, rather than being unreflectively rejected and removed outright. We have been experiencing a paradigm shift which has both shattered previous understandings and stimulated us to reconsider them in light of contemporary, unexpected realities. In some ways this parallels the shift that was required when our ancestors thought their worldview and their lives were secure in the era of the First Temple and later the Second Temple until each was destroyed in turn. In our own lifetime, our experience of Nazi Germany's genocide of Jews in death camps such as Auschwitz and Treblinka shattered whatever social and spiritual security we thought we had enjoyed. Today, too, we are in a previously unexperienced *Weltanschauung* in which not only is all humanity threatened with decimation and even extinction, but the Earth, our home, is endangered. We are challenged in this socially, psychologically, and spiritually stressful situation to rethink our understandings of and interactions with who we are and who we should be in this time and this place, while being aware that this place, too, is not frozen in time.

In light of the pressing social issues that imperil human community and the possibility of achieving just relationships among all people and peoples, and ecological crises

The Wiley Blackwell Companion to Religion and Ecology, First Edition. Edited by John Hart.

that threaten the survival of humankind, all living beings, and planet Earth, our common home and the common ground for our encounters and relationships, we need as a species to find concord. This should be sought not only politically and economically, but also on a spiritual level that enables us to overcome interreligious conflicts. Human, biotic community (community of all life), and Earth survival and wellbeing will depend to a great extent on how we work together in a relational community. If we cannot progress beyond doctrinal and religious wars and embrace a consciousness that does not just tolerate but accepts or at least accommodates and respects culturally distinct (but often morally and ethically complementary) creeds and practices, we will not eliminate other areas of disagreement. Our species', our biotic community's, and our planet's survival all are at stake.

In 1990, I was part of a Jewish religious leaders' delegation, which included Rabbi Arthur Waskow,[2] which traveled to Dharamsala to dialogue with the Dalai Lama and other Buddhist monks in their community-in-exile. The monks had fled the religious persecution that followed the imperialist expansion into Tibet of the People's Republic of China, spearheaded by its army. China had invaded their homeland, claimed it as their own, and systematically destroyed the majority of Buddhist temples and monasteries or converted them into tourist centers, devastated villages and cities, occupied on an apparently permanent basis a previously independent nation, and forcibly brutalized the Tibetan people, committing cultural genocide and seemingly striving for ethnic genocide. The Dalai Lama was aware of the millennia during which Jews had lived in exile after similar destruction by invading armies. He wondered what Jews might teach Buddhists about how to endure and ultimately overcome religious and ethnic oppression and enforced exile. He hoped that he would find Jewish insights, religious understandings, and cultural practices that had enabled Jews to live in exile that would help Tibetan Buddhists and Buddhism to survive well in exile while awaiting their return to Tibet. He hoped, too, that the end of exile would occur in his lifetime and not be as prolonged as had been the periods in which Jews experienced it. The direct, congenial, open, and inspirational dialogue was mutually instructive and spiritually exhilarating as participants compared complementary understandings and teachings and considered insights new to them.[3]

Today, all humanity, not solely Jews and Buddhists who seek to preserve historically and culturally sacred traditions, is threatened by political and economic—and sometimes military—invasions, and environmental devastation resulting from human need and greed. These events have catalyzed culturally disruptive and even life-threatening exile not solely away from peoples' familiar national homelands, but from the Earth, their shared geophysical homeland. Mother Earth is threatened with geocide: human-caused and human-exacerbated global heating is causing droughts, wild fires, extreme weather events, loss of agricultural land needed to feed our species, and consequent human conflicts over land and water.[4] Peoples are being forced to leave intergenerationally occupied places—witness, for example, island peoples who are forced into permanent exile by rising seas because of heat-expanded water around the globe, such as the 10,000 people of the island of Lohachara, in the Sundarban Islands of West Bengal, and five unoccupied Solomon Islands in the Pacific Ocean. Pollution of land, air, and water is worldwide. Global forests, whose trees are the Earth's lungs, continue to be irresponsibly, relentlessly, and recklessly felled on a massive scale by transnational corporations' clearcutting; fracking techniques to acquire natural gas are causing visible damage such as sinkholes in some towns, and are evident, too, in multiple earthquakes in regions where they had previously never been experienced. Such Earth impacts from fracking prompt the question: What damage is being done to the Earth's crust that will not be felt until the future? The same question can be asked about global heating's long-term effects.

All these ecologically destructive practices are caused by efforts to meet the needs of an exponentially increasing human overpopulation and, to a greater extent, to match the greed and meet the wants of the middle classes and the wealthiest 1% in our consumerist society. We are faced, as a species-extincting species, with our own destruction as places of exile for even the most affluent disappear before the onslaught of fire and flood. Unlike previous exiles, when displaced peoples were forced to leave their homeland, in the ecological exile already initiated humanity will continue to live on their alienated Earth homeland: there will be ever-fewer places that could serve as their secure shelters. Humanity will be, as a whole, environmental exiles, forced to live with polluted air, poisoned water, and smog-filled skies, the result of ecologically devastating emissions, effluents, and chemical residues.

Religion can have a profound impact on ecology in our time and places. People in faith traditions must look to their sacred texts for insights that affirm the divine Spirit's solicitude not only for all humans, but for all living beings and the Earth—witness the Covenant God makes with all Creation at the end of the Flood story, in which God saves all Earth creatures; and human responsibilities for God's Creation as humans seek to image God with a like solicitude. The ancient instructions of the Spirit of the universe to the first humans, as expressed in the biblical Creation stories, must be contemplated in their literal meaning: people are not told to "subdue the Earth" but to conserve and serve the Garden that symbolizes the Earth as a whole. "Serve" is used elsewhere in the Bible to indicate human relationships with the Most High. Genesis teaches, then, that people are to serve the Earth just as they serve the divine Spirit, who called all Creation "very good." Imagine the difference an accurate translation of these Hebrew phrases into other languages, if taken to heart, would have on our thinking about and attitudes toward the Earth and all living beings!

We need to think here and now about what is happening to our planet and what are our understandings of ourselves, yes; but we need to think too about what might happen there and then—that is, in the future, in the new presents that fast approach and will succeed each other in turn.

As I reflect on these present and future matters, I have decided to go back to my considerations in the recent past, thereby integrating in my consciousness the past, present, and future. In particular, I have pondered anew themes that I explored and thoughts I expressed in "Renewing God."[5] I draw on that essay here, recalling and renewing what was presented earlier. I reflect further on these themes and elaborate them in greater depth. In the present chapter, I go beyond my previous thinking. For in only little more than a decade much has transpired and much more is imminent that has influenced where we live and what we think about life and the places and historical eras in which it emerges. We need to remember our presence in a living sacred Being, whether understood and revered as a Creator God or in another way. Divine Being has distinct names in diverse religions and cultures, each of which has settled upon a name that best expresses, and by which to address, particular cultural or individual understandings of and belief in a transcendent-immanent entity not limited by material existence or by any religious communities' doctrines as they claim that they can describe divine characteristics and divine action in the universe.

The "constant" for our time and all time, no matter the type or content of paradigm shifts, is to remember and be faithful to the divine Being, including with respect to our perhaps ever-developing and transformed belief in and understandings of God, based on new experiences, new knowledge, and new social environments. In that remembrance we are called to renew the Earth in our time while putting in motion an enduring understanding of our relationship with and responsibility to the Creator and to Creation or to the Being of a cosmos that did not have a specific moment of divine creativity. We must bear in mind, in our reflections, our complementary knowledge that future paradigm shifts might prompt changes in our current relevant thinking such that it becomes then irrelevant thinking in future times and places. Such is the ebb and flow of life and thought—and spiritual consciousness—through the ages.

Today, in the months leading up to my 90th birthday, I am pondering anew ideas and insights I developed in dialogue with the treasures of Jewish traditions, excavating their depths to provide, from the riches of our religious narrative, seeds that might present ever-evolving sources of spiritual and social renewal—in our understandings of them and through our openness to radical new perceptions of what they reveal and teach. We need a new icon, a symbol of our time and our historical place.

The present era is characterized by a greater consciousness of our planet and the peoples who populate it in all their diversity and interdependence. Earth consciousness—with Earth understood to be not only the planet as a whole, but all who live on it and benefit from its nourishing waters, cleansing and refreshing wind, and warmth-providing fire, in whatever form they take—is a fruitful icon, a *partzuf*, for our era. The Living Earth icon is beneficial to the extent that we respond, too, to the presence from whom it emanated and in whom all life has life, and to all other beings—living and, for some believers and scientific thinkers, non-living—with whom we are intimately related and mutually dependent.

Remember the One from Whom the Cosmos Emanates/Emerges/ is Born

Remembrance should imply "be faithful to." This means, for some, retaining unchanged the understandings of "divine Revelation" received millennia in the past, as if thinking about and perceptions of the sacred were available to people only during previous historical epochs. "Being faithful" should mean, I suggest, being willing to listen to the divine voice speaking not solely to Abraham, Moses, and the ancient prophets, but to people since, especially in our own time as we experience a shifting and even shifted paradigm. Did God, called by whatever name, not speak to diverse peoples in the past, since well before the stories of Genesis were recounted? Did God, called by whatever name, not speak to the Buddha, to Mohammad, to seers and sages of cultures and traditions other than Judaism and Christianity? Does God not speak to us today, in the twenty-first century? Or, does divine Being indeed communicate, but the divine "words" are not heard because we believe that the voice that spoke to our ancestors does not address us, an idea that stimulates a false consciousness that prompts us to block out or even drown out the new words by repeatedly uttering the old?

To say that God did not speak solely to our ancestors means that while acknowledging ancient expressions and interpretations of the words' meaning by sages through the ages, we must reflect anew on those words today. In our reflection, we must be open not only to the inspiration that our predecessors had, and their insights about what the words meant then, but also to new inspiration and insights presented to us—a contemporary divine Revelation. This will become more evident as we reflect on what was discerned by those who preceded us and relate it to our new consciousness in our new paradigm.

The one in whom the cosmos originates might be understood in the long tradition of Jewish, Christian, and Muslim thought developed over the millennia of Western history as a Creator whose explosive burst of creative energy—symbolically, over six days—began the world, near and far, that exists today (Genesis 1, cited by Jews and Christians); the Creator of a primeval atom that came into existence on a "day without yesterday" (in George LeMaître's phrase) and exploded and extended into space (the "Big Bang"); a Creator knowing the past, present, and future, who, when the time is appropriate, creates material forms for pre-existing spirits and places them on Earth (Islamic Sufism). In the spiritual traditions of the Americas, the union of Father Sky and Mother Earth long ago brought into being the origin creatures whose descendants live today (early and ongoing native peoples' traditions).

I have become familiar with several religions' cosmological understandings through my immersion in the religious and spiritual thought of diverse cultures. I became through this immersion a sheikh in the Sufi lineage of Hazrat Inayat Khan in 1975, and co-founded a Sufi–Hasidic, Inayati-Maimuni Order with my student Netanel Miles-Yepez in 2004; I enjoyed conversations with His Holiness the Dalai Lama in Dharamsala, in 1990.[6] In all of this, I studied the mysticism of diverse traditions and found a complementarity that unites, and can overcome doctrines that divide.

For my part, I have evolved intellectually and spiritually to the point that I have a commitment to the Earth and Earth's wellbeing that surpasses my commitment to a particular traditional philosophy or belief system. As noted in my *Tikkun* article years ago, I entered the first stage of a Gaian initiation and have strived to deepen my commitment to Gaia and Gaia's living beings ever since. I experienced an "identity shift from ethnic to global" in order to live into my Gaia initiation. I am guided from beyond who I am or who I think I am. I seek to be led always by Wisdom, Hokhmah, Sophia, who constantly emerges from the Earth's mind. We must all be open to "the possibility of accessing on the inner-net, the inner internet" what is required of us by the *melekh-ha-olam* (the Spirit of the Universe or, in native peoples' traditions, the Power of the Universe).

In exploring our own and other traditions we must be faithful to a practice of hearing, recognizing, and responding responsibly to the Revelation that we hear, see, and experience today, sometimes in most unexpected ways. The core of the universe expects us to live in harmony. We are intentionally integral to cosmic being, not an accident of time and chance events. We humans have evolved to fill our particular niche in all that is, to use our unique attributes and abilities to make responsible contributions to the whole. We have a right to be here when we seek and strive, however haltingly, to become gradually who we are, which is visible now only in shadow form, in transparent moments. We are called to recognize the spirit of who we are, the Spirit who is in us individually and communally because we are one of many temples of the Spirit in the cosmos. In the words of Maximus (580–662 CE), an early Christian mystic, all beings in the cosmos, not just beings regarded as "living" in traditional and scientific perspectives, are *logoi* of the divine *Logos*, the Creator and creating Word whose voice in the Genesis 1 Creation story "said," and creatures came into existence; the divine voice said further that all beings are "very good," something we are finally acknowledging, and have begun to act accordingly. The *Logos* and *logoi* are in constant dialogue throughout the cosmos and through time; divine self-communication was not a one-time act. The Hindu greeting *Namasté* expresses this well: the spirit and Spirit within each of us as individual beings greets and engages with the spirit and Spirit within all of us, individually and communally.

We are simultaneously children of Being, children of the universe, children of Mother Earth (as stated in native peoples' traditions and by Francis of Assisi in the Christian tradition), and children of our human parents in a human family that has come to have a place in biological evolution. We are children, too, of our cultural environment, and children of the diverse faith traditions in which we were born and raised, in which we have chosen to live our social identity, or into which we have chosen to place our spiritual being and our lives as we seek an ever-closer relationship with the divine within and around us.

Epiphanies Rather than Theophanies

The biblical narrative relates that Moses had a great theophany, a magnificent, singular experience of God's Revelation on Sinai. My own experience has been decidedly different in that I have had, over the decades, a series of epiphanies, intimations of God's Revelation at significant moments in my life and the life of Judaism. These were "Aha!" moments, in today's parlance, which began to come together for me over time, even though when a revelatory moment occurred it seemed isolated, perhaps a sudden insight. When considered together their meaning and message became more profound, and I was moved to integrate them holistically and express them in my publications and public presentations.

If all we do in seeking a new divine Revelation in this historical time is to expect and await a Moses-like theophany, a dramatic event from the heavens, we will miss ongoing epiphanies. These might not be as grand as the theophany. Rather, they will speak to us in diverse, at times commonplace, situations as well as in spiritually distinctive times and places. Unlike Elijah who knew better than to seize on dramatic Earth natural phenomena and interpret them as divine manifestations but instead awaited direct divine engagement, we have been hoping to see God in the dramatic, rather than listen for, or hear even without listening. But by being open to it, that "still, small voice" within us that softly teaches us we will hear if we are willing to be learners.

In the new paradigm, we must not wait expectantly yet blindly for a grand theophanic Revelation while numerous epiphanic revelations provided for us pass before our eyes and through our minds unnoticed or disregarded. We need to pause periodically in our hurried and harried lives for Sabbath moments in which we make time for the voice speaking not loudly and dramatically, but softly and insistently. It seeks to provide support in our struggles to comprehend the shift in consciousness that we are experiencing, despite our efforts to ignore or deny it as we cling to what was instead of considering what is, will be, or might be.

Prophets' Voices in the New Paradigm

In our new paradigm, we must learn to discern divine Revelation when we listen to and for contemporary prophetic voices, acknowledging that Revelation is being expressed in distinct cultures and tongues. We Jews are comfortable with Revelation in Hebrew; but it might be disconcerting and even troubling to our way of thinking and doing when the language that we hear and the culture from which it comes did not exist when the prophets spoke, or even when the Bible was written. What might we hear and learn if we listen attentively to a Martin Luther King, Jr., an Oscar Romero, or a Mohandas Gandhi, among others who criticized what is, and offered what is not yet, but could be? How might we express from our Jewish culture what we learn from such voices, as we integrate their insights? God speaks to those whom God chooses around the world and through time. Solomon affirmed at the Temple dedication that God's presence is not confined to a particular location, even a place of worship, when he said, "But will God really dwell on earth? Even the heavens to their uttermost reaches cannot contain You, how much less this House that I have built!" (1 Kings, 8: 27; *The Jewish Study Bible*, 691).

Just as God's Presence is not contained in a particular human-fashioned structure, neither is God's voice or divine words limited to a particular people or sacred book. The Presence in whom we live expresses principles and projects through selected prophets from specific peoples. Each of us honors, and should heed, the prophets in our respective traditions. We must listen also for prophetic voices from other traditions that express complementary insights, culturally expressed, and respond to them as insights for all peoples regardless of the diversity of cultures and traditions from which they emerge and the distinct languages in which they are expressed.

We learn, too, from great souls and from souls in process who are struggling to deal with the changes in their world which have been so unsettling. In Jewish mysticism, especially in the ancient, insightful, and inspirational Kaballah, I was particularly helped to deal with times and events troubling to my spirit and my security in times past, a security that had seemed to be time-tested and helpful for later moments. However, some of those ideas and beliefs no longer passed the tests of time.

The Kaballah is not, despite what its critics declare, reality-denying. Rather, it leads us to different dimensions of reality that are not available to us when we hold fast to our materiality. Mystical experience does not contradict "reality" or even materiality: it gives it greater depth through a profound experience of the Presence immanent in the energies and matter of the cosmos. The Kaballah was not dictated by a divine voice, as some claim when they interpret, seemingly literally, the narratives of the Torah; it was born from an intuition that discerned, experienced, and expressed a spiritual communion and communication understood without words when an open-minded seeker of the divine Presence and ultimate cosmic meaning engaged in a special way the totality of Being.

Renew Creation

When we experience the Presence that permeates all that is, we want to make those parts of Creation for which we are particularly responsible—our homes, places of work, and recreational sites, for example—expressive of the divine within them, for which they are transparent to those who have eyes to see. Earth, whose soil is laden with dangerous chemicals, whose waters are tainted by harmful effluents, and whose air is polluted by toxic emissions, all of which have led to species extinctions and the Earth's degradation, does not mediate the Creator to the extent it once did, nor is it able to reveal its own inner reality and what it has evolved to be. Creation needs renewal. What God called "very good" might more often be "very harmful" in our age. In eons past, in our own era, and in eons in the future the cosmos, Earth, and all therein, when pristine or when renewed, are revelatory: they mediate the Presence immanent in them and all being, and present who they are in themselves, in all their beauty, complexity, and depth and dimensions of being.

It is difficult if not impossible to renew what we regard as the created world—or as the world which emerged from a different grand cosmic event or process—if we assume that we humans are situated, by divine placement, atop the world in which we live, to have dominion over it rather than responsibility in it. Our being is intimately integrated with all being and beings. We have our role in the world and each other being has theirs. We must seek the integration of our roles for our mutual benefit and the wellbeing of the whole. Genesis teaches that Yahweh looked at the entire Creation and called everything "very good." We can do no less.

As we seek to fulfill our human role we should remain conscious of the role of Being. In a cosmic dance of being we can seek joyfully to be guided by the One who brought all into being and brings everything into Being over eons of existence.

Renewing the Earth so that it becomes resplendent in all its beauty of place and places requires that we seek kinship with the Earth and all life on the Earth, recognizing and acting as if we are Earth's children. We must respect our sacred Mother and our siblings if we are all not only to survive but to thrive.

We must do more than imagine a renewed Earth and renewed relationships with all life. Our imagined future will remain an unfulfilled dream if we do not go beyond hoping that it will happen. We must aspire to make Earth's better future; we must act to make it a reality such that the imagined future will be the present for our children's children. We are in this together, people of every spiritual and religious tradition or of none.

The One who calls us is the One who will guide us; we must learn anew to read the signs in the heavens and listen to the sounds of the Earth's creatures. On occasion, often unexpectedly, we might well see events and hear voices that suggest ways to get from here to there together, not only as a human family but as an intentional interrelated Earth family.

Restore Community

In the US and elsewhere, communities are fractured internally and divided internationally. "Wars and rumors of wars" have continued incessantly in human history, despite World War I, the "War to End All Wars," the even more devastating World War II, and the "shock and awe" of succeeding wars. It has been said (by Albert Einstein if I recall correctly) that in the disastrous direction in which we are heading, while we do not know what armaments will be used in a third world war, we do know what will be used in a fourth world war and its successors: sticks and stones.

Today, in the US and other Western nations in particular, and externally in the economic and political relationships these nations have with countries that are less developed technologically and whose economies are struggling due to domestic and foreign exploitation of their labor and resources, the gap is growing between rich and poor, those who have too much and those who lack even the necessities of life. Racism and ethnocentrism are on the increase globally, violating any notion of a common humanity and a common heritage of being God's children. Religious conflict, often due to hidden political and economic forces, increases too; in this area, shared moral values and complementary mysticism provide common ground that is solace from and contrasts with notions of peoples' "fighting turf," and indicates possibilities for overcoming "business as usual."

We need not continue down the path of self- and other-destruction. Divine Revelation in distinct religious traditions and secular humanist ideas provides us with new yet traditional ways of resolving our differences and meeting everyone's basic needs. As I said earlier, I have developed a Gaia consciousness as I have newly interpreted and integrated my own prayer, meditation, and thinking about past Jewish tradition and its insights as expressed through the ages, and what I have learned from the spiritual writings and spiritual people in other traditions. I have kept one foot in the past while simultaneously extending the other foot toward the future and to other traditions. It has proven to be quite a stretch, and I have gradually brought forward the foot dragging in the back while ensuring that it carried with it the dust and muddy soil of past paradigms; these provide fertile ground to plant what will be needed in the present paradigm and its successor paradigms.

Spiritual teachers, through both formal and informal educational venues, should encourage rather than discourage those from their own tradition who value insights from other spiritual elders and have found helpful teachers in other traditions. Spiritual leaders who embrace mystical elements of their tradition will find complementary insights in mystical teachings from others: God is One, not multiple, in Jewish and other traditions. The divine Revelation from one Being and the immanent Presence of Spirit

Being are offered to diverse people in diverse cultures, and expressed by them in the ways and languages characteristic of their cultures, intergenerationally. Sacred encounters that are experienced by every seer and seeker are honored, not denigrated, by spiritual teachers who are comfortable in their tradition but open to the Presence evident in, revealed through, or expressed by other teachers and traditions.

Partzufim through Time: Both Place-Specific and Intergenerationally Significant

In kabbalistic traditions, people throughout the ages have dreamed of mythic icons, *partzufim*, that provide bases from which to reflect on and respond to dramatic historical change. Effectively, each *partzuf* provided a "reality map," a means of assessing the terrain, possible future paths to follow because of what has been given, and permissible alterations to prior paths by revising existing road maps and developing maps—and, eventually, a common map—adaptive to and transformative of the present situation (the site and social-spiritual realities and insights of the present era).

A *partzuf* appropriate to be our present paradigm emerges from an organic understanding of what is. We have learned that our Earth is a living Earth (an insight held by indigenous peoples around the world for millennia). Native traditions refer to her as a nurturing Mother Earth. The sciences of quantum physics and ecology (as well as spiritual perceptions through the ages, in all cultures) teach that, to use a Lakota phrase, *Mitakuye oyasin*: "we are all related." All biota in what has been called the great chain of life, the *tz'ror hachayyim*, are integrated, interdependent, and interrelated; no part can survive alone. This insight requires rethinking how to replace social structures that no longer work for the mutual benefit of all peoples; how to eliminate environmental practices that harm the organisms and places that have flowed from the cosmic Being's original and ongoing creativity; and how to transform or transcend religious traditions that do not provide instruction for a global society that is different from when they first emerged. We humans need a new mythology for our new millennium, and we must be open to those who discern its possibilities in "Aha!" and "Eureka!" moments.

Right Brain and Left Brain Observation and Consideration

In the twentieth century, physiologists and psychologists began to note that the right and left hemispheres of the human brain have distinct but complementary purposes and abilities. Simply and allegorically put, the right brain observes with the heart, the affective aspect of human being; the left brain observes with the head, the analytical aspect of human being. People considering what they are observing or have observed will base their reflections and subsequent actions on which approach is most fundamentally theirs. As noted earlier, the Kaballah describes what are ineffable events experienced without words; culturally, the experience can be expressed only through words, since we cannot transmit directly one to another what we have encountered, in a moment of whatever duration, as we participated in and became one with the spiritual dimensions of our existence. When we experience such moments we do so through perceptions from the right side of our brain, the hemisphere that appreciates, accepts, and appropriates realities inexpressible in language, written and spoken. We cannot, however, pass on such experiences to others except through words, through activation of the left side of our brain, that hemisphere that analyzes and expresses in a communicable way—however partial, and approximate rather than entirely accurate—what we have seen and heard through our spiritual faculties.

Consideration of two viewers' respective and diverse considerations of a forest that they encounter unexpectedly when they round a bend on a mountain walk together will illustrate how they can see the same forest, from the same observation point, in radically different ways. The right side of the brain has to do with the heart, which is characterized by openness to the wonder of the cosmos and to compassion for all being. The left side of the brain has to do with the head, and is characteristic of someone who interprets the visual analytically and concretely, materially. The right brain-seeing person will note the beauty of the forest, and its expression of its own vibrant life integrated with other vibrant lives and the world around them. The left brain-seeing person will calculate how the forest might be beneficial for commercial purposes in terms of the board-feet that might be converted when the trees are felled to provide lumber for residential, commercial, and industrial purposes. The two perspectives are not mutually and continually exclusive. The left brain-influenced person can come to have some heart consideration: to use lumber derived from the living forest to build homes for impoverished people or hurricane victims, for example. The right brain-oriented person can realize that compassion for some members of the human community might mean that some trees must be selectively harvested to meet basic human needs, but that this must be done in a manner that respects the inherent rights of trees to life and the overall integrity of the forest as a whole, and so ensures the forest's ongoing life. The head, too, must consider whether or not it is realistic to use the species in this forest to construct homes, if needed, and thereby eliminate selected parts of the forest that are appreciated by the heart. A respectful dialogue between the two travelers—representative in microcosm of what can occur in macrocosm—might result in a balance of the two approaches and to overall conservation of trees and their forest communities.

The right hemisphere of the brain enables us to "see" with our heart and to be drawn to relationships with the cosmos in its entirety, its complexity, and its wonder. The heart experiences the interrelatedness of all that is, Being and beings. The left hemisphere allows us to process what we see and experience, to some degree, so that we might express our visions and our relatedness in language and symbols that those who are open to this experience of reality and relatedness—and perhaps are seeking to live in it also—might have a sense or at least an inkling of what the heart has come to understand. When a critical mass of people share common heart experiences and relationships, the Earth can be transformed and renewed. The sages, seers, and seekers plant social and spiritual seeds in words that can be grasped by the less adept, and thereby guide others to enter upon and walk along the heart path of mystical experience, leading to community and planetary wellbeing. In community, they will relate well with the Being who is the center, heart, and spirit of the universe, and therefore with each other. A new song will arise from a cosmic chorus that will melodically permeate the cosmic community and stimulate cosmic harmony and an intricate and joyful cosmic dance of all-that-is.

The mystically experienced spiritual reality of the right brain is imperfectly expressed in the words of spiritual traditions such as the Kaballah, which translate it into concepts understood in material reality in order that others might, even at secondhand, have glimpses of what the seer experienced firsthand. Such translations of a theophany can stimulate a change of spiritual consciousness and of relationships in material reality. The theophany of the seer prompts, even in the incompleteness of its transmission, new ways for others to respond to mystical communication, making the seer's vision and message their own, in a derivative way. When a critical mass of seers enables others to see with new eyes the deeper dimensions of the world around them, that very world can be transformed.

Dreaming Dreams and Seeing Visions

We do not know from whom will come or from where will emerge a unifying mythology to inform our present paradigm, our moment of altered consciousness. It almost assuredly will not come from philosophers who are self-sequestered in ivory towers; it might well come from mystics who pass back and forth in different dimensions of reality. It might come from someone regarded as unexceptional. Who would have imagined in ages past that a shepherd boy would become King of Israel, that an agricultural laborer would become a great prophet, or that a carpenter's son would be regarded as a special envoy from God, and even as a unique divine manifestation in the material world?

We all should be comfortable with dreaming dreams, including those that are very remarkable and even unsettling; from such dreaming new realities might be conceived and developed. We should be open to visionary experiences, moments in which we seem to transcend our materiality and dwell in spiritual realms, as we metaphorically "have a foot" in both realities simultaneously. On the ashes of older traditions a new mythology might soar, crossing cultures and previous understandings to provide an icon that will lift our spirits (in several senses), our civilizations-become-one in community, and our spiritual depth. As we travel we must look through the windshield to see what lies ahead and will be surprised to see signs not yet written placed on poles yet to be posted that can guide our journey rather than look constantly in the rearview mirror for signs and messages we have passed, thereby endangering our vehicle and all within. When we reconcile ourselves with learning from our present time without being constrained by what it teaches, we will be able to learn for and eventually learn from future times.

The new *partzuf* for our time might emerge in and be expressed by the integral impact of several *partzufim* that are voiced in different tongues from different cultures and religions. The words of the prophet Joel (3: 1) instruct us still today, but in a new way in that regard: "I will pour out My spirit on all flesh; Your sons and daughters shall prophesy; Your old men shall dream dreams. And your young men shall see visions" (3: 1; *The Jewish Study Bible*, 1172).

Our efforts might mean that, in the concept of relationship presented by Jewish thinker and mystic Martin Buber, we come to understand and accept those whom we have feared and even hated. We will relate to them as "Thou" and learn from those who previously were regarded as "It," the "Other"—including, perhaps especially, those who have harmed or threatened us in the past by embracing them in an "I–Thou" relationship. The riches of religious insights from diverse traditions might then inspire us as we reflect on our own tradition. Further, as Buber writes, this I–Thou relationship of interactive subjects should be sought not only with human beings, but with other living beings, the Earth, and the Presence who embraces us all. He elaborates, along these lines, his consideration of an I–Thou relationship with a tree as he consciously communed with it wordlessly. This caused him to wonder if the tree, too, had consciousness and a spirit.

The Torah that Transcends Yet Carries Tradition

In our altered consciousness, we learn what the past cannot teach us even as we envision how the current paradigm shift can teach us. The customary Jewish prayer, "Blessed are you, God" has a deeper meaning when the phrase "King of the Universe," *melekh ha-olam*, follows it. We acknowledge thereby God's cosmic and timeless Presence while our new understanding of the Earth as a personal being, a beautiful and nurturing Gaia, becomes integrated into our consciousness today. Having seen astronomers' and astronauts' images of the Earth in immense space, and the Keppler and Hubble telescopes' photographs of other planets, asteroids, and the birthplaces of stars in distant space, we come to know well how the Earth is an organic unity, despite national borders and topographical boundaries, and that its unity is integrated within the vast organic unity of the dynamic, interacting cosmos. We are one in the One. We are all children of God and children of the cosmos. This is our new Torah, our new Revelation, our *mattan torah*. We who are Jews are called to be a blessing to the Earth and cosmos, an organ of Jewry in the organism of the Earth in the organism of the universe.

Embracing the *mattan torah* and our organic unity with all-that-is, we understand that we are called to a shared spirituality with all people. The old religions must find common ground—literally and figuratively—to express the new beings we are becoming. All people must likewise acknowledge that we are citizens of the Earth, not of distinct, diverse, and dividing nations; the political is transcended in the spiritual, especially in our cosmic mysticism that cannot be confined to a particular place or guide but is open to divine Revelation everywhere and from all deeply spiritual teachers. *Hashgahah*, Divine Providence, Earthmind is deep within us, not external to us, and commissions us. We are inspired by and follow *Hokhmah*, Sophia, Wisdom.

Beyond False Images

We need to transform our understanding of God and our abuse of the very word and concept "God." Over time, "God" has become overlaid with false images that exist as residual *partzufim* from past ages. As I said earlier, each paradigm needs an icon. "God" often conjures images and understandings limited by a past (and false) consciousness of the Divine. Consider, for example, art in Christian churches depicting the Trinitarian God: the Father is seated on a throne, has a long white beard and is clothed in a long robe; the bearded Son is in the human material form that Jesus is believed to have had; and the Holy Spirit is a dove hovering overhead. Many Christians, when they think of "God," imagine an old man with a long beard. This is not a teaching of the Christian churches; it is artists' symbolic depiction of God that has become a reality in the minds of some. The same is true of angels. Artists painted angels, spiritual beings, with bodies and wings to represent that they were divine messengers who could travel swiftly from the heavenly to the earthly realm. In the public mind today, angels have a material form and wings. Films released in recent decades have reworked artistic angelic images too, from the angel Clarence in *It's a Wonderful Life* (1946) through to the Archangel Michael in the film *Michael* (1996), and continue to do so. Similarly, false images of God are readily described in philosophical, theological, and political discourse. The word "God" comes to the lips, too, in often less-than-reverential and less-than-prayerful evocations and appropriate places and circumstances. We might hear "God damn it" about something God is not likely concerned with, or "Oh, God" when a prayer to Providence is not what the speaker had in mind.

In religious contexts too, from individual through ritual prayers "God" is cited in sterile ways that represent misleading understandings. People's consciousness of who they think "God" is colors the way they pray and the words they use—words taught them by parents, rabbis, and other teachers in our Jewish tradition. Often those who teach children prayers have the same limited and limiting views of God and Divine Revelation that have persisted for millennia, often solely because "that's 'tradition,'" without seeking the meaning behind the "tradition," meanings that have attached to the "tradition," and alternative descriptions of what the "tradition" might mean today, in our time of a substantial paradigm shift.

Toward a Global, Universal, and Evolving Spiritual-Social Consciousness

The Age is upon us when we can think no longer in a narrowly confined doctrinal and dogmatic manner. We must not only "think" outside the box; we must "believe" outside the box. The paradigm shift in our consciousness must be extensive, in depth, and total. We cannot reserve particular traditions for ourselves; we must develop, discover, and disseminate universally agreed, creative new ways of expressing the best of earlier traditions while integrating insights from those traditions and from our own and others' spiritual experiences (perhaps as expressed particularly in mystical thought) in the world in which we live, with its multiple dimensions of reality.

The *partzuf* for our time might have its early expressions in *The Wiley-Blackwell Companion to Religion and Ecology* for which I am writing this. Distinctive voices from diverse traditions offer glimpses of creative and correlative thinking and spiritual insights that provide the seeds of particular *partzufim* from and for particular religious and spiritual understandings; these might evolve toward a common understanding of social realities, spiritual consciousness, and spatial awareness that can come to be presented in a first attempt at a single *partzuf* that speaks to and attracts people from each of the *partzufim*. If this were to become a commonly accepted initial *partzuf*, which might evolve collaboratively over time as an ongoing, adaptive *partzuf*, then indeed we humans might come to aspire for and work toward constant consciousness of the Presence in which we exist and with which we are engaged as we live in a revived Earth and restored and global human community.

In my own life, I have experienced the "Being who is the center of the universe, the volition, the mind center of the universe, the heart and love center of the universe" (*Tikkun*, 2001). The word "God" cannot capture, try as its proponents may, the magnitude, magnificence, and munificence of this Being. The Being who is Love calls us all to love, to live in love, to be in love. We are called to go beyond mere Earth-bound and doctrine-confined religion to a holistic cosmic spirituality in which we relate to all-that-is, including the Earth, all life, and the Being of the universe. In a new way, we must become "images of God," in the phrasing of Genesis: not placed over Creation but in Creation, called to be solicitous of all we meet, and to respond responsibly to each other and all that exists. In this way, we can come to experience engagement with and the embrace of Being and beings.

It has been and will be difficult for many people of diverse faiths, as it was for me, to make a break from the confinement and constraints of their traditional religion. The Judaism into which I was born, which had been handed down intergenerationally over millennia, initially called and embraced me fully. However, as I realized that spiritual treasures are to be found in diverse spiritual traditions, I gradually became transformed into someone who was able to accept reflectively the insights of all traditions, and therefore to make a break from attachment to one tradition, however revered. It has been difficult. Ultimately, however, it has proved to be a correct decision as I have grown into a universal spirituality that integrates and unifies the best of all religions and seeks the wellbeing of all beings and Being; of the Earth and all life and lives; and of the interrelated spirits of the Earth and cosmos. I wish others well who are about to begin or who have already begun to follow this way into the heart of the Earth and the heart of the cosmos, and the heart of all beings that dwell on and in our planet and universe.

In this era of social turmoil evident, too, in the world's religions' search for spiritual meaning that will be clearly expressed in a faith perspective and cultural commitments that address our age, acceptance that the human world needs a new *partzuf* to share as a common guide and catalyst will prompt community building across nations, cultures, and faith traditions. We can no longer self-confidently, and religiously serene and secure, proceed as usual, teaching and embodying the *partzufim* of previous ages. Jewish Renewal, Christian Renewal, Islamic Renewal, and Buddhist Renewal, among others, have the capacity to formulate the new *partzuf* together. As I observed more than a decade ago, "we are now privy to information which floods us with wonder at the view of a wider and ever more complex cosmos, and we don't want to put our minds in pawn as the price of staying wedded to our tradition" (*Tikkun*, 2001). Cosmic Being is providing us guidelines for a new marriage of minds, born from a cosmically arranged wedding. The progeny of this marriage will set aside dividing doctrines and embrace a unifying consciousness in a unified community. They will seek a new community road map, one that is organic and dynamic. At times, pilgrims following this map might build new roads even while on their journey. They will come to acknowledge that they are living cells of the living Earth and a living cosmos. Their shared worship and words will express their heart's understanding, not parrot their head's safe, stable, secure, and sterile supposed sureties.

As my 90th birthday approaches, I have come to a place and state of peace in my life. I have reflected on who I have come to be through the decades that I have walked on the Earth, absorbing from so many sources but particularly in mysticism and through mystical experiences the spirit of Gaia and the Spirit of the universe. I have encountered others on similar journeys, some of whom have arrived on their life journey where I have come to be on my life's journey. We are all part of one Being, one Spirit, one Universe Power. It is my hope that people throughout the Earth and in generations to come will experience and be guided by this Source of all-that-is, as we evolve together in our Earth life while being conscious of the spiritual dimensions of the reality in which we are immersed. The spiritual reality embraces us at every moment—even when we do not see or sense our relationship to and in it. In such an envisioned time or, perhaps, beyond time we will relate to each other as one community in the One from whom all has come to be and toward whom all that is journeys through time and space.

Notes

1 Rabbi Zalman Schachter-Shalomi and John Hart met in 1987, when Reb Zalman accepted John's invitation to give an address on Religion in the 21st Century, at Carroll College, Helena, Montana. They formed a friendship and conversed periodically over the years, including at the 1992 Rio Earth Summit. This chapter began when Reb Zalman accepted John's invitation to write for the *Companion*, sent him a draft article, and invited him to work together on it via Skype. Reb Zalman sent his final edits and approval to John on June 30, 2014; he passed on to a new reality a few days later, on July 7.

Reb Zalman, a founder of the Jewish Renewal Movement, was its much-beloved spiritual guide. His roots are in the Chabad-Lubavitch tradition, an offshoot of Hasidism. He welcomed insights from all religious and spiritual traditions; promoted women's equality in Judaism, social justice, and environmental wellbeing. He earned an MA degree in the psychology of religion at Boston University and a doctorate in theology at Hebrew Union College-Jewish Institute of Religion. His books include *A Heart Afire* and *From Age-Ing to Sage-Ing*.

John Hart, Professor of Christian Ethics, Boston University School of Theology, is author of six books and editor of the *Companion to Religion and Ecology*. He earned his Master of Sacred Theology degree and PhD at the Union Theological Seminary, New York. He has lectured on socioecological ethics on five continents, in eight countries.

2 Arthur Waskow, *Wiley-Blackwell Companion to Religion and Ecology*, chapter 27: "Prayer as if the Earth Really Matters."

3 The Jewish–Buddhist dialogue is elaborated and analyzed in great depth in Kamenetz, Rodger. 1995. *The Jew in the Lotus—A Poet's Rediscovery of Jewish Identity in Buddhist India*. New York: HarperOne.

4 See the numerous books by award-winning environmental activist Bill McKibben for an insightful discussion of global heating and its impacts.

5 Schachter-Shalomi, Zalman. 2001. "Renewing God." *Tikkun*, September/October. This dialogue is described and discussed by the Dalai Lama. 2012. *Towards the True Kinship of Faiths. London: Abacus*; and by Kamanetz (1995) and in his movie by the same name.

Reference

Berlin, Adele, Brettler, Marc Zvi, & Fishbene, Michael (Eds.). (2004). *The Jewish Study Bible: Featuring the TANAKH Translation of the Jewish Publication Society*. Oxford: Oxford University Press.

Afterword

John B. Cobb, Jr.

Today there is a vast literature about "religion and ecology" of which the chapters in this volume are excellent representatives. Most are written by people of faith in diverse traditions who show how their traditions do or could contribute to better attitudes toward the natural environment and better practices as well. Much of it rightly recognizes that while religious teachings and attitudes sometimes have been a positive impetus in promoting ecological responsibility, they have been also, and to some extent continue to be, obstacles to moving forward.

Sadly, the attitudes toward religion and its teaching about the natural world were more shaped by an earlier stage of the discussion than by the current literature. Today, discussion of these topics is largely relegated to the religious community. In the early spurt of discussion in the late 1960s and early 1970s, the general public was involved and the messages that stuck were largely negative.

The negative message focused on Christianity, which was also condemned for its teaching of patriarchy and its heterosexism. One reason for the decline of old-line Protestantism is the negative image it acquired among the thoughtful young. With respect to ecology, the image of Buddhism fared much better, as did Taoism and indigenous thought.

In my opinion the single most important essay on religion and ecology, "The Historical Roots of Our Ecologic Crisis," was by Lynn White, Jr. and first published in 1967 in *Science*. It was written for a meeting of scientists, and by arguing that the deeper roots of the crisis lay in religious teaching, it challenged their assumptions about the irrelevance of religion. At the same time it deeply upset Christians. White's paper was carefully and accurately nuanced. Its interpreters and popularizers, of course, were not.

White was an historian of technology. He was impressed by the technological prowess of Western Europe during what are called "the Dark Ages." They increased the yield

The Wiley Blackwell Companion to Religion and Ecology, First Edition. Edited by John Hart.

of the land by using new types of plow that dug deeper into the soil. They harnessed the energy of running water and wind. When he asked why the culturally laggard Western Europe developed technology, while Eastern Europe, which preserved classical learning and culture did not, he developed a rather surprising explanation.

White noted that monasticism and its spirituality in Eastern Europe, like spirituality in India, tended to separate spirituality from physical considerations. On the other hand, Western monks had to do much of their own manual labor as well as study and pray. They connected these activities and used their creative skills to make their work more efficient.

Their study centered on the Bible, and one verse played a significant role for them, a verse that was not singled out for emphasis elsewhere in spiritual or biblical literature. In Genesis 1, after God creates human beings, He instructs them to be fruitful and multiply and fill the Earth. The monastics passed over this command, but they emphasized the next. Human beings are to subdue the Earth. White found evidence that this idea that humans are obeying God when they exercise control over the Earth and all its creatures was highlighted in the West in a unique way.

The result may be called the technological attitude, and it is this attitude that White considered responsible for the ecological crisis. Instead of adjusting to the pattern of a healthy ecology, humans began to impose a different order on the natural world, an order that most benefited themselves. This did little damage when human technology was limited. And in any case, during the Middle Ages no one raised the subduing of Nature as God's overarching purpose for human beings. More important by far would be love of God and love of neighbor. The Creation story that authorizes the subduing of the Earth also makes it clear that all the creatures have value in themselves and in God's sight.

As far as I know, the Western Europeans did not disrupt the ecology of their environment significantly more than Eastern Europeans, Indians, or Chinese disrupted theirs. However, I believe that White was correct that the technological attitude that developed in Western Europe is the root of the ecological crisis. During the Enlightenment this attitude was liberated from the broader Christian context in which it was found and became increasingly central to modern culture. The clock may have been the most complex creation of medieval technology. Craftsmen delighted in embellishing the clocks with lifelike figures that came out and danced to celebrate each new hour. These clocks were generally placed on cathedral walls and people understood them as celebrating the glory of God. But during the Enlightenment they began to play a different role. They showed that machines could cause behavior that is generally attributed to purpose. René Descartes, father of modern philosophy, taught that the plants and animals that make up the ecology are no more than machines.

An accurate judgment of the role of the Western reading of the Bible in bringing about the technological attitude requires a second step. This is universalizing the model of the machine that is the product of technology. Without the technological attitude, based on the call to subdue the Earth, the idea that all Nature is machine-like could not have arisen. But it is equally true that this is a huge leap unsupported by anything in the Bible or in Christian theology. The contribution of the Western reading of the Bible is a necessary, but far from sufficient, cause of the ecological crisis. The doctrine that all

Nature is mechanical is a second contribution, dependent on, but by no means necessitated by, the first. This second contribution, including and reinforcing the first, has become basic to the modern university. The importance of this distinction can be shown by the difference in the responses of the churches and the universities.

Consider, first, the response of the churches. Remarkably rapidly the major bodies of Christendom, both Western and Eastern, have disavowed the teaching that has led to the ecological crisis. Biblical scholars have shown that the biblical teaching about humans' relationship to other creatures does justify use of the natural world and adapting it to human need, but it gives no justification for the rape of the Earth or for treating other creatures as existing only for our benefit.

When the destructive consequences of the one-sided Western emphasis on mastery are called to their attention, Christian leaders have consistently striven to free their teaching from what they see to be errors. This is not easy because it requires freeing themselves from Western scientism, dualism, mechanism, materialism, individualism, and anthropocentrism. Much work is needed and in fact continues. But *metanoia* (a changed mind) has occurred in the leadership and to a considerable degree in lay people as well.

I want to be clear. There are still important issues to be discussed by Western Christians and by others. No tradition has a perfect record, even if Western Christians have been the worst. The Bible unquestionably assigns human beings the dominant role among creatures, but it calls on us to use our power wisely and sensitively. Sadly, even though we have changed our rhetoric, our practice remains bound to excessive anthropocentrism. Our theology and our churches say very little about how we should deal with the animals we rear for our food. We tolerate treating them as if they had no value in themselves, as if their suffering did not matter. Teaching and preaching on this topic remain scant. Even those Christians who have become sensitized to the suffering of animals have generally come to this independently of church teaching. There is still much of which we need to repent.

I hope readers will not consider my focus on Western Christianity insensitive to the broader concern of this volume. It is, of course, partly because I am a Western Christian. But it is chiefly because Western Christianity has borne the brunt of the criticism and has had the most of which to repent. Perhaps I should add that I am a liberal Protestant, and that we bear the most guilt of all. I hope it is not boasting to claim that now, at last, we have given some leadership in the work of repentance.

But we are not alone in the need to repent. Destructive relations to the environment characterized civilizations long before the biblical scriptures were written. Many cultures have destroyed the ecosystems about them. We find ruins of ancient cities that were abandoned when exploitative farming destroyed the arability of the land. Even indigenous people have damaged the local ecology, and pastoral nomads have created deserts.

Western Christianity contributed to the rise of modernity and then adjusted to its teaching. It is this modernity that has created the global crisis. Overall, Western Christians, especially Protestants, have accepted modernity and participated in it. Its missionaries contributed to its spread. Most of us have appreciated the achievements of modernity and thought that bringing them to others, along with distinctive Christian teaching, was a gift. I have called attention to the important fact that Western Christian churches have repented, and this includes both Catholic and Protestant. No other institutions have produced so many excellent statements as have the Vatican, the World Council of Churches, and many individual denominations.

I have focused on repentance and therefore on Western Christianity. The global crisis has evoked new statements and leadership from traditions that did not have the same need for repentance. Buddhists and Hindus, Muslims and Sikhs, Taoists and Confucians have all shown their commitment to contribute to solutions of global problems. Among Christians the Patriarch of Constantinople, Bartholomew I, has been an outstanding leader.

I set out to contrast the response of the churches and the response of the universities. On the side of the churches we can generalize by saying the Western churches have verbally repented and are trying gradually to turn their new affirmations into deeply changed action. Those traditions that have not shared in responsibility for the crisis have also been stimulated to accent their useful teachings. What now of universities?

Universities have a far more direct responsibility for the global crisis than do any of our wisdom traditions. The modernity that has brought about the global crisis owes more than it wants to admit to Christian teaching. But whereas Christians are repenting, global modernist leadership continues to affirm the modern vision. And modern universities are the institutions most responsible for preserving, implementing, and transmitting modern thought and practice.

Sadly, there has been virtually no repentance on the part of universities. They continue to measure "excellence" by just those standards that are the cause of the ecological crisis. The most prestigious universities are the worst and the least likely to express even an interest in repenting.

Modernists in universities and elsewhere often blame the Church, and it is good for us to be reminded. But their charges would have more credibility if they recognized the repentance of the churches and their own greater guilt. Christians have rightly concentrated on their needed repentance, but that has now gone far enough that we have not only the right, but also the duty, to point out the damage being done by the worldview that governs the universities. At this juncture blaming us for their bad teaching is no longer helpful. We should encourage them to take responsibility for their destructive teaching and criticize their refusal to take responsibility for the consequences of their actions. Such a new stance on the part of the universities might begin with those closest to churches, especially Catholic ones.

In June 2015 an event took place that may be of great importance. Pope Francis issued an encyclical, *Laudato Sí.* There is little in it that had not been present at least implicitly in previous Catholic teaching, but this encyclical brought it together in a way that deeply communicated the interconnection of all things. Especially it united the cry of the Earth and the cry of the poor. It identified the forces that stand in the way of healing action, and it pointed to the need for an integral ecology.

The pope sought the best scientific advice in order to put an end to any idea that the Christian message requires resistance to scientific advance. He addressed the encyclical not only to Catholics but to all of us. Without criticizing any of us, he made it clear that we need to move from good statements about our traditions and how they can now guide us, to join with him in what Thomas Berry called the "Great Work."

To follow Francis does not require that we agree with him on all matters. Some of us think that stabilizing the world population is a primary goal, whereas he treats that dismissively. Some of us would speak not only of the cry of the Earth and the poor, but also of the cry of women and girls. To join in work for integral ecology does not lead some of us to abandon these struggles. Instead, it calls us to intensify them. But even this will be part of that great movement to which the pope calls us and of which, intentionally or not, he is the leader.

For half a century we have held conferences, published books, and written declarations about helping our diverse traditions to care deeply for the Earth and all its inhabitants. We have done much to overcome the obstacles to cooperation among the world's great wisdom traditions. Now let us direct our thought and energy to the task for which we have prepared ourselves—working together to ameliorate the now inevitable disasters and constructing an integral ecology to replace our suicidal society.

Index

The Wiley Blackwell Companion to Religion and Ecology, First Edition. Edited by John Hart.

TJI55154-9781118465561-22-05-17